Fourth Edition
Developing Communities for the Future
Susan Kenny

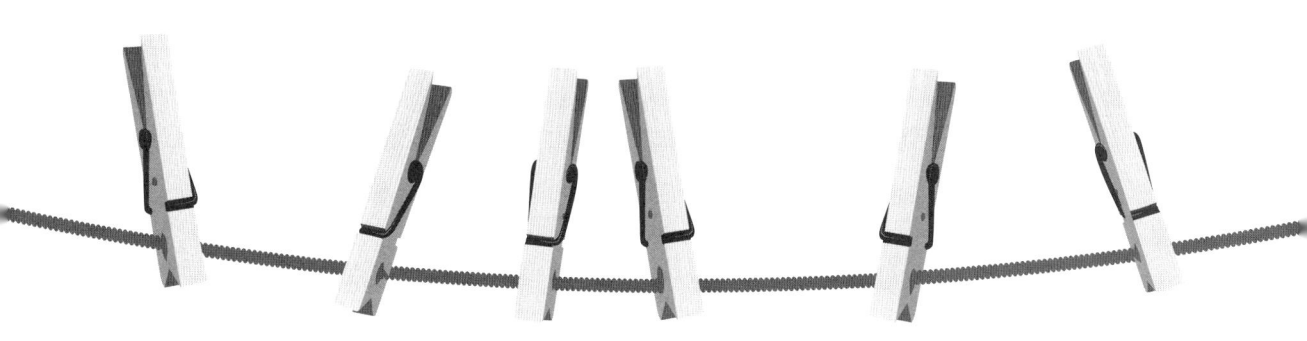

CENGAGE
Learning

Australia • Brazil • Japan • Korea • Mexico • Singapore • Spain • United Kingdom • United States

Developing Communities for the Future
Fourth Edition
Susan Kenny

Publishing manager: Alison Green
Publishing editor: Ann Crabb
Project editor: Michaela Skelly
Publishing assistant: Miriam Allen
Cover design: Ami-Louise Sharpe
Text design: Danielle Maccarone
Editor: Gill Smith
Proofreader: Greg Alford
Indexer: Julie King
Reprint: Magda Koralewska
Typesetter: KnowledgeWorks Global Ltd

Any URLs contained in this publication were checked for currency during the production process. Note, however, that the publisher cannot vouch for the ongoing currency
of URLs.

The third edition was published in 2006

Acknowledgements
Cover image by Getty Images

© 2011 Cengage Learning Australia Pty Limited

Copyright Notice
This Work is copyright. No part of this Work may be reproduced, stored in a retrieval system, or transmitted in any form or by any means without prior written permission of the Publisher. Except as permitted under the Copyright Act 1968, for example any fair dealing for the purposes of private study, research, criticism or review, subject to certain limitations. These limitations include: Restricting the copying to a maximum of one chapter or 10% of this book, whichever is greater; providing an appropriate notice and warning with the copies of the Work disseminated; taking all reasonable steps to limit access to these copies to people authorised to receive these copies; ensuring you hold the appropriate Licences issued by the
Copyright Agency Limited ("CAL"), supply a remuneration notice to CAL and pay any required fees. For details of CAL licences and remuneration notices please contact CAL at
Level 15, 233 Castlereagh Street, Sydney NSW 2000,
Tel: (02) 9394 7600, Fax: (02) 9394 7601
Email: info@copyright.com.au
Website: www.copyright.com.au

For product information and technology assistance,
in Australia call 1300 790 853;
in New Zealand call 0800 449 725

For permission to use material from this text or product, please email aust.permissions@cengage.com

National Library of Australia Cataloguing-in-Publication Data
  Title: Developing communities for the future
  / Susan Kenny
  Edition: 4th ed.
  ISBN: 9780170186704 (pbk.)
  Notes: Includes index.
  Subjects: Community development--Australia.
  Dewey Number: 307.140994

Cengage Learning Australia
Level 7, 80 Dorcas Street
South Melbourne, Victoria Australia 3205

Cengage Learning New Zealand
Unit 4B Rosedale Office Park
331 Rosedale Road, Albany, North Shore 0632, NZ

For learning solutions, visit cengage.com.au

Printed in China by RR Donnelley Asia Printing Solutions Limited.
2 3 4 5 6 7 8 15 14 13 12 11

Brief contents

Preface x
Resources guide xvi
Introduction xviii
About the author xxiv
Acknowledgements xxv

Part 1 Background and basics 1

Chapter 1   The nature of community development 2
Chapter 2   The context 41
Chapter 3   Theoretical perspectives and concepts 83
Chapter 4   The role of the state 137

Part 2 Processes and practices 173

Chapter 5   Practical foundations 174
Chapter 6   Community organisations 228
Chapter 7   Activities and practices 266
Chapter 8   Understanding and responding to difference 307
Chapter 9   Funding and research 342

Part 3 Contradictions 397

Chapter 10 Difficulties and dilemmas 398
Chapter 11 Challenges for the twenty-first century 424

Appendix and references

Appendix 433
References 439
Index 451

Contents

Preface	x
Resources guide	xvi
Introduction	xviii
About the author	xxiv
Acknowledgements	xxv

Part 1 Background and basics — 1

Chapter 1 The nature of community development — 2
Overview	2
Introduction	2
Defining community development	8
Community development work and community organisations	13
The roles of community development workers	17
Principles	21
Processes	32
Summary points	38
Key terms	39
Exercises	39
Further reading	40
Weblinks	40

Chapter 2 The context — 41
Overview	41
Introduction	41
The welfare backdrop	43
The community backdrop	44
The political backdrop	53
The global backdrop	58
The policy backdrop	65
Summary points	79
Key terms	80
Exercises	81
Further reading	81
Weblinks	82

Chapter 3 Theoretical perspectives and concepts — 83
Overview	83
Introduction	83
Theoretical perspectives	86

Contents

Language and discourse	115
New themes, concepts and theories	121
Summary points	131
Key terms	133
Exercises	133
Further reading	134
Weblinks	136

Chapter 4 The role of the state — 137

Overview	137
Introduction	137
Approaches to understanding the state	139
The welfare state	155
Models for the future	164
Summary points	168
Key terms	169
Exercises	169
Further reading	170
Weblinks	171

Part 2 Processes and practices — 173

Chapter 5 Practical foundations — 174

Overview	174
Introduction	174
Professionalism	175
Competency	176
Empowerment	179
Participation	187
Empowerment in practice	190
Community capacity building	193
The social inclusion agenda	202
Strategy development	204
Summary points	224
Key terms	225
Exercises	225
Further reading	226
Weblinks	227

Chapter 6 Community organisations — 228

Overview	228
Introduction	228

Contents

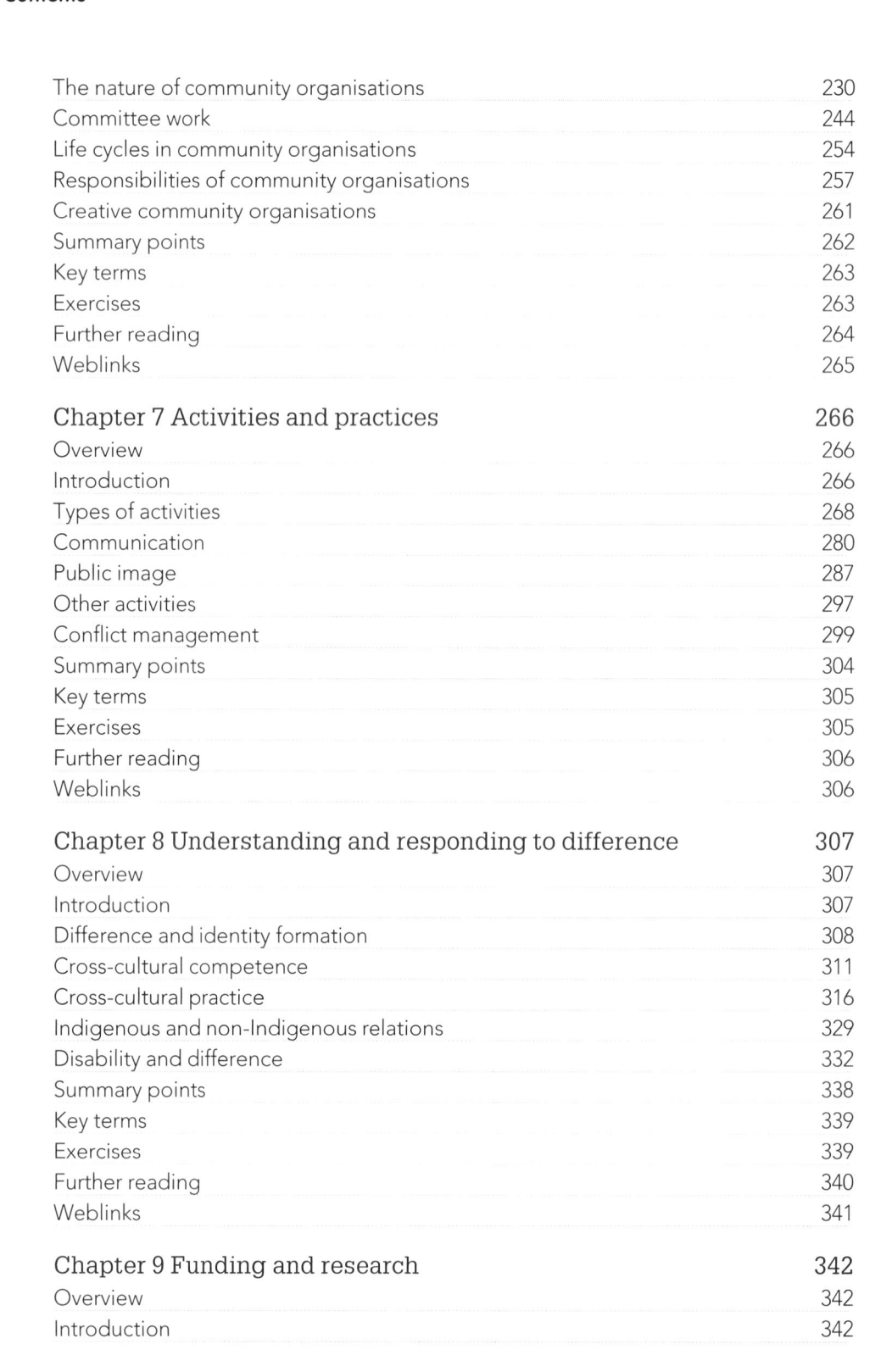

The nature of community organisations	230
Committee work	244
Life cycles in community organisations	254
Responsibilities of community organisations	257
Creative community organisations	261
Summary points	262
Key terms	263
Exercises	263
Further reading	264
Weblinks	265

Chapter 7 Activities and practices — 266
Overview	266
Introduction	266
Types of activities	268
Communication	280
Public image	287
Other activities	297
Conflict management	299
Summary points	304
Key terms	305
Exercises	305
Further reading	306
Weblinks	306

Chapter 8 Understanding and responding to difference — 307
Overview	307
Introduction	307
Difference and identity formation	308
Cross-cultural competence	311
Cross-cultural practice	316
Indigenous and non-Indigenous relations	329
Disability and difference	332
Summary points	338
Key terms	339
Exercises	339
Further reading	340
Weblinks	341

Chapter 9 Funding and research — 342
Overview	342
Introduction	342

Accountability, relevance and effectiveness	343
Funding and resource allocation	344
Types of funding	347
Preparing submissions	361
Competitive tendering	367
Research	371
Evaluation	386
Summary points	391
Key terms	392
Exercises	392
Further reading	393
Weblinks	394

Part 3 Contradictions 397

Chapter 10 Difficulties and dilemmas — 398

Overview	398
Introduction	398
'Pure' community development	398
Contradictory themes and expectations	400
Summary points	421
Key terms	422
Exercises	422
Further reading	423
Weblinks	423

Chapter 11 Challenges for the twenty-first century — 424

Overview	424
Introduction	424
Constraints and challenges	426
Directions for community development	428
Summary points	430
Exercises	431
Further reading	431

Appendix and references

Appendix	433
References	439
Index	451

Preface

I began writing this preface to the new edition at the time of the United Nations Climate Change Conference, which took place in Copenhagen between 7 and 18 December 2009. The international interest in the conference indicates the shift in thinking about the key issue facing humankind at the end of the first decade of the twenty-first century. For the moment, international anxieties about the possible collapse of capitalism generated by what has come to be known as the 'global financial crisis', and the politics of fear that have focused on Islamic fundamentalism, have become background noises. For much of the world, the real and most urgent changes required revolve around how human activity is threatening the survival of our planet and consequently our lives as we know them. Yet, in Australia, there remains a significant minority of the population who deny that climate change is upon us or reject the idea that climate change will have devastating effects or simply argue according to the principle of providentialism that 'all will turn out alright in the end'. It is worth reflecting on the extensive range of views on climate change held by Australians. The majority view, which is expressed by the Australian Labor government, is that indeed climate change is upon us and that it will affect our region in many ways, bringing more extreme weather (more rain in the north of Australia and more drought in southern Australia) and rising sea levels, which threaten the very existence of some Pacific Islands, such as the Marshall Islands, Kiribati and Tuvalu, and the lives and livelihoods of millions in Bangladesh, India and Vietnam. The minority viewpoint, held by the climate change ' deniers' or 'doubters', holds variously that the idea of climate change is a left conspiracy, even a socialist plot to undermine capitalism, or is a diversionary tactic to draw attention away from more pressing threats to Australia, such as the flood of refugees from developing countries preparing to enter Australia 'illegally'. The latter anxiety, which involves a rerun of the panic generated by the seafaring endeavours of asylum seekers to reach the shores of Australia in the years of the Howard prime ministership, is a depressing reason to pause about how far ordinary Australians continue to be influenced by populist politicians and the right-wing media.

Yet against this often discouraging picture, we can identify some significant changes. On 24 November 2007, a federal Labor government was elected under the leadership of Kevin Rudd, in a victory that saw the conservative prime minister, John Howard, actually lose his own seat. The Labor Party came to power amid high expectations regarding Indigenous reconciliation, restoration of workers' rights, reversal of the harsh treatment of asylum seekers, policies for action on climate change, the softening of neo-liberal policies and a halt to what had seemed like the inexorable processes of privatisation. Many expectations have not been fulfilled, perhaps most notably the hope held by many for a curbing of neo-liberalism and a reversal of policies on asylum seekers. However, one of the first actions of the former prime minister, Kevin Rudd, was an historic apology to Indigenous

Australians and subsequent (although often misguided) attempts to address their poverty and marginalisation. The years 2007 to 2009 saw the teetering of the global financial system in the global financial crisis. Australia has stood out as one country that seems to have weathered the storm of this crisis. Strategies dealing with climate change have posed a real challenge for the Labor government. With the federal Liberal National coalition shifting to the Right, its hostility to Labor's views and strategies for responding to climate change, and particularly the emissions trading scheme, has hardened, while at the same time the public at large seem to be a little confused, not so much in regard to whether or not there is climate change (most people agree), but in regard to what to do about it.

From the point of view of the Labor supporters in Australia, evaluation of the overall performance of the Labor Party under Kevin Rudd was mixed. Of course, governments never deliver fully on all the expectations and promises and the Rudd Labor government was no exception. However, there is considerable support for Labor policies for the community sector. Two initiatives stand out. The first initiative concerns the social inclusion agenda, which sets out the need, principles and strategies for social inclusion. Social inclusion would seem to be a central part of community development. However, as will be argued in chapter 2, it depends on what we mean by social inclusion and how social inclusion takes place. The second initiative has been the recognition of the importance of the third sector, or not-for-profit sector, in Australia. This recognition has been demonstrated by the Productivity Commission's research into the contribution of the not-for-profit sector and the scoping of a national compact between government and the third sector. In February 2010, as I was well into revising the third edition of this book, the Productivity Commission released its report *The Contribution of the Not-for-Profit Sector* (2010). This report is the most comprehensive study of the not-for-profit sector so far undertaken in Australia. Within this report there is a proposal for the establishment of an Office for the Third Sector, whose brief it will be to document, assist and monitor the third sector. We examine these initiatives in this book in discussions of the role of community organisations in Australia and in the analysis of state and community sector relations and partnerships.

Of course, state and community organisation relations do not only take place at the national level. While the federal government might set the broad backdrop to policy development affecting the community sector, state and local governments play a critical role in supporting (or otherwise), funding and partnering the community sector. At both state and local government levels there are now numerous programs concerned with community capacity building, community strengthening and neighhbourhood renewal. Some governments have established departments for community development, community planning and social inclusion. As remarked in the book, the romance with the idea of community has certainly not diminished. It continues to be used for its medicinal qualities, as Mowbray (1985) argued so eloquently over 20 years ago.

Preface

On the world stage we have a black man, Barack Obama, with a background in community development (or what is called community organising in the USA) as the leader of the most powerful country in the world. This is truly remarkable and has been cause for celebration among many left-inclined people globally. Within community development networks we have probably not sufficiently considered how President Obama translated his insights and strategic skills as an organiser in poor neighbourhoods in Chicago into a national political agenda for change. Even in a country that worships at the twin shrines of individualism and turbo capitalism, it is necessary to work collectively to get things done. Looking at the way that Obama, together with his supporters, developed his political base, we can learn about his strategies for utilising the power of new means of communication such as Facebook, his grassroots organising skills and extensive network of alliances cross-cutting class, gender, ethnicity, 'race' and age. We can identify the ways that he has operated across four spheres: the state, the market, the family and civil society. As a salutary lesson for community development practitioners, we need to remember the power of alliances between those working in the context of powerful political, business and civil society institutions. Yet like Kevin Rudd, Barack Obama has disappointed many of his supporters. He has appeased the Right, while being implicated in a constant struggle to keep American liberal (or left) agendas alive.

Like any political endeavour, the successes of community development, like the successes of politicians, are always double-headed. With every success comes more expectations, many of which can never be fulfilled. And for every success we might ask of ourselves: Has this win been at the expense of some other issue? Have we compromised too much? For example, there are many apparent successes for community development since the first edition of this book was published in 1994. In its various forms (as community engagement, community capacity building and social inclusion, for example), the presence of community development in public policy, transnational relations and local politics is much stronger than in 1994. There are probably many more champions of community development. But in some cases, their understanding of community development is different to mine. For example, their partisanship to disadvantaged and marginalised groups is much more ambivalent. In some cases, community workers talk about community empowerment while at the same time employ an individualistic, competitive approach to their work, as is evident in prize-giving nights for the 'best volunteer' or 'best social entrepreneur' in the community. While it is important to avoid drawing out territory that is 'pure' community development, there is a point at which practices and policies undermine the principles of community development. As with previous editions, this issue is taken up in this edition.

What have strengthened since the last edition are the technologically facilitated interconnections between people, organisations and institutions, which are understood in the framework of globalisation. Globalisation increasingly affects us all, whether it be in the borderless impacts of climate change, the expansion of knowledge and information through the Internet or our vulnerability to the self-interested decisions of global financiers. Community development practitioners have responded differently to this globalising world. For example, for some, globalised communication opens up new ways of relating to each other and sharing information, and strategies never dreamed about several decades ago. For others, interconnections in industrial and agricultural production have led to new forms of environmental degradation, exploitation and dependence, as local production and consumption have been eroded. As local economies become unviable, the very existence of many small towns is under threat. We see such devastation in our own Indigenous communities. Local autonomy is lost as governments strengthen their regulatory and monitoring regimes. In the wake of these forms of globalisation has come the movement back to relocalisation. These shifts are considered in this edition.

One of the new elements of contemporary life that is a corollary to the growing awareness of the vulnerabilities of our physical environment is the growing interest in natural disasters and their effects. During the past decade, Australians have shown considerable interest in assisting communities affected by natural disaster, not only in Australia but in the Asia Pacific region as well. A particular catalyst for this interest in Australia was the Black Saturday bushfires in Victoria in February 2009. In the aftermath and the reconstruction efforts, the importance of a community-based response has been emphasised. Indeed, in a way, post-disaster reconstruction offers an exemplary site for community development practice. Yet for all the rhetoric of community involvement in the post-bushfire recovery, the process of recovery and reconstruction was, in general, set up and controlled by government with only tokenistic input by the communities affected. Chapter 1 includes a composite case study, drawing on different examples of community development practice, that demonstrates how community development processes can be used in a post-disaster situation. We consider ways that survivors can take significant control of the recovery effort, as opposed to the more common post-disaster recovery and reconstruction, which is top-down and offers, at best, tokenistic involvement by the communities affected. In chapter 5, we reflect on the forms of participation and the issue of tokenistic consultation.

For those of you who are familiar with previous editions of the book, in this edition you will find some stronger emphases on certain ways of framing community development. These shifts are the result of some important learnings, debates, reflections and self-criticisms and, most of all, some hard lessons learnt in the field of community development practice. Five emphases can be noted here. First, I have made more of the asset-based approach to community development. But this does not mean that I have fully embraced all aspects of the asset-based community development (ABCD) model that is championed by Kretzmann and others (Kretzmann & McKnight, 1993). Second, I have tried to take more account of the diversity and 'messiness' in community development, in communities, practice and strategies. Third, I have paid more attention to the international nature of community development, which is manifested in the growing interconnections across the globe and facilitated by new forms of technology and communication. For example, the term 'community' traditionally has referred to groups of people involved in face-to-face relations. However, with the realisation of the interconnectedness of all life on the planet, the idea of community is being extended to groups of people who share an identity and interest across regions and national borders, who might be networked as 'virtual communities'. Fourth, this book is a little more strident in its criticism of the community-oriented practices of government, however well intentioned, that function to control and co-opt civil society and the community sector through regulation, monitoring and spin. I have become more concerned about the culture of performance management over the past few years whereby, often in the name of transparency, the methods of regulation and monitoring have become a normal part of our everyday lives. They undermine the critical edge of community development as they naturalise the role of government in setting the terms of reference for social inclusion, community engagement and community capacity building, for example. Such state control diverts attention away from careful thinking about, and sensitivity to, the people we work with on the ground to how we construct our relationship with government. Finally, while I continue to be wary of the motives of corporations in setting up corporate social responsibility policies and community-based activities, I can now identify a number of projects that are based on sound accountability to communities and have involved good partnerships arrangements. In some cases, then, I am less strident in my criticism of community-oriented business activities.

Like earlier editions, the ideas in the book have many origins. I would like to thank colleagues at Deakin University for their constant intellectual challenges. My understanding of community development principles comes from the inspiring work of countless people in Indigenous communities in Australia, in the fire-ravaged outskirts of Melbourne and in the untiring work of multicultural communities throughout Australia, as well as from the courageous survivors of the devastating tsunami in Aceh and the 2009 earthquake in Padang, Indonesia, and finally from farmers' cooperatives in France.

I would like to acknowledge the Australian Research Council for supporting my research into the role of community organisations in developing civil society both in Australia and internationally. The international research has assisted me to locate Australian community development activities in a wider international framework. Many of the ideas in this book have been presented in articles and at conferences where I have had the privilege of discussing and debating my views.

In regard to the presentation of this book, I thank Linette Hawkins, Jim Ife and Martin Mowbray for gently forcing me to consider the heavy normative baggage that I have a tendency to load onto community development: Linette for her enlightened common sense, Jim for reminding me of the complexities of community development and Martin for his continuing rigorous exposure of the ideological uses of community development.

As with the earlier editions of the book I would also like to acknowledge the patience of my family for all their support of my community development activities.

During the writing of this edition three important people passed away: my mother, Margaret Pullman, who instilled in me a belief in humanity and believed that 'girls could do anything', and who always encouraged me to 'live life to the fullest and seize opportunities'; Caty Kyne, who dedicated her life to community development and had been an Australian 'living treasure' of community development; and Mark Lyons, whose contribution to the study of the third sector in Australia and steady gaze was an inspiration to researchers. All three people were warm, generous and intelligent, and in different ways, were blessed with keen sense of humour. This book is dedicated to them.

Postscript

As I submit this manuscript in the first half of 2010, concern about global warming has slipped backstage as political parties flirt with the media to secure the best spin on their policies leading up to the federal election to be held later in 2010. Part of this spin revolves around the renewed demonisation of the asylum seekers, which the two dominant political parties, together with a complicit media, are constructing in a way that can only be judged with contempt.

Resources guide for students

As you read this text you will find features in every chapter to enhance your study of community development and help you understand its wider context.

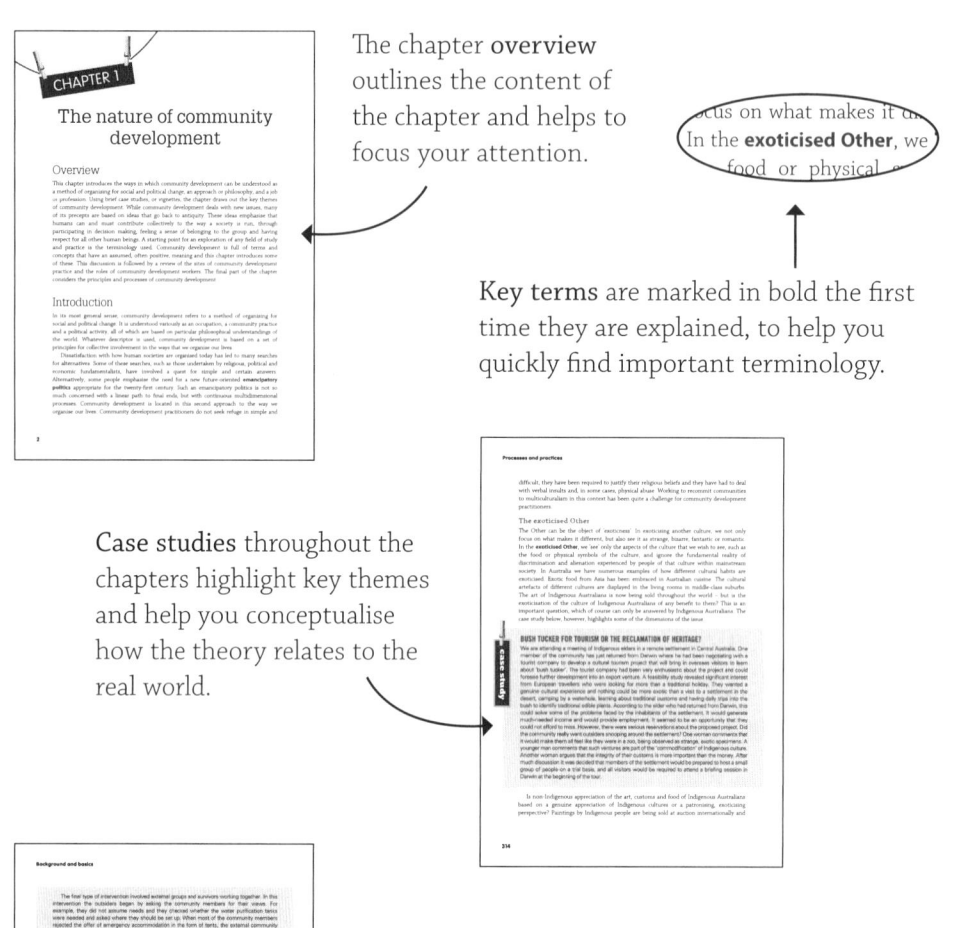

The chapter **overview** outlines the content of the chapter and helps to focus your attention.

Key terms are marked in bold the first time they are explained, to help you quickly find important terminology.

Case studies throughout the chapters highlight key themes and help you conceptualise how the theory relates to the real world.

At the end of each chapter you'll find more learning tools to help you review the chapter content and extend your learning.

The list of **summary points** gives a concise recap of major concepts covered in the chapter as a starting point for your own review.

Resources guide

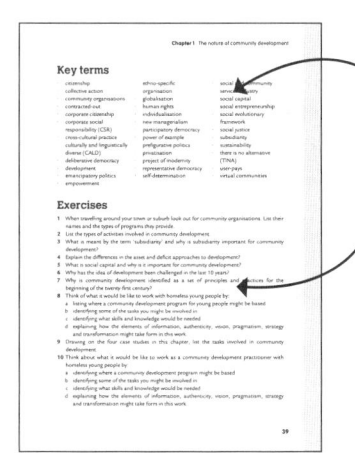

A **list of key terms** highlights important terminology to know.

The end of chapter **exercises** enable you to consolidate your knowledge and apply the theory you have learned.

The **further reading** section provides an opportunity to extend your depth of knowledge and understanding of the key concepts of the chapter.

The **weblinks** section lists selected key sites as a starting point for further online research.

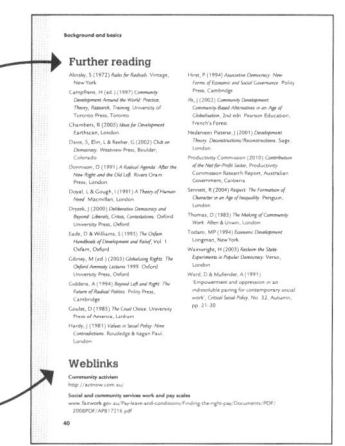

To help you get more from your text, visit the companion website at

www.cengage.com.au/kenny4e

Resources for students include the weblinks from the text and internet exercises to extend your knowledge.

Introduction

Community development is an area of study and a set of approaches, principles and methods to assist ordinary people to work together to take control of their futures. It proposes the development of structures, resources and processes by which communities can collectively identify and address their own development, including the identification of needs and assets, and the resolution of issues and problems. The study of community development promises to show how different forms of development can be constructed and implemented, including development that takes account of the diversity of assets, needs and views between and within communities. In responding to difference, community development methods also offer new ways of dealing with disagreement and conflict, which start from the principles of deliberation and mutual respect.

This book introduces the reader to the practices and principles of community development in general, because these have universal application. But it also argues that understanding the various contexts in which community development operates is essential for community development practice. While the focus of the book is Australian community development, community development in this country is no longer just about activities in the nation state called Australia. More and more Australians are working both in Australia and with colleagues internationally, and this trend is reflected in discussions and case studies in the book.

An overview of the past 15 years since the first edition was published reveals many continuities, but also some important discontinuities. The practices that were constructed for the purpose of empowering ordinary people have not lost their potency. Overall, the difficulties and dilemmas facing community development practitioners have changed little.

However, the contexts in which community development is practised in Australia have shifted considerably, as governments, international power configurations and theoretical understandings have changed. Over the past two decades, we can track a whole host of reflections, themes and concepts that have provided new insights into the challenges facing humankind. These in turn have influenced community development strategies for empowering people to take control of their lives. For example, a whole body of literature around the idea of civil society has provided a new launching place for critiques of state- or market-controlled development of societies. Interest in civil society has been complemented by the development of a new field of research, the study of what are variously known as third sector organisations, non-profits or non-government organisations (NGOs) as key sites of civil society activity. The concept of social capital has become a 'frontline' tool to demonstrate the power of community ties, and the importance of mutuality and cooperation. The concepts of risk and risk society have drawn attention to our preoccupation with identifying, pre-empting or managing the many threats facing human existence. Importantly, the idea of risk took on a new intensity after the attacks on symbols of American power in September 2001 and the bombings of the London transport system in July 2007. Since that time, state power has been harnessed further to implement new methods of surveillance and control, and we seem to be witnessing the genesis of new forms of the authoritarian state. Since the last edition, the apparent indestructibility of neo-liberalism has been potentially challenged by what has come to be known as the global financial crisis, or the GFC. This crisis, together with the realisation of the speed at which human-caused global climate change is moving, exposes the reality that we exist in a globally connected world and it is incumbent upon all of us to actively respond. And many people are actively responding.

Indeed, at the same time as new risks seem to be posing a threat to the so-called 'global order' in the form of the global financial crisis and climate change, ordinary people are working together across the world around visions of a better society. For example, the whole concept of community development as operating only within a local neighbourhood has been shaken by the appearance of new networks across the world in what has come to be known as transnational action. For a new generation of activists, the term 'community' can now refer to 'virtual communities' just as much as it refers to the local neighbourhood. Virtual communities comprise networks of people who know each other well and work on the basis of shared interests and identity, mutuality and trust, but operate through videoconferencing using tools such as Skype^{TM}.

People working together in these networks come together on projects to save rainforests across the world, to support asylum seekers and to organise campaigns around civil rights. Thus another of the changes in community development since 1994 is the significant rescoping of community development arising out of the shifting conceptions of community. The classic views of community development as predominantly face-to-face neighbourhood work in rundown working-class, village or peasant communities whose residents share much the same culture have been expanded to include diverse cultures and activities that extend beyond traditional ideas of neighbourhood and even beyond nation states.

In many ways the growth of community development during this period is a clear success story. There has been increasing interest in community development as an approach to social problems, as an alternative to passive welfare and as a method for generating social capital and strengthening social cohesion. Indeed community development is now identified as a key practice in social development. Yet from some standpoints there has been an unacceptable price to pay for these successes in so far as they have often blunted the critical edge of community development practice.

The view taken in this book is that community development is multifaceted. It operates at a number of different levels and in different settings. It can be both radical and conservative. In some instances, community development processes radically challenge dominant power relations. In many other instances, community development works well to develop social capital, through social engagement and social inclusion projects. In yet other cases, community development practices can empower communities in some respects by giving them more say in the economic development of their communities, for example, while at the same time they are unwittingly co-opted to the needs of those in power.

Purpose of the book

The purpose of this fourth edition, as with the previous editions, is to explicate the components of community development and to open up discussion of the issues and dilemmas in community development work in Australia. Like earlier editions, this book covers the intellectual, political and social contexts in which community development is performed. It explores the principles of community development and explains the skills, abilities, tasks and roles undertaken by people involved in community development. Case studies illustrate the ways that community development practitioners operate in everyday situations.

Because the contexts and practices of community development are ever-changing, this edition offers new material and new insights. The new and supplementary material includes updates on green perspectives; discussion of new public policies and precepts, such as social inclusion and participatory practices; recognition of the contribution of third sector/not-for-profit organisations to Australian society, and new forms of information technology and their role in community development; further discussion of social enterprise and corporate social responsibility; and additional material on difference and Indigenous approaches.

As with earlier editions, this book has been written for people who are engaged as community development practitioners and those who wish to undertake community development work, such as students. The material will be informative for those who are concerned to apply community development approaches in a wide range of unpaid and paid activities. For example, it is hoped that people organising a project such as a refugee support program, a community garden or an international human rights campaign will find some useful ideas in the community development approaches elucidated in the book. Lawyers working in legal aid, architects involved in post-bushfire reconstruction and medical doctors working with remote Indigenous communities might find an understanding of community development approaches and methods useful in their everyday work.

As a learning aid, I hope the book will be used in the spirit in which it was written, providing reference points for thinking about community development. It has been written as a facilitating document to be interrogated and challenged, rather than a text to be learnt for exams.

Orientation of the book

The book presents my understandings and my emphases. Rather than being seen as prescriptive material, the themes, interpretations and arguments are intended to generate the dissent necessary for a living discipline. We all bring a range of learning experiences to situations and reading a book should be no exception. Community development, by its nature, rejects authoritarian teaching models in which all that is required is regurgitation of the views of an 'expert'. As a corollary, it is important that this book be used in a non-coercive learning environment.

Of course, there will not be complete agreement by either practitioners or teachers with all that is in this book. This is because of differences in assumptions and theories and the various ways that goals, tasks and practices are prioritised and developed. Such disagreements are an inherent part of community development work. They stem from disparate perspectives and experiences, and in many cases they cannot be resolved. However, it is possible to identify the sources of these disagreements and to discuss ways of dealing with them.

While I am not committed to a narrow line, my views are underpinned by some specific reference points and allegiances. It may, therefore, be useful for the reader to know what experiences and perspectives guide my approach to community development. My views on community development are influenced by involvement in a range of community projects and political and social justice campaigns. I have also been influenced by a range of sociological, left and feminist theories, and more recently, the concept of cosmopolitanism and the critical understandings of risk society. I have come to the view that community development work must be guided by an understanding of the theories and politics that constrain and facilitate action and that it requires a critical understanding of everyday tactics and practices. Without such understandings and critique, activities within communities lose emancipatory potential and tend to become no more than shallow formula-based practices.

I am committed to the view that it is necessary to be vigilant in analysing the changing contexts in which we operate. We must develop strategies that are appropriate to the context and time. But we also need to base any new directions on understandings of where we have come from, what we have done right and what we could have done better. I hope this book contributes to both reflection upon the past and the breaking of new ground.

Difficulties in introducing community development

Community development is not an easy field in which to practice. It is full of ambiguities, contradictions and paradoxes. Because it is driven by politics and passion, and because it brings together values, principles and practices, it is not the sort of job or activity that easily separates one's identity as an ordinary person and one's identity as a worker. Community development work is not of the type where you can close the office door at 5.30 pm and turn off.

It is difficult to take on community development tasks in a half-hearted way, for they require a commitment to the continual search for better ways of doing things. Those who expect simple instructions for 'doing' community development will be challenged and perhaps provoked by this book. While it is possible to identify principles, strategies and actions that work in specific situations, no magic formula can be applied in all situations. Indeed, community development is a confronting, living set of activities that defies simple answers.

Organisation of the book

Some of the material covered in this book is quite difficult. I have tried to make it more accessible in a number of ways. At the beginning of each chapter is a brief overview of the themes covered in the chapter. The use of bold type draws attention to key terms as they are introduced. At the end of each chapter is a list of the major points covered, suggestions for further reading, some links to useful websites, and several exercises or questions that can be used to reflect on what you have learnt in the chapter. Each chapter contains descriptive examples and, where appropriate, case studies.

Part 1 comprises four chapters that together are an account of the general characteristics of community development and the intellectual, political and social contexts in which it operates. Chapter 1 introduces the reader to the distinguishing features of community development, including the settings, roles, tasks, processes and principles. Chapter 2 discusses the broad contexts of community development. In chapter 3 the theories relevant to community development are elaborated on. Chapter 4 examines interpretations of the state and the relationships between the state and community development.

In Part 2, chapters 5 to 9, the processes and practices of community development are examined in detail. Chapter 5 is concerned with broad practice concepts, such as empowerment, participation, capacity building, social inclusion and strategy development, and discusses the issues of professionalism and competency. The nature and tasks of community organisations are explained in chapter 6. In chapter 7, key activities of community development work are examined in detail. In chapter 8 issues of diversity and difference are explored, and principles and strategies for responding to difference are analysed, including a review of cross-cultural competence. Chapter 9 is concerned with funding and research issues as key aspects of survival for community organisations. In Part 3, the two concluding chapters elaborate on the critiques and dilemmas that face community development workers. Chapter 10 discusses the critiques, difficulties and dilemmas in community development theory and practice. It includes a discussion of our own assumptions and orthodoxies and the issues associated with the idea of 'pure' community development. A major issue covered in this book is whether community development offers practices and principles that contribute to the social needs of contemporary society and provide a new form of politics that is appropriate to our time, or whether it involves misguided 'heroic' attempts to change power structures that are doomed to failure because they always operate at the margins of the major determining power struggles. Chapter 11 revisits this challenge and reviews community development in the current period. It concludes by identifying some possible directions for the next decade.

About the author

Professor Susan Kenny is the Director of the Centre for Citizenship, Development and Human Rights at Deakin University. She has extensive practical research and consultancy experience in community development in Australia and internationally, and has published extensively on issues in community development and community organisations, including *Rhetorics of Welfare: Uncertainty, Choice and Voluntary Associations*, with Kevin Brown and Bryan Turner (2000), *Post-disaster Reconstruction: Lessons from Aceh*, co-edited with Matthew Clarke and Ismet Fanany (2010), and *Challenging Capacity Building*, co-edited with Matthew Clarke (2010). She has many years' experience in constructing and teaching community development courses at both undergraduate and postgraduate levels. In this fourth edition of *Developing Communities for the Future*, she brings together her insights from research, practice and teaching to provide an accessible, comprehensive and highly relevant analysis of the contexts, issues and everyday practices of community development, focusing on Australia.

Acknowledgements

Cengage Learning would like to thank the lecturers who provided comments on the previous edition or reviewed draft chapters, including those who provided anonymous feedback as well as the following reviewers:

Dr Uschi Bay – Deakin University
Dr Phil Connors – Deakin University
Claudia Cunningham – Metropolitan South Institute of TAFE
Dr Mike Dee – Queensland University of Technology
Jan Falloon – University of Western Sydney
Joseph Fleming – University of Tasmania
Dr Kalpana Goel – University of South Australia
Maurice Hanlon – Australian Catholic University
Jenny Jakobs – Massey University New Zealand
Associate Professor Philip Mendes – Monash University
Dr David Palmer – Murdoch University
Cathy Trembath – Monash University
Dr Anthea Vreugdenhil – University of Tasmania

PART 1

Background and basics

Chapter 1	The nature of community development	2
Chapter 2	The context	41
Chapter 3	Theoretical perspectives and concepts	83
Chapter 4	The role of the state	137

CHAPTER 1

The nature of community development

Overview

This chapter introduces the ways in which community development can be understood as a method of organising for social and political change, an approach or philosophy, and a job or profession. Using brief case studies, or vignettes, the chapter draws out the key themes of community development. While community development deals with new issues, many of its precepts are based on ideas that go back to antiquity. These ideas emphasise that humans can and must contribute collectively to the way a society is run, through participating in decision making, feeling a sense of belonging to the group and having respect for all other human beings. A starting point for an exploration of any field of study and practice is the terminology used. Community development is full of terms and concepts that have an assumed, often positive, meaning and this chapter introduces some of these. This discussion is followed by a review of the sites of community development practice and the roles of community development workers. The final part of the chapter considers the principles and processes of community development.

Introduction

In its most general sense, community development refers to a method of organising for social and political change. It is understood variously as an occupation, a community practice and a political activity, all of which are based on particular philosophical understandings of the world. Whatever descriptor is used, community development is based on a set of principles for collective involvement in the ways that we organise our lives.

Dissatisfaction with how human societies are organised today has led to many searches for alternatives. Some of these searches, such as those undertaken by religious, political and economic fundamentalists, have involved a quest for simple and certain answers. Alternatively, some people emphasise the need for a new future-oriented **emancipatory politics** appropriate for the twenty-first century. Such an emancipatory politics is not so much concerned with a linear path to final ends, but with continuous multidimensional processes. Community development is located in this second approach to the way we organise our lives. Community development practitioners do not seek refuge in simple and certain answers. From a community development perspective, while it is important to understand the lessons of history, these do not necessarily apply to contemporary contexts.

Community development involves the quest for processes and structures that as far as possible ensure that people who are affected by decisions have collective ownership and control of, and responsibility for, those decisions, and that they are based on mutual respect and trust, and sharing of knowledge, ideas and resources. Community development practitioners work alongside communities to identify community members' collective needs and priorities; to develop assets, talents and resources; and to access new resources. While the starting point for community development is the assumption that all communities have existing assets, talents and resources, community development is also based on an understanding that communities can also be resourced and facilitated by governments, statutory bodies and private institutions.

The long vision of community development is to establish societies in which existing knowledge and expertise is validated and in which people have much more control of their lives. For many community development practitioners, we can broadly visualise this society today. While we do not seek a blueprint for such societies, because community development involves continuing processes, we can envisage the principles of such a society. It would:

- redistribute resources more equitably and sustainably
- maximise opportunities for people to work together to identify goals, develop assets and fulfil needs
- embrace choice, difference and respect
- be underpinned by the principles of human rights
- be more tolerant, cooperative, creative, democratic and ecologically sensitive than existing societies.

Importantly, this society would not be a static one. It would be a society in which members have learnt to live with uncertainty, continual change and diversity. It would be based on an emancipatory politics that recognises the complexity of our daily life.

In general, people working in community development tend to be modest and make no grand claims about solving the problems of the world. They promise no blueprint or definitive agenda for social change. Instead, community development is conceptualised as a living, dynamic and challenging endeavour, sometimes simple and coherent, but usually complex, contradictory and full of dilemmas. While this book engages with the broad claims of community development, it also considers the more modest everyday activities of community development work and the contexts that facilitate and hinder these activities.

We can begin with a discussion of where and how people undertake community development work. People engage in community development as unpaid members of a local community group; as full-time paid workers in roles in neighbourhood houses; undertaking community development roles as part of a job description (for example, working for a local council in fire-affected rural communities); or working for and alongside refugees as a community lawyer. At any one time, thousands of people in Australia are involved in community development work, beavering away on projects that take many forms, which might be tucked away in ordinary houses in suburban streets, or in old office

Background and basics

blocks in the central business district of a capital city, or shopfronts in a small rural town. We drive past the signs outside these premises, which say, for example, Refugee Support Group, Environment Hub, Heritage Centre or Gay Action Group. Not only are the locations of community development programs well known, but also the issues, practices and processes embodied in community development are in some ways recognisable to us all.

Community development projects have been established in Indigenous communities, international aid agencies, neighbourhood houses, **culturally and linguistically diverse (CALD)** groups, public housing communities and programs developed by local and state governments. They include women's projects, disabilities rights projects, community legal and community health organisation, self-help groups, community education and arts projects, international aid programs and environment action campaigns.

Let us consider some specific settings of community development in Australia. Like the other case studies in this book, the following case studies are amalgams of several projects and are presented to show the range of community development activities.

case study

SOUTHSIDE GARDENERS

The site is a community garden located on a housing estate in an inner urban suburb in a capital city. An elderly man is taking a group of primary school children around the garden, explaining how to grow vegetables, an expertise he has built up over 70 years of gardening. For some of the children this is the first experience of a fruit and vegetable garden, and they are fascinated, especially when they are given the opportunity to pick and eat fresh raspberries. The garden exists because a group of residents in the estate put a proposal for a community garden to the Minister of Planning when they heard about plans to sell off part of the housing estate land. With the help of their own Southside Tenants' Association and the state-based Tenants' Advice and Advocacy Coalition, the residents drew up plans for a garden as an alternative to commercial development. Today the use of and responsibility for the garden is in the hands of a democratically elected group who call themselves the Southside Gardeners, with the support of the Southside Tenants' Association. The garden is now regularly profiled as an example of what local people can do when they act collectively. Members of Southside Gardeners, many of whom are elderly, have set up a website explaining how they campaigned for the garden and offering suggestions about what to plant and when, and sharing recipes for great vegetarian meals. These participants from the community are involved in community development.

ROCKY HILL REFUGEE ACTION GROUP

This second community development setting is the small shire hall in a relatively isolated mining town, where a meeting of residents is organising a multicultural night to be held the following month. The chair of the meeting is an Iraqi woman and the organising committee comprises people of diverse backgrounds. While those involved in the community activities are not formally described as community development practitioners, they are undertaking community development. The meeting has been convened by the Rocky Hill RAG, or Refugee Action Group, a group affiliated with the national body, the Coalition for Refugee and Asylum Seekers. The aims of the Rocky Hill RAG are to support refugees in the community, encourage good intercultural relations in Australia, raise public awareness about the Australian Government's obligations to give refuge to asylum seekers, and ensure humane and dignified treatment of asylum seekers and refugees. Before any refugee families had arrived in town, many residents had been apprehensive about how they should react to 'people of different cultures'. However, these anxieties evaporated quickly once the families arrived. The Rocky Hill RAG immediately organised English classes and found part-time employment for many of the newcomers. The first meeting place had been in the local schools and it was discovered that some of the refugees had been teachers before they came to Australia. They volunteered to help in the primary schools as teachers' aids, and they were warmly welcomed. The children struck up friendships too. Today, refugee families now comprise the majority of the members of Rocky Hill RAG. Many new social connections have been established, and this is clearly demonstrated by the ease with which people talked to each other at the meeting, and debated and argued in the spirit of mutual benefit and learning.

ARTS IN THE COMMUNITY – THE NARBARONG THEATRE GROUP

The setting of the third example of community development is a central Australian town, characterised by a dwindling population, high suicide rates, family fragmentation and high bankruptcy and unemployment rates. The community arts worker for the region spent several months visiting and talking with a range of people in the area, as well as organising a public meeting and local workshops to hear what people wanted from a community arts worker. As a result, a community arts liaison group has been developed. It has taken a lease on a local hall and established a community arts program that incorporates several projects.

A group of young Aboriginal people, with the assistance of an Aboriginal community development worker who has worked closely with the Aboriginal community, has established its own band, with instruments and audio technology provided through an arts grant. Another group of young people of diverse cultural backgrounds has established a street theatre group that performs at the local shopping centre and schools. In addition, people of various social and ethnic backgrounds and ages have participated in the production of a play. In six months they conceived a theme, scripted, cast and produced a satire about the demise of the town. Throughout this process all members of the theatre group participated in making decisions about such matters as the style of props and lighting and the choice of director. In the overall process, the community developed a renewed sense of identity and solidarity. With the success of the play in Australia, a number of international visitors have come to the town and the Narbarong Theatre Group have joined an international network of Indigenous actors. They are now embarking on an international exchange program.

Key themes

Each of these case studies demonstrates aspects of community development. Community development takes place among groups of people. Sometimes formal organisations are established for and by a group of people; at other times organisation is very loose, such as in the case of the Southside Gardeners. In all cases, however, the people involved share some common interest and are sufficiently motivated to come together to act on it. These groups of people who join together are identified as communities, although the term 'community', like community development itself, can be problematic as it is often based on unarticulated assumptions and can carry a range of meanings. These difficulties are discussed in chapter 2. In each of these examples people are being given more control of aspects of their lives. There is sharing of information, skills and resources. Each group works with existing assets. The projects described in the case studies involve the principles of collective action and solidarity and bring people together. They all illustrate the importance of practising by example.

For the Narbarong Theatre Group, solidarity extends beyond face-to-face relations and involves cross-cultural solidarity beyond traditional ideas of community. As will be discussed in this book, community development encompasses more than the traditional idea of homogeneous geographically based communities. It increasingly operates cross-culturally, transregionally and transnationally, as projects and campaigns are organised around national and global networks.

Each project reflects a commitment to the idea of **subsidiarity**; that is, that power should be devolved to the grassroots, so that decisions are made in a bottom-up rather than a top-down manner. As Hirst puts it, as far as possible, welfare should be organised around and controlled by self-governing associations, consistent with the effective governance of the affairs in question (Hirst, 1994:20). The idea of change from below, as Ife (2002:101) points out, is at the heart of community development. Today, the idea of subsidiarity is manifested in the hundreds of thousands of community empowerment projects being undertaken throughout the world. Strengthening the principle of subsidiarity requires structural and institutional changes. It requires the deepening of democratic politics to ensure the meaningful participation of community members.

Community development work is premised on the need to redress the imbalance of power between groups in society. It is committed to empowering those who lack resources and opportunities and those who suffer isolation. Each of the projects in the case studies encourages the development of resources, skills and opportunities for ordinary people. The activities in the case studies operate on the principle of community-generated social inclusion. Each involves attempts to overcome community fragmentation and isolation by providing opportunities for participating in community activities and programs.

Community development is committed to the idea that people can and should take more collective control and ownership of their resources and their future directions. These case studies show ways that people can have more control over their lives. For example, even in modest ways, they can take responsibility for identifying their own needs, developing their own strengths and assets, and managing their own welfare, resources and directions. Ownership and control is facilitated by establishing supportive communities based on developing and sharing resources, social participation and mutual support activities.

While community development principles are invoked in grassroots projects and campaigns, community development activities are not necessarily part of a formal project, nor do they necessarily require the employment of a paid community development worker. People come and go as part of a community group.

Community development practitioners in the case studies identify with, and participate in, the community with which they are working. That is, they work with, and for, communities. This means that they usually do not work primarily from a private office. Their work involves outreach activities, meeting the community on their own territory, for example.

The case studies demonstrate that the role of community development is to help communities to identify strengths, projects, issues and needs – as they themselves see them, in their terms of reference – and to facilitate the collective development or resolution of these. Thus, when community development workers work with and for people, they do this not from a patronising perspective as outside experts, but on the basis of mutual emancipation.

Shared contexts

Community development workers are subject to the very political, social and economic systems that constrain and facilitate the community they are working with. This can be expressed as:

- If you are here to help me, you are part of the problem.
- If you are here because you understand that your emancipation is inextricably tied up with mine, then we can get on with it (see Wadsworth, 1991).

It is important to acknowledge that community development activities do not take place in a vacuum. While community development operating at the local level can make a real difference to people's lives, broad structural, political, cultural and social contexts can constrain or facilitate community development activities and programs. Consequently, one of the key aims of community development is to build structures that facilitate participation in decision making at all levels of social development. This requires processes to be established that enable a community to have access to and, as far as possible, democratic control of knowledge, resources and power structures. Hence, community development is based on a commitment to the empowerment of ordinary people in such a way that they have real options for their future. A key concern is with powerless people, including those who do not own or control the means of production, traditionally known as the working class; women; unemployed people; people with disabilities; and people who have been rendered marginal through age, gender assignment, sexual preference, 'race' or ethnicity.

From a broad perspective, the rationale of community development interventions is to alter the way things are done in general and to change the structures of society. That is, community development intervenes in the processes of social change and development to initiate forms of social organisation that are sensitive to social justice issues and the collective needs of communities. The idea that community programs change the way things are done draws our attention to the fact that community development can also be conceptualised as a form of politics.

Community development interventions aim to change the way groups of people relate to each other and to their physical habitat. While these interventions generally occur on a small scale, they are based on ideas of a better and mutually enriching society, one that rejects an emphasis on individual competition for wealth, status and power, and unlimited exploitation of the natural environment. This view of an alternative society draws on a specific approach to what it is to be human. Over 150 years ago, Karl Marx pointed out that humans are productive, social and creative beings who enter into relationships with other humans in order to produce their world (see Marx, 1977). From this perspective, human capacities are best nurtured in societies in which they can be sustained physically, in which they have personal autonomy and in which they have an equal say in the way society is run. Collective endeavour is facilitated when people have collective control of society's resources and can deliberate and negotiate rationally when there is disagreement and conflict. In such a society people participate actively and responsibly in decisions that affect their lives and they have a sense of commitment to the wellbeing of others.

Generating social capital

One idea that has helped to highlight the role of **community organisations** in society, and the positive contribution of community development, is **social capital**. This term, which has now entered common discourse, refers to the way that certain types of social relationships are beneficial to social cohesion and social development. Such relationships are based on trust, mutuality, sharing and cooperative effort. They generate networks of people prepared to work and act together; in effect, generating solidarity as well as greater trust and mutuality. The link between community development and social capital is important. The principles and practices of community development – such as the principles of **social justice** and **human rights**, for example – require mutuality. Processes and practices invoked to facilitate the fulfilment of the needs of a community, such as meetings and collective action, involve trust and cooperation. More is said about social capital in following chapters.

Defining community development

Following the discussion above, we can summarise community development as a method for empowering communities to take collective control and responsibility for their own development. Effective control requires the development of ongoing structures and processes by which communities can identify, develop and address their own strengths, issues, needs and problems within their own terms of reference. Effective community control requires adequate resources, including income, material resources and knowledge and a strong skills base.

Terminology

The power of language and terminology to set agendas and give specific meanings to words should never be underestimated. As Chambers (2005:187) points out, understandings and use of terms can change how we think and act. At the same time, language is not static. Words and meanings continually change and reshape how we perceive the world. As with any human endeavour, understanding terminology is critical to grasping the nature of activities and issues in community development. Indeed, as noted above, the term 'community' is beleaguered by a range of meanings, many of which carry strong ideological connotations. In community development work, the term 'community' is used in a broad sense. It refers to a group of people who share a common identity, which might be based on geographical location, class or ethnic background, or a special interest, such as a common concern about the destruction of rainforests. Traditionally, the term has referred to groups of people involved in face-to-face relations. However, with the realisation of the interconnectedness of all life on the planet, the idea of community is being extended to groups of people who share an identity and interest across regions and national borders, who might be networked as **virtual communities**. The idea of community is discussed in detail in chapter 2.

The term **development**, like the term 'community', also has different meanings. While development is a generic term, referring to change in general, when it is put into a social context it is often seen in a **social evolutionary framework**. The social evolutionary framework considers the direction of change to be towards increasing differentiation and complexity, and integration of the parts of society that enable a continuing adaptation to changing conditions. The effect of this process is to enhance the resilience of society (Spencer, 1964). Growing complexity and adaptation are also often seen within economic terms of reference and linked with increased economic growth and higher material standards of living, which purportedly enhance the resilience of the economic system. In turn, increasing national economic productivity, more sophisticated information technology and exploitation of natural resources have been seen as indicators of development. This understanding is linked to Western ideas of the value of modernity and economic growth, or more specifically, growth of capitalist economies.

However, as the United Nations Development Programme (UNDP) and Nederveen Pieterse (2001:6) point out, the lineages of the concept of development are quite mixed. The United Nations Development Programme (1996: iii) acknowledged the need for different conceptions of development in its 1996 report:

> The paradigm shift is still in the making. But more and more policymakers in many countries are reaching the unavoidable conclusion that, to be valuable and legitimate, development progress, not nationally and internationally – must be people centred, equitably distributed, and environmentally and socially sustainable.

While the term development refers to the interventions in different societies that are propelled by the desire to apply science and technology and neo-liberal economics, it also refers to managing the changes arising from such applications. Goulet (1985) has noted the ambiguities of the term, highlighting how it can refer either to a process or to certain objectives. The idea of development as a process tends to emphasise the importance of quantification and the use of statistical indicators, such as incomes, literacy rates and productivity, to demonstrate the extent of development in a community or a nation. The idea of development as an objective is to overcome the degradation that is seen to come from underdevelopment. Here, development evokes ideas of a qualitatively better life. The desirability of development as a goal – involving higher standards of living, economic growth and evermore sophisticated technology – is usually taken for granted.

It is probably no exaggeration to say that the traditional idea of development is in considerable trouble today. There are many reasons for this. First, if we examine the values on which development as a goal is usually based, we have, in the past, generally found unquestioning acceptance of unrestrained 'development' of the natural environment, such as the exploitation of natural resources. However, we are now finding a growing awareness of the ecological limits to growth, and the human causes of climate change. This awareness has resulted in unease regarding the 'business as usual' approach to economic growth, and its corollaries, the increasing release of carbon emissions, and the impending disastrous consequences on climate change (Stern, 2006).

Second, the idea of development as linear cumulative progress, which is embedded in what has come to be known as the **project of modernity**, has lost credibility. As Nederveen Pieterse (2001:1) argues, the primacy of modernity has come into question:

> The classic aim of development, modernization or catching up with advanced countries, is in question because modernization is no longer an obvious ambition ... in view of ecological problems, the consequences of technological change and many other problems. Westernization no longer seems attractive in a time of reevaluation of local culture and local diversity.

The promise of modernity was that by applying modern methods of science, technological development and rational thinking to all human activities, the wellbeing of all humankind would continuously improve. We do not have the evidence that all human life has improved, and with the dark clouds of global warming upon us, it is now looking more like the promises of modernity have backfired, and are heralding a decidedly poorer outlook for human existence. Third, taking a Western capitalist idea of progress or growth as the benchmark for development is ethnocentric. Even within this ethnocentric viewpoint, there are inconsistencies. Some commentators have pointed out that it is possible to have high national economic growth with declining living standards for the majority of the population (Goulet, 1985; Seers, 1969). More recently, Ife (2009) has pointed out that in the context of the ecological crisis facing the world, the idea of development as growth is quite problematic. Community development recognises the effects of a naive faith in the so-called benefits of development as unrestrained economic growth. Indeed, 'Too much growth produces negative rather than positive consequences' (Ife, 2009:19). Ife explains how growth can be simply equated with quantitative changes, such as getting bigger, while (human) development can be connected with qualitative change, or in Ife's words 'getting better'. Getting better, of course, is not the same as 'getting bigger'. Thus there is a clear contrast between the idea of development as economic growth and the idea of development as the strengthening of human relationships. The uncoupling of the ideas of growth and development is well overdue in the broad development arena.

Fourth, even now as the folly of defining development through Western eyes is apparent, mainstream development discourse and practice persist in carrying the legacies of their colonial past, as Nederveen Pieterse (2001:28) and Kothari (2005:143) point out. Western nations continue to impose structures and ways of doing things that are (often falsely) presented to be in the interest of those who are powerless. Mainstream development discourse and practice continue to provide examples of techniques for establishing particular mindsets that legitimate the actions of the powerful. Fifth, whether it involves control by Western 'experts', or by local 'experts', the history of 'development projects' is a history of intervention by outsiders in the ways that a group of people 'do things'. Such interventions have usually been undertaken in a top-down manner, often completely ignoring the strengths, resources, skills and expertise in the 'recipient' community. In ignoring the existing assets of the recipient populations, such interventions have often had destructive outcomes.

Finally, an obvious difficulty in these formulations of development is how to discern the bases upon which to judge desirable change or development that in the past has been known as 'progress'. Hundreds of factors could be taken as indicators of progress in a society, including the Western economic benchmark, gross national product (the monetary value of the total amount of goods and services produced within some boundary, such as a nation state or a region) and its derivatives, including an increase in number of consumer goods available, a decline in crime rates, an increase in a community's self-sufficiency, an increase in equality of opportunity, an increase in adequate housing, or a decrease in the occurrence of racial conflict. A number of questions arise: How do we decide which indicators to use? Can the indicators be ranked in order of importance? How do we measure the indicators in a rigorous comparative framework? These are complex issues that require discussion of issues of philosophical, anthropological and sociological significance.

In the light of the critiques and complexities identified above, notions of development based on ideas of a 'good and fulfilling life' have been proposed. Here, we can refer to some of the key ideas that are embodied in the concept of 'humanness and human fulfilment'. Goulet (1985) has identified three core values that are important to human fulfilment. These are sustenance, which includes access to nourishing food, good health, shelter and protection; self-esteem, which involves a belief in one's own value, a sense of worth and self-respect; and freedom from servitude, which involves having real choices in one's life. Working from Goulet's formulation of human needs, Todaro (1994:18) identifies development as

> both a physical reality and a state of mind in which society has, through some combination of social, economic and institutional processes, secured the means of obtaining a better life.

For Todaro, the three key objectives of development are to increase the availability and widen the distribution of basic life-sustaining goods, such as food and shelter to raise the levels of living, including greater attention to cultural values, as well as higher incomes and more jobs to expand the range of economic and social choices in society. A similar view of human need is proposed by Doyal and Gough (1991), who extend the focus on cultural values. They argue that to be fulfilled, humans not only need physical sustenance, but also the capacity to participate in social and cultural life.

However, these broad views still leave the questions of how to decide what are the indicators of cognitive and emotional competence, and how political freedom to choose lifestyles and participate in society is measured, which brings us to the question of who decides what is a better lifestyle and a better society. For the influential Bangladeshi writer Amartya Sen (1999), it is the people themselves who decide. The key is to understand the concept of freedom. In his seminal book, *Development as Freedom* (1999), he explores the relationship between freedom and development, and argues that development is about expanding the choices people have to lead lives they value. For Sen, freedom is both a basic constituent of development in itself and also a way of achieving development. Real freedom must also involve capabilities that enable people to do and be what they want. Development is a matter of eliminating the obstacles to freedom.

Drawing on ideas from Sen, from a community development perspective, the answer to these questions cannot be made just by expert economists, social scientists or politicians, although such people might be called upon to provide information on an issue in their specialist field. Instead, it is up to the members of a community themselves to decide what constitutes a qualitatively better society and work out ways to facilitate such a society. Relying on the people themselves to decide what constitutes a qualitatively better society, of course, involves bottom-up development. This is use of the term development adopted in this book.

It is important to note also that the term 'community development' rather than 'community work' has been adopted in this book, because it focuses on the importance of change in society. Implicit in the notion of development are ideas about transformation. The concept of community development stands in strong contrast to the way the concept of community work is now often used by authorities. Government and education officials commonly use community work to refer to 'voluntary' activities engaged in by unemployed young people and schoolchildren. The judiciary and correctional service officers identify community work as community service for offenders – as an alternative to a period in prison, for example. Thus, as noted above, in community development circles, the term 'community development' refers to

- an approach or philosophy
- a job or profession
- a method of organising for change
- an intervention or political activity.

Familiar principles

Community development deals with new issues, but many of its precepts are based on ideas that go back to antiquity. These ideas emphasise that humans can and must contribute collectively to the way a society is run, through participating in decision making, feeling a sense of belonging to the group and having respect for all other human beings. While these ideas or principles have never been fully achieved in any society, they have existed throughout human history. An important notion underlying community development is the **power of example**. By demonstrating that things can be done differently or that things can work effectively in other ways, community development shows that ordinary people can have real choices in their lives. The belief that ordinary people can and should take responsibility for the direction of society has underpinned movements for deepening democratic principles through deliberative democracy; for example, the people's struggles for democratic change in Eastern Europe and Asia in the 1990s, as well as the protests against the undemocratically based power of the World

Economic Forum and other institutions of global capitalism. It underpins support for the green and environment groups. The importance of participation in decision making underlies the demands of workers for industrial democracy and control in the workplace, and demands by women for the control of their own bodies.

Community development work and community organisations

A useful starting point for a discussion of what community practitioners 'do' is to differentiate between community development methods and activities that are found in any community, and employment as a community development worker. Community development methods are used in many activities in Australia today, whether they are utilised by unpaid activists, in unpaid participation in international exchanges, in unpaid civic activities, in paid neighbourhood-strengthening projects or in paid advocacy work. In Australia, the major employers of community development workers have traditionally been community organisations. Community organisations are non-profit organisations and fall within what is known as the third, community-based or non-government sector. The most recent study of the non-profit or third sector reports that there are 889 900 employers in the sector and 4 616 100 volunteers (Productivity Commission, 2010, p. xxviii). While we do not have information on the number of community development practitioners in either paid or volunteer positions, the figures indicate the growing employment in the sector overall.

However, local governments are increasingly also employing community development practitioners to work with communities, community groups and community organisations in a range of ways, as general facilitators and researchers, and in community building and capacity building programs, in such positions as liaison officer in a Vietnamese cultural centre or a tenants' organisation.

In the neo-liberal climate dominating Australian economic and political life, there has been a continued commitment to reduce direct government services for community affairs by such means as the introduction of a **user-pays** approach to welfare services and the **privatisation** of government programs. That is, community programs that were once run by government departments are now often **contracted-out** to what is known as the private sector, comprising both for-profit and not-for-profit organisations.

Privatisation policies are a double-edged sword for community organisations. On one hand, privatisation means that governments contract services, projects and programs to not-for-profit community organisation, which means that the organisations are able to make these services more responsive to the grassroots community. Contracting-out can also mean that community organisations have access to more funds. Winning government contracts to deliver community programs, then, can give more resources and control to community organisations. However, there is often little room to manoeuvre within a government contract, especially when it is based on a competitive tender, and community organisations end up becoming agents and risk managers for governments. Because government funds are increasingly attached to projects, 'core funding' to maintain infrastructure costs such as rent and a coordinator's pay has become more difficult to obtain.

One resolution to the problem of reliance on government funds has been for community organisations to develop small business enterprises on a cooperative basis, for example. One approach is to argue for community development to be moulded in a way that stimulates social entrepreneurship. In the **social entrepreneurship** approach, business strategies are adopted. Community development workers are constructed as leaders who are able to seize opportunities and use their initiative to develop creative community-based projects that can become sustainable through the generation of financial surpluses.

In summary, community development workers include:

- paid workers in specific community development positions – these people might come either from outside or within the community
- unpaid 'organic' workers who are part of the community and work from the ground up – these people devote much of their time to community activities and are respected as part of the community
- people employed in other occupations who undertake some community development activities as part of their job description.

The social and community services industry

Community development in Australia is often understood as part of what has come to be known as the **social and community services industry**. There has been considerable debate about what actually constitutes the social and community services industry. However, a general consensus focuses on human service work, which provides a range of services designed to enhance the quality of life of those using the services, or provide personal or family support to consumers of services, or advance the interests of a group within society, such as in a neighbourhood (Social and Community Services Industry Training Board, 1990:28). The name 'industry' is a reminder of the shift from traditional notions of welfare as charity to modern notions of welfare programs based on service delivery, community needs and strategic planning. Within an industry framework, programs are to be provided by a professional workforce, working according to industrial awards or contracts with regulated or contracted wages and working conditions, industrial and training policies and unionisation.

As Bryson (1989) has pointed out, being identified as an industry links the social and community services to the economic system. In view of the esteem in which economics is held in contemporary society, this gives it added status and (potential) political and industrial muscle. The sector has traditionally comprised a largely female workforce, with poor working conditions and low pay rates. Unionisation, the establishment of industrial awards and the development of education and training opportunities significantly changed the profile of the sector during the 1980s.

Overall, community development has a mixed reputation within the social and community services industry. To some, it has taken on the spectre of a revolutionary front, the harbinger of radical action groups that are seen to challenge the very foundations of society. To others, community development work represents a nostalgic and naive longing for a romanticised sense of community, a panacea used to calm and subdue the working class and the powerless. Between these two extremes is the view that community development work is a modest attempt to facilitate people's efforts to gain control of their lives. As we will see in later chapters, all of these views have elements of truth. Community development aims to, and does, empower ordinary people by facilitating participation in, and ownership of, community programs and directions. Today, many social and community service jobs acknowledge the importance of community participation, and accountability to service users is an important aspect of service provision – although most community participation remains symbolic and there is scarcely any real ownership of programs and projects by communities themselves. Community development in the social and community services sector is identified with these empowering aspects of new ways of thinking about the social and community services. It can give ordinary people the knowledge and the skills to work collectively to resolve issues of everyday life. Community development can also significantly radicalise people, and demands for social justice and human rights can threaten the status quo. Yet community development can certainly also be co-opted by the powers-that-be. It has been used to deflect people's attention from issues regarding a fair distribution of resources and to delude people that they have complete control of their lives.

The range of community and human service jobs available is illustrated in classified advertisements in newspapers and on the Internet in 'community', 'government' and 'local government' sections, under the specific headings of 'community development', 'community', 'policy', 'youth', 'human services', 'health and local government', for example. A cursory glance at these advertisements indicates the range of positions available, such as campaign coordinator, disability recreation coordinator, outreach worker, environment worker, project officer in women's health, Aboriginal development worker, community support and access worker, Indigenous rights worker, community arts project worker, housing worker, rural women's outreach worker, youth worker, police community liaison officer, legal aid worker, environment centre project worker, community planner, diverse sexualities access worker and community services policy officer.

Other occupations that use community development

In addition to specific community development positions, there is now a wide range of jobs and occupations that use community development approaches and methods. Community development workers and community development approaches are now being employed at different levels of government and also in some parts of the for-profit sector as part of a new approach that focuses on the links between financial profit, social development and environmental impact – or what has come to be known as the 'triple bottom line'. This approach is located in the idea that businesses and corporations have a general social responsibility (sometimes known as **corporate social responsibility, or CSR**), as well as a responsibility to shareholders and owners to make a profit. Following a number of overseas programs, such as those run by the Body Shop, in which corporations commit to social good or **corporate citizenship**, some Australian corporations are committing substantial resources to developing social and environmental responsibilities. There are also practical reasons for employing community development workers, as large corporations such as mining companies need to liaise with local Indigenous communities, and where social impact research is a legal requirement. It should be noted that there is some debate about these new ways of community development, including whether corporate 'giving' is just a clever marketing strategy. We discuss this issue further in the following chapter.

Community development as international practice

In Australia, working as an employee in the social and community services industry or as an unpaid participant in a small group in an isolated community, it is easy to forget that community development has international dimensions. In this section, we note three of these dimensions:

- the international acceptance of the importance of community development
- how community development is affected by global forces
- how globalisation also opens up new opportunities for community development.

The first dimension draws our attention to the idea that community development comprises practices and pursuits that are internationally recognised. Rossouw (1996:2) has drawn out the following definition of community development from United Nations documents:

> The term *community development* has come into international usage to connote the process by which the efforts of the people themselves are united with those of governmental authorities to improve the economic, social and cultural conditions of communities, to integrate these communities into the life of the nation and to enable them to contribute fully to national progress.

In 1995 the Non-Government Organization Forum at the World Summit for Social Development in Copenhagen, Denmark, argued that social (or community) development is a

> question of innovating and devising local answers to community needs, promoting the skills and energy of women in full equity with men, and benefiting from valuable traditions, as well as new technologies ... The keys to effective development are equity, participation, self-reliance, sustainability and a holistic approach to community life (United Nations Development Programme, 1996:2).

In his comparative review of community development, Campfrens (1997:23) has identified common social values and principles that inform community development internationally. These include a commitment to cooperative, responsible and active communities; the ideal of **participatory democracy** and the enhancement of political participation; the development of the community's capacity to identify and solve problems; the resourcing of communities, including those that are most marginalised, to fulfil their needs in their terms of reference; and a commitment to community integration.

Commitment to changing values, structures and institutions to facilitate the empowerment of ordinary people has been championed in an increasing number of international projects and forums. For example, in a statement that resonates with the discussion above of community development understandings of 'development', Eade and Williams (1995:9), authors of the *Oxfam Handbook of Development and Relief*, state:

> Strengthening people's capacity to determine their own values and priorities, and to organise themselves to act on these, is the basis of development. Development is about women and men becoming empowered to bring about positive changes in their lives: about personal growth with public action; about both the process and the outcome of challenging poverty, oppression and discrimination; and about the realisation of human potential through social and economic justice. Above all, it is about the process of transforming lives, and transforming societies.

The second dimension draws attention to the many ways in which global forces impact on community development. Campfrens (1997) argues that while it is useful to place community development in a national context, it is also important to understand how unprecedented mega-level changes are affecting communities across the globe. These mega-level changes include the tenacity of neo-liberal policies, and the exploitation of workers and their communities in developing countries. Other forms of **globalisation** have been made possible through new technologies. The Internet has facilitated the establishment of international networks of community organisations. New global politics concerned with environmental, social and human rights issues have developed. These other international links open up new ways of accessing information and new forms of cooperation for community development workers.

The third aspect of community development as international practice focuses on the ways that globalisation can also provide significant opportunities for community development. For example, globalisation can mean that struggles that were once with national governments and businesses are now with international government bodies and businesses. But this does not mean that the local community struggles are necessarily becoming less important or obsolete. Nor does globalisation mean that a process of homogenisation in community development is taking place. In fact, as the powers of nation states are weakened by the forces of transnational business and other international political players, diverse actions at the community level can become more significant. While often affected by international forces, community struggles and programs are also set in the context of local conditions.

The roles of community development workers

Community development aims to provide ordinary people with maximum control over their lives. This requires intervention in existing structures and 'ways of doing things' in order to facilitate access to, and control of, resources and the development of new processes that can enhance the lives of powerless and disadvantaged people. The following discussion sets out some of the actual tasks of community development practitioners, providing a taste of the everyday work of community development. It is an introduction only, because community development will be practised differently in different contexts. Moreover, as Ife (2010) points out, rather than working from easily learned rules of practice, community development practitioners need to understand principles and processes at a more theoretical level, more like a 'street-level' intellectual than a technician. As street-level intellectuals, they will need to be able to understand and assess a situation in its many dimensions and work collaboratively and imaginatively with the other members of a community, in the spirit of mutual and continual learning and reflection.

Tasks

Community development workers undertake a range of tasks with and for communities. These tasks include:

- researching and analysing community issues, needs and problems
- identifying existing community assets, including knowledge, resources, skills and capacities
- preparing policy and issue-based submissions
- developing and maintaining community resources
- identifying innovative programs
- identifying innovative ways of developing resources
- developing, maintaining and evaluating community programs
- strategic planning
- developing, interpreting and implementing community policy
- developing and maintaining democratic and participatory decision-making processes within the community
- representing, advocating, negotiating and mediating within and between communities, agencies, institutions and government
- developing and maintaining networks and liaising with community groups, other workers and professionals, agencies and government
- developing and transferring skills and knowledge in community organisation, advocacy, resource development, cultural awareness and other relevant areas within the community
- developing ways of obtaining access to external resources and external decision-making processes
- educating the community about their rights and responsibilities
- preparing and distributing written and audiovisual material, and developing media contacts
- undertaking the administrative tasks associated with the maintenance of community projects, such as lobbying and preparing funding submissions, reports and financial documentation
- assisting members of a community in relation to other professionals, institutions, community agencies, government and other bodies
- developing community campaigns.

Abilities

In order to perform these tasks, community development workers must be able to:

- work with and for people in a self-reflective, creative and flexible way
- facilitate, in a range of ways, the empowerment of powerless groups in society
- identify the existing skills, knowledge and resources in a community
- transmit skills and knowledge
- draw on the skills and experiences of others
- think strategically
- engender a commitment to the possibility of significant change in the lives of disadvantaged people
- be sensitive to the dilemmas and contradictions of community development and to the manner in which they use their knowledge and skills.

In applying these abilities, community development workers must at all times be sensitive to the needs of the people with whom they are working.

Knowledge

It is essential that community development workers understand the general economic, social, cultural and political contexts within which they work, including:

- relevant social, economic and political theories and concepts
- the sites of community development work, including government and community organisations
- the roles of community development in these institutions and the industry, the industrial relations system and the industrial awards affecting their working conditions
- policies affecting their work
- organisational structures, processes and forms of decision making within government and non-government sectors
- the various ways in which community development operates in concrete situations, including how activities and practices are constrained by a variety of contextual factors
- where and how to obtain funds
- research methodology
- the history of community development
- the required abilities and knowledge base that is the background for the skills required to undertake community development work
- the difficulties and dilemmas in undertaking community development work.

Key skills

Key skills include:

- *Facilitation skills*: an ability to practise different techniques to help a community identify assets and issues, analyse issues and fulfil its needs. Specific skills include resource

Background and basics

development, negotiation, representation, advocacy, lobbying, delegation and submission writing.
- *Organisational skills*: an ability to manage, develop and maintain information systems, committee structures and meeting processes; set priorities; implement tasks; develop policy; schedule work; and manage finances.
- *Strategy skills*: setting goals, developing strategies, reassessing goals and evaluating progress.
- *Networking skills*: fostering and maintaining networks through liaison with other groups and individuals, and constructing alliances between groups.
- *Communication skills*: listening and responding effectively, articulating ideas, presenting points of view.
- *Research skills*: the ability to find information, make sense of it and use it, and the ability to evaluate programs.

Examples of roles

Let us look at how some of these skills might be combined in typical situations.

- A community development worker is required to prepare information for the community about specific topics, such as how to obtain emergency accommodation or what self-help groups exist. The worker must know how to collect data and present it in an accessible form with appropriate graphics. The worker will also ensure that information is presented in the languages spoken in the community.
- A community development worker in a CALD or **ethno-specific organisation** forms a network to lobby politicians about issues of relevance to their community; for example, changes to immigration policy. The worker requires strong networking, organisational and lobbying skills.
- A community development worker is employed by a municipal council to work with local community groups to establish an employment program. For this project, the worker needs research, organisational and networking skills, as well as knowledge of small business operations and financial management.
- A community wants a hazardous chemical dump removed from its locality and the site cleaned. It forms an action group that obtains funds to employ a part-time community development worker. The worker needs to be knowledgeable about political processes and key political players and able to facilitate protest action, including civil disobedience, if necessary.
- A community development worker is employed by a refugee action group to prepare information on the effects of new policies on asylum seekers and prepare press releases on how the new policies contravene human rights.
- Workers in a women's refuge are preparing a submission for funding the building of an additional bedroom for the refuge. They need to know the funding guidelines and how to demonstrate the need for a new room.
- Members of a local Australian community want to work with a small overseas NGO to provide assistance after an earthquake. A community development worker is employed

to make contact with NGOs in the earthquake-stricken province to see how the two communities could work together, focusing in the first instance on the immediate needs of the earthquake survivors.

Diversity in community development

Community development takes place in a range of sites and with a diversity of groups. Community development projects could include the following:

- an Aboriginal cooperative that operates cultural tourism programs from a shopfront in a central Australian town
- a tenants' association project situated on a public housing estate
- an ethnic group that operates a program through a local community health centre
- a group of older people running a project at several elderly citizens' clubs
- a program specifically developed as a response to rural isolation, located in a caravan
- a community radio program for gay men.

Because of the diversity of immediate contexts in which community development takes place, it is sometimes suggested that different forms of community development are required for different settings. The position taken in this book is that community development comprises general practices and principles. Practices are not set in concrete and will be modified in response to an immediate situation or cultural context. The importance of understanding cultural context and developing cross-cultural competence is discussed in chapter 8.

Principles

While there is a variety of community development activities, and there are many debates and controversies about practice, it should now be evident that some key values form the basis of community development theory, objectives, tasks, processes and practices. In this section we draw these values together to identify the key principles of community development, and we explore some of the implications of adopting these principles.

Values underpin the everyday activities, assumptions, commitments and principles of community development. It is important that community development workers are self-conscious about their principles and are aware of how these determine attitudes and practices. This is not to argue, however, that a community development worker must be a narrow ideologue. As pointed out by Thomas (1983), a community development educator in the United Kingdom, such people generally make extremely bad community development workers because they are too concerned with imposing their own views on a community. He comments that the best way a community can develop is through experience and understanding rather than having ideas imposed by someone such as a highly educated community worker, who is articulate and able to impose their views (Thomas, 1983:138–9).

Background and basics

The principles of community development are in some ways so accessible that they appear obvious. For example, we have already discussed the view that people should take control of and responsibility for their own resources. In other ways, however, the principles can be remote and intimidating. They are based on views that challenge many of the commonly held notions about society and social problems. For example, community development rests on the view that disadvantaged people can ultimately have full control of their own lives only when social structures and institutions are changed. To change institutions is to challenge existing power structures and wrest forms of power from dominant groups. For example, changing the traditional male domination of family or legal institutions requires that women challenge men's power and wrest power from men.

The community development approach to the problem of disadvantage in our society also challenges the commonsense framework in which social problems are often conceptualised. The usual response to social problems is not the restructuring of society but careful counselling of individuals who experience 'the problem' for the purpose of adapting them to their situation. This commonsense view is sometimes identified as 'blaming the victim'. It locates the cause of disadvantage within individuals themselves. It has been the traditional way of dealing with people living in poverty, with the so-called Aboriginal problem and with survivors of domestic violence. The most recent incarnation of the 'blaming the victim' approach has been in processes of **individualisation**. In contemporary societies, in which people are deemed to have unlimited choices in their lives (in conditions that have already been set), failure to 'do well' is sheeted home to individuals themselves for not making the right choices in their lives, for example. We discuss the culture of individualisation in chapter 2.

In contrast to the 'blame the victim' and individualised approaches to organising for social development, community development locates the cause of disadvantage in the entrenched and systematic inequalities of our social system, in which gender, class, race and ethnicity are key determinants of one's life chances. From this perspective, social problems such as poverty, racial discrimination and family violence cannot be fully resolved unless the very structures, institutions and beliefs that give rise to them are eliminated. For example, Australian Government policies dealing with unemployment have focused on the individuals who are unemployed, involving training, counselling and instilling a work ethic based on accepting their so-called 'mutual obligation' to society to ensure that they are motivated and 'ready for work'. This is at a time when the number of people looking for paid employment is in excess of the number of jobs available to them.

Community development opens up thinking about how to change structures, institutions and beliefs. Methods include:

- challenging existing structures; for instance, campaigning against a tax that favours the wealthy
- resourcing people who are disadvantaged; for instance, ensuring that Aboriginal communities have legal ownership of their traditional land
- establishing choices; for instance, providing the option for a survivor of family violence to remain unmolested in her own home or to move into a women's refuge.

Community development probes inequalities based on power and difference in order to reveal underlying structures and ideologies, and consequently it has natural links with critical social theories such as Marxist theory, feminist theory and theories of cultural difference. These theories are discussed in chapters 3 and 8.

Objectivity and impartiality

Community development begins with the assumption that ultimately there is no value-free objective interpretation of society and that all intellectual, practical and personal actions are guided by values and interests. Community development practitioners attempt to reveal values and articulate them clearly.

However, while it is important to understand that no selection of data or interpretation is entirely interest-free or value-free, in the actual collection and analysis of information community development practitioners must be rigorous, impartial and self-critical. It certainly does not serve the interests of a community if knowledge is deliberately distorted. For example, when undertaking research, community development workers identify different viewpoints, including those of opponents, and gather and analyse empirical data dispassionately, but in their actual use of the data they are partisan: they use it in the interests of the community that they are working with and for.

What then are the key principles underpinning community development practice? We answer this question by listing the principles first, then discussing each in turn.

The principles involve a commitment to:

- powerless people and social justice
- citizenship and human rights
- empowerment and **self-determination**
- sustainability
- collective action
- diversity
- change and involvement in conflict
- liberation, open societies and participatory democracy.

Powerless people and social justice

Community development work is committed to improving the lot of ordinary people. In the framework of community development, the terms 'ordinary people' and 'powerless people' refer to those who do not hold powerful positions in society, who are disadvantaged and who do not have ease of access to power structures.

The use of the terms 'powerless people' and 'ordinary people' is not a rejection of the class nature of most inequality; rather, it acknowledges that there are categories of disadvantage that cannot be neatly reduced to class categories, such as disadvantage accruing from gender, disability or ethnicity. Community development is concerned with ordinary people's lives, their experiences, their hopes and their visions. People are not conceptualised as objects to be studied, rescued, corrected or controlled.

Background and basics

Disadvantage, marginality, exclusion and oppression have multiple forms. They can involve a state of affairs or a process by which privileged groups or individuals systematically limit and control the lives, experiences and opportunities of groups or individuals with less power. Actions that are exclusionary and oppressive are embedded in institutions, language, behaviour, processes and practices. Presumptions in favour of men, white people and other dominant groups encode exclusion and oppression and skew all social relationships in favour of the dominant groups (see Ward & Mullender, 1991). For example, some feminists argue that the whole concept of 'woman' has come to encode oppression. That is, just to be a woman has tended to mean denial of access to the resources and power structures controlled by men. Disadvantage can be manifested in a number of ways, such as the lack of equal opportunity. This includes lack of equal access to education and cultural institutions, and exclusion from rewarding socially useful work and a liveable income.

People are also disadvantaged and exploited when they have little or no control over the means of production. The working class serves society, either by directly producing through paid or unpaid employment or by supporting producers (in families and in friendships, for example). The Marxist viewpoint is that because workers work for bosses who make large profits but pay low salaries, they are exploited. When workers cannot gain employment or are made redundant they form what Marxists have called 'the reserve army of the unemployed', who can be brought in to service the needs of capitalism when required.

A society in which groups of people are oppressed, excluded or disadvantaged, and in which there is inequality of power and resources, is one in which social justice is denied. Social justice expresses the values of equity and fairness and is concerned with:

- equal distribution of economic resources
- equality of civil, legal and industrial rights
- fair and equal access to services such as housing, health and education
- equality of opportunity for participation and decision making in society.

Commitment to powerless people and social justice requires that community development practitioners always respect the people in the communities with whom they are working, even when they might not agree with all the views of community members. Respect is a very important part of community development. In an interesting critique of the erosion of respect in contemporary society, Sennett (2004) examines the links between powerlessness and lack of respect. He comments how, when people are rendered dependent, they lose the respect of others. They become 'spectators to their own needs', experiencing 'that peculiar lack of respect which consists of not being seen, not being accounted for as full human beings' (Sennett, 2004:13). He emphasises the importance of mutual respect but points out, however, that this does not 'just happen'. It means building up trust and finding the words and gestures 'which make it felt and convincing' (2004:207). Learning how to make mutual respect happen is part of what makes a good community development worker. It is important in communities in which we are familiar with the normal ways of doing things, but it is equally if not more important in communities in which the normal ways of doing things are unfamiliar. We discuss ways of responding to unfamiliar and different situations and expectations in chapter 8.

Citizenship and human rights

A commitment to powerless people can be linked with the notion of citizenship and human rights. **Citizenship** is about what it means to be a member of society and how we contribute to the continual making of society, how we are resourced to be a member of society, what rights we have and should have as members of society, and what obligations we have to society. We can begin to unravel the concept of citizenship by drawing on the sociological discussion initiated by Marshall (1950) in Britain in the 1950s. Marshall argued that there has been a gradual extension of citizen rights, from civil rights (such as the right to free speech) to political rights (such as the right to vote) to social rights (the right to welfare). The extension of rights can be seen as part of a class compromise through which those in power extend rights to the working class in exchange for working-class acceptance of class-based economic inequalities (Turner, 1986). If we add economic rights to the list, then the rights of workers in their place of work or even to control the processes that drive the means of production can be brought into the equation.

While Marshall's formulation opened the way to a broader understanding of citizenship in the English-speaking world, it has been criticised for its ethnocentric, patriarchal and somewhat simple evolutionary approach to citizenship rights. More rigorous approaches have pointed to the highly differentiated access to rights experienced by women and minority groups, and Indigenous Australians, as an obvious example in Australia. What Marshall's discussion did set out, however, was a framework for describing the elements of membership of society and how compromises between the classes may be struck, and an analysis of how certain groups are systematically excluded from full membership and participation in society. The broad sociological concept of citizenship helps us to understand how people can be included in social, political, cultural and economic life.

One way of understanding the contemporary constructions of citizenship is to differentiate between passive and active citizenship. Passive citizenship emphasises rights and duties that are given from above, whether they be in such areas as welfare rights based on principles of social justice or citizenship obligations to obey the law based on principles of moral duty, for example. While passive rights are a necessary component in the development of citizenship, they are not enough in themselves. To ensure full citizenship, people must be empowered to participate in the continual processes of shaping their society, their communities and their identities.

Community development is concerned with ensuring that citizenship rights in the Marshallian sense are guaranteed. But it is also concerned with the obligations of citizens to treat others with dignity, to respect differences and to participate in the shaping of society. Perhaps, most importantly, community development is concerned with active citizenship, involving the active participation of communities to define issues and problems and to identify options and shape their futures. That is, while both passive citizenship based on social justice and active citizenship based on the empowerment of communities to control their own destinies are central aspects of community development, it is the active form of citizenship that nurtures community development.

Equal access to and control of resources, opportunities, knowledge and structures are needed for equal participation in decision-making processes in a society. Participation in society, access to the resources necessary for a sustainable existence and control of one's life are human rights. Equal participation in decision-making processes is a human right. Human rights include those rights derived from what it is to be human. They are designed to protect the integrity of this humanity. They refer to actions and attitudes about how people ought to be treated by other people, institutions and governing bodies – for example, the right not to be tortured – and what they are entitled to do – for example, the right to freedom of association and the right to a secure livelihood (Gibney, 2003:5). The distinguishing characteristics of rights include the assertion that they are irreducible, inalienable and indivisible. This means that one right cannot be reduced to another right and individuals cannot give up their human rights (see Ife, 2002). These include the right to:

- life, liberty and human security
- equal recognition before the law
- be treated with dignity
- freedom of thought, movement, association and speech
- take part in the conduct of public affairs
- non-discrimination
- social participation
- economic wellbeing.

Human rights are enshrined in United Nations' treaties such as declarations, covenants and resolutions. A list of human rights is found in the Universal Declaration of Human Rights (see the Appendix).

There has been an increasing focus on the importance of linking community development and human rights. Those who put a human rights lens over community development work, such as Ife (2002; 2004; 2010), point out that much of community development practice is concerned with human rights. For example, community development work in legal aid centres is premised on the right to legal justice. Disability groups employing community development workers to assist them in campaigns for access to public transport and employment argue that wellbeing, dignity and freedom of movement are all human rights. Survivors of domestic violence identify their struggle as a struggle for freedom from assault and harassment.

For Ife (2004:84), while community development might be understood as developing and affirming community, human rights are also concerned with establishing our common humanity. Miller (2004b), drawing on the approach of Pin-Fat (2000), comments that universal human rights articulate a normative (or value-driven) commitment to the equal moral worth of all human beings. Much of the discussion of human rights in Australia is concerned with the rights of individuals. In contrast to the individualistic approach to human rights, community development focuses on collective rights and collective obligations to ensure that human rights are met, and a bottom-up approach that involves discussion and identification of human rights by ordinary people themselves, rather than by politicians, journalists, lawmakers and opinion leaders.

Empowerment and self-determination

It is not enough for community development workers to be concerned about citizenship and human rights issues or be committed to working with ordinary people and people who are disadvantaged and oppressed. Many jobs, including those of doctors, lawyers, traditional social workers and even politicians, claim to be based on the same commitment. The difference between such traditional professions and community development lies in a commitment to the collective **empowerment** of ordinary people and to transforming social structures, relations and processes. For example, many lawyers are committed to human rights. For them, legal rights are particularly important but, as the English commentator Donnison (1991:63) points out, the law and the court system are 'a bewildering and expensive jungle' dominated by middle-class men. Only when lawyers work to demystify the processes of law courts, and endeavour to provide ordinary people with real input into the processes and practices of the law, are they engaged in community development work. Community development also differs from traditional service professions in its commitment to developing lasting structures that help people to collectively identify and meet their own needs. It is only when there is an active process to empower others that a community development perspective is evident.

It is important to acknowledge that communities are never 'blank slates'. As discussed in this book, any one community will already have a wealth of skills, knowledge, social capital and material resources. Hence, community development practitioners, whether they are already part of a community or are newcomers, approach issues in a collaborative way and eschew the role of an expert who provides solutions in a top-down manner. Communities must be able to do things in their own way. While a community development worker's job is to work with communities to determine goals, issues and strategies, the ultimate power to accept or reject these lies with the community members. In the final analysis, it must be the community's views or interests that prevail. In colonised societies, empowerment can require the colonisers to give back to the Indigenous people what is rightfully theirs so that they have legal ownership and control. In the case of the ownership of tribal land, it means the right of the tribe to make its own decisions about how the land is used.

It is important to note that while community development rejects the view that humans are inherently self-seeking individuals, it does not subscribe to the opposite view that humans are naturally altruistic. Rather, if human life is to be sustained in anything like a satisfactory way during the twenty-first century, ordinary human beings must choose to participate in society on an equal basis and be able to make their own history.

Sustainability

As indicated previously, in the last two decades there has been growing critical evaluation of the ways in which humans think about development. In particular, the idea of modernity pays scant attention to the limits of growth and development. For example, 'modernisation' in the forms of technology and economic development have failed to understand the ecological impact of growth, and development projects have been set up without any consideration as to whether they can be sustained. The principle of **sustainability** is important for community development in two main senses. First, we need to be clear about whether there is a genuine ongoing need for the continuation of a community program, project or organisation. If there is not a clear need, or if the program, project or organisation is not fulfilling a need or draws on too many resources to keep going, then it might not warrant continuing support. That is, it is likely to be unsustainable. Second, of course, is the question of environmental sustainability. While there are many definitions of environmental sustainability, in this book we take a broad approach. A program, project or organisation can only be considered sustainable if it meets the needs of the present without compromising the ability of future generations to meet their own needs. We discuss the issue and ideas of sustainability further in chapter 2.

Collective action

From a community development perspective a corollary to the principle of empowerment is the recognition that people's lives are interrelated. The wellbeing of each person depends on the welfare of society at large. As suggested above, this is not to argue that people are or should be selfless, but to emphasise that each human is a social being; individuals are able to communicate, produce, reproduce and create their environments only because they are part of society. In entering into relationships, we constantly work upon and transform our very existence. While problems might at first appear to be individual ones, the task of the community development worker is to identify common themes and structural underpinnings and to develop networks and alliances.

Thus, another principle of community development is the commitment to **collective action**. Community development rests on the view that people can collectively bring about real change in society for the benefit of all. Collective endeavour and action involves a deeper commitment to the principles and processes of mutuality than just participation or consultation. For example, a person can say that they are a participant in an international activist organisation when they might do no more than subscribe to an annual newsletter. While this might be participation, it is of a shallow kind. The collective endeavour in community development requires a different level of commitment. It involves mutuality, trust and solidarity, the sharing of information and a strategy for activity and action that draws on the combined wisdom and abilities of all members of a group. Only by acting together can we change society.

Diversity

In some ways, commitment to diversity appears to contradict the principle of collective action, which implies unity and sameness. Collective action, however, is not forced upon communities. When people take part in collective action, it is because on a particular issue they have chosen to do so. The same people might not agree on another issue.

Community development accepts that people are both similar and different. Its practitioners should not expect conformity and agreement on all issues. Community development is based on the premise that people have different viewpoints and opinions and it encourages a diversity of views, lifestyles and cultures. As we have already seen, community development is committed to providing people with real choices about the way they live their lives, which are based on control of the conditions of their existence. These choices should be premised on an acknowledgment of the differences between people. Community development workers must be careful not to silence or undermine the language of diversity.

Commitment to diversity allows for different ways of doing things using various community development practices, depending on the immediate context and issue. Community development work requires a willingness to learn from the community, respect for the culture of the community and sensitivity to the way things are done.

Cross-cultural practice is one manifestation of the commitment to diversity. It is premised on an understanding of, and sensitivity to, different cultures. Cultural differences can be manifested in attitudes to the family and the aged, ideas of what constitutes respectful behaviour and gender roles.

When working with Indigenous groups in Australia, it is important to respect the diversity of cultural traditions and not to homogenise Indigenous cultures. The requirement to respect and understand Indigenous communities might mean that only Indigenous workers are employed by these diverse communities, or that a process of positive discrimination in favour of Indigenous communities prevails. The requirement for respect and understanding can also mean accepting or taking up new values that might contradict the cultures of non-Indigenous or even other Indigenous groups. This can challenge some of the community development principles and strategies discussed in this book. For example, hierarchical structures based on respect for elders and tribal traditions can undercut commitment to collective decision making and giving voice to all members of a group. The strategic process for organising action and change, as outlined in chapter 5 of this book, may not be appropriate to the customs of an Indigenous community. These kinds of tensions draw our attention to the many dilemmas facing community development workers, which are discussed in chapter 10.

Change and involvement in conflict

Community development aims to transform unequal, coercive and oppressive structures in society. To fulfil this aim it confronts, provokes, presents unpalatable information and even disturbs. Here, community development overlaps with new social movements, such as human rights and peace movements. Like them, community development challenges the presumed inevitability or naturalness of existing power structures and social systems.

The commitment to disadvantaged and oppressed people, to empowerment and social change can make life difficult for the community development worker. Those who side with the underdog are sometimes vilified as agitators and are ostracised or even threatened. Such responses come not only from people in power but also from disgruntled communities. A community development worker cannot shy away from conflict. It is often through conflict that we move into different forms of social relations and structures. Drawing on his experience as a community organiser in the United States of America, Alinsky (1969) distinguishes between those who are prepared to fight for the rights of the underdog (whom he calls radicals) and those who are morally indignant but are not prepared to act on their outrage (whom he calls liberals). Working in the 1940s, Alinsky argued that without active opposition, we perpetuate existing unequal social and political relations. In a discussion of the difference between liberals and radicals, Alinsky (1969:21–2) comments:

> Society has good reason to fear the radical. Every shaking advance of [humankind] toward equality and justice has come from the radical ... Liberals fear power or its application. They labour in confusion over the significance of power and fail to recognise that only through the achievement and constructive use of power can people better themselves ... They talk glibly of people lifting themselves by their own bootstraps but fail to realise that nothing can be lifted or moved except through power.

While involvement in conflict is an inevitable part of community development work, community development requires much more than a preparedness to 'get one's hands dirty'. It requires the development of and involvement in processes and strategies that move beyond conflict. There are basically two levels of conflict in the context of community development work. First is conflict that arises through competing ideas of development, and competing needs and expectations. At the local level, compromise is theoretically possible in resolving this form of conflict. We discuss the forms of conflict management around issues of needs and expectations in chapter 7. The second level of conflict comes about through a clash of values. Compromise at this level is much more difficult. Giddens (1994) points out that there are a limited number of ways that a clash of values can be dealt with: first, geographical segregation; second, exit or banishment of one group, such as occurs when people become political refugees; third, use of force in which one side is physically victorious; and finally, dialogue and understanding of difference and the development of strategies for intercultural understanding and coexistence. Community development practitioners are increasingly required to facilitate the management and resolution of conflict and incompatibility in regard to values and cultures. Dealing with cultural and value differences without hostile conflict is one of the major challenges facing community development workers in the first decades of the twenty-first century. We discuss the importance of understanding and responding to cultural and value difference in chapter 8.

Liberation, open societies and participatory democracy

Underpinning the importance of collective action is a particular interpretation of liberation. In analysing the contradictions in welfare policy, Hardy (1981) argues that liberation is reactive against forms of authority, servitude and oppression. Liberation requires empowerment and autonomy. It involves struggle against, and freedom from, domination by powerful individuals, ideologies and structures. Liberation is ultimately something that groups or individuals do for themselves: one cannot be liberated by someone else. This has important implications for community development work. It provides a foundation for the view that the community development worker is a facilitator rather than a leader, expert or agitator.

Individually and collectively, liberation can only take place in a free and open society. An open society is one that has an active citizenship. It rejects dogma and nurtures diversity, unrestricted discussion and open debate at all levels and on all topics. Debates, as far as possible, must be accessible to all people.

An open society must have open politics. While there is considerable debate about what constitutes open politics, there is broad agreement that it must involve some type of participatory democracy, involving an informed public who have time for open discussion.

Democracy is based on the view that all people in a society have an equal right to determine how the society should be run and what its ultimate aims and purposes should be. In a **representative democracy**, people elect other people to represent them and make decisions on their behalf. Formally, people have a direct say in how society should work at election time once every few years. The choices people make are influenced by their resources and values and by media representations.

In a direct participatory democracy, people do not elect others to represent them. They take part in identifying, articulating and presenting issues, policies and problems in their society and make decisions about the strategies to be used to overcome the problems. People directly participate in and jointly control the decision-making processes. In Australia today, representative democracy prevails in formal politics; some elements of direct participatory democracy are found at the local level in schools, community groups and, where possible, in community organisations. The development of direct participatory democracy is constrained in the current political context in Australia, where it is deemed to be unwieldy, slow, ineffective and inefficient. The dominant view is that the most effective decision making is done by strong political leaders, who might consult the populace through market research, for example, but who must make the 'hard decisions' on the basis of their own knowledge and skills. In this view of democracy, people are regarded as consumers of politics rather than participants in the process.

The creation of a participatory and open society would require a freeing up of the political processes and the establishment of more accessible forms of democracy. It would need a different political culture or way of thinking about politics, and new attitudes, such as the view that genuine participation is both a right and an obligation. Participants would expect to take part at every level of decision making, in government departments, workplaces, schools, universities and neighbourhoods. Decisions about what would be produced and when, where and how would involve all participants in the process. On one hand, the prospects for this type of democracy in Australia are poor. Yet there have been some interesting developments in the form of **deliberative democracy**. Deliberative democracy establishes processes whereby people come together to learn, share understandings and strategies and discuss ways of thinking about and acting upon specific issues. Only after this process of deliberation can decisions be made. Decisions must be made on the basis of the power of deliberation rather than coercion, manipulation or deception (Dryzek, 2000). Deliberative democracy can be complemented by new sources of information and new mechanisms for exchanging views such as the Internet, which allows people to source information without the gatekeepers of mainstream media, education institutions and political spin (Davis, Elin & Reeher, 2002). Deliberative democracy was practised in some of the deliberations in the Constitutional Conventions organised before the referendum in 1999 on Australia becoming a republic. It has been practised in other contexts as well, such as a people's convention in South Australia in 2003. More shall be said about participatory democracy in chapter 6.

Challenging 'TINA' and practising the power of example

Given the pressured work environment, the immediacy of problems and the need to focus on everyday activities, it is easy to forget that there are many ways of thinking about issues and many alternatives to the ways that societies and communities in Australia are currently organised. It is also easy to turn a blind eye to the profound environmental problems facing the earth today. In a world that is based on the view that the earth is an infinite resource to be plundered by humans, it is easy to overlook the importance of developing sustainable programs. As will be discussed in following chapters, the neo-liberal environment in which community development operates is based on a commitment to continual growth without full replenishment of the world's resources, competition as the driving force of economic and social development, and privatisation of state activities. In this context it is generally assumed that a continuation of neo-liberal policies is the natural development of Australian society – that is, **there is no alternative** (**TINA**).

There are, in fact, many alternatives to neo-liberal policies. We tend to forget that history is the story of changes to what people once thought of as the natural way of things. Even today, in the first part of the twenty-first century, we can find alternatives in European countries. The social democratic tradition in northern Europe offers a much softer and more circumscribed approach to economic development than we are experiencing in Australia. Community development stands out as an approach and set of practices that is prepared to engage alternatives. Throughout the world there are many alternative examples of ways of organising culturally, politically, economically and socially that do not accord with the requirements of neo-liberalism and **new managerialism**. We are beginning to learn about such projects in recent publications and forums; for example, in the World Social Forums and through publications such as *Reclaim the State* by Wainwright (2003). Thus, community development is committed to the power of example. It can play its part in showing that there are always alternatives by demonstrating different ways of organising at the local level through what I have called **prefigurative politics**. More will be said about prefigurative politics in chapter 3.

Processes

It is one thing to talk about the ideas, values and principles of community development work and the world we would like to live in. But community development is not just ideas, values and aspirations for a better world. It concerns itself with how people live their lives in the real material world. It confronts power and influence as they are constructed and maintained in concrete situations. Yet the world we live in is a patriarchal class-based one, full of inequities, exploitation, intimidation and downright repression.

How do we negotiate this tension between the world as we want it and the world as it is? One way is to conceptualise community development as a process that works both with and against existing social forms. It is important to work within an existing situation, while at the same time challenging and transforming it according to community development principles.

On first appearances, these precepts seem inconsistent. However, it is possible to hold onto the principles of community development, yet continue to live in the real world. The first way of doing this is through developing demonstration projects that show that things can be done differently. Ways of doing things that are different to mainstream, welfare-based or managerialist approaches are discussed in case studies in this book.

However, in order to develop alternatives, it is also important to understand and critique existing ways of doing things and to have the tools to conceive and implement different ways. This is what this book is about. Its aim is to equip people interested in community development to collectively construct their own communities.

We can begin with the idea of community development as a process consisting of six interrelated elements or stages: information, authenticity, vision, pragmatism, strategy and transformation (see table 1.1). These elements generally overlap. At times they occur

Table 1.1 *Elements of community development*

Element	Characteristic	Question
Information	Theories Concepts Research reports Australian Bureau of Statistics surveys Budgets People's own experiences	What do we know?
Authenticity	People's own knowledge and viewpoints	What do the people think?
Vision	Alternative views of how things could be done	How could things be different? What would we like to happen?
Pragmatism	Existing structures, processes and practices	What are the facilitating or constraining factors? What are our choices? What can we do?
Strategy	Plans for getting to where we want to be	How to get from A to B? What is to be done and who will do it?
Transformation	Changes to existing structures, processes and practices	What changes have taken place?
Evaluation	Evaluating the changes to existing structures, processes and practices	What do we think of the changes that have taken place?

simultaneously; at times they follow a clear sequence. Sometimes certain elements are more clearly developed than others. In a particular project the element of strategy might not be fully or successfully developed and the element of transformation might not come. Evaluation is the final stage in this cycle, but the evaluation of one cycle will influence the next cycle.

Information

A community development worker facilitates access to both formal and informal information. This includes broad understandings about how society works and how things could be done differently, as well as specific information such as analyses of government policies, availability of resources and reports. These may be provided through international environment reports, local government documents, legislation or Australian Bureau of Statistics research. Although in Australia, the policy of user-pays is being applied in regard to access to much government information, such as detailed census data collected by the Australian Bureau of Statistics and information available through freedom of information (FOI), a considerable amount of information is now becoming accessible on the Internet.

In regard to their everyday work, community development workers are required to access such data and make it relevant and accessible for specific purposes. It is for information that community development workers might refer to 'experts': that is, they might need to ask economists to clarify different economic predictions for the development of a city in which a community development project is underway; they might refer to a demographer to explain different predictions of demographic changes in a rural area; or they might seek advice from a lawyer on a matter of human rights.

Part of a community development worker's job will be to provide verbal or written summaries and reports of critiques and new theories, legislation or other formal documents. People need access to wide-ranging information and time to reflect on it in order to make informed choices about their lives.

Authenticity

Community development accepts the experiences and views of ordinary people and their knowledge of the world, based on their experiences. Alinsky (1972), while warning against 'enshrining the poor', always enjoined activists to trust the people. Donnison (1991:126) urges:

> If you want to know what should be done about depressed cities and impoverished cities and impoverished neighbourhoods, start with the people who live in them and listen carefully to what they say – respecting and tolerating the anger that is often the first response of the oppressed.

Community development workers always begin at the point known as 'where people are at'. They ensure that the disadvantaged and the powerless can speak and be listened to. They provide people with a forum and a voice to challenge conventional wisdom.

Pragmatism

Pragmatism emphasises practical values and attention to what are usually understood as facts, or pieces of information that are strongly backed up by the evidence available. A pragmatic approach will take into account the political and ideological contexts and the interests of various stakeholders. It can require community development workers to work within existing structures and with those who hold power.

Vision

Community development is premised on the importance of understanding the world as it is and people's real experiences of this world, as well as the need for philosophical awakenings of alternative constructions or visions of what we would like the world to be. Vision implies open discussion of values and principles: What do we really want? What are we working for? People must consider alternative constructions if they are to think in terms of choices and control over their lives. Here, the idea of the community development worker as facilitator is especially important.

Strategy

Strategy begins with the question, what are we going to do? Participants define their aims and objectives, and plan specific strategies and tactics to achieve them. Strategy development takes into account the factors that hinder or help the achievement of aims and objectives. The processes involved in strategy development are explained further in chapter 5.

Figure 1.1 *Domains of community development*

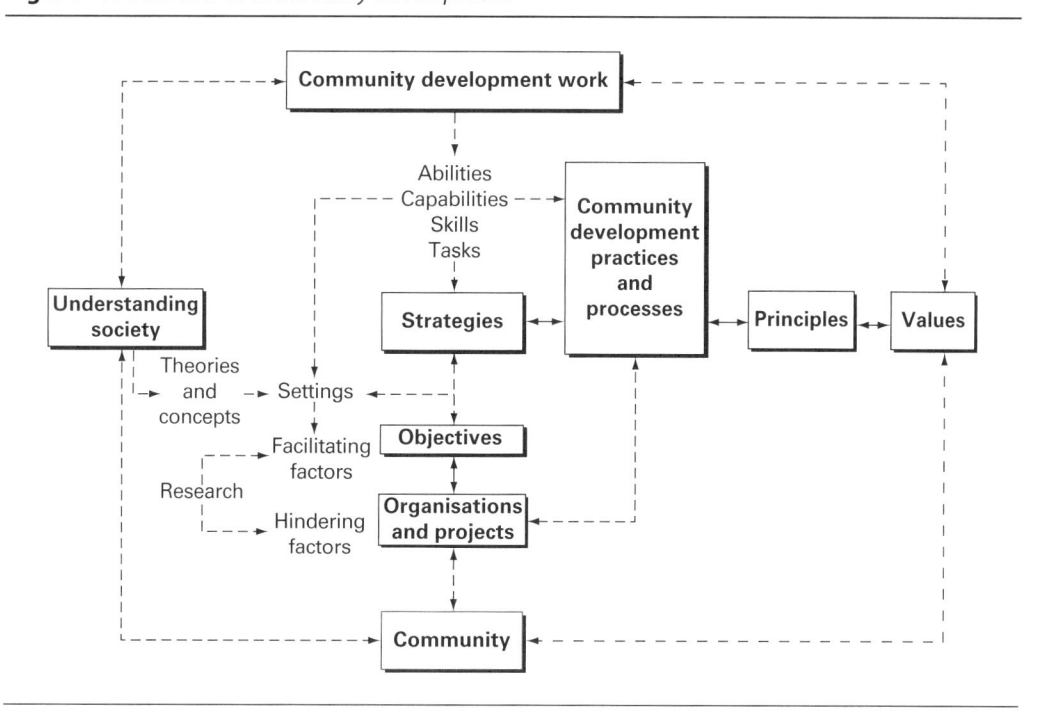

Transformation

Transformation involves something as small as a minor change in attitude to something as large as a major policy change. But insofar as change occurs all the time, the element of transformation can be discerned throughout the community development process. An understanding of these six elements is important to the concept of community development that is presented in this book. Figure 1.1 above is an overview of all the major domains in community development.

To conclude this chapter the following case study is presented as an example of how elements of community development can come together in a post-disaster situation.

BUSHFIRE RECOVERY THROUGH COMMUNITY DEVELOPMENT – RATHDONE CREEK

We have already noted how the opportunities for showcasing community development in the post-bushfire recovery following the devastating bushfires in Victoria in February 2009 were largely overlooked. Consultations with affected communities were mostly tokenistic. However, this is not to argue that there have been no community development responses in times of natural disaster.

The setting is a small town community called Rathdone Creek, which has been overcome by a bushfire. The town and its surrounding district, an area of about 20 square kilometres, has been devastated. Out of a population of nearly 15 000 people, 37 people have lost their lives and 72 have been hospitalised with burns and other injuries, some in a critical condition. The surviving townspeople people are extremely traumatised.

The conventional wisdom has been that in such circumstances the 'victims' are immobilised. This wisdom holds that it is not appropriate to start thinking about how the 'victims' can take charge or to consider how community development approaches and methods might be applied. Indeed, it is only through a massive external effort that there can be any recovery or reconstruction. However, what this case study shows is that not only is community development possible in such circumstances, but also it perhaps offers the best route to recovery and reconstruction.

When we visit the town to assist relatives, it is 48 hours since the fire has gone through, and the most obvious presence is of the police and the media. As one local community member comments: 'Natural disasters are spectacular media events. Journalists and news teams rush to the site and provide graphic pictures of the helpless "victims" and the media run stories on how grateful we should be for the help we are getting.'

When we return four days later we realise how inaccurate the media coverage is. In contrast to the media portrayal of the aftermath of the fire, and the continual framing of the event in terms of victims and deficits, our friends and family members who have survived the fire outline the importance of community development principles, methods and processes for restoring the dignity of the survivors.

In talking to survivors in the first few months after the disaster, it was apparent that there were three types of post-disaster intervention. First was the intervention by the 'expert' outsiders, including government, community organisations and church groups, who assumed what was needed and acted on behalf of the survivors. Second was the intervention controlled and undertaken by the survivors themselves. And finally was an intervention involving both external groups and survivors working together in a partnership model. We will consider each of the types of intervention in turn.

Chapter 1 The nature of community development

In this first type of intervention, the state government called and chaired the meetings, set the agendas and decided what funds would be available. Local and state governments and the police decided what tasks were necessary and used their own workforce to undertake all jobs and tasks. This intervention operated on the basis of a deficit approach to relief and recovery, whereby 'victims' were passive and had no usable capabilities, skills or resources. What was required was outside professional experts taking charge. These experts provided medical supplies, professional trauma counselling and water purification systems; they ran church services; they brought in truckloads of food and clothing; and they set up tents. Some of the services and resources were well received in the community, especially the water purification systems. However, survivors commented that they felt disempowered by the patronising attitudes of the experts; there had been little acknowledgement of what locals had done themselves. They were angry that none of the experts actually asked them about what they already had and what they needed.

The second type of intervention was based on the community development principle of self-determination. In this intervention the community members themselves took control. The disaster was a powerful catalyst for getting the community to work together to respond to the disaster. Within 24 hours, community members had met in the one surviving hotel and had begun to collectively identify the different needs of the community and to prioritise these needs. They also identified the assets and resources still existing in the community. One of the strongest assets was their substantial bond of trust and mutuality (social capital). The community also had many physical resources that could be shared, such as spare rooms in houses that had survived the fire, cars and vans for transport, and food and clothes.

The second community meeting decided to divide the town and its environs into geographical areas. They set up a taskforce in each area, which, as a first step, began to identify priorities and assets. As a second step they identified the various skills that they could share. For example, there was an insurance broker and a solicitor, who could help with insurance claims; a plumber, who could check leaks in roofs; and an electrician, who could advise on the safety of buildings. The school had burnt down, but the schoolteachers organised a classroom in the back of a local shop and afternoon classes were held as part of a policy 'to get things back to normal as soon as possible'. Parents and teachers had contacts in the local city and they were able to get books and writing material, and even several laptop computers. A group of women, led by a 90-year-old survivor, decided to set up a 'baking group' that would ensure that survivors had good home-baked bread and cakes. They brought in the children who enjoyed baking (and eating) biscuits. A local psychologist spoke with families who had lost their loved ones to identify their needs. There were very different responses: some people just wanted to be left alone; others wanted counselling. The dignity and personal choice of all families was respected.

The dominant issue at the third community meeting, which had now named itself the Community Recovery Action Group, was concern that the views of the most disadvantaged and marginalised in the community were not being heard. They developed strategies to ensure that all community members had a say and were listened to. The meeting deliberated about how the Community Recovery Action Group could be as representative as possible. It was decided that they should only be a steering group until a proper democratic process involving elections could be held. Disagreement about priorities was beginning to emerge. For example, some community members wanted a 'back to normal' approach to reconstruction, while others wanted a 'build back better' approach. The 'build back better' supporters argued that the community now had an ideal opportunity to challenge the TINA (there is no alternative) approach to development. The group needed a democratic and effective way of dealing with such disagreements.

The final type of intervention involved external groups and survivors working together. In this intervention the outsiders began by asking the community members for their views. For example, they did not assume needs and they checked whether the water purification tanks were needed and asked where they should be set up. When most of the community members rejected the offer of emergency accommodation in the form of tents, the external community organisations worked with the survivors to identify alternative forms of accommodation. They worked in a partnership model, in teams comprising members of the Community Recovery Action Group, government representatives, community organisation and business representatives, as well as journalists and other individuals. The Community Recovery Action Group and government representatives drew up a list of tasks and allotted personnel to carry them out. For example, one team chose some empty portable school classrooms. Perhaps most importantly, the teams understood that people respond differently at different times. While most local people wanted to be involved immediately after the fire, after a few weeks many had withdrawn due to sheer exhaustion. At this point, a number of community survivors asked some of the external members of the working teams to advocate on their behalf. Several survivors withdrew participation from the relief efforts, as food and clothing donations were not always suitable (some tinned food was out of date and some donated clothes were unusable).

In the two last types of intervention we can see community development principles at work. We can clearly see the elements of empowerment, collective action, respect for people's (diverse) views, commitment to powerless people, democracy and the challenging of TINA.

What this case study reveals is that even in what might seem to be the most disempowering situations, community development is still possible, and preferable, as a way of proceeding to ensure the best chances for future development.

Summary points

- Community development can be variously described as an approach or philosophy, a job or profession, a method and an intervention or political activity.
- Community development is premised on the need for continual critical assessment of the ways we organise our lives and relate to each other and to our natural environment.
- Community development deals with new issues but many of its precepts are based on ideas that go back to antiquity.
- The issues, practices and processes embodied in community development are in some ways familiar to us all.
- In Australia, community development is often understood to be part of what has come to be known as the social and community services industry.
- Community development is also an international practice.
- Community development work consists of specific tasks and requires specific abilities and skills.
- Community development work traditionally has taken place almost solely in community organisations, but today it is also located in government, particularly local government, and to a lesser extent in the business sector.
- Community development is based on a number of principles.
- The community development process consists of the elements of information, authenticity, vision, pragmatism, strategy and transformation.

Key terms

- citizenship
- collective action
- community organisations
- contracted-out
- corporate citizenship
- corporate social responsibility (CSR)
- cross-cultural practice
- culturally and linguistically diverse (CALD)
- deliberative democracy
- development
- emancipatory politics
- empowerment
- ethno-specific organisation
- globalisation
- human rights
- individualisation
- new managerialism
- participatory democracy
- power of example
- prefigurative politics
- privatisation
- project of modernity
- representative democracy
- self-determination
- social and community services industry
- social capital
- social entrepreneurship
- social evolutionary framework
- social justice
- subsidiarity
- sustainability
- there is no alternative (TINA)
- user-pays
- virtual communities

Exercises

1. When travelling around your town or suburb look out for community organisations. List their names and the types of programs they provide.
2. List the types of activities involved in community development.
3. What is meant by the term 'subsidiarity' and why is subsidiarity important for community development?
4. Explain the differences in the asset and deficit approaches to development?
5. What is social capital and why is it important for community development?
6. Why has the idea of development been challenged in the last 10 years?
7. Why is community development identified as a set of principles and practices for the beginning of the twenty-first century?
8. Think of what it would be like to work with homeless young people by:
   a. listing where a community development program for young people might be based
   b. identifying some of the tasks you might be involved in
   c. identifying what skills and knowledge would be needed
   d. explaining how the elements of information, authenticity, vision, pragmatism, strategy and transformation might take form in this work.
9. Drawing on the four case studies in this chapter, list the tasks involved in community development.
10. Think about what it would be like to work as a community development practitioner with homeless young people by:
    a. identifying where a community development program might be based
    b. identifying some of the tasks you might be involved in
    c. identifying what skills and knowledge would be needed
    d. explaining how the elements of information, authenticity, vision, pragmatism, strategy and transformation might take form in this work.

Further reading

Alinsky, S (1972) *Rules for Radicals*. Vintage, New York.

Campfrens, H (ed.) (1997) *Community Development Around the World: Practice, Theory, Research, Training*. University of Toronto Press, Toronto.

Chambers, R (2005) *Ideas for Development*. Earthscan, London.

Davis, S, Elin, L & Reeher, G (2002) *Click on Democracy*. Westview Press, Boulder, Colorado.

Donnison, D (1991) *A Radical Agenda: After the New Right and the Old Left*. Rivers Oram Press, London.

Doyal, L & Gough, I (1991) *A Theory of Human Need*. Macmillan, London.

Dryzek, J (2000) *Deliberative Democracy and Beyond: Liberals, Critics, Contestations*. Oxford University Press, Oxford.

Eade, D & Williams, S (1995) *The Oxfam Handbook of Development and Relief*, Vol. 1. Oxfam, Oxford.

Gibney, M (ed.) (2003) *Globalizing Rights: The Oxford Amnesty Lectures* 1999. Oxford University Press, Oxford.

Giddens, A (1994) *Beyond Left and Right: The Future of Radical Politics*. Polity Press, Cambridge.

Goulet, D (1985) *The Cruel Choice*. University Press of America, Lanham.

Hardy, J (1981) *Values in Social Policy: Nine Contradictions*. Routledge & Kegan Paul, London.

Hirst, P (1994) *Associative Democracy: New Forms of Economic and Social Governance*. Polity Press, Cambridge.

Ife, J (2002) *Community Development: Community-Based Alternatives in an Age of Globalisation*, 2nd edn. Pearson Education, French's Forest.

Nederveen Pieterse, J (2001) *Development Theory: Deconstructions/Reconstructions*. Sage, London.

Productivity Commission (2010) *Contribution of the Not-for-Profit Sector,* Productivity Commission Research Report, Australian Government, Canberra.

Sennett, R (2004) *Respect: The Formation of Character in an Age of Inequality*. Penguin, London.

Thomas, D (1983) *The Making of Community Work*. Allen & Unwin, London.

Todaro, MP (1994) *Economic Development*. Longman, New York.

Wainwright, H (2003) *Reclaim the State: Experiments in Popular Democracy*. Verso, London.

Ward, D & Mullender, A (1991) 'Empowerment and oppression in an indissoluble pairing for contemporary social work', *Critical Social Policy*, No. 32, Autumn, pp. 21–30.

Weblinks

Community activism
http://actnow.com.au/

Social and community services work and pay scales
www.fairwork.gov.au/Pay-leave-and-conditions/Finding-the-right-pay/Documents/PDF/2008PDF/AP817216.pdf

CHAPTER 2

The context

Overview

In this chapter we discuss the social, economic and political contexts in which community development operates. We identify five main backdrops: welfare, community, political, global and policy. The chapter begins with a brief history of community development in Australia and its location in the social and community services industry. We then discuss the debates that surround the concept of community and the political and ideological implications of the use of the term. The relation between community development and political action is deliberated. The rest of the chapter discusses insights into the contexts of community development in recent years, drawing on discussions of globalisation, cosmopolitanism, neo-liberalism, enterprise culture, social inclusion, risk society and new political forms that are relevant to the practice of community development in Australia today, including the demise of the traditional Left and traditional working-class politics, the rise of human rights and the idea that we live in a postmodern society.

Introduction

In chapter 1 we indicated that while community development is based on values and principles, its practices and strategies can vary according to context. In this chapter we consider in some detail how community development is affected by specific contexts. We begin the chapter with a brief overview of the history of community development, before considering the welfare backdrop of community development in Australia. These discussions lead to an examination of the specific community contexts in which community development takes place.

Brief history of community development

We can trace the rise of community development as an approach and a method to the idea of bottom-up development. **Bottom-up development** is premised on the argument that people who are affected by decisions about their future should be empowered to collectively control or influence such decisions. This argument is based on the view that there are alternative, or supplementary, ways of organising society to the traditionally dominant view that decisions about people's lives and options should be set by those in authority in a hierarchical system and by people who are outside 'experts'.

We can identify different ways this idea has been developed through community development. One of the first practical explorations of bottom-up approaches developed in British territories in post–Second World War colonial settings, particularly in Africa, where the introduction of ideas of self-help and the mobilisation of local resources took hold (Scott, 1981). By the 1970s, community development methods were being considered as a way forward for international development projects (Nederveen Pieterse, 2001:75). As British administrators returned from the colonies in the 1960s they asked whether such methods could or should be applied in the 'developed world', and in particular to Britain (Mayo, 2008; Popple, 2008; du Sautoy, 1966). The answer was 'yes'.

So the second way the idea of bottom-up development was constructed was through its application in the 1970s in Britain (Craig, Derricort & Loney, 1982; Craig, Mayo & Sharman, 1979; Jones & Mayo, 1974), where bottom-up community-based projects were offered as an alternative to the passive welfare controlled by external professionals (Jones & Mayo, 1974). In these settings, the idea of bottom-up development drew on the leftist arguments for working-class struggle and the active empowerment of disadvantaged groups. In Britain this trajectory of a critical community development was linked to the critique of traditional social work as a form of control. It was expressed in proposals for new approaches to welfare (Curno, 1978).

The third way the idea of 'bottom-up' development has been constructed has been in rural and regional development, which in Australia has a trajectory running through farming communities (such as the Country Women's Association) to the Australian Assistance Plan, which we discuss below, and the Landcare program, whereby local communities have taken responsibility for rural conservation by getting together to protect and repair the natural landscape, including rivers, bushland and farming and coastal areas.

Fourth, there are two traditions of community involvement in the USA: community economic development and community organising. Some of the projects within these two traditions are bottom-up in orientation, and involve what are known as local leaders, while others rely on outside leadership (Rubin & Rubin, 1992:49–50). The work of Saul Alinsky (1972) in the 1940s to the 1970s stands out as the prime example of community organising, involving both outside leadership and locally generated activism. The community organising methods developed by Alinsky have been applied by activist groups (including those led by the current president of the USA, Barack Obama) ever since. The left tradition also found expression in the work of Paolo Freire (1972), who has profoundly influenced how we think about knowledge and education as a way of liberating rather than controlling and domesticating people who are powerless and disadvantaged.

The fifth way that bottom-up approaches to development have been manifested is in the idea of civic engagement. This approach draws on the civil society and communitarian themes such as cooperation, rootedness, mutuality and common identity and interests. We discuss communitarianism in some detail below. The communitarian approach has been embraced in many of the community engagement and neighbourhood renewal projects undertaken by local, state and national governments in Australia since the 1990s. This approach can sit ambiguously within community development, because it does not necessarily work to empower people or to challenge existing power relations; rather, it fits people into existing structures.

These five approaches to bottom-up development have provided broad frameworks for understanding how community development has unfolded in general. In the following section we delve further into the history of community development in Australia. We begin with the important welfare backdrop.

The welfare backdrop

The social and community services industry grew out of the traditional welfare approach to issues of poverty and disadvantage. The general history of welfare shows elements of genuine compassion for the poor as well as deliberate attempts to control and incorporate them. In his discussion of Australian welfare history, Kennedy (1982) argues that historically there has been little difference between charity and philanthropy. He points out that charity refers to Christian love but in the Middle Ages it became almsgiving to save one's soul. Similarly, while the concept of philanthropy was based on a love of humanity, it has been used by those in power to save their property by buying off the poor. The welfarist idea of helping the poor may be well meaning, but it adopts a patronising and controlling approach to those who are disadvantaged in society. In this tradition, the helping person or professional is viewed as a superior person or an expert; their job is to provide individuals and families with material relief or counselling so that they may more easily cope with their situation.

Community development is at odds with this welfarist tradition, for a community development worker does not aspire to be an expert, superior to the community. Community development workers provide education and information, but they argue that counselling and direct material relief do not change the overall situation in society that has produced poverty and disadvantage. The traditional ideas of welfare have also been challenged from within the social and community services industry; notions of social justice, community participation and accountability to service users are important aspects of this industry.

There has always been some community involvement in municipal councils, sporting groups, historical societies and fundraising for schools and churches, for example. But such activities have generally worked to support existing social structures and power relations rather than to give real power to local people. In Australia it was not until the 1970s that community development was identified as a strategy for social change and as a way of dealing with social and economic problems by involving those affected by these problems in decision making. In 1970, the Brotherhood of St Laurence, a Melbourne church welfare organisation, evaluated its welfare program. It rejected the bandaid and individualistic approach to social problems whereby people were blamed for their own poverty. The Brotherhood established the Family Centre Project, later to become the Action and Resource Centre for Low-Income Families, which was initiated on the premise that structural and economic factors – such as unemployment, poor housing, low wages and poor education – cause and perpetuate poverty. The Family Centre Project provided disadvantaged people with more control over their lives, better access to participation in decision making, a guaranteed minimum income and improved access to education and health services.

Of particular significance is the establishment of the Australian Assistance Plan (AAP) in 1973. The Whitlam Labor government introduced the AAP as an experiment in social development. It provided direct subsidies to local governments and small assistance grants to community groups. Regional Councils of Social Development, comprising representatives of community organisations and governments, were established. The AAP aimed to encourage people at local and regional levels to participate in the planning and development of their communities.

The AAP provided a setting for innovative thinking (see Thorpe, 1985). It opened up discussion about the community as a tool for the achievement of broader social change (Mune, 1989) and focused on regional decision making as a basis for the empowerment of ordinary people. Yet the AAP was plagued by controversy and was shortlived.

In commenting on the strengths and weaknesses of the AAP, Graycar (1976) notes the tension that continues to lie at the heart of community development. When community participation becomes more than tokenistic it can result in attacks on the inadequacies of government structures. Participants must choose whether to continue with their aim of real empowerment and redistribution of resources, and the consequent exposure of government inadequacies, which might cause a loss of government funding. If they become more compliant and docile, they are more likely to retain funding but they can lose their effectiveness. As will be discussed in chapter 5, since 2002 there have been significant efforts by state governments in particular to reinvigorate communities through specific community building strategies. It is interesting to note how those involved in these strategies do not seem to have reflected on the experiences of the AAP in the 1970s.

The position taken in this book is that community development is both part of the social and community services industry and also goes well beyond this industry. Community development principles and practices are now being used in a range of paid and unpaid activities and in a number of occupations. Community development is therefore at once much broader and more universal than Western human service or social work. It is now found in international political movements, in environmental planning and in business enterprises in the form of corporate citizenship, for example, as well as in the social and community services.

The community backdrop

When we ask what is the context of community development, a common answer is, of course, that the immediate context of community development activities is a community. But there are a number of meanings of the term 'community'. In this section we explore in some detail the meanings, contestations and functions of the term 'community'.

The concept of community

As mentioned in chapter 1, the meaning and use of the term 'community' is the subject of considerable discussion and debate. Traditionally the term has referred to groups of people involved in face-to-face relations. This has been the most common use applied by community development practitioners. They have used a working definition that starts with the idea of a group of people with a common identity, which may be derived from class position, geographical location, cultural values, gender, race, ethnicity, disability, workplace or age, or it may be self-defined on the basis of shared political or other special interests.

However, even this simple working definition is not without its difficulties: it is significantly overburdened with positive value and it embraces many ideas. Over the last 100 years social scientists have attempted to extract the elements of the term. Hillery (1955) identified 94 definitions and found many inconsistencies between them. As Bauman points out, 'community' has a central place in our world view as a 'feel good' concept:

> Community is a warm place, a cosy and comfortable place ... in the community, we can relax – we are safe ... We are never strangers to each other ... we can count on other's good will (2001:1–2).

The following discussion draws out the many ways the concept has been applied. We begin with the idea of community as an object to be studied.

Community as an object of study

The term 'community' might refer to an object of study rather than a method of study. There are two key themes in this approach. The first categorises different kinds of communities; for example, urban and rural communities. The urban and rural continuum, as it came to be known, set the framework for many of the early studies of communities in the early twentieth century in the USA. The second theme considers how local social systems work (Wild, 1981). Interestingly, Stacey (1969) pointed out that while they used the term 'community', many studies were actually researching local social systems. This underpinned discussions about 'localism' and 'local socialism' in the United Kingdom in the 1970s and 1980s (Gyford, 1985; Boddy & Fudge, 1984) and is embedded in the American tradition that studies community politics and power structures (Alinsky, 1969). From this perspective, the boundaries of a community are less important than the way power is distributed.

Community as a site

'Community as a site' has both a physical and a conceptual meaning. As a physical site, community has boundaries, specific demographic features and usually some idea of a shared history (Wild, 1981). However, it is important to acknowledge that even physical communities are not fixed entities. They can establish themselves slowly or quickly. They can grow and shrink as people move locations. Their boundaries are porous. In the idea of community as a conceptual site, community is an abstract concept referring to networks of social relations based around common attributes and interests shared by people as a collective entity, rather than just geographic proximity (see Chaskin et al., 2001:8).

Yet the popular constructions of community as a site carry more than just a description of a group with a commonality. The idea of community as a site of people's power has been associated with the radical nature of community development. When identified as the *site of people's power*, community can be seen to be a harbinger of radicalism. Here, community development becomes synonymous with community activism.

In this approach, the community is a *site where relations of power are constructed and controlled*. According to Mune (1989), it is also a site where the distribution of goods and services takes place. Mune points out that the distribution of goods and services takes different forms and involves different processes in the various sectors of society:

- in the state, distribution is through the political bureaucratic process
- in the family, distribution is through obligation and kinship
- in the private sector, the market economy distributes goods and services through entrepreneurial mechanisms
- in the community sector, distribution is through exchange, mutuality and gift relations.

Community in sociological theory

Community has been the subject of a considerable amount of theoretical inquiry, especially in sociological theory. Particular theoretical understandings orient conceptions of community. Take, for example, the idea that members of a community have a mutual commitment and sense of belonging. This approach to community is connected with writers who were concerned about the social changes that took place as a result of the development of industrial society. Toennies (1987) and Durkheim (1960), for example, constructed typologies or contrasting pairs of concepts as analytical tools to explain the changes that took place in nineteenth-century Europe. Toennies distinguished between:

- **gemeinschaft**, or community, which is self-contained, united by kinship and common bonds and predominantly rural
- **gesellschaft**, or society, which is competitive, individualist, impersonal and based on contractual ties.

Durkheim identified two forms of social solidarity:

- **mechanical solidarity**, in which social relationships are intimate, personal, all-encompassing and based on common identity, values and beliefs
- **organic solidarity**, a solidarity not based on commonality, but on difference.

Increasing division of labour makes people interdependent. Durkheim argued that although industrial societies had lost a sense of common identity and values, new interrelationships had developed through the specialisation of roles and the need to rely on other people. Thus, for both Toennies and Durkheim, the onslaught of industrialisation caused the collapse of traditional values and ways of doing things. As geographical and social mobility increased, intimate and enduring social relationships disappeared, along with rigid patterns of morality and authority based on religion and family power structures.

Ironically, with the accelerating changes taking place in industrial society, there has been some nostalgia for traditional relationships and values. This nostalgia lingers both in academic circles and in popular views of contemporary industrial society (see Etzioni, 1993). It is both a burden and an advantage for the theory and practice of community development. The nostalgia is a burden when it expresses a desire to return to more traditional social life, based on enduring, authoritarian and apparently conflict-free social relations. Such societies were dominated by one gender and one class, and this domination was generally viewed as unchallengeable. Traditional societies were also hierarchical and based on patronage. While conflict might have been hidden, these societies were never completely conflict-free.

Where the term 'community' is used to connote a desire to return to these types of traditional ways, the implied values are ultimately antagonistic to community development. However, the nostalgia for idealised relationships and values based on a common identity can also draw our attention to the collective nature of the construction of identities and human endeavour. It places the sharing of interests, resources and ideas at the centre of the discussion of social development. Collective decision making and the sharing of resources and ideas are central goals of community development.

Recently a number of discussions have been concerned with developing a more complex understanding of the types of social relationships that are created in communities, an understanding that moves beyond the simple gemeinschaft/gesellschaft dichotomy. These discussions revolve around theoretical understandings of the different forms of association within and between groups, and the importance of these forms of association. For example, one strain of this discussion revolves around ideas of *thick* and *thin* types of social relationships, solidarity and trust. Thick solidarity and thick trust develop through deep, lasting and all-embracing relationships. They are evident in deep feelings of solidarity found among, for example, ultra-nationalist and racist groups, as well as in feminist organisations and oppressed minority groups. Thick social solidarity occurs when a person becomes an active member of an organisation by participating in all aspects of decision making in the organisation, for example. Thinner forms of solidarity and trust have developed as new types of close relationships are established in broader and even global settings, rather than in immediate localist communities. Thin social solidarity occurs when a person identifies with and becomes a member of an organisation just by paying a membership subscription.

Community and communitarianism

Another discussion regarding the forms of association and the importance of these forms is found in the framework of **communitarianism**. Communitarianism attempts to reinvigorate the theories and practice of community involvement as a foil to the disintegration of traditional community life, but without all the pitfalls of a naive nostalgia (Tam, 1998; Etzioni, 1995). In particular, communitarians have challenged the neo-liberal ideas of competition, individualism and self-interest as the driving forces of society. While there is not always agreement about the theoretical underpinnings and practices of communitarianism, in a very useful book, Tam (1998:7) offers three central principles. First is the viewpoint that we can only accept a claim for truth (and commitment to values) when developed through cooperative enquiry. Second, the common values that have been validated by communities of cooperative enquirers should form the basis of mutual responsibilities, which are practised by all members of the community. Finally, power relations at every level in society must be reformed so that those affected by them can participate as equal citizens in determining how power is to be exercised. The aim of these principles is to build inclusive communities.

> This means that questions about what collective action is to be taken for the common good are not to be left either to political elites who are rarely answerable to their fellow citizens ... or to individuals in the marketplace, but are considered through informed community discussions (Tam, 1998:7).

While it has a close affinity with community development, there are a number of critiques of communitarianism. First is the view that the emphasis on collective activity undermines individual incentive and creativity. Second, a related criticism is that the emphasis on inclusiveness can be taken in an authoritarian way, whereby all community members must be involved in and agree on any decisions made. Third, communitarianism begs the question about what constitutes the community and how one becomes a member of a community. Notwithstanding the claim that communitarianism is not based on a naive longing for the past, it can tend towards the idealised notion of a homogeneous community. This idealised notion finds expression in the romance of gated, patrolled middle-class communities. And, as pointed out by many writers from the Left, the idea of community glosses over class, gender and ethnic inequalities. In fact, as noted above, communities are diverse, they overlap, and we are members of a number of communities. Fourth is the question of how far a communitarian structure can overcome cultural inequalities – such as linguistic skills, confidence and knowledge – and ensure that all participants really do have an equal say in things. And, even if cultural inequality can be redressed, this does not mean that power and economic inequalities disappear. Fifth is the question of practicality. How can society be structured in a way that facilitates equal involvement by community members (and the knowledge required) to participate in effective decision making? Finally are the critiques of the ways that communitarian ideas of community have been adopted and used in third-way politics. While there has been debate about the meaning of the concept of 'third way', its proponents, such as Giddens (1998a), argue that it involves an approach to policy development that moves beyond both the Left notion of social democracy and the Right notion of neo-liberalism, thus reconstructing active, self-reliant communities. In third-way approaches, community becomes both a 'thing' to be treated and governed and a moral imperative. For example, communities become sites to be managed and bureaucratised.

There are also important and, in many ways, obvious responses to these critiques. First, even if we take the view that both collective–cooperative endeavour and individual–competitive endeavour can drive our actions as humans, then in the ascendancy in the Western world is an emphasis on the view that individual–competitive endeavour is the key to human and social development. It is therefore necessary to tip the balance back to emphasise collective–cooperative endeavour. As Tam (1998:7) points out, 'All that is distinctively human is only realised when human beings interact with each other as members of shared communities'. Indeed, it is certainly possible for humans to be both creative individuals and part of cooperative collectives.

Second, communitarianism does not have to be taken up through authoritarian pressures. There should be room for non-involvement (this point is taken up in chapters 5 and 10). Third, communitarianism does acknowledge that communities are diverse and we are members of several or many communities, and this does not undermine its principles. The key is to identify sites where people can come together to share knowledge and make decisions and to organise appropriate structures. Educational institutions, including playgroups, kindergartens, schools, colleges and universities, are such sites, as are workplaces and community organisations. Fourth, the problem of cultural inequalities can be overcome through education. Cooperative decision making can begin to make inroads on power and economic inequalities. Finally, there are now a host of new techniques and processes for organising collective and cooperative decision making, including the Internet and deliberative democracy. More shall be said about these in chapter 6.

Whether these responses are adequate or not depends to some extent on one's values and theoretical position. Perhaps the most damaging of the criticisms remains the claim that cooperative enquiry cannot redress socioeconomic and political inequalities. This criticism is perhaps best understood as part of the socialist critique of community to which we now turn.

Community from a socialist perspective

The socialist analysis of the idea of community was clearly articulated during the 1970s. Cockburn (1977) argued that the idea of community had been hijacked by those in power and used in a sense that obscures the massive inequalities existing in society. From a socialist viewpoint, the term 'community' can be used to legitimate a whole range of controlling activities by the state, as in the ideas and practices of community surveillance, community psychology and community care, for example. According to Cockburn, such labelling has electoral appeal and is cynically used by political parties without any real concern for the interests of community members.

Cockburn is concerned that the terms 'community' and 'community politics' can distort our understanding of power relations in capitalist societies. Politicians use these terms opportunistically to centre social issues and problems in the community. Community problems are seen not as the result of inequities in the distribution of resources and power, but as problems that the community itself must resolve without proper resources. Cockburn argues that such a view camouflages the structured inequalities inherent in capitalist society. In her critique of the use and meaning of the concept of community, Cockburn argues that the term should be rejected altogether, because it has been co-opted by a capitalist state. Cockburn suggests that it be replaced by the notion of *struggle in the field of capitalist reproduction*.

Repo (1977), drawing on her experiences as a community worker, identifies two uses of the term 'community': a geographical area and a client group. Both, according to Repo, view people as having common interests and common goals. They assume that everyone is equal and that problems can be sorted out through cooperative effort. She points out that community control denies the existence of class, yet it actually often involves middle-class people whose efforts result in the undermining and fragmenting of the working class.

Similarly, Bryson and Mowbray (1981) comment on the ideological usage of the term 'community', in which it is constructed in an apolitical and romanticised form that ignores class interests and assumes that significant decision making can take place at the local level. In fact, Mowbray (1985:41) identifies what he calls localist practices, such as occur in community action and community development, as 'orthodox elixirs for invigorating the democratic state'. He argues that community participation has become a modern panacea that uses the rhetoric of cooperation and harmonious relations, while servicing and legitimating the needs of those in power. For Mowbray, community participation can conceal the actual conflicts of interest that underlie our society. Following up on his earlier critique, Mowbray (2004) has analysed the idea of community in community strengthening programs. It still has ideological efficacy and Mowbray argues that the term 'community' continues to be effective in promoting affirmative messages.

This linking of community with ideology is also discussed in the context of the emphasis on organisational participation and user involvement 'in the community', which constructs people as individual consumers and glosses over their lack of real political power (see Croft & Beresford, 1989).

Cockburn, Repo, Mowbray, Croft and Beresford express significant views regarding the ideological nature of the term 'community'. It is important to note here that they reveal theoretical, ideological and strategic implications in the privileging of communities as the key sites of conflict, struggle and, ultimately, the emancipation of humanity.

Feminist critiques

The feminist critiques of the ideological use of the concept of community are also unforgiving. In particular, feminists have pointed to the imputed natural relationship between community as an associational form and women's types of association. Both are designated as secondary to the 'real business' of organising society, which operates through men's power relations in male-dominated institutions such as political parties, large corporations and trade unions. Community, when constructed in this framework, is complicit in circumscribing the limits of women's activity, defined through ideas of cooperation, informality and trust, and renders women's relationships as subordinate to the competitive, professional and formal types of relationships that dominate men's business. More shall be said about feminist perspectives in chapter 3.

Virtual communities

In contrast to the face-to-face gemeinschaft notion of community, we have new ways of associating, using mobile telephones and the Internet, which have led to different thinking about what constitutes a community.

This thinking reflects on new relationships formed around a common identity and shared interests, in what have come to be known as virtual communities. The organising idea of virtual communities is a social network. While all communities have social networks, the networks in virtual communities are mediated by information and digital technologies. Virtual communities are formed around discussion groups and chat rooms. That is, they are 'extraterritorial and do not necessitate the face-to-face contact, which is conventionally seen as central to community relations' (Blackshaw, 2010:104). Virtual communities are, in a strong sense, communities of choice because people can easily choose their degree of involvement in virtual communities (Wellman & Gulia, 1999, in Blackshaw 2010:106). As Blackshaw (2010) argues, virtual communities enable people to join communities of their own volition.

Virtual communities are usually 'thin' communities. The relationships formed are unlike the multidimensional relationships of the older gemeinschaft-type communities. That is, people do not present themselves in many dimensions as friends, partners, relatives, workers, and such. This anonymity opens up possibilities for more egalitarian relationships and the traditional, ascribed identities can be challenged or undermined. For example, in virtual communities people have more room to experiment and 'play' with their identities. Virtual communities open up opportunities for the empowerment of marginalised groups that have been frozen out of traditional community power structures (Blackshaw, 2010). However, such communities usually provide no more than 'thin' support for people wanting to share many aspects of their lives. Indeed the traditional idea of community solidarity can look very weak in the context of a virtual community. Moreover, searching out people (on the Internet) to share your specific ideas can lead to narrow enclaves with particularistic interests. Do these virtual communities challenge the conception of community-based solidarity and comfort of the thick face-to-face relationships of the traditional community? In some ways yes, because the time we spend 'online' and in chat rooms, linking with people around the globe, affects the amount of time we have to talk to our neighbours, for example, in face-to-face relationships. However, as Blackshaw (2010) contends, the Internet does not necessarily provide a separate reality; it is more likely to supplement existing relationships. For example, Facebook and Twitter are used to support existing relationships, rather than replace them.

A useful concept?

At the end of this section, we come to the question 'Is "community" a useful concept in the contemporary world?' How this question is answered is profoundly important for community development practitioners, because 'community' sets out the sites upon which they work and frames the scope of their activities. Most writers seem to be ambivalent about the meaning and value of the concept today. Certainly there seems to be some agreement that the traditional ideas of community, especially those embedded in some kind of 'gemeinschaft' concept, are outdated. For example, in a moving critique of the traditional community, Bauman (2001:3) states:

> What the word (community) evokes is everything we miss and what we lack to be secure, confident and trusting. In short, 'community stands for the kind of world which is not, regrettably, available to us but which we would dearly wish to inhabit and which we hope to repossess.

Similarly, MacCannell (1992, in Blackshaw, 2010:8) has argued that the idea of community in its orthodox sociological understanding has ceased to be of any use and in its place we have ersatz or manufactured substitute communities, based on illusion. Community, in this way, has been so hollowed out that it is no more than an empty shell.

While these critiques, as well as the socialist and feminist critiques discussed above, are considerable, the position taken in this book is that such critiques do not render the concept unusable. What is required, however, is thoughtful and informed use that takes account of the realities of life in the first decades of the twenty-first century. In the following discussion, six suggestions for dealing with the concept of community today are proposed. First, it is important to sort out the ideological uses of the term. For example, it is useful to distinguish between the idea of community that is used to identify the context of an activity (physical and conceptual) and the idea of community that is nostalgic and ideological in its use. For example, it is important to be mindful of how the idea can involve appropriation, such as often occurs in its placement alongside other terms in way that serves to 'soften' the concept, as in 'community playground' and 'community policing', or marketing ploys such as 'community supermarket' and 'community plumber', in which, as Mowbray (1985) has pointed out, it has a 'medicinal effect' to legitimate existing structures, market activities and power relations.

Second, even in its value-laden or normative use, the concept of community draws attention to the human quest for mutuality, trust and collective endeavour, as discussed above. The importance given to community views – for example, through community consultations organised by government (even when these are tokenistic) – validates the important role of the bottom-up processes that are central to community development. The role of community politics as a training ground for politicians who later become involved in wider politics (such as in the case of President Barack Obama), and as a significant site of power itself, has not diminished. It continues to have a role in the overall transformation of society. The views of Cochrane (1986) remain relevant today. As he pointed out in the 1980s, community politics

> begins to redefine politics as a process which stretches from the daily experience of ordinary life to wider decisions about resources. It implicitly challenges the notion that certain areas can be defined out of political discussion and that other areas of decision making, namely government, have to be left to political experts, whether bureaucrats or party politicians (Cochrane, 1986:52–3).

Third, the term continues to have meaning for ordinary people, in both its descriptive and normative sense. It continues to carry with it important understandings of the ways that individuals share common experiences, goals and interests; develop shifting but common identities; cooperate to achieve goals; and construct a collective existence. What is important about the concept of community in this sense is that it reflects a reality constructed by people themselves. People identify with communities on the basis of their own concrete experiences and relations. That is, people develop their own social ties and their own identities, and these are meaningful to them. Communities provide reference points for their lives. We can specify groups of people who share sufficient elements of commonality that they think and act as a community in the sense of shared relations of trust and mutuality. For example, for people who voluntarily get together at the neighbourhood level to work for their local state school, or people who share a passion for saving the world's wilderness and who communicate consistently via the Internet, the idea of community has resonance. Communities in this sense, of course, are not constructed for all time. For example, they can arise when a common threat is perceived, develop a strong sense of solidarity and then dissipate when the threat dwindles. Communities change and disappear as their constituent identities and social relationships change, fragment and disappear.

Fourth, we are beginning to think about how we can refashion the concept to make it appropriate to our understanding of new forms of association and collective endeavour, such as virtual communities and transnational organising via the Internet. We are witnessing the appearance of new types of communities, organised around new types of networks, that are not face-to-face or 'once and for all' communities. These new communities are fluid networked communities. They are what Bauman (2001, 2000) identifies as 'liquid communities', continually changing and taking new shapes.

Fifth, overall, when speaking about community it is important to be aware of where common interests may or may not lie. The commitment to diversity means that we must be sensitive to the coexistence of multiple communities. For example, a number of communities exist in any one locality.

Finally, one useful approach to community is to avoid the notion of an abstract community and instead link community with a specific descriptor, which might be geographical, interest-based or culturally based, for example. Such an approach can draw our attention to the source of the shared interest, identity or identities, whether they are based on locality, class, gender, age or ethnicity, for example. Thus, we speak about the rural community, the gay community, the Koori community or, more specifically, the youth community in Port Augusta or the elderly Greek community in Brisbane. But we should also remember the fluidity of groups, the multifaceted characteristics of communities and the porous nature of the boundaries of communities. For example, ethnicity is not a straightforward concept. In the framework of multiculturalism we identify 'blended communities' involving groups of people with two or more identities. For example, there are Arab–Australian communities and Vietnamese–Australian communities. This terminology draws our attention to the fact that people belong to more than one community and can draw on many cultural traditions. Once we start thinking in terms of identity it is clear that all of us have multiple identities.

Before we leave this, we consider on page 54 how one community development worker thinks of her 'community' in a multidimensional sense.

The political backdrop
Political action

Above we noted that community development is often located in the social and community services industry, although its identity as a political practice can make this location problematic. In this section we focus on community development that emphasises its role as a form of political struggle and political activism, by considering its connection to **class** and **patriarchy**.

Background and basics

> **INTERVIEW WITH MARIA**
>
> We asked Maria, a community development worker in a Greek Community Centre, what she identified as her community. 'I don't have just one community, but many,' she replied. 'First and foremost, I am a Greek Australian, therefore I identify as a Greek Australian. This is my primary community. I also work in a Greek–Australian community organisation and therefore I have many co-workers who also form part of my community. My mum and dad are retired now, but they were factory workers, and they made many friends in this [working-class] suburb, and I still visit their friends and I think of their friends as my community as well. My kids go to Glen Ryan State School. I am on the school committee. We are currently organising the school fete and are working closely together on this. This is also my community. But we have a relationship with a school in East Timor, and we have an exchange with this school in place. I have visited our partner school on several occasions and its teachers have come to Australia. We work closely together and we exchange ideas on the Internet so I also think of them as my community. There is also a group of us, mainly women, who meet as a book group, and I now think of the members of this book club as my community. So you see, I have many communities and many identities.'

case study

Class struggle

When community development first found political expression in Australia it was linked with struggles against the state. As we will discuss in the following chapter, those influenced by Marxist theory have argued that what goes on in the state is circumscribed by the economic system, and that the key players in the struggle for power are classes. Metcalfe (1990) points out how the Marxist concept of struggle has been identified only as **class struggle** and has been expressed in the metaphor of war. This metaphor leads us to think in terms of a 'one-off' cathartic event. It conjures up notions of the actors as armies, facing each other in violent battles in public places such as battlefields and in the streets. This effectively rules out the notion of struggle in more private places such as in neighbourhood houses and in the home. The imagery of struggle as a war also embodies a zero-sum concept of power in which there are only two sides: one that wins and one that loses. This zero-sum approach to conflict oversimplifies both power and social change, yet it sets the political agenda for many people involved in struggle. From a community development perspective, politics is manifested at all levels of human life. All institutions, all social structures and all social relations are political spheres.

Struggle against patriarchy

Community development owes much of the understanding of political power to the insights of feminism. While feminism will be discussed in detail in the following chapter, it is worth considering some of its key tenets here. Feminism has revealed that the pervasiveness of patriarchy, involving structures, values, beliefs and practices, sets the context in which the oppression of women takes place. Feminists have also argued that *the personal is political*. They have shown that practices and processes such as the household division of labour, friendships and sexual relationships, child rearing and childcare are central sites of the domination of women (see Rowbotham, Segal & Wainwright, 1979). In the past, such everyday activities were not regarded as part of politics. Feminists have explained how everyday life and everyday institutions reinforce inequality. One such institution is the family, an important agent that limits women's life choices and transmits existing beliefs about how society should work (Wilson, 1977).

The crisis of the Left

During the last century, the working class and the oppressed tended to turn to leftist and socialist parties, socialist movements and the trade unions for support in their struggles against the powerful. However, by the beginning of the twenty-first century, there is general agreement that the Left in Australia has suffered a series of serious defeats. Its relevance for the contemporary period is very much in question. But what do we mean by 'the Left'? There are countless discussions of the definition and meaning of the Left, in the contexts of etymology, political theory, social movement analysis, philosophy and history, just to name a few. A useful starting point is provided by the Italian writer Norberto Bobbio, who identifies the Left with egalitarianism and distinguishes left-leaning positions, which support equality, from right-wing ones, which support inequality (Bobbio, 1996). Thus, in its broadest form, the term 'left' refers to ideas and philosophies, people, groups and political and social movements whose normative base is embedded in a commitment to an equalitarian society. An equalitarian society is based on the principles of equality of opportunity, sustainability for future generations (in both the social and physical sense), sharing of resources, productive activities, skills and knowledge and, as far as possible, collective endeavour and self-determination.

In Australia both the Labor Party and the unions have moved away from traditional left agendas. The Labor Party has departed from socialist objectives and shifted to the right. The trade union movement has placed itself in an awkward position in regard to its links with working-class action. The leadership of the union movement has tended to become more technocratic and bureaucratic. The union movement is now caught up in the momentum of neo-liberal policies that are further undermining the traditional principles of trade unionism. Given the practical weaknesses of the left agenda for equality and the failures of socialist states, there has also been theoretical discussion of the ways the dichotomy of left and right has lost its heuristic value. Indeed, it leads into a political one-way street, with no room for about-turns or compromise. According to this view, the activities and beliefs of human beings are messy and often contradictory. They cannot always be placed into neat categories of left or right (Giddens, 1994). Often they are both. For example, a government policy commitment to community capacity building can be based on both a commitment to equality through strengthening the resources and power of communities, and a commitment to lifting the competitive edge of a community and engendering further inequality. As a champion of this third-way approach to policy, Giddens (1998a) has argued that third-way politics and thought offer a route for breaking through the binary way of thinking presented in the left/right dichotomy. The construction of third-way politics can be seen as part of a search for new political and social forms, to which we now turn.

The search for new political and social forms
Rethinking politics

In recent years we have seen the construction of new terms of reference for the debate about how we are to organise socio-political structures. This debate is propelled by the search for new processes for development and emergent and feasible institutions that offer paths to more equalitarian and just societies. While this has a long way to go, it is useful to note some key themes. First, we will consider how two influential writers, Giddens and Hirst, have begun to conceptualise and map new forms of social and political organisation. Second we will consider the rise of human rights discourse and understanding.

We begin with the theme of **generative politics** developed by Giddens. For Giddens (1994:15):

> Generative politics is a politics which seeks to allow individuals and groups to make things happen, rather than have things happen to them, in the context of overall social concerns and goals ... It works through providing material conditions and organisational frameworks, for the life–political conditions taken by individuals and groups in the wider social order.

Culturally and socially, generative politics requires the creation of situations in which active trust can be built and sustained. It also requires the giving of autonomy to those who are affected by specific programs or policies. Economically, the development of generative politics requires generating resources that enhance autonomy. Structurally, an effective generative politics requires the decentralisation of political power (Giddens, 1994:93). Generative politics is the kind of politics that underpins the activities of many self-help groups, for example, for such groups are self-determining organisations. They are concerned with the development of self-understanding and autonomy. They seek to 'make things happen' by providing democratic structures, material conditions and organisational frameworks that can facilitate the achievement of the members' goals.

A second theme we consider is associative democracy, which has been most comprehensively elaborated by Hirst (1994). **Associative democracy** involves shifting the control of, and responsibility for, social development from the social administrative institutions of the centralised state to self-governing voluntary associations (or community organisations). Self-governing voluntary associations can be organised around any range of interests, projects or services. For example, they might involve community development, welfare service delivery, not-for-profit community enterprise, advocacy or community education programs.

Hirst (1994) argues that self-governing voluntary associations have the potential to be principal organising forces in society, the key institutions that provide public welfare and other public services and the primary means of democratic governance. He envisages that voluntary associations will be funded primarily through mechanisms of public finance established by the state and regulated by some common public rules and standards. Voluntary associations would be democratically accountable to both the publics they serve for the relevance and effectiveness of their programs and to common public power for their expenditure. Associative democracy offers a mechanism for individual and collective responsibility and empowerment that is necessary for active citizenship and a strong public sphere. It promises to combine a deepening of citizenship choice with strong public welfare.

The concepts of generative politics and associative democracy have much appeal for community development. Community development, like generative politics, encourages self-determination and autonomy. It aims to provide material conditions and organisational frameworks that facilitate people taking action on their own behalf. Similarly, associative democracy offers a new way of thinking about how to develop political and social forms appropriate to different social conditions. For example, a system based on associative democracy offers an alternative to contemporary welfare regimes by cutting through the separation of welfare, governance, social change and empowering institutions. It offers democratic and self-determining processes that could replace welfare regimes based on the top-down welfare provided by centralised bureaucratic states, the private welfare programs constructed around market principles and the private non-market provision of welfare based on concepts of familial duty, which bear heavily on women.

For the moment, the ideas of generative politics and associative democracy remain mostly theoretical endeavours that set out frameworks for change, but require political will on the part of both citizens and politicians to be implemented. However, this is not to deny their potential to open up debate about the need to supersede both the egoistic individualism that underpins economic rationalism and the formal state collectivism of communism. An understanding of the ideas of generative politics and associative democracy can also open up discussion of alternative ways of organising our socio-political structures.

The rise of human rights

A third theme that is influencing our thinking about how to develop social and political organisation is that of **human rights**. As discussed in the previous chapter, human rights begin from some understanding of what it is to be human and what makes a decent and fulfilling life. Discussion of what constitutes a decent and fulfilling life has taken place throughout human history. However, this discussion has generally been particularistic, insofar as it has dealt with the rights of the privileged. It has not included the rights of the underprivileged, disadvantaged and marginalised people in society. In fact, one way that elites have historically maintained their power has been to deny that the powerless of society have any rights at all. What characterises the rise of human rights discourse as we know it has been the idea that human rights apply universally. For example, all human beings have the right to live in a peaceful world; to have liberty and security; to be free from servitude and degrading treatment; to have freedom of thought, opinion and expression; and to have a standard of living adequate for health and wellbeing (Universal Declaration of Human Rights, 1948; see the Appendix). A corollary to the identification of universal human rights is the obligation to guarantee these rights. Thus, within the human rights framework, the institutions of government, business and civil society must operate in ways that reinforce the rights of their constituents.

Human rights discourse has set up a framework in which those in power can be made to account for abuses to people who challenge their power or are deemed to be inferior. It calls for citizens to respect others and exercise their own rights. It provides a rallying point for community organisations concerned with exploitation, disadvantage and oppression. For example, Australians challenging the incarceration of asylum seekers in detention centres point out the many ways that both Labor and Liberal and National Party policies on asylum seekers are an abuse of human rights.

In the last 50 years there has been considerable discussion of the claims, promises and failures of the rise of human rights discourse and practice. The major critique holds that notwithstanding the discussion of human rights over this time, the identification of human rights abuses, the establishment of human rights courts and the discourses, policies and laws established to guard against abuses really have no teeth. Despite the use of sanctions and stern United Nations' directives, there is often little that can be done to stop oppressive regimes short of an invasion, and invasion poses problems in terms of other forms of human rights abuses of a country's right to sovereignty and self-determination. This paradox has been poignantly illustrated in the case of the US-led invasion of Iraq. While this criticism of the failures of human rights discourses is important, it does not negate the importance of consistency in dealing with human rights issues and the need to strengthen the processes we have developed to protect human rights.

The global backdrop

In this section we survey some of the features of the wider environment in which community development operates in the first decades of the twenty-first century. We begin with the important concept of globalisation.

Globalisation

It is impossible to discuss the contemporary context of community development without mentioning **globalisation**. In recent years, the idea of globalisation has captured the imagination of political commentators, business executives and social critics alike. For the Left, globalisation can mean new international networks of workers and political activists. But it can also mean strengthening the monopoly of multinational capitalist enterprises. It can lead to the deepening exploitation of workers and new forms of ideological and material control of disadvantaged people. For the Right, globalisation, particularly when manifested in free-trade policies, can mean the opening up of lucrative markets and the supply of cheap and non-unionised labour. Globalisation can also mean weakening the sovereignty of nation states.

But what is globalisation? There are many views. McGrew (1992:65–75) understands globalisation to refer to the multiplicity of linkages and interconnections that transcend nation states. Steger (2003) notes that globalisation is used to describe a process, a condition, a force, a system and an age. For example, it is a process through which events, decisions and activities in one part of the world affect individuals and communities in another part of the world. Through globalisation, economic, social, political and environmental aspects of human life interconnect in a way that both strengthens interdependences and overrides traditional borders and boundaries. That is, it opens up new ways of relating to each other as humans. In an everyday sense, globalisation means that elements of our existence, including ideas, goods, money, pollution, disease, crime, terrorism, information, entertainment, and even people, are now crossing the world on an unprecedented scale and speed (Held, 2004).

According to Giddens (1994:4–5), globalisation should be understood as the transformation of time and space. That is, globalisation involves not only the creation of large-scale systems, but also the transformation of local and personal contexts of experience. What is often of interest to community development is the idea that globalisation can simultaneously strengthen and weaken the powers of local communities. What is happening in one city of the world can be influenced by an event somewhere else in the world. A currency crisis in Japan can affect Australian exports to Japan, which in turn can mean an increase in the number of jobless in an Australian regional city, which puts more pressure on local community services. But the economic behaviour of consumers in an Australian regional city can also affect the jobless rate in an Asian regional city. As Giddens points out, a decision to buy a shirt made in the sweatshops of Asia can also have implications for the international division of labour.

A dominant critical view from the Left has been that globalisation has three core interpretations. First, it is essentially neo-liberalism gone global. Second, it is a manifestation of American economic and political hegemony. Third, it is a continuation of Western colonialism (see Gibney 2003:7). From this perspective, the forms that globalisation has taken since the 1980s are different from previous forms of internationalisation such as inter-country trade. But more importantly, neo-liberal globalisation involves the intensification of threats to the security, autonomy and, indeed, the human rights of much of the world's population. The neo-conservative image of a world progressing in unison in a developing global utopia has been undermined by the reality of the marginalisation of the poor and disenfranchised, and increasing inequalities of power and wealth, driven by the prerogatives of global corporations and Western foreign policy (Gibney, 2003).

The much-flaunted international free-flow of capital between the middle classes and the wealthy of the (usually Western) world has been profoundly shaken by the global financial crisis of 2008–2009. It has certainly not been matched by a free-flow of the poor or other global actors such as asylum seekers. In a provocative book, Ritzer (2004) has taken the neo-liberal meaning of globalisation a step further. He argues that much of what is actually being 'globalised' is 'nothing'. That is, globalisation involves 'social forms that are centrally conceived, controlled and comparatively devoid of distinctive substantial content' (2004:xi). His analysis of 'nothing' focuses on the proliferation of goods and services that are produced for consumption, such as standardised logo-based T-shirts, shopping malls and ATMs. These goods and services lack unique, authentic and local features. They are not planned individually and there is no organic development, care or local ownership involved in their operations, as there is in farmers' markets and cooperatives. From this viewpoint, 'nothingness' erodes cultural richness and diversity. Ritzer's theory throws out a number of challenges to think about in terms of how community development could become a generic global practice, or even a 'brand name' that could be used cynically to gain legitimacy for global programs. As a global brand, instead of facilitating cultural richness, community development could undermine the authenticity of local cultures.

Another form of globalisation draws on these Western structures and processes, but with different intents and outcomes. This form of globalisation involves the transfer of capital, information and a 'select few' global actors. But its powerful and wealthy are the leaders of international networks of religious fundamentalists, some of whom have become international terrorists. The terrorism these international actors practise in some ways mirrors the state terrorism practised by some governments. International terrorism of both state and religious groups invokes the use of violence or threat of violence against civilian targets and for political objectives (Barker, 2003). Consciousness of Islamic terrorism, in particular, and the threats and actions of radical Islamists have been ratcheted up since September 2001. The backdrop of their actions, as Ali (2002) points out, was the very actions of the agents of global capitalism, such as the neo-liberal economic prescriptions handed down to developing countries by the International Monetary Fund and the World Bank, for these actions helped to unlock the space for political Islam. The political oxygen that allowed the minorities who have engaged in politico-religious extremism to grow has been provided in the context of corrupt regimes in the Middle East and Africa, often backed by the West, and indecisive leaders flirting with fundamentalist elements that they thought they could control to their own advantage. This form of globalisation, while often ignored in the discussion of globalisation and human rights, also poses a significant threat to the autonomy and security of much of the world's population, and particularly to the populations of the developing world. In our discussions of difference and diversity in chapter 8 we discuss how the actions of radical Islamists and the media response to these actions have affected multicultural communities in Australia and how community development practitioners are responding to the new forms of nationalism and xenophobia.

Notwithstanding these extensive critiques, it is important to remember that globalisation is not a single process, but a complex mixture of processes that may be conflicting (Giddens, 1994). For example, McGrew (1992:74–5) draws our attention to the contradictory processes that are taking place within the framework of globalisation. These include:

- *Universalisation versus particularisation*: globalisation both universalises aspects of life (such as the experience of watching the world through the eyes of CNN journalists and working on an assembly production line making Ford cars) and simultaneously encourages particularisation, as communities react to universalism by accentuating differences and uniqueness (as manifested in the resurgence of regionalism and ethnic identity and the identification of niche markets in the manufacturing industry).
- *Homogenisation versus particularisation*: globalisation involves an emphasis on the sameness of experience (such as eating a McDonald's hamburger, staying in a Hilton hotel, walking through a street of skyscrapers in a modern city) and claims for the

universal application of rights (for example, 'The Universal Declaration of Human Rights'), that exist alongside the construction and re-articulation of the global in relation to local circumstances (for example, new hotels and skyscrapers might attempt to present a local cultural decor in their interior design; human rights are given different emphases in different cultures).

- *Integration versus fragmentation*: globalisation means new political and social alliances that integrate cultures and societies (for example, transnational corporations, multilateral agreements on trade, international trade unions), as well as the fragmentation of social formations, including nation states torn by racial and ethnic conflicts (as groups search to reinstate deep identities so that they may overcome the alienation that results from their distance from universal powers) and the fragmentation of class and labour solidarity as workers fight for jobs in fragmented labour markets.
- *Centralisation versus decentralisation*: while forces for universalism and integration facilitate the increasing concentration of power, knowledge, information and wealth, they also generate a reaction to centralisation, through both central governments divesting powers and decision making to regions and communities in a top-down fashion (such as has occurred in Britain where Scotland has been given limited self-government) and bottom-up movements and demands made for self-government by local regions (for example, Quebec in Canada) and often violent struggles for independence (such as have occurred in East Timor and Bougainville, and by the Kurdish people in Iraq and Turkey). Similarly, while many social movements, including women's, peace and green movements, have centralised global offices and policies, they also have autonomous decentralised structures and policies that operate very much within local areas and constraints and use local strategies.

There continues to be vigorous debate about the strength and effects of globalisation. In their book, *Globalisation in Question*, Hirst and Thompson (1996) have subjected the idea of globalisation to critical scrutiny. They contend that, while there are trends towards internationalisation, the strong globalisation thesis that leads to the conclusion that distinct national economies are being dissolved is not supported by their analysis of the data.

Understanding the debates about globalisation is important for community development. The question of the degree of autonomy at local, regional and nation-state levels is profoundly important to community development practitioners. As Hirst and Thompson (1996) point out, if the image of global economic processes is strong, it can paralyse radical national reforming strategies. Governments can invoke the need to be economically competitive in the globalised economy as a way of disciplining the workforce. They can also repress political opposition and local struggles in the name of political stability and so ensure investment by multinational companies.

At the same time, the globalisation of communication systems such as the Internet opens up possibilities for the exchange of information between those involved in different local struggles (across nation states for example) in ways that were unimaginable 30 years ago. Indeed, there are many liberating elements of globalisation. Globalisation can mean the development of new international networks and alternative sources of information. The unprecedented access to information provided by the Internet includes uncontrolled information exchanges between ordinary people. For example, in the United Kingdom political parties are taking notice of discussions in a 'mums' website, called Mumsnet, which at first glance appears to be little more than advice to 'mums' about babies and recipes, but is actually wielding quite significant policy influence in its informative online discussions. There are now many websites – such as Democracywatch, Human Rights Watch, Wikileaks, Witness and hurisearch (a human rights search engine) – that subvert ideas and practices that support anti-democratic behaviour, exploitation and avoidance of human rights obligations. The power of the Internet is also evident in the Chinese government's need to black out what it considers to be subversive websites.

Globalisation also engenders the new forms of transnational solidarity necessary for global movements, such as those fighting for an environmentally sustainable world. International NGOs and networks of NGOs are key forces in international politics (DeMars, 2005). The meanings, forms and enforcement of human rights are being discussed and debated within these networks.

Overall, globalisation seems to offer a mixed bag of opportunities and dangers, depending on one's theoretical and value standpoint. As pointed out above, from a community development perspective, globalisation can mean that many community struggles must be waged on new international fronts. And, as the reach of international capital spreads, this can weaken the power of local people in their struggles for self-determination. Yet globalisation can also mean that new opportunities for international cooperation between diverse communities can be opened up.

Risks, contradictions and crises

While many philosophy and sociology books have analysed the profound global crises and challenges over the past 50 years, one concept has come to prominence in the last 20 years, and this is the concept of risk. For example, Beck (1992:19–20) argues that the production and distribution of wealth in contemporary societies is systematically accompanied by the production and distribution of risks:

> Questions of the development and employment of technologies (in the realms of nature, society and personality) are being eclipsed by questions of the political and economic management of the risks of actually or potentially utilised technologies – discovering, administering, acknowledging, avoiding or concealing such hazards with respect to specially defined horizons of relevance.

Since September 2001, with the intensification of world focus on terrorism, border protection and environmental risk, there has been growing interest in the idea that our existence has become more hazardous and our world is 'out of control' or at least dangerously unpredictable. One way of understanding this view is the idea of a particular type of society, which Beck describes as **risk society**. We discuss the theoretical concept of risk further in the following chapter.

In the context of risk society it is easy to understand how there is increasing focus on risk assessment and risk management in the work of community development practitioners. Verity (2004) points out that a trigger for establishing formal risk management systems has been the rise of public liability insurance. Verity's research has revealed how the growing costs of insurance products have affected community organisations. A vicious circle of fundraising and insurance requirements and regulations has profoundly affected smaller organisations that have to secure public liability insurance to receive government funds. To pay for the insurance they need more fundraising activities, which in turn require additional public liability insurance and thus more fundraising. Verity describes how in some cases the need for public liability insurance has sometimes meant the demise of a community organisation altogether. As well as bringing about funding crises, insurance requirements mean that organisations focus on establishing a risk-averse environment at the expense of initiating new and innovative projects. Risk management courses abound, including those offering guidance to non-profits in selecting the best risk management and insurance packages.

The following case study indicates the extent to which risk management affects our daily activities.

INTERVIEW WITH A MIGRANT RESOURCE CENTRE WORKER

Working in a Migrant Resource Centre, I am continually reminded of the so-called 'riskiness' of our activities and the lack of trust in what we do. To begin with, when I enter the foyer to the office in the morning, I am greeted by a security guard. Even though he knows me, I still need my 'smart card' to get through the first door. My every move in the foyer is also monitored by a security camera. Of course, this is not as bad as getting into a government department, where I need my ID card all the time and have to go through three safety checks. The red tape has increased exponentially in the last five years. For most of our funds we now need to apply through a competitive tendering process. If we win a tender we have to use lawyers to assist in drawing up a detailed contract. The government funding department has the right to inspect our premises and all our files at any time they like. We are required to develop detailed strategic plans for our activities, with KPIs (key performance indicators), and we need to account for which KPIs we have not fulfilled and why. All our staff and even our volunteers need to be cleared through police checks – they could be paedophiles or potential terrorists! Because we work with Islamic communities, and Australia has adopted profiling to identify possible 'terrorists', we are required to report anyone suspicious in these communities. All our programs require a monitoring and evaluation process to be put in place. Our lives now seem to be run on the basis of a continual charade of risk and audit (interview, October 2005).

Here, the community development worker is under surveillance, both physically and bureaucratically, in her activities of arriving at work and managing a contract and funds. She is monitored and audited through complex reporting systems. She is also required to monitor the activities of the people she works with, be they volunteers or paid workers.

Cosmopolitanism

Sitting alongside ideas of globalisation is an approach to understanding and responding to the diversity of social, cultural and political life that has come to be known as **cosmopolitanism**. Like globalisation, forms of cosmopolitanism have always been with us. Also, like globalisation, the cosmopolitanism of today is deeper and more pervasive than in the past. The concept begins from the premises of the interdependence of humans globally (Beck & Sznaider, 2006). It applies this premise to the notion of a world citizenry that transcends the interests of the nation state (Beck, 2006). While the idea of cosmopolitanism comprises elements that are similar to those embodied in the idea of globalisation, the two concepts are not synonymous. Cosmopolitanism involves what Beck (2006:7) identifies as the 'melange principle': 'the principle that local, national, ethnic, religious and cosmopolitan cultures ... interpenetrate, interconnect and intermingle'. Thus it eschews the distinction between us and them and the dualisms of 'local and global' and 'national and international' that underpin much of the discussion of globalisation (Beck & Sznaider, 2006; Tomlinson, 1999). As Fine (2007:x) comments:

> the appeal of cosmopolitanism has to do with the idea that human beings can belong anywhere, humanity has shared predicaments and we find our community with others in exploring how these predicaments can be faced in common.

Community development practitioners who are equally at home whether they are working with anti-logging groups in South-East Asia or in Australia, and identify equally with both groups as their community, can be understood as 'cosmopolitan citizens'.

To complete this section, it is worth noting a plea for cosmopolitanism by Václav Havel (1997), a former president of the Czech Republic:

> There are countless types of responsibility, perceived as either more or less pressing, many of which vary naturally among individuals. We feel responsible to ourselves or for ourselves, for our health, our performance, our welfare; we feel responsible for our families, our companies, our communities, our professions, political parties, churches, regions, nations or countries; and somewhere in the background of all these feelings of responsibility there is, in every one of us, a small feeling of responsibility for the world as a whole and for its future. Don't we all feel that the world does not end at the moment of our death and that it is wrong to act as if we do not care if the floods come after we are gone? Nevertheless, it seems to me that this last and deepest responsibility, that is responsibility for the world, is very low for a number of reasons and is actually dangerously low against the background of the fact that the world today is a more interlinked place than ever before in history and that we are de facto living one global destiny and that almost anything that happens anywhere in the world may in one way or another affect the lives of us all.

Sustainability

We should not leave this discussion of globalisation, risk and cosmopolitanism without mentioning the global issue of sustainability. We listed sustainability as a key principle of community development in the previous chapter. Here we return briefly to the concept. There are different forms and definitions of sustainability. As discussed in the previous chapter, in the community development context there is a commitment to sustainability in two main senses. Community development programs and all community development activities need to be environmentally sustainable. In this book we refer to sustainable development generally as development that meets the needs of the present without compromising the ability of future generations to meet their own needs, as defined by the World Commission on Environment. Even according to this most simple definition, the ways we practise development today are alarming. As Ife (2009:2) points out, the social, economic and political system that has driven this world in recent decades is unsustainable. The ecological crisis facing humanity challenges us to rethink our relationship to each other, our relationship to the natural world, our lifestyles, and indeed our very ways of thinking about humanity and whatever meaning human life has. We take up the issue of sustainability in our discussion of green approaches in the following chapter. To end this section, we consider a case study of a transnational non-government organisation that has elements of both cosmopolitanism and sustainability.

MUTUAL LEARNING THROUGH BOOKS FOR SCHOOLS

Ten years ago, Polash was studying a postgraduate course that assisted him to undertake an in-country placement on the Burma–Thai border, where thousands of Burmese refugees had settled. In the school he was placed in, very few students had access to books. On returning to Australia he spoke to his friends about the desperate need for books in these schools. Together they set up a foundation, 'Books for Schools', whose purpose was to liaise with the teachers in the refugee schools in Thailand to establish a process for purchasing and sending much-needed books. They approached Burmese refugees in Australia, who also joined the foundation. These Burmese refugees, together with Australian teachers, visited the refugee camps in Thailand to find out what would be of most benefit to the schools. After visiting these schools, the foundation realised that there were many, many schools that could be assisted by having a small collection of books, and developed a plan to establish small libraries. But they also realised the wealth of the traditional Burmese culture and how much they could learn from the people in the refugee camps, who had lived in a sustainable way for many generations. They raised money for exchanges of students and teachers with the aim of mutual learning. Some schools had access to the Internet and here the libraries offered computer access and training. Now some of the refugee students have access to off-campus courses in Australia and the USA. Several graduates have set up Burmese cultural exchanges. The aim of the foundation is for all involved to learn from each other, treat each other with respect and learn to live sustainably. All parties realise that they have much to learn and a long way to go – but they have set up a program to do this.

This foundation is a cosmopolitan organisation in several respects. It involves the 'melange principle' by bringing together traditional Burmese and Thai cultures with modern Western learnings. It is strongly based on cross-cultural respect and identity. It has developed a cosmopolitan culture insofar as the different cultures 'interpenetrate, interconnect and intermingle'.

The policy backdrop

With the election of the federal Labor government in November 2007 there have been some interesting reconfigurations of issues in Australian communities, resulting in some new emphases in social policy. Perhaps the most important of these has been the emphasis on social inclusion.

Social inclusion

One of the most important initiatives setting the context for community development in the second decade of the twenty-first century involves the adoption of social inclusion policies by various governments in Australia. Commitment to social inclusion begins with concern about those who are excluded from meaningful participation in society. Academic analyses of the meaning of social inclusion trace its history back to French Republican thought whereby socially excluded people were deemed to lack the rights of citizens (Pierson, 2002). This tradition placed citizenship rights at the centre of analysis. In contrast, a dominant policy driver today is neo-liberalism. Rather than focus on citizenship rights, neo-liberalism focuses on how individuals make inappropriate choices that result in disadvantage (Buckmaster & Thomas, 2009).

Social exclusion both causes and results from a breakdown of the bonds and social connections between the state, individuals and society. Contemporary government policy initiatives to tackle social inclusion are based on the belief that it is the responsibility of the state to bring disconnected people back into the (social) fold (see Buckmaster & Thomas, 2009) and secure a socially inclusive society. In Australia the government approach to social inclusion moves between the citizen rights approach (where inclusion is a right and must be facilitated by state action) and the neo-liberal approach (where inclusion is the responsibility of individuals, through gaining employment, for example) noted above; that is, the need for structural change towards more equality, which is sometimes known as the redistributionist approach (Pierson, 2002; Levitas, 1998) and the need for personal initiative to overcome social exclusion.

The idea of government involvement in social inclusion strategies was evident in South Australia in 2002 (Buckmaster & Thomas, 2009) and was picked up by the Rudd government in 2008. Under this government it was translated into national government policy and managed by a Social Inclusion Board and a Social Inclusion Unit in the Department of the Prime Minister and Cabinet, as well as a minister and a parliamentary secretary for social inclusion. At the most general level, the goal of social inclusion policies in Australia is to ensure that people are able to participate fully in the economic, political, social and cultural life of their society. The social inclusion agenda is concerned with identifying factors that hinder social inclusion and the groups that are socially excluded, and to develop strategies for their inclusion. In so doing it involves the construction of indicators of social exclusion and inclusion, and a research program to measure whether particular interventions have increased levels of social inclusion. The Australian Government has published a comprehensive set of research reports on the forms and extent of social exclusion and strategies for tackling social exclusion. What these reports highlight is the extent to which many Australians are trapped in a 'spiral of disadvantage' caused by such factors as family circumstances, low level of education, long-term unemployment, low expectations, chronic ill health, community poverty and lack of suitable and affordable housing (Australian Government, 2009b). The key aims of the federal government's social inclusion policy are to improve the quality of essential government services, ensure that these services work more effectively in the most disadvantaged communities, and to develop partnerships with business, community organisations and disadvantaged communities to find solutions and to address needs (Australian Government, 2009b).

To understand what underpins this agenda it is useful to draw on citizenship theory and the claims about the value of social capital. As discussed in chapter 1, citizenship is concerned with what constitutes membership of a society. Citizenship can be passive or active. Passive citizenship is constructed and maintained in a top-down manner. That is, rights and obligations of citizens are decided by those in power and then often passed on from generation to generation. Citizens are passive recipients of these rights and obligations. In contrast, active citizenship involves citizens themselves participating in the construction and maintenance of their rights and obligations. Different societies have different mixtures of these two different forms of citizenship. People are excluded as passive citizens when they cannot access their rights (such as a right to decent shelter), or do not fulfil their obligations (such as the obligation to obey the law). They are excluded as active citizens when they do not participate in social, political, economic or cultural life; for example, when they live an isolated, lonely existence. The social inclusion agenda concerns the identification of people who are excluded from society, the development of ways of facilitating the activities demonstrating passive and active citizenship for these 'excluded' individuals and the reduction of the obstacles inhibiting their citizenship roles. As indicated above, as a strategy for addressing the 'cycle of entrenched and multiple disadvantage in particular neighbourhoods and communities', the federal government proposed partnerships between government, business, the **not-for-profit sector** and the community sector, and the establishment of new 'innovative community-based employment projects' (Australian Government, 2009b).

Interest in social capital, defined as relations and norms of trust, mutuality and cooperation (Putnam, 2000), also sets up a framework for understanding the embracing of social inclusion agendas. In some ways, the social inclusion agenda is a logical extension of claims about the value of social capital. That is, because social capital theory proposes that when people are involved with each other in networks of trust and mutuality, social cohesion is enhanced and this in turn is a stabilising force for society.

At one level the development of this social inclusion agenda is to be welcomed. It acknowledges the structural nature of social, economic and political inequalities, the interconnections between them, the need to redress these inequalities and the need to provide opportunities for the most disadvantaged groups in Australian society. In this context, the social inclusion agenda can be seen to be a validation of the human right to citizenship. However, as Spandler (2007) points out, social inclusion policies are paradoxical. They express a genuine demand to tackle the consequences of social inequality, but at the same time they are a way of regulating, or even socially engineering, groups of people who are understood to be excluded from society. Importantly, social inclusion policies are based on a number of quite problematic assumptions. First, they assume that social inclusion is self-evident and is a desirable, even a moral imperative (Spandler, 2007). Second, in much of the policy discussion of social inclusion it remains an abstraction. It is very important to consider the reference point of social inclusion, which can be drawn out by asking 'inclusion into what?' Not all sites for social inclusion will be acceptable to governments. Some sites, such as a criminal gang, might be very socially inclusive in their own way. Indeed, they might provide strong bonding social capital, but as discussed in chapter 3, this form of social capital is inward looking and characteristic of closed groups. It would seem that most of the policy initiatives around social inclusion assume that there is an acceptable 'mainstream society' that people want to be part of (see, for example, Australian Government, 2009b) and presuppose a general consensus about the basic values of this society, such as the value of paid and volunteer work, family and community.

Third, social inclusion policies as constructed in Australia assume a top-down approach to policy development and implementation. They work on the basis of the right of people in power to define what constitutes social inclusion and exclusion and a 'healthy and normal life' (Spandler, 2007). The focus on what politicians or experts think is necessary for social inclusion ignores the subjective dimensions of belonging and identity, which are critical to our understanding of whether people are prepared to become active citizens. Fourth, linked to the idea of a 'healthy' and 'normal' life is the assumption that it is possible to define two categories of people: those who are excluded (and dissatisfied) for whom intervention is needed to include them in society, and those who are already included (and are satisfied) for whom no intervention is required. Such an approach invokes an insider–outsider binary logic (Buckmaster & Thomas, 2009) and is constructed around a deficit-based understanding of the outsider. It assumes that groups that are deemed to be marginalised in Australia, such as some Indigenous groups, refugee groups and people with a disability, have no social connections and no community identity or support. It is appropriate to identify how some communities in Australia are systematically excluded from access to resources and opportunities and to propose measures to address these systemic inequalities. However, it does not necessarily follow that because people are unemployed, have a low level of education, bad health and poor government services, they are not socially included. There are many forms of social inclusion and different kinds of social ties.

Fifth, while outsiders might be identified as a particular category of 'risky people' that form a group, socially excluded people are largely treated as individuals who must learn to function in 'mainstream' society. Sixth, much of the analysis of social exclusion and inclusion focuses on the role of paid work as the route to social inclusion. While there is considerable discussion of the effects of exclusion from paid work, the overemphasis on employment as the source of wellbeing confuses social inclusion with employment. Such an approach reinforces the idea that unemployed people cannot be full members of society (Buckmaster & Thomas, 2009). From this vantage point, to be included in any form of paid work will bring about social inclusion, and the exclusionary effects of social divisions and social inequality within paid employment are ignored (Levitas, 2004). When involvement in paid employment is taken as the determinant of social inclusion, neighbourhoods with high unemployment rates are, by definition, socially excluded neighbourhoods, regardless of whether they share their resources, have strong networks or organise together on a community issue, or whether the inhabitants feel subjectively part of an active community. Finally, the social inclusion agenda works to secure 'buy-in' to, and conformity with, the putative 'mainstream' of society. It does this through framing the way we think about social inclusion. For example, the policy of social inclusion might be applied through encouraging people to 'join society' (by engaging in paid work, for example), and through reinforcing the view that there is something wrong with people who operate outside this mainstream. In this way social inclusion agendas can legitimate existing political and social arrangements and institutions.

However, as noted above, commitment to social inclusion can draw attention to the blockages to individual fulfilment that exist in society and the need for strategies to overcome such blockages. We will consider the theme of social inclusion again in chapters 5 and 7, in which we discuss community development approaches and understandings of social inclusion strategies.

Neo-liberalism

In the late 1980s, an economic and government policy agenda known as **neo-liberalism** was taking root in most developed countries, although with different levels of enthusiasm. This agenda is known in Australia as both neo-liberalism and **economic rationalism** (see Pusey, 2003; 1991). The dominance of this agenda has had profound effects on the political and social sphere, and the context in which community development has had to operate. In this section we identify the key tenets of neo-liberalism and the associated concept of the New Right.

We begin with the idea of *governance*. The neo-liberal agenda has changed the face of governance. In its broadest sense, governance refers to the processes by which authority is exercised. This includes both formal and informal actions and practices by which a group makes decisions. It covers traditions, norms and rules through which a group distributes and exercises authority and power, regulates, monitors behaviours and assigns responsibility. Governance protocols shape the forms that organisational structures take, how agendas and expectations are set, and how public affairs are planned and steered.

The proponents of neo-liberal policy argue for the diminution of the role of government in delivering services and decreasing union power in the name of individual choice. Governments operating with neo-liberal agendas have argued that they have 'deregulated' corporations, financial institutions and the labour market to make these more 'economically efficient' or 'rational'. They have developed industrial relations strategies that include winding back the rights of workers, excluding unions from negotiating for workers and allowing employers unilaterally to withdraw from awards.

Neo-liberalism and economic rationalism are linked to new right thinking. While espousing deregulation of business and the labour market, there is a new right dimension of neo-liberalism that invokes authoritarian attitudes of social control in regard to education and welfare, such as tightening the regulation of childcare, and promoting the need for a strong police force to maintain so-called law and order. New right thinking involves a broad approach to organising society that rejects the traditional left emphasis on equality, human rights and collective endeavour. The rejection of collective endeavour was expressed in the statement made by the former prime minister of Britain, Margaret Thatcher, that there is 'no such thing as society'. Former Australian prime minister John

Howard and his supporters attacked the Left's commitment to human rights and equality as unsupportable 'political correctness' and refused to apologise to Indigenous Australians for the oppression practised by non-Indigenous Australians.

Proponents of neo-liberalism have been vocal in their attacks on the welfare state. Where a welfare state has been established, the government takes responsibility for the wellbeing of all its citizens and ensures access to health facilities, housing, education and welfare. The neo-liberal agenda is to wind back these state responsibilities, arguing that individuals and communities should take responsibility for their own destinies. Here, there is an ironic convergence between community development and neo-liberal agendas. Both argue for empowering people to take control of their own destinies. However, the neo-liberal approach emphasises responsibilities over rights and sets the terms of reference for gaining the so-called 'control', which is individualist in orientation and based on a commitment to individual entrepreneurship. For example, in emphasising the importance of responsibilities over rights, the Liberal National Party coalition government introduced policies of so-called mutual obligation, including 'work for the dole'. Members of the Australian Labor Party, too, have invoked ideas of the New Right in originally introducing and maintaining the policy of mandatory detention for asylum seekers.

Although neo-liberal ideas have held sway in Australia over several decades, the superiority of neo-liberal programs has not been fully accepted by everyone. In an important study, Pusey (2003:15) documented the responses to economic rationalism from what he calls middle Australia – the people who recognise themselves as middle Australia (those in the middle range of income earnings). Pusey (2003:171–2) found that:

> For many of our middle Australians and many people of goodwill who have sometimes been its reluctant advocates, the promises of economic reform have now gone sour. We are becoming aware that, delivered in this form, economic development fights with quality of life.

Pusey (2003:71) points out that a constant theme in discussions with middle Australia is that economic 'reform' is bad because it

> unjustly undermines employment and work, whether through deregulation of the business sector, the consequences of privatization, competition policies, or ... globalisation, or through a combination of these.

Community development practitioners have responded to the rise of neo-liberalism in different ways. On the basis of the incompatibilities between neo-liberalism and community development, some practitioners have decided to withdraw from formal community organisation involvement altogether. They point out that neo-liberalism is individualistic in both style and practice, while the community development approach is collective. Community development champions a form of self-determination that involves communities collectively setting their goals, and it supports the development of a welfare state that facilitates collective endeavour. Such practitioners eschew government, business and philanthropic funding. Other community development practitioners have adapted to neo-liberalism by formally changing how they work to be more 'business-like' in approach and presentation – for example, by focusing their activities around business plans, unit costs and outputs – while still retaining a commitment to empowering the people they are working with. Others have become more entrepreneurial in style, seeking funds from different sources and even setting up small businesses. Indeed, there has been increasing pressure, especially from governments, for community programs to operate more as though they were small entrepreneurial businesses. We discuss the idea of enterprise culture later in this chapter.

Individualisation

Neo-liberalism also draws on what sociologists have identified as **individualisation**. Individualisation is a process that involves individuals taking responsibility for their own destinies. According to Beck (1992:135):

> Individualization means that each person's biography is removed from given determinations and placed in his or her hands, open and dependent upon decisions.

In a world dominated by individualisation, old solidarities collapse. As discussed in this book, people are no longer simply identified through their families or other collective and determined structures or communities in which they can rely on the certainty of traditional ways of doing things. They must look to their own decisions and their own resources to survive. The stories of the self-construction of our identities and life chances are played out in all aspects of life. We are required to take responsibility for our own health by choosing the appropriate food, exercise and therapies. We are required to take responsibility for our own income by choosing the right strategies for maximising our wealth. Indeed, we are required to take responsibility for our own happiness by making an informed decision when choosing a partner or spouse.

In one way, individualisation is a logical response to risk society. As Mythen (2004:118) points out, in risk society 'everyday life becomes contingent upon an infinite process of decision-making'. We are continually caught up in a reflexive process of gathering information, decision making, engaging and responding, and more decision making. This individualisation of responsibility has been an important factor in shifting blame and responsibility away from the collective actions of governments and corporations to individuals. For example, in Australia today a stable of norms and regulations make individuals the guardians of the environment through such practices as household-waste recycling and water conservation. As the welfare state has been wound back, the most disadvantaged and marginal groups in society have been enjoined to 'pull themselves up by their bootstraps'. For example, 'welfare to work' and 'mutual obligation' policies are premised on the view that the individual's own future is 'up to them'.

The rise of enterprise culture

One of the questions considered by those associated with New Right and neo-liberal thinking is: What is the best way to engender a competitive and productive society in which individuals are equipped to make choices and take responsibility for their own actions? The answer is often presented through the idea of **enterprise culture**. Enterprise culture can be understood as a culture constructed around values, behaviours and attitudes that promote hard work, competition, motivation, self-reliance, flexibility, boldness, daringness, innovation and success (see Fairclough, 1992; Keat, 1991).

These values, behaviours and attitudes are identified as pertaining to the entrepreneurial individual. They are the essential components of private enterprise. The idea of developing enterprise culture in Australia has been supported in various ways by business elites, the National, Liberal and Labor parties and key policy makers. The current commitment to enterprise culture developed around the imperatives of competition policy set out in the Hilmer Inquiry in the early 1990s (Hilmer, 1993). From the perspective of neo-liberalism, competition (between individuals, groups, organisations and institutions) would increase efficiency and unleash creativity. It should be facilitated by freeing business and strategic activities from regulation, government control and trade union interference. Enterprise culture was championed strongly by the previous Liberal prime minister, John Howard, who supported the development of Australia as a nation of shareholders in private companies. The federal Labor government has continued strong support for the development of an enterprise culture. Securing an enterprise culture is championed as a necessary part of the positioning of Australian capitalism to make it viable in an increasingly competitive international arena.

New managerialism

There is some disagreement about the most suitable processes and practices for fostering enterprise culture. For some, enterprise culture is best facilitated through specific management practices that have come to be known as **new managerialism**. While there is some debate about the different types of managerialism and the implications of new managerialism (see Considine & Painter, 1997), the concept of new managerialism, as used in this book, is constructed around a number of principles:

- the enhancement of managerial leadership, autonomy and initiative, including performance initiatives and rewards
- the devolution of managerial responsibility, including financial management and performance review and risk management
- streamlined decision making, including freeing managers from regulations that are deemed to constrain innovation and productivity
- a competitive attitude
- a preparedness to make hard decisions
- individual rewards for individual hard work
- the weakening or elimination of the power of unions
- a commitment to flexibility in regard to employment practices, and working conditions and practices
- the development of a 'can-do' mentality
- a focus on output and outcomes rather than process
- increased efficiency and productivity
- a commitment to clients and customers by providing 'best practice' services and 'best quality' products.

A noticeable omission in these principles is specialist knowledge of the area or sector that the manager administers. In fact, it is often argued that managers administer better if they do not have such specialist knowledge. This view has led to the appointment of 'generic managers' who are skilled in the processes of management rather than having knowledge of the minutiae of the areas or sectors that they manage. Such managers are said to be 'value-neutral'. They perform their tasks with a technical expertise that allows no room for values or principles. For example, a 'generic manager' should be able to shift from administering a large private profit-making office-cleaning company to a human services public-sector department without requiring any detailed knowledge or experience of the 'coalface' activities undertaken by the workers that they are managing. New managerialist approaches have been implemented in workplaces in both the private and public sectors.

The adoption of new managerialist practices means more responsibility and less control for workers in community organisations. In its strongest form, new managerialism renders those who do not have a competitive businesslike approach to their work redundant to the needs of contemporary society. It is the workers who are independent individuals, self-reliant, competitive, ambitious and prepared to make the 'tough' individual decisions when they reach the top (such as selecting people to be made redundant) who are deemed to be successes in the new managerialist work environment.

The commitment to new managerialist structures that underpins this work environment is profoundly problematic for community development. For example, collective organisational structures are rendered obsolete and community control inefficient under managerialist strategies. Within a new managerialist framework, committees of management made up of local community representatives and participants in programs are viewed as 'unbusinesslike' by government funding bodies and may be replaced with government appointees or even abolished altogether.

There is another approach to establishing enterprise culture. This approach is based on a commitment to construct a facilitating, empowering (Scott & Jaffe, 1991) and even 'enchanted' workplace (Gee & Lankshear, 1995). In this type of workplace, hierarchy is eliminated to be replaced by multiskilled workers, operating in teams, who not only undertake the everyday tasks required but also identify and solve problems (Gee & Lankshear, 1995; Reich, 1992; Scott & Jaffe, 1991). It is only in a collaborative environment that the creative talents of individual workers can be unleashed. For Scott and Jaffe (1991:4), the key to this kind of enterprising workplace is empowerment, which means that:

- Employees feel responsible not just for doing a job, but also for making the whole organisation work better. The new employee is an active problem solver who helps plan how to get things done and then does them.
- Teams work together to continually improve their performance, achieving higher levels of productivity.
- Organisations are structured in such a way that people feel that they are able to achieve the results they want and can do what needs to be done – not just what is required of them – and be rewarded for doing so.

This approach to enterprise culture is more 'community friendly'.

Assessments of enterprise culture

The analyses of the push to enterprise culture and the development of new workplace environments are mixed. There is support for the development of an environment that encourages and facilitates creativity, innovation, autonomy and productivity. The argument that Australian workers need to embrace an ethos of hard work and competition has gained considerable support in both the main political parties, particularly in the context of the claim that Australian workers must become more internationally competitive.

Yet the harsh effects of these changes have not been completely hidden by the lexicon of new managerialism and the so-called entrepreneurial or **enchanted workplace**. For example, downsizing and rationalisation might sound quite neutral – in fact, they are not. They often mean increased profits for shareholders in large public companies and performance bonuses for chief executives, for example, while at the same time they spell out a decline in male earnings, increasing insecurity of work (Pusey 2003:80) and unemployment for 'downsized' workers, more work and uncertainty for remaining workers, and often poorer services for customers. Similarly, the outsourcing of work in government departments means that the 'insourced' work in these departments disappears, as do workers. Outsourcing does not guarantee better services. Indeed, workers and others have understood and questioned the price of these changes (Pusey, 2003).

While often appearing to offer correctives to some of the stifling and outworn procedures that can inhibit workers' self-determination, new managerialism actually constructs new methods of hierarchical control. It tends to engender uncertainty in the workforce and constrains innovation among workers (see Rees & Rodley, 1995).

International assessments of the effects of enterprise culture and neo-liberalism have been quite bleak. Sennett (1998) paints a grim picture of a regime that is based on individualism, competition and 'winner takes all'. Enterprise culture based on individualisation and neo-liberalism lead to situations in which failure and dependency render people 'parasites' of the system. Indeed, for Sennett (1998:146), this system

> radiates indifference in the organization in the absence of trust, where there is no reason to be needed. And it does so through reengineering of institutions in which people are treated as disposable. Such practices obviously and brutally diminish the sense of mattering as a person, of being necessary to others.

The idea that people are disposable is taken up in a recent book by Bauman (2004). With economic globalisation and economic 'progress' has come a new category of redundant humans or, as Bauman calls them, **wasted humans**: humans who are 'out of place', 'unfit' or 'undesirable' (2004:5). Redundant humans are cast adrift because they are not needed by others: 'they can do as well, and better, without you. There is no self-evident reason for your being around and no obvious justification for your claim for the right to stay around' (Bauman, 2004:12). The most obvious example of redundant people are refugees, 'the outsiders incarnate' (Bauman, 2004:80).

The winners and losers approach to life is now permeating most of the world. Beck (2000) argues that the basic existence for the majority of people is fast becoming one marked by endemic insecurity. What he calls the 'political mantra' of labour market flexibility means that risks are being redistributed away from the state and business towards the individual in a no-win situation for ordinary people, because skills and knowledge become obsolete and jobs on offer are short-term and easily terminable (Beck, 2000:3). Pertinent to this discussion, Beck accepts that there is value in the idea of entrepreneurship, but it must be associated with the common good. For example, what he calls 'welfare entrepreneurs' must work inclusively and for publicly useful ends (Beck, 2000:129).

From the standpoint of community development, the shift to an enterprise culture is like a double-edged sword. Some of the characteristics of enterprise culture are consistent with the principles of community development and suggest a symbiosis between the two. For example, there are good reasons for linking the commitment to innovation, creative problem solving, autonomy, flat organisational structures and teamwork with the practices of community development. Scott and Jaffe's (1991:4) argument that empowerment is the key to a creative work environment sits quite comfortably beside the community development commitment to empowerment and self-determination, and those who champion **social entrepreneurship** often argue that such entrepreneurship is primarily a form of community development. But the question must be asked: In the context of enterprise culture, who is actually empowered?

Corporate social responsibility

Before we finish this investigation into the contextual factors that have set the backdrop for community development activities, we should note the shifting relationships between the business and the community sectors. In the discussion above we considered how business ideas of innovation and creative leadership have entered into community activity through the concept and application of social entrepreneurialism. The movement has also been the other way in the sense that civil society commitments have also entered into business activity. The major concept used to explain this latter movement is corporate social responsibility, or CSR.

Corporate social responsibility (sometimes also known as **corporate citizenship**) is based on the view that businesses and corporations should engage and support civil society as an integral part of their 'business'. Many large corporations, in particular, have established departments for corporate social responsibility. Four ways of demonstrating commitment to CSR are commitment expressed in mission statements, commitment to sustainability, adoption of what is known as the 'triple bottom line', and working formally and informally with NGOs and communities. As Manteaw (2008:429) states, 'The overall net profitability, which is usually perceived as a money figure, is now expanded to encompass economic, social and environmental imperatives of business operations'. Manteaw notes that there are, of course, significant differences in interpretations and approaches to CSR, depending on a particular corporation's motive in any given situation. For example, it is important to understand how far a company has a CSR strategy in place because this is a statutory requirement or is good public relations and assists the company to become more competitive, or because it assists local communities to identify assets and needs.

Indeed, the motive for involvement in CSR activities can affect the way in it is received in a community and the method by which it is implemented. Cynics argue that CSR is largely a public relations exercise on behalf of a company, which displays only a superficial commitment to civil society. For example, giving their products or money to local charities, supporting schools, organising for employees to do volunteer work and providing advertising billboards for local festivals and school fetes are excellent ways of showcasing a company and giving it a competitive edge. Such activities are nothing more than elaborate facades designed to conceal the operations 'backstage' (Manteaw, 2008). This does not necessarily mean that communities should reject such assistance but instead awareness of the charity-giving assumptions underlying this type of CSR should be urged and the several functions of such support acknowledged.

Laufer (2003) comments on how such 'backstage' activities are a form of environmental corporate deception, sometimes known as **greenwashing** and **bluewashing**. In the environmental context, greenwashing involves a pious, but deceptive, concern for the environment, public health and people's wellbeing so as to present an environmentally responsible public image (Corpwatch, 2010). In a broad context, the term is also used to describe how products are presented as 'green', 'organic' and 'healthy' when they are not. Bluewashing refers to the way that companies, often with dubious human rights, labour rights and green credentials, have signed up to the United Nations Global Compact. Under this Compact, firms commit to nine principles, distilled from key environmental, labour and human rights agreements, and to implementing these principles in at least three ways. First, they commit to promoting the principles in mission statements and annual reports. Second, they will post specific examples and lessons learnt in applying the principles. Finally, they will participate in partnerships with the UN at both the policy level and 'on the ground'. Corpwatch (2010) criticises the lack of any regulatory force in the Compact and the way that corporations can bluewash their image by 'wrapping themselves in the flag of the United Nations'.

There are other ways companies can work with local communities, most notably in local partnership arrangements. Some companies now employ community development workers to liaise with local communities; identify needs; analyse social, cultural and environmental impacts; and negotiate between the company and community over claims about land, land usage and compensation, for example. The importance of community-development-based negotiation is especially acknowledged by those mining companies concerned about environmental effects and the impact of their activities on local communities. As with working as an employee of the state, the question arises as to how far community development workers can be accountable to the communities they are working with when they are paid by external agencies. This is an important question. At one level, of course, it is clearly in the interest of corporations to have good relations with local communities and to be seen as a company with demonstrated integrity. Yet it is difficult to fool increasingly savvy local communities about the operations and impact of corporations, in the same way that communities find it difficult to bluff their way through deals with corporations.

Manteaw (2008:430) poses the question, 'is CSR just another name for corporate posturing – a way to let their presence be felt or a genuine attempt by businesses and corporations to make a difference in communities where they operate?' Using a case study of failed CSR in a foreign-owned company in Ghana, Manteaw reflects on what can be done to redress the gap between the promises made for CSR and what actually happens backstage. He argues that CSR must shift from an externally generated to a collaborative learning agenda based on the principle 'give and take' rather than 'take and give'. Such an approach requires recognising and engaging local people as stakeholders and authentic participation based on mutual respect. While there is growing interest in such an agenda (Demetrious, 2004), there is also continuing concern about the possibility of genuine CSR. Demetrious (2004) argues that, in some quarters, there is a genuine shift in corporate thinking about civic, human rights and environmental responsibilities that would involve real accountability to communities. From a community development perspective, probably the most unproblematic type of CSR is a relationship whereby all the participants work together on a project and have a stake in the outcome. Often such a relationship is not known as CSR and the idea of triple bottom line is not even mentioned. Such a relationship is evident in the following case study.

CSR IN MT JANOOK

The setting is a mining town in Western Australia. The major mining company has officially done all the right things in regard to CSR. It has CSR aims in its mission statement and has signed up to the United Nations Global Compact. But its employees, including its senior executives, are cynical about what is written on paper and see it as just a piece of window-dressing. What they actually participate in involves authentic commitment to the local community. Such a commitment is not written down and is not the outcome of formal meetings, statements of intents or the strategic plan. It is a part of what they do at the everyday level.

A member of a family who has lived in the town for several generations is doing her PhD on the town. Armed with all the criticism of the tokenistic nature of most CSR, she undertakes a survey of CSR activities in the town. Much to her surprise she receives glowing reports about what she identifies as CSR. However, neither the townspeople nor the mining company use the terminology of CSR. They talk about 'people getting together as one community and the company learning from us and helping us'. The townspeople give a number of examples, including the decision of the top executives to live in the town, rather than commute back to the capital cities. They send their children to local schools, sit on school councils and financially support community events. The company has provided free water tanks for the elderly, while a group of employees and some local people have set up a project to write the history of the town, including an analysis of how the company has operated and contributed both positively and negatively.

Privatisation

As indicated above, in Australia the type of enterprising organisations that have been deemed to be most 'internationally competitive' are those in which highly motivated managers are given a free rein to be productive and efficient, relatively unrestrained by government regulations or bureaucratic structures. These institutions are the private for-profit institutions. During the 1990s and into the 2000s there have been shifts in ownership and control of government instrumentalities into the hands of private companies, subcontracting of the delivery of services and programs to private for-profit and non-profit organisations, and significant deregulation of their activities in a general process that has been referred to as *privatisation*. However, in light of the need to reassess the role of government regulation in stemming the capitalist excesses that contributed to the global financial crisis and the extensive bail-out of banks internationally, there has been rethinking about how far governments should limit their oversight and regulatory control of the private sector overall (including in both for-profit and non-profit organisations). This rethinking has resulted in government re-regulation of the corporate sector internationally. At the same time, governments have been averse to re-nationalising private institutions such as power companies, public transport and telecommunications industries.

The culture of performance management

As we move into the second decade of this century, we continue to observe a paradox; a paradox that confuses how citizens perceive their governments. On one hand, governments support the neo-liberal principles of freedom, enterprise culture and competition. On the other hand, we have a strengthening of the **culture of performance management**, or what is sometimes called **performativity**. Performance management involves governments setting agendas, categorising actions, setting 'quality' performance indicators, checking and monitoring progress (surveillance), and putting (often punitive) measures in place for required output and outcomes, all in the name of transparency and (upwards) accountability. For community development, with its emphasis on process and its acceptance of the 'messiness' of development processes, the culture of performance management is problematic. Public institutions, including schools, universities, hospitals and the not-for-profit sector, are all increasingly affected by this culture, which has been embraced enthusiastically, especially by the federal Labor government. While these contradictions have been apparent for some time – they exist in the tensions between New Right and neo-liberal principles – government initiatives to manage the performance of public institutions have strengthened since the 1990s, as evidenced in the federal Labor government's detailed monitoring and auditing (and reporting of results) of the performance of schools and hospitals. There is, however, one way that governments are able to present as facilitators, initiators and collaborators while also having regulatory and monitoring oversight, and this is through partnerships with both government and non-government organisations.

Private public partnerships

One way of strengthening government oversight of the private sector, while encouraging enterprise culture, has been to enter into partnerships with the private sector in what is often known as **private public partnerships (PPPs)**. PPPs are established to facilitate funding, secure regulation and establish facilitating infrastructure arrangements for strategic development. Mostly PPPs have been developed around specific business enterprises, such as housing development, for which government and companies both contribute funds. However, many of the principles of PPPs can also apply to the non-profit community sector. We discuss the idea of partnerships further in chapter 4.

We should note that the federal government has signalled its interest to become more engaged with the third sector of non-profit organisations, and to be more involved in collaborative partnerships. In February 2010, the Productivity Commission released its report of research into the contribution of the not-for-profit sector, commissioned by the Australian Government (Productivity Commission, 2010). The study assessed the overall contribution of the sector to Australian society, examined tax arrangements and the ability of the sector to raise funds, identified ways that the effectiveness and efficiency of the sector can be improved and examined relations between the not-for-profit sector, government and business. As we will discuss in chapter 4, the study was framed by a commitment to improve government policy and programs. While there were important findings and supportive statements about the not-for-profit sector in the report, including an updated analysis of the size and scope of the sector and recommendations for the streamlining of reporting on activities, it argued for closer relations between government and the not-for-profit sector and was concerned with such matters as how to effect government oversight, monitoring and regulation. The extent to which the recommendations of the report will be picked up by government, including those about streamlined funding and establishing a framework for performance management, is yet to unfold.

One of the central arguments of this book is that to understand the aims, roles, successes and disappointments in community development it is necessary to analyse the contexts in which it operates. In this chapter we have considered some of the major contextual factors that have affected the growth of community development as an approach, a job and an intervention or political activity in Australia. However, it is not enough to just identify the contexts and themes. To fully comprehend how these themes affect what community development practitioners and community organisations do, it is necessary to explain the theoretical and conceptual frameworks that are used to analyse social and political environments. While we have touched on a number of these theoretical and conceptual frameworks in this chapter, the following chapter elaborates these further by focusing on the major theoretical perspectives and conceptual themes that elucidate the insights necessary for effective community development work.

Summary points

- We can trace the rise of community development as an approach and a method to the idea of bottom-up development.
- Community development has a short history in Australia. Community development organisations as we know them today developed only after the 1970s, with the establishment of the Australian Assistance Plan.
- To be able to operate effectively community development practitioners need to understand fully the contexts in which they are working.
- Five contextual factors, or backdrops to community development work, are identified: the welfare backdrop, the community backdrop, the political backdrop, the global backdrop and the policy backdrop.

Background and basics

- Community development is at odds with the traditional welfare approach, which holds that the way to respond to poverty and disadvantage is to establish charity organisations to help the 'deserving poor'.
- 'Community' is a difficult concept to define. It carries with it a remarkable array of meanings that are politically loaded and often contradictory.
- Community development is a political activity and, as such, is concerned with understanding new ideas of social and political organisation, such as generative politics and associative democracy.
- The context in which community development takes place at the beginning of the twenty-first century is one of uncertainty, crises, fragmentation and cynicism.
- A number of new concepts are used to understand this context, including the idea of risk society and the concept of individualisation.
- Community development practitioners who are equally at home whether they are working with anti-logging groups in South-East Asia or in Australia, and identify equally with both groups as their community, can be understood as 'cosmopolitan citizens'.
- Sustainable development, which can be defined as development that meets the needs of the present without compromising the ability of future generations to meet their own needs, is an increasingly important part of community development.
- As many of the old left approaches have been eroded, neo-liberalism has come to the ascendancy. Neo-liberal philosophy comprises a mixture of authoritarian attitudes to social control and deregulation of businesses and the labour market to ensure competition. It is based on the idea that key aspects of society should be structured to maintain an efficient economic system and that the welfare state should be wound back.
- The imperatives of performance management and entrepreneurship are contradictory and pose a difficulty for governments when they are forming policy.
- One way of dealing with this difficulty is for government to strengthen its oversight of the private sector while at the same time encouraging enterprise culture by entering into partnerships with the private sector.
- The idea of corporate social responsibility based on the view that businesses and corporations should engage and support civil society has opened up opportunities for partnerships between community organisations and the business sector.
- In a recent report the Productivity Commission has identified the contribution of community organisations and the third sector as a whole. The report recommends how government and the third sector can work together better.

Key terms

- associative democracy
- bluewashing
- bottom-up development
- class
- class struggle
- communitarianism
- corporate citizenship
- corporate social responsibility
- cosmopolitanism
- culture of performance management
- economic rationalism
- enchanted workplace
- enterprise culture
- gemeinschaft
- generative politics
- gesellschaft
- globalisation
- greenwashing
- human rights
- individualisation
- mechanical solidarity
- neo-liberalism
- new managerialism
- not-for-profit sector
- organic solidarity

- patriarchy
- performativity
- private public partnerships (PPPs)
- risk society
- social entrepreneurship
- wasted humans

Exercises

1. Identify three ways that bottom-up development has been applied in community development.
2. Explain three ways the term 'community' has been constructed.
3. Ask your friends and colleagues to describe their idea of who constitutes their community or communities.
4. Why is the welfarist tradition problematic for community development?
5. In what ways is community development part of the social and community services industry?
6. In what ways is community development involved in political struggle?
7. What is meant by the idea of the crisis of the Left?
8. What are some of the ways there has been a rethinking of political processes and organisation?
9. List the various meanings of globalisation.
10. What is cosmopolitanism and in what ways can community development be cosmopolitan?
11. What is risk society and why is it important for community development?
12. What is neo-liberalism and how do neo-liberal policies affect community development?
13. What is new managerialism and how has it affected community organisations?
14. Why is social inclusion important today? What do you think are the indicators of a socially inclusive society?
15. What is corporate social responsibility? Why do you think some community development practitioners are ambivalent about it?
16. What do you think are the most important contextual factors affecting community development today? Give the reasons for your answer.
17. In the case study 'Interview with Maria', Maria identifies six groups as her community. Make a list of the groups that form your community.

Further reading

Bauman, Z (2000) *Liquid Modernity*. Polity Press, Cambridge.

Bauman, Z (2001) *Community: Seeking Safety in an Insecure World*. Polity Press, Cambridge.

Bauman, Z (2004) *Wasted Lives: Modernity and its Outcasts*. Polity Press, Cambridge.

Beck, U (1992) *Risk Society: Towards a New Modernity*. Sage, London.

Beck, U (2000) *World Risk Society*. Polity Press, Cambridge.

Curno, P (ed.) (1978) *Political Issues and Community Work*. Routledge & Kegan Paul, London.

Etzioni, A (1993) *New Communitarian Thinking: Persons, Virtues, Institutions and Communities*. University Press of Virginia, Charlotteville.

Etzioni, A (1995) *The Spirit of Community*. Fontana, London.

Fukuyama, F (1992) *The End of History and the Last Man*. Hamish Hamilton, London.

Gee, CD & Lankshear, C (1995) 'The new work order: critical language awareness and "fast" capitalism texts', *Discourse: Studies in the Cultural Politics of Education*, 16(1), pp. 5–14.

Giddens, A (1994) *Beyond Left and Right: The Future of Radical Politics*. Polity Press, Cambridge.

Havel, V (1997) Statement delivered at Forum 2000, 4 September.

Hirst, P & Thompson, G (1996) *Globalization in Question*. Polity Press, London.

Huntington, S (1996) *The Clash of Civilizations and the Remaking of World Order*. Simon & Schuster, New York.

Manteaw, B (2008) 'From tokenism to social justice: rethinking the bottom line for sustainable community development', *Community Development Journal*, 43(4), pp. 428–43.

McGrew, A (1992) 'A global society?', in S Hall, D Held & T McGrew (eds) *Modernity and its Futures*. Polity Press (in association with The Open University), Cambridge, pp. 61–116.

Mowbray, M (2004) 'The new communitarianism: building great communities or brigadoonery?', *Just Policy*, No. 32, June, pp. 11–20.

Pusey, M (1991) *Economic Rationalism in Canberra*. Cambridge University Press, Cambridge.

Pusey, M (2003) *The Experience of Middle Australia: The Dark Side of Economic Reform*. Cambridge University Press, Cambridge.

Putnam, R (2000) *Bowling Alone: The Collapse and Revival of American Community*. Simon & Schuster, New York.

Rees, S & Rodley, G (eds) (1995) *The Human Costs of Managerialism*. Pluto Press, Leichhardt.

Tam, H (1998) *Communitarianism: A New Agenda for Politics and Citizenship*. Macmillan, Basingstoke.

Turner, BS (1999) 'McCitizens: risk, coolness and irony in contemporary politics', in B. Smart (ed.) *Resisting McDonaldization*. Sage, London, pp. 83–100.

Weblinks

Bluewashing
www.corpwatch.org/article.php?id=996

Greenwashing
www.corpwatch.org/article.php?id=242

Social inclusion
www.socialinclusion.gov.au/Resources/Pages/Resources.aspx#board
www.medicalsociologyonline.org/archives/issue22/spandler.html

CHAPTER 3

Theoretical perspectives and concepts

Overview

In the previous chapter key contextual factors affecting community development in Australia were considered. In this chapter we examine theories that frame our contextual analyses and explore some of the key conceptual tools that are used to analyse social and political conditions. We discuss the importance of linking theory with practice and note the way that theories and concepts move in and out of fashion. Key theoretical perspectives and how they influence or affect community development practice are examined. This is followed by a discussion of new and renewed themes, concepts and theories that are currently influencing social analysis.

Introduction
Perspectives on the world

A key theme of this book is that community development practice is not just a set of technical procedures, but is embedded in specific values and theoretical understandings about the way society works. Community development draws on a number of theories and uses specific concepts. It is important to understand how theories and concepts shape our world and how they influence the everyday activities of community development work. This chapter introduces theoretical themes that are relevant for understanding the everyday work of community development practitioners.

Theoretical perspectives (sometimes called theoretical traditions, frameworks or approaches) involve broad orientations to subject matter. They make certain assumptions about the way the world works and they reveal people's interests. While theoretical perspectives provide intellectual maps for making sense of general contexts and set out frameworks for interpreting the world in general, specific theories are concerned with explanations of less abstract experiences and issues, such as why there might be an increase in racist attacks on minority groups in a particular neighbourhood or why suicide rates among certain groups in society are higher than in other groups. Specific theories attempt to explain particular social conditions and tell us how and why particular social occurrences happen. Specific theories, of course, are influenced by broad theoretical perspectives. Theories also carry with them concepts. An example of how theoretical perspectives, specific theories and concepts might be brought together can be seen in the following critique of a male-dominated workforce.

ANGELA'S CRITIQUE OF A MALE-DOMINATED WORKFORCE

Angela holds a broad feminist perspective. She has a general view about how society works, about women's material lives and how and why women are treated in certain ways. This theoretical understanding informs her specific understanding of why men dominate her particular workplace. She uses the concept of patriarchy to explain how an entrenched work culture has developed in the work situation whereby men are favoured over women in job selection for senior positions, although formally her employers must abide by the legal requirement of equal opportunity.

It is important to note that theoretical frameworks, theories and concepts go in and out of fashion. Hancock and Garner (2009:1) point out that two forces influence changes in social theory: internal critique in a field or discipline and external contextual factors. They reflect on the contribution of Kuhn (1962) in understanding how theoretical frameworks (or paradigms) change. Referring to changes in the natural sciences, Kuhn argued that theories change when they are no longer able to make sense of the changed reality and when they are inconsistent with other theoretical frameworks and concepts. Kuhn's ideas equally apply to the social sciences. Hancock and Garner (2009) discuss how different social theories and concepts are developed in attempts to make sense of changing social, economic and political conditions. For example, as we saw in the previous chapter, a general interest in the nature of industrial society underpinned Toennies's (1987) and Durkheim's (1960) views of 'community'. Analysis of the nature of industrial society also set the context of early Marxist theories.

A question that exercised the minds of theorists during much of the twentieth century was how it was, given the profound structural inequalities arising from capitalism, that those who were unequal and disadvantaged continued to support it. By the 1970s the question of how inequality was maintained was taken up by the feminists, focusing on the unequal power of women. While not using an analysis of capitalism as his starting point, Foucault (1980) was nevertheless interested in the practices of social control and regulation that worked to reinforce unequal power relations. During the 1970s, Marxism and feminism provided both the key theoretical frameworks and the conceptual armory for understanding the contexts in which community development practitioners worked, and broad-stroke answers to such questions as 'why does social inequality persist?' By the beginning of the twenty-first century, the idea that one all-encompassing theoretical framework, sometimes called a **metanarrative** (or grand narrative), could provide an overall explanation of events lost ground. However, with the international focus on global environmental threats, and particularly climate change, we have seen a resurgence of the grand narrative in reconstructed green theories.

At the beginning of the twenty-first century, Marxism and feminism continue to form some of the theoretical background of community development. But these theoretical perspectives are complemented by new frameworks, such as those constructed through such notions of identity, difference and social capital, which we discuss elsewhere in this book. Hancock and Garner (2009) comment on how we have learnt to question basic assumptions, historical labels and identities. One approach, for example, has come to be known as **deconstruction**, involving the critical analysis of a 'text' – which might be a book, behaviour, a practice or even society itself. Deconstruction challenges the view that the meaning of something is fully transparent and can be understood completely.

The relation between theory and practice

When we bring the two terms 'theory' and 'practice' together, we are talking about the links between theories, explanations and perspectives on the one hand, and everyday activities, processes, tasks, skills and strategies on the other. Thus, community development integrates theory and practice. This integration is sometimes referred to as **praxis**. The idea of praxis draws our attention to the idea that people are not just objects of study, but also agents of history. Thought and action are always interrelated and people should live their lives in ways that are consistent with their values and beliefs.

For community development, the integration of theory and practice brings together our theoretical understandings of how society works, and our vision of how we would like it to work, with specific strategies and tasks. It is not easy to do this, as social theories are a different type of thing to our everyday practices. They are abstractions based on general views of society. They provide general explanations as to how society works and of the underlying factors that influence and determine our lifestyles. Community development is based on a wide range of theoretical perspectives about how society does and could work.

As implied in the idea of praxis, community development workers, of course, must do more than clarify other people's theories. They must make explicit their own assumptions and theories about such phenomena as the feminisation of poverty and racial discrimination, and subject them to critical analysis as well. For theories guide community development workers' methods and their responses to the attitudes and practices of others. They influence the development of our goals and how we evaluate what we are doing. As indicated above, our everyday activities are always throwing new light on our theories.

Theories are important to our practices and everyday activities because they explain why things are the way they are. For example, they can help us to understand how structures of society frustrate people in their daily life. They explain how the context of our work shapes what we do and how we do it. They are the assumptions that provide the backdrop for our beliefs and our values; in fact, our whole lives. Yet in many cases we are not aware of the whole host of assumptions we are working from when we go about our daily activities. To do this properly, it is necessary to understand the theories that can be used to make sense of a situation. Take the case of a community development worker negotiating with an official to have a lift in a public-housing estate repaired. Knowing that 70 per cent of the tenants are unemployed women and their children, the official comments that, 'Because the tenants are mainly women and children on welfare, and not employed, they have plenty of spare time. Thus they can afford the time to walk up the stairs. Moreover, if they were real women, they would have got a husband to look after them'.

How could the community development worker make sense of such a view? They could begin by clarifying the assumptions that underlie antagonism towards women as welfare recipients. Such assumptions are embedded in patriarchy, functionalism and neo-liberal theories of how the social world should be organised. A range of feminist and Marxist theories explain how **feminisation of poverty** has developed and the ways that people have responded negatively to single mothers on welfare.

The lack of respect for Indigenous Australians and their cultures, manifested in desecration of Indigenous sites, has been underpinned by social Darwinist, functionalist and neo-liberal theories. At the beginning of the twenty-first century Australians have been instructed on their involvement in fighting a 'war on terror'. This so-called war draws on residues of social Darwinism and functionalism, and mixes these with what Huntington (1996) has called a 'clash of civilisations'. The power of stereotypes, or generalisations, such as those used when referring to Aboriginal peoples or peoples of the Islamic faith, needs to be understood by community development workers.

Thus it is not enough just to know the theoretical perspectives that positively inform our theory and practice. Different key assumptions and theories underpin understandings of society but present views of the world that are, at least in part, contrary to the views and principles of community development. These are social Darwinism, functionalism and what has come to be known generally as neo-liberal theory. We consider these below.

Theoretical perspectives
Social Darwinism

Social Darwinism developed from a more complex theoretical perspective called **social evolution**, first put forward by Herbert Spencer, who postulated that the degree of complexity in society indicated progress. Complex, differentiated societies with many specialised functions had evolved from simple, undifferentiated ones. Social Darwinism drew on this idea, claiming that changes that increased a society's ability to adapt made that society more viable. But those holding social Darwinist views also argued that intelligence and the capacity for moral action, rational judgement and general success in society were not distributed evenly among 'races' or groups within society. Evidence for this argument was presented in claims that Indigenous people were inferior to Europeans in their capacity for rational thought and moral conscience. Because social Darwinism espoused the doctrine of survival of the fittest, people who did well in society – by becoming powerful and wealthy, for instance – could justify their position by arguing that they had been chosen by natural selection.

Social Darwinism has been discredited as a pseudoscience. Its arguments have been convenient for legitimating discriminatory treatment of minority groups, the poor and non-Europeans. They have underpinned the welfare approaches to Aboriginal people, migrants, convicts and women during the years of European settlement in Australia. They continue in the form of verbal and physical attacks on minority cultural and racial groups in Australia today. They are manifested, for example, in patronising or abusive treatment of Aboriginal peoples, in discrimination against Asian migrants and the belief that the fabric of Australian society will be weakened if asylum seekers from the Middle East and Asia are permitted sanctuary on Australian soil.

An understanding of how social Darwinist theory has developed and been applied can help a community development worker make sense of how certain groups in society are treated as inferior by others.

Functionalism

Functionalism starts from the assumption that the various parts of society are interrelated and, when put together, form a complete whole. The parts of society include institutions such as the family or religious institutions. The function of these institutions is to maintain a healthy society. Drawing on biology, functionalists have sometimes compared society to the human body. To understand how the human body works, it is necessary to examine its various parts, such as the heart, brain, kidneys and lungs, both in themselves and in relation to other parts and their contribution to the whole body. Like the human body, society is seen as a system that requires its parts (such as social institutions) to contribute to its smooth working. This comparison of the body with society is called the **organic analogy**.

Those holding implicit functionalist views often argue that the family is an integral part of the social system, in the same way as organs are integral to the human body. The family is a building block of society: it is a key institution responsible for socialising children and ensuring that they become useful members of society. The family is also seen as an institution through which to organise the roles of women (such as childrearing and housekeeping) and the roles of men (such as breadwinner).

From the perspective of functionalism, if a society is to be maintained, social institutions must contribute effectively to its smooth functioning and people must willingly carry out designated roles. Overall, the various parts of society must work together and there must be some sort of consensus regarding values. If the parts of society change, if the required degree of 'working together' or integration does not occur or if there is no general agreement regarding values (value consensus), the stability of society can be threatened. To ensure that society does not break down, it is important to take measures to reintegrate the parts (to ensure social inclusion), minimise change and emphasise value consensus.

This functionalist line of argument has important implications for community development. Community development emphasises change, diversity and choice, rather than stability and conformity. Thus, in contrast to functionalism, changes in or even the breakdown of family life, are not necessarily seen to be problems because they threaten the stability of society, but rather are seen to be part of the development of society. Indeed, feminist community development workers view the breakdown of the traditional male-dominated family as a development that can liberate women.

While there is virtually no discussion of the way functionalism underpins assumptions about 'how society works' today, a functionalist perspective still underlies much of our attitudes to society. Law and order campaigns rest on the view that there must be value consensus and people should know their place in society. Functionalist views underpin arguments that those who are different are deviants and must be brought into line with the rest of society. Gay men and lesbian women, for example, are often labelled as deviants by those arguing for more conformity and law and order in society. Another functionalist view is that benefits paid to unemployed people should never be sufficient to live on comfortably, because this will make people work-shy and discourage them from getting a job, thus allowing them to withdraw their contribution to the smooth functioning of society.

Yet for all the commitment to diversity, several elements in community development practice can slide into a functionalist perspective. First, functionalist views of how society should work can be embedded in the community development commitment to consensus decision making, cohesion and harmony. Second, there is an argument that the rhetoric and practice of community building and capacity building are forms of neo-functionalism. For example, in one of the key texts on capacity building, Chaskin et al. (2001:7) describe capacity building as 'what makes communities "work". It is what makes well-functioning communities function well'.

Liberalism and neo-liberalism

We have already discussed the ascendancy of neo-liberal policies in the previous chapters. In this chapter we outline the intellectual background to neo-liberalism, namely liberal theory. **Liberalism** is deeply embedded in Australian culture and politics. Liberal theories first emerged in Europe at the end of the eighteenth century and were associated with radical political views, struggles for political rights and self-determination. While there are various strands of liberalism, it is possible to identify some key themes. Classic liberalism had a vision of open, meritocratic, competitive and tolerant societies in which free-thinking, enterprising individuals compete and achieve success. In this vision, societies aspire to maximise the liberty of individuals. Governments interfere as little as possible. Individuals are free to associate with whom they wish, have freedom of thought, religion and opinion and are free from arbitrary arrest. Thus, all aspects of civil rights are assured. There are some consistencies between liberalism in its classical sense and community development. For example, the commitment to tolerance, freedom of thought and action are central to both community development and classic liberalism. However, there are points of inconsistency such as in the narrow liberalist position whereby competition and meritocracy are emphasised as the basis for social organisation. Indeed, competition is the lynchpin of the new strand of economic liberalism that we have come to know as economic rationalism or neo-liberalism.

In its economic form, strong liberal theory enshrines the individual as someone who has the right to own property, to buy and sell, to employ others and to make profits. Governments should have little say in the productive actions of 'free' individuals and overall there should be minimal government intervention in the workings of the economy.

This laissez-faire approach to organising society is linked with the view that individuals are naturally self-interested, and that competition between self-interested individuals is the motor of growth and development.

As indicated, while community development is based on a commitment to human and civil rights, the civil rights notion of equality before the law is a sham unless it is accompanied by equality of access to resources and power structures through which one can present one's case in a courtroom. Community development also draws apart from liberalism in this view of individualism. Community development does not enshrine the individual, nor does it use this vision of a meritocratic, competitive society. The basis of community development is collective decision making and the development of options that are based on community need, rather than on individual self-advancement.

The free market

For neo-liberal theorists, the key mechanism that ensures competition and guarantees freedom is the so-called free market. The market is a site or a process where people buy, sell and exchange livestock, goods, skills, services, stocks and shares. For Friedman (1962), the economic marketplace is meritorious because it is based on free competition and it rewards initiative, hard work, talent and self-sufficiency. The market is free in the sense that individuals are free to enter, or not, into any particular exchange, so that any transaction is voluntary. For example, the exchange of goods is voluntary and the choice of employers and employees is voluntary. From this viewpoint, the market maximises individual choice and minimises the need for government intervention. Neo-liberal theorists argue that the free market encourages plurality of power and opinion. However, Hancock and Garner (2009:27) note that markets are social constructs. They are not, as implied by those who support neo-liberal ideas, 'natural' forms of development.

The New Right

As indicated in the previous chapter, neo-liberalism is a body of thought that draws its precepts from liberal philosophy, but it is not synonymous with the New Right. Neo-liberalism is premised on the view that the economic system and economic power, based on the principles of the free market, should be a dominant force in society. New Right thinking also supports the free market, but at the same time it is committed to a disciplined society in which law and order are maintained through government intervention in social institutions. While those supporting neo-liberalism argue for small government and a minimal state, New Right thinking sees the state as a disciplining force, which should be responsible for the implementation of disciplining policies such as 'work for the dole' and mandatory detention for asylum seekers. In contrast, neo-liberalism does not necessitate an authoritarian state. We pick up the threads of the influence of neo-liberalism at different points in this book.

A critique of neo-liberalism

It is important to understand the appeal of neo-liberal and New Right theoretical perspectives and policies. At first glance, the populist notions of autonomy appear to be consistent with community development. This is because of the presence of traditional liberalism in some neo-liberal thinking. However, neo-liberal theory has shifted considerably from classic liberal philosophy. Ultimately, in a society that enshrines individual freedom and competition (in rhetoric, if not always in practice), individuals are led to see other individuals not in terms of collectives to work with for the greater good of the group, but as obstacles to their own interests. New Right thinking draws on a concept of duty: duty to work, duty to society and duty to family. The notion of duty, in fact, is often underpinned by a narrow authoritarianism.

Battin (1991) points out that, while economic rationalism (or neo-liberalism) presents economics as being above philosophical, social and political issues, and portrays its own doctrine as being value-free, it *is* strongly ideological. It has a narrow view of individuals as fundamentally selfish, and it assumes that they should be free to pursue their own free will as economic agents. Singer (1993) makes the point that economic self-interest is not enough – humans have other needs, such as cooperation, durable social relationships and social harmony. Moreover, the emphasis on self-interest is invoked selectively. For example, when workers request a wage rise, if such a request is perceived by employers to be excessive, which it often is, workers are then condemned for their selfishness.

Neo-liberalism presents the market as independent of political interests and manipulation. However, the market is not neutral. It never exists in a political vacuum. Its very functioning occurs on terrain in which some players are privileged and others are frozen out through lack of bargaining power (based on such things as money, skills and credentials). The market is influenced by monopoly power and interfered with through the machinations of paybacks and favours.

As a theory of political philosophy, neo-liberalism is at a loss to account for altruism: for example, a mother's sacrifice for her baby. A theory that purports to explain society and cannot account for social bonds is deficient. In practical terms, also, neo-liberalism has deficiencies. Its preoccupation with immediate dollar savings may obscure other productivities and efficiencies, and it diminishes goodwill. For example, permanent school cleaners identify as part of the school community and contribute to this community. Contract cleaners are less likely to feel part of and contribute to the school.

There are continuing criticisms of neo-liberalism, including about the harmful effects of unfettered markets such as have been evident in the global financial crisis. However, the global financial crisis has been explained as a result of excess, and not as an indictment of neo-liberalism as a whole, and commitment to the principles of neo-liberalism continues in mainstream political and economic spheres in Australia. How long neo-liberalism will maintain its presence in Australia is uncertain. It is clear that both the Labor Party and Liberal National coalition have been guided by its ideas since the 1980s. It has set agendas for governments and it has permeated economic and social policy in both the public and the private sector in ways that will not easily be undone.

Social interactionism

The theoretical starting point of **social interactionism** is that society is best understood as a multitude of small-scale interactions between people. Interactionists argue that it is through these interactions that we construct meaning and, in fact, our whole notion of what reality is. One of the most influential theorists working in the symbolic interactionist tradition was Goffman (1967, 1961a, 1959). From Goffman we have learnt that to understand social relations we can invoke what he calls the 'dramaturgical model' in which we conceive of the self as a performance and society as a theatre production with roles, masks and scripts (Hancock & Garner, 2009). The performance space is 'everyday life' (Goffman, 1959). Structures set up the framework for the performance.

Given the importance of interactions in social life, we construct a very complex repertoire of objects (or props), language and mannerisms that assist us in defining our roles and positions in regard to other people. Professional people such as lawyers, doctors and social workers often use props to present themselves as powerful. They can construct an image of an important person, for example, by sitting behind a large desk in a formal office and having a 'client' ushered in by a secretary.

As we pick up symbolic messages in verbal and non-verbal interchanges with other people, we develop our own self-identity. Through long processes of interactions we become labelled. We may be identified as 'honest', 'intelligent' or 'reliable', for example. If we are given a stigmatising label, such as 'stupid', 'neurotic', 'dishonest' or 'unreliable', this can have a powerful effect on the way other people see us and on the way we see ourselves. Cooley (1909) coined the term 'looking-glass self' and argued that someone who is continually defined in a certain way will act accordingly. Goffman (1961b) pointed out stigma is set contextually. For example, community development practitioners have noted how the idea of someone being disabled is set within a context that, in a particular situation, makes someone disabled (an example being where there is no wheelchair access to public transport). Fear of being stigmatised (as a troublemaker or an outcast, for example) is a regulatory device that operates through self-management. In emphasising what are sometimes known as micro-practices and micro-power, Goffman's work has similarities with the ideas of Foucault, whose work we consider later in this chapter.

Stereotypes

As emphasised above, social interaction does not take place in a vacuum. Interpretations of our experiences and relationships are often based on stereotypes, which generalise about a group on the basis of selective and usually one-sided interpretations. For example, the stereotype of Asians as 'working for peanuts and taking the jobs of non-Asian Australians' is one rationale for hostility to Asian migrants. Stereotypes form the basis of prejudice and discrimination. Prejudices are preconceived views about an individual or group. For example, people who are paraplegics are sometimes seen as being helpless, or a physical disability may be taken as a sign of mental disability. Discrimination occurs when people are excluded from, or included in, activities on the basis of their membership of certain groups. Negative discrimination occurs, for example, when Indigenous people are excluded from certain activities on the basis of their race and when a paraplegic cannot attend a meeting because there is no wheelchair access to the meeting room. An example of positive discrimination in favour of women is when a number of places on a committee are reserved for women solely on the basis of their gender.

Stereotypes are often expressed in a way that engenders hostility. Minority groups with different customs or beliefs to those of the dominant group are often stereotyped and labelled as unintelligent or stupid. Those in dominant cultures interpret and evaluate different customs, values and beliefs in terms of their own culture, which tends to be accepted uncritically. The term **ethnocentrism** is used to describe this tendency.

Racism attributes differences in cultures and social groups to physical features such as colour of skin and shape of eyes. While there is no scientific basis to the concept of 'race' and to the claim that physical features such as skin colour determine a person's or a group's capabilities, racists believe that people are inferior or superior because of supposed racial differences and treat people differently on the basis of race.

Those involved in community development should be conscious of the ways that stereotyping, prejudice, discrimination and ethnocentrism are manifested in society. They should also have a critical awareness of their own prejudices and ethnocentrism. Merton (1949) draws our attention to the various ways that those in majority groups approach minority groups. He identifies four categories in the case of racism:

- *All-weather liberals* are prepared to take a stand against racism, even when the personal consequences are harmful.
- *Fair-weather liberals* present themselves as anti-racist, but weigh up the consequences of any action and withdraw from their anti-racist position when deemed necessary.
- *Timid bigots* hold prejudices but because of their interests, such as concerns about money or status, they act in a friendly way towards minority groups, while criticising these groups behind their backs.
- *Active bigots* are prejudiced against minority groups and actively discriminate against members of these groups.

Community development workers must be sensitive to the forces at play in the complex interactions of their work. They must understand that the processes discussed above can render members of minority groups powerless. Later in this chapter and in chapter 8 we discuss the importance of working with difference and the dangers of stereotyping people because they look different.

Marxism

The large and various body of theory known as Marxism is perhaps the pre-eminent theoretical perspective to have influenced community development, although not without debate and dissent. Marxism not only offers a grand theory that sets out a whole program for critique, but also the ideas, methods and concepts of Marxism, many of which are discussed in this book, have 'seeped out of their container' and while coming from the Marxist lineage, are often no longer understood as Marxist (Hancock & Garner, 2009:77).

Marxism does not provide a singular coherent body of thought: several strands have developed over the past 150 years, some of which are contradictory to community development. Here, we will discuss five interrelated ways that Marxism has influenced community development and outline debates within the Left that are important for community development strategy.

1 Community development has drawn on aspects of Marxist philosophy, and particularly the early writings of Marx and Engels, about what it is to be human and what constitutes the basis of an alienating or fulfilling life.
2 Marxist conceptions of society and social change have set the context of debates in community development about the sources of inequality and the general processes of change.
3 Community development work has been influenced by the Marxist critique of traditional social work and the identification of social workers as agents of control.
4 Western Marxist discussions of ideology, power and political struggles have contributed to the way in which community development theorises its own role as an agent of change.
5 Community development practitioners might draw on Marxist analyses of capitalism as a basis for their critiques of neo-liberalism and the 'free market' and their concerns about the way commitment to unrestrained economic growth leads to environmental crises.

Marxist philosophy

In their early writings, Marx and Engels founded an approach to an understanding of society that has come to be known as **historical materialism**. They explained that people are creative, productive beings, who enter into relationships with other humans in order to produce their material world and, in doing so, they fulfil themselves as human beings. While Marx and Engels rejected the view that there is a definitive 'human nature', they did argue that what and how people produce is the key to understanding the varieties of human beings and societies.

> As individuals express their life, so they are. What they are, therefore, coincides with their production, both with what they produce and how they produce. Hence what individuals are depends on the material conditions of their production (Marx & Engels, 1976:37).

In what is known as the humanist tradition in Marxism, there is a focus on how, in capitalist society, the relationships between humans and what and how they produce have become distorted, as have relationships between humans themselves. Human beings have become alienated in a number of ways. Workers who make products have no say in what they produce, how they produce or what happens to a product after it is made. Thus they are alienated from the process of production, the product itself, other humans and their overall humanness or **species-being**. In the period in which we now live – late capitalism – millions of workers have no employment and thus can play no part in the process of capitalist production, except as 'reserve' workers (the industrial reserve army) and passive consumers of handouts provided by relatives, the state or charity.

A school of thought, known as **critical theory**, emphasises how the working class has come to be incorporated into the capitalist system through cultural and ideological processes. Two contributors to this school of thought, Horkheimer and Adorno (1972), argue that capitalist culture is essentially one of manipulation and control.

If human beings are to overcome alienation and fulfil themselves, they must construct economic and social systems that realise the ability of all human beings to contribute to the productive activities of society, and in which workers collectively decide what, where, how and when things are produced. Those influenced by Marxist theory argue that ownership and control of the resources, equipment and know-how for production must be in the hands of the direct producers, the working class, or what Marx and Engels identified as the **proletariat**. These arguments are important for community development workers. They are consistent with the view that human fulfilment rests on collective control of productive activities.

The structure of societies and social change

These ideas of what it is to be human underpin a specific interpretation of the structure of societies and social change in general, and the nature of capitalist societies in particular. They constitute the second way in which Marx's ideas have influenced community development. Struggles over resource distribution, equal opportunity and consumption issues, such as access to adequate health care and housing, and opportunity for employment in fulfilling jobs, cannot be understood without reference to the way production is organised.

We have identified above the importance of the productive capacities of humans in understanding what it is to be human. Marxist theories conceptualise the social system in terms of the notion of **mode of production**. While there is considerable discussion about the specific use of this term, it is generally conceived of as a combination of the forces of production and the social relations of production.

- The **forces of production** comprise all the knowledge about how to do things, and the actual instruments of production. Of course, this includes science and technology (such elements as principles of mechanical engineering), as well as factories and tools.
- The **social relations of production** comprise the ways we organise ourselves to produce. They include the tasks we assign to managers, supervisors and shopfloor workers, and the relationships between them. They include the arrangements through which some people sell their **labour power**, or capacity to produce, to people who own and control the means of production. They deal with what people actually do in employment and how some people physically produce goods and services, and others do not.

The mode of production comprises the particular social relations of production and the forces of production, and the way they go together in any one society. According to Marx, different epochs are characterised by different modes of production. For example, in feudal times, the mode of production was based on an arrangement whereby peasants owned their own tools, but the feudal lord had control of the disposition of their produce. Where a capitalist mode of production prevails, the capitalist owns and controls both the tools and the disposition of the products. The mode of production is taken to be the key factor that influences, or determines, human life. This economic level of society is usually identified as the base upon which rest all other aspects of society, such as social values and beliefs and political power (or the superstructure). Because this view regards economics as the determining factor in human life, it is known as **economic determinism**.

There is some debate within Marxism about what is actually meant by 'determinant', and most Western Marxists have rejected the notion of economic determinism in the sense that everything that humans do is caused by the economic system. While they generally agree that the mode of production sets the stage on which political power and social institutions are constructed, they argue that it does not narrowly determine everything else that goes on in society. According to an approach identified as **structural Marxism**, the economic is determinant only in the last instance and the superstructure has a relative autonomy.

The argument that the economic level sets the stage for all other aspects of society has important implications for understanding the processes of social change. If the mode of production is taken as the crucial influence or determinant, then real change cannot occur unless a particular mode of production – in our case capitalism – is overturned.

Capitalism, according to Marx, rests on the **capital–labour relation**: one class (the owners and controllers of the means of production, or the **bourgeoisie**) exploits another class (the direct producers, or proletariat), who produce the goods and services but neither own nor control the means of production that enable society to continue to exist. The direct producers or proletariat have no real control over the means of production, how they produce or what they produce. They are forced to sell their labour to the bourgeoisie in order to survive.

In capitalist societies, because the bourgeoisie derive their power and wealth from their ownership and control of the means of production, it is not in their interests to have this system undermined or changed. According to Marx, the capitalist system is inherently exploitative and exploitation cannot be removed until the system is replaced by an alternative one based on communism, in which the workers own and control the means of production. (Communism in this sense should not be confused with the economic organisation that existed in the USSR.)

Why do the working class and those who are disadvantaged and oppressed in capitalist society accept their lot in life? A wide range of Western Marxists, including those associated with structural Marxism and critical theory, have argued that the working class has become integrated into capitalist society through subtle means of control. This leads us to the third way that Marxism has influenced community development: the exposé of traditional social welfare work as a control mechanism.

Critique of social welfare programs

Marxists have identified social welfare as a mechanism of control, whereby governments use programs and policies (such as those associated with unemployment benefits) to keep the poor in their place and willing to be exploited in the capitalist system. Any small improvements in the living conditions of the working class only serve to gloss over the inequities of this system. Inequities are integral to the capitalist system and cannot be eliminated until the whole system is changed. In their critique of traditional welfare, **orthodox Marxist** theorists have contended that the overall life of the working class cannot be improved by small welfarist changes or by counselling and casework.

Social reforms and social welfare function to ensure the continuation of the existing unjust and exploitative capitalist system by hoodwinking members of the working class into believing that their lives are getting better. Welfare institutions are part of the state, and like other institutions in capitalist societies, they work in the interests of those who already own and control the means of production.

In some ways, of course, community development also reproduces the capitalist system by militating many of the effects of capitalism, such as disempowerment and a feeling of lack of worth. However, the welfare state provides important infrastructure support to the disadvantaged and marginalised in society. Moreover, poverty rarely brings with it a preparedness to challenge the structure of capitalist societies. And as we will discuss in the next chapter, the state is not so monolithic that all its aspects are oppressive, either by stealth or by explicit force. It is full of contradictions and ambiguities. Indeed, societies that have attempted to develop socialist systems have experienced their own social problems.

Political struggle

Can we support the best aspects of an existing society while at the same time challenging some of very foundations of that society? The orthodox Marxist response to this question is no. Orthodox Marxists have argued that real change can only occur when the whole system of society is overthrown. Other left theorists, including **Western Marxists**, have a more nuanced picture of political struggle. That is, strategies for change call for working with and accepting the existing terms of reference through which a society operates, while at the same time challenging its very structures and processes. It is this left viewpoint that has influenced community development. Moreover, both the left (Marxist-influenced) viewpoint and community development hold that effective strategies for change need a vision and a transformative strategy. They entail opening up new forms of politics, new ways of thinking about human life and social relationships and an alternative economic system. Community development is committed to developing new political processes in the form of what is sometimes known as *prefigurative politics*. Prefigurative politics show how, even within existing societies, things can be better. Consistent with the commitment to fighting TINA (there is no alternative), community organisations and community development workers try to show that there are other ways of doing things in their everyday relations, tasks and processes. Prefigurative politics can help develop an alternative political culture, one that rejects the view that we must continue to be controlled by 'the way things are'. It emphasises that things can be different. Even in a modest way, workers in community organisations often begin to explain how things could be done differently by describing issues in their own way and defining them in their own terms. They can organise different ways of 'doing things', such as was evident in the bushfire case study in chapter 1.

Here, it is important to understand that, although community development draws on many of the Marxist insights into social change, it is often not in agreement with

Marxist views of political struggle. For example, community development has always been at odds with those Marxists who see oppression and conflict only in terms of capital and labour, and who argue that real struggle exists only between classes at the place of production, the workplace. Later Marxists such as Gramsci (1971) reject the economic determinist reading of Marx, whereby economics determines everything else in society. Gramsci (1971) points out that power relations are very complex and that any society comprises a balance of class and social forces, leading to a variety of forms of oppression. He emphasises that popular democratic struggles cannot be neatly reduced to class struggles.

Western Marxists have generally extended the sites of power to what they identify as the superstructure, which includes the political system and social institutions. In particular, power is held by what they call the **ideological state apparatuses** such as the media, educational institutions and trade unions (see Althusser, 1977), which, although set in economic contexts, have a relative autonomy from the economic base. **Ideology** refers to practices, beliefs and social relations that conceal alternative ways of acting and thinking, and close off a thorough understanding of future options and the realities and possibilities for human society. Practices and beliefs that are ideological become 'natural' to our ways of acting and thinking. Ideological apparatuses are important as they enable powerful groups to control through consent rather than coercion (Gramsci, 1971).

The critical theory tradition of Western Marxism provides other insights into the ideological incorporation of the working class in late capitalism. Habermas (1971) points to the importance of the depoliticisation of the mass of the population, whereby parliamentary democracy provides only the illusion of participation in political decision making, and politics becomes defined in terms of solutions to technical problems. Western Marxism has thus extended the view of where power lies and, in this, it has influenced community development. From a community development perspective, important political struggles can occur in any institution that produces or reproduces existing relations of power.

Restructured Marxist theory and practice

In the light of the collapse of Soviet communism, a number of those influenced by Marxism sought to reconstruct Marxist theory and practice in ways that have rendered it more sensitive to contemporary socio-political conditions. What could a renewed Marxist theory look like? It should perhaps be thought of more as a *socialist* theory or a Marxist-*influenced* theory than a Marxist theory per se. Such a theory needs to account for the collapse of communist regimes, as well as the problems with attempts to provide overarching theories and resolutions to human problems. It must explain how human societies are constructed around differences (such as between men and women and between different cultures), as well as similarities. It must accept that different groups of people have different ways of seeing things and different interests. It should continue and extend its critique of the capitalist forms of production and unfettered economic growth, including the pervasive inequality and human and environmental degradation that result from global capitalism, to include strategies for sustainable societies. A renewed Marxist theory, of course, must consider ways that humans can collectively participate in the making of their own, sustainable, history.

For Blackburn (1991:13), a renewed Marxist theory can offer a critique of 'the exercise of arbitrary power in all walks of life – in factories, offices, schools, and wherever else power affects people's existence'. In *Reinventing the Left* (Miliband, 1994), a number of authors offer insights into ways the Left can develop a new identity. They argue for the necessity of addressing the pressing problems that face the world as it changes and tackling the weaknesses of traditional left analyses and approaches. The themes of the Miliband book are, first, that the Left's traditional emphasis on the importance of equality and solidarity must be supplemented by renewed commitment to personal autonomy; second, that the role of socialist politics is not to abolish markets altogether, but to organise and regulate them; third, that politics, while including conflicts in the workplace, covers all the struggles that occur in both private and public life; and, finally, that the concept and practice of politics should be extended to include democracy as a process and an end in itself, and to cover modes of political organisation both within and beyond the nation state. In an interesting discussion of ways of reinvigorating the Left from the perspective of democratic renewal, Wainwright (2003:183) documents how local communities are working to develop a new bargaining power that is embedded in a robust participatory democracy. This bargaining power provides new leverage over local state institutions, private developers and even national and global players. In the light of the growing awareness of the harmful environmental consequences of the commitment to economic growth and ever-increasing profit, a reconstructed Marxism needs to bring the issue of sustainability to the fore. It needs to rethink the idea of economics organised around growth that involves unfettered exploitation of the earth's finite resources and insufficient regard for the harmful effects of the output of such exploitation, such as greenhouse gases and the many forms of environmental pollution.

While many left theorists remain to a large extent within the Marxist stable, a significant number of writers who began their careers under the influence of Marxism have moved significantly away from it. Take, for example, Castells (2004, 2000), who began his sociological career as a Marxist, as Elliott (2009) points out, and understands the capitalist principles underlying the new global economy, but argues that today it is information technology, communication and computers, rather than manufacturing, that are driving global production. New communication technologies, in particular, are transforming our relationships and networks. Our new technologically advanced and information-rich society has meant different types of organisations are possible: ones that have no clear centre and porous boundaries. Indeed, the whole idea of boundaries is being challenged daily through new processes of globalisation, as individuals and organisations connect across the world in real time and politicians are searching for ways of recapturing the old security of the nation state (and loyalty to the nation state). Community development practice has already been altered significantly by the massive technological changes since the 1970s, and continues to do so. We consider the effects of new technology on communication, identity and organisation in following chapters.

Feminism

Feminism, like community development and Marxism, is based on an inextricable linkage of theory and practice, and it is concerned to change the world, not just understand it. Like Marxism, feminism comprises different schools of thought or traditions, each proposing specific interpretations and explanations of the roles of women in society. As with Marxism, there are some central theses. The history of the development of feminism is based on observations of the inequalities in society that relate to whether one is male or female. Feminists make critical analyses of the subordination of women in society. Feminist theories set out to explain the enduring nature of sexual inequalities – how and why women are exploited, suppressed, repressed and oppressed. They are concerned with such questions as how sexual stereotyping occurs and how societies are constructed so that males are dominant.

Feminists challenge the main ways that women's identity and women's roles have been historically constructed. They emphasise the importance of giving women a voice and authenticating women's experiences. They aim to eliminate the conditions that are responsible for women's oppression, to empower women and to change how societies have been constructed in the interests of men.

There are two key concepts in feminist theory: **gender** and **patriarchy**. The social construction of gender involves society's prescription of the situations, values, attitudes and imagery for male and female roles. Identification of gender determines how we feel, act and relate to one another as men and women. It is a fundamental organising principle in our society, which sets the limits of what is acceptable masculine and feminine behaviour. An understanding of the construction of gender and gender relations is essential for community development workers. For example, social issues are often expressed in apparently gender-neutral terms, although in fact they are gender-based. Terms such as 'family violence' and 'spouse abuse' conceal the fact that these offences are nearly always committed by men against women and, furthermore, are embedded in the power relations of patriarchal society. Feminists are concerned to study and explain the systematic nature of the domination of men over women.

Patriarchy refers to the structures, values and relations that reproduce and reinforce male power. Patriarchy is also evident in the way we think about spheres within society. For example, activities in our society have been associated with two broad domains or spheres: the public or the private.

- The public sphere is the world of paid work, politics, technology, bureaucracy, business and economics, and impersonal relationships. This is the sphere of men's activities.
- The private sphere is the world of home, reproduction, childcare, unpaid work, sociability and personal life. This is the world of women.

Politicians, businessmen and the media generally focus on the public sphere as the one where the most important things in society take place. For example, the 'real' politics and the 'real' productive activities are said to take place in the public sphere. The private sphere of the family and interpersonal relations is popularly characterised as secondary. Feminists have pointed out that the construction of these two spheres has been an important factor in women's subordination and in the inferior status of the 'caring professions'.

Feminists have argued that patriarchy is the basis of women's subordination and oppression, and is manifested in all aspects of our existence. For feminists, societies are patriarchal because they bestow power and status upon masculine values, such as hierarchy, authority, domination and competition. These values systematically discriminate against the feminine gender, which is regarded as weak and inferior. **Existentialist feminism** points out that women are defined in terms of men, as the 'other' to men. Women are oppressed because they are 'not-men'. The meaning of women's existence is determined by men (de Beauvoir, 1972). According to **psychoanalytic feminism**, women's roles, submission and oppression are deeply embedded in their psyche, and women fear their own power. From this viewpoint, women's submission and oppression give men satisfaction.

Patriarchy is inherent in the way we think about and organise work. Men have controlled the definition of work as paid employment, the allocation of rewards and resources in jobs and occupations. Paid employment in what continues to be male-dominated masculine work, such as engineering and accounting, is identified as more valuable than domestic labour and gives men power and privilege. Even in paid employment, women are over-represented in low-paid inferior jobs and are under-represented in highly paid high-status jobs. Within the family, men throughout history have had unchallengeable rights and domination over women. These rights and domination continue today, although, in Western societies, mostly without legal sanction.

Patriarchal relationships are also constructed by and reflected in language. The English language is patriarchal. Women are often either systematically ignored or subsumed under masculine terms. We have 'mankind', 'workmanlike', 'man's inhumanity to man', just to give a few examples. Similarly, the English language reinforces the imagery of women as inferior and weak: such terms as 'effeminate' denigrate feminine traits.

Like Marxism, there are different viewpoints within feminism; for example, in regard to exactly how and why masculine and feminine genders have been constructed and in regard to what should be done about women's oppression. Feminist practice explores ways of overcoming the oppression of women in attitudes, structures and relationships. In the following section, we consider some of the key feminist theories that are relevant to community development.

Liberal feminism

There are historical links between **liberal feminism** and liberal philosophy. Mary Wollstonecraft, in the late eighteenth century, was concerned about contradictions between commitment to democracy and liberalism and the actual subordination of women. The suffragettes in the late 1800s invoked the liberal principles of freedom of speech, equality, laissez-faire policies and the importance of individual development in their struggles for votes for women.

Liberal feminists aim to reform society and improve the social system. From their perspective, the subordination of women is rooted in laws and in social relations and customs that block or hinder women's chances of success. They argue that because women have been subdued by legal constraints and norms, and because they have been excluded from the public (men's) world, their true potential and fulfilment have not been achieved. They point out that just to be a woman results in certain restrictions, regardless of interests, abilities and needs. Thus, liberal feminists have fought for laws to ensure women's rights in the workplace, such as for maternity leave and equal pay. Equal access to traditionally male jobs can be achieved by equal opportunity programs and anti-discrimination legislation. Liberal feminism criticises the 'glass ceiling' – the obstacles that prevent women from undertaking senior roles in government and management.

Liberal feminists also emphasise the influence of socialisation in developing sex roles and sexist attitudes, and work to change existing attitudes and practices that discriminate against women. For example, they stress the importance of unlearning traditional sex roles. Programs to improve women's assertiveness, esteem and competitiveness are thus part of the liberal feminist agenda. Educational institutions can play a role here by developing non-sexist curricula and by developing traditionally male skills in girls and female skills in boys.

Marxist and socialist feminism

Marxist feminism and **socialist feminism** link patriarchy with a critique of capitalism. According to this approach, women's oppression and class oppression mutually support each other. Both are inherent in the structure of our society. That is, women's subordination is set alongside the subordination of the working class.

Engels (1884) argued that women's oppression originated from the introduction of private property and the rise of capitalism and the bourgeois family. Private property meant ownership of the means of production by men and the development of capitalist class relations. Along with the bourgeois family came the privatisation, isolation and devaluation of women's life and work at home. With the development of industrial capitalism, production outside the home began to outstrip production within the home, where women had been very significant. As the production of goods moved from the private to the public sphere, so too did men's productive activities. Men dominated the public sphere and were seen as the productive wage-earners. Women remained in the home or private sphere as unwaged workers, and their role was restricted to child-rearing, unpaid housework and the provision of emotional and sexual comfort for their husbands.

For capitalism to continue, there must be a continual supply of willing workers. That is to say, there must be motivated able-bodied workers who are willing to sell their labour. The major role of women in capitalist society is to help ensure the availability of labour through producing children and nurturing, socialising and motivating them. The key institution in which they do this is the nuclear family, in which women have always borne the brunt of unpaid domestic labour. Some feminists argue that women's domestic labour also produces **surplus value** for it adds to the profits of capitalists, who would have to increase wages if workers had to pay for domestic labour.

Other Marxist feminists argue that women's exploitation cannot be explained simply by reference to the needs of the capitalist system, nor by the prevailing ideas and images of women as inferior to men because they are biologically different. They argue for a more complex relationship between class and patriarchy (see Barrett, 1980). Patriarchy has set the scene for the development of a pool of disposable poorly paid women workers.

It legitimises men's privileges and enshrines ideas that men should wield power over women. In these ways patriarchy splits working-class men and women and is thus not in the long-term interests of the working class. For Marxist feminists overall, the two central and mutually reinforcing sources of inequality and oppression are class and patriarchy. The construction of an equal and just society requires the abolition of both capitalism and patriarchy.

Radical feminism

A third feminist view on sexual inequality has been identified as **radical feminism**. While there are also wide-ranging debates within this approach, there is general agreement that patriarchy is an autonomous system and that unequal relationships between men and women are the most fundamental and enduring of all. Biological differences between men and women have led to the construction of a patriarchal society in which women are seen as physically and psychologically dependent on men. The domination and oppression of women by men is more important than any other form of domination, including class and racial oppression.

Moreover, no area of society or human relationship is free from male definition and dominance. 'Real work' is men's work and 'the truth' is men's truth, including male (malestream) knowledge and science. The apparently universal categories of 'human', such as worker and individual, are constructed on the basis of male attributes. Women's culture, women's experiences and women's knowledge are all devalued or denied by men. Thus, all aspects of women's lives are subject to male control; they must be critically analysed, questioned and changed. Therefore, to the radical feminists, men are the agents of oppression and women must challenge male power at all levels.

To some radical feminists, men can liberate themselves from their role as oppressor. To others, the oppressor role of men is so strongly biologically determined that it cannot be overcome. This difference in view has led to different strategies for overcoming women's subordination. One strategy is to challenge the whole patriarchal social system with the aim of establishing a different, non-patriarchal society. In this approach, women must struggle to overthrow all manifestations of patriarchy. While there is discussion about what this requires, there are some general views. They include:

- overthrowing the existing conceptualisation of the public and private spheres
- demolishing hierarchical and authoritarian structures, including traditional religious organisations, the family and legal, political and educational institutions
- undermining the often ruthless competitive business ethic that underpins the capitalist economic system.

A non-patriarchal society would be based on different principles for human relations and human endeavour, aimed at establishing a culturally enriched, nurturing and humanising environment. It requires new structures, such as collective decision making and power sharing, which encourage creative resolution of problems. To some feminists, this society would blur or minimise gender roles and divisions and become androgynous. Feminists argue, of course, that there would need to be a significant weakening of masculine values and a significant strengthening of feminine values. In such a society women would take responsibility for their own destinies.

To other radical feminists, because men's oppressive role is biologically determined, women can escape oppression and take responsibility for their own destinies only by excluding men altogether from their lives. Only when women develop separate existences can they have absolute control of their minds, bodies, productive and reproductive activities. Medical technology, such as artificial insemination and in-vitro fertilisation, can free women from the need to have heterosexual relationships for the purpose of procreation. There has been considerable criticism of the biological determinism of this approach.

Postmodernist feminism

In contrast to the idea that the concept of 'woman' is clear-cut, and the claim that what defines women is their biological make-up, for some feminists the concepts of 'women' and 'men' are socially constructed in ways that render the terms fluid and ambiguous. It might well be that it is impossible to find any immutable characteristics of 'woman' at all. Other feminists express concern over such attempts to provide an explanation of women's subjugation. These concerns led to whole new trajectories of feminist thought. For example, one important trajectory involves the idea of deconstruction, which we touched on at the beginning of the chapter. From this perspective, understanding the position of women involves exposing the hidden assumptions of a text (such as a marriage) and rejecting the idea that there must be a unified meaning. Another trajectory involved reflections upon who defines and controls feminist understandings.

During the 1980s and 1990s, some women began to reflect on how traditional feminist analysis was constructed by white, middle-class Western women, presenting their view of women's oppression as the 'correct view' and, moreover, speaking for all other women. This criticism tended to draw on postmodern ideas of difference and plurality, which formed the basis for the argument that there could be many feminisms. Thus **postmodern feminism** rejects the view that women are destined to have a specific self-identity based on a specific nature or 'essence'. Reducing any category of people to specific characteristics or 'essences' is identified as 'essentialism' and is discussed in chapter 8.

Much feminist theory has worked with overarching theories, through which aspects of women's lives are interpreted and explained. In contrast, central to postmodernism is the view that overarching and all-encompassing theories have no use and no meaning. There is no ultimate truth, and it is human weakness and insecurity to search for it. Yet, this very rejection of overarching theories opened the way for a convergence between feminism and postmodernism. Overarching theories have been traditionally constructed by men for men. They belong to a world that is elitist, authoritarian and inflexible. This world is rejected by feminism and postmodernism alike. The cutting edge of postmodern feminism lies in its subversion of all self-righteous givens about how society should work. From a postmodernist perspective, no value, principle, moral code or theory is sacrosanct.

Postmodernist feminists celebrate difference and diversity, and reject forced unity and closed totalities (see Young, 1990). Hence, there is no one correct form of feminism. Women should be free to choose their own female selves.

In Australia today we can find all of the feminist perspectives discussed above. Feminist agendas are being maintained, although these are mainly framed by liberal feminism, such as expressed in concern about the 'glass ceiling' that hinders aspiring managers. From a more radical perspective, there has been some disquiet regarding the avoidance of the discourses of feminism by young Australian women. Perhaps more troubling, though, is the failure of Australian women to work in solidarity with those women struggling against their own traditional misogynist cultures both internationally and within Australia.

The feminist contribution to community development

The trajectory of community development since the 1970s owes a lot to the various streams of feminist thought, and feminism continues to be relevant to community development today. For example, community provision of services continues to occur in the context of the existing sexual division of labour and all too often this means an unquestioned reliance on the unpaid labour of women (Doyal & Gough, 1991). Community development work, like that in other sectors of the social and community services industry, is characterised by **vertical gender segmentation**, such that men are over-represented in positions of control and management and under-represented in subordinate positions. For example, community care for the elderly is underpinned by women carers, who often live in conditions of near servitude.

The following points set out some of the key learnings from feminism for community development practice. In their activities, community development workers should:

- make conscious their views of patriarchy, class and ethnicity and relate them to their life experiences
- challenge the idea that there is one definition of 'woman' and one way of being a woman
- draw attention to the lack of resources for women and how this restricts women's lives
- work to expand real options and choices for women
- treat women's lived experiences with respect
- encourage women to articulate and define issues in their own terms
- be conscious of everyday language that perpetuates women's oppression and the feelings of inferiority felt by women. For example, the comment 'I'm only a housewife' should be challenged, as it belittles housework and women.

All these considerations are important in analyses of where women's problems lie and in developing strategies for change. Of course, where one stands in regard to specific feminist theories and strategies varies significantly in community development work. The important thing, however, is that community development workers are conscious of and able to explain why they hold particular theories and why they subscribe to specific strategies.

Social movement theory

The idea of linking theory and practice has been central to both Marxist and feminist perspectives. However, while the application of Marxist theory has focused on class struggle, feminist theories have generally been understood as a new **social movement theory**. New social movements have different aims to class movements. They are forms of collective action aimed at social reorganisation and/or social change, but they do not propose revolutionary class struggle in which the proletariat comes to power. Indeed, notwithstanding the way socialist feminism links patriarchy with a critique of capitalism, the discourse of revolutionary class struggle conceptualises the agents of change as men.

Thus, in contrast to Marxism, new social movements are organised around social, cultural and environmental concerns that became central issues in contemporary political life from the 1950s onwards. New social movements include human rights, environmental, gay and lesbian, democratic, alternative lifestyle and animal liberation movements. New social movements might be organised around a campaign for change, such as a feminist campaign for equal pay for men and women, or they might be reactive, such as movements aimed at stopping the development of nuclear power.

While there are significant variations between the various new social movements, they share some central characteristics (see Feher & Heller, 1983). They are specifically issue-based and, as indicated above, they tend to cross class lines. They do not aim to seize political power in the traditional sense of overthrowing the state. Instead they aim to mobilise the populace in support of the right to participate in or control decisions that are related to a specific issue or cause.

A key theorist of new social movements, Touraine (1988), argues that the chief characteristic of contemporary societies is an increasing capacity to act upon themselves. He suggests that new social movements represent a new stage in the development of societies. They are authentic sources of opposition and radicalism. They exist in a field of social action in which the contestation is about cultural orientations and the self-determination of society. He identifies the notion of people making their own history as the self-production of society or **historicity**. His view is that 'social life is produced by cultural achievements and social conflicts, and at the heart of society burns the fire of social movements' (Touraine, 1981:1). For Touraine, social movements are the agents of collective action and political struggle. At stake is the social control of a new culture, of society's ability continually to re-create and act upon itself through collective challenges and conflicts.

Another influential social theorist, Habermas (1981), locates the activities of new social movements within concerns about what he calls the **grammar of life**. Habermas identifies a thematic change from old politics to new politics: from issues of economic, social, domestic and military security to issues of the quality of life, equality, individual self-realisation, participation and human rights. He emphasises the defensive role of new social movements as reactions to the 'colonisation of the life world'. Unlike Touraine, Habermas does not identify new social movements as the highest form of social action. Yet they do signal possibilities for new forms of interaction and a search for personal and collective identity. New social movements are sensitive to what he identifies as the self-destructive consequences of the growth in complexity (Habermas, 1981).

In her discussions of new social movements, Cohen (1983, 1982) emphasises the importance of the themes of self-defence and democratisation of society and, like Habermas, she is interested in the way that new social movements can foster and coordinate new meanings and defend and expand social spaces in the public sphere.

Community development and social movements

Community development has a symbiotic relationship with new social movements. Community development practitioners often begin as activists in a social movement and then move into paid work in community development. For example, people working in disability organisations sometimes come from disability activist groups; people working in environmental education programs might have begun as members of green organisations or parties; and a woman working in a prostitutes' collective might have developed organisational skills participating in a social movement about gay and lesbian issues. Similarly, the experience of working in a community organisation can influence a person's decision to become a member of a social movement. However, new social movements are not synonymous with community organisations and community development work is rarely the same as participation in a social movement. We need to be clear about the similarities and differences between community development and new social movements. These are:

- *Central concerns*: both are premised on the interrelationship between theory and practice. Both community development and new social movements challenge conventional ways of seeing and acting in the world. Community development shares with new social movements the idea of humans collectively creating their own destiny, a commitment to transcending established norms and an interest in the promise of social emancipation. Community development is issue-based and may transcend traditional class divisions. For example, like social movements, it is concerned with quality of life and human rights issues.
- *Permanence and professionalism*: as Donnison (1991:116) suggests, community development is often nurtured by new social movements 'giving people the capacity to mobilise and work together, and the confidence to challenge authority'. Yet community development comprises a set of clearly articulated practices and services that are associated with specific tasks, usually operating under an industrial award. It is, therefore, in its own way a profession.
- *Social movements*, or elements of new social movements, sometimes become political parties, which contest electorally based power. In such circumstances they can no longer be thought of a social movement. Community development does not aspire to be a political party or contest political power.
- *Leadership*: members of new social movements attempt to persuade ordinary people to join their movement. They generally have clearly identified leaders, who can be ideologues. In fact, the strength of a leader's conviction can be the driving force behind a movement. Community development does not have the same kind of leaders as social

movements do. Community development workers emphasise empowerment rather than leadership. Empowerment occurs when community members themselves identify needs and develop their own strategies for change. From this perspective, community members are not followers and 'joiners' in the same way the members of social movements are. They do not rely on charismatic leaders.
- *Radicalism:* a defining characteristic of social movements is that they exist outside institutions and mainstream political processes and parties. This allows possibilities for radicalism and a political freedom that community development does not have. Most community development work takes place within, or is auspiced by, existing institutions such as local government and this circumscribes its radicalism.

Green perspectives

To illustrate the power of new social movements we will consider in some detail the theory and practice of what has come to be known as the **green movement**. The green movement has been one of the most active social movements since the 1970s. Understanding green perspectives begins with an analysis of how humans conceive of, and relate to, their physical environment. Human history, particularly as it has developed since industrialisation, has largely been the history of the exploitation of the natural environment, whereby nature becomes purely a matter of utility, a 'stratagem' designed to subdue human requirements, whether as the object of consumption or as the means of production (Bookchin, 1986).

Of course, disquiet about the destruction of the environment, overpopulation and how industrialisation affects nature is not entirely new. As Giddens (2009:50) points out, green thinking is actually an outcome of the industrial revolution. It was expressed in nostalgia for leafy fields outside the cities in the nineteenth century and deepened during the twentieth century, especially after the Second World War. Green perspectives today begin by focusing on the profound environmental crises facing the world. Understanding how these crises have occurred has led to a sense of urgency about the need to change the ways that humans organise their lives and relate to nature (see Ife, 1995).

Environmental concerns now include the depletion of the earth's resources; pollution of water, air and soil; extinction of species; shrinking of biodiversity; global warming; nuclear waste; and most importantly and urgently today, climate change through global warming. If the earth's ecosystems are under stress or in a state of collapse, then humanity cannot afford to ignore analysing the ways that they organise its relationship to its physical environment. There are several schools of thought on how we should analyse our relationship to our environment and respond to environmental issues and crises. While there is no complete agreement on the terminology for identifying the different types of interpretations and responses to environmental issues, writers often distinguish between environmentalist responses and ecological or green responses.

Environmentalism is generally seen as being less radical and less holistic than an ecological or green approach. Environmentalist approaches compartmentalise environmental problems and seek specific solutions within the terms of reference of an acceptance of continuing industrialisation and technological progress. That is, they do not seek to shift our thinking about our relations with nature or change how societies are organised in any fundamental way. For example, while faith in science contributed to (or caused) many of the environmental problems we are now facing, the environmentalist perspective holds that science can also be harnessed to begin to undo or control the harm it has caused over the past few centuries. Environmental solutions revolve around modifying how we use science and/or around drawing on the right experts. For example, the solution to the problem of global warming is to reduce greenhouse gases; the solution to the problem of the depletion of earth's resources is to develop alternative technologies; the solution to water shortages is to legally restrict water consumption (see Ife, 1995). From this perspective, nature is something that is separate from human beings – a resource, preferably treated with respect, or maybe an object of beauty and comfort, but not to be thought of as an intrinsic component of human social life (see Giddens, 1994).

In contrast, ecological responses (sometimes also identified as green responses) to environmental crises place humanity's relation to nature at the centre of understanding of human social life. Rather than relying on piecemeal alterations directed by scientific experts to modify the damage we have done to our environment, greens are concerned with how to ensure the complete retrieval of nature by changing how we think about and organise our lives. Some writers take the approach that the value of nature is that it is the source of human existence itself (see Goodin, 1992). The Norwegian philosopher Arne Naess (2002, 1989) argues for **ecological wisdom**, a philosophy that understands the value and interrelationships of all forms of life. Ecological wisdom rejects the anthropocentrism that places the immediate satisfaction of human needs above all other values. It is based on a concern that anthropocentrism is impacting dramatically on the planet's resources, and in so doing is threatening the whole ecosystem. From this vantage point we must act immediately to halt the ruination of the natural environment, whatever the circumstances. This approach, sometimes also known as **deep ecology**, requires humans to radically change the way they live and interact with the natural environment.

Failing to understand how nature is intrinsically woven into human life has led to an attitude that constructs nature as an object to be continually exploited for the purposes of human gratification. From a green perspective, environmental crises are the result of the way we think about and structure human societies, not just of some erroneous applications of science. The resolutions to environmental problems require fundamental changes in how we organise our lives. For some, this means the organisation of a non-violent effort to overthrow materialistic industrial society and replace it with a new type of society in which humans live in harmony with nature. Yet this begs the question as to what nature actually is. In the following section, we briefly consider this question.

What is nature?

The idea that the green movement tends to sanctify nature has been taken up by a number of writers. For example, Beck (1994:65) comments:

> Nature is not nature, but rather a concept, norm, memory, utopia, counter-image ... The ecology movement has fallen prey to a naturalistic misapprehension of itself.

One approach is to render what humans have done to their habitat as unnatural because it interferes with the unfettered development of nature. The extreme resolution to this problem is to eliminate humans altogether. But this viewpoint fails to understand that humans, being biological organisms, are part of nature. The things that they produce are, by and large, part of nature. While cities, being built of concrete rather than unadulterated twigs, may be seen as less natural than other forms of habitat, does this makes cities less 'natural' than, say, a twig dwelling? In fact, humans live in settings that are continually changing, both through human intervention and through the so-called natural cycles of seasons, weather, life and death. Humans interact with these settings and other biological organisms. Humans affect these organisms in the same ways that these organisms affect humans. Moreover, does leaving nature alone always have better results for the environment than human intervention? For example, should bushfires started by lightning always be left to run their own course because they are natural events? And, as Giddens (1994) points out, human intervention, such as the development of reforestation projects to prevent erosion after a cyclone or mudslide, can actually protect nature, rather than destroy it.

Critiques of growth and technological progress

There are several areas of focus for green analyses. Here, we consider two of these. First, is the idea of growth, which was introduced in chapter 1. The positive value given to the idea of growth is expressed in how we talk about human growth, economic growth, growth in business and growth in prosperity, for example. We have assumed that growth is both good and inevitable. But, of course, there is nothing intrinsically good about growth per se. For example, growth based on exploitation of the earth's resources is not a positive when the earth's resources are finite (see Meadows et al., 1992).

Second, is the idea of technological progress. The promise of technological development was that the 'mastery' of the physical and natural environment by humans would reap unlimited material benefits for humankind. Instead, as green activists point out, technological development has unleashed uncontrollable (and often unknown) destruction. They cite the effects of modern warfare, disasters at nuclear power stations (for example, Chernobyl) and nuclear tests, the pollution of waterways and oceans, greenhouse gas omissions, the building of massive dams and sophisticated deforestation technology. In addition, technology is now servicing the needs of the powerful to control the mass of ordinary people in ways that were not possible in the past. New and sophisticated forms of control and surveillance have been developed, such as the extensive use of video cameras, computer records on citizens and even new techniques of torture. The solution is to radically alter the way we think about and use technology and technological experts. All technologies should be investigated to find out if they are appropriate to the needs of the communities in which they are used. Audits of technological innovations should be undertaken to discover their disadvantages and advantages.

Eco-socialist approaches

What is the basis for the emphasis on growth? The **eco-socialist perspectives** point to how capitalism is underpinned by a commitment to the accumulation or growth of capital and production, not because these serve the real needs of all humans, but because they provide the 'motor' or rationale for the whole capitalist system. The result of the capitalist emphasis on growth is overconsumption, pollution and, of course, depletion of the earth's resources. The solution lies in changing the very mode of production from a capitalist to a socialist one, in which there will be collective ownership and control of the means of production. In this society, people will be educated about the devastating effects of capitalist production processes, and production will be more restrained and will take place through appropriate technology and only to satisfy the needs of people, not to make profit for the minority.

There are several issues in the eco-socialist approach to environmental problems and crises. First, it is not capitalism alone that places such a value on growth. The havoc wreaked on the environment by Soviet-style communism has been equal to if not worse than the havoc brought about by capitalism. Second, the idea of production taking place only to satisfy the needs of people begs the question, what are the needs of the people? It can be argued that capitalism is doing no more than responding to real needs, because if people didn't want the goods that capitalism produces, they wouldn't buy them. However, these issues do not negate the argument that capitalism is premised on the idea of growth and, as such, has contributed significantly to the environmental problems that confront humankind today.

Eco-feminist approaches

There is another way of explaining why humans relate to their environment in terms of it being a resource to be mastered and exploited. This way of thinking opens up the question of who it is that is doing the mastering and exploiting and why. From the **eco-feminist perspectives**, the answer to this question is that it is men who are doing the mastering and exploiting and they are doing it because of the patriarchal values and structures that dominate society. These values and structures emphasise control, oppression, competition and acquisitiveness. The environment is an object, separated from humans, to be dominated and exploited. In contrast, eco-feminist approaches see another kind of relationship between earth and women in which women, with their values of sharing and caring for all things (as opposed to dominating and exploiting them), nurture the environment. In its more romantic form, eco-feminism sees women as having an almost spiritual relationship with 'Mother Earth' in which they become the protectors of the environment. As for the eco-feminist solution to environmental destruction, if the root cause is patriarchy, with its emphasis on exploitative and competitive mastery of the environment, then the solution is to eliminate patriarchy and replace it with structures that are based on nurturing, caring and sharing values.

One of the key issues in the eco-feminist approach is that it raises issues about the characteristics of 'nature' and the symbiotic relationship between nature and feminism. It tends to be based on sentimental and nostalgic assumptions about the idea of nature. For example, the construct 'Mother Earth' has had religious and feminine connotations. Today, this idea has taken new spiritual forms that sanctify the natural over the unnatural in a way that has become an act of faith. This act of faith is expressed in claims about the superiority of 'being close to nature' and 'living naturally'. But the question of what nature actually is, and what it means to live in harmony with nature, is still debated.

Eco-anarchist approaches

Eco-anarchist perspectives also focus on how the structures of domination have caused humans to exploit and deplete their natural habitat. But it is not just a matter of singling out capitalist or patriarchal structures. It is the very nature of organisations and structures themselves that are the problem. Organisations and structures always mean control and constraint. That is, organisations and structures deny humans the freedom to express themselves as humans; they prevent people from understanding their relationships to each other and their relationships to their natural habitat. The solution to environmental problems is to minimise the degree of organisation and structures in society as a whole, and maximise decentralisation and autonomy for communities and individuals. One vision is to establish small, autonomous and self-sustaining communities. Another vision is to eschew both modern technology and the quest for growth and to get 'back to nature'. As with some of the critiques of eco-feminism, eco-anarchist views have been criticised for their romanticised and nostalgic assumptions about an ideal world where humans live in complete harmony with nature.

Environmental authoritarianism

Following the logic that it is the way we live our lives that causes environmental collapse, some writers have argued that it is the culture of respect for everyone's views that underpins liberal democracies that has led to the environmental crises of today. From this perspective, environmental destruction is the logical outcome of the liberalism of freedom of speech and freedom of action (Shearman & Smith, 2007). Respect for everyone's views is now a luxury. Because of the urgency of the situation, we need a new type of deep ecology solution, based on **environmental authoritarianism**. We need strong governments that will punish, in no uncertain terms, those who are involved in acts that wreak havoc on the environment. This viewpoint, proposing an environmental authoritarianism, of course runs counter to the principles of community development.

Green perspectives and community development

Incompatibilities

As with the discussion above concerning new social movements in general, we can find significant similarities and differences between the green movement and community development. We consider the significant influence of green perspectives on community development in the following section. But before we do this, we note four aspects of green approaches that are at variance with community development. First, the perspectives that prioritise 'nature' over humans are problematic in several ways. They challenge the community development focus on human societies. They undermine the responsibility of human agents. And they are premised on a clear distinction between a discrete phenomenon that is called 'nature' and the discrete phenomena of human beings – they are based on a dichotomy between humans and nature. Yet humans, being biological organisms, are part of nature. Humans live in settings that are continually changing, both through human intervention and through the natural cycles of seasons and weather, life and death, any of which can be environmentally destructive. Humans interact with these settings and other biological organisms and affect these organisms in the same ways that these organisms affect humans. What this viewpoint does offer community development is the reminder of the dangers of the naive anthropomorphism that continues to dominate how many people live their lives.

Second, many ecological perspectives tend to be top-down, insofar as knowledge and direction come from 'experts'. For example, it is the 'activist' or 'expert' who articulates the issues, makes decisions, takes control, initiates action and even speaks for communities. Such a viewpoint is at odds with the bottom-up approach of community development. Third, many environmentalists focus more on working with large corporations to deal with environmental issues, under the banner of corporate social responsibility, and avoid working with local communities altogether (Buckman, 2004). The irony in such an approach is not lost on many community development practitioners, who see such partnerships as little more than a public relations exercise, because large corporations are often the biggest emitters of greenhouse gases, through their promotion of continued reliance on oil, for example. The question of how and when to work with large corporations is a complex one for community development practitioners, and is taken up in chapter 10. Finally, environmentalists are largely silent when it comes to the issue about which groups of people carry the burden of environmental destruction. It is people who are disadvantaged and marginalised who bear the brunt of environmental damage.

Compatibilities

Notwithstanding the tensions described above, community development has been profoundly influenced by green perspectives, particularly over the past two decades. There are four key trajectories in community development that provide alternative, and somewhat contradictory, approaches to ecological issues. The first trajectory is organised around the theoretical position known as the **environmental justice/distributive justice framework**. The second is the **fair trade approach**. The third is organised around **participatory justice** and the final approach we discuss is **relocalisation**.

The environmental justice viewpoint is that in focusing on the physical effects of damage being done to the physical environment, some environmentalists ignore the unequal distribution of these effects and the unequal culpability for environmental destruction. Underlying the environmental justice perspective is the idea that the distribution of benefit and harm in regard to the natural environment should be governed by principles of social justice. This perspective holds that every individual, regardless of gender, ethnicity, race or class, has the right to be free of ecological harm and deserves equal protection (Jamieson, 2007). Supporters of the environmental justice movement point out that environmentalism can in fact increase global injustice. For example, by preventing poorer countries from developing, it increases the inequality between rich and poor nations. To redress this inequality, the allocation of allowances for greenhouse gas emissions could be organised within the framework of *distributive justice*, which would include a calculus of forgone development opportunities, and economic and social restructuring costs (Jamieson, 2007). We also need to take seriously the weightings of global footprints from the perspective of producers, and not just consumers. Of course, strategies must be developed that protect the natural environment, but at the same time they should ensure that the distribution of environmental harm and responsibility for redressing environmental degradation do not fall unfairly on poor nations and poor people. Of course, from a community development perspective also, poorer countries and poorer communities need to be protected against the unequal distribution of environmental destruction.

One example of the distributive justice perspective is that of those anti-globalisation protesters who argue that rich countries owe poor countries an 'ecological debt'. Ecological debt has been accruing over many centuries, as rich countries have plundered the resources of poorer countries, including their minerals, agricultural products and labour power (Buckman, 2004: 92–3). Ecological debt also accumulates as polluting industries owned by Western-based corporations are established in developing countries. Similarly, the NIMBY (not-in-my-backyard) policies of middle-class areas in developed countries means that they, too, owe an ecological debt to those living in less powerful and poorer working-class areas.

While the ecological debt approach is linked with those organising *against* existing economic globalisation, there is another approach that also begins with the view that the developed countries have exploited poorer nations, but argues that economic globalisation can be redeemed in a way that supports distributive justice. This approach has come to be known as the 'fair trade school' (Buckman, 2004). It holds that if world trade was conducted on the basis of distributive justice, and if the export subsidies for rich countries were abolished, then poor nations and poor people would be lifted out of poverty. Interestingly, the fair trade movement does work with large corporations to ensure access of exports from the developing world to the developed world. In order to defend themselves from subsidised 'dumping' of overseas products, poorer countries should be able to protect their own products, which satisfy local needs and assist the cause of self-sufficiency. More shall be said about the arguments for domestic self-sufficiency below.

The environmental justice and the fair trade approaches, based as they are on the principle of distributive justice, are in many ways appropriate from a community development perspective. However, from a community development perspective, there is a weakness in the ways the environmental justice and the fair trade approaches are implemented, because they still tend to be top-down. That is, decisions about what constitutes justice and fair trade and how policies are applied are made by experts, and do not allow for input from ordinary community members. More consistent with community development is an approach that brings *participatory justice* alongside environmental justice (see Jamieson, 2007; Young, 1983). Participatory justice requires empowering community members in poorer communities to participate in decisions that have environmental impacts. From a community development perspective, the processes for environmental justice must always be based on the principle of participatory justice.

Taking environmental and participatory justice standpoints not only requires understanding the effects of environmental policies on disadvantaged and marginalised communities, both nationally and internationally, but also ensuring that local communities have information about the environmental effects of decisions, and can also participate meaningfully in policy development. Overall, the environmental and participatory justice approaches offer a strategy that is compatible with community development, although they do not, by themselves, reconcile competing needs for community empowerment and environmental sustainability.

The relocalisation approach

Perhaps one approach that promises to reconcile the competing needs for community empowerment, environmental justice, participatory justice, environmental sustainability and socialist- and feminist-influenced green perspectives is found in the relocalisation movement. At the centre of this movement is the view that the resolution to environmental destruction lies in the rejection of economic globalisation. We need to relocalise and radically restrict our global ecological footprint by developing local economies and local solutions. The keyword of localisation is self-reliance. That is, local economies, based around the principle of self-reliance, should be at the centre of productive activity. The relocalisation approach, of course, draws on the community development perspective, which takes the view that the identification of and responses to local problems must be controlled locally (Kenny, 2008; Ife, 2002). From this perspective, control of economic activity should be in the hands of local communities in whose interests it is to nurture their own natural environment and live sustainably. Living sustainably can mean giving equal weighting to both the environmental priorities and the needs of local communities, or it can mean prioritising environmental needs over community wants or short-term needs. From a relocalisation perspective, the local economy should be reconstructed around forms of local production that are sustainable and minimise harm to the environment. Dumping of products should be refused and local production nurtured and protected. The 'slow food' movement is a good example of relocalisation. As Burkett (2008) points out, there has been growing interest in this movement, which celebrates the virtues of local food systems, including local farming, local production, local markets and slow on-site cooking, all of which are counterposed to the fast-food industry.

The relocalisation approach is bolstered by two important critiques of the growth–development agenda. First, it draws on the left critiques of global capitalism, in particular the view that it is the power of global corporations that drives environmental destruction (see Sarkar, 1999). The quest for profit has driven the intense capitalist development since the Second World War, in which nature is seen to be no more than a resource to be exploited to increase the wealth of the few. From this perspective, community development practitioners' struggles at the local level should be part of the wider battles against rampant capitalism (see von Kaufmann, 2002). Second, some supporters of relocalisation now argue that Western science and modernity are the key problems (see Mander & Goldsmith, 1996). We need to validate an education that challenges mainstream knowledge, particularly knowledge based around economic 'science'. For some commentators this means authenticating Indigenous people's knowledge and their relation with their natural resources (Johnson & Murton, 2007; Powell, 2006).

The main weakness of the relocalisation approach lies in its rejection of global engagement. If global capitalism in the form of huge and powerful corporations, with their quest for growth and consumption, is the main contributor to environmental destruction, then withdrawing into a local community with a self-reliance agenda can do little to stem global environmental decline. It might be a start, and if a large enough number of citizens joined the relocalisation movement it could have important effects, but on its own it is not enough to challenge the might of global corporations and restrain the environmental destruction perpetrated by the industrial military states.

To conclude this discussion of green perspectives and community development we can identify some of the small ways that community development practitioners can incorporate green attitudes and orientations in their everyday activities.

Community development practitioners can include green perspectives in their practice by:

- understanding that questions about how we organise our lives include the question of how are we to sustain our physical environment
- facilitating communities to make informed choices about how they will respond to environmental issues; for example, sharing information about how humans are destroying their environment, and explaining the different perspectives on why this is happening and the ways communities might respond to environmental issues
- working with local communities in activist campaigns about environmental issues
- ensuring that in their everyday activities people take a holistic approach to practice, one that requires paying attention to such matters as recycling, sharing of resources and sensitivity to the use of energy, while at the same time thinking and acting globally by engaging with and sharing ideas in the international arena
- being sensitive to the tensions between the community development quest for improved living standards for humans and the limits to growth in a world of finite resources.

Language and discourse

During much of the twentieth century there was considerable theoretical debate in the social sciences around what was known as the structure–agency debate. This debate focused on the question of whether it was the structures that set up what we do and how we do it – indeed, our life chances – or whether it is what we actually do that shapes social structures, our role in society and our life chances.

Yet by the 1980s a quite different view of what we see as social reality was gaining ground. This view acknowledged that we cannot understand reality without the intervention of language. While this emphasis was not entirely new, it radically shifted some of the trajectories of conventional social theory, particularly through the work of French theorists Derrida (1978) and Foucault (1980, 1969). Of these two theorists, it is the work and influence of Foucault that is the most important for community development. As Elliott (2009:71) comments, by using texts, discourses and doctrines used in the production of knowledge, Foucault attacked taken-for-granted concepts, ideas and structures that have served to legitimise Western knowledge and philosophy. Foucault produced 'powerful insights into the systems of power that people make to entrap themselves' and particularly the power of discourses (Elliott, 2009:71). For example, Foucault investigated how ways of thinking about and talking about a phenomenon such as madness, and the practices for dealing with madness, are used to disempower those labelled as 'mad'. At various times in history 'madness' has been seen differently and associated with different discourses. These discourses have drawn on different manifestations of reason and patterns of domination (Foucault, 1979). Arguing that there is no totality and no truth – only truths – Foucault developed a radical methodological approach, identifying the social sciences themselves as forces of domination. The following case study provides a brief glimpse of how one person applies a Foucauldian analysis.

THE LANGUAGE AND PRACTICE OF DOMINATION

The scene is a meeting room in the local council chambers of an outer suburb of a capital city. The meeting has been called to discuss a council proposal to establish a volunteer program. There is a heated discussion between steering committee members about whether to employ a coordinator who has undertaken a formal community development course or not.

Rob, a local businessman, has two major concerns about the proposal: first, the whole idea of 'volunteering' reinforces existing forms of domination; and second, if the program goes ahead, then who should run it? A member of the steering committee, Costa, argues that a person trained in community development should be appointed to the position of coordinator. Rob disagrees, arguing that formal training, even in community development, is just another form of domination as it trains people to use a particular language. Terms such as empowerment, social inclusion and community strengthening are used in a way that glosses over the real underlying inequalities; meanwhile, community development practices actually patronise and disempower people who lack the language, tools and knowledge that trained community development workers have.

While Rob himself has an Arts degree, he would prefer to recruit someone from the business world who has common sense and doesn't have a degree. Rob had studied the work of Foucault at university, and argues that by applying a Foucauldian analysis it is possible to understand how the social sciences are forces of domination in themselves. Moreover, he argues, when the whole idea of volunteering is considered, it can be seen that it is yet another way of getting the population to support society – and do it for no pay. It is no more than another (subtle) way of self-governing and self-regulating society.

In contrast to the narrow Enlightenment view (more on this below) of the positive value of the social sciences, Foucault argues that these sciences have come to dominate rather than liberate us and he is interested in revealing the mechanisms of this domination. Foucault's approach to history is a radical break with conventional ideas of history. History involves events that are singular, discontinuous and unsynchronised, rather than a linear succession of grand events. His studies emphasise the contingency and ultimate fragility of all historical forms, often focusing on previously neglected or discredited phenomena, such as the uses and meaning of the body and punishment.

From the perspective of a community development practitioner we can draw out four challenging insights from Foucault's work. First, we need to critically interrogate the discourses and assumptions embedded in Western knowledge, and be sensitive to how these assumptions can themselves be the bases of domination. For example, the contemporary discourse of 'disability' has profound implications for how people labelled as 'disabled' are treated in general. Second, Foucault's approach can remind us that insofar as community development constitutes itself as a specific form of knowledge, or a discipline, it can become a form of domination by setting up boundaries and closing off challenge and change. Third, Foucault's message that change is contingent and unsynchronised reminds us of the folly of understanding the history of a community as a simple linear one with discrete events, and of straightjacketing the community development activities of planning, evaluating and social action as if processes and tasks were simple technical procedures. Finally, Foucault's ideas on governance, and particularly self-governance, are especially important for community development. Without us realising it, we live in societies with ever-increasing forms of subtle control. For example, the ever-growing virtual methods of control or surveillance, through security cameras, for example, mean that are constantly controlling and constraining our own behaviour. Through self-regulation we become complicit with the oppressive structures of society, making the effort to become involved in social action and social protest ever more difficult. These insights are taken up in various parts of this book.

Modernism and postmodernism
The project of modernity

Most of the principles of community development identified in chapter 1 – commitment to ordinary people, liberation and empowerment, human rights – are the principles of humanism and part of the **project of modernity**. They are based on a belief in the power of humans to control their own destiny, which was proposed by the Enlightenment thinkers over two centuries ago. While there is debate about the exact meaning and period of the concept of **modernity**, there is some agreement that the project of modernity developed in Europe during the eighteenth century in the period known as the **Enlightenment**.

In the Enlightenment view of the world, humans can work creatively, freely and intelligently to construct a universal morality and humanity that is committed to human fulfilment. Indeed, the accumulation of human knowledge could lead to the enrichment of life.

Modernity is characterised by particular types of activity, or what German sociologist Max Weber identified as social action. Weber (1946) identified four types of social action:

1. **Traditional action**, which is based on customs and habits.
2. **Affective action**, based on emotions.
3. **Wertrational action**, based on values; that is, it is oriented to some ultimate value or end, such as a religious end.
4. **Zweckrational action**, which is goal-oriented; it is the most rational of these types of action because it is based on a calculation of the most efficient means to an end.

Weber pointed out that Western societies have become increasingly based on *zweckrational* action. Indeed, the preoccupation with goal-oriented rational action now influences all aspects of our lives. It is evidenced in our concern for strategic planning and efficiency; in the increasing interdependence of science, technology and industry; and in the role of the state bureaucracies in controlling our activities through a myriad of rules and regulations.

Instrumental rationality and technocratic consciousness

This preoccupation with goal-oriented rational action has been a central concern of theorists connected with critical theory, and in particular it has been pivotal to the work of Habermas (1971). Habermas pointed out that the ascendancy of thinking that is goal-oriented and rational has undercut our understanding of the political and moral bases of decision making. He uses the term **instrumental rationality** to describe how modernity is concerned to utilise the most efficient and instrumentally useful (rational) means to achieve an objective. We construct decisions as if they are scientific technical matters that are value-free and out of the scope of ordinary people.

Habermas (1971) constructed the term **technocratic consciousness** to refer to the way ideological control is maintained through technological justifications of the social order and political decisions are dressed up as technical decisions. Because of the tendency to define problems as technical we begin to think of solutions to problems only in technical terms. For example, a government budget is presented as an impersonal technical document free from the political considerations that might affect the electoral standing of the government. The annual federal budget in Australia is couched in terms that convey the idea that decisions about where federal funds are distributed are not political.

We live in a world in which technocratic consciousness undermines our capacity to take a critical view of our own culture. In this world, ordinary people have themselves become categories and statistics – such as users, consumers or the disabled – to be targeted and prioritised. Instrumentalism has reached the point at which efficiency and productivity become ends in themselves, replacing goals of human fulfilment and liberation. In this view of modernity, the Enlightenment vision of humanity is completely undermined. A society based on technocratic consciousness actually becomes depoliticised.

Postmodernism

The critique of modernity discussed above not only found expression in academic circles, but also in a range of discontents about the failed promise of an enlightened world in which there would be no wars, no acts of barbarity, and in which science and reason would resolve human and environmental problems. As Harvey points out, these concerns led to an all-out assault on the Enlightenment legacy, which by the 1970s had

> spilled over into a vigorous denunciation of abstract reason and a deep aversion to any project that sought universal human emancipation through mobilisation of the powers of technology, science, and reason (1989:41).

This denunciation ushered in a very different way of thinking about the world and looking at society, a way that has come to be called **postmodernism**. Like the other approaches considered above, postmodernism has many viewpoints and themes within it. But unlike these theoretical approaches, postmodernism has no coherent framework, for totalising theoretical schemata are contradictory to the whole idea of postmodernism. The world is conceptualised from the viewpoints of fragmentation, discontinuity, plurality and even chaos. It is perhaps most appropriate to think about postmodernism as a device that is useful for describing (selected) experiences of the world rather than providing a definitive approach or explanation, for it rejects the very causal premises upon which social science has been constructed. Postmodernism provides no clear answers and no truths. It subverts all self-righteous claims to knowledge, and exposes and pulls apart (deconstructs) the bits of our existing knowledge. Thus for postmodernists, the overall theoretical frameworks, or grand narratives, are at best misplaced and, at worst, they become tyrannies of their own.

There is debate about whether postmodernism constitutes a complete break with modernism or is an extension or deepening of many of its theories. Whatever position one takes in this debate, from the perspective of postmodernist critique, the modernist project has been a dismal failure. Some say that modernity was predicated on a misguided belief in the possibility of universal truth, the domination of nature and the expectation of moral progress, and so was doomed from the very beginning. Others argue that modernity has been subverted by a range of deviations, such as the spell of instrumental rationality, but it remains a continuing and unfinished quest. From this viewpoint, postmodernism may be characterised as a response to the deviations and crises of contemporary economics, culture and science.

Some writers see postmodernism as symbolic of the demise of European power. Smart (1990), for example, has located the ascendancy of postmodernism in concern about a post-European and post-Western era when 'other voices' are the voices of black people and developing countries.

Community development, modernity and postmodernity

Community development workers have certainly been critical of the expressions of instrumental reason as they are manifested in program budgeting, service agreements, auditing and performance indicators, for example. They understand that decisions made on political grounds are often dressed up as technical decisions and that so-called consultation is often just window-dressing. Many of them have discovered how easy it is to be co-opted by bureaucracies, so that they actually become part of the forces of domination themselves. Thus, community development can be very critical of the instrumentalist elements of modernity. There are clear reasons for embracing the debunking elements of postmodernity. Yet postmodernism has strong critics as well as strong supporters. In the following section we consider some of the key evaluations that are important for community development.

In a positive appraisal, postmodern approaches:

- provide new ways of thinking about and responding to the precarious state of humans and the earth, insofar as they face up to the disjointed, indeterminate nature of society and offer a realistic assessment of the possibilities for human development
- respond to the diversity and heterogeneity that are increasingly part of our cultural and social experiences, including, for example, the idea that Australia is a multicultural society

- offer a counter-practice to traditionally based official culture
- challenge the pretensions of the traditionalist elite culture and the assumptions of truth upon which it is based (see Lyotard, 1984)
- can make sense in a diverse, rapidly changing and uncertain world
- overall, have a radical appeal, as explained by Harvey (1989:353):

> The odd thing is how radical some of these diverse [postmodernist] responses appeared … On reflection, the oddity disappears easily enough. A mode of thought that is anti-authoritarian and iconoclastic, that insists on the authenticity of other voices, that celebrates difference, decentralisation, and democratisation of taste, as well as the power of imagination over materiality, has to have a radical cutting edge.

In a negative appraisal, postmodern approaches:

- are one-sided in their reading of modernity; for example, as well as oppressing people, new technologies can also give them power (over knowledge and over decision making, for example) in completely new ways
- place too much emphasis on discontinuity and fragmentation – our lives work on the basis of continuity and not everything is fragmentary
- create a defeatist and individualistic world, in which individuals abrogate their responsibility to collective processes and wellbeing, lest they should be seen as subscribing to metanarratives
- are based on hesitation, uncertainty and even political nihilism, which erodes the determination of political activists, when those who have power in society rarely experience hesitation or uncertainty
- lead people to people abandoning political principles, goals and strategies for a better society and this leaves a political vacuum, which can be filled by those seeking power.

However, as noted above, the principles of community development are also located in the project of modernity; that is, community development simultaneously embraces principles that are drawn from both the project of modernity and the postmodern critique of modernity. In this section we explore this apparent paradox.

One way of sorting out the modernist precepts in community development is to differentiate between two idioms of modernity: the instrumentalist idiom and the humanist idiom. Humanist modernity emphasises the themes of demystification and emancipation and instrumentalist modernity emphasises rationality and efficiency outcomes. The latter, manifested in economic rationalism, seeks to increase efficiency and productivity in the workplace. Community development is most strongly committed to the idiom of humanist modernity. Community development assumes that people have both the capacity and the will to control their own destinies. They are able to do this through a mixture of vision, reason and skills, through using science and through developing new ways of thinking about human relations and political forms. An expression of this is the practice of prefigurative politics.

Community development also operates with the instrumentalist idiom of modernity. Instrumental modernism is apparent in the identification of community development as an industry and a profession, and in the extension of instrumental rationality and technocratic consciousness. Instrumentalism is evidenced in the emphasis on training, competency skills, managerialism, goal clarification, strategy development, service agreements, performance indicators and evaluation.

Community development workers might also draw on the ideas of Habermas (1983), who takes the position that the project of modernity is incomplete. Habermas accepts that there have been diversions to this project that, during the twentieth century, shattered the optimism once felt about its promise. He rejects several aspects of modernism: the oversimplified commitment to a unitary metanarrative; the breaking up of science, morality and art into autonomous spheres separated from the life-world and administered by experts; and what he identifies as the deformed realisation of reason in history. However, he retains a commitment to the qualities of human communication that allow reciprocal understanding and the universalising of reason. He characterises postmodernism as reactionary opposition to the emancipatory project.

Community development is also incompatible with many postmodernist views. For example, postmodernism pushes us towards cynical, relativist and even nihilist views of the world and thus loses any commitment to, and any practical program for, improving the human condition. Rather than accepting postmodernist relativism, community development theory and practice invoke principles for adjudicating between competing views of how society does or should work. Moreover, community development does engage in global projects and argues for linking struggles with the common purpose of developing a program for a better and sustainable life on earth. In broad terms, then, community development accords with the modernist project and, in fact, a theme of this book is that it is part of the modernist project. Like the project of modernity itself, it is full of contradictions and dilemmas. And, like the project of modernity, it is still unfinished.

However, it is also important for community development workers to understand the importance of the correctives to modernity provided by postmodernist critiques. Postmodernism offers a radical critique of the authoritarian and elitist tendencies in mainstream social theory. It rejects the notions of ultimate truth and value-free objectivity. It accepts the integrity and authenticity of ordinary people, the oppressed and those who are disadvantaged in society. Community development workers also reject authoritarian and elitist constructs and practices. They reject the idea of the all-knowing intellectual or expert practitioner. They also acknowledge that societies are continually changing. For them, there are multiple sites of power and sources of oppression, and struggles occur on all levels. They emphasise responding to domination and control in the multiplicity of ways they occur in their everyday work and they encourage a plurality of viewpoints and practices. In all these ways, there is a meshing of the principles of community development and the themes of postmodernism.

New themes, concepts and theories

At the beginning of this chapter we emphasised that theoretical frameworks, theories and concepts are not static. They change, they can fall into disuse and they can be renovated and renewed. For example, at the beginning of the twenty-first century, while Marxist theory forms the backdrop of the continuing left critique of inequality and global capitalism, much of the Marxist language has slipped from use. Similarly, reference to specific feminist theories has slipped into the background of discussion of inequality between men and women. Indeed, there is much less interest today in mapping society from one consistent theoretical perspective. People endeavouring to analyse society as a whole, or concerned to make sense of a particular situation, are more likely to select a range of concepts, theories and ideas, often drawing these from different traditions, rather than locating their approach, concepts and explanations within one theoretical tradition alone.

There are several related explanations for the way that theories and concepts are now used in a much less holistic fashion than they were 20 to 30 years ago. First, as society and our material environment change, our knowledge and information base expand, and our views of what constitutes the 'truth' or the 'facts' begin to change as well. Because our experiences are mediated by our ideas, concepts and theories, our understanding of reality changes. We now have unparalleled growth of information, made possible through the use of information technologies such as the Internet. And as we noted at the beginning of this chapter, the usefulness of theories and concepts is challenged when they no longer help to make sense of a changed reality and when they look out of place beside theoretical frameworks and concepts.

Yet some theories retain their utility. As Ritzer (2000:xix) points out, as time goes by, some social and political theories lose their appeal and currency; some theories stay put, reminding us of the usefulness of their core concepts; and others are new developments that become 'hot' with immediate explanatory purchase. From the perspective of community development practitioners, understanding new and 'hot' ideas can equip them to engage – critically or positively – with proponents of these ideas in public forums and with journalists, politicians and policy makers, for example. In the following discussion we explore some of these new and renewed ideas. What is particularly interesting about the new concepts that are relevant for community development is that they are usually drawn from modernist frameworks rather than postmodernist ones. We begin with the theme of risk society.

Risk society

The theory that risk is an important aspect of recent societies was most clearly developed through the work of the German sociologist Ulrich Beck. Beck set out the idea of risk society in the 1980s in the seminal book *Risk Society: Towards a New Modernity*. The core thesis of **risk society** is that more and more aspects of our lives are framed by an awareness of the dangers confronting humankind at the individual, local and global level, and that humans need to develop strategies to confront these dangers.

As Giddens (1998b:64) points out, risk refers to dangers that we seek actively to identify, confront and control. Humans have always faced hazards and dangers, but our understanding of the ways we respond to these is new. Risk society can only take hold in situations where people are future-oriented, where the future is conceptualised as a territory to be conquered (Giddens, 1998a) and where there is a commitment to the efficacy of human agency to influence or control the future. Indeed, the idea of risk offered a major new frame of reference by which to understand contemporary society, and by the beginning of the twenty-first century, ideas of a risk-based society had begun to gain support among both academics and policy makers.

It is because we live in a society based on knowledge, information and ever-developing new technologies that we can envisage what Beck calls the 'threatening sphere of possibilities' (1999:141), for Beck believed that

> risks are the whip to keep the present day moving along at a gallop. The more threatening the shadows that fall on the present day from a terrible future looming in the distance, the more compelling the shock that can be provoked by dramatizing risk today ... Established risk definitions are thus a magic wand with which a stagnant society can terrify itself ... (1999:137–8).

Of course, humans have always faced hazards and dangers, and all societies have developed ways of identifying and responding to risk, but our contemporary understandings of risk, and the ways that risk assessments permeate both the choices we make in our everyday lives and public policy, are new.

Giddens (1994) points to the paradox that as humans have sought greater and greater certainty through the advance of human knowledge and intervention into society and nature, in many ways they have actually deepened the unpredictability of things. He identifies this human-made or human-exacerbated risk as manufactured uncertainty (Giddens, 1994:4). Increasingly, the role of politicians and elites is one of risk management. But, so too, community development can be identified as a form of risk management. Community development involves practices that ensure that communities take responsibility for their own welfare and thus shifts responsibility and risk from the state or the corporate world to the grassroots.

The perception of risk can evince different kinds of interpretations, some of which see risk as harmful to society (threatening security and wellbeing), while others are identified as creative or beneficial to the development of society (unleashing entrepreneurial activity). The interpretation of risk as creative is demonstrated in the idea that the business and social world, in particular, must be freed up from government intervention to allow for the unleashing of entrepreneurial and innovative capacity. As an effective 'risk responder', community development can involve identifying and implementing creative and strategic responses to risk. The other side of deregulation, of course, is re-regulation, which becomes necessary as the risks resulting from deregulation accumulate and explode. Much of contemporary social and fiscal policy, and thus the context of community development, is shaped through radar designed to pick up and respond to risk, hazard and danger. Increasingly, community development practitioners are required to put risk management strategies into place, and to succumb to a whole new range of bureaucratic checks, including performance reviews, monitoring and evaluation, and audits, which are presented in the name of probity and accountability – to bureaucrats and funding bodies, not the community.

Since 11 September 2001, the view that contemporary society is full of risks has deepened. The view of the world based on the construction of 'them and us' has been reactivated and strengthened. It is being nourished by a fear of attacks by crusading terrorists or crusading nation states (or coalitions of nation states). As with other forms of risk, the threat of the risk of terrorism, foreign intervention or invasion is sufficient to increase the anxiety levels of whole countries.

One of the most ominous effects of the construction of our existence within the framework of risk is the increasingly sophisticated way that surveillance mechanisms have developed. Surveillance today is mostly practised by governments as part of maintaining order or 'national security', but it is also practised by those wishing to threaten or intimidate citizens for other political purposes. Lyon (2001) discusses how daily life today is closely monitored by governments and private businesses. Soon, the personal data that is collected through security cameras and computer databases of medical and financial activity will be supplemented by databases of citizens' fingerprints, retinal scans and DNA.

While power elites have always used the idea of threats – to sovereignty, internal security or religious purity – as the basis for surveillance and oppression, new technologies offer the means of effective monitoring, categorising, intimidating and punishing, where deemed appropriate, in ways previously unknown. We are just beginning to understand the meaning of the concepts of risk and surveillance as they affect our lives today. There is a multitude of issues to consider that will, in the coming years, impact upon the theory and practice of community development. We can already identify a number of ways that the construction of risk society impacts on community development work, through being alerted to risk or through regulations ostensibly put in place as risk management strategies. Some of these impacts are listed in table 3.1.

Table 3.1 *How the theme of risk affects communities and community development*

Children at risk
Neighbourhood houses offering childcare facilities are required to have extensive protocols in place (including police checks of staff) to protect children against physical, emotional and social harm, and also to protect the neighbourhood houses in any situation of litigation by parents or guardians.
Reporting suspicious behaviour
Communities are encouraged to report any suspicious behaviour or packages to police in the campaign against terrorism in Australia.
Risk assessment and risk management strategies
Community organisations are increasingly required to prepare risk assessment and management strategies as part of their planning.
Redefining problems as 'community problems'
Social problems are being defined as community problems, thus shifting the responsibility for problems away from governments to the community; that is, the solution is seen to lie within communities not governments.
Developing databases
Ostensibly in the name of 'accountability and transparency', community organisations are required to develop databases on their programs and participants. These databases allow officials and funding agencies to audit and check on their activities in order to prevent fraud and corruption.

Difference and identity

One of the themes of this book is the importance of understanding that community development takes place in a world that has many cultures, many ideas and many ways of doing things. But within this diversity there are also some principles that are part of our common humanity, including a commitment to human rights and the empowerment of marginalised people. Understanding the types of difference is important for community development practitioners and is taken up in chapter 8. Here, we note how ideas of difference shift. Indeed one of the significant developments in our thinking about diversity and identity has been the realisation that identities are fluid, fragmented and not territorially based (Hancock & Garner, 2009). While we have always had different identities, these have tended to be constrained by social position, gender, age, ethnicity, place and space. Today all these categories are much more fluid. Even the ideas of what it means to be a 'man' or a 'woman' can change. Because we can conduct social relationships across the world, we can identify with many more people instantaneously, in a virtual space (through the Internet, Facebook and Twitter, for example). The 'destabilisation' of identity is extremely important for community development. It undermines the argument that we do or can live in self-contained, homogeneous and territorial-based communities throughout our lives.

Social capital, active citizenship and civil society

Several other key conceptual developments that have led to a renewal of interest in strengthening active engagement in society are significant for community development. These are the concepts of social capital and **active citizenship**, which we have already mentioned, and the concept of **civil society**. We begin this section with a discussion of the concept of social capital. As indicated in previous chapters, the term 'social capital' has gained popular attention through the work of Putnam (2002, 2000, 1993) in his studies of the ways that social bonds and communal activity influence the quality of personal and civic life and economic development. Since the mid 1990s in Australia, we have witnessed a steady growth in discussion and debate about the meanings and importance of social capital (see, for example, Winter, 2000; Cox, 1995). The idea of social capital begins from an interest in people's ability to associate with each other. It refers to features of social organisation – such as trust, reciprocity, norms and networks – that facilitate coordination and cooperation for mutual benefit and increase a society's productive potential (Putnam, 1993). As Winter (2000:xviii) points out, a common feature of the understandings of social capital is 'the vital role that the quality of our social relationships and engagement in civic affairs plays in creating a good society'.

Social capital is a resource that can be developed through particular types of social relationships. It can be drawn on, increased or depleted (Jochum, 2003). It is also reflexive in that it both causes or strengthens networks of trust and mutuality and is the effect of networks of trust and mutuality. A group, community or society is deemed to have high levels of social capital when it has strong networks of social relations between its members, when members trust each other and engage with each other, and cooperate through reciprocal sharing of tasks and responsibilities, for example. The most common ways of measuring social capital focus on levels of trust (general and specific) and civic participation (Yates & Jochum, 2003). In their study of the levels of social capital in five Australian communities, Onyx and Bullen (2000) use these indicators of social capital and two others: proactivity in a social context and tolerance of diversity. Their study reveals the importance of social capital for economic, social and political wellbeing; how methods of social capital generation can vary across communities; and the importance of trust in developing connections and encouraging participation.

In his study of the different regions of Italy, Putnam (1993) discovered those regions that were most effective in their form of government and more advanced economically were also the most civic-minded regions, in the sense that the habits of cooperation and an appreciation of shared responsibility for collective endeavours dominated social relations. Civic engagement in these regions was also facilitated by strong horizontal social networks. The least civic-minded regions were dominated by vertical networks and authoritarian social relations that were constructed around dependent, personalistic patron–client networks. Putnam argued that social capital, embodied in norms and networks of civic engagement, is a precondition for economic development and effective government. That is, it is social capital that lubricates both democracy and commerce and not the reverse (Putnam, 1993:176). Moreover, social capital is self-reinforcing and cumulative and is enhanced by use.

The dominant view of social capital accumulation has been that it works for the good of society. However, some forms of social capital can be located in very introspective communities in which a 'them and us' view of the world prevails. Where this form of social capital exists, it can lead to exclusionary practices. For example, the exclusionary and racist views of neo-Nazis and the Ku Klux Klan in the USA are nourished through strong social capital. High levels of exclusionary social capital within a community can lead to xenophobia and fear of both external and internal threats. When the solidarity of the 'in-group' appears to be or is threatened, one response is to establish an authoritarian structure through which tight control over members is maintained (see Jochum, 2003). As Putnam (2000) points out, social capital can be directed towards malevolent, antisocial purposes as well as the common good.

To make sense of the different contexts and outcomes of social capital, Putnam and others have identified two different types of social capital. First is 'bonding social capital', which is inward-looking and tends to reinforce exclusive identities and homogeneous groups (Putnam, 2002:11). It can have either harmful or good effects. For example, as well as sectarian groups, ethnically based women's groups tend to have high levels of bonding social capital that help them to retain their identity and support each other. In contrast to bonding social capital, 'bridging social capital' occurs when networks develop between groups; when social relations are established between people of different backgrounds such as ethnicity, age and country. These contacts and ties connect people to different social circles and different sources of information and knowledge. Bridging social capital can generate broader identities and forms of reciprocity than bonding social capital (Putnam, 2002:11). While both forms of social capital tend to refer to bonds that are horizontal in nature, there is another form. Woolcock (2001) has identified what he calls 'linking social capital'. Linking social capital refers to networks and bonds between people who have different access to resources and power. For example, it occurs when relatively powerless people link up with people who have leverage over resources, ideas and information. Such a relationship can weaken reciprocity between groups. However, the key is to find some way that reciprocity can be developed, as in the case of Indigenous communities who can offer non-Indigenous communities new and challenging cultural experiences in exchange for 'non-Indigenous resources' such as access to the Internet.

There is growing interest in the argument that community organisations provide the sites, par excellence, for the civic engagement required for the development of social capital. This argument rests on certain interpretations of the characteristics of community organisations. For example, community organisations exude the essence of civic engagement. The engine of community organisations is citizenship participation, which inculcates skills in cooperation and a sense of shared responsibility for collective endeavours. The voluntary and generally egalitarian structures of community organisations facilitate the trust, reciprocity and open communication that are necessary for a sense of shared responsibility and a willingness to find innovative and collective resolutions to social and political problems.

The whole idea of social capital is a useful theme for developing our thinking on the forms of social relationship and communities, and the intersections between the activities of community groups and the practices of community development. However, some nagging issues remain in the linking of social capital with community development, which rehearse the earlier socialist arguments against the concept of community. The first issue concerns the argument that the concept of social capital, like the concept of community, glosses over existing inequalities, thus making the achievement of real mutuality and reciprocity across significant inequalities of wealth and power very difficult, if not impossible. For example, communities that already have more wealth, power and social capital will be able to develop their stocks of social capital further than those communities with low stocks of wealth, power and social capital. There is no level playing field when it comes to the spread of social capital across communities. Some communities have more social capital to start with than others. Indeed, the different starting points for social capital accumulation, like cultural and economic capital accumulation, contribute to the reproduction of general inequalities (see Bourdieu, 1985). Second, in some versions of social capital, communities with strong social capital are characterised by a homogeneity engendered by norms of mutuality and trust. But what this picture of a homogeneous community tends to leave out is the importance of diversity and the role of tension and conflict in challenging the status quo and shifting thinking. In fact, conflict is ubiquitous. A fully harmonious community is impossible to achieve. Indeed, in other versions of social capital the idea of tolerance of difference is central (see Onyx & Bullen, 2000).

These issues are significant, but they do not undermine the relevance of social capital as a way of drawing attention to the role of social connections, trust, mutuality, proactivity and tolerance of difference. Differential access to social capital and the resulting inequality are germane in understanding social capital, but this does not negate the importance of understanding social capital as a way of reinserting 'the social' into our understandings of what is precious in human existence. From a community development perspective, social capital can be seen as a resource that communities draw on and use as they work towards self-determination. It is not an end in itself.

The growth of discussion of the role of social capital in social and community development can be understood in the context of the renewal of interest in civil society. We can understand the notion of civil society by reference to the idea of spheres of social activity. There is a fairly long history in social theory that divides social life into three spheres: the sphere of the state, or government; the sphere of the market, or for-profit business; and the sphere of the civil society: for example, non-profit and community organisations. Some people add a fourth sphere, that of the family and close personal relationships. While this differentiation of society into different spheres provides a useful analytical model, it is also important to note that the boundaries between the spheres are porous. For example, under the principle of corporate social responsibility, some businesses, such as the Body Shop, work for civil society causes.

Since the late twentieth century, trust in state and business spheres has declined, particularly in developed countries. Interest has increased in the idea that the sphere of civil society will provide a better mechanism than the state or market-based sectors for steering social change. Civil society also promises to deliver innovative welfare, reinvigorate democracy and ensure that elites are accountable to the populace. We can trace some of the key claims about the merits of civil society to the writings of a French aristocrat, Alexis de Tocqueville, who visited America in the 1830s. His view of the importance of civil society in 'skilling citizens in the democratic arts' remains relevant today. Among some parts of contemporary society is growing interest in civil society as providing the 'best bet' for 'humanising' society on the basis that a vibrant civil society is a foil against the unfettered state or market (Salamon et al., 1999:4–5).

But what is civil society? While there has been much debate over the meaning of the term 'civil society' (Cohen & Arato, 1995:18–23), in its most general sense it can be identified as a sphere in which people come together freely and independently to discuss issues and work collectively to influence and shape their society. It is the site for political assembly and debate in much the same way the agora was in Ancient Greece (Geoghegan & Powell, 2009; Bauman, 1998). As suggested above, civil society is a sphere inhabited by non-government and non-profit organisations, public activities such as public protest and public media such as public broadcasting services.

Within the framework of this interest in civil society has come the idea of the importance of people associating freely and taking responsibility for their own lives. This idea involves the conception of humans as autonomous self-conscious beings. In some ways this is a new understanding of humans and human society. For most of human history the dominating view has been that individuals' lives are determined by an other-world power or by the settings and structures that they are born into, as peasants or kings, for example. The tension between these two ways of thinking – about whether humans create their world or are determined by it – has come to be thought of in terms of agency versus structure. In developed countries in particular, the pendulum has swung towards the agency side of the debate. Humans are being identified as agents who shape and change society – through social movements, for example – and in so doing they are also agents of their own fortunes (Touraine, 1988:1–2). This contextual factor emphasises that people are the agents of their own destiny. They are engaged in active citizenship.

Active citizenship can refer to individuals alone taking responsibility for their wellbeing, as a form of individualised action, or it can mean collective collaborative endeavour (Kenny, 2004). Community development is concerned with this latter understanding of active citizenship. It involves active citizenship in a number of ways. First, communities seek to control their own agendas in the sense that it is they who decide what are their problems and needs and goals, for example. Second, communities will demand resources when necessary. The activism in community development usually involves some reference to the redistribution of wealth to the poor through such mechanisms as higher progressive taxes and death duties, and increases in social and hospital services and income support for the poor. Third, community development practitioners will engage in political protest, when appropriate, to express their concern and give voice to those who have no other outlets and, for strategic reasons, to gain political leverage, for example. Fourth, community development in the very act of mobilising around issues also develops the solidarity and mutuality that underpin active citizenship. Finally, active citizenship requires the development of skills and capacities, involving listening and respecting others, informed discussion and democratic decision making. Community development passes on these skills in the very processes of collective organising, in which the sharing of experiences and knowledge are vital ingredients for success.

Beck (2000) has brought together the two dimensions of life – civil society and active citizenship – to propose what he calls a **multi-active society** in which work is reconceptualised and restructured. The features of this society would be a reduction of hours for full-time workers; availability of work for every woman and man wishing to be employed; the construction of a new category of work, which Beck calls **civil labour**, involving work in civil society and in cultural, family and political activities; and simultaneous involvement in conventional paid labour and civil labour (Beck, 2000:6–7).

Civil labour is not to be confused with volunteerism or 'work for the dole'. It would be socially recognised and rewarded through what Beck calls 'civic money': qualifications, credits for community services and pension entitlements, for example. The values upon which civil labour would be premised are consistent with community development values, for civil labour is voluntary in the sense that people have the option of undertaking civil labour or not, and it is self-organised in the sense that what should be done and how it should be done are in the hands of those who actually do it (Beck, 2000:127). Civil labour is evident in the work of non-government organisations (NGOs) and citizen action groups, as well as festivals and cultural projects. Thus, for Beck:

> Civil labour is also wherever eyes flash and people act, a concrete labour of criticism and protest. It takes up issues that have been neglected, bungled or suppressed by administrators and politicians. In particular, civil labour espouses the civil rights of minorities and the excluded (2000:127–8).

The renewal of interest in the important role of civil society institutions and the focus on active citizenship are important and positive components of the context in which community development workers practise in the twenty-first century. But there are also negative assessments of active citizenship and civil society. Here, we note two. First, encouragement to be an active citizen, for example, can be read as a call to take control of and responsibility for all that happens to you. This involves the privatisation of responsibility: if things go wrong for you through forces beyond your control, it is your responsibility to work out how to respond and take control (see Kemshall, 2002). Second, unlike involvement in paid work, involvement in civil society does not bring home the necessary income to survive. The civil sphere is, at best, secondary.

These sceptical evaluations of active citizenship and civil society are important. However, taken with the growing interest in social capital and prefigurative politics, this emphasis on the civil not-for-profit sphere provides a corrective to the unproven view that all society's welfare depends on the vigour of the for-profit business sector. As Beck (2000), Putnam (2000), Hirst (1994), Bauman (2004) and a host of other writers demonstrate, civil life is just as important to a society's and an individual's wellbeing as is involvement in paid work in the labour market, and in some ways is even more important, because civil labour and involvement do not have the appalling effects of diminishing human dignity and, as Sennett (1998) has put it, the 'corroding character'. We will reflect on some of the choices opened up by these new social and political themes and the implications for community development in the final chapter of this book.

Southern theory

Before we finish this chapter it is important that we acknowledge a way of thinking that not only critiques the dominant theoretical perspectives and concepts within their own Western terms of reference (such as occurs within the modernity–postmodernity debates), but also challenges the very foundations of Western thought. It does so in a way that is much more radical than the approaches understood as postmodern. This strand of theoretical thinking attacks the privileging of certain conventions in theoretical discussion. Connell (2007) identifies this challenging theory as **southern theory**, drawing on the categorisation of societies into developed societies of the 'north' and underdeveloped societies of the 'south'. She argues that we must accept that there are many forms of knowledge (Connell, 2007:viii). In our interconnected world of transnational relations, transnational employment, transnational cultures and transnational identities, we need to understand that Western knowledge does not exhaust all that humans need to know. Other theories of reality, ways of knowing and uses of information are now accessible to increasing numbers of people. For example, Indigenous traditions offer different ways of knowing that can enrich human life and cultures across the globe. Southern theory resonates with many people working with Indigenous communities in Australia, who begin from the principles of recognition and respect (discussed further in chapter 8).

However, we must also acknowledge the criticisms of southern theory. It validates the binary divide between the north and south, ignoring the complexity and fluidity of all forms of knowledge and assuming homogeneity in the two sides of this divide. It also opens the way for superstition and the total rejection of science. Discussion of this debate is beyond the scope of this book. However, the idea of the integrity of other systems of knowledge is important and Connell's arguments are important reminders to engage with other forms of knowledge.

This discussion of theoretical perspectives, frameworks and concepts should convey the great richness and diversity of the ideas, themes and polemics that inform community development theory and practice. While further reading should be undertaken, it is hoped that this survey has provided a map for understanding the theoretical contexts in which community development takes place.

Theories offer ways of thinking about or explaining how and why things happen the way they do and what we can do about these happenings. Theory is not a separate activity, lying only in the realm of academia, but is informed by lived experience and actual events. It is continually reflected upon, criticised, renewed and reformulated. Community development workers must be conscious of and be able to explain the bases of their own ideas, views, practices and strategies.

Summary points

- An understanding of community development requires an appreciation of theories about how society works.
- People involved in community development work should be familiar with a number of key theoretical perspectives and concepts.
- It is important for community development practitioners to understand how theory and practice are linked.
- Social Darwinism holds that the capacity for moral behaviour, rational judgement and general success in society is not distributed equally among groups or 'races' and that those who are the fittest in society will and should survive.
- Functionalist theory views society as made up of interrelated parts, such as the institutions of the family and religion, that, when put together, form a complete whole. For functionalists, a healthy society is one that is based on value consensus. Stability and conformity are emphasised. If society is to be maintained, people must be prepared to carry out their designated roles.
- Liberalism, in its classic form, emphasises the value of an open, competitive and meritocratic society that aspires to maximum liberty for individuals.
- Neo-liberal theories are based on the view that governments should not intervene in society as this interferes with individual freedom and incentive. Individuals should be free to compete with others for goods and resources in the 'free market'. In practice, neo-liberal policies are a somewhat contradictory mixture of deregulation of businesses and labour-market activities, and a tightening of the policy control of social institutions.
- Social interactionists reflect on the ways reality is constructed in everyday interactions. As we pick up symbolic messages in verbal and non-verbal interchanges, we develop our self-identity. We communicate to people in a number of ways that reinforce this identity.
- Identity is also formed through stereotypes, which generalise about a group on the basis of selective and usually one-sided interpretations. Stereotypes form the basis of prejudice and discrimination.

Background and basics

- Marxism is a complex and non-unified body of thought. It is based on several key tenets. First, understanding the way people produce their world is central to an understanding of how society works. Second, when production and ownership of the means of production are separated, then a class system based on exploitation of the working class by the bourgeois class must exist. Thus, the classes are always in an antagonistic relation to each other. Third, the only way to eradicate disadvantage, poverty and oppression in capitalist societies is to change and overthrow the whole capitalist system. Some of these tenets have been developed and modified by later Marxists.
- Feminism, like Marxism, comprises a number of strands. Feminists are concerned with the subordination of women in society. They set out to critically analyse and explain the nature and origins of gender-based inequalities, exploitation and oppression. The way they analyse and respond to gender issues depends on which feminist standpoint they take.
- Social movement theory rests on the argument that contemporary societies are characterised by an increasing capacity to make and remake themselves. This self-making is expressed in new social movements. Far from being aberrant aspects of societies, new social movements are now an essential part of contemporary life.
- From the perspective of community development, there are four important frameworks in what is known as green or ecological theory: environmental justice/distributive justice, fair trade, participatory justice and relocalisation.
- Understanding the power of language to shape our thinking has led to the view that it is necessary to critically interrogate the discourses and assumptions embedded in language.
- The project of modernity is based on the idea that humans can work creatively and intelligently to control their own destiny and construct a universal morality. It promises a world based on rational thought and science that is free from scarcity and irrationalities.
- Social theorists have pointed out that the project of modernity has its own dark side. For example, the dominance of instrumental rationalism, which is a key part of modernity, has led to new forms of domination and dehumanisation, and science has unleashed environmental problems of immense proportions.
- Criticism of the project of modernity opened the way for a different view of contemporary society altogether: postmodernism. Postmodernists reject overarching theories. They do not attempt to speak for others. They do not seek to uncover 'the truth' or a universal strategy for human emancipation.
- The contemporary world is conceptualised as one of fragmentation, discontinuity and plurality.
- One of the most important new perspectives on contemporary life is what Beck calls risk society. The risk society perspective holds that more and more aspects of our lives are framed by an awareness of the dangers confronting humankind at the individual, local and global levels, and that humans need to develop strategies to confront these dangers.
- Several other key conceptual developments – social capital, active citizenship and civil society – have led to a renewal of interest in strengthening active engagement in society and are significant for community development.
- In recent times there has been an emphasis on thinking about identity as fluid, fragmented and not territorial.
- Beck (2000) has brought together the two dimensions civil society and active citizenship to propose a 'multi-active society'.

- From the perspective of southern theory, Western knowledge does not exhaust all that humans need to know. It is important to recognise that there are different ways of knowing, and there is a wealth of knowledge produced by Indigenous cultures.
- How we think about the world is embedded in theories about the way the world works. Theories are not static once-and-for-all things. They are both informed by and inform our everyday experiences and, as such, are living and dynamic parts of our lives.

Key terms

- active citizenship
- affective action
- bourgeoisie
- capital–labour relation
- civil labour
- civil society
- critical theory
- deconstruction
- deep ecology
- eco-anarchist perspectives
- eco-feminist perspectives
- eco-socialist perspectives
- ecological wisdom
- economic determinism
- Enlightenment
- environmental authoritarianism
- environmental justice/ distributive justice framework
- environmentalism
- ethnocentrism
- existentialist feminism
- fair trade approach
- feminisation of poverty
- forces of production
- functionalism
- gender
- grammar of life
- green movement
- historical materialism
- historicity
- ideological state apparatuses
- ideology
- instrumental rationality
- labour power
- liberal feminism
- liberalism
- Marxist feminism
- metanarrative
- mode of production
- modernity
- multi-active society
- organic analogy
- orthodox Marxist
- participatory justice
- patriarchy
- postmodern feminism
- postmodernism
- praxis
- project of modernity
- proletariat
- psychoanalytic feminism
- radical feminism
- relocalisation
- risk society
- social Darwinism
- social evolution
- social interactionism
- social movement theory
- social relations of production
- socialist feminism
- southern theory
- species-being
- structural Marxism
- surplus value
- technocratic consciousness
- traditional action
- vertical gender segmentation
- wertrational action
- Western Marxists
- zweckrational action

Exercises

1 Why is an understanding of theories and theoretical frameworks important in community development work?
2 How can an understanding of social interactionism assist in community development work?
3 What assumption underpin the theoretical perspectives of functionalism, neo-liberalism and the New Right?

4 In what ways did Marxism and feminism influence community development in the 1970s? How influential are they today?
5 There is general agreement that new social movements are now an essential part of social and political life. Identify some ways that new social movements are part of contemporary Australian life.
6 What are the different types of green perspectives and why are they important for community development?
7 What is meant by 'risk society'? How is it used to explain some of the contextual factors affecting community development today?
8 What is meant by the terms 'social capital', 'active citizenship' and 'civil society', and why are these concepts important for community development?
9 'Postmodernism grew out of the problems with modernism.' Discuss this statement.
10 'Contemporary Western social science is a basis for both enlightenment and domination.' Discuss this statement.
11 Identify several social problems in Australia today. Think about how the theoretical frameworks discussed in this chapter offer different views on the nature, causes and contexts of these problems.
12 Refer to the case study 'Angela's critique of a male-dominated workforce' on page 84. Angela is actually a nurse. Think about how she might apply the various feminist theories outlined in the chapter to her everyday work.
13 Referring to the case study 'The language and practice of domination' on page 116, think about how you would respond to Rob's arguments about the language and practices of community development and volunteerism.

Further reading

Ali, T (2002) *The Clash of Fundamentalisms*. Verso, London.

Bauman, Z (2004) *Wasted Lives: Modernity and its Outcasts*. Polity Press, Cambridge.

Beck, U (1992) *Risk Society: Towards a New Modernity*. Sage, London.

Beck, U (1994) *Ecological Political Politics in an Age of Risk*. Polity Press, Cambridge.

Beck, U (1999) *World Risk Society*. Polity Press, Cambridge.

Blackburn, R (ed.) (1991) *After the Fall*. Verso, London.

Bobbio, N (1996) *Left & Right: The Significance of a Political Distinction*. Polity Press, Cambridge.

Bookchin, M (1986) *Toward an Ecological Society*. BlackRose, Manfred-Buffalo.

Buckman, G (2004) *Globalization: Tame it or Scrap it?* Zed Books, London.

Cohen, J & Arato, A (1995) *Civil Society and Political Theory*. MIT Press, Cambridge.

Eliot, A (2009) *Contemporary Social Theory: An Introduction*. Routledge, Abingdon.

Foucault, M (1980) *Power/Knowledge: Selected Interviews and Other Writings, 1972–1977*, (ed.) C Gordon. Harvester Press, Brighton.

Giddens, A (1994) *Beyond Left and Right: The Future of Radical Politics*. Polity Press, Cambridge.

Giddens, A (1998a) *The Third Way*, Polity Press, Cambridge.

Giddens, A (1998b) 'Risk society: the context of British politics', in J Franklin (ed.) *The Politics of Risk Society*. Polity Press, Cambridge, pp. 23–34.

Goodin, RE (1992) *Green Political Theory*. Polity Press, Cambridge.

Hancock, B & Garner, R (2009) *Changing Theories: New Directions in Sociology*. University of Toronto Press, Toronto.

Harvey, D (1989) *The Condition of Postmodernity*. Basil Blackwell, London.

Hart, SL (2007) *Capitalism at the Crossroads: The Unlimited Business Opportunities in Solving the World's Most Difficult Problems*, Wharton School Publishing, Philadelphia.

Huntington, S (1996) *The Clash of Civilizations and the Remaking of World Order*. Simon & Schuster, New York.

Ife, J (1995) *Community Development: Creating Community Alternatives – Vision, Analysis and Practice*. Longman, Melbourne.

Jochum, V (2003) *Social Capital: Beyond the Theory*. National Council for Voluntary Organisations, London.

Kemshall, H (2002) *Risk, Social Policy and Welfare*. Open University Press, Buckingham.

Lee, D & Newby, H (1983) *The Problem of Sociology*. Hutchinson University Press, London.

Lyon, D (2001) *Surveillance Society: Monitoring Everyday Life*. Open University Press, Buckingham.

Manteaw, B (2008) 'From tokenism to social justice: rethinking the bottom line for sustainable community development', *Community Development Journal*, 43(4), pp. 428–43.

Marx, K (1976–80) *Capital*, 3 vols. Penguin, Harmondsworth.

Meadows, DH, Meadows, DL & Randers, J (1992) *Beyond the Limits: Global Collapse or a Sustainable Future*. Earthscan, London.

Miliband, D (ed.) (1994) *Reinventing the Left*. Polity Press, Cambridge.

Miliband, R (1994) *Socialism for a Sceptical Age*. Polity Press, Cambridge.

Onyx, J & Bullen, P (2000) 'Measuring social capital in five communities', *Journal of Applied Behavioral Science*, 36(1), pp. 23–42.

Power, M (1997) *The Audit Society*. Oxford University Press, Oxford.

Putnam, RD (2000) *Bowling Alone: The Collapse and Revival of American Community*. Simon & Schuster, New York.

Ritzer, G (2000) *Contemporary Sociological Theory and its Classical Roots: The Basics*. McGraw Hill, New York.

Salamon, LM, Anheier, HK, List, R, Toepler, S, Sokolowski, SW & Associates (1999) *Global Civil Society: Dimensions of the Nonprofit Sector*. The Johns Hopkins Center for Civil Society Studies, Baltimore.

Swingewood, A (1991) *A Short History of Sociological Thought*. Macmillan, London.

Tong, R (1989) *Feminist Thought*. Unwin Hyman, London.

Wainwright, H (2003) *Reclaim the State: Experiments in Popular Democracy*. Verso, London.

Winter, I (ed.) (2000) *Social Capital and Public Policy in Australia*. Australian Institute of Family Studies, Melbourne.

Weblinks

Social capital
www.abs.gov.au/websitedbs/c311215.nsf/22b99697d1e47ad8ca2568e30008e1bc/
   3af45bbd431a127bca256c22007d75ba!OpenDocument
www.socialcapitalresearch.com/

Fair trade
www.fta.org.au/
www.fairtrade.asn.au/pfft/products.htm

Relocalisation
www.relocalize.net/about/relocalization
www.relocalize.net/how_do_we_relocalise

CHAPTER 4

The role of the state

Overview

In this chapter we explore the role of the state and its importance for community development. We begin by identifying the ways community development is linked with the state. We note that the relationship between community development work and the state is complex one, and understanding the nature of the relationship to some extent depends on how the state is theorised. We differentiate between the state as a *concrete* object and as a *theoretical* object and discuss seven theoretical approaches to the state. This discussion is followed by consideration of the welfare state. The welfare state has provided an important framework for the positioning of community development work. The importance of neo-liberal policies in refashioning the welfare state is then discussed in some detail. In the final section of the chapter we consider some scenarios for future state formations, several of which could facilitate community development work.

Introduction
Community development and the state

In Australia, state institutions operate at three levels: the federal level, covering all of Australia; the level of Australian states and territories; and the local government level, at which local councils operate. Many government activities take place on at least two levels, such as the provision of education, and some activities take place at one level only, such as the defence forces (national) and garbage collection (the responsibility of local government).

Community development workers are linked to these levels of government in different ways:

- *as paid workers* in programs set up by governments, undertaking activities that are often identified as part of the social and community services industry: for example, working in disability programs or in women's programs (Productivity Commission, 2010:68)
- *through funding* – community development workers in community organisations are often funded by the state, either directly or through government funding to their employer organisations (see Productivity Commission, 2010:72; Lyons, 2001:40; Brown et al., 2000:146–7)
- *fulfilling reporting and accountability requirements* – community organisations and community development practice operate under increasingly demanding regulations and accountability procedures (Productivity Commission, 2010:129)

- *through partnership arrangements* between the state and community organisations
- *as advocates* for disadvantaged and marginalised groups, such as asylum seekers in detention
- *as activists and protesters* against government policies and activities.

Over the past 30 years, the local government level has been the major site for initiating community development programs at the government level. Recently, however, there has been growing interest in sponsoring programs for community strengthening, community renewal and capacity building at the state and national level, within the policy contexts of social cohesion and social inclusion.

The orientation of many local councils, in particular, is to facilitate local communities to develop their own programs. An example of how they might do this is provided in the following case study.

SOUTH BRIDGE MULTICULTURAL ARTS PROGRAM

The setting is a shopfront owned by the local council in the northern suburbs of a capital city. Operating out of the shop is a multicultural arts program, which was established five years ago. At that time, three local cultural organisations approached the council for funds to set up a new arts program. As a result of their lobbying, local councillors provided funds to the organisations to undertake a needs analysis to discern how they could best nurture the rich cultural life of the suburb. The needs analysis revealed that the overwhelming majority of local residents thought that the best way to develop the community and to engender a sense of pride in the cultural mix was to celebrate its diversity through a multicultural arts program. The local council established a multicultural committee to liaise with the three community organisations. It appointed two community development workers to work with the various culturally and linguistically diverse (CALD) groups to identify the assets (including skills, knowledge and resources) already existing in the neighbourhood, the needs of the residents, new proposals of how to develop a multicultural program and the ideas of the community members, and to work with the various groups to develop multicultural arts projects.

The program today runs free workshops for the community on such topics as jewellery making, clothes making, music, use of the Internet and banner making. The most popular project is the annual multicultural festival, involving two days of events. In the lead-up to this event, the shopfront is a hive of activity. Community members are putting the last touches to the colourful banners that will be hung from the light poles in the main shopping centre. Children are finishing their posters that will be put in all the shop windows. Women are framing their quilts, which will be placed in the local council buildings, hospitals and schools. The shopfront has a buzz of excitement.

It is important to note that there is debate about how far community development projects initiated by government can retain the autonomy necessary for the independent action required in community development practice. Community development work is distinguished by the loyalty of the community development worker to the community they work with and for. One view here is that community development cannot take place in government bureaucracies because, as government employees, community development workers are primarily accountable to the bureaucracy itself through its managers. This has caused many community development practitioners to refuse to work within government bureaucracies.

A group calling themselves the London Edinburgh Weekend Return Group took issue with this viewpoint in their seminal little book *In and Against the State* (1980). They argued that struggling in and against the state is not only important but also is crucial to the transformation of existing societies. The authors were either employed by the state or worked in organisations that were directly funded by the state. They believed that any struggle for an alternative society must include struggles *within* the state. This meant being sensitive to all the activities of state workers, whether they were dealing with students, applicants for licences or welfare recipients. They argued that their position as state workers enabled them to understand the processes involved in state control and to intervene and interrupt power relations within the state. Such a view of change is premised on an understanding of society which holds that while relations, decisions and actions are circumscribed by existing structures and forms of domination, they are not immutable.

Overall, the relationship between community development work and the state is a complex one, and understanding the nature of the relationship to some extent depends on how one theorises the state. In the following section we review the different theories of the state.

Approaches to understanding the state

In the previous chapter we discussed how theories come in and out of fashion, adapting to shifting contexts. For most of the twentieth century there was considerable interest in the role of the state as controller, regulator and facilitator of community activities, and much theoretical and political debate about what the role of the state should be. During the 1980s such interest waned, largely because of the influence of the neo-liberal argument regarding a (putative) diminishing role for the state in both economic development and civil society. However, with the focus on crises such as the global financial crisis, climate change and terrorist activities, there have been calls for the state to step back in to ensure the wellbeing and security of its citizens. There has thus been renewed interest in the role of the state, both in terms of the expectations placed on the state to support the major institutions, but also from a more critical perspective that focuses on the failed expectations and promises of governments and the camouflaging role of 'spin'.

From one community development perspective, the withdrawal from state analyses and critique demonstrates a failure to understand the power of state institutions to facilitate or profoundly frustrate and hinder community development practice. For example, a sound grasp of the many debates about the state, the diversity of state institutions, the functions of the state and the efficacy or otherwise of different forms of state power is important for decisions about when and where to enter into partnership arrangements with different state instrumentalities.

What is the state?

Preoccupation with theories of the state has often glossed over the issue of what are to be specified as state institutions. It is important to distinguish between the **state as a**

Background and basics

concrete object and the **state as a theoretical object**. The conventional approach to the state draws on classical political science and contrasts the state with civil society. As a concrete object, the modern state consists of the judiciary, the legislature, bureaucratic administrative apparatuses, the police and the armed forces. These form state institutions that are public institutions and are not privately owned and controlled. State activities encompass the administration of numerous services, policy development and implementation, and legal, military, educational and cultural activities, as well as the development of social and physical resources and infrastructures.

The actual details of the form and content of the concrete state institutions vary within and between societies. The state legally is the supreme power in a territory – the ultimate authority for all law. Functional definitions of the state focus on the role of the state as carrying out particular goals and purposes, and as stabilising and organising society. It is when considering the functions of the state in detail that the theoretical issues arise.

From a community development perspective, it is helpful to understand seven broad positions in regard to the relationship between state institutions and the rest of society. These are presented in figure 4.1. It is important to understand that these are only models to be used for the purpose of understanding. In reality the state is, of course, not a monolithic structure. It is complex, multi-level and often contradictory in its logic and functions.

Figure 4.1 *Theories of the state*

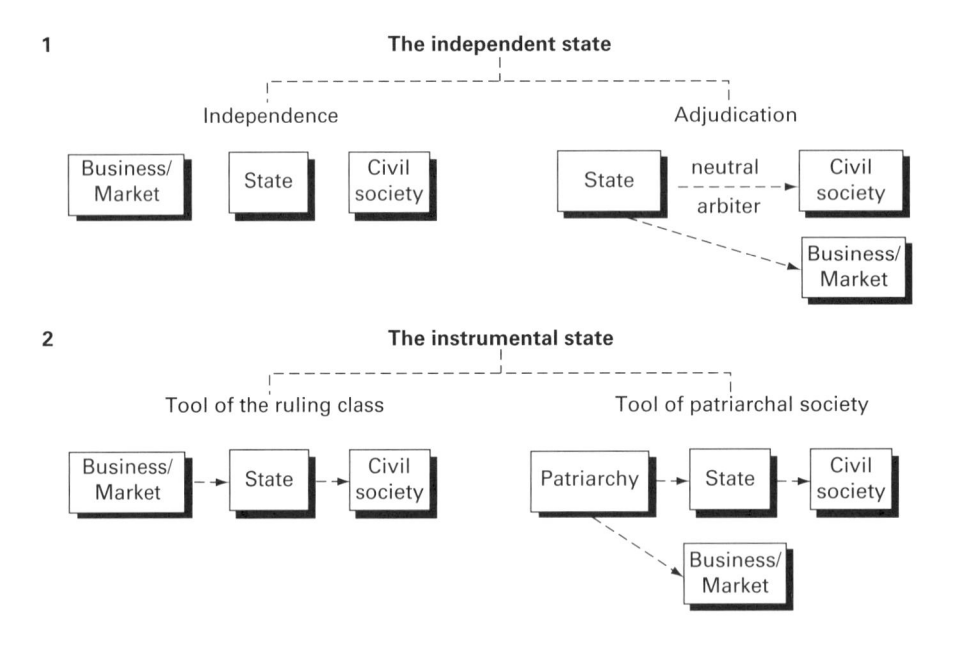

1   **The independent state**

Independence   Adjudication

[Business/Market] [State] [Civil society]   [State] —neutral arbiter→ [Civil society] / [Business/Market]

2   **The instrumental state**

Tool of the ruling class   Tool of patriarchal society

[Business/Market] → [State] → [Civil society]   [Patriarchy] → [State] → [Civil society] / [Business/Market]

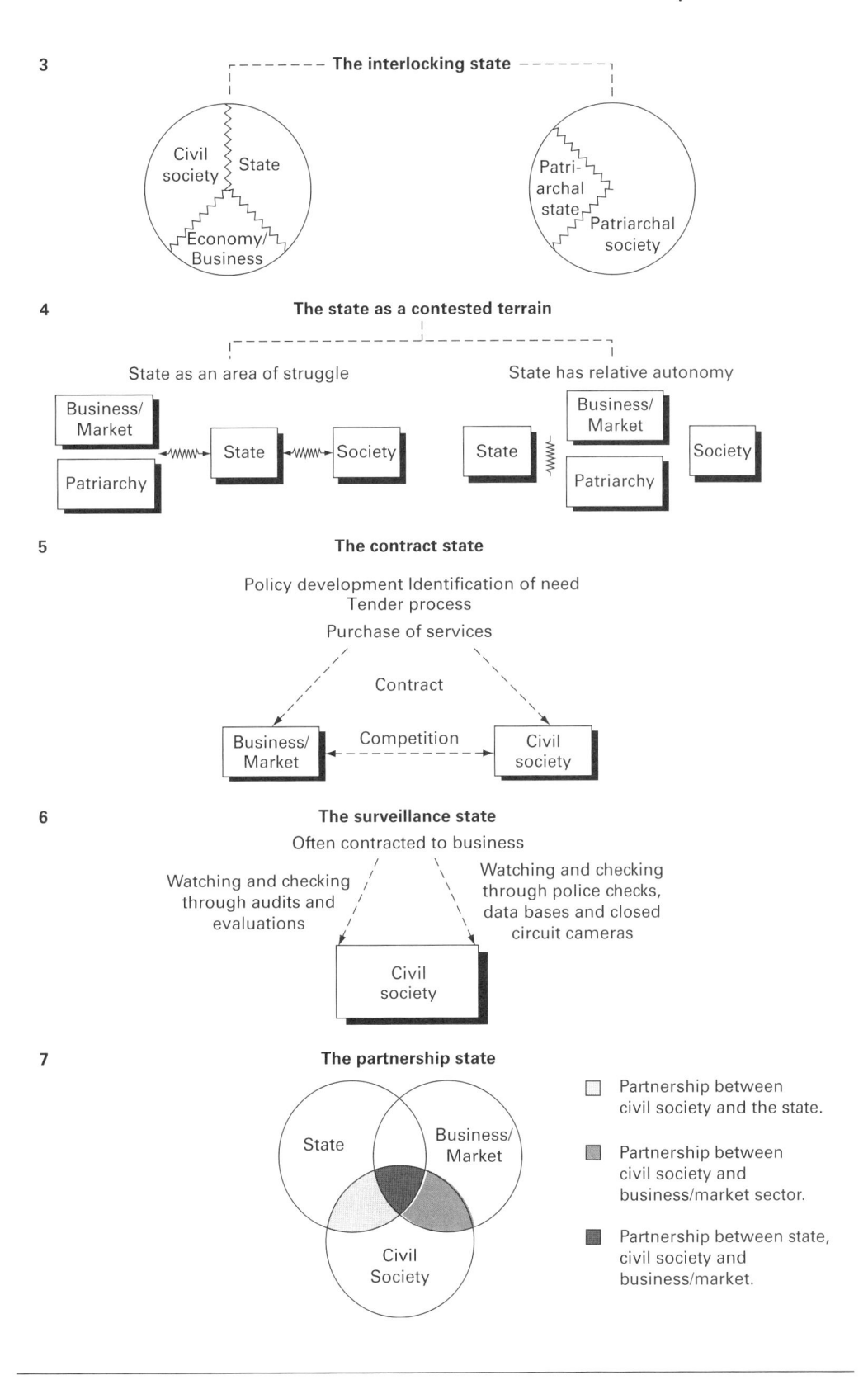

Chapter 4 The role of the state

3   ---- **The interlocking state** ----

- Civil society / State / Economy/Business
- Patriarchal state / Patriarchal society

4   **The state as a contested terrain**

State as an area of struggle   State has relative autonomy

- Business/Market — State — Society; Patriarchy
- State ~ Business/Market; Patriarchy — Society

5   **The contract state**

Policy development Identification of need
Tender process
Purchase of services

Contract

Business/Market ←— Competition —→ Civil society

6   **The surveillance state**

Often contracted to business

Watching and checking through audits and evaluations   Watching and checking through police checks, data bases and closed circuit cameras

Civil society

7   **The partnership state**

State / Business/Market / Civil Society

- ☐ Partnership between civil society and the state.
- ▒ Partnership between civil society and business/market sector.
- ■ Partnership between state, civil society and business/market.

Each diagram in figure 4.1 indicates how the different theories conceptualise the relation between the state and civil society, and the state and the business sector, or what is sometimes known as the market sector. In the previous chapter, we described the nature of civil society as the sphere or sector in which people come together freely and independently to discuss issues and work collectively to influence and shape their society. **Civil society** is the sphere of non-government, non-profit organisations; public activities such as public protest; and the public media such as public broadcasting services. Civil society is contrasted with the spheres of the state and with the market in which for-profit business takes place. It is sometimes also contrasted with the sphere of close and intimate relations, such as those in the family.

The independent state

There are two components to the idea of the state as independent from the rest of society. The first component holds that the state is, or should be, minimally involved in everyday social and economic activities. This view has been described as a **laissez-faire** (or 'leave well alone') approach. In its strongest form, the laissez-faire approach sees the state as an alien power that inhibits people's freedom and ability to achieve (see Hayek, 1960). This approach has been championed by supporters of neo-liberalism. It was been particularly strong in the post–Second World War period in the USA, whereby supporters of the Republican Party, in particular, have argued that intervention in civil society should be minimal and the state's role should be limited to such activities as providing national security through the military and ensuring the rights of individuals to pursue their own interests. The independent laissez-faire state encourages self-help, whereby individuals should themselves strive to improve their own welfare. We discuss this self-help approach in our discussion of the welfare state below.

The second component of the idea of the independent state involves the concept of a neutral umpire. This understanding of the state rests on the view that state institutions act in the public interest. They can ensure that existing rules are maintained, and they are able to adjudicate between conflicting groups when necessary. Overall, the neutral state works to preserve stability and legitimacy in society. A variant of the neutral state approach is found in some elite theories. **Elite theory** is based on the view that society is, or should be, ruled by a small elite group. Michels (1959) argues that the masses are psychologically incapable of making complex decisions and need to be organised by leaders. Leaders are necessary to shake ordinary citizens out of their apathy and to organise them. From this perspective, rule by elites can provide stability for the whole society.

Pluralists take the view that power should be diffused throughout society, which comprises a multiplicity of institutions, interests, beliefs, political groupings, practices and values. From a pluralist point of view, the state's role can remain minimal, as discussed above; it can intervene on behalf of society as a whole as a neutral harmoniser or it can simply be an independent vehicle (a weathervane) that reflects the balance of forces in a society.

In a system based on **liberal democracy**, rule is a result of a range of political inputs – in which case, the state acts as a filter for competing interests. However, some theorists also argue that liberal democracy is ultimately a sham; it always works in the interests of a small group, because skilled leaders are able to manipulate state institutions for their own purposes.

The minimal, neutral and weathervane concepts of the state have been attacked from a number of sides. Activities of state institutions are not selfless or disinterested. Bureaucrats in state institutions become guardians of their own processes and momentum and, when politicised, become the agents of the agendas and policies of governing political parties. Moreover, it is argued that state bureaucracies are responsive to strong pressure groups in society: they act to appease powerful groups rather than act in the interests of society as a whole. At the same time, the concept of the interests of society as a whole is problematic if not actually contradictory to the concept of a pluralist society.

Marxists and feminists have argued that the interests of society as a whole are really the interests of (patriarchal) capitalism. In addition to these difficulties, the concept of an independent state involves **reification**; that is, it is based on the view of the state as an entity in itself – as a unitary, thinking, independent 'thing' that seems to be immutable and beyond human control. Of course the state is a construction of human beings; it is not immutable and beyond human control.

The instrumental view

The instrumental view holds that the state is a tool or instrument of the ruling class, ethnic or religious group or gender, and it is used to reinforce the interests and power of these groups. Government policy decisions that frequently support male-dominated big businesses (such as the mining and media industries, for example) are cited as evidence of the way governments work in the interests of wealthy elite males.

Critiques of state instrumentalism

There are several critiques of **state instrumentalism** that are important from a community development perspective. The first is the anarchist critique. Anarchists argue that the very existence of the state – which by definition is a controlling apparatus – must negate the possibility of individual freedom. In order to have a non-authoritarian, non-hierarchical society, any structure resembling the state must be abolished and replaced by federations of communities and workers' cooperatives that are voluntary, non-coercive and respond to the immediate needs of individuals. Parliaments, governments, bureaucracies, political parties and trade unions are repressive. As Woodcock (1962:15) points out:

> In fact, the basic ideas of anarchism, with their stress on freedom and spontaneity, preclude the possibility of rigid organisations, and particularly of anything in the nature of a party constructed for the purpose of seizing and holding power.

Because of its radical rejection of forms of large-scale organisation, its emphasis on individual spontaneity and its commitment to political propaganda and disruption as central tactics, **anarchism** rejects the notion of a political program that could lead to an alternative society. During the nineteenth and twentieth centuries, anarchism was associated with terrorism and it has had a very small following in the period since the Second World War. It was seen to be incompatible with the highly organised industrial societies of the late twentieth century and its conception of a society without any centralised coordinating institutions appears unrealistic.

Unlike anarchists, Marxists do not believe in abdicating all forms of large-scale organisation. Yet Marxist views of the oppressive nature of the (capitalist) state are similar to those of the anarchists. In the Marxist formulation, the key level of power is not the state but the economic base. Thus, state institutions are actually determined and controlled by those who own and control the means of production. According to this approach, the key controlling groups in Australia are those involved in big business, both within and outside the country. Marxists thus see the state as an instrument of the ruling class: 'a committee for managing the common affairs of the whole bourgeoisie' (Marx, 1977:223) or, as Lenin (1971) saw it, a machine for the oppression of one class by another, through such institutions as the army, the judiciary, prisons and the police force.

There are two broad concepts of state power in Marxist literature. The first is the narrow instrumentalist position discussed above. The second is a more complex position which holds that state institutions have relative autonomy and can take different forms in different societies. According to this second view, the state can retain a degree of independence from the ruling class. However, while policies developed by state institutions may be in conflict with the interests of the ruling class at a particular time, the state overall acts as a **master capitalist** to ensure the maintenance of the capitalist system, and hence the future of the capitalist class as a whole. In this approach, the state can be seen as either 'a reified thing' – an active subject that has a will of its own – or as a set of institutions that follow the logic of capitalism. Althusser (1977) identified two kinds of state apparatuses that follow the logic of capitalism: **repressive state apparatuses**, which include the military and police forces; and **ideological state apparatuses**, which include educational, cultural and religious institutions, trade unions and the family.

These state apparatuses together work to maintain and reproduce the whole capitalist system. The notion of social reproduction is concerned with society's methods of continuing the social organisation and setting that is necessary to maintain the capitalist mode of production. This social organisation involves the social reproduction of a disciplined, fragmented and willing labour force.

The interlocking state

The two views of the state that we have discussed so far generally rest on the separation of the state from other institutions in society. A number of left writers in the 1970s argued that the state and the economic institutions have become so reciprocally interlocked that the state cannot be clearly separated from the economy. Habermas (1974:195) points out that the economy

> requires so much centralised organisation and administration that bourgeois society, once left to private initiative operating according to the rules of the free market, is forced to resort to political mediation of its commerce in many of its branches.

This approach holds that state institutions and economic and social systems (civil society) are organically fused. In the case of the Marxists known as **stamocap** theorists (from **state monopoly capitalism**), the giant industrial corporations in the monopoly stage of capitalism are fused with the bourgeois state so that economic exploitation and political domination are merged. In this approach, state intervention with and on behalf of monopoly capital is the key force of domination in contemporary capitalist societies. Most recently, stamocap theory has been evidenced in the response to the global financial crisis that developed during 2008, as governments stepped in to shore up many of the large banks. In the USA this meant actual transfer of large sums of money. In Australia it has meant government guarantees for the banks and banking system. To the stamocap theory, it is possible to add patriarchy to theorise a general patriarchal monopoly capital state fusing political, social, economic and masculine domination.

The state as contested terrain

A key difficulty with the interlocking approach, as with other broad theories of the relationship between the state and society discussed above, is its determining and largely abstracted starting point. Such determinism conceals the diverse activities and forms of state institutions and leaves little or no room for resistance to state power. This, then, leads us to the fourth position in the relationship between state institutions and the rest of society. It is based on the view that the state is not unitary or even coherent. There are many forms of the state, and our experience of state institutions is variable and often contradictory. State institutions include progressive elements as well as oppressive ones. As the London Edinburgh Weekend Return Group (1980:79) put it:

> The state is not like a pane of glass – it can't be smashed in a single blow, once and for all. We are entangled in the web of relations it creates. Our struggle against it must be a continual one, changing shape as the struggle itself, and the state's response to it, create new opportunities.

The group argues that as soon as the idea of the state as an abstraction or institution is abandoned, and the state is conceptualised as a form of relations, then the possibility of the state as an arena of change and struggle is opened up. For them, opposition must not only be at the level of ideas and argument but also at the material level – in the provision of resources, options and skills, and in all our social relations.

The contract state

In the context of the neo-liberal commitment to the development of enterprise culture and the winding down of roles and responsibilities of the state under neo-liberal policy regimes, the relationship between the state and civil society has been remodelled to establish yet another form of the state. This form has come to be known as the **contract state**. The contract state is constructed around the idea that the state should withdraw as far as possible from the actual delivery of services and programs and take on the role of policy making or 'steering'. Depending on how one interprets the injunction for the state to 'take a back seat' in regard to the actual provision of services, the contract state approach to state–civil society relations can be interpreted within the framework of the independent state or the interlocking state.

The idea of the contract state is premised on the view that many social, economic, cultural and environmental activities have been wrongly undertaken by the state. It begins with the contention that optimal output and efficiencies are not possible when there is monopoly state control and management of resources and instrumentalities. The bureaucratic nature of the state ensures a focus on procedural rules and problem-finding rather than outputs and outcomes and a can-do approach to problem solving. From this perspective, the bureaucratic state hinders creative solutions to problems.

The contractual model has a number of key themes. These include:

- maintaining a distinction between 'rowing', or delivery of services, which is to be undertaken by businesses and non-profit organisations; and 'steering' of overall policy and direction, which is to be undertaken by the state
- reducing the size of the public sector overall
- reducing the size of the public service by focusing on the 'core' functions of government, such as policy, resource allocation, standard-setting, monitoring and evaluation
- devolving service delivery functions to separate public agencies that have some autonomy over how they deploy resources, including outsourcing activities to private contractors
- establishing contractual relationships between the government purchasers of services and other government or private providers
- wherever possible, subjecting contracts for service delivery to competition
- within the public service, establishing contractual relationships between superiors and subordinates
- focusing on clear responsibility and accountability for results
- preferring market mechanisms, involving outsourcing or contracting-out of government services and exposing government-funded activities to competition
- ensuring business-like management of the public sector (Alford & O'Neill, 1994:4–5).

Linked to the idea that the role of the state is to facilitate, or steer, is what has come to be known as the **governance** or **governmentality approach** to organisation and management. The idea of governance refers to the (formal and informal) processes and structures by which a group makes decisions, distributes and exercises authority and power, develops rules, regulates and monitors, and assigns responsibility.

In this approach, the state develops policies and oversees the direction of society in a hands-off manner. The theory of the governance approach can be linked to the work of Foucault, who argued that a critical understanding of power relations requires an understanding of the 'conduct of conduct'. We consider governmentality further in the following chapter.

As pointed out by Alford and O'Neill (1994:6), the contractual model actually covers different types of contracts:

- employment contracts – between parties within the same public sector organisation, such as between superior and subordinate; they can cover work tasks, performance outcomes and performance indicators

- intra-public-sector service contracts – between separate sections of the public service, involving agreements between one section as purchaser of the service and another section as provider of the service
- public–private service contracts – between public sector organisations (as purchasers of the service) and private organisations (as providers of the service); private organisations might be for-profit private businesses or non-profit community organisations, for example
- contracts between individual consumers and private organisations – in which private individuals are the purchasers and private organisations are the providers.

A central component in the contractual model of the state is the separation of the activities of funding, policy development, regulating, standard-setting, monitoring and evaluation from the activities of providing a service. This separation has come to be known as the purchaser–provider split or the steering–rowing distinction. It is based on the belief that the private sector is the best site for developing a society's resources. The function of the state is only to steer the activities of the private sector. According to this view, it is the role and responsibility of the rowers (those directly operating the programs) to ensure that they provide a quality service. The government, as purchaser of the service, has responsibility for developing policies that will steer the activities (see Osborne & Gaebler, 1993).

Analyses of the contract state vary. Those committed to the establishment of the contract state support the idea of the independent state. They argue that the advantage of the contract state is that it strengthens the independent role of the state by ensuring the neutrality and transparency of state activities, particularly when there is competitive tendering for services. Setting out publicly the criteria for being awarded a tender means favouritism and 'insider knowledge' are eradicated.

The surveillance state

The **surveillance state** is both 'watcher and carer'. That is, it both controls and cares for its citizens. First, the state implements a whole range of regulations aimed at ensuring compliance with its policies, accountability (usually to government) and transparency. For example, community development workers have noticed an increase in the ways that governments check on their activities through such mechanisms as audits and evaluations. It works subtly, through state regulations and the processes of documentation, reporting, and monitoring and evaluation. Second, in the context of the 'war on terror', the controlling and protecting state has been revived, particularly in some English-speaking countries. Lyon (2003) contends that after the attacks on American institutions on 11 September 2001, surveillance of ordinary citizens has been increased in most of the world. State institutions such as the police, military and intelligence agencies gain greater powers, as anti-terrorist legislation is passed. New information technology such as iris scans and biometric data is being introduced. State access to personal information through databanks has become easier and more secretive.

From the perspective of community organisations, the compliance pressures are increasing all the time. Community organisations are required to undertake police checks on many of their workers, they are given information on racial and ethnic profiling and they must report suspicious behaviour. The surveillance state extends the control and reach of the state into all aspects of life, not necessarily in the interests of any special group or class, but in the mixed interests of both its own power and the care of the populace. The 'care of the populace' reading of the surveillance state assumes the independent neutral state. But as Lyon (2003) points out, there is always a tension between the role of the surveillance state as watcher and carer and as controller and punisher. From the perspective of community development, the ability of the surveillance state to protect is yet to be borne out and, in the meantime, the effects of surveillance, draconian anti-terrorism laws and their infringement of human rights undermine many of the basic principles of community development practice.

The partnership state

As discussed in this book, one way of understanding how society works and community development's role in society is to divide society into spheres or sectors. The division commonly invoked involves four spheres or sectors: the state sphere; the economic, market or business sphere; the civil society sphere; and the sphere of intimate relations, such as those within the family. Community organisations and community development are located in the sphere of civil society. Over the last two centuries, there has been discussion and debate about how each sphere contributes to society as a whole, and which sphere is the most important for determining the development of society, or which can be identified as the key steering mechanism of society. During the twentieth century, the emphasis shifted back and forth between the state and the market as the key mechanism, depending on the era and the ideology of the analyst. With the dominance of neo-liberalism in the last decades of the twentieth century, particularly in the English-speaking world, emphasis on state responsibilities lost ground to the view that the market is the most important steering mechanism for society. However, in the last couple of decades there has been unease about reliance on either the market or the state as the dominant steering mechanism, leading to a focus on the ways in which civil society, including community or civil society organisations contribute to the general wellbeing of the populace. Most recently, the Productivity Commission has been investigating the role of community organisations, or what it identifies as the not-for-profit sector, in Australian society as a whole.

Out of this discussion has come the view that one of the best ways of organising social development is to harness the attributes of civil society alongside one or more of the other spheres. The favoured approach is to bring community organisations together with government departments, and often also business organisations, in **partnership** arrangements. The body of discussion of the pros and cons of partnership arrangements is growing (see, for example, Mayo & Taylor, 2001; Balloch & Taylor, 2001; Lyons, 2000; Leat, 2000; Jones & Novak, 1999). As with the contract state, assessments of the partnership state vary. For example, from the vantage point where the state is seen to be independent, partnerships between government departments and local governments bring together two autonomous agencies. From the perspective of the instrumental and interlocking views of the state, community organisations entering into partnerships with the state just add another element to the sphere of influence of the state. For example, partnership represents a new narrative of governance in which community development is at risk of becoming a paid arm of the state (Powell & Geoghegan, 2006). Ling (2000) argues that partnerships work to bring civil society into a new 'strategic arena' that both includes citizens and also shapes them within authoritarian control. However, if the state is seen as a **contested terrain**, then a more nuanced and ambiguous reading of the links is possible, in which there is a more complex relationship. In the following section we discuss partnership arrangements in some detail.

Partnerships between community organisations and the state

The idea of community organisation and state partnerships has two important dimensions. First, in their broadest sense, partnership arrangements can be based on genuine commitment to sharing of knowledge and viewpoints, as well as establishing structures and processes that can facilitate joint decision making. This approach to partnership promises a corrective to the traditional power relations between community organisations and the state, based on the unilateral power of the state. This promise can be located in the search for ways of invigorating democracy and developing new relationships between sectors that can strengthen social inclusion and cohesion. It involves sharing knowledge and decision making on matters that affect society and the community sector in general; for example, in regard to the development of public policy. A second dimension focuses on securing agreement about how the two sectors should treat each other and work together. For example, agreements embodied in compacts and accords involve ideas about mutual respect and protocols for the types of relationships between the state and community organisations.

When there is discussion of partnership in Australia, it is generally concerned with this second dimension. It is restricted to matters that directly affect community organisations; in particular, when governments fund community sector programs. For example, partnership arrangements involve commitment to exchanging views (on problems and issues in the community sector) and taking joint responsibility and accountability for programs in the sector.

The various approaches to partnership can be manifested practically in different ways. For example, a minimal partnership arrangement can involve no more than a verbal agreement to share information and respect each other's sphere of influence. Alternatively, a partnership arrangement might be based around fiscal and skill-resourcing requirements, whereby government provides seeding money for a community program, government representatives and community organisations develop both a business plan and a strategic plan, and a joint committee of management is formed. A variant of this approach is when the community provides seeding resources, such as skills and start-up capital, and the state provides a matching grant. Another form of partnership might extend sharing of expertise to exchange of staff between community organisations and government.

A formal construction of the notion of partnership is found in the idea of a **compact**, which deals with such matters as understanding of priorities of the partners, types of consultation between the partners and acceptable levels of resources and information provided by government. Formal compacts have now been developed in the United Kingdom and Canada and in some parts of Australia. For some time in Australia there have been significant tensions in the relationship between community organisations (or the third sector) and governments, particularly at the national level (Productivity Commission, 2010). It would thus seem appropriate to introduce a national compact that would set out agreements and expectations between the state and third sector organisations nationally, and there is evidence of broad support for a compact as a step towards transforming the relation between the government and the third sector (Productivity Commission, 2010; Australian Government, 2009a). Consultations regarding the desirability and possible content of a third sector and national government compact were undertaken in 2008 and 2009. In summary, the consultations revealed expectations that the compact would be jointly owned by government and the third sector, would acknowledge the need for appropriate resourcing of the sector and would actively engage all parts of the sector. It would be committed to diversity in the sector, particularly including and valuing the smaller organisations and volunteers; it would reinforce the sector's independence and its ability to advocate and participate in policy and program decisions would be respected (Australian Government, 2009a). The consultations also identified priority areas for action, including documenting and promoting the value and contribution of the third sector; improving information-sharing, giving greater access to publicly funded research and data; reducing red tape and streamlining reporting; simplifying and improving consistency of financial arrangements; attending to paid and unpaid workforce issues; and improving funding and procurement processes. A key criticism of partnership arrangements is that because governments hold key aspects of power, partnerships are no more than tokenistic sharing of information or consultation. This criticism has force in some forms of partnership. Whether this inbalance of power can be addressed in the proposed national compact remains to be seen.

While we discuss some of the different ways of gaining equal power in decision making in the following chapters, it is useful to identify some of the forms of partnership arrangements and decision making in this chapter. Examples of the various ideas of partnership are illustrated in table 4.1. The importance of the actual relationship is underscored by the range of metaphors that can be used to explain the idea of partnership.

Table 4.1 *Different forms of partnership*

Government 'consults'	Government consults	Government and community	Government and community	Community sector
Government tells community what to do and community responds	Government sets terms but listens to community, with some negotiation of parameters	Government and community agree on parameters, but government still controls the partnership	Government and community jointly set parameters, including agenda, funding and actual project	Community sets parameters and tells government what it wants and expects government to respond

For example, the Oxford Dictionary identifies partnership within the context of a relationship of shared risk (one who shares or one who shares in crime) and a relationship of play (player associated with another in a game and scoring jointly, or a companion in dance).

For those promoting the role of community organisations, the appeal of community–state partnerships lies in a number of directions. First, partnership arrangements acknowledge the central role of community organisations in the development of society. Second, community–state partnerships promise a way of strengthening the accountability between partners, particularly accountability of the state to the community. Third, they promise a corrective to the one-sided power relations whereby the state maintains its control of community programs through acting unilaterally to establish policy, determine funding and monitor compliance with bureaucratic requirements. Fourth, community–state partnerships can serve to empower communities when they open up new spaces for dialogue between government and community organisations (Fairclough, 2000; Clarke & Neuman, 1997). Fifth, insofar as partnership arrangements are oriented to what Giddens (1994) calls 'generative politics and positive welfare' that 'make things happen, to create the conditions in which people can become active citizens', they present the key role of the state as facilitation, rather than surveillance. In this context, the state becomes an investor, 'enabler' or empowerer (Clarke & Neuman, 1997:134). Finally, partnership arrangements promote the power of collaboration and mutuality, which undermines the neo-liberal tenet of competitive behaviour as the basis for a better society and reinforces the value of the trust and reciprocity necessary for building social capital.

We conclude this section with an example of a positive experience of a partnership arrangement between a community organisation, a local council in Australia and a regional government in tsunami-affected Indonesia.

PARTNERSHIP THROUGH TWINNING

A local council, Bambridge, established a tsunami relief fund in January 2005 after the Boxing Day tsunami hit large parts of South-East Asia, but was not sure about the best way of using these funds. At the first meeting to discuss the issue, the council discovered that a member of council had spent time in Sumatra with representatives of an Australian community organisation, and the Australians had developed a close friendship with a local village that was subsequently affected by the tsunami. Having discovered that the survivors had lost all their possessions, the community organisation and the council member set out to establish a 'twinning relationship' with the Indonesian village. Rather than 'twin' with just one village, they decided to establish a three-way relationship between the parties: the council, the community organisation and the Indonesian villages. The partnership was based on community development principles and methods and involved mutual visits, sharing of cultural understandings, exchanges of teachers and TAFE college students, and the re-establishment of an arts industry in the Indonesian villages, through which local products were made and then sold in Australia. This project involved new thinking about partnership arrangements and is now held up as an example that could be followed for other more expansive partnership arrangements.

The social investment state: the third way

A variation of the partnership state is what Giddens (1998a) identifies as the **social investment state**, which is based on the idea that the role of the state is to facilitate citizen initiative and ensure that both the citizen and the state accept their rights and responsibilities. The social investment state is a central component of what has come to be known as third way politics. The **third way** approach to politics

> seek[s] to preserve the basic features of the left – a belief in a solidary and inclusive society, a commitment to combating inequality and protecting the vulnerable. It asserts that active government, coupled with strong public institutions and a developed welfare state, have an indispensable role to play in furthering these objectives ... [It aims to reform] the state, not in order to diminish public institutions and services, but to renew and enhance them (Giddens, 2002:15).

In proposing a third way approach to policy development, Giddens argues that (state) authority must always be underpinned by democracy. For him, it is the responsibility of the government to strengthen entrepreneurial culture through fostering partnerships between the state, community and business sectors. At one level, third way politics is very appealing. However, there have also been a number of weighty criticisms of third way politics. Fairclough (2000) points out that third way politics maintains all the elements of the neo-liberal agenda that support the reduction of welfare spending and the expansion of global capital, and all that this engenders in terms of growing inequality and continuing social exclusion, but dresses up its neo-liberal agenda with a rhetorical commitment to social justice. For Fairclough, the language of the third way is a 'rhetoric of reconciliation' based on the claim that economic dynamism is fully compatible with social justice, and strengthening central government is fully compatible with dramatic devolution of power to the local level.

From the perspective of community development, there is awkwardness in responding to the promises and weaknesses of third way agendas. As indicated above, the third way has many appealing aspects: in particular, the idea of an enabling and facilitating democratic state. However, it is incumbent upon community development practitioners to distil the principles underpinning third way politics and to sort their way through its rhetoric to the practices. Much of its potential revolves around the extent to which there really is a shift in power from the state to citizens and whether third way policies actually reverse the gross inequalities that permeate societies – and indeed the world at large. If there is no evidence of these changes in the country where it has been most clearly practised – namely Britain, which appears to be the case (see Callinicos, 2001) – then there is a strong case for the view that third way politics is just another stage of (more sanitised) neo-liberalism.

Of course, none of these theoretical approaches to understanding the role of the state is sufficient in itself, including the last approach, which assumes a one-sided power relation between the state and the sector. Yet all approaches offer insights to the developing relationship between the state and community organisations that will inevitably affect the practice of community development.

THEORIES IN PRACTICE

As an interesting case study we can see how some of these theories underpin the analysis and recommendations in the Productivity Commission's 2010 report *Contribution of the Not-for-Profit Sector*. People in the sector were asked to comment on the roles of the state that were envisaged in the report. First, they agreed that the report correctly assumes a symbiotic relationship between the not-for-profit sector and the state, and in so doing it also reflects on the tensions between the sector and the state. They argued that governments did acknowledge that not-for-profit organisations must be accountable to the communities they serve, yet at the same time government funding agencies assume that because not-for-profit organisations receive taxpayers' money, priority must be given to government demands and regulations. Many of the interviewees in the community sector expressed antagonism towards government bureaucrats because of their heavy-handed treatment of workers and volunteers in the sector. They also questioned the complex and often inconsistent reporting requirements. Such tensions reveal a questioning of state power on the part of some community organisations and suggests the theory of a contested state.

Second, many of the interviewees noted the assumption of the contract state that underpins the analyses of the not-for-profit sector in the report. The report accepts the role of the state as one of developing policies and steering the not-for-profit sector at arm's length. A key issue considered in the report is how to steer the sector in a way that stimulates productivity growth and social innovation.

A third understanding of the role of the state in the report, commented on by several interviewees, is that it has a 'caring' role, as a supporter and protector of the not-for-profit sector; for example, by streamlining the burden of duplication in reporting requirements and ensuring more equality between the state and the sector.

The fourth understanding of the role of the state was the partnership model. For example, the report supports the development of a 'compact' between the state and the not-for-profit sector and touches on the need for greater mutuality between the partners.

Finally, most interviewees commented on how the report sets out the ways the state could have oversight of the sector; for example, by establishing an Office for Not-for-Profit Sector Engagement, which would drive the creation of a position of a registrar of not-for-profit organisations and a Centre for Community Service Effectiveness (Productivity Commission, 2010:369). The Office for Not-for-Profit Sector Engagement would 'pursue implementation of reforms related to government funded not-for-profit services, pursue agendas in relation to efficiency and effectiveness of the sector, including regulatory reform, and drive development of a knowledge base, including promoting performance measures for the sector. The Registrar will provide organisational financial probity information for line agencies ... for contracting purposes' (Productivity Commission, 2010: 371).

Underlying these recommended initiatives is the idea of surveillance at a distance. By documenting, monitoring, setting regulatory frameworks, developing contract specifications, preparing contracts and evaluating, the state is able to watch and shape what the community sector does, not so much through direct control but through moulding activities and the mindsets of workers and volunteers in the sector. The interviewees agreed wholeheartedly with transparency and fiscal and community accountability; however, they were concerned about the lack of real transparency in government departments and that accountability would be predominantly to government bureaucrats – and not to the community.

Feminist views of the state

We now consider how feminists have drawn on the different notions of the relation between the state and society. Women are linked to the state in several ways: as state workers they are over-represented in low-status and low-paid jobs, and state policies and laws impinge on their lives in various ways.

Some liberal feminists look to the state as potentially a neutral arbiter that can work towards a just society and dispense assistance and resources fairly, but most feminists emphasise that the state is an instrument that is used to maintain patriarchal society. Feminist approaches conceptualise the state as working in the interests of men. That is, the state supports and reinforces male power and it acts on behalf of men. They point out that women's experiences of state institutions have largely been as victims. The state plays an important role in women's lives by controlling and withholding resources, oppressing women and exploiting them as underpaid or unpaid (volunteer) labour.

To most feminists, it is important to identify sites where the disciplinary state intervenes in the lives of women, such as the social security office and the family court. Feminists also point to the feminisation of poverty. They argue that women now largely constitute 'the poor' and are more likely to be exploited by the state than men. Women's lives are more dependent on and determined by state policies than are men's lives. In everyday contact with state institutions, women are still disparaged in a variety of ways: through language and attitudes, for example, and in blame-the-victim policies that punish and oppress single mothers. When men's natural role is seen to be the breadwinner, women's natural role, in both paid and unpaid work, is seen to be the nurturer. This ideology has restricted women's opportunities overall (see Barrett, 1980).

Community development and theories of the state

Whichever way the relation between the state and society is theorised, community development is at odds with the view that the nexus between state power and dominant groups in society is immutable, because, as we have seen, it is premised on the possibility of changing existing power relations and social structures. Thus, for community development there must always be the prospect of the state as a facilitator on contested terrain that holds varying actualities and possibilities for struggle and resistance. In their daily activities, community development workers are involved in a range of interactions with state institutions: in responding to social policies, in negotiating for funds, acting as advocates for their communities or working in partnerships, for example. They know that in many ways they rely on state workers who are sympathetic to the principles of community development. From their own experiences, then, community development workers generally come to think of the state as comprising elements that both support and oppose community development.

Working with local government

At various points in this book we discuss the ambiguities of the relations between communities and local government and the issue of how far community development practice is circumscribed when it operates within a local government setting. One way of thinking about this issue is to identify different forms of relations between communities and local government councils. Table 4.2 is a matrix for thinking about the types of relations with local government within the specific stages of project development.

Table 4.2 *Types of community project development*

Involvement	Initiate	Plan	Implement	Maintain	Evaluate
Community control Community owns the process and project development	Community initiates action alone	Community plans alone	Community implements alone	Community maintains alone	Community evaluates alone
Partnership Shared decision making, activities and responsibilities	Local government and community jointly initiate action	Local government and community jointly plan	Local government and community jointly implement	Local government and community jointly maintain	Local government and community jointly evaluate
Consultation Local government sets terms of reference and asks community for their views	Local government initiates after identifying needs, setting objectives and consulting community	Local government plans after consulting community	Local government implements after consulting community	Local government maintains with consulting community	Local government evaluates after consulting community
Top-down information giving Local government informs community	Local government identifies needs, sets plans and initiates action alone	Local government plans alone	Local government implements alone	Local government maintains alone	Local government evaluates alone

Source: based on Wates, 2000:10

The welfare state

Since the mid 1970s there has been increased scrutiny of the role and efficacy of the **welfare state**. This has taken place in a context of debate about the definitions and nature of the welfare state and, of course, it has been conducted within the overall theoretical frameworks for analysing state power discussed above, changing political agendas and the shifting configurations of the relations between the state, business and civil society.

The idea of the welfare state

The concept of the welfare state rests on the view that responsibility for the wellbeing of citizens does not, and should not, lie essentially with the individual, the private entrepreneur or corporation, the family, or philanthropy or community organisations. While all these institutions can contribute to people's wellbeing, the state has an overall responsibility to ensure the welfare, security and prosperity of citizens by establishing protective structures, processes and institutions, such as a universal medical insurance scheme like Medicare, and providing back-up whereby individuals in need are supported through public housing and social security mechanisms, such as unemployment benefits and income supplements. The strategies and processes whereby governments ensure the wellbeing of their citizens are articulated in social policies.

Some writers extend the concept of the welfare state and social policy to take in all government involvement in civil society, including nationalised industry; government policies covering trade and industry (through industry policy, for example); employment awards and conditions; recreation, leisure and culture policies; public intervention into scientific research and development; and public regulation of private capitalist enterprises. That is, the welfare state has come to stand for the general expansion of the networks of administrative state power into civil society (see Keane, 1988; Offe, 1984; Mishra, 1984).

A failed promise?

It is no overstatement to say that the welfare state has come into disrepute since the mid 1980s. While the attacks upon the welfare state come from all political directions, there is some agreement that the promise of the welfare state to look after the wellbeing of all its citizens has not been fulfilled. Keane (1988) points out that the welfare state assumed that state power could become the caretaker and moderniser of social existence to ensure the welfare of all. But it has been unable to fulfil its promise. Critics have also argued that the postwar welfare state has not significantly reduced inequality, nor has it eliminated poverty (see Hindess, 1987). In addition, welfare bureaucracies have used the poor to maintain the 'welfare industry'. They have constructed people as 'target groups' and 'statistics'. Rules and conventions in welfare bureaucracies are seen to have been developed to meet the needs of their staff, legislators, taxpayers – everyone, except the clients (see Donnison, 1991). From this critical perspective, by the 1980s, the welfare state had become a huge, unwieldy, centralised bureaucracy that has lost touch with the real needs of people. And not only as an amorphous bureaucracy – it was now penetrating and interfering with all aspects of the lives of its citizens.

Theoretical critiques

According to proponents of neo-liberalism, the welfare state shackles personal initiative and private enterprise in a way that can lead to the strangulation of the whole economic system. Their view is that the welfare state is not only wasteful and inefficient, but it also limits people's freedom (see Hayek, 1960). Neo-liberalism draws on people's often heartfelt concern about the unresponsive, even coercive nature of the welfare state, whereby individuals are forced to pay through taxation for unsatisfactory state-provided services that they have no control over, that they have not chosen and which do not meet their needs.

Many Marxists and feminists, of course, argue that the welfare state was a sham from the beginning. From an instrumentalist viewpoint, the welfare state is interpreted as functioning to incorporate the poor and the working class and has been largely responsible for the feminisation of poverty. Seabrook (1982) argues that, while the welfare system in advanced capitalist societies has provided enough for the physical survival of the poor, it has been in the context of a deepening subordination of the working class. Seabrook (1982:xiii) states:

> The price paid by working people of the 'successes' of capitalism has been in terms of the breakdown of the old neighbourhoods, the destruction of human associations, the loss of solidarity, indifference between people, violence, loneliness, mental illness, alcoholism, drug-dependency, a sense of loss of function and purpose.

That is, the welfare state has been responsible for disorganising the working class and obscuring the true nature of capitalism. For example, welfare policy generally constructs poverty as an individual condition. Policy responses to unemployment in the form of unemployment benefits, mutual obligation and work for the dole locate the problem of unemployment in individuals. Training and work motivation programs ensure that the individual remains 'motivated for work'. In these situations, the victim is blamed for the failure of the social system.

Workers in the welfare state are seen as lackeys of the state, paid to control the poor, women, minority groups and the working class. They practise the ideology of blaming the victim by continuing to see social problems as individual social inadequacy rather than as the workings of the patriarchal capitalist system. Feminists point out that the whole development of the welfare state was premised on the division of labour whereby women's role was as dependent wife, carer and unpaid domestic, and men's role was as breadwinner and worker.

Others see the welfare state as a concession of the capitalist system, or even as a significant achievement of the working class. One viewpoint here has been that the welfare state is an island of socialism in capitalist society. From the contested terrain perspective, others see the welfare state as a relatively autonomous and somewhat contradictory institution in relation to the economic sphere. This viewpoint rests on the insight that problems and contradictions lie at the very heart of the welfare state. In explaining the disarray of the welfare state during the 1980s, Hindess (1987:1) comments:

> The expansion of the welfare programs came to a halt at the same time as increasing demands were made on the welfare services. Improved welfare could no longer be financed out of the increment of economic growth, and the level of welfare expenditure became a matter of political dispute. The question was raised in some quarters whether we could really afford a welfare state on anything like its present scale, and there were fears of taxpayers' revolts.

Thus, while state intervention in the form of the welfare state can hide the real nature of capitalist exploitation and soothe the working class, it in turn has become a problem for the capitalist economy. O'Connor (1973) has suggested that the major functions of the state are to ensure both capitalist accumulation and state legitimation, and that these two functions are often mutually contradictory. The state must try to create or maintain the conditions by which profitable accumulation of capital is possible, while at the same time creating and maintaining the conditions for social harmony. When a democratic capitalist state openly uses its coercive forces to help one class accumulate capital at the expense of another class, it undermines the basis of its support and loses legitimacy. But if it does not assist the process of capitalist accumulation, it risks the drying up of the economy's surplus production and the taxes drawn from private enterprise. For example, if the state withdraws support and subsidies, big business enterprises can shift their activities to other countries that do provide subsidies, with subsequent loss of tax revenue for the state and unemployment for the workers.

Forms of crisis

There has been considerable discussion about the crisis tendencies in late capitalism and how the state has been given responsibility for **crisis management**. In general terms, a crisis may be set off by a catalyst; a crisis is a turning point, a new direction, or even the collapse of a whole system.

In his book *Legitimation Crisis*, Habermas (1976) discusses crisis tendencies in late capitalism. Four types of crisis have emerged:

- economic crisis: lack of the requisite quantity of consumable values
- rationality crisis: lack of the requisite quantity of rational decisions
- **legitimation crisis**: lack of the requisite quantity of generalised motivation
- **motivation crisis**: lack of the requisite quantity of action-motivating meaning (Habermas, 1976:49).

According to Habermas, economic crises and rationality crises emerge in the political–economic system. The modern state has two tasks: to sustain capitalism and to maintain a certain level of mass loyalty and commitment to the system. Since the state is merged with all aspects of life, including the economy, economic crises can be displaced by rationality crises in which the state fails to make sufficient rational decisions. A rationality crisis occurs when 'the administrative system does not succeed in reconciling and fulfilling the imperatives received from the economic system' (Habermas, 1976:46). If the administrative system cannot satisfy demands within the legitimate alternatives available to it at the same time as avoiding crisis, the penalty is the undermining of the legitimacy of the state. Legitimation and motivation crises tend to be crises of social integration of individuals. They withdraw from the existing social system of support and loyalty, and their motivational commitment breaks down.

In the context of tendencies towards crisis, there are a number of ways in which the modern state is maintained. Habermas argues that the public realm has been structurally depoliticised, through the fostering of leisure and consumption and emphasis on the atomised life, the family and individual vocation. Dominant class interests are justified and hidden through technocratic consciousness, whereby practical issues, underpinned by particular class interests, are defined as technical issues.

By the 1990s there was an accepted argument expressed by both the Left and the Right that given the logic of the crisis tendencies in late capitalism, the forms of state organisation and particularly the welfare state, as we now know it, cannot be expected to continue. Moreover, as Pusey (1991:19) puts it: 'The "crisis of the state" has, with the benefit of hindsight, turned out to be a "crisis of society".' Something had to give, and this was the whole concept of increasing state functions and responsibility, as we see in the following section.

The neo-liberal view

New Right and neo-liberal theories reflect on the issues facing the state and see the problem as lying in the nature of the welfare state itself. The welfare state is seen to provide too much government support for individuals. This support hinders the development of the self-reliant and competitive individuals who are required for the economic development of society.

Lee and Raban (1988:220) have identified six elements in the neo-liberal position on welfare:

1. Unrestrained competition (for jobs and contracts to undertake work, for example) would unleash sufficient entrepreneurial energy to increase productivity and jobs for the benefit of all, and this would help the poor through the so-called 'trickledown effect'.
2. The notion of the right to welfare is dangerous, because it leads to ever-increasing expectations and demands for resources that are finite. When increasing expectations and demands are unfulfilled, it leads to frustration, anger and social disruption.
3. Demands for welfare are fuelled by welfare professionals, who are parasites on the system and are the real beneficiaries of the welfare state.
4. The welfare state is inefficient in its own terms; it does not redistribute wealth to the poor.
5. The welfare state undermines social justice by its coercive nature; only the market can secure freedom and justice.
6. Lowering taxation, because it encourages personal incentive, is far more likely to benefit the poor than the welfare state and central planning.

Thus a key plank of neo-liberal thinking is that private individuals, private initiative and the private sector are more effective and efficient 'drivers' of society than collective endeavour supported by a strong state and guaranteed welfare. This view has led to what is known in Australia as privatisation.

Processes of privatisation and marketisation

The idea that the private sector is the best site for the development of a society's resources has been developed around two broad processes. The first process is that of **devolution of responsibility** from the state or public sector to the private sector. The second process is that of **marketisation**. Devolution of responsibility is evident in the privatisation of public utilities such as power and water. Yet devolution through privatisation is not necessarily linked to marketisation. Privatisation can actually refer to situations in which social issues are identified as a community or family responsibility, and as such should be dealt with on the basis of unpaid volunteer work or family duty, rather than through a program funded, delivered and controlled by the state. The devolution of responsibility of so-called 'social problems' to families always bears heavily on women, of course.

Background and basics

A commitment to marketisation is based on the view that it is more desirable for the private sector to operate programs than the public sector, as the market mechanism that operates in the private sector ensures a competitive work environment, a more flexible and responsive workforce and a focus on efficiency. Following the National Competition Policy Review, or the Hilmer Inquiry (Hilmer, 1993), 'competition' has become the panacea for economic problems and issues in Australia. Thus, policies and regulations have been introduced to maximise competition within and between public utilities for contracts between Australian and overseas companies for an increasing share of the market, and competition between workers for jobs, for example. In regard to welfare programs, competition between agencies wanting to deliver welfare programs, engendered through such mechanisms as competitive tendering or user-pays programs, maximises efficient program delivery.

We can discern three forms of marketisation operating in community organisations that can come together in different configurations of the processes of devolution of responsibility from the state to the private sector and marketisation. First, marketisation can refer to the quasi-markets of internal marketisation of welfare programs within the public sector (Le Grand, 1990). This involves selling and buying programs and skills within the public sector. Second, marketisation can entail a deepening of the market principle by putting the operation of a welfare program out to the private sector through a competitive tendering process that may be open to all interested players or to only a select few. Finally, privatisation can involve welfare programs being sold in toto to companies in the private sector, which then operate them on the basis of user-pays (and sometimes government-provided subsidies), such as in the operation of nursing homes and childcare centres.

Marketisation of welfare programs means a deepening **commodification** of programs. Commodification takes place as markets and quasi-markets are developed through which contracts to operate welfare programs are traded and the access and use of welfare programs is bought by welfare consumers.

The market model is also concerned with the politics of need, difference, identity and recognition to the extent that a diverse private sector is 'free' to pursue a plurality of needs and interests, or the market is left 'free' to respond to the diverse needs of welfare consumers. There is a view that as the processes of marketisation are embraced, both institutional and individual asymmetries of power will be redressed. When the full market mechanism is put in place, community organisations will be empowered to develop, choose and operate their own programs. Once welfare recipients are constructed as consumers, they will have the power to enter or not enter the welfare marketplace and to choose whatever service they want. The devolution of responsibility to direct service providers for the delivery of programs can enhance responsiveness to consumer needs and good quality programs (Paddon, 1993; Sanderson, 1993).

But we need to unpack further the processes of devolution of responsibility and marketisation of welfare to consider how far these processes operate and facilitate empowerment through the mechanism of consumer power. Under neo-liberal policy regimes, devolution of responsibility means that governments retain the overall command of projects, including policy directions (the steering process) and, where government funds are required, overall fiscal management. Yet the task of administering and delivering the programs within policy guidelines and fiscal constraints (the rowing process) is the responsibility of those directly operating the programs, whether community sector workers, private contractors, community volunteers or families (see Ernst, 1994; Osborne & Gaebler, 1993).

In fact, for all the rhetoric of diminishing state intervention, businesses need a strong interventionist state to protect markets and corporations (against labour collectives and anti-competitive practices, for example). The capacity of 'the rowers' to respond to the active citizenship of welfare consumers is therefore quite circumscribed. Indeed, marketisation sees relations between humans as commodity relations rather than sharing reciprocal relations. The privileging of contractual relations over relations of mutuality weakens other dimensions of civil society, such as trust, cooperation and solidarity (Cox, 1995; Muetzelfeldt, 1994). In addition, welfare recipients are only quasi-consumers. They are not the actual purchasers of the services; the government or other funding bodies are actually the purchasers. Thus, welfare recipients do not have the fiscal power to demand 'quality' service. Welfare consumers have little or no choice of welfare program or service provider.

It is ironic that, while welfare consumers actually have little choice in programs once the concept of competition between providers is established, public relations and marketing strategies become increasingly important.

The New Right resolution of the crisis of the welfare state is to abolish the welfare state as we know it. This means shifting coordinating functions in society away from states and bureaucracies in two directions: first, to families and communities, and second, to (efficient) economies and markets, so that the economic system and economic power unequivocally dominate both the state and society (see Pusey, 1991). This shift involves such measures as identifying social problems as community and family problems, to be solved at these levels; privatising government assets and programs, including the tendering out of projects; deregulating the economy; abolishing the rights of workers, such as the right to work, to a basic wage and to strike; and destroying the power of trade unions. New Right governments have taken an authoritarian stance in respect to control over social institutions and law and order issues.

Supporters of neo-liberal policies argue that welfare institutions should be run along the same lines as private enterprise in order to provide streamlined, efficient organisations, with few resources from government. Thus neo-liberalism draws on the New Right philosophy that individuals, being calculating economic agents, should be free to pursue their own interests in a neutral, open forum.

In this view, the logic of capitalist competition and individual incentive should be applied to public institutions: they must be run along the same lines as private enterprises to ensure lean, efficient functioning. It is thought that both the private and public sectors have the same functions. Both should operate along competitive, profit-oriented lines and ultimately embrace competition for contracts to undertake work and require users to pay for their services. Concerns about social justice and state activities for the general public benefit are not part of this thinking.

Proponents of neo-liberalism use apparently neutral terms such as 'saving the taxpayer's dollar', 'streamlining the public sector', 'making tough and realistic decisions', 'ensuring that the user pays', 'corporatising government departments', 'freeing up labour markets', 'increasing productivity' and the 'level playing field'. In the social and community services industry, economic rationalist views are manifested in shifts to **corporate management** structures and in moves to privatise social security programs and the prison system. Models of efficient business enterprise are often invoked in attempts to encourage or force community organisations to develop new management techniques. These organisational techniques and structures are drawn from the private sector and focus on output, strategy, competition and entrepreneurship. Hierarchical line management is often invoked as being the most efficient form of management. Operations based on rules and precedents, which have dominated the social and community services industry in the past, are seen as obsolete. For example, funding on the basis of historical precedent is increasingly identified as inefficient. It is being replaced by submissions, service agreements, contracts and tenders, whereby community organisations compete with each other for funds. Economic rationalism is enmeshed with technocratic consciousness. For example, everyday transactions that result in cost cutting and redundancy are carried out in the name of efficiency and productivity, and are presented as technical solutions to problems rather than as political decisions about who gets what.

It is important to understand why neo-liberal arguments appeal to the general public. Many people welcome the idea of increasing accountability and effectiveness through privatisation, contracting of work to the private sector and selling of state-owned property and businesses to private enterprise. Together with the emphases on problem solving, strategy and output, this all suggests more responsive social and community services, in which people will have greater choice and more control. For example, Papadakis (1990) comments on the popular appeal of Thatcher's policy of selling council housing in Britain, which enabled some of the working class to fulfil their aspiration of home ownership. However, it is important to understand the negative effects of privatisation.

The effects of neo-liberalism

What have the effects of neo-liberal policies been? First, reforms in the name of neo-liberalism, even in their own terms, have failed to increase choices for most people or to fulfil the utilitarian principle of the greatest happiness for the greatest number. They have certainly failed to redistribute income equally. Instead, there has been significant redistribution of income upwards; that is, the rich have got richer (see Pusey, 2003, 1991). A whole host of writers and studies have revealed the extent of social alienation, disruption and fragmentation engendered by economic rationalist policies. For example, Pusey (2003:184), summarising the views presented in his research on 'middle Australia', comments:

> Now that economic reform appears to have run its full term, the nation reflects on what it has adopted with increasing misgivings. The international comparative evidence shows that economic reform has for the most part failed in its own terms.

Both Pusey and Keane argue that neo-liberalism must fail in the long run. Keane (1988:9) comments:

> Aside from worsening ecological conditions, the strategy of resuscitating market forces and encouraging business at any price is based on a false premise. It assumes that private capitalist firms will rush to occupy the newly available market territory by making new investments and hiring new workers, thereby restoring economic growth, 'full employment' and price stability. This typically generates uncertainty and 'holding back' among capitalist investors. Free-market capitalism is self-crippling because it tends to increase many investors' reticence to invest in growth and employment-oriented business strategies.

Sennett (1998) has documented the ways that the commitment to flexibility (in time and work), which is a key plank of neo-liberalism, has eroded people's security, identity and a sense of personal worth. It 'corrodes their character'. He states:

> The system [of modern capitalism] radiates indifference. It does so in terms of the outcomes of human striving, as in winner-take-all markets ... It radiates indifference in the organization of absence of trust, where there is no reason to be needed. And it does so through reengineering of institutions in which people are treated as disposable. Such practices obviously and brutally diminish the sense of mattering as a person, of being necessary to others (Sennett, 1998:146).

Bauman has analysed how modernity and 'economic progress' in the form of global capitalism have led to an unprecedented growth of **superfluous populations**, who are 'supernumerary, unneeded, of no use' (2004:12). These 'superfluous' populations comprise those who have no means of survival. They have no jobs, no orientation points and no control over their lives. They lose dignity and self-esteem. They have 'wasted lives'. Wasted lives are evident in Sennett's study of the effects of 'flexible' labour, but they are also evident in the people who are discarded within their own country on the basis of race, ethnicity or religion, and in the desperate bids of refugees and asylum seekers to find a way to claim (or reclaim) their dignity and identity.

The corrosion of character and the growth of wasted lives occur when the principles of the market reign supreme, when the state is primarily an agent of business, as in the instrumental and interlocking model of the state. It is ironic that many in the Left are calling for a renewal of the state as an independent or contested entity, with the powers to build structures and processes for the purpose of engendering equality and social justice, and regulating capital. The state that was once the enemy of the Left is now being seen in some quarters as the only institution able to oversee the development of a fairer society.

Before we finish this discussion, we should reflect on how far centralised state power and responsibility is sustainable. As pointed out by some on both the Left and the Right, there needs to be devolution of power and responsibility from the centralised state to other levels of decision making. The configurations of the relation between the state, the market/business and civil society are continually unfolding. The neo-liberals hold that the configuration should be dominated by the market/business, with civil society and the state acting largely as market supports. The Left, in general, sees an important role for the state, and supports more state control of the market and the continuation of the welfare state, although those promoting left policies have different views about the details of this role. According to those defending third way agendas, commitment to the market and most neo-liberal principles, such as those championing enterprise culture, should be maintained. The role of the state is to 'civilise' neo-liberalism by encouraging an inclusive social system, enabling environments, a vibrant civil society based around active citizenship such as volunteerism, and the fostering of market competition against monopolies (see Giddens, 2002, 1998a; Latham, 2001, 1998).

Models for the future

What sort of state might we see in the coming decades of the twenty-first century? And what sort of relationship between community organisations and the state can we envisage for the next decades? Four broad models can be identified. These models are based on a unitary state. In reality, of course, the state is not unitary; it has diverse values and different ways of operating. Thus we will probably experience a mixture of the four models.

A neo-authoritarian state

In the first model, authoritarian tendencies in the state are strengthened, both ideologically and in practice. While trust in the state, and particularly the welfare state, has lost some legitimacy over the past 20 years, this does not necessarily eliminate the possibility of a strong authoritarian state rising from the ashes, as it were. The renewal of a large, strong centralised state could direct Australian society's journey along the path of the centrally controlled brave new world. In this scenario, central planning in the economic sphere is strengthened, and existing control of social and political life is tightened. The state intervenes at all levels of civil society. The state is reinvested with its power as guardian of the nation against internal as well as external enemies (see Keane, 1988). Overall, there is a shift away from representative bodies to a bureaucratised executive that further extends the depth and scope of state intervention (see Pakulski, 1991). The discourse of rights will be swamped by the discourse of obligation, particularly obligation to the state. In Australia, neo-authoritarian individualism is becoming most obvious in the program for Indigenous 'welfare reform', set up by the Howard government in 2003, whereby required behaviours of Indigenous Australians are policed by the state, and state welfare support is only forthcoming when these behaviour targets are met.

A neo-authoritarian state can be a logical response to a putative need for security and certainty in an anxious, fragmented and pluralist society, and to popular demands for law and order, so-called 'border protection' and defence against 'terrorists', and for the clear direction of society by strong leaders. New technologies of power are brought into the service of the state for the purpose of further standardisation and conformity, and to extend existing surveillance of tax files and banking transactions, for example, and surveillance methods such as identity cards, police checks and security cameras. The forms of post–September 11 surveillance promise to control risk through new and increasingly sophisticated procedures for assembling data, and classifying and cross-referencing in ways to which none of us are immune. It is to these new forms of surveillance that Lyon (2003) alerts us. He comments that neglecting the need for ethical care for the objects of surveillance is a serious mistake, with ramifications that we may all live to regret. However, 'In the current climate it is hard to see how calls for democratic accountability and ethical scrutiny of surveillance systems will be heard as anything but liberal whining' (Lyon, 2003:39).

A strengthening of the authoritarian, bureaucratised, centralised state would marginalise most community development practitioners and push them further into usually unpaid advocacy and activist roles, which would be circumscribed according to political conditions and, in the extreme, could become illegal. However, for those workers in community organisations prepared to act for the state, there could perhaps be an extended role in service delivery.

A strengthened neo-liberal state

The second model continues and extends neo-liberalism. There is a strengthening of the position in which state institutions, along with other public utilities, are privatised and in some cases phased out. Privatisation requires the reorganisation of social and community services to make them more amenable to the logic of capitalism. Resources are allocated through the market. The welfare state as we know it disappears. Welfare institutions are largely replaced by religious and private charity organisations and private enterprise, as well as families that take responsibility for the welfare of relatives.

Residual social problems require some state programs as a safety net to prevent end-of-the-line destitution and to maintain the legitimacy of governments. Government funds for community programs are provided either on a contract basis or through vouchers to the deserving poor, who are expected to shop around for the best services and programs.

A strong emphasis on tendering for contract funding extends the existing practices of funding agreements and service agreements. All community organisations are expected to tender for programs, thus constructing community service programs around the concept of the marketplace.

The process could work in several ways. On a grand scale, it is possible to imagine a government identifying social problems or issues of concern by contracting private research agencies to undertake public opinion polls. Such issues could include youth homelessness or high rates of unemployment. Once an issue is identified as being of public concern, decision makers call for submissions. These set out a detailed program – including aims and objectives, a strategy plan, expected outcomes, processes for evaluation and a budget – for dealing with the issue or solving the problem. This approach reduces social issues to technical problems, which are resolved through appropriate strategy alone.

On a less ambitious scale, existing community organisations could continue only if they successfully tendered to operate programs. For example, governments call for tenders to run a range of programs, and private profit-making companies compete in the so-called open market against other organisations and community groups to win the contract.

Community development programs, therefore, continue to have a place in this scenario. There is an increased reliance on volunteer labour. Unemployed people and retirees are supposedly integrated into society by participating in community organisations and activities on an unpaid basis. There is increased demand on charitable trusts and corporate sponsorship to keep programs going. Many community programs that, at present, operate with government funds are forced to become privatised, user-pays organisations – or else collapse.

Community organisations are also required to develop programs for self-funding, including independent economic activities. This could result in cooperative community-based ventures, which would facilitate autonomy, but it could also lead to a preoccupation with raising funds and enterprise development. Yet community development, located at the periphery of the state, might be able to utilise the notion of 'minimal state' in new ways, and play a role in mitigating the harshest effects of neo-liberalism.

In the short term, this scenario is consistent with third way and neo-liberal government agendas. A further shift against the traditional welfare state is highly probable, although it will be dressed in the rhetoric of self-management of welfare programs and devolution of decision making to local levels. Governments will need to present imagery of people being in control of their own destinies to maintain their legitimacy.

A supervising state

The supervising state brings together the neo-liberal and surveillance state. Privatisation and contractualism continue, with the terms of reference set by the supervisory state that monitors, checks and supervises. The major role of the state is, in fact, to supervise. But it does so at arm's length and thus presents as a neutral arbiter in the interests of the whole society and might be seen as a re-run of the idea of the independent state. However, the supervisory state is not an independent laissez-faire state. It sets up the terms of reference of state–civil society relations, it has oversight of society as a whole, and when deemed necessary, it will intervene. At different times it will work to support different interests in society, often in arbitrary ways. In this way the state is understood as both a controller and a carer/protector. We can find an implicit carer/protector role for the state in the social inclusion agenda, which has been constructed and is driven by government. The government assumes the role as the prime agent for social integration, insofar as it builds individual and community strengths, develops services tailored to the needs of communities, and undertakes early intervention and prevention (to prevent social exclusion) (Australian Government 2009b).

It is also evident in the ways partnerships are constructed. Governments set the policies for partnership arrangements and monitor the application of these. As indicated in the earlier case study, the 2010 Productivity Commission report into the not-for-profit sector suggests some of the ways the state can have a supervisory role in the development of the sector, both as a carer/supporter and a controller/regulator. Like the two models discussed above, the supervisory state is certainly not the optimal model in which to practise community development. The major issue to be confronted in such a model is that, ultimately, it is premised on the need for community organisations to work within terms of reference set by the state. A term that is used to explain how community organisations accept state control of framing of their activities is *governmentality*. As mentioned above, governmentality works to secure compliance on the part of the community sector by shaping the roles of citizens in their everyday activities. The concept explains how the sector has become compliant. For example, it refers to how we govern ourselves, how we are governed and how to be the best governor (Foucault, 1991, in Elliot, 2009:81). As Ling (2000) argues, partnerships are good examples of governmentality at work; they secure the legitimacy of the actions of the state by agreement and consent to specific methods of governance.

A decentralised democratic and facilitative state

The final model rethinks the concept of a neutral state. It also sees the state as relinquishing some of its powers, and decentralising and de-bureaucratising many of its activities (see Hirst, 1994). Thus, this model requires the diminution of the welfare state as we know it. However, unlike the neo-liberal version of a minimal state, in this scenario the state does not minimise funding of welfare programs. Nor is the political sphere placed at the service of the capitalist economic system. The state maintains some central coordinating functions: it guarantees security of the natural environment and it ensures a more equal redistribution of wealth and resources, rather than further concentration of wealth in the hands of a few (see Camilleri et al., 1989).

The state ensures that the social wage and citizens' rights are maintained and strengthened. Marshall (1981) defines three kinds of citizens' rights: civil rights, which are embodied in the legal system; political rights, which ensure the right to vote; and social rights, which guarantee access to a society's resources through, for example, the social wage.

In this model, the running of many programs is contracted-out by governments to both community organisations and the for-profit sector. All programs are democratically accountable to their workers and users as well as funding bodies. The state retains some mediating roles in regard to civil society. Yet it also facilitates the development of an independent public sphere. In a sense, this reverses the economic rationalist assumption of primacy of the economic over the socio-political sphere. This reconceptualisation of the state could go some way to ensuring that the economic system serves society as a whole, rather than the interests of some groups.

Extending democracy

Extending democracy would be a key element of this decentralised state. Keane (1988:12–15) presents a case for re-emphasising the traditional goals of equality and liberty. He shows that the neo-liberals have capitalised on the popular view of the welfare state as taking away people's freedom, initiative and choice. Keane explains why the left goal of equality should be maintained. Multiple mechanisms for the production and distribution of goods should be established, so that different goods can be distributed to different people, in different ways, for different reasons. In order to increase liberty and enlarge choices, citizens must be given maximum opportunity to participate in decision making through a variety of institutions within and between civil society and the state. Autonomous spheres would be established through which civil society would become a 'permanent thorn in the side of political power'.

A similar point about the extension of democracy is made by Hirst (1994), Mathews (1989), Bobbio (1986) and Cochrane (1986). In the context of 'local politics', Cochrane shows that community politics is an autonomous sector of politics, which promises to democratise civil society through its emphasis on the direct involvement of people in collective decision making.

Bobbio seeks to extend democracy to many locations in civil society, including the workplace, school councils, hospital boards, bureaucracies and technocracies. Mathews develops a concept of what he calls associative democracy, in which a strong ideological offensive democratises all economic and social life. He emphasises collective activity, via existing associations of workers and citizens, to release the energy and imagination of the membership, while bringing that collective strength to bear on political issues (Mathews, 1989:12).

Community development is in a good position to participate in this push to extend democracy and establish a new political configuration. In various ways it can be conceptualised as a practice and a structure in civil society that mediates between the individual large bureaucracies, the economy and the state. This model of a decentralised state presents a scenario that is the most compatible with community development. It remains to be seen how plausible it is.

Summary points

- In Australia state institutions operate at three levels. Community development workers are involved in working in all three levels.
- In concrete terms, the state consists of the judiciary, the legislature, bureaucratic administrative apparatuses, the police and the armed forces. These form state institutions, which are non-privately owned and controlled. State activities can involve administering numerous services; developing and implementing policy; legal, military, educational and cultural activities; and maintaining and developing social and physical infrastructures. In classical political science, the state is differentiated from civil society.
- In recent years there has been a number of intense debates about the state, focusing on such areas as the identification and derivation of the state, the functions of the state, the efficacy of state power and the strategic implications of the different theories of the state.
- From a community development perspective, it is important to understand seven broad positions in regard to the relationship between state institutions and the rest of society.
- Individual community development workers identify patterns of determination of state power according to their own theoretical stance. However the relation between the state and

- community development is conceptualised, community development cannot see state power as immutable, because community development practice is premised on the possibility of changing existing power relations and structures.
- The concept of the welfare state rests on the view that governments should ensure the security and wellbeing of citizens by establishing protective processes, structures and institutions, such as public housing and social security.
- There is some agreement that the welfare state has been in a period of crisis over the past 20 years.
- The neo-liberal solution to the crisis of the welfare state is to abolish the welfare state as we know it, while at the same time taking more control of social institutions through, for example, law and order campaigns. According to the proponents of neo-liberalism, welfare institutions should be run along the same lines as private enterprise to provide streamlined, efficient organisations with limited resources from the state. There are some serious weaknesses and profound dangers in neo-liberal thinking.
- In regard to future configurations of the relation between the state and the rest of society, four broad possibilities can be identified: first, a continuation of differing degrees of state intervention into economic and social matters, with residual welfare state activities; second, the establishment of a strong authoritarian state; third, the continuation and extension of neo-liberalism; and, finally, the decentralisation and devolution of state powers to the local level. This final model is compatible with community development.

Key terms

- anarchism
- civil society
- commodification
- compact
- contested terrain
- contract state
- corporate management
- crisis management
- devolution of responsibility
- elite theory
- governance or governmentality approach
- ideological state apparatuses
- laissez-faire
- legitimation crisis
- liberal democracy
- marketisation
- master capitalist
- motivation crisis
- partnership
- reification
- repressive state apparatuses
- social investment state
- stamocap
- state as a concrete object
- state as a theoretical object
- state instrumentalism
- state monopoly capitalism
- superfluous populations
- surveillance state
- third way
- welfare state

Exercises

1 The state impinges on our lives in many ways. List the ways you engage with the state in the course of a week.
2 All three levels of government in Australia affect community development. List how each level influences community development programs. General information can be sourced through the Internet and at local council offices.

Background and basics

3 To understand the state it is important to grasp the different theories of the role of the state. Identify a specific example of a way you have engaged with the state. Which of the theories, or combination of theories, can be used to explain your encounter?
4 Think of examples of operations of the welfare state and how the value of the welfare state is being questioned.
5 What are the neo-liberal criticisms of the welfare state?
6 What are the criticisms of the neo-liberal views of the welfare state?
7 Some people argue that the neo-authoritarian state is the most likely option for the development of the relationship between the state and society. What do you think?
8 Why are decentralisation and the extension of democracy important for community development?
9 Referring to the three case studies in this chapter, identify some of the ways that local councils and the federal government might facilitate different forms of community development.

Further reading

Alford, J & O'Neill, D (1994) *The Contract State: Public Management and the Kennett Government*. Centre for Applied Social Research, Deakin University Press, Geelong.

Balloch, S & Taylor, M (2001) 'Conclusion – can partnerships work?', in S Balloch and M Taylor, *Partnership Working: Policy and Practice*. Policy Press, Bristol, pp. 283–8.

Bauman, Z (2004) *Wasted Lives: Modernity and its Outcasts*. Polity Press, Cambridge.

Brown, K, Kenny, S & Turner, B (2000) *Rhetorics of Welfare: Uncertainty, Choice and Voluntary Associations*. Macmillan, London.

Callinicos, A (2001) *Against the Third Way*. Polity Press, Cambridge.

Clarke, J & Neuman, J (1997) *The Managerial State*. Sage, London.

Cox, E (1995) *A Truly Civil Society: 1995 Boyer Lectures*. Australian Broadcasting Corporation, Sydney.

Dunleavy, P & Hood, C (1994) 'From old public administration to new public management', *Public Money and Management*, July–September, pp. 9–16.

Ernst, J (1994) 'Privatisation, competition and contracts', in J Alford and D O'Neill (eds) *The Contract State: Public Management and the Kennett Government*. Centre for Applied Social Research, Deakin University Press, Geelong, pp. 101–35.

Fairclough, N (2000) *New Labour, New Language*. Routledge, New York.

Giddens, A (1994) *Beyond Left and Right*. Polity Press, Cambridge.

Giddens, A (1998) *The Third Way: The Renewal of Social Democracy*. Polity Press, Cambridge.

Giddens, A (2002) *Where Now for New Labour?* Polity Press, Cambridge.

Hirst, P (1994) *Associative Democracy: New Forms of Economic and Social Governance*. Polity Press, Cambridge.

Keane, J (1988) *Democracy and Civil Society*. Verso, London.

Latham, M (2001) 'The third way: an outline', in A Giddens (ed.) *The Global Third Way Debate*. Polity Press, Cambridge, pp. 35–45.

Leat, D (2000) 'Making partnerships work: typologies and conditions', in *Third Sector and State Partnerships: Conference Proceedings*. Centre for Citizenship and

Human Rights, Deakin University, pp. 51-62.

Lee, P & Raban, C (1988) *Welfare Theory and Social Policy*. Sage, London.

London Edinburgh Weekend Return Group (1980) *In and Against the State*. Pluto Press, London.

Ling, T (2000) 'Unpacking partnerships: the case of health care', in J Clarke, J Gewirtz and E McLaughlin (eds) *New Managerialism, New Welfare?* Sage, in association with the Open University, London.

Lyon, D (2003) *Surveillance after September 11*. Polity Press, Cambridge.

Lyons, M (2000) 'The impossibility of public-private partnerships under quasi-market funding regimes: Australian case', *Fourth International Research Symposium on Public Management*, April. Erasmus University, Rotterdam.

Lyons, M (2001) *Third Sector*. Allen & Unwin, Crows Nest, NSW.

Mayo, M & Taylor, M (2001) 'Partnerships and power in community regeneration', in S Balloch and M Taylor, *Partnership Working: Policy and Practice*. Policy Press, Bristol, pp. 39-56.

Mishra, R (1984) *The Welfare State in Crisis*. Harvester Press, London.

Muetzelfeldt, M (1994) 'Contracts, politics and society', in J Alford and D O'Neill (eds) *The Contract State: Public Management and the Kennett Government*. Centre for Applied Social Research, Deakin University, Geelong, pp. 136-57.

Osborne, D & Gaebler, T (1993) *Reinventing Government: How the Entrepreneurial Spirit is Transforming the Public Sector*. Plume, New York.

Paddon, M (1993) 'Taking contracting seriously: the current debate in the UK and Europe', in J Coulter (ed.) *Doing More with Less: Contracting Out and Efficiency in the Public Sector*. Public Service Research Centre, Kensington, NSW, pp. 62-71.

Productivity Commission (2010) *Contribution of the Not-for-Profit Sector,* Productivity Commission Research Report, Australian Government, Canberra.

Pusey, M (2003) *The Experience of Middle Australia: The Dark Side of Economic Reform*. Cambridge University Press, Cambridge.

Sennett, R (1998) *The Corrosion of Character: The Personal Consequences of Work in the New Capitalism*. WW Norton, New York and London.

Woodcock, G (1962) *Anarchism*. Penguin, London.

Weblinks

Government–community sector compact
http://fahcsia.gov.au/sa/communities/pubs/national_compact_consultation/Pages/p1.aspx

Public private partnerships
www.aph.gov.au/library/pubs/rp/2002-03/03RP01.htm

Surveillance state
www.caslon.com.au/surveillanceprofile1.htm

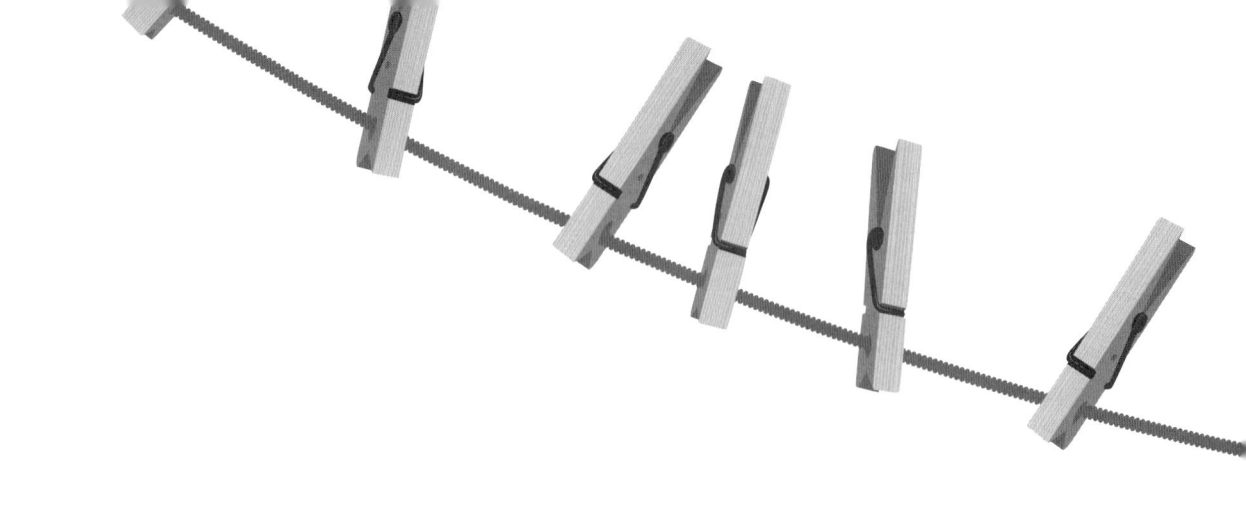

PART 2

Processes and practices

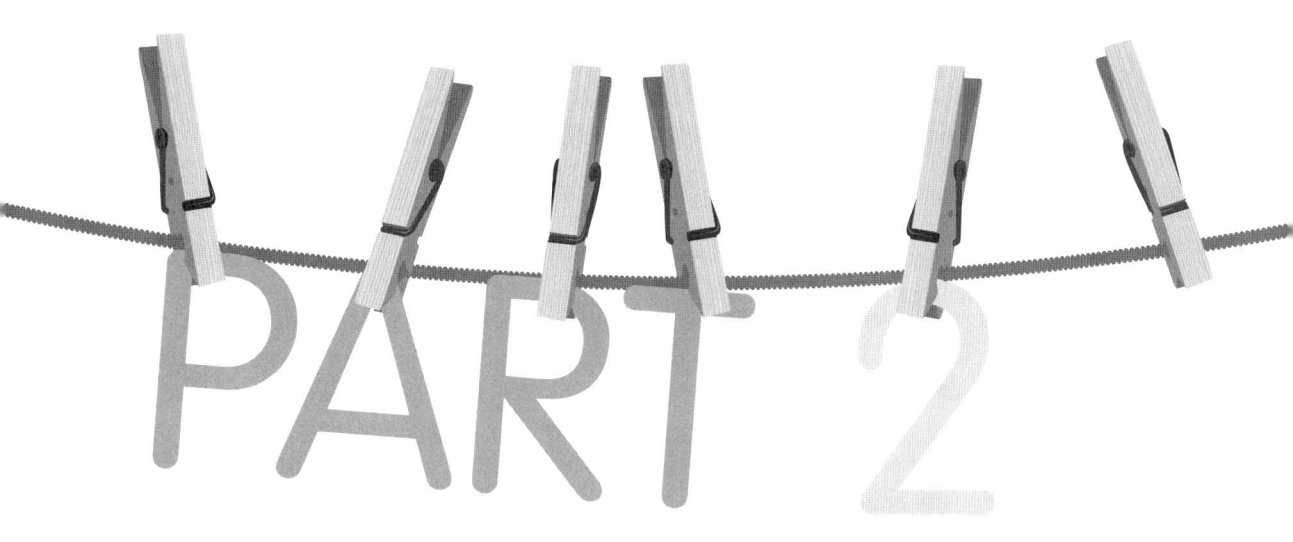

Chapter 5	Practical foundations	174
Chapter 6	Community organisations	228
Chapter 7	Activities and practices	266
Chapter 8	Understanding and responding to difference	307
Chapter 9	Funding and research	342

CHAPTER 5

Practical foundations

Overview

This chapter examines the practical foundations of community development. We begin by examining the ideas of professionalism and competency and the uneasy links between the common construction of these concepts and community development. Empowerment is a central concept in community development and we explore the meanings of power and empowerment in some detail, referring to the various ways that community development practitioners might apply these concepts. Community development is premised on the value of participation in society; however, there are different forms of participation, some of which are tokenistic or manipulative. The idea of participation and different forms of participation are discussed, and the issue of 'non-participation' is considered. This is followed by an examination of community capacity building, which over the last 20 years has shaped many development programs, both in Australia and overseas. As mentioned in chapter 2, alongside capacity building, an important focus of government policy has been social inclusion. We undertake a critical analysis of this concept and its applications. The final part of the chapter focuses on the importance of strategy development. Approaches to strategy development, and levels and types of strategic plans, processes and steps in developing a strategy are elaborated, followed by a discussion of key issues and the criticisms of strategy development.

Introduction

This chapter considers the practical foundations of community development. Community development practice today is framed by the somewhat contradictory imperatives of neo-liberalism, including a commitment to self-determination, new managerialism and increasing government monitoring and regulation. At the same time it is encouraged to be more 'professional' and more strategic. All of these themes are, in various ways, concerned with issues of power. A considerable amount of community development practice is constructed around challenging the different dimensions of power, through empowering communities, developing assets, facilitating social inclusion and strengthening civil society. In such a climate, there is pressure on communities and community organisations to become more professional, to build their capacity, to clarify their goals and to develop strategic plans. We consider all of these activities in this chapter. We begin by considering the idea of professionalism.

Professionalism

It is sometimes said that community development work is anti-professional, but of course this depends on the definition of **professionalism**. There are two main uses of the term:

- a commitment to a profession or occupational grouping
- attitudes and skills, including an approach to tasks.

The notion of commitment to a profession has developed out of the new occupational hierarchies that have been characteristic of industrial societies during the last 100 years. Professionalism in this sense refers to how occupational groupings form, maintain and protect their identities. A profession tends to be thought of as a relatively closed occupational grouping of people who have specific skills and knowledge, an identity as experts and an aura of respectability. One becomes a 'professional' after a period of socialisation, usually involving education or training and gaining a qualification.

Most professions form professional associations, which are held responsible for maintaining standards, developing rules of conduct, protecting members, developing codes of ethics and scrutinising potential members. Thus, professionals develop formalised and often elaborate systems of behaviour to regulate and protect the reputation of their profession. They regard themselves as repositories of specialised knowledge and reinforce this view through the use of exclusive terminology. Thus professionals are involved in the construction and circulation of the knowledge that comprises their 'discipline', such as economics or medicine. In his discussions of the idea of 'discipline', Foucault (1980) focuses on how power and knowledge are interrelated. He points out that knowledge is never neutral or arbitrary. It is produced, worked on, circulated and used for specific purposes (Hancock & Garner, 2009).

While the professional has a duty to carry out the work in a way that respects clients and consumers, loyalty and commitment are to the profession itself – and hence to other professionals. The corollary of this is that professionals must not get 'too close' to clients or consumers, for this is said to impinge on their ability to work objectively. In the case of social services work, identifying too closely with a client cuts across the detachment necessary in professional counselling, for example. Community development workers do not aspire to be professional in this sense. They shy away from this use of the term for several reasons. First, community development rejects the idea of social services work based on an elite group of people who have privileged knowledge and skills and a technical language that sets them apart from others and enables them to have power over others. Community development, of course, promotes the sharing of knowledge and skills. It is not a closed club, with its own standards of admission and rules of conduct. Second, loyalty of community development workers is not first and foremost to other community development workers and to maintaining the standards and reputation of the profession. Community development workers have no pretensions to impartiality in the interests of the profession. They accept that all humans carry with them the baggage of values, assumptions, ideologies and desires. Their task is to make these explicit: to communities, other workers and themselves. Rather than distance themselves, community development workers form part of, and identify with, communities.

While community development workers tend to be ill at ease with professionalism as gatekeeping, as discussed in previous chapters, they understand that community development work requires specific commitments, attitudes, capacities, knowledge and skills. Here, there is some overlap with ideas of ethics in other professions. For example, in community development, a professional worker is someone who respects the people with whom they work, who listens attentively, who is trustworthy and who honours requests for confidentiality. However, they generally reject the view that professional associations should be formed to protect the standards and interests of community development work. The view that community development work takes place in a myriad of ways, and does not necessarily require formal credentials, does not mean that community development can be undertaken by anyone in any way. Indeed, there is a significant debate about where to draw the line between community development work and welfare work and how far it is meaningful to talk about 'pure' community development, for example. These issues are taken up in chapter 10.

Competency

The term **competency** has come into use to describe desired levels of skills in professional work; it is sometimes used interchangeably with the term 'professionalism'. Generally, competency in a task means that it has been performed effectively and efficiently, with the appropriate use of skills. While competency levels for community work and community development have been specified within a competency framework (through, for example, Social and Community Services Industry Training Boards), there has not been strong enthusiasm for the application of competency models by employers, especially in community-based employment. Community development workers themselves are ambivalent about the practice of specifying competency levels. On one hand, they accept that they must be effective and efficient, and that they must know when and how to use their skills. On the other hand, the notion of competency levels is full of difficulties, both political and practical. Discussion of competency standards often uses neo-liberal rhetoric that focuses narrowly on productivity, on output that is measurable or quantifiable and on the completion of discrete tasks rather than complex interrelated processes. The consultation and collective work of community development are difficult to measure in terms of output, and thus can be seen as inefficient in both cost and time. Rees (1991:114) criticises this preoccupation with skills or competency in terms of efficiency:

> Skills will contribute to cost-effectiveness and efficiency but may divert attention from the questions of whether saving money contributes to empowerment. The importance of these questions gives reason to ponder the relationship between skills and the ideology and objectives of empowerment. Students, practitioners and an even wider public can easily become fascinated with *skills as though developing them is an end to itself*. If that happens it may soon be accompanied by sterility of thought and boredom with practice. It would represent some vacuous idea of efficiency without equity, of management without the wit or patience to consider management to what end.

There are also the questions of who sets the standards, who judges workers' competencies and how such judgments are made.

Different types of competency

To get insights into how ideas of competency must be understood in the context of the types of work being considered, it is useful to refer to a discussion by Reich (1992). Reich, an American political economist and one-time adviser to President Clinton, argues that three broad categories of work have emerged: **routine production work**, **in-person services** and **symbolic–analytic services**. Routine production work dominated the industrial activities of the twentieth century. It involves the repetitive tasks of production and supervision that are performed by blue-collar workers, clerks, data processors and line managers, for example, typically working in large bureaucracies, guided by standard procedures and codified rules. The workers' pay is generally based on hours worked and sometimes on a piece-rate based on their output. Their skills can be used worldwide. Competency for routine production workers is seen in terms of their ability to continuously perform routine tasks. They must be reliable and loyal and able to carry out instructions. In the social and community services industry, clerks, data processors and line managers in human services bureaucracies perform routine production work.

Workers involved in in-person services must also be able to carry out routine tasks and they are paid according to hours worked or the amount of work performed. However, unlike routine production work, in-person services involve direct contact with those people who are the beneficiaries of their work. Workers include hairdressers, house cleaners, nurses, childcare assistants, car mechanics and flight attendants. As well as being reliable, these workers need to be courteous to their customers. Because of language and other cultural factors, workers undertaking in-person services are restricted in their work location. Conventionally, human service professionals (including social workers and community development workers) working face to face with clients would be placed in this category. Usually routine production work and conventional in-person services require some level of formal training, inculcating predefined skills and taught by experts (Miller, 2010). As Miller (2010:31) states, when it is constructed as professional training, the competency-based approach to learning is driven by technical and instrumental rationality and coexists alongside neo-liberal discourses that emphasise competitiveness, performance and target-driven measurements and regulation.

The third category of work is still developing and is becoming more important and powerful; it entails what Reich calls symbolic–analytic work. Symbolic–analytic workers may be trained as scientists, lawyers, accountants, graphic designers or engineers, for example, but what they provide that is of special interest to their clients are problem identification, problem solving and strategic brokering skills. What they trade is the manipulation of symbols, including data, words, and oral and visual manipulations. The tools they use may be mathematical formulas, legal arguments, psychological insights or marketing symbols, for example. In Reich's (1992:178) discussion, symbolic analysts

Processes and practices

> simplify reality into abstract images that can be rearranged, juggled, experimented with, communicated to other specialists, and then, eventually transformed back into reality. The manipulations are done with analytic tools, sharpened by experience.

Symbolic analysts tend to work alone or in teams, rather than as bosses or under bosses. Much of their work might be done in meetings, on the telephone or through email. They produce reports, strategies, designs and scripts, for example. They tend to be paid as consultants, according to the originality and quality of work and their ability to broker or solve problems quickly, rather than through any quantitative measure such as hours worked. While they do not have neat or set careers, they can work internationally. According to Reich, the motivations of symbolic analysts may be to make as much money as possible, to gain power or to cause people 'to reflect on their lives or on the human condition' (Reich, 1992:178).

The idea of symbolic analysts reflecting on the human condition and responding to problems in strategic ways resonates in community development. Problem identification and problem solving is what community development workers do, as will be discussed later in this chapter. An important component of both symbolic–analytic and community development work is the ability to analyse and respond effectively to changing conditions. Moreover, community development workers act as symbolic–analytic consultants to communities, but there are some significant differences between the position of symbolic analysts as described by Reich and the position of community development workers. According to Reich, the motivations of symbolic analysts are often money and power, for themselves. The motivations of community development workers are, in altruistic terms, typically the enhancement of empowerment in communities and redundancy for themselves and, in less altruistic terms, probably employment for self-fulfilment. While Reich presents symbolic analysts as experts and quite distant from the ultimate beneficiaries of their work, community development workers eschew the idea of becoming distant experts who may never meet with the people they are ultimately working with and for. Reich emphasises how for symbolic analysts the idea of community means commitment to other symbolic analysts, thus undermining the possibility of other definitions of community. From a community development worker's perspective, commitment is rather to the community they work with than to other symbolic analysts.

If there is any accuracy in Reich's analysis of the three job categories and the growing importance of symbolic–analytic skills, then it is important to understand the nature of the different types of skills and how these influence one's conception of competency.

The notion of competency helps community development workers analyse their own actions and skills, and encourages clarity about possible options and outcomes in their work. Nevertheless, community development workers will probably remain suspicious about attempts to measure their competency in terms set by professional bodies or government bureaucrats. They do not necessarily endorse the requirements for increased productivity, efficiency and accountability in terms of reference set by governments. Yet, they will continue to demand of themselves high levels of commitment to empowering ordinary people, for this is central to all community development work. They will also need to be increasingly flexible and creative, understanding that empowerment has many dimensions, can be fulfilled in a number of ways and requires a wide range of knowledge, self-knowledge and skills.

In the following sections we consider the notions of power and empowerment and discuss strategy development and the skills required for the purpose of empowering ordinary people.

Empowerment

The term **empowerment** is found throughout the language and literature of community development. Indeed, the idea of collective empowerment is understood to be the lynchpin of community development and, as we have seen, distinguishes it from other approaches to working with people. Sometimes the goal of empowerment is stated explicitly in community development work, as in the mission statement of a community organisation or in a duty statement. At other times, collective empowerment is an implicit goal of an organisation or project. For example, a community development worker taking up a new job with a community house may be given a duty statement that sets out tasks in terms of maintaining programs, employing staff, networking, advocacy work and producing a newsletter. These tasks are (or should be) part of a strategy to empower people in a community.

But what does empowerment actually mean and is it as simple as it appears? Empowerment is a complex notion and, like the term 'community', it has a strong value overlay. Over the last 20 years it has also become one of those loaded 'buzzwords' (Cornwall, 2008). At its roots it is based on philosophical views about what it is to be human, and it involves processes that are full of dilemmas and contradictions. We briefly considered empowerment in chapter 1; here we probe the concepts of power and empowerment in some detail. We begin by examining the concept of power and how it is exerted through coercion and ideology. We discuss the concept of empowerment and the importance of empowerment as a central theme in human fulfilment, after which we consider how empowerment takes place through community development.

Ideas of power

Power is a ubiquitous part of our lives, yet the more we try to understand it, in many ways, the more illusive it gets. In a recent study of power in Britain, Leighton (2009:13) explains some of the difficulties in defining power:

> In daily life people discuss the location of power and its extent, who has more or less, and how to gain, resist, seize, harness, secure, tame, share, spread, distribute, equalize or maximize it. In addition, there are long-running theoretical debates about whether social power should be derived from individual agents or from social structures, and whether it is a 'zero sum' game of symmetrical and conflictual relations between winners and losers, or a 'plus sum' communal phenomenon where power is a collective resource more closely related to consensus than conflict.

Simply put, empowerment involves the achievement of power through participating in power relations – being given it or taking it. But what is power? A common response to this question is that it is possible to have 'power to' (power to decide one's own life) and 'power over' (power to be involved in shaping the wider society: 'to have a voice'). In the first sense, power involves such attributes as shaping one's own life and resilience in the face of setbacks and arbitrary power of others. In the second sense, power can mean the capacity to impose one's will against the will or interests of others. According to this viewpoint, 'A exercises power over B when A affects B in a manner contradictory to B's interests' (Lukes, 1974:34). A dominant person or group maintains power over other people or groups in a variety of ways. Power can be explicit, as in winning a situation of overt conflict, or implicit, as in being able to set agendas and ignore alternatives, limit the range of alternatives to be considered or mask conflicts of interest. There is another less obvious form of power. This involves the shaping of people's goals and desires, such as the desire for consumer items (see Lukes, 1974).

It is important to distinguish between two types of power or control:

- *Coercion:* a dominant group maintains its power by forcing people to do things against their will, such as through the threat of violence.
- *Consent:* a dominant group maintains power by gaining the consent of subordinate groups. It can do this by distorting, concealing and deflecting a real understanding of power relations and how things work. Subordinate groups can unwittingly enter into an alliance with dominant groups, and this allows unequal relations of power to be maintained. At other times, subordinate groups are complicit in their own subordination because they believe that they are inferior or have no right to power and that this stage of affairs is natural, legitimate and inevitable.

In different societies, combinations of coercion and consent are used by dominant groups to maintain their power or hegemony. In contemporary Australia, dominant groups largely maintain their power through consent, rather than coercion, and it is the forms of power that come through consent that are most important for community development in Australia. In the following section we consider how power is maintained by consent.

Ideology

Some of the most important insights into why people comply with their own subjugation draw on ideology. **Ideology** comprises beliefs, practices, attitudes and relationships that support existing relations of power. As Marx and Engels stated in *The German Ideology* (1976:67):

> The ideas of the ruling class are in every epoch the ruling ideas: that is, the class which is the ruling material force of society is at the same time its ruling intellectual force.

Of particular importance is Gramsci's development of the idea of ideology. Ideology constrains the everyday practices of community development. By means of ideological control, or hegemony, dominant groups set agendas; they stage, frame and contain alternatives; they identify what is realistic and reasonable; and they maintain fatalistic views among subordinate groups. Because existing ways of acting and thinking become naturalised and appear inevitable, people do not have the language or the option to imagine other ways of thinking about and doing things. Drawing on the earlier ideas of Marx and Engels, Gramsci provided a deeper understanding of how ideology works, especially in his work on **ideological hegemony**. From Gramsci's writings we learn how subordinate groups enter into alliances with ruling groups in ways that reinforce their subordinate positions. Gramsci uses the term *direzione* (direction, leadership) interchangeably with *egemonia* (hegemony) to denote these alliances.

The Marxist tradition of critical theory discusses the power of capitalist ideology to insert human beings into the consumer society, where identity, wellbeing and status are seen in terms of the ownership of consumer items such as clothes, cars, housing and jewellery. All aspects of life can become commodified in a consumer society. Everything, from culture and sport (pop music, festivals, football players, and so on) to sexual relations (through singles clubs, online dating agencies and brothels), becomes a commodity to be sold for profit. Popular culture reproduces and strengthens the views of reality constructed by dominant groups, through film, television and music. Horkheimer and Adorno (1972) use the term 'culture industry' to describe the culture in capitalist societies that is produced for mass consumption and integrates people into society from above. In capitalist societies, culture does not arise spontaneously from the masses; it is not a product of genuine demands, but is a result of demands that are evoked and manipulated. So-called 'popular culture' masks special interests. As well as consumer ideologies, religious and cultural beliefs also serve to mask hidden interests and to close off different ways of looking at the world. Fundamentalist religious views, for example, provide only one way of interpreting events in the world and prescribe set behaviours in ways that present certain ideas and beliefs as natural. Cultures, for example, become ingrained in individuals as cultural dispositions, which set up the taken-for-granted world in which we all live and work to legitimate existing social and political systems. To explain this type of power, Bourdieu (1977) used the concept of *habitus*.

Needs discourse

Another important insight into the way power is exerted in everyday life focuses on what has come to be known as the **discourse of needs** (Fraser, 1989). In everyday life, we habitually talk about people's needs. For example, governments talk about the need for the populace to feel secure, conservative politicians comment on how children need discipline and businessmen talk about their need for a flexible workforce. The question of who has power over the definition of needs is an important one. As Fraser points out, there are a number of assumptions embedded in the discourses of needs and numerous disputes about 'what exactly various groups of people really do need and about who should have the last word in such matters' (1989:161). Fraser elaborates how 'needs talk' becomes an arena through which political power is constructed and applied. For example, in the welfare arena, what is designated as a need has important effects economically and socially. Who defines the needs of disadvantaged groups? Is it the government, individuals or communities who have the need; the media; or the professionals who deal with the need or other so-called experts, such as academics or religious leaders? Governments might define the need of disadvantaged unemployed people to be 'actively looking for work' within the context of 'mutual obligation'. Professional welfare workers might emphasise the importance of income support as the primary need of people who are disadvantaged. These instances illustrate how others speak for the people with a need. In community development work, the focus is on communities and people themselves deciding their needs and their priorities. From the perspective of the politics of needs, when people make claims about their own needs and talk about the needs of others, they become involved in ideological and practical struggles over power. We further consider how needs have been defined in our discussion of needs assessment in chapter 9.

Challenging ideology

These views about the strength of ideology and the hegemonic power of the ruling groups in society present a rather dismal scenario of the opportunities for the empowerment of ordinary people. But is the ideological hold of dominant groups in contemporary societies really so strong? Abercrombie, Hill and Turner (1980) draw our attention to the plurality of views in human history. Their research reveals that not all subordinates accept the views of dominant groups and of those who do, many negotiate the dominant value system adding their own subordinate and even oppositional values. Abercrombie, Hill and Turner comment: 'The actuality of obedience and satisfactory role-performance is all that the dominant groups require of subordinates, not the internalisation of an ideology' (1980:142). Clarke et al. (1976:43) argue that subordinate working-class groups have the capacity to find their own spaces and identities. These spaces are both physical (the networks of the streets, houses, corner shops, pubs and parks) and social (the networks of kin, friendship, work and neighbourly relationships). Fiske (1989:159) also points out: 'Under certain historical and social conditions this submerged (oppositional) culture can break through the surge into visible political action.' In these spaces and cultures, subordinate groups construct their own cultures, values and ways of doing things. Community development – in the form of grassroots action, for example – often begins in these spaces.

Activist writers such Wainwright (2003) and Chomsky (2003) have identified the many ways that communities, organising collaboratively, have made a difference to the way people live their lives. In a timely discussion of 'where to start' collectively as activists, Chomsky (2003:191) comments:

> Well, everything can be done – everything can be done up to the point of eliminating all structures of authority and repression: they're human institutions, they can be dismantled … You work on the things that are worth working on. If it's taking control of your community, it's that. If it's gaining control of your workplace, it's that. If it's working on solidarity, it's that. If it's taking care of the homeless, it's that.

Thus ideological hegemony is not immutable. It is made up of situations and relations that may at one time favour one group, but can later favour another. Although the dominant ideologies that reinforce the ideas and practices of dominant groups prevail and perpetuate the incorporation of subordinate groups, ideological hegemony must be continually propped up through negotiation and struggle. It also changes, and in the processes of reconstruction, subordinate groups can define new values and meanings, and identify other options and new ways of doing things. New ways of looking at things open the way to resisting the dominant groups' definition of what is proper and reasonable. Developing new ways of looking at the world is a central aspect of empowerment.

In their everyday work, community development practitioners are well aware of the many small ways in which ordinary people resist the forms of domination that we have discussed above. For example, ordinary people refuse to comply with campaigns urging the populace to 'dob in a welfare cheat'; they sabotage the efficacy of databases of personal data by providing incorrect information; they refuse to abide by local government bylaws; they refuse a stereotype used to describe them such as the 'frail elderly' by joining 'bikey' clubs; they fail to be intimidated by protocols in bureaucratic hierarchies by demanding to see the head person.

Practices and processes of power

The previous discussion draws attention to the point that rather than being a one-off experience, power is exerted in myriad ways in everyday life and it can also be challenged in myriad ways. One of the most influential writers on this topic is Michel Foucault. While Marxists tended to focus on the ways groups and structures are organised to ensure the ideological hegemony of the ruling classes, Foucault's work emphasised the ways that we regulate and control ourselves, in our everyday language and practices, and in activities that seem to us as 'normal' (Elliott, 2009:71). For Foucault there is no conspiracy of powerful groups deliberately setting out to control us, as some Marxists have argued. Indeed, there is no unitary state or capitalist class that can be branded as the 'enemy of the working class'.

For Foucault, power is not a thing to be possessed or taken. Power relations are not a matter of overthrowing the state or seizing power. Nor are they congealed in large-scale confrontations such as class struggle. They are constituted at the innumerable points of confrontation in society. The study of power should concentrate on how it operates and is experienced in everyday life 'at the level of on-going subjugation, at the level of those continuous and uninterrupted processes which subject our bodies, govern our gestures, dictate our behaviours' (Foucault, 1980:97). Analysis should be concerned with how power is exercised through the apparatuses of knowledge and through dispositions, manoeuvres, tactics, techniques and functioning at the micro level. Foucault analyses different techniques of domination. Advanced capitalist societies are characterised by technologies of power that are based on the manipulation of information.

Yet rather than seeing power as an impenetrable, irresistible force, Foucault argues that wherever there is power, there is resistance. Power and resistance are inseparable because the very existence of power relations presupposes forms of resistance. Foucault's ideas provide useful correctives to the narrow focus of power as essentially an attribute of macrostructures, such as the state and classes.

Let us pick up these last two points in regard to the exercise of power and resistance to power, in regard to community development. As Foucault argues, power is exercised through manipulation of information, manoeuvres and tactics. Community development workers involved in humanitarian resettlement of asylum seekers find that they have to deal with these forms of power daily. For example, they can point to how politicians and the media are complicit in demonising asylum seekers as 'queue jumpers' and potential terrorists, threatening the Australian 'way of life', or as passive pawns of international traffickers and secret agreements by international governments. Each of these images stereotypes asylum seekers, who comprise very diverse groups. There have been many manoeuvres to reinforce the stereotypes. The personal stories of the asylum seekers are rarely known. There are few opportunities for friendships with Australian citizens when asylum seekers are locked away in detention centres in remote locations, offshore on Christmas Island or, in the case of the so-called Pacific solution, outside Australia. In contrast to the numbers of asylum seekers in Europe, numbers attempting to enter Australia are relatively small. Community development practitioners working with asylum seekers also point to how a group of Sri Lankan Tamils in Merak, Indonesia, articulated their rights and refused to leave the boat they had contracted to take them to Australia in 2010. And asylum seekers who have been granted asylum organise their own advocacy organisations.

Governmentality

A concept that encapsulates how power works subtly, through different relations and techniques, is governmentality. **Governmentality** involves the shaping, framing and directing of conduct or 'the conduct of conduct'. It includes governance or 'control at a distance'. Governmentality turns people into active subjects who take initiative and make choices in a way that aligns their directions with the goals of government. It sets up practices through the regulatory frameworks of the modern state and the activities of self-governance, such as the shifting of responsibilities for wellbeing to individuals. For Foucault, governmentality provides the dominant logic of contemporary political systems. When, for example, Indian students in Australia have been assaulted, one response has been to advise them to 'look poor' and 'avoid travelling on their own at night'. That is, they are advised to be more vigilant in their self-governance. Community development practitioners working on a contracted project to report on how juvenile delinquents should be retrained (to be self-constrained) in a particular region are implicated in governmentality logic when they have little scope to challenge the definition of juvenile delinquency or the assumption that young people should be retrained. They are participants in the circulation of power that reinforces ideas of self-governance.

An important example of the processes and practices of subjugation in Foucault's work is found in his discussion of a method of organisation and control that has come to be known as the **panopticon vision** (Foucault, 1979). In his discussion of the panopticon, Foucault (1979) draws on the design for prisons developed by Jeremy Bentham in the late eighteenth century. Bentham developed a particular structure and system of prison surveillance that enabled the guards to see the prisoners without the prisoners seeing the guards, through back-lighting and a system of blinds and observation posts. The effect of this one-way vision was to induce self-monitoring by prisoners. The idea of panopticon vision has not only been taken up by prison systems, but also is used as a method of controlling the general populace through surveillance cameras, databases and auditing mechanisms, which allow those in power to monitor us without us seeing them, knowing who they are or knowing when we are being monitored. Like Bentham's prison, this one-way vision induces us to self-monitor our actions (Lyon, 2001).

Community development practitioners can find value in Foucault's methodological rule that an understanding of power begins from an analysis of the multiplicity of forces and practices at the micro level of everyday life. Take, for example, the following case study.

COMPLIANCE WITH A TENDER AT THE WONBRAC MRC

A migrant resource centre (MRC) has won a tender with a government department that specifies that the MRC is required to keep confidential files on all migrants who visit the MRC and describe the reason for the visit and the action[s] taken. Where migrants run volunteer groups, the MRC is required to undertake police and psychological checks to ensure their suitability. The tender also specifies that the MRC must provide audited accounts and an evaluation of all its services for migrants. The government department can call for reports on all or any of these activities at any time, and can visit the MRC and demand to see the files.

Knowing that this elaborate checking process is set out in the tender, the MRC ensures that it abides by every aspect of the tender. Yet at no time in the three-year contract do representatives of the government department visit the MRC or request to see the detailed files. All that is required each year is the annual report, with audited accounts, and the yearly evaluation report. Moreover, as there is no feedback on these reports, the staff at the MRC suspects that no-one in the government department actually reads the reports.

This experience of self-monitoring happens throughout Australia, probably thousands of times every year. Why do community organisations such as the MRC actually comply with government requirements if no-one is actually going to check? There are two answers to this question. First, there is always the possibility of a visit or query from the government department. As Foucault points out, people self-monitor when they are not sure if they are being watched – and this is a very effective form of control. Second, community organisations follow the requirements set out in policies and of funding bodies as a form of insurance; that is, to guard against 'being caught out' when something goes wrong. In a society alerted to risk, there is always the threat of litigation. One apparent safeguard against such litigation is to ensure that correct protocols and policies have been followed. These understandings of power show that community development workers must always be sensitive to the many manoeuvres, techniques, dispositions, tactics and languages through which power relations are expressed, maintained and altered.

Empowerment and the human condition

The concept of empowerment brings to our attention the view, already noted, that power is not just a negative phenomenon. In the context of community development, empowerment is used in a positive and collective sense. It refers to the ways that power relationships are changed in the interests of disadvantaged, oppressed or exploited groups. It distinguishes between 'power over' and 'power to' – the two dominant conceptions of power previously discussed – and the idea of 'power with'. Community development emphasises 'power to' and 'power with'. Empowerment raises awareness of the ways power is exerted and of the identities and rights of subordinate groups. But empowerment is not just a matter of consciousness-raising. It requires changes to the material living conditions of those who are oppressed and disadvantaged in society; it requires access to resources; it alters the balance of power towards subordinate groups, who increase their access to, and control over, assets and information.

Without using the terminology of empowerment, many social theorists and philosophers have been concerned with issues of empowerment, albeit in quite different ways. For example, Touraine (1988, 1981) argues that society always acts upon and makes itself historically on the basis of its self-knowledge. For Touraine, attempts to transcend existing values and ways of acting are essential components of human life. Marx and Engels were concerned with how humans create societies and transform themselves. In their early writings we find the view that humans are distinguished by their ability to make and remake their own material world and, in so doing, create and transform themselves. It is in this process of production that humans enter into relationships with other people and develop their own identity (Marx & Engels, 1976). In a society in which the producers do not own or control the means of production, such as a capitalist society, humans are stunted in their capacities to be fulfilled. For Marxists, people cannot be fully human unless they collectively own and control the means of production, including what and how they produce.

What Marx and Engels overlooked was the additional requirement for empowerment; that is, that disadvantaged groups must have confidence in their ability to manage their own affairs and increase their levels of democratic participation. People must develop a belief that they actually can collectively control their lives. People need to have a sense of their own history and society; they need to overcome pessimism and fatalism; they need to see new possibilities for human societies. Underlying all these requirements for empowerment is the principle of *human agency*. Indeed, human agency is central to human rights. When people are abused and oppressed, when they are denied knowledge, when they are starving and have no political or associational freedoms, their ability to be agents of their own destiny is denied (see Ignatieff, 2001). In a philosophical sense, empowerment enables people to fulfil themselves as humans.

This philosophical view is based on arguments about human needs or 'what it is to be human'. In fact, there are dimensions to humanness. First, in order to survive, humans require sustenance and maintenance: food, water, shelter, clothing and protection from physical harm. Physical survival is a necessary condition of being human, but it is not sufficient. Doyal and Gough (1991:69) point out that humans also have to be able to participate in a cultural form of life. In practice, this means that they must have the physical capacity to interact with fellow humans over sustained periods in ways that are valued and reinforced. For this, humans need to be able to reflect critically upon their situation and to change the rules of their social environment. Doyal and Gough term this 'critical autonomy'. They argue that critical autonomy comprises cognitive and emotional competence and the political freedom to participate in democratic political processes.

In a similar vein, Nussbaum and Sen (1993) have argued for what is known as the 'capabilities approach'. Most simply, this approach considers the importance of the capabilities that people need to have to lead dignified autonomous lives. To the idea of capabilities we can add Goulet's and Maslow's views of what it takes to have human fulfilment. Goulet (1985) argues that, as well as physical survival and autonomy, humans need a sense of self-esteem, dignity and self-worth. Maslow (1962) argues that humans need a sense of fulfilment and what he calls 'self-actualisation'. These dimensions – physical survival, personal autonomy and the capacity and environment for fulfilment – must be considered in any discussion of ways of ensuring human empowerment.

Freire (1972) suggests that humans can be fulfilled only when they are liberated from oppression. This requires a critical awareness of the world in which they live and their role as agents in this world, and they must also be prepared to act upon this critical awareness (education for liberation). He points out that control over decision making must also include control over problem-posing. That is, ordinary people must be able to identify problems as they see them, and not as selected by those in power. Control over problem-posing can be even more important than control over problem solving. Freire developed the term **conscientisation** to describe the process by which people discover the meaning of humanity. Conscientisation is a change of consciousness, producing an accurate, realistic awareness of one's place in nature and society. It includes the capacity to analyse society and one's place in it, to compare one's own position with the positions of others and to envision and act upon logical programs for transformation.

It should now be clear that human fulfilment and empowerment are inseparable. They both require access to resources, knowledge, decision making and enriching social relationships. They both rest on notions of freedom from material deprivation, ignorance and alienation. They both assume that people are able to explore their intellectual and emotional capabilities and have real choices in their lives. Ultimately, real choices can occur only in a thoroughly democratised society in which people are free from ignorance and can participate in all aspects of social life.

Participation

One of the defining features of community development is that it is a bottom-up, participatory form of development. However, like empowerment, participation is a loaded word, with implied meanings and assumptions of its intrinsic benefits (Cornwall, 2008). In this section we consider the forms of participation and suggest some cautions in developing participatory programs.

Forms of participation

To appreciate the role of participatory approaches it is important to understand that the idea of participation does not rest on one unitary process. Participatory processes have been developed for instrumental purposes, such as to obtain 'buy-in' to policy changes and to bring about satisfactory outcomes in a planning process, but they are also ends in themselves (Taylor & Mayo, 2008). They are important, of course, for validating the contribution to society of people who are marginalised and disadvantaged.

A number of commentators have pointed out that there are different forms and levels of participation and different reasons for developing participatory programs (Cornwall, 2008; Cooke & Kothari, 2001; Smith, 1998; Pretty, 1995; Eade & Williams, 1995; Arnstein, 1969). The work of Arnstein (1969), in particular, has been influential in setting out 'a ladder of participation' that ranges from non-participation (therapy and manipulation) to tokenism (including informing and consulting) to citizen power (including partnership and citizen control). From a community development perspective, we can begin by identifying forms of participation on a continuum (see table 5.1), moving between four positions in a similar way to which partnerships between the state and community can be conceptualised (see chapter 4, table 4.1). First, at one end of the continuum there is participation as *manipulation*, whereby agendas are set externally and so-called consultation is tokenistic. Community development practitioners are only too aware of situations in which participation is a pretence, where 'community representatives' might sit on official boards but are unelected and have no power (Cornwall, 2008). Second, there is *consultation*, whereby agendas and plans are set externally, but authorities allow for comment. While there might be some modification of original plans, for example, authorities have no obligation to respond to people's views. Third, participation can mean *partnership*, whereby, for example, people might take the initiative in proposing a program and work with government and business in developing it. Finally, participation can involve *self-mobilisation and ownership* of the whole process by those who are affected. As Pretty (1995) and Cornwall (2008) argue, self-mobilisation may or may not involve challenging existing distributions of wealth and power.

Table 5.1 *Forms of participation*

Participation as manipulation	Participation as consultation	Participation as partnership	Participation as self-mobilisation and ownership
Externally set agendas Tokenistic communication with the community	Agendas and plans set externally Authorities allow for comment but have no obligation to respond	Communities take the initiative in proposing a program and work with government and business to develop it	Communities initiate and own the process

Many factors influence how participation works in practice. For example, in regard to participation as a means, even participation based on the most transformational of intentions can meet a dead end when it is hijacked by special interest groups, or when 'intended beneficiaries' choose not to take part because they foresee no useful outcome (Cornwall, 2008). From a community development perspective it is important to be clear about who participates. There might only be a small group of people involved in the full participation process (identifying a project, setting up a process for participation and seeing the project through to fruition), while other community members come and go, participating only at certain stages. That is, there might only be a few people involved at a deep and full level of participation, but many more involved at a shallow level (Cornwall, 2008). It is important for community practitioners to be sensitive as to who actually is involved and understand how governments can claim that there is 'full' participation of 'stakeholders' when in practice only a few people are involved at a deep and broad level and they are not necessarily representative of all 'stakeholders'. They are, as Cornwall (2008) notes, de facto representatives.

Non-participation

An argument presented in this book is that participation and empowerment are pivotal to democratic societies and community development. However, it is important that we consider a critical dilemma in participation and the quest for empowerment. The dilemma is that some people do not wish to participate in civil society. For example, they do not want to become involved in decision making or participate in collective control of local resources. Many people are quite happy to let others control their lives and take responsibility for the workings of and activities in their communities. The desire not to be involved in decision making or other community activities must be taken seriously, lest we slip into a 'dictatorship' over participation. It is important to consider people's reasons for remaining outside community processes.

In an informative discussion about this issue, Goulet (1985:144) refers to the argument that people find it satisfying to take part in decisions only within a narrow sphere of activity in which they have had experience or feel competent. When people lack confidence or have no immediate experience or interest in an issue at hand, they may be happy to transfer responsibility to others, especially those whom they perceive to be above them in a hierarchy. In addition, many people just do not feel that they have the time to get involved in the community, particularly when they see that such involvement is time consuming.

Some people do not participate in decision-making processes because they see involvement as a sham. This is particularly so in regard to participation whereby mainstream politics is involved. An inquiry in 2006 into the state of democracy in Britain, the Power Inquiry, revealed a profound disengagement with political parties and the electoral system. So-called community consultation, for example, is sometimes pseudo-participation (participation as manipulation) whereby the views of the community are sought mainly to legitimate decisions made by those in power. Similarly, there are many anecdotes about community consultation programs in Australia in which community representatives have sat on committees in the belief that their views were being taken seriously by powerful decision makers, only to realise in retrospect that they were manipulated by group pressure and hidden agendas. Such experiences have led some community development workers to reflect on how co-option takes place, and how people are more likely to go along with unpalatable decisions if they feel they have been part of a 'democratic' decision-making process.

Withdrawal from both national and local politics can be understood in the context of the general political environment in late capitalist societies, such as exists in Australia.

Responses

How can activists, community development workers and those arguing for full democracy respond to these arguments? Three points need to be made.

- Participation requires 'power to' – that is, power to 'do something', to lead a life of one's own choice: a life that is of value to the individual. Without removal of the sources of 'unfreedom' a person cannot have real freedom and participation is tokenistic (Sen, 1999). From a community development perspective, it is important to be able to identify the sources of freedom, such as having the time and energy to be involved in a community or political event, or the capability to plan one's life and engage in critical reflection. We need to be convinced that all efforts have been made to ensure that involvement in decision-making processes is both possible and meaningful and is not a sham.
- It is important to remember that theoretical understandings, experience and involvement in action all combine to set the ground for commitment to collective participation. We need to ensure that people have, and believe that they have, the knowledge and confidence to participate. The more knowledge, experience and power you actually have, and the more you see the possibility of changing your lot in life, the more likely you are to be involved. Held and Pollitt (1986:1) point out that, 'Not surprisingly, perhaps, those closest to both power and privilege are the ones who have most interest in and are most favourable to political life.'
- People must always be given the choice as to the extent to which they participate in decisions that affect their lives. As Goulet (1985:168–9) puts it,

    > if a population, after having been respectfully confirmed and consulted about changes affecting its vital future, chooses to delegate its responsibilities to its own hierarchical leaders, so be it. People will not have something imposed on them by leaders not of their choosing or, at least, tacitly accepted by them ... [This choice is based on] the desirability of respecting the preferences of a populace, whatever these may be.

Empowerment in practice

In this section we consider the everyday practices of empowerment and community development's role in empowerment. To begin with, there is an argument that people cannot be empowered by others; they can only empower themselves. In one sense, of course, this is quite true. However, this is not to argue that others cannot assist or facilitate the empowerment of others. They can do so, but with two very important provisos. First, effective facilitation requires humility. Because working with and for communities requires mutuality and trust, relationships must be built on a commitment to shared learning and mutual respect. It is not a matter of 'a knight in shining armour' turning up one day to 'empower the locals'. This point can be linked to the second proviso, which concerns the question of whether facilitators take a deficit-based approach or an asset-based approach. A **deficit-based approach** treats communities as if they have no resources, capabilities, knowledge, skills or social capital – as if they are 'blank slates'. An **asset-based approach** accepts that all these attributes exist in a community in various ways. It involves understanding attributes and working with communities to develop these, while at the same time offering, when appropriate, additional resources, knowledge and skills.

Understanding power in a given context enables community groups to develop appropriate strategies for the contexts in which they are working. For example, in their activities, community development workers need to be sensitive to the many forms of power based on coercion and consent that are manifested in beliefs, values, language, practices, relationships and everyday processes. In their everyday activities, they can raise people's consciousness of their rights and help to develop new ways of thinking about situations by prefiguring other, more equal, social relationships. They can analyse how power relations are developed and maintained, and challenge assumptions about the apparent natural right of dominant groups to have control over the lives of others. Community development workers can also help communities gain control of resources and develop real options for their members. This means ensuring access to information and, when appropriate, to interpreters.

Signs of empowerment

Following are two checklists that community development workers could use when analysing the extent to which the communities are empowered. Do the community members have power in regard to:

- identifying their needs as they see them?
- identifying their assets, including skills, knowledge and resources?
- how they utilise assets, including skills, knowledge and resources?
- developing plans for their future?
- the way they obtain their income (for example, the type of job)?
- their financial resources in general (for example, adequate to needs)?
- decision making that affects them?
- the appropriate education for their needs?
- the use of commonly owned resources?
- real choices in life direction and lifestyles?

Do community members:

- have access to open and democratic community structures?
- have optimum and meaningful participation?
- believe in the right to control their own destiny?
- have the physical health and energy to participate?
- have a real voice of their own, with the right to speak in their own words and be listened to?
- have access to different sources of reliable information?
- trust each other and share resources?
- have access to resources that positively affect their wellbeing?
- have control of their own assets?

- collectively decide on and prioritise community needs, issues and problems?
- collectively decide how to resolve needs, issues and problems?
- have self-esteem?
- have reason to believe that participation in decision-making processes is meaningful and productive?
- work and live in non-authoritarian environments?
- have the right not to participate in community decisions and processes?

In a modest sense, we can identify indicators of whether communities increase their control of resources over a period of time. For example:

- We can monitor whether community needs are being met, such as through shorter waiting lists for childcare or increased numbers of playgroups.
- We can examine increases in government budgets.
- We can identify the effects of community participation, such as a change in policy.
- We can identify increases in participation in international networks, such as the establishment of a 'sister cities' program with a city in a developing country.
- We can see whether communities have more information at their disposal: for example, when a community that has learned of government plans to establish a power station in its locality has access to researchers who undertake social, economic and environmental impact studies.

For feminists, the indicators of empowerment are whether women have control over their own bodies and their own resources and are able to set their own agendas based on their knowledge, their lived experience and their language. As indicated in chapter 3, there are also ways of assessing levels of participation and trust through, for example, research to measure the levels of social capital (see Yates & Jochum, 2003; Onyx & Bullen, 2000; Putnam, 2000). To conclude this section we consider an example of modest empowerment.

BRANLEA COMMUNITY ARTS

The council of Branlea, a small regional city, has decided to relocate the shire offices to an area where they have more room to build and more car-parking spaces.

The local community arts group has been operating in a large garage behind the house of one of its members. This garage has been the venue for meetings, storing of artworks and files, and even exhibitions of the members' work. On hearing about the move of the shire offices, the group decides to see if there is any interest in applying for space in the old shire offices. They agree that securing such a space would not only benefit their members but also the wider artists' community in Branlea by demonstrating the value of art to the community. Several members visit their local councillor to see if they can have a space in the old offices rent-free. They are encouraged to submit a proposal to the council. Buoyed by the possibilities, the members decide to share the writing of the proposal, drawing on the group's existing expertise. They work with much enthusiasm to prepare a submission, asking all those who have been involved in the arts group over the past 15 years to sign a letter of support. They fully expect a positive response to their request.

Many weeks after submitting their proposal, the group receives a formal letter stating that their proposal has been unsuccessful. At first the group is despondent, but after talking to community arts organisations in other parts of the state, they decide to continue their efforts. They rewrite their proposal but again it is unsuccessful. Undeterred, they decide to campaign for an artists' space in the council elections, bringing in several well-known Australian artists to support their cause. They are joined by the other artist groups in the city and, after a rowdy meeting in the town hall, all the groups decided to work together, demanding even more space. Together the arts groups argue that the shire offices are a community asset and should be owned by the community. Senior arts students in the local schools join the campaign, suggesting that an arts precinct be established in the old shire offices. This vision of an arts precinct galvanised the community of Branlea. Meetings are held. People speak positively about the role of the arts in the shire and they share ideas and plan new exhibitions. Just before the local elections, the arts group is informed that an arts precinct, with all the features requested by the community and more, would be developed. In their election platform all the candidates support the arts precinct. The test, of course, is whether the new council will follow through with the promises made. To everyone's delight, 18 months later the arts precinct is up and running, offering a vibrant location for a thriving arts scene.

In what ways was the success of the Branlea community arts group a case study of empowerment? The group collectively decided on its needs and was able to tap into an opportunity when it arose. It identified its assets and resources and developed a vision with the broader community using democratic processes. The group argued that shire offices were community assets and should be owned by the community. The group's success validated its views that the arts are important in all communities. When interviewed, group members felt that they had learnt the power of trust and working together. One person commented that 'believing that you can win' is essential. At the same time, they understood that their success was based on their ability to develop different strategies and seize opportunities.

Community capacity building

While the term 'empowerment' still has explanatory and strategic value, it has somewhat slipped out of use in official policy and planning rhetoric. In its place the terms **community capacity building** and **community building** are used, and these are sometimes linked with **neighbourhood renewal** and **rural renewal**. In Australia, these terms are sometimes used interchangeably. What is interesting about the use and popularity of these terms is how they silence or sideline issues of power. In *community capacity building* and *community building*, for example, the use of the term 'community' draws our attention to place and, while it often it refers specifically to communities or neighbourhoods that are disadvantaged or deemed to be rundown, the discourse of community capacity building rarely mentions capacity in the sense of empowerment or eliminating 'obstacles to unfreedom' (Sen, 1999) and instead tends to focus on training and on those individuals volunteering to strengthen their community. Capacity or community building projects require community members, groups and community organisations to develop their capacity to operate more 'effectively' and/or achieve certain ends.

Is it possible to have community building, neighbourhood renewal and rural renewal without any capacity building? One answer is yes – as in the case of a government supplying funds for a community hall. But a community hall may offer a (modest) way of increasing a community's capacity by providing a location for meetings, and so enhancing levels of social capital. Most community building, neighbourhood renewal and rural renewal projects involve some form of capacity building as a process through which communities increase their competence to function better and/or achieve specified goals. It is therefore important to understand the meanings, approaches and frameworks, processes and indicators of capacity building.

Capacity building projects

Capacity building has been in vogue internationally since the beginning of the 1990s. For example, capacity building features in many international aid programs, including the United Nations Development Programme (UNDP) and those of the World Bank, and in many state-government programs aiming to reinvigorate rural communities. Its appeal lies in its contrast with traditional welfare and aid programs, which have been donor-driven and input-oriented. At their best, capacity building practices promise long-term self-determination and self-management, respect for local knowledge, and local participation and control (United Nations Development Programme, 1997).

Most simply, capacity building involves increasing the capacities of individuals, communities, community organisations and governments to do things. Increasing capacity involves changes in structures, resources, behaviour and skills. Chaskin et al. (2001) point out that the term 'capacity' includes the ideas of both containing and ability. Capacity implies that an individual, group or community can act in particular ways. It has the powers to do certain things. Chaskin et al. (2001:7) define capacity building in terms of

> the interaction of human capital, organizational resources and social capital existing within a given community that can be leveraged to solve collective problems and improve and maintain the well-being of that community. It may operate through informal social processes and/or organized efforts by individuals, organizations, and social networks that exist among them and the larger systems of which the community is a part.

There are a number of ways that we can think about and categorise approaches to capacity building.

- First, capacity building can be seen as a means to something else – a means to a specified end (Eade, 1997). There are different manifestations of this approach. For example, capacity building can refer to specific approaches, strategies and methodologies used for the purpose of improving the performance of individuals, communities, community organisations and even countries to carry out particular functions (see Morgan, 1998). 'Improving performance' usually involves increasing abilities through developing skills, knowledge, attitudes, values, relationships, conditions and behaviours that enable groups and individuals to generate benefits for stakeholders over time. Morgan (1998) emphasises

the importance of 'performance monitoring' in capacity building programs; that is, of being able to identify increased capacity. The importance of changing values and behaviour is also assumed in international programs that emphasise the development of skills and values competencies so that individuals have the capacities to implement policies developed by governments or non-government funding agencies. Here, changing individuals so that they can function well in the existing conditions is the goal, rather than working with communities for the purpose of collective control to change these conditions.
- Second, capacity building can be an end in itself. This approach rests on a more philosophical idea of capacity. Here, capacity building is understood as a generic phenomenon that is important for all human endeavour, not just endeavours by disadvantaged individuals and groups. It is more important to continually extend and strengthen capacities in general than to develop specific capacities for specific purposes. This leads us to the third way of thinking about capacity building.
- The third way begins with the questions: who needs their capacity developed and who is involved? These questions might seem naive, but are important because the implied answer is that disadvantaged communities need their capacity developed, and by outsiders, who do not need their capacity developed. But it can also mean that it is the external agencies that need their capacities developed, such as in the situation of post-disaster recovery (see Kenny, 2007). Capacity building here is one-way. Mostly, this approach involves prompting, stimulating and training by outside agents who build capacities *for* communities, not *with* communities. This deficit approach to development is problematic from a community development perspective.
- Fourth, it is important to remember that capacity building can and does take place without any intervention from outside the community. Communities can do their own internal self-capacity building. For example, capacity building in Indigenous communities can mean relearning traditional ways of doing things (Leggett, 2009). Unfortunately, many aid agencies and governments forget this fact. From a community development perspective, it is important to remember that intervention to assist and facilitate democratic capacity building should only take place if a community requests assistance.
- Fifth, thinking about capacity building requires identifying whether the approach is top down or bottom up. O'Shaughnessy (1999:5–6) argues that the top-down approach improves people's capacity to carry out preordained functions and objectives more effectively and efficiently. Here, capacity building is 'designed at the top and delivered to the targets whose capacity is seen to require development' (O'Shaughnessy, 1999:7). This approach is manifested in many capacity building projects of the UNDP and the World Bank. The UNDP has identified capacity building as a way of levering scarce resources and reacting to changing needs of partners in developing countries (United Nations Development Programme, 1997). The World Bank has identified effective structural adjustment of labour markets as a key indicator of successful capacity building. People might participate in project development but as a means of assisting project designers rather than as an end in itself. These approaches are both top down and instrumentalist.
- The sixth approach involves a bottom-up orientation, or what O'Shaughnessy (1997) calls the democratic approach to capacity building. This approach is evident in the

capacity building programs of Oxfam. Eade (1997:2) locates Oxfam's approach to capacity building in the framework of its commitment to the right of all people to an equitable share in the world's resources and to be the *authors of their own development*. This requires strengthening people's capacity to determine their own values and priorities, and to act on these. Eade argues that capacity building is an approach to development rather than a set of discrete or pre-packaged interventions.

- In contrast to approaches that distinguish between bottom-up and top-down orientations is an one that starts with the premise that all parties involved – including governments, funding bodies and community members – share a need to improve their capacities; that is, mutual capacity building. This approach tends to see capacity building as a multidirectional, multidimensional process (see Eade, 1997). It can be initiated democratically or bureaucratically. It can be thought of as the mutual capacity building approach.
- This brings us to the eighth way of thinking about capacity building, based on whether the approach is a deficit-based or an asset-based one. The deficit-based approach begins not with the capacities that a community has, but with what it does not have. This approach is consistent with the instrumentalist top-down approach. In contrast, the asset-based approach begins with the many assets that already exist in the community. As Eade (1997) points out, people always have many existing capacities. To ignore these is disrespectful and it can leave communities even more vulnerable.
- The final category for making sense of capacity building is whether it deals only with a specific project and identifies specific capacities needed for this project, or if it is based in a more holistic approach that locates the project in the wider economic, social and political context, and involves identifying how these contextual factors can facilitate or hinder the capacity building. For example, Eade (1997) states how capacity building cannot be abstracted from social, economic and political environments. It is important to understand how environments can hinder or facilitate the opportunities for acting on existing capacities and developing new capacities. From this perspective, capacity is meaningless without appropriate resources and structural conditions. Below is a vignette, drawn from several cases, of an instrumentalist, top-down, one-way deficit-based approach to capacity building.

A DEFICIT-BASED APPROACH TO CAPACITY BUILDING

A funding agency is concerned about young people using their leisure time in 'destructive' ways, such as graffiti writing. It provides a grant to develop and implement a youth recreation plan. The funding agency does not believe that the community has the capacity to develop and implement a plan and so requires as a condition of the grant that community 'leaders' attend training courses at which they will be provided with the skills to undertake the project. This scenario assumes that existing leisure activities are not desirable and it assumes that the community needs a formal recreation plan. The community is conceptualised as an empty vessel, lacking existing capacities to organise its own recreation. It does not start with community views, existing capacities or community ownership of the project.

Criticisms of capacity building

Most Australian states have now adopted policies supporting capacity building or community building programs, and community practitioners are now reflecting on their experiences of these programs, many of them quite critically. For example, the top-down deficit approach to capacity building can leave communities denuded of confidence and community pride. The 'short-termism' of most government funding programs undercuts the possibility of long-term and sustainable self-development. As Cauchi and Murphy (2004) point out, the process of understanding a community takes time. Cauchi and Murphy also reflect on the complexity of community self-determination and lament the failure of the 'community builders' to understand these complexities, pointing out the gap between the rhetoric of community and capacity building and the 'successes'. They contend that government funding bodies seem more interested in efficient fiscal management than the ability of funded agencies to develop community capacity for self-determination.

Ife (2010) comments critically on how capacity building is seen as a linear process, as if capacity building proceeds in an orderly, linear fashion that is planned in advance by external experts who know what capacity is to be built, where a community should be headed and how to 'get there'. In contrast, Ife points out, community development is an organic process that is messy and contradictory, and is more likely to be cyclical than lineal. Equally problematic for Ife is the selection of what capacities are deemed to be desirable, such as the capacity for better management and for constructing stronger institutions. He points out that capacities to engage in political action, to take responsibility for the local environment, for cultural expression and for safeguarding human rights are usually excluded from this list. Mowbray (2004) has critiqued the Community Capacity Building Initiative in Victoria for its failure to attend to its socioeconomic context. He identifies the ideological opportunism evident in the top-down approach of the Victorian government and its 'cut-rate, short-term, boosterist' frame of reference.

Another problem with the idea of capacity building in communities is the simplistic and unexamined use of the term 'community'. Smith (2004) discusses the difficulties that arise when there is a mismatch of assumptions about what constitutes a community. For example, in remote Australia, a community development worker might work with people who define their communities as a 'clan' with little reference to place, while government funds are allocated to a community based on location. As Smith points out, community building involves joint problem solving and equitable access to resources by the community. But what is the community? Does it comprise all the people living in a local area or all the people who live in a wider region but identify with a particular clan?

Capacity building in practice

In understanding capacity building in a practical sense, we can see that it involves a range of processes and mechanisms that are used to develop capacities. Below is a list of key elements, which draws on the work of Eade (1997:36). Capacity building involves

- identifying and accessing opportunities
- monitoring the context

Processes and practices

- developing a strategy
- drawing on existing experiences, skills and capacities
- drawing on existing resources
- providing knowledge, workshops and training
- developing bonding social capital
- developing bridging social capital
- learning problem-solving skills
- learning advocacy skills
- working on projects with governments and/or business
- learning organisational, planning and evaluation skills
- learning political acumen
- developing and implementing strategies
- having evidence that these strategies can work
- establishing new community organisations
- learning financial skills.

These elements can be understood within three frameworks, as set out in table 5.2.

Table 5.2 *Capacity building framework*

Infrastructure (physical capital)	Skills and knowledge (human and cultural capital – public sphere)	Social capital (networks)
Material resources: for example, buildings, furniture, computers, printing, paper	Examples are: • knowledge • democratic processes • open information • Internet • confidence	Examples are: • bridging and bonding • solidarity and linkages
Non-material resources: for example, money, credit, policies, practices, active public sphere	Examples are the capacity to: • define own needs • prioritise goals • identify facilitating and hindering factors • implement actions • problem solve • advocate • communicate (write reports and submissions) • run meetings • do public speaking	Examples are: • reciprocity • trust • mutuality • tolerance of diversity

Capacity building and community development

Capacity building seems to be new and innovative because it is contrasted with the dominant development paradigms located in the welfarist or aid traditions, in which professionals provide services to poor and disadvantaged people in a top-down fashion. Importantly, the discussion of capacity building above shows that there can be overlap between capacity building programs and community development: for example, where there is commitment to capacity building programs that ensure a community's self-determination and sustainability and where external facilitators in capacity building programs focus on making their role redundant. Capacity building is also consistent with community development when it uses the self-capacity-building approach, the bottom-up democratic approach, the assets-based approach, the holistic approach and the two-way and mutual capacity building approach. An example of the way that the mutual asset-based approach might work is when a doctor provides paramedical skills for an isolated Indigenous community and, in turn, is herself trained in the administration of local herbal medicine.

However, while there is significant overlap, capacity building and community development are not synonymous. This is for several interrelated reasons. Unlike community development, much capacity building is one way and top down, involving external experts making decisions about what is best for a community, what a community's goals should be and how a community should reach these goals. Community development begins with a commitment to community control, involving members of a community collectively defining their goals, needs and priorities. From this standpoint, it is not a matter of external experts foisting capacity or community building on a community from outside, but more a matter of community members deciding on what they might need from others, if anything, to assist them.

Moreover, the role of a community development worker is not to make decisions for the community. It is to facilitate community power and responsibility in regard to what is best for a community and decisions about how to achieve its goals. Some capacity building starts from a deficit base. Often the focus of capacity building is on how individual failures hinder the development of a specific project, without any reference to the wider context and structural, economic and political factors impeding opportunities. When individual failures are seen as weakening community capacity, then capacity building programs will focus on behavioural and attitudinal changes. This in turn can mean building the capacity of individuals to help themselves, to 'pull themselves up by their bootstraps', so to speak. Community development is about collective endeavour, involving people working together to share information and resources and to develop actions that will benefit the community as a whole.

Given the issues in undertaking capacity building projects and the similarities and differences between capacity building and community development, should community development practitioners steer clear of capacity building? The answer to this question is no, but with several caveats. In deciding whether to get involved in any capacity building program, it is important to examine the program in order to unpack the meanings and approaches to capacity building. Capacity building can certainly be compatible with community development, but it is incumbent upon community development practitioners to check this. Below is a list of principles for a community development approach to capacity building, a set of questions to ask that could aid community development practitioners when deciding whether or not to engage in a capacity building project, and a list of capacity building indicators.

Capacity building principles

As previously discussed, from a community development perspective, what is of particular interest in capacity building is a collective and democratic approach. There are a number of ways of thinking about this. It is worth first thinking about the principles of the collective and democratic approach to capacity building. These begin with a commitment to:

- community self-determination
- making a positive difference to the community
- community ownership: for example, the community identifying its issues and priorities
- identifying a community's assets and existing capacities, not its deficits
- human rights for women, men and children
- the view that there are many starting points for needs and capacities
- people's capacity to determine their own values and priorities and to act on these
- ongoing learning
- developing the capacities of all involved, including the capacities of relevant sections of government and funding agencies
- all forms of sustainability, not just economic and financial
- working with people willing to be involved.

When undertaking a capacity building project, some key questions could be asked, as listed in table 5.3.

Table 5.3 *Questions for capacity building*

What do we mean by capacity?
For example, knowledge, skills, structures, resources, networks
Whose capacities are we talking about?
For example, individuals, groups, funding agencies, government
For what purposes are we undertaking the capacity building program? And who decides this purpose?
What capacities and assets do we already have?
How do we build on these?
What new capacities and assets do we need?
How will we get these?
Will our project really enhance the community?
What evidence do we have that it will?
Who will work on getting this?
What resources and structures do we need?
How will we get these?
Who will work on getting these?
How will we decide what to do?
What evidence do we have that what we want to do will work?
Who will decide?

Table 5.4 presents one community organisation's schedule for a series of workshops that indicate how a community might develop a capacity building program. Of course, each stage involved review and a feedback loop whereby participants would reflect on the previous workshop and add or delete topics for discussion and even change direction if necessary.

Table 5.4 *Fourteen workshops for capacity building*

Workshop 1	To discuss ways that communities could be better and where people want to go (for example, the goals and aims)
Workshops 2–3	To identify the ways of getting there and what is needed (for example, resources, skills, structures)
Workshop 4	To identify assets in the community (for example, resources, skills, structures)
Workshop 5	To identify assets in the community that do not exist (for example, resources, skills, structures, interest in the project)
Workshop 6	To identify facilitating and hindering factors (for example, government policies, regulations)
Workshop 7	To work out ways of accessing facilitating factors and overcoming hindering factors
Workshop 8	To prioritise what is needed
Workshop 9	To draw up an action plan: what are alternative ways of getting there?
Workshops 10–13	To monitor the action plan and identify assets in the community that do not exist (for example, resources, skills, structures)
Workshops 14	To evaluate the project

Indicators of increased capacity

Eade (1997) provides a list of changes that communities might use to indicate an increase in capacity. In general they are subjective but, as Eade argues, they are no less important because of this and because they are not readily measured according to objective external indicators. How people actually feel is very important for sustainable change. The indicators include:

- increased collective and individual confidence in assessing and finding solutions to social and political problems
- increased participation in decision making, especially among those who were previously excluded
- increased ability to make the connections between day-to-day living conditions and the wider socio-political and economic context
- greater ability to organise to press the authorities for better living conditions or respect for civil rights
- better knowledge of other relevant organisations (for example, NGOs)
- collective acquisition of specific skills, together with increased political awareness and skills in social analysis

- better social relations within the community or organisation
- improved conflict-prevention and conflict-resolution skills
- higher self-esteem and an ability to challenge negative stereotypes
- more awareness of others' needs and greater willingness to cooperate (Eade, 1997:83).

We may note similarities between these indicators and the indicators of empowerment, demonstrating the overlap between the two.

The social inclusion agenda

As discussed in chapter 2, social inclusion has been one of the most important policy developments and government interventions in the last few years. In this chapter we consider social inclusion from the perspective of community development practices. In chapter 2 we commented that, notwithstanding the ways that the social inclusion agenda can acknowledge the importance of redressing inequalities and providing opportunities for the most disadvantaged groups and draws attention to the obstacles to individual fulfilment that exist in society, it also carries with it some quite problematic assumptions and approaches. These include how social inclusion is conceived as a requiring top-down intervention, the focus on individuals, the homogenisation of the putative mainstream of society, the binary conception of insiders/outsiders upon which social inclusion agendas are based and the emphasis on paid work as the path to social inclusion. We also commented on the possible ideological functions of the social inclusion agenda. The question we introduce in this chapter is how social inclusion might be understood and responded to within a community development practice framework. As a preface to the following discussion it is important to note that the concept 'social inclusion', as it is used in social policy today, does not always fit comfortably in the community development lexicon, in the same way as, say, 'participation' or even that overused concept 'empowerment'. The question 'are you socially excluded?' calls for the qualifier 'from what?' The answer to the question varies. Rather than starting from the insiders/outsiders distinction that identifies the disadvantaged as a 'ghettoised risk category' (Daly & Silver, 2008), lacking their own social networks and sense of belonging, it is important to understand that people can be simultaneously both socially included and socially excluded, depending on the group and the context.

A more useful starting point is the concept of human fulfilment. As indicated in chapter 1, human fulfilment requires human dignity and a sense of self-worth and belonging. In some ways this is consistent with the conventional social inclusion agenda. However, where the community development approach is different from the conventional social inclusion agendas is that the meanings of, and strategies for, human fulfilment are not assumed or defined in a top-down manner. There are different ways of thinking about fulfilment and many paths to fulfilment, and 'social inclusion through paid employment' may not be one of these – for example, in the case of self-funded retirees – let alone the main one.

One of the appeals of social inclusion is that it suggests ways of ensuring commitment to society and agreement with the values of mainstream society. Much of the policy discussion identifies having a job, a good education, appropriate housing, quality social services, a supportive family and cohesive communities as providing the environment for social inclusion (Australian Government, 2009b). However, there are different ways of facilitating social inclusion and 'buy-in'. For example, buy-in to society in general can be the effect of empowerment and collective self-determination. Collective endeavour, empowerment and self-determination, of course, are principles of community development. And while these principles can mean commitment to a local group or community, at the same time they can also mean disagreement and resistance to mainstream structures and values. That is, in the context of empowerment and collective self-determination there is more room for a diversity of viewpoints and activities than in social inclusion agendas. Empowerment and collective self-determination lead us to a different way of thinking about social inclusion. From this community development orientation, social inclusion comes about when people are active citizens, and when they are not the objects of top-down policies that define who is socially excluded and how they should be socially included. It comes about when people define what they want to be included in, and how. Buy-in to the activities of society or its component parts is more likely to come about when people have real control over where they want to belong and when they identify what resources they need to feel socially included than when a government decides this for them. Moreover, the choices people make about these dimensions of social inclusion change over time. They are not 'once and for all' or linear.

Thus, the approach to social inclusion in the community development context is quite different to the approach within a formal government policy framework. For example, it could start with the questions 'What makes the people in this community feel involved?' 'Why do they become involved?' Community members will answer these questions, of course, and will probably give different answers in different situations. For example, answers to the question of why people are involved in their society or community include:

- because I feel comfortable
- because I feel welcome
- because we trust each other
- because I am valued
- because it is worthwhile
- because I can contribute
- because I can learn there.

A research project investigating the background to active citizenship in six countries including Australia asked people involved in community organisations to identify the most important factors that influenced their decision to join a particular community organisation (Brown, Onyx & Kenny, 2008). Of the 1610 respondents, 44.2 per cent replied 'to help those in need', 36.3 per cent replied 'to learn new things' and 33.5 per cent replied 'to meet different people'. An additional question, 'What is the most important aspect of community involvement for you?', was answered by 1573 respondents of which 53.1 per cent stated that it was 'to work with others to make a better world' and 20 per cent responded that such involvement helped them to be 'to be aware of what is happening in the community'. However, this data does not probe directly for an answer to the question of how far

Australians feel they are able to have a say on important community issues. Such data is available in the Australian Bureau of Statistics 2006 *General Survey Data Report,* which notes that just 29 per cent of a representative sample of Australians aged 18 and over said that they felt that they were able to have a say on communal issues of importance.

These answers suggest that obtaining buy-in to society is a much more complex process than creating policies to improve employment rates and employability, increase educational opportunities and outcomes, and improve housing. The answers indicate that the social and group settings in which people operate are important for whether people are involved or committed. They also suggest the importance of bridging social capital. Situations in which there are high degrees of trust, mutuality and openness are more likely to attract people who want to and can be socially included. Thus, social inclusion is more likely to occur when people are valued and can see good reason for participating than when they feel they are outsiders. This is not to argue that subjective attachment to a group or society is sufficient for social inclusion to occur. However, it is to argue that indicators of social inclusion constructed around expert calculations of what should be important for individuals provide only a partial understanding of social inclusion.

Strategy development

Although rarely noted, underlying much of the work involved in empowerment and capacity building, and indeed much of the activity of community development work, is the idea of **strategy development**. Strategic planning can be a formal process, required for the purpose of receiving funds, or it can be a more informal process. For example, strategic planning in community development can involve formally identifying ways of dealing with racial tensions or informally developing ways of saving lives and property during a bushfire. It can involve developing a strategic plan for a whole organisation or it can be an activity undertaken by a small part of a community or organisation to develop a strategic plan to provide nutritious food at a local school or to attract more students to a literacy program in a neighbourhood house.

The pervasiveness of strategic thinking

Strategic thinking in the form of thinking about and planning what we want and how will we get there is a central part of contemporary human existence, as pointed out by Weber (1946) in the twentieth century. We are engaged in strategic planning and decision making on a daily basis. For example, a strategic plan might include weighing up options and ramifications when we have conflicting demands on our time – such as whether to attend a community meeting, a work meeting or spend the time writing a report – or it might be a matter of how to prioritise money available for the development of public-health programs when the need to employ outreach paramedics competes with the need to improve a regional hospital's facilities. Or strategic planning could just be a matter of which public transport to use when trying to reach a destination in a hurry.

An overview of recent publications on strategic planning reveals a plethora of 'how to do it' strategy manuals and analyses of strategic management in the context of organisational change, corporate planning and business plans. Government and other funding bodies are asking community organisations to prepare strategic plans, often in the context of a business plan, as a condition of funding. One view is that to be effective, community organisations should adopt the same strategic planning principles as are employed in the business for-profit sector (see Joyce & Woods, 1996; Bowman, 1990). However, from a community development perspective, of course, the principles and goals of community organisations are very different to those of for-profit enterprises.

Most discussions about the processes of strategic planning begin with the questions 'why plan?' or 'why develop a strategic plan?' Strategic planning enables communities to think about what they are doing and why, to focus their activities, to clarify their aims and objectives, and to develop ways of achieving these aims and objectives. Strategic planning is a way of thinking systematically about what we are doing in community programs and whether we are using resources effectively. But it should not be systematic in any sterile and one-dimensional way. While providing systematic analyses of situations, a strategic plan can also provide ways of responding to opportunities and for thinking creatively. Strategic planning is future-oriented, but this does not mean that strategic planners believe that they can predict or control the future in any absolute sense. For Eade and Williams (1995:406), strategic plans can set parameters by which community organisations can respond flexibly to unforeseen events. For example, well-laid plans offer a framework by which an organisation's staff can make decisions and respond flexibly to the unexpected according to agreed parameters and priorities.

However, to understand strategic planning from a community development perspective we also need to be aware of what might be identified as the 'mistake of lineality'. We have touched on the 'mistake of lineality' above. It refers to the assumption that change and development always proceed in an orderly, predictable way. As Ife (2010) points out, it is the *processes* of development and change, and who controls these, that are central to community development. Importantly, effective community development needs to operate within a world that allows for spontaneous and unexpected directions and that does not necessarily follow in an expected direction.

Also, from a community development perspective, strategic planning should also be reflexive and proactive in the sense that it is not just a (knee-jerk) reaction to things that happen to communities and community organisations. Strategic planning also involves creating new opportunities and reviewing aims and objectives to decide whether these are appropriate and, if necessary, jettisoning them. In the following section we consider five elements of strategy development that are employed in community development practice: the asset-based orientation, the activist orientation, the systematic planning for effectiveness approach, the strategic thinking approach, and the strategic questioning approach.

Elements of strategy development
The asset-based approach

In chapter 1 we introduced the distinction between the asset- and deficit-based approaches to community development. We have described a deficit approach as focusing on the problems and issues in a community. It is oriented to working with 'needy' and 'problem' communities in a way that is akin to the labelling approach to 'problem' individuals. In contrast, an asset-based approach to community development, sometimes known as *asset-based community development* (ABCD), is oriented to identifying assets in a community. The asset-based approach recognises that members of communities have skills, knowledge, talents, resources, networks and experiences that they can use to make their communities better places to live in. However, this is not to present a 'Pollyana' view of communities, which denies that communities have unmet needs, internal tensions and unresolved issues. Nor does it rest on the view that all of the resources used by communities can be generated internally. While it is important to work with assets this does not mean that the different levels of governments can abrogate their responsibilities to their constituents. What it does contend though is that community assets should never be overlooked or forgotten in strategy planning and development.

The activist approach

There is a long history of strategic thinking in the context of struggle and conflict, and social action campaigners tend to draw on this for practical insights and inspiration. One way of understanding this history is to see it through the metaphor of war (see chapter 2). The metaphor of war draws on the etymology of the concept of strategy. The English term 'strategy' is derived from the Greek word *strategos*, which means generalship or art of the general. In this approach to strategic planning, strategy involves coordination and manoeuvring of units or armies. Good strategy is a matter of outwitting competitors or enemies, and developing adroit leadership, involving an ability to 'deploy available manpower [*sic*] and other resources to best advantage' (de Wit & Meyer, 1994). The metaphor of war approach to strategic planning is also evident in Gramsci's writings on relations of power and class struggle in the 1920s and 1930s. Gramsci (1971) discusses strategy in terms of a *war of position* and a *war of movement*. For Gramsci, when bourgeois civil society is undeveloped, a frontal attack on centralised state power, or what he called a war of movement, could succeed. But where civil society is well developed, the working class must build alliances with other forces that are striving to change the existing power relations. This strategy is based on the idea of a war of position, which involves the working class building up 'a bloc of social forces cemented by a common (alternative) conception of the world' (Simon, 1991:63).

Underpinning these conceptions of strategy are ideas of leadership, strategic alliances, tactical manoeuvres and ideological struggle. These conceptions of strategy have informed many of the programs of political activist groups throughout the world, community organisers and much of the development of strategic management in business. In Australia, struggles of activist groups – green, women's, Aboriginal and Torres Strait Islanders, gay and lesbian – have often been constructed around notions of tactics and strategic alliances (see Burgmann, 1993; Baldry & Vinson, 1991). In community development theory and practice, these conceptions of strategy found expression in the work of Alinsky (1972). Alinsky was a community activist who organised around issues of disadvantage and oppression with poor communities in the USA from the 1940s until the 1970s. For Alinsky, having a good grasp of available tactics is an important attribute for community organisers and a key part of strategy development.

> Tactics means doing what you can with what you have. Tactics are those consciously deliberate acts by which human beings live with each other and deal with the world around them. In the world of give and take, tactics is the art of how to take and how to give. Always remember the first rule of power tactics: Power is not only what you have but what the enemy thinks you have (Alinsky, 1972:126–7).

Here, strategy and tactics are located in the context of a contest with enemies, manoeuvring (giving and taking) and threatening. But Alinsky's approach is also one that invokes the importance of community empowerment. A community development approach is evident in much of Alinsky's attitude to organising. His major concern was to bring people together in activist campaigns. Strategies were a means of mobilising people. As discussed in chapter 2, Alinsky worked in the USA in the 'community organising' tradition, which focuses on community deficits and external leadership and has a number of features that we would not recognise as being entirely compatible with community development today. Nevertheless, Alinsky's argument for empowerment and activism has inspired many community development practitioners since his time.

The systematic planning for effectiveness approach

In the context of increasing concern with efficiency and effectiveness of programs, community development practitioners are being urged to think more systematically about what they are doing and why they are doing it. Much of the strategic development that takes place in this context is concerned with organisational development and change. Here, strategy is thought of in terms of articulating a project's or organisation's purpose or mission, establishing aims and objectives, developing action plans in order to fulfil aims and objectives, monitoring changes and responding appropriately to the changes. The central focus of this approach is organisation. For Burkhart and Reuss (1993:x),

> all long term organisational success begins with an organisation successfully positioning itself: that is, being in a position to take advantage of a variety of critical opportunities ... Positioning is a function of all of the elements (of strategy planning) ... for the ideal organisation: clear purpose, adequate resources, enthusiasm, and commitment.

This approach draws on management texts that emphasise the need for organisations to be flexible in order to cope with the ever-changing contexts in which they operate. Carr, Hard and Trahant (1996:ix), for example, argue for the establishment of improvement-driven organisations 'that are equipped to renew themselves on a continual basis and can cultivate the habits of organisational resilience'. Hatten and Hatten (1988:xii) point out that 'effective strategic action requires an ability to respond to opportunities and to recognise the organisation's strengths relative to its competition'.

While organisational effectiveness is an important component in community development, maintaining an organisation is not an end in itself. That is, a community organisation is only a means for resourcing and skilling a community. Indeed, some of the most effective community development projects and community action have taken place through informal networks that are well organised – but do not have formal structures – with membership lists and formal decision-making and meeting structures, for example (Piven & Cloward, 1971; Alinsky, 1972). Moreover, insofar as strategic planning is located in the framework of instrumental rationality, it is important to be sensitive to how instrumentalism can fall into the trap of expecting that problems can be solved by the use of formulas and organisations managed according to set rules, procedures and plans.

The strategic thinking approach

In the **strategic thinking approach**, effective responses to all the challenges facing human beings today require not only organisational strategy and flexibility, but also a particular type of also strategic thinking, involving planning for uncertainty. Coote (1998:29) argues that thinking strategically requires planning for uncertainty, stating:

> Planning for uncertainty involves, firstly, a clear understanding of the principles that guide policy making. We may not know the shape of things to come or where we want to end up, but we can decide how we are going to travel, and why.

The emphasis on strategic thinking for uncertainty, rather than on strategic organisation, is expressed in the idea that strategic planning involves the seizing of opportunities when they arise. Understanding new conditions and identifying new ways of thinking require symbolic–analytic work and open the way to creative solutions. Joyce and Woods (1996) encourage us to think about strategic planning not as a set recipe, but as an emergent process, combining foresight, chance, incrementalist decision making and experimentation.

The strategic questioning approach

A related approach to strategy, and one that is clearly pertinent to community development, is the **strategic questioning approach**. As Peavy (1994:86), a key proponent of this approach, points out:

> We approach problems with a constantly changing body of knowledge about the issues at stake. The amount of information that is known by human beings now doubles every five years … The rapid turnover of knowledge in every field requires a new understanding of information and the way that questions relate to problems … Asking the same question today elicits a different answer than yesterday … You find one piece of information and from that piece of information new questions arise … So it goes on – discovery, new questions, new discovery, and new questions, and on and on.

Peavy argues for the use of strategic questioning as a way of developing local strategies for change. Strategic questioning involves opening ourselves up to another point of view, shifting our own ideas to take account of new information, new possibilities and new strategies for resolving problems. Peavy's idea of strategic questioning demonstrates some of the possibilities for more creative and reflexive approaches to strategic planning.

The context of community development

From a community development perspective it is important to acknowledge that there is a range of different approaches and starting points in developing strategic plans. While community development practitioners might take some pointers about strategic planning from for-profit organisations (such as ways of budgeting for strategic actions), the position taken in this book is that it is essential to distinguish between strategy planning in for-profit organisations and not-for-profit organisations. It is also useful for community development practitioners to understand the criticisms outlined above of the conventional ways of thinking about strategic planning. For example, the community development approach does not see the prime purpose of strategic planning as improving the performance of an organisation; rather, it seeks to strategise to empower communities to take collective control of and responsibility for their own development, and sometimes this will involve the development of formal organisations and sometimes it will not. It is important to remember that improving the organisation is not an end in itself. The strategic thinking and strategic questioning approaches can be very useful for community development practitioners, because community development involves problem posing, problem articulation and problem solving, and workers need symbolic–analytic skills. In addition, while any community development approach might involve monitoring organisational activities, responding to change and developing a learning culture, it is prudent not to slip into an 'ideology of progress' whereby any change is seen as progress.

Before we conclude this section, it would be helpful to consider a case study of one community's thinking and planning organised around an asset-based approach to community development.

DINGLEFORD PARKLAND

We are at a workshop in the shire offices of Dingleford, an outer suburb of a capital city, where community members have come together to draw up a register of community assets. Once they have constructed the register they then hope to identify a project that will demonstrate the asset-based community development approach to planning. The workshop begins with a discussion of the talents, experiences, skills and knowledge that members of the community possess. The participants are enthusiastic. They identify a range of skilled tradespeople, including builders, carpenters, plumbers and electricians, who could advise on the building of a new community centre. There are also professional gardeners who could assist in the construction of a community garden. The list goes on and on. Indigenous families have an appreciation of their traditional culture and their relationship with the land. There are people with graphic design, legal, financial and journalism skills. Discussion then turns to the young people in the community. They have skills in the use of computers and mobile phones, which they can pass on to others. Older people have life experience and a sense of history and will be able to recall their stories in an oral history of the area. The culturally and linguistically diverse communities have a range of cultural contributions to make, including different cuisines, stories, dress and dance. Many are adept in two or more languages.

The workshop participants then begin to identify physical assets, adding the local community houses, the council-owned community hall and the large parkland in the centre of the suburb. Several asset-based projects are considered, such as a cultural festival and the refurbishment of the community hall. But what captures the imagination of the participants is the considerable area of parkland in the centre of the suburb. As it is a publicly owned site, participants feel that communities should collectively be able to decide how it should be used. There are many options. The bushland area, the participants argue, must be kept as native vegetation as it could be used to teach local schoolchildren about preserving native flora. The Indigenous members of the community could facilitate an education program about maintaining the local landscape. The landscape architects and gardeners could work with interested community members to draw up a design for the remaining land.

The lawyers offer to look into the legal requirements for setting up a community garden. A wall at one end of the park could be used for a community mural. The rather neglected formal children's playground could be replaced with an adventure playground constructed by community members, guided by the builders and carpenters who offer their time. A small area of the parkland could be set aside for a community flower and vegetable garden. A member of a Chinese community offers to establish an old-fashioned Chinese market garden. This discussion jogs the memory of an elderly couple, who remember that they have photos of the area in the 1900s, with what looks like a market garden at the edge of it. The young people attending the meeting offer to set up a website for Dingleford parkland while Meg, a journalist, will use her networks to get the message out through the community that the group welcomes new members.

In the final part of the workshop the participants work on an outline of the strategy plan to be put to the community as a whole. They also discuss ways of encouraging new people to be involved. Importantly, as with all community assets, the participants note that the Dingleford parkland project should not be seen as a once-and-for-all development. Communities change, they agree. The various uses of the spaces can change too.

Levels and types of strategic plans

We can think of strategic plans in terms of a descending level of abstraction. In community development we can identify long-term aims based on vision and commitments that guide action, but may not be achievable in the immediate future, such as a commitment to alleviate poverty in a local region or to prevent youth suicide or domestic violence. While these are very long-term objectives, we can set achievable medium-term and short-term objectives and milestones, or indicators, to measure the degrees of success in achieving objectives. We can also think of strategic planning as an activity undertaken by a whole community or community organisation or as an activity undertaken by a small part of a community or organisation. Some writers distinguish between strategic and tactical, or operational, plans. Here, strategic plans are seen as addressing long-term issues, say over a five- to 10-year period. Tactical or operational plans are short-term plans, specifying what is to be done within a year, for example.

When to undertake strategic planning

There are several ways of starting strategic planning processes. For example, some groups only begin when 'things just don't seem to be going right', such as when membership of a social action group seems to be drifting away. This is sometimes seen as crisis-management strategic planning. In contrast, another view is that it is just when 'things are going right', when people feel comfortable, that it is important to undertake strategic planning. Another approach is to undertake regular strategic planning exercises – for example, on a six-monthly or annual basis or at the end of a project – as part of a review and planning exercise. Increasingly, community organisations with some form of external funding are required to follow such timing of strategic planning. In these situations, the focus of the strategic plan is how the organisation or a campaign is going.

Where to begin the strategic planning process

Some strategic planning processes begin with an analysis of the external environment to identify opportunities and constraints. When assessing the environment, many organisations use a **SWOT analysis** (discussed below). Others begin with an analysis of the internal environment, by analysing the organisation, part of an organisation or a campaign itself. After linking these two analyses, gaps can then be identified and acted upon.

Wadsworth (1991) distinguishes between two different starting points, based on an **audit review** or an **open enquiry**. The audit-review approach examines practices in the light of aims and objectives. It asks such questions as 'What are we trying to achieve?' and 'How far did we achieve our aims and why?' The open-enquiry approach does not check action and outcomes against specific aims and objectives to see if they are being achieved. It probes practices in order to extract assumptions and intentions and to open up new ways of thinking about the organisation. Whatever general approach a group or organisation decide to take when commencing a strategic planning process, they need to understand the environment in which they are operating. SWOT analysis is a popular technique for doing this.

Visions, missions, rationales and aims

The idea of linking the strategic planning process with the identification and clarification of visions, missions, rationales and aims has been the dominant approach in strategic planning. One of the first things you notice when reading vision and mission statements, rationales, purposes, aims, objectives and goals is the way that the terms are used differently by different writers and in different contexts. Thus, it is important for any community organisation to be clear about its use of the terms. The process of identifying and developing visions, missions, purposes and rationales, of course, is based on values and assumptions. Many of the publications on strategies for non-profit organisations suggest that the process of strategic planning should always begin with a discussion of values and assumptions. As Davis-Meehan (1996:41) points out:

> Reflecting on values helps members of the organisation to determine whether or not they are operating with the same set of assumptions ... Values clarification is an examination of the current values of the organisation, the organisation's philosophy of operations, the assumptions that the organisation ordinarily uses in its operations, the organisation's preferred culture and the values of the stakeholders, such as the funding body.

For example, visions, missions and rationales can be seen as the very broad statements about a group's or an organisation's reason for being. One way of distinguishing between the terms is to identify a vision, or 'the what', as a picture of the future that we wish to create, asking such questions as:

- How would you like to see this organisation in, say, five or eight years?
- What is our ideal future state in X number of years?
- Where would we really like to be in X number of years?

Visions embody the shared aspirations of the whole group, community or organisation.

The purpose or mission involves the question 'why?' For example, 'Why does our group or organisation exist?' A mission statement sets out the group's, campaign's or organisation's reason for existence, its purpose and ways of fulfilling the purpose. As noted above, some writers use the term 'purpose' or 'long-term aims' rather than mission to explain the idea. Other writers, such as Migliore et al. (1995), use the terms 'mission' and 'purposes' interchangeably. Mission statements are a general outline of 'reason for being'. While there is agreement that mission statements should be clear, compelling, brief and simple, there are different understandings of what is meant by 'brief and simple'. A mission statement should be able to answer a number of questions about a group, campaign or organisation.

The term 'aims' is often used interchangeably with the term 'purpose' to refer to long-term goals. Objectives are often identified as shorter-term goals. They are usually identified as things that are clearly achievable, have clear outcomes and are in some ways measurable. Action plans (sometimes called tactics or operations) set out the actual ways that the objectives will be achieved. The whole process of strategic planning has often been summarised as *why, who, what, when, where* and *how*. The 'why, who, what, when, where and how' process involves identifying and clarifying values and assumptions, visions, missions and purpose, aims, goals, objectives and action plans.

Processes and steps in developing a strategy

As indicated above, there are a number of approaches and starting points when undertaking a strategic plan, and a number of elements to any planning process. And, like any other community development process, of course, the reality of strategy development and planning is always going to be messy and complex. Having stated this, it is informative to try to identify the elements and their links. Figure 5.1 is a diagrammatical representation of the elements of strategic development and some of the ways they are linked.

This diagram shows some of the ways that the process of strategy development could take place. It is important to remember that this is a model or guide to the activities involved in strategising, planning and acting. In addition, the ongoing reflection that occurs in all community development methods will mean that some directions might be abandoned altogether, and certainly decisions made earlier will be revisited and revised.

In the final part of our discussion of strategic development, we consider these elements and trace out how a strategic plan might take shape:

- clarifying reasons for undertaking and developing a strategic plan
- clarifying aims and objectives
- analysing the current situation

- developing the action plans
- carrying out the action plans
- evaluating.

We consider these elements in some detail below.

Figure 5.1 *Strategy development*

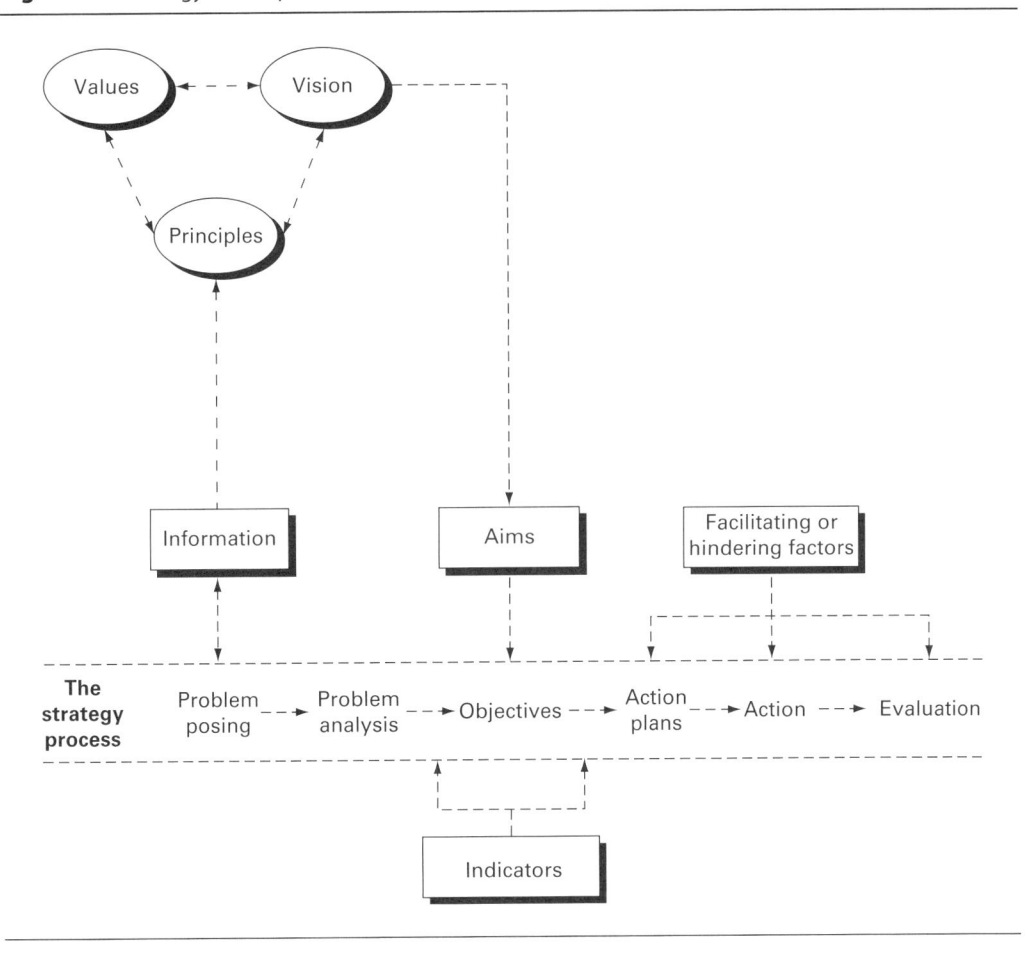

```
        Values  ←--→  Vision
           ↘         ↙    ╲
          Principles        ╲
              ↑              ╲
              │               ╲
              │                ╲
       ┌────────────┐    ┌────────┐   ┌──────────────────┐
       │Information │    │  Aims  │   │  Facilitating or │
       └────────────┘    └────────┘   │ hindering factors│
              │              │        └──────────────────┘
              │              │              │
  The         │  Problem    Problem              Action
  strategy    │  posing  →  analysis → Objectives → plans → Action → Evaluation
  process     │
                                        ↑       ↑
                                        │       │
                                    ┌───────────┐
                                    │ Indicators│
                                    └───────────┘
```

Reasons for undertaking and developing a strategic plan

It is important that the reason for undertaking a strategic plan is clarified at the beginning. As indicated above, community development work involves different types of strategic planning. For example, strategic planning can be part of a campaign or event such as organising a protest rally. Community development practitioners are also required to develop strategic plans as part of funding requirements or other bureaucratic obligations (the systematic 'planning for effectiveness' approach). As part of their work, practitioners are involved with developing a strategic plan to deal with some problem or issue. Strategic planning for the purpose of responding to a problem or issue is one of the most important activities that a community development practitioner does. It involves identifying and naming the problems and issues. Communities are generally aware of their own issues and problems, although their exact nature may not be clear or concisely articulated. The role of a community development practitioner is to help the community name and describe these issues and problems by providing information and facilitating discussion. Sometimes, this process is relatively formal through, for example, a community needs assessment. However, it is usually a more informal process initiated by the community itself. For example, a community development worker in a rural community becomes aware that people are expressing vague concerns and even hostility about the closure of a nearby regional institution for people with intellectual disabilities. In discussions with community members, the worker brings to light fears that deinstitutionalisation will mean a loss of resources for people with disabilities or that the former clients will be forced into town and will be 'a threat' to the town's people and the 'harmony' of the town (a functionalist view). In the stage of problem posing, the role of the community development worker is to facilitate the naming of the problem, identifying and articulating the concerns and their manifestations, including those expressed in gossip and rumour.

Aims and objectives

One way of thinking about aims and objectives is to pose the question 'What will the strategic plan achieve?' Aims and objectives can be attached to an organisation, a campaign or a problem-solving exercise. When people talk about aims and objectives, they often use terms such as 'goals', 'outcomes', 'priorities' and 'options'. Because these terms are vague, it is important to define their meaning.

In this book, 'aims' refer to long-term visions or ends, and statements about general direction. For example, the aim or vision of community development is the establishment of a world society in which all people are actively involved in programs to maintain the earth's ecological system, and in which the social, economic and political structures ensure maximum equity of access to basic goods and services. Such a society would be based on thoroughly democratised decision making and resource control, cultural and social diversity and choices in lifestyle. All these are large issues that require large-scale changes in social structures and political and economic systems. Because much of the everyday strategy of community development is based on a community's own problem-solving ability, it does not focus on broad aims. Rather, its focus is on objectives or goals. Objectives or goals are more specific than aims. They specify what we believe we can achieve in the foreseeable future and thus allow us to set up specific processes and tasks. An objective may be a successful submission or establishment of a democratic process in an organisation. Objectives have observable results; they consist of activities that can be clearly identified, analysed and reflected upon. That is, we must identify, at different levels of abstraction, what we wish to achieve. In the development of a strategic plan, communities often prioritise objectives. They might do this so that the most important ones are tackled first, or the most difficult ones are left to last. Like aims, objectives are not once-and-for-all. They are often modified or even rejected as strategies throw new light on issues and lead us to think about problems in different ways. Objectives may be long term, medium term or short term. Long-term objectives generally require a number of different strategies and are often set out in stages. Medium- and short-term objectives are on a smaller scale. In understanding and constructing our aims and our objectives for the long, medium and short term, we move from the broad to the specific and from the abstract to the concrete. This is sometimes called the 'descending ladder of abstraction' (see figure 5.2).

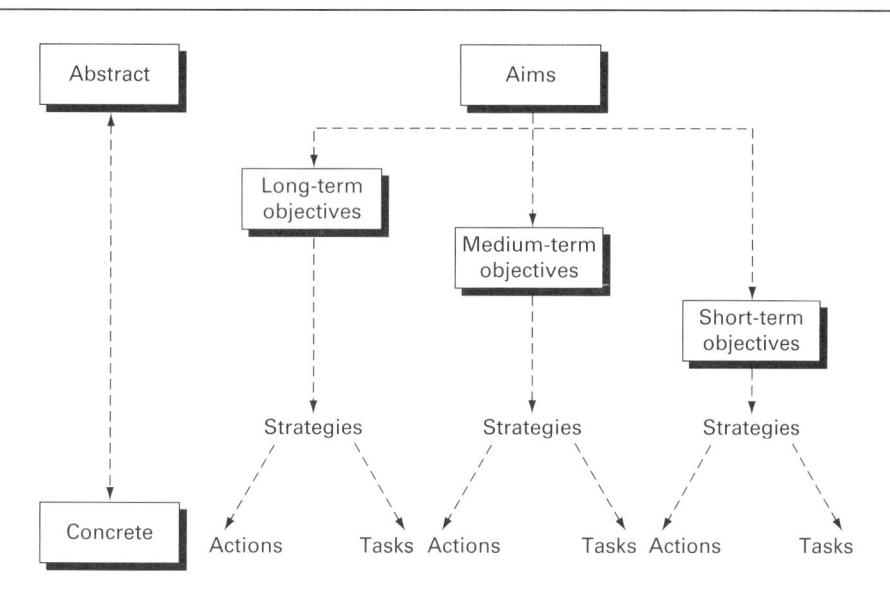

Figure 5.2 *Descending ladder of abstraction*

[Diagram: Abstract ↔ Concrete on the left; Aims branching down to Long-term objectives, Medium-term objectives, and Short-term objectives, each leading to Strategies, which branch into Actions and Tasks.]

In fact, the difference between short-term and long-term objectives, for example, depends on one's viewpoint and the timescale of the particular strategy. A medium-term objective to one person may be a short-term objective to another. This does not matter, as long as people are clear about what they are trying to achieve and how. In community development, a long-term objective might be a choice of housing for all people in a rural town. This could involve a variety of household structures, including the single, communal, extended and nuclear family. It could also involve a choice between public and private housing, and between high-density living (flats or communal houses, for example) and lower density single dwellings. Another example of an objective is the actual maintenance of a community project or organisation, which, in turn, is part of a strategy to achieve the aim of community empowerment. The everyday activities of a community development worker are important in maintaining a community project or organisation. These, in a way, also constitute the action plan.

The context

From a community development perspective, analysing a context in which a strategy is developed involves collecting information, making it accessible and then identifying how this information could assist in deciding what to do. There are several approaches to context and problem analysis. First, a key technique for analysing the context is a SWOT analysis. This involves identifying *strengths*, *weaknesses*, *opportunities* and *threats*. In identifying strengths, for example, an organisation or group might reflect on its positive standing in the community or any actions undertaken by the organisation that have worked; or consistent with the assets-based approach, it might identify the resources and skills in a community. In reflecting on weaknesses, an organisation might consider its failure to attract new community members to its management committee or it might consider its lack of funding for a project (although lack of funding could also be considered as an opportunity, as it might be a stimulus to rethinking its priorities). A newly elected government or council or an increase in funds to employ more workers could also provide opportunities. Threats could include the 'opening up' of council or government-funded community projects to competitive tendering, so that new private and profit-based organisations with more resources can now compete for the contract to develop a community project (although again to some this could also be seen as an opportunity). As Migliore et al. (1995:62) point out, the major value of a SWOT analysis lies in its ability to 'match vital operational strengths with major environmental opportunities ... [and provide] a basis for improving our weaknesses or at least minimising them and avoiding and managing environmental threats to our operations'.

A somewhat different approach might be used when dealing with a specific problem or issue. For example, a community development practitioner would provide information on the type, size and scope of the issue or problem, what is at stake and, if applicable, the antagonists. In the case of the rural community mentioned above, information is needed about the number of people with concerns, the numbers of clients, the date of the closure of the institution and what arrangements, if any, are in place to help the former clients to adjust. The community development worker seeks out any plans to establish halfway houses, hostels or disability resource centres. Public meetings would analyse and discuss the issues in the light of such information and perhaps establish a local action group that comprises both current clients at the institution, caregivers and other local community members.

Let us look at another example. A group from a Kurdish community approaches a local council to request that all publications about local council activities be translated into Kurdish. The local council refuses this request on the basis of cost, because the local Kurdish community numbers only 312 people. Feeling a sense of injustice, the Kurdish community seeks help from the community development worker employed by the regional migrant resource centre.

Problem analysis begins when the community development worker checks on the number of Kurdish and Kurdish-only speakers, the cost of translating and printing leaflets, the stakes involved and the antagonists. What is at stake could be more than Kurdish leaflets: it could be the integrity of the Kurdish community. The community development worker passes information on to the Kurdish community and, if requested, assists in its deliberations on how to proceed. This assistance may involve helping to organise a meeting place or a public forum, identifying the key players on council and publicising the issue through the local paper.

While many issues can be resolved by strategies at the local level, there are, of course, some that cannot. For example, while local councils may establish local employment programs, in a situation of high unemployment it is impossible to create jobs for all who need them. What is the role of a community development worker in this situation? It is to provide accessible information about unemployment for the community, including:

- the various structural reasons for unemployment
- the number, age and gender of unemployed people, and the number and type of job vacancies in the local area
- social security and unemployment benefit policies
- the rights of the unemployed
- possibilities for the community to develop its own employment scheme and government programs that support such a scheme
- successes and failures of similar programs.

Finally, a detailed plan of action would need to be drawn up in collaboration with the community at large.

Action plans

Action plans or strategy plans set out actions that are designed to achieve objectives. Regardless of whether the community begins with a problem that they have identified, or are considering action plans to further develop the existing assets in the community, action plans set out the specific activities and tasks and who will do them. This is the crucial point for strategy development, because it specifies the means by which we intend to get from one point to another. In most cases, there are several ways of getting from A to B. It is an opportunity for creative thinking.

Once a range of possible actions has been suggested, a number of questions can be asked:

- Are the actions realistic, considering the resources available (workers, equipment, contacts, money, space, information)?
- Are the actions feasible in the amount of time available?
- What are the hindering factors?
- What are the facilitating factors?
- What are the issues at stake?
- What are the actual tasks involved?
- Who are the key players (groups and individuals)?
- Who are the people with a significant stake in the outcome (the stakeholders)?
- Are there dilemmas or contradictions: for example, tensions between means and ends?
- What are the possible results of the action? Could it have any disastrous consequences?

Having considered these questions on the basis of the widest information available, a community is in a position to make a decision about which actions to undertake. There is often a temptation to think that we never have sufficient information. It is important to be sensitive to this thinking. Some community initiatives have been undermined by fragmentation resulting from some members wanting to act immediately and others

Processes and practices

wanting to spend more time on planning. The process of preparing the details of an action plan is complex. However, there are some guides to follow. One simple method of evaluating action plans is the **SMART analysis**:

- *Simple*: straightforward, easy to understand
- *Measurable*: we have some way of finding out if we achieved what we wanted to
- *Achievable*
- *Realistic*: we can do it with the resources available
- *Time-related*: it can be done within the given amount of time.

This approach can also be used when evaluating submissions, negotiations and research. As long as the whole process is flexible and the principles of community development are maintained, it is a useful checklist for action plans.

The following chart sets out a simple action plan schedule. There are now quite complex computer-based flow charts for action (which can be accessed on the Internet) that allow for many more categories and actions than does this diagram. In particular, community development practitioners can access what are known as Gantt charts or action plans. Like the chart in figure 5.3, a Gantt chart is a graphic representation of a project, setting out the sequence of tasks, when they are performed and who is responsible.

Figure 5.3 *Schedule for an action plan*

Task	March	April	May	June	July	August	Person(s) responsible	Date completed
Gather information on the issue							John, Margaret	3 May
Prepare publicity leaflet							Joyce, Li	28 August
Draw up petition							Van, Maria	14 June
Visit local doctors							Ahmet, Con	12 April 2 June 8 July
Organise protest							Con, Barry	6 August
Talk to women outside workplaces							Tanya, Maria	2 June 28 June 25 July
Speak to local media							Li, Van	26 April 17 May 22 July
Write letters to politicians							John, Tan	3 May 29 July

Alinsky (1972:126) set up a framework for thinking about tactics, using a language of war strategy. He sets out 13 rules:

- Power is not only what you have, but what the enemy thinks you have.
- Never go outside the experience of your people.

- Wherever possible, go outside the experience of the enemy.
- Make the enemy live up to their own book of rules.
- Ridicule is the most potent weapon. It is almost impossible to counter-attack.
- A good tactic is one that your people enjoy.
- A tactic that drags on too long becomes a drag.
- Keep pressure on, with different tactics and actions, and utilise all events of the period for your purpose.
- The threat is usually more terrifying than the thing itself.
- The major purpose of tactics is to maintain constant pressure on the opposition. It is this unceasing pressure that results in the reactions from the opposition that are essential for the success of the campaign.
- If you push a negative hard and deep enough, it will break through into its counter-side, based on the principle that every positive has its negative.
- The price of a successful attack is a constructive alternative.
- Pick the target, freeze it, personalise it and polarise it.

Whenever action plans are discussed, it is important to keep in mind the principles of community development. For community development is not just a matter of achieving certain ends; it is more than a list of tasks and activities. It requires sensitivity to the way we do things. It works through processes that are empowering in themselves, as well as being instruments for achieving results.

Let us again consider the case study of the rural community concerned about the closure of the regional institution for people with intellectual disabilities. Assume that this community has decided on two objectives: to establish a disabilities resource centre and to set up a housing cooperative for people with a mild intellectual disability.

A public meeting is held and establishes a small working party of clients, community members, institution staff and the community development worker. The working party studies possible actions and presents its findings to another public meeting. The actions they suggest include identifying the resources and funds needed to establish the resource centre and the housing cooperative, identifying key players and powerbrokers and obtaining widespread publicity and support for the whole project.

Action plans often include actions to influence decision makers. Pressure can be applied by various tactics, such as lobbying, petitions, posters, media coverage and behind-the-scenes networking and persuasion. It can also include direct action, such as rallies, sit-ins, pickets and boycotts. Publicity is a powerful form of pressure and will be discussed in detail in chapter 9. In evaluating each of these actions, the elements listed on page 212 should be considered. In the case of the Kurdish community, similar action plans could be considered to gain publicity for the community's needs and to put pressure on decision makers.

Taking action

We are not able to predict absolutely the results of our actions and there are often some unintended consequences. Nevertheless, it is useful to think about the possible consequences of direct action and to consider possible wins and disasters. For example, suppose a

Processes and practices

community has as its aim the elimination of high unemployment rates in its area. Its objective is to get the local council to establish a job creation scheme, and one of its strategies is to hold a rally outside the town hall. The organisers should consider what they will do if very few people turn up, or if the media interview people who say they don't want to work or if the rally becomes violent. They should find answers to these questions before they decide to proceed. It is important to stop and think about all aspects of our proposed activities. Table 5.5 sets out how an action plan might work in practice.

Table 5.5 *An action plan, with examples of its use*

Stage	Example	
Problem: name it and describe it	The local neighbourhood house is under-utilised.	
Options: describe suggested actions and explain how they will resolve the problem	**Option 1** close the neighbourhood house	**Option 2** neighbourhood house to offer more community programs
Resources needed: list expertise, money, equipment, etc.	accountant to check books	more money and staff to organise, publicise and run programs
Resources available: list expertise, money, equipment, etc.	money and expertise for wind-up	money, volunteer staff
Group contribution: describe what the group can offer: e.g., political power, social-development experience, communication channels, financial resources, leadership, attitudes	paid time for wind-up	goodwill, access to decision makers, experienced staff
Time scale: decide how long will it take to put into effect	three months	lobbying, three to six months; establishment (hiring staff, publicity), three months
Action: list tasks	seal assets, close books, liaise with authorities, distribute assets	write funding submissions, train volunteers, devise programs, hire staff
People: list the people who will carry out the tasks	coordinator of neighbourhood house	all staff – tasks to be allocated, approximate total time 30 hours per week
Indicator: ask how will we know when we have resolved the problem	all programs cease	neighbourhood house is used to capacity

Evaluation

It is useful to have in place some way of evaluating the use and success of the strategy. An evaluation can be a formal activity or it can be quite informal. Some community development workers argue that evaluations should be carried out in a formal or semi-formal way at the end of a set of processes, while others favour a continuing informal evaluation that might be performed at the completion of an action or as a regular occurrence: monthly, weekly, or even daily.

As evaluation is considered in some detail in chapter 9, an overview only is provided in this chapter. As a more formal process, evaluation often begins with restating the objectives of the strategic plan and posing the questions, 'What did we set out to achieve?' and 'What did we achieve?' As discussed previously, Wadsworth (1991:28) names this the audit approach to evaluation.

It is useful to draw upon the principles of social research in understanding evaluation. When studying social phenomena, researchers identify indicators of their object of study. These may or may not be quantifiable, yet there will be some way of detecting changes that have taken place as a result of an intervention. An indicator of family breakdown is divorce rates; an indicator of the failure of small business is bankruptcy rates; an indicator of the success of a community program is its general reputation in the community.

In other words, social research shows us the value of operationalising and observing what we want to achieve, and how we are going to achieve it, by identifying observable indicators. If the objective of a strategy is to make public housing available to all who need it, one indicator of the success of the strategy is the number of people on waiting lists for public housing. Like many indicators, though, this may not tell the whole story; people may not put their names on a waiting list as they may believe that they will never obtain public housing.

Measures show the nature and extent of achievements. Measures can be qualitative (such as opinions, feelings and impressions) and quantitative (such as the number of people attending a meeting or using a resource centre). Quantitative measures allow us to present statistical data on activities such as the percentage of participants who are single parents.

What needs to be said here in regard to evaluation is that at each stage of strategy, the participants should reflect on what they did, how they did it and what the results have been. They may need to modify objectives and strategies in the light of unexpected results. This, in turn, could lead to a new direction (because the original objectives were misguided) or even abandonment of the project. In fact, termination at an appropriate time can be less disastrous than trying to see a project through. Even when a project appears to have been a total disaster, people may have learned useful lessons from it.

There is a cookbook approach to strategy development that sees it as a matter of getting aims, objectives and action plans together, identifying means and ends and then following a formula. In fact, there is no simple formula for achieving objectives. Strategy development is rarely a tidy package. It is messy and full of misplaced goals, mistakes, wrong directions and even dead ends. The fluid nature of strategy development is to be expected; it is a healthy part of a changing and creative society.

Sometimes, as our strategy takes effect, we realise that an achievable or more appropriate objective should have been constructed. A flexible approach, when controlled by the community itself, opens up new ways of thinking about issues that are consistent with community development principles.

On means and ends

Traditional approaches to strategy development clearly separate means and ends: actions, processes, practices and strategies constitute the means; and goals, objectives and aims constitute the ends. Once means and ends have been separated, do the ends justify the means?

In community development, this question is wrongly framed, because it assumes that means and ends can be neatly divided. As we have seen, objectives and strategies overlap; what is an objective (or end) in one context is a strategy (or means) in another. For example, maintaining a community organisation can be both an objective (end in itself) from the perspective of the management committee and a strategy (means) for empowerment in the view of the community development worker.

Alinsky (1972) makes pertinent remarks about what he calls the ethics of means and ends. He identifies a number of rules that should be considered in discussions of the means and ends of strategies. He argues that the more intensely one feels about an issue, the less one is concerned about ethics. Judgement of ethics depends on the political position of those sitting in judgement and the context and time in which the judgement is made. Alinsky (1972:34) comments that the success or failure of a strategy is a 'mighty determinant of ethics'. He also points out that concern with ethics increases with the number of means available. If one lacks a choice of means, then ethical questions are less likely to arise.

Alinsky's views are important reminders of the need to be pragmatic in strategy development and to understand the interests of oppositional forces and the political context in which strategies are applied. But his arguments do not absolve community development workers from ensuring that community development principles permeate both means and ends in strategy development.

The discussion so far could give the impression that strategy development is a foreign and tedious aspect of community development. In fact, it involves familiar ways of thinking about what we want to do and what we are actually doing or have done. We develop strategies in much of what we do every day. In informal ways we think about what we want to do and achieve, and we develop action plans. We also reflect on what we have or have not achieved on a daily basis, and why – this is the basis of evaluation.

When we consider writing a letter to the local council about the need for a pedestrian crossing in our street, we are thinking strategically. Writing a letter is a step towards influencing an outcome: the provision of a pedestrian crossing. When we make a decision about whether to walk or go by public transport to the supermarket, we think strategically.

In our deliberations we probably consider such factors as how much time we have and how much we have to carry. We could also consider the environmental impact of driving a car or travelling by train. We weigh up the factors and decide on an option on the basis of the information available.

Thinking in terms of strategy is a natural part of community development work. For example, female community development workers who refuse to answer to 'girlie' are rejecting a misleading and pejorative label; they are refusing to be defined in patriarchal terms. This is one small tactic in a larger strategy: to construct a new way of thinking about the role of women in society and relations between men and women. Suppose a community is asked to send one paid worker to negotiate with a funding body for a community project, but instead sends a group of participants. It is rejecting official procedure as part of a strategy to show that there are other ways of doing things.

Issues and criticisms

It is useful to be aware of some of the things that can go wrong or slow down a strategic planning exercise. In many situations these things are just not predictable or avoidable. They can result from changes to the external environment that are not within the control of a community group or organisation, or unexpected changes within the group or organisation, such as changes in participants. Yet some issues can be pre-empted by both sensitivity to their possibility and taking steps to avoid them. Some of the common things that can go wrong or slow down a strategy process are:

- people in the community group or organisation are not committed to the strategic plan, because there has been insufficient involvement of all the members
- the strategic planning exercise becomes an end in itself
- the aims are not sufficiently operationalised (given a concrete form through which observable indicators are identified), and thus the tasks and activities are not developed in sufficient detail to be able to be carried out
- the timing of the planning and implementation is too ambitious
- external events overtake the strategic plan
- the strategic plan was appropriate, but there is now an insufficient number of people to carry out the actions
- while the plan was going well the community wanted to own it, but when the plan runs into difficulties, or fails, the community no longer wants to own it or take any responsibility for what happened. Community members search for someone to blame.

The importance of strategic planning in community development also comes with four important caveats, which are based on particular approaches to strategic planning. The first caveat applies to situations in which strategic planning becomes a protracted ritual: it is 'done' because this is 'what a professional organisation does'. There are, of course, times when strategic planning is a hindrance to 'getting things done' such as when discussion becomes bogged down without any agreement as to aims and action and when it undermines the sense of urgency required immediately after a disaster. For example, it is often the small immediate actions that make the difference in post-disaster recovery, not the longer-term strategic plans (Kenny, 2010).

The second caveat applies to situations in which preoccupation with preparing a good strategic plan can focus attention on instrumental activities at the expense of everyday relations of trust and care that have no instrumental motive. This instrumentalism can become technocratic; that is, as though strategies were simply technical procedures designed for specific outputs. In the context of community development, strategies should take into account the complex nature of intervention, and the contextual factors that affect empowerment. The community development approach does not conceive of strategy as a single process that produces changes that can be measured by quantifying output. The value of a process can be much more elusive and is usually quite modest.

The third caveat concerns the need for community development practitioners to be sensitive to the way that strategy development is constructed within a framework in which the development of a community organisation becomes an end in itself rather than being a means or conduit for community empowerment. A fourth caveat is based on the proposition that while we can identify elements in developing a strategic plan from a community development perspective, strategic planning is not a one-off singular exercise. A key theme in this book is that community development at the beginning of the twenty-first century takes place within a 'risk society'. A community development approach to strategic planning involves processes that are messy and full of misplaced goals and dead ends. This approach needs much more than traditional instrumental thinking. It requires new forms of thinking such as strategic questioning.

The final caveat concerns the mistake of lineality. In reality, few strategic plans develop completely as expected. As indicated at various points in this book, reality is always messy and contradictory. It is for this reason that some community development practitioners will argue that strategic plans can be little more than rough guides to where a group might want to be. They must always be challengeable. Moreover, from a community development perspective there is a tension between a messy democratic process that undermines the strategic plan and the effective achievement of the plan. This tension is discussed in chapter 11.

Summary points

- The current climate of community development practice in Australia puts pressure on community development practitioners to be professional, competent and strategic in their activities.
- Community development practitioners are professional in the sense of having specific commitments and attitudes, and competency in their activities.
- The idea of collective empowerment is central to community development work and distinguishes it from other approaches to working with people.
- Grasping the concept and practice of empowerment requires understanding the different views of what power actually is, and how power is manifested, challenged and maintained.
- Like empowerment, 'participation' is another word with implied meanings and assumptions about its intrinsic benefits.
- There are different forms and levels of participation and different reasons for developing participatory programs.
- Some people do not wish to participate in civil society and it is important that community development practitioners respect and understand this.
- Increasing community capacity – which involves changes in structures, resources, behaviour and skills – has become a central part of social development policies and strategies in Australia and internationally.

- It is important for community development practitioners to understand the different approaches to, and elements of, community capacity building.
- Over recent years, the social inclusion agenda has set the framework for a number of government policies in Australia.
- From a community development perspective, social inclusion comes about when people are active citizens, and when they define what they want to be included in and how.
- The development of strategies is a central element in the empowerment of communities. There are different approaches, levels and types of strategic plans.
- Community development practitioners need to be able to develop and implement strategy plans. They also need to be aware of key issues in strategy development.

Key terms

- asset-based approach
- audit review
- community building
- community capacity building
- competency
- conscientisation
- deficit-based approach
- discourse of needs
- empowerment
- governmentality
- ideological hegemony
- ideology
- in-person services
- neighbourhood renewal
- open enquiry
- panopticon vision
- professionalism
- routine production work
- rural renewal
- SMART analysis
- strategic questioning approach
- strategic thinking approach
- strategy development
- SWOT analysis
- symbolic–analytic services

Exercises

1. In what ways can community development be seen to be professional or anti-professional?
2. Explain the different ideas of competency in community development.
3. In what ways does community development work involve symbolic–analytic work?
4. What is meant by ideology? Why is understanding ideology important for community development work?
5. What is needs discourse and how does it become an arena through which political power is constructed and applied?
6. 'Empowerment is based on philosophical views about what it is to be human, and it involves processes that are full of dilemmas and contradictions.' Discuss this statement.
7. Identify three dimensions of power and discuss ways in which community development practitioners might challenge or use these dimensions.
8. 'Some approaches to participation are problematic from a community development perspective.' Discuss this statement.
9. Identify four ways that we can think about and categorise approaches to capacity building.
10. What are some of the difficulties in capacity building from a community development perspective?
11. Why is strategy development important for community development?

Processes and practices

12 Describe some of the different forms of strategy development.
13 Identify some of the issues and dilemmas in strategy development.
14 Using the case studies in this chapter identify some of the elements of empowerment and disempowerment in community development.

Further reading

Alinsky, S (1972) *Rules for Radicals*. Vintage, New York.

Burkhart, PJ & Reuss, S (1993) *Successful Strategic Planning: A Guide for Nonprofit Agencies and Organisations*. Sage, Newbury Park, California.

Carr, DK, Hard, KJ & Trahant, WJ (1996) *Managing the Change Process: A Field Book for Change Agents, Consultants, Team Leaders and Reengineering Managers*. McGraw Hill, New York.

Cauchi, J & Murphy, J (2004) 'What's wrong with community-building!: It's much worse than we thought', in *Community Development, Human Rights and the Grassroots Conference Proceedings*. Centre for Citizenship and Human Rights, Deakin University, Geelong, pp. 44–66.

Chaskin, J et al. (2001) *Building Community Capacity*. Aldine De Gruyter, New York.

Chomsky, N (2003) *Understanding Power*. Vintage, London.

Davis-Meehan, E (1996) *The Power of Positive Planning: A Strategic Planning Kit for Even Better Service Delivery*. Family Support Services Association of NSW and ITRAC, Wyong Shire, NSW.

de Wit, B & Meyer, R (1994) *Strategy, Process, Content, Context: An International Perspective*. West, St Paul.

Doyal, L & Gough, I (1991) *A Theory of Human Need*. Macmillan, London.

Eade, D (1997) *Capacity Building: An Approach to People-Centred Development*. Oxfam, Oxford.

Foucault, M (1979) *Discipline and Punish: The Birth of the Prison*. Allen Lane, London.

Foucault, M (1980) *Power/Knowledge: Selected Interviews and Other Writings, 1972–1977*. C Gordon (ed.), Harvester Press, Brighton.

Fraser, N (1989) *Unruly Practices: Power, Discourse and Gender in Contemporary Social Theory*. University of Minnesota Press, Minneapolis.

Freire, P (1972) *Pedagogy of the Oppressed*. Penguin, Harmondsworth, Middlesex.

Ignatieff, M (2001) *Human Rights as Politics and Idolatry*. Princeton University Press, Princeton.

Joyce, P & Woods, A (1996) *Essential Strategic Management: From Modernism to Pragmatism*. Butterworth Heinemann, Oxford.

Lyon, D (2001) *Surveillance Society: Monitoring Everyday Life*. Open University Press, Buckingham.

Migliore RH, Stevens, RE, Loudon, DL, Williamson, SG & Winston, W (1995) *Strategic Planning for Not-for-Profit Organizations*. The Haworth Press, New York.

Mowbray, M (2004) 'The new communitarianism: Building great communities or brigadoonery?', *Just Policy*, Vol. 32, June, pp. 11–20.

Nussbaum, M & Sen, A (eds) (1993) *The Quality of Life*, Clarendon Press, Oxford.

O'Shaughnessy, T (1999) *Capacity Building: A New Approach*. World Vision, Melbourne.

Pasmore, WA (1994) *Creating Strategic Change: Designing the Flexible, High-Performing Organisation*. Wiley, New York.

Reich, R (1992) *The Work of Nations*. Vintage, New York.

United Nations Development Programme (1997) *Capacity Development, Technical Advisory Paper 2*, July. Management Development and Governance Division, New York.

Wadsworth, Y (1991) *Everyday Evaluation on the Run*. Action Research Issues Association, Melbourne.

Wainwright, H (2003) *Reclaim the State: Experiments in Popular Democracy*. Verso, London.

Weblinks

Community builders NSW
www.communitybuilders.nsw.gov.au/builder/what/capb_progs.html

Community capacity building
www.illawarraforum.org.au/assets/files/Discussion%20paper%20CCbuilding.pdf

Community capacity building toolkit
www.getinvolved.qld.gov.au/assets/pdfs/ccb-on-line-toolkit.pdf

Gantt charts
www.gannt-chart.com/gnIndex.asp
http://toolboxes.flexiblelearning.net.au/demosites/series9/906/map_respak/map_e1/html/map_e1_ganntchart.htm www.freedownloadmanager.org/downloads/gannt_software/

CHAPTER 6

Community organisations

Overview

Community development involves collective endeavour. This means, of course, that community development programs and activities take place in, or through, some type of community group. The role of a community development practitioner is to work with a group to help facilitate its goals. Some community development practitioners will already be part of the community and may operate as unpaid or paid workers. Other community development practitioners will be employed in agencies originating outside the community, such as local government, international development agencies or activist organisations, but they will still be working with and for community groups. In this chapter we consider the nature of community groups, focusing on the more formal type of group, generally known in Australia as a community organisation. We begin by noting the scope of community organisations and the terms used. We briefly consider the available data on community organisations. We proceed to elaborate a typology of community organisations in Australia, based on the idea of operating rationales. This is followed by consideration of the types of organisational structures and management principles adopted by community organisations and the decision-making processes, life cycles and the responsibilities of people involved in community organisations. The issues of industrial disputes and resource sharing are also discussed. The chapter concludes with an enjoinder to consider possibilities for developing creative organisations.

Introduction

Community development takes place through groups of people who come together because of a common interest or concern. These groups might begin quite small and informal, and remain informal in character. Alternatively, relatively informal groups might develop into larger formal organisations. Formalisation of a group's activities into a legally constituted organisation is often a matter of government requirements and regulations (such as the requirement to be incorporated to receive government funds). Whatever direction a group takes, the basis of the association is one in which people come together out of choice. While the focus of this chapter is the more formal community organisations, much of the discussion in the chapter – such as that concerned with commitment to collective models of organisation, committee work, meeting structures, decision-making processes and life cycles of organisations and groups – can be useful for informal groups.

As mentioned in chapter 1, formal community organisations refer to not-for-profit or third sector organisations that are autonomous or semi-autonomous from governments and business, and are constructed around issues and programs that are relevant to the communities with which they are working. They include community arts groups, refugee organisations, single-parent organisations and local organisations for the unemployed, for example. Several terms describe what we in Australia generally refer to as community organisations. These include **voluntary associations**, **non-profit** or **not-for-profit organisations** (while they can generate a financial surplus, this surplus cannot be distributed as personal profit), **third sector organisations**, **non-government (or non-governmental) organisations (NGOs)** and **civil society organisations**. Involvement in a community organisation can be on a paid or unpaid basis. For unpaid positions and many paid positions, participation in a community organisation is on the basis of common identity and interests. From a community development perspective, the purpose of such is to be a site for organising and supporting the empowerment of communities.

Internationally, community organisations are seen as part of the third sector of society (Salamon et al., 1999; Salamon & Anheier, 1996), which is conceptualised as a distinct sphere that operates in the interstices between formal state institutions, the market or for-profit sector and the informal relations in household and other private spheres. In international literature, third sector organisations are recognised by certain organisational features: they are formally constituted, not-for-profit, voluntary (in the sense that members are free to join or exit the organisation), self-governing and organisationally separate from government (Salamon & Anheier, 1996:xvii–xviii).

Community organisations are found in small rural towns and in large cities. They might be in suburban or inner-urban areas. Because they want to identify with community interests, they are usually located in ordinary suburban houses, local halls or shopfronts, rather than in large office blocks or government departments. However, with the emphasis on 'being more businesslike' that goes with neo-liberalism and new managerialism, and when securing large funding support from government, public philanthropy and corporative sponsorship is a priority, some community organisations have opted for corporate-style offices in the large cities of Australia.

The following case study is a description of a community house in a regional city.

TOOLAC COMMUNITY HOUSE

The community house is an old Victorian house with a large garden. One side of the house is now partitioned off into a community childcare cooperative. The other side of the garden has been set aside as a communal vegetable garden. On the gate is a large sign saying 'all welcome'. It lists the programs operating from the house and the opening hours. Both the front gate and the front door have disability access. The house comprises a passageway, four large rooms and three smaller rooms, a kitchen and a bathroom.

Inside the front door is a large noticeboard that is used by community members for notices of meetings and items wanted and for sale. Along the passageway a smaller noticeboard displays detailed information about the activities of the centre, such as community classes and the names of self-help groups and advocacy groups that use the centre, with times of meetings and details of contact people. The centre's hours of operation are listed, together with a timetable that sets out the hours of the tenancy worker and financial counsellors. There are details of the resources available to community groups, such as the photocopier and computers. This information is in English, Greek, Turkish, Arabic and Vietnamese.

On the left is an enquiries table and, next to it, a large stand and table displaying leaflets about such things as a local employment program, social security entitlements, welfare rights and legal aid. There are also notices of meetings and pamphlets about campaigns, including an environmental campaign, and a public meeting sponsored by the local Justice for Refugees Group. Around the table are armchairs and a couch. A person who deals with enquiries sits beside the table, working at a computer. The house is a hive of activity. It is 3 pm. In the four large rooms are meetings and classes: a meeting of a local pensioners' association, a self-defence class for women and a class for people returning to study. In the largest room is a meeting to organise a forum on domestic violence. The small rooms contain a photocopier, printing machine, computer and layout table, and there is a darkroom. The kitchen is open to all users and, at present, a group of mothers is having an informal discussion there.

There are four workers. One is on the phone, responding to a request for information on youth crisis accommodation in the area. One is typing a new timetable for the use of the house, agreed on at a meeting of all users the night before. The third is collating the monthly survey of participants in the centre's programs, which elicits views on how these programs and the centre's activities could be improved. The fourth worker is meeting with a group of local residents to help them prepare a submission to the local council for funding a bilingual youth outreach worker. If the submission is successful, the youth outreach worker will be located at the community centre and be accountable to a committee comprising representatives from the community, the government department that funds the project, the centre's committee of management and young people from the area.

It is now 7.15 pm. In one of the large rooms, a group of lawyers, teachers and other local people are meeting to prepare for a large public forum to discuss a nationwide proposal for a bill of rights, as part of the response to new surveillance methods that have been imposed under the 'war on terror'. In one of the other large rooms, a workshop is being held to help local people fill out their tax returns. In another, an English class is taking place. In the fourth room is a meeting to discuss a draft paper prepared by the local council in response to a state-government initiative for community building.

What is going on at this centre is a whole range of community development processes: the development and maintenance of community resources and programs, advocacy, networking, community education, cultural awareness, publicity and campaign organisation. The Toolac Community House is only beginning to open up participation and control of community resources, decision making and power sharing. But it is beginning.

The nature of community organisations
The size of the sector

As international and Australian data on the third sector becomes available we are beginning to get a picture of what the community organisations look like comparatively. For example, researchers with the Johns Hopkins Comparative Nonprofit Sector Project (see Salamon et al., 1999; Salamon & Anheier, 1996) provide some interesting data on third sector organisations. Their research in 22 countries reveals that the third sector is a major economic force. It is a USD$1.1 trillion industry, employing 19 million workers and another 10.6 million full-time-equivalent unpaid volunteer workers (Salamon et al., 1999:8).

Estimates of numbers of community organisations in Australia vary considerably, because of the difficulty in obtaining data on the small, unincorporated organisations that do not have paid employees and lack a legal status, and because of the different definitions of the sector and different methods of counting. Lyons and Hocking (2000) estimate that there were 380 000 not-for-profit organisations overall in 1995–96, while Brown et al. (2000:128) estimate that there were 94 000 organisations in the community welfare sector alone in 1994–95, employing 542 000 paid workers (2000: 145).

In the Productivity Commission report *Contribution of the Not-for-Profit Sector* (2010:xxiii), the authors calculate that there are 600 000 not-for-profit or community organisations in Australia, of which 59 000 are economically significant, contributing nearly $43 billion or 4 per cent to Australia's GDP in 2006–07. Since the 1990s, the average annual growth in number of employees has been 5.7 per cent, with an estimated total number in 2006–07 of around 890 000 paid workers, equivalent to 8.5 per cent of total Australian employment (Productivity Commission, 2010:69). By 2006–07 the gross value of the sector (the output of goods and services less the value of intermediate consumption inputs used in producing the output) was $55.6 billion, doubling that of 1999–2000 (Productivity Commission, 2010:64).

These figures indicate the scope of the third sector, but it should be remembered that much of the data gathered, including data collected by Lyons (2001) for the Johns Hopkins Project and the Productivity Commission (2010), is from a wide range of organisations that we would not conventionally include as community organisations in Australia, such as independent schools and professional associations for lawyers and accountants, and, of course, we do not have data on the extent to which third sector organisations practise community development. Yet the sheer size of the sector – which is still growing – also indicates the extent of potential sites for community development.

Types of community organisations

There are several ways we can differentiate community organisations. First, it is possible to distinguish between organisations that are member-serving and organisations that are public-serving. Member-serving organisations include the University of the Third Age and self-help groups such as for breast cancer survivors or refugees. Public-serving organisations include neighbourhood houses, community legal centres and community arts clubs.

Of course, many community organisations are both member- and public-serving; an example is a disability action group that serves the interests of its members as well as champions the rights of all people who have a disability. A second way is to identify the major purpose, function or theme dealt with by the organisation. For example the Johns Hopkins Comparative Nonprofit Sector Project (Salamon et al., 1999; Salamon & Anheier, 1996) uses what it calls the International Classification NonProfit Organizations (ICNPO) system. This system differentiates between culture and recreation; education and research;

health; social service; environment; law, advocacy and politics; religion; and business and professional categories.

A third way of thinking about the varieties of community organisations, as such, is to differentiate between the operating rationales of organisations. An **operating rationale** sets out (either formally or informally) the overall rationale for the organisation and ways that it operates. The operating rationale includes the principles and organisational structures of the organisation, the way the participants in the organisation relate to each other, the way it deals with other institutions such as the state, and how everyday practices are organised. There are five general models of operation in community organisations in Australia: charity, activist, welfare state industry, market and social entrepreneurship models. The models are not exclusive and they can operate concurrently. It is important to understand these models because community development workers often have to construct what they do within and against these models, and community development practices are often laid on top of them. With some clear exceptions, these different models of operation have generally constrained rather than facilitated community development work. The five dominant types of community organisations and their operational rationales are discussed below.

The charity model

Central to the charity model is the idea of the 'more fortunate' members of society giving to the 'less fortunate'. The principles of this model were set out at the beginning of white settlement in Australia (Macintyre, 1985; Kennedy, 1982; Dickey, 1980). They are usually based on a conceptual distinction between the 'deserving' and 'undeserving' poor, which was developed around commitment to the work ethic and linked to class, gender and race inequalities. The early charity model of community organisations predates the welfare state and is linked to an approach to welfare whereby responsibility for welfare provision lies outside state institutions with the family and, in the case of charity, with church institutions. However, the style of operation of the charity model can exist under regimes of state intervention in which relations between state actors and welfare recipients can be influenced by the charity ethos.

The welfare approach employed in the charity model rejects any structural or collectivist solution to issues of social justice and inequality in favour of relationships that are based on the patronage of individuals. There is a clear distinction between the provider and the recipient of welfare. In this model, community programs are developed to help individuals cope with their situation. There is no interest in issues of redistribution and no concern with either equality of services or equality of outcomes. Citizenship tends to be expressed in terms of obligation and duty, rather than rights. For example, charity givers tend to deliver welfare as a duty or obligation, rather than because the recipient has a right to charity. Contemporary constructions of the charity relationship are manifested in the strengthening of what has come to be known as the 'ethos of volunteerism' in community organisations. The ethos of volunteerism has underpinned the quest for unpaid workers. The moral arguments for volunteerism are usually couched in terms of moral obligation to help 'the needy' and the self-development of unpaid workers. In fact, the charity principles are eroded when instrumental factors come strongly into play, such as when volunteers are brought into community organisations to undertake tasks for which there is no money for paid work and when volunteers take on volunteer work in the hope of gaining experience that will give them some leverage in the job market.

In some ways, the new charity-based institutions have become a charity industry in which 'the poor and disadvantaged' are like products to be marketed through advertising agents in order to raise money for the organisation. Moreover, as charity organisations become increasingly corporatised, many have embraced new organisational themes that are based on ideas of new managerialism and enterprise culture. The charity model of community organisations lacks empowering and democratic forces. It is a long way from the community development approach to the operation of community organisations.

The activist model

The activist model is the one that is most clearly associated with community development. Its ascendancy took place alongside the political and intellectual reinvigoration of the Australian Left in the 1970s. It begins from a strong value base (drawn from feminism, socialism or environmentalism, for example), a commitment to structural and collectivist strategies for change and acceptance of the community sector as a site for effective struggle. The welfare sector is conceptualised broadly as a site that embraces a whole range of activities that can enhance wellbeing, including activities organised around environmental issues, cultural development and international aid. In the 1970s and early 1980s, community organisations dominated by the activist model operated against the backdrop of a popular acceptance of state responsibility for welfare provision. However, activist community organisations have always been divided in their response to the welfare state. Some workers in activist organisations argue that advocacy for community requires working both 'with and against the state' (see London Edinburgh Weekend Return Group, 1980) and identify their activities as mediations between the state and civil society aimed at strengthening civil society. Some activist organisations emphasise the co-optive implications of dependency (on the capitalist and patriarchal state, for example) and eschew state funds. Yet other activist organisations invoke concepts of state responsibility and citizen rights and argue for the use of state funds, even when the price to pay is increased control by state institutions.

The activist model that prevailed in the 1970s focused on the issues of equality, redistribution and ecology. In the early 1980s there was a shift to the question of social justice, which has included issues of social and human rights and recognition of claims for the development of separate identities among minority and Indigenous groups. The concept of citizenship informing the activist model of community organisations emphasises rights rather than obligations and duties. The rights discourse and the rhetoric of empowerment and self-determination imply active citizenship principles at work.

Many activist community organisations profess commitment to non-hierarchical structures and open decision-making processes. They appear to exude democratic principles. Lines of accountability are primarily to co-members of the organisation, which, because the distinction between providers and recipients is weakened or non-existent, will include both co-workers and recipients of programs. In their passion against formality, some activist organisations have rejected the imposition of any policy that stipulates formal decision-making processes, preferring to work along loose collectivist lines. Yet a lack of formal structure can actually conceal the relations of unequal power and provide a framework for undemocratic relations of power (see the discussion of the dilemmas of democratic decision making later in this chapter). Bureaucratic structures, enterprise culture and managerialist approaches to community organisation have been derided in activist community organisations. Yet, while activists have generally had no truck with issues of professionalism, competency, bureaucracy, enterprise culture and managerialism, some activist left groups epitomise the bureaucratic and hierarchical approach to organisation and develop their activities in the framework of corporate planning.

With its promise of collective empowerment and self-determination, the activist model rejects the construction of the distinction between the provision and consumption of welfare, and appears to replace the hierarchical dependency relationship between client and patron with relations of trust and mutual support. Yet the commitment to trust and mutual support can be quite tenuous. As critics have stressed, authoritarian tendencies lurk within the preoccupation with securing commitment to a 'cause' and can generate leadership and organisational styles that prohibit the extension of mutual relationships to those not committed to 'the faith'.

The welfare state industry model

The welfare state industry model signals the high tide of the modernist welfare state. As discussed in chapter 4, the idea of the welfare state sits comfortably in the theoretical framework of the neutral independent state and it privileges state responsibility for provision of community services. That is, community organisations are agents of state provision, funded and largely controlled by centralised welfare bureaucracies. Their activities and organisational forms are based squarely on the idea that social and community services are an industry. A strong commitment to the welfare state industry model can be manifested in a preoccupation with procedural form and an emphasis on following rules (Considine, 1996), and in the adoption of the authoritarian principles of new managerialism.

The focus of this model is on the politics of equality and distribution, rather than on the politics of difference and identity. Concern with equality of welfare provision is manifested through the standardisation of programs and welfare delivery practice. Ideas of redistribution are implicit in a commitment to residual welfare, or welfare as a safety net for those who are unable to fend for themselves, and are manifested in the targeting of programs. In this model, welfare services are best delivered by an expert, professionally trained workforce. The concept of empowerment may be invoked, but it is constructed in an individualist rather than a collectivist way. For example, empowerment may involve a professional worker identifying strategic lifestyle choices for the welfare recipient in the course of professional counselling.

State control is maintained through a variety of mechanisms that are embedded in instrumental rationalism and a commitment to professionalism. During the 1980s in Australia, the strength of the instrumental welfare state industry model meant that community organisations had to learn how to operate within guidelines, and injunctions required them to clarify their performance indicators, measure output and outcomes and evaluate the effectiveness of their programs. The ethos of professionalisation has been maintained through the development of competency standards for workers and the strengthening of professional organisations as guardians of standards and ethics.

The welfare state industry model presents a clear configuration of citizenship rights. The right to welfare is supported by the state. However, in Australia the right to welfare is not universally guaranteed to all members of society. Welfare programs are carefully targeted and recipients have to fulfil obligations in order to receive welfare benefits. Overall, the extent to which welfare rights are secure will depend on the government policies in place at any one time. In the case of community organisations, while welfare programs might be provided by the organisation, they are funded by the state and operate under strict guidelines set by the state. The separation of provider and clients and maintenance of the professional ethos ensure that welfare recipients are the passive consumers of welfare. In fact, welfare rights are circumscribed by the residual nature of welfare provision in Australia; eligibility requirements, especially those based around concepts of duty (such as the 'work test' for receipt of the various forms of unemployment benefit); and the targeting of recipient groups.

There is much about the welfare state industry model that does not sit easily with the principles of community development. It is top-down in approach and is based on a passive form of citizenship whereby rights are decided upon from above. When operating through tight bureaucratic regulations, community organisations can be hampered in their attempts to respond to diverse needs. Centralised control also impedes efforts to develop flexibility in the delivery of programs. While attention is paid to issues of equality through, for example, the standardised formula according to which welfare programs are delivered, institutional asymmetries of economic and political power are not redressed. There is little or no room for the extension of democratic processes.

Yet some of the principles of the welfare state industry model and community development do overlap. Both sets of principles retain important roles for the state, although with significant differences in emphasis. Most community development programs are premised on some form of government funding for community welfare. Both the welfare state industry model and community development seek state mechanisms to ensure quality of welfare provision. However, from the welfare state industry perspective, quality assurance is linked to the procedural and regulatory functions of the state and a professionally trained workforce, for example, while from the perspective of community development the value of programs is not linked to technical tests, but to the level of community participation and whether programs empower the communities they serve. Thus, there are profound differences in degree and type of acceptable state intervention in the two approaches to community organisation.

The market model

The market model differs radically from other models. It is based on a commitment to the idea of the market and the principles of neo-liberal economics. Thus it is strongly anti-collectivist and premised on the view that competition is the motor of progress. The market model is concerned with the politics of need and difference to the extent that a diverse private sector is 'free' to pursue a plurality of needs and interests, or the market is left 'free' to respond to the diverse needs of welfare consumers. The market model is organised around the idea of choice. There is a view that, as the processes of marketisation are embraced, both institutional and individual asymmetries of power will be redressed. When the full market mechanism is put in place, community organisations will be empowered to develop, choose and operate their own programs. Once welfare recipients have been constructed as *consumers,* they will have the power to enter or not enter the welfare marketplace and to choose whatever service they want. The devolution of responsibility to direct service providers for the delivery of programs can enhance responsiveness to consumer needs and good quality programs (Paddon, 1993; Sanderson, 1993). Importantly, the privatised way of delivering welfare does nothing to correct asymmetries of power or the passive welfare citizenship found in welfare state industry models.

There are interesting similarities and differences between the market model and the principles of community development. In terms of similarities, both the market model and community development are committed to pluralism. For example, they emphasise responsiveness to diverse needs and flexibility in the delivery of programs and they both allow community organisations to develop their own programs free from the constraining red tape of state bureaucracies. However, in the market model that dominates in Australia policy, control remains in the hands of the state (the steering process) and the tight fiscal controls and constraints that set the terms of the relationship between community organisations and the state are not conducive to autonomy and self-determination for community organisations. The requirement that community organisations operate along new managerialist lines and compete with each other, often as though they were for-profit businesses, also undermines the commitment to devolution of decision making, collaboration and sharing principles of community.

The social entrepreneurship model

The social entrepreneurship draws on many of the ideas of the market model but emphasises the social mission of community organisations. We have engaged the idea of entrepreneurialism in chapter 2, where we identified social entrepreneurship as a key element of the context in which community development works today. In this chapter we discuss in more detail the different themes in social entrepreneurship and their application to community organisations. There are now many enjoinders for community organisations to embrace the idea of social entrepreneurship (Productivity Commission, 2010; Social Enterprise Coalition, 2010). From a community development perspective, we can identify two themes in social entrepreneurship. First is the idea of social enterprise organisations as businesses trading for social and environmental purposes (Social Enterprise Coalition,

2010). Here the market model discussed has a clear resonance. Second is the idea of creating leaders and animators who are driven by a social mission, but are entrepreneurial in their endeavours. We will consider each of these themes in turn.

Social entrepreneurial businesses, like all businesses, compete to deliver goods and services. Unlike most community organisations, they seek to eliminate or significantly reduce reliance on government and other funds. While they adopt traditional business tools, they also challenge conventional structures and identify new opportunities (Skoll Centre for Social Entrepreneurship, 2009).

Social entrepreneurial organisations see their activities as social investment and seek a social return on such investment. For example, they investigate the social and environmental impact of their endeavours. As the UK-based Social Enterprise Coalition (2010) states, the difference is that social purpose is at the very heart of what social entrepreneurial businesses do, and the profits they make are reinvested towards achieving the social purpose rather than being driven by the need to maximise profit for shareholders and owners. While the description of businesses as social entrepreneurial appears new, a number of such organisations operated 30 years ago, such as Community Aid Abroad. Today, social entrepreneurial businesses range from small stalls in markets selling products for local or international cooperatives, such as those run by Aboriginal peoples and East Timorese selling handicrafts, to large global enterprises, such as the *Big Issue*.

The second theme involves the idea of social entrepreneurs working in community organisations to initiate innovative projects that can generate new activities and new sources of funds. Social entrepreneurs are enjoined to use their skills to make a difference, to 'make things happen'. As Stewart-Weeks (2001:23) comments:

> [Social entrepreneurship] combines the passion of a social mission with an image of business-like discipline, innovation and determination commonly associated with, for instance, the high-tech pioneers of Silicon Valley ... Entrepreneurs are prepared to leverage resources, energy and vision to make ideas happen, to exploit opportunities that others either don't or can't see or don't or won't execute.

Thus, social entrepreneurship has a strong emphasis on individual leadership, and in this sense it can sit uneasily with community development. Rather than operate within a community's terms of reference, social entrepreneurs set themselves apart from the community. The effect of embracing the principles of social entrepreneurship, albeit usually unintended, is to free government from its responsibility to provide financial and other support for community organisations, which are so necessary for the development of the non-profit activities that maintain community infrastructure.

Structures of community organisations

Every organisation has a structure that sets the organisational parameters, including how it works: who does what, why, when and where; how decisions are made; and the nature of authority in the organisation. The 'way things are usually done' varies significantly between organisations. Some organisations develop **policy and procedures manuals**, which set out how the organisation functions. Policy and procedures manuals are discussed below. Other organisations have informal processes, which are passed on by word of mouth. Increasingly, community organisations are required to put in place some kind of formal policy protocols and even to embrace some formal management practices.

There are many textbooks on formal organisational structures and organisational behaviour, which, from varying perspectives, analyse and instruct on management structures in large and small organisations. Community development practitioners are critical of much of this instructional literature because it tends to reinforce hierarchical bureaucratised structures and new managerialist processes. Below we sketch out the features of bureaucratic and new managerialist structures and processes to highlight why they are antithetical to community development.

Bureaucracy and scientific management

Early in the twentieth century, Weber (1946) constructed an ideal type, model or abstracted definition of a **bureaucratic organisation**, which is still relevant today. Bureaucracy is an administrative structure that is designed for the rational and efficient pursuit of organisational goals. It has set rules to govern its operation, directed towards organisational ends. Administration is based on standardised documents. There is a hierarchical structure of power, with clear channels of command and responsibility. Tasks are specialised in a bureaucratic organisation and roles are clearly defined. Tasks are distributed as official duties, and relationships between organisational members and clients are impersonal. Personnel are recruited on the basis of skills and technical knowledge, and promotion is on the basis of seniority or merit. The process of working through official channels in which responsibility and accountability are held at the top of a hierarchy and instructions are passed down from each level to the subordinate level is called **line management**. Organisational forms that separate production activities from coordination activities, and divide tasks into small discrete actions in which each worker's job is simplified, are based on an approach to organisation called **scientific management** (or **Taylorism** after FW Taylor, who proposed this form of organisation to increase profitability). Such an organisational structure is not compatible with the principles of community development. Bureaucratic organisation through its administrative operation has been important in the development of the modern state and in expanding such institutions as the welfare state. The emphasis is on formal rational action, which is calculable and systematic. Concerns about maximising the calculability of means, legal formalism, appropriate rules and administrative procedures replace values and ethical considerations. Even within its own terms of reference, a bureaucratic organisation does not necessarily fulfil its purpose. The specialisation of tasks means that most workers have no overview of the working of the organisation; they often ritualistically adhere to rules without understanding why or they bend the rules to make their working lives easier. The rules and hierarchy constrain flexible and creative responses when circumstances change. Specialisation and hierarchy can direct loyalty to co-workers rather than to the organisation, undermining the authority of senior management.

From a Marxist perspective, bureaucracies and scientific management are methods of increasing control over and deskilling workers (see Braverman, 1974). These developments have led to the establishment of a managerial class, distinct both from those who own the means of production and from the working class. Bureaucracies also control workers by setting rules and through the power of management prerogatives.

In a bureaucratic structure, the real goal tends to be the maintenance of the organisation itself, while the workers come to see adherence to the rules as their goal. Workers become isolated, and depersonalised relationships prevail. Rules can disguise the underlying relations of domination and subordination. The specialisation of tasks means that each worker is expendable. In this context, those who are 'soft' on subordinates are seen as 'bad managers'.

Ferguson (1984) argues that bureaucracies are a primary source of oppression of both women and men in capitalist society. They destroy personal relations and the very foundation of self-identity:

> Bureaucracy separated people from one another in their activities, and from themselves in their roles: our lives are fragmented into partial actions and needs (for example, citizen versus taxpayer versus unemployed person versus old person) and our dependency on the very organisations that spawn this fragmentation is perpetuated (Ferguson, 1984:13).

Feminists point to the patriarchal nature of bureaucratic organisations: their hierarchical, authoritarian, rule-based structures; their competitiveness; and the self-interested career orientation of workers. Moreover, as Watson (1990:9) comments, 'Bureaucracies operate on a closed system of favours, shared perspectives and values, deals, hierarchies of knowledge, and mystification'. Female employees in bureaucracies are commonly in subordinate (often part-time) positions. 'Women are much more likely than men to be face-to-face "clients" of government bureaucracies, on the receiving end of social services' (Sassoon, 1987:78).

The rise of new managerialism

Overlaid on the traditional form of bureaucratic organisation are both the consistencies and inconsistencies of new managerialism. We have already discussed new managerialism in previous chapters. In this chapter, we discuss the links between new managerialism and bureaucratic organisation. Commitment to managerial policy setting (at the top of an organisation), goal-directed behaviour and value neutrality are themes that are found in both bureaucracies and new managerialism. However, while the conventional bureaucratic form has emphasised set procedures and rules, in a number of bureaucracies there has been a shift away from a focus on process to a concern with output and outcomes and a commitment to managerial leadership, autonomy and initiative. In place of stability and certainty for the workforce, an increasing emphasis has been placed on flexibility in working conditions and work practices. As discussed in chapter 2, new managerialism is consistent with the individualist and 'can-do' approach of enterprise culture, based on the principles of overcoming or even ignoring problems or difficulties in order to 'get things done'. The traditional rule-governed or procedurally based bureaucracies are characterised as slow nit-picking 'problem finders' rather than as 'problem solvers'. Considine (1996) sees much of this shift in bureaucratic organisations in terms of a movement from **procedural bureaucracy** (focusing on procedures) to what he identifies as the **corporate bureaucracy** (concerned with the achievement of goals).

However, it can also be argued that community organisations now have to work under a type of regime that requires both procedural accountability and achievement of goals. In the context of the risk society that we discussed in chapter 3, community organisations are required to have risk-management strategies in place and they must have satisfied insurance and legal requirements in order to operate. In addition, community development workers comment on how the reporting requirements for governments and funding bodies have become more onerous, as are the extensive policy and performance protocols (see Productivity Commission, 2010). While there is general support for transparency and accountability in community organisations, participants and workers question both the level and direction of accountability. That is, accountability is seen to be insured through reporting, based on performance (sometimes known as **performativity**), and it is based on systems that require reporting to the state or funding bodies, rather than to the community or communities with whom the organisation is working.

As discussed in chapter 2, there is much that is anti-democratic and disempowering for ordinary rank-and-file workers in new managerialism. By giving (often more) power to managers to manage as they see fit, new managerialism is essentially a form of autocratic management. The emphasis on flexibility in the labour process and labour force engenders fear and uncertainty among workers, rather than unleashing creativity and enterprising behaviour, as the rhetoric of new managerialism seems to promise. Sennett (2004, 1998) and Bauman (2004) have pointed out that workplace flexibility comes hand in hand with a 'winner takes all' approach, whereby workers are subjected to the whims of institutions manoeuvring around the principle of market advantage. Workers are brought in or discarded by managers at will. They lose value, dignity and control of their lives. Ironically, in contrast to the 'can-do' approach of new managerialism, there has been some reconsideration of the positive outcomes for the community of an approach that identifies problems before they arise and emphasises standardisation of processes and procedures. In contrast to the insecurity in the new workplace, some workers are favourably reviewing the security and career paths provided by the old bureaucratic structures of state institutions.

Yet as also discussed in previous chapters, new managerialism can be seen as part of a shift in thinking that emphasises outcomes, streamlined decision making, innovation, commitment to service users and strategic thinking, and which can be compatible with community development practice.

Vertical and horizontal structures

In the light of the difficulties of new managerialism, bureaucracies and scientific management for community development, we will now consider what types of organisational structure are appropriate to community development. Perhaps the best way of conceptualising appropriate organisational structures is to think about them on a

Chapter 6 Community organisations

continuum. At one end is the formal, closed, hierarchical bureaucratic model discussed above and, at the other, a flat, open, democratic, collective, cooperative mutually supportive model.

It is informative to contrast different organisational structures in diagrams. Figures 6.1 and 6.2 show the main differences between **vertical and horizontal organisation**. These

Figure 6.1 *Hierarchical organisation*

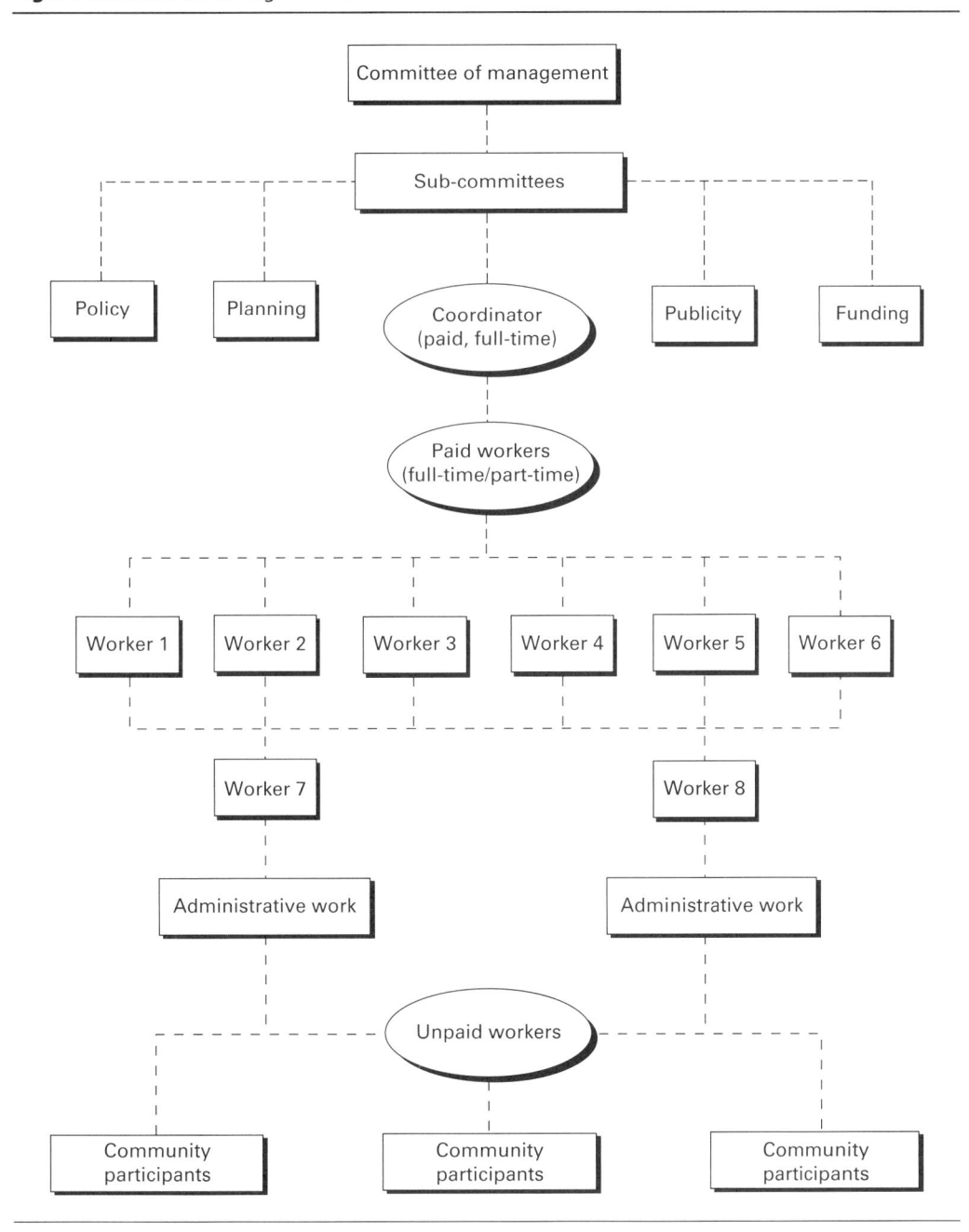

Processes and practices

Figure 6.2 *Non-hierarchical organisation*

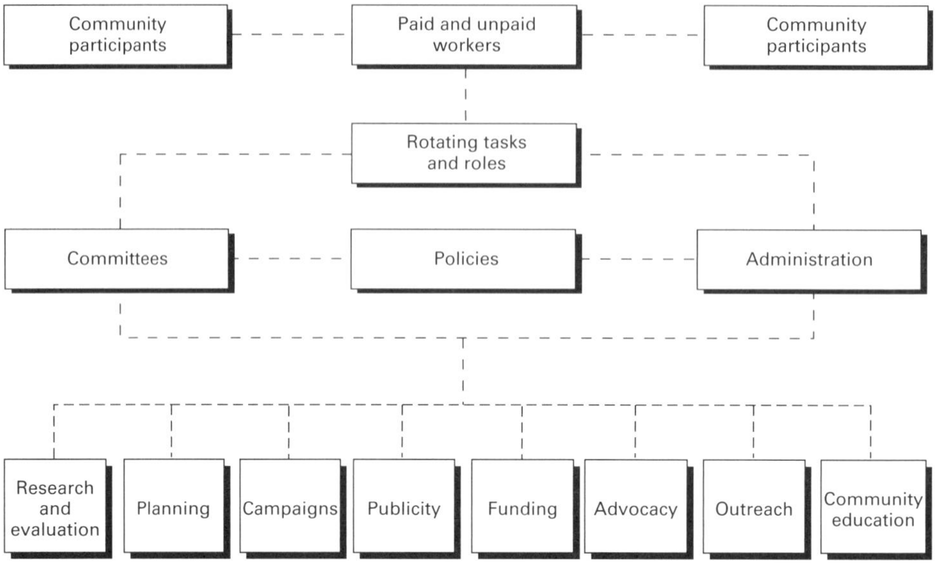

```
    Community          Paid and unpaid         Community
    participants  ---    workers       ---    participants
                            |
                       Rotating tasks
                         and roles
         ----------------------------------
         |                  |                  |
      Committees  -----   Policies   -----  Administration
         |                  |
    ---------------------------------------------------
    |       |        |        |       |       |      |       |
 Research Planning Campaigns Publicity Funding Advocacy Outreach Community
   and                                                          education
 evaluation
```

models, of course, can be mixed. For example, workers may work on a day-to-day basis as a collective, but also have a **committee of management** that comprises all the workers, participants and users.

An appropriate committee of management alongside a collective can help to ensure that a collective is accountable to the community and participants in a program at the same time as it facilitates a less hierarchical working situation interest in collective structures.

Collective models

As shown in figure 6.2, the cooperative, a **collective model** has no hierarchy; decision making is equal and everyone is welcome to participate in it. It attempts to ensure that the voices of those who are marginal in society are heard, and encourages spontaneity, flexibility and assertive solutions to problems. This model of organisation is based on the view that an organisational structure should facilitate equality in power, status, tasks and responsibilities for all the participants. Responsibility is to the group of people involved in the organisation or group. Ideally, where people are in paid employment, everyone is paid the same. Decision making begins from open discussion in an open meeting, roles such as notetaker and facilitator are rotated, the agenda is informal and a process-observer ensures that all participants have a say.

Agreement is by consensus and written up in notes of the meeting, rather than formal motions. In such situations, meetings are held regularly. Everyday activities are halted to facilitate full participation, and full reporting ensures that each member of the collective is informed of all that is going on. All members' voices and skills are taken as having value. Indeed, in a collective organisation it is assumed that everyone has something to offer; members are required to contribute and share their skills with other members. Staff are encouraged to learn new skills and share information, and this is seen to foster common bonds and a caring environment.

In contrast to formal bureaucracies, informal collectives often shift strategy away from emphasising the efficient achievement of measurable objectives and towards increasing involvement of all participants in the processes. Also, unlike bureaucracies, no one person has authority over another. A collective approach to decision making requires that people can work together cooperatively as a group, for the benefit of the whole organisation or group. This means respecting and trusting others in the organisation and declaring and negotiating conflicts, including conflicts of interest. Within collectives there is no manager, and roles and responsibilities should reflect both the existing and potential abilities of individual workers. Positions such as spokesperson, treasurer and receptionist are rotated. Decisions about hiring staff, budgets and policies are made collectively at meetings.

Limitations and criticisms of collective models

Collective organisations appear to be consistent with community development principles. They prefigure a social system that is non-authoritarian, non-hierarchical and egalitarian. Yet Landry et al. (1985) argue that while collective decision making is appropriate for a small group of, say, four to six people (for example, in a modest campaign in which a collective is much more effective than a national organisation), a long-term campaign requires more formal structures, lines of responsibility and a clear division of labour. And Twelvetrees (1982) points out that if a community is mounting a campaign that requires tight coordination and planning, roles and responsibilities need to be clearly delineated.

Other important issues and criticisms should be considered when developing collective structures. For example, such organisations can become closed and parochial. Denial of power structures does not eliminate underlying power relations. In fact, denial may obscure them. Elites can take over a collective without the members being fully aware of it; and even if they do realise it, there is no process for dealing with the unequal power. In fact, as Landry et al. (1985) argue, the breaking down of hierarchy and denial of unequal skills can cause an organisation to work at the lowest common level of skills and it can become bogged down with inefficiency and trivia. A loosely organised collective can actually be a less effective way of making democratic decisions than a more formal community organisation. For example, in unstructured meetings, the strongest personalities can dominate. If membership and decision making become too casual, decisions can be overturned by any new group of people who attend a meeting.

In such a situation, it is often believed that 'as long as we fight in the right way we are bound to win'. From here it is only a short step to thinking that it doesn't matter if we win, as long as we've played the game in the right spirit (Landry et al., 1985:13). The same authors point to the inbuilt structural delays or 'bias against action' of collectivism. It takes time to let everyone have a say and reach consensus; it may not be possible to wait until the next meeting before action can be carried out. Because a collective gives equal power to those who are skilled and unskilled, activities may not be completed. It is necessary to assign responsibility for ensuring that tasks such as the preparation of a submission are allocated and fulfilled. Consensus decision making, whereby members try to find a decision that is acceptable to everyone, can be long and arduous. Conflicts of interest and personal and political sensitivities arise when workers participate in decisions on matters such as wage rises and sackings. Landry et al. (1985) argue that collectives are prone to personal conflict and have a tendency to individualise and personalise issues. In fact, a collective can actually be less accountable to a community than a more hierarchical organisation.

There are two related responses to these criticisms of collectives.

- We live in a social and political environment that is hostile to the development of cooperative non-hierarchical organisations, so there is little room for practising to make different processes work. We have to make spaces in which we can practise new forms of organisation.
- Many of the critiques of collectives, including that of Landry et al., contrast what they see as the inadequacies of existing collectives against an idealised version. This point is strongly made by Stanton (1989), who argues that we should be much less ambitious in our expectations of collectives, particularly in regard to the grand claims of workplace democracies that they are prefiguring future socialist societies.

Appropriate structures

In fact, most community organisations have a mix of structural arrangements, depending on such factors as their stage of development, the programs and services they operate and their objectives. What is clear, then, is that there is no one model structure for a community organisation, because an appropriate structure depends on the needs and stage of a community organisation or project.

When deciding upon or analysing and evaluating the structure of a community organisation, it is important to keep in mind that organisational structures are there to get things done and to empower people. The structure must help the organisation to make decisions in an effective and democratic way, to facilitate the involvement of all members of a community, to build on strengths, to identify objectives and carry out strategies to achieve them; that is, the structure must facilitate the (democratically decided) wishes of the community members. There is a range of organisational arrangements to do this and some general elements facilitate the effectiveness of the organisation's ability to empower ordinary people. These are discussed in the following section.

Committee work

We can identify two rationales for committee work. First there is increasing emphasis on committee work that is necessary part of compliance with the regulatory framework. For example, committees oversee the processes of fiscal reporting, risk assessment and insurance claims. Second, committee work is part of the democratic governance of the community sector. Yet, while community development requires transparency and accountability as part of its adherence to the regulatory framework, and is based on a commitment to facilitating participatory decision making, workers often complain that too much of their time is spent in fruitless committee work and meetings. Some workers believe that too much is expected from committees. They argue that, rather than being neutral forums for democratic discussion and the allocation of tasks, committees are sites where people compete with each other for power and status. Many people have experienced ineffectual or overbearing committees, and bullying tactics in meetings. Yet subgroups and committees are essential for both accountability processes and democratic decision making. If procedures are clearly set out and followed, and decisions are carried out, the experience can be empowering. Of course, clear procedures cannot guarantee effective or democratic decision making, but they can help to make an organisation, committee or meeting function more smoothly.

Meetings

The usual method of sharing information; clarifying, discussing and making decisions; negotiating; and reviewing the progress of a committee is a meeting. It is interesting to reflect on how attitudes to meetings have changed. In the 1970s, workers in community organisations tended to see meetings as a way of ensuring that information was available to all and that democratic decision-making processes were in place. Meetings were seen as an effective way of ensuring the smooth functioning of an organisation. In the twenty-first century, this enthusiasm for meetings has dissipated. Workers complain of time-wasting and ineffective meetings that do not provide information or use democratic processes. They often argue that meetings have become forums for ratifying decisions that have already been made and for political point-scoring. In this context it is wise to think about whether a meeting is really called for. Indeed there are occasions when decisions and information sharing can effectively take place without a meeting. Thus, it is always important to ask why a particular meeting is needed at a particular time and for what purpose.

There are several different types of meetings, including large public meetings, annual meetings of the whole membership and monthly committee meetings. The difference between an effective and ineffective meeting often lies in the abilities of the facilitator or chairperson. A good facilitator or chair respects the members of the group, is interested in what people have to say and offer, can summarise well and is assertive without being overbearing. Beaumont (1987) has identified 'rules' for achieving productive meetings:

- *planning:* arranging the venue, agenda, etc.
- *informing people:* making sure that everyone knows about the meeting
- *preparing:* for example, timing and prioritising items on the agenda
- *structure and control:* clarifying the scope, aims and decision-making capacity of the meeting
- *summarising and recording:* making an accurate record of discussion motions and actions to be taken, including who is responsible for what.

From a community development perspective, these rules should be subject to democratic discussion and scrutiny. Clear meeting procedures that everyone understands are an essential part of a good meeting. As Roberts (1991:29) states:

> Knowledge and use of procedures are often used either as tools of war or peace. Ignorance and misuse of the procedures can be used similarly. However ... meeting procedure is the

responsibility of *every person* at the meeting ... Every person has the responsibility to assist the chairperson if her/his skills or confidence are not great. And any person can question or challenge an overconfident or officious chairperson during a meeting.

From a community development standpoint, a good meeting as one that is open, cooperative and collaborative, with everyone contributing, feeling respected and learning something useful. Within these general principles, however, there is scope for a range of purposes and styles. For example, a meeting might be called for no other reason than to share information and ideas. Alternatively a meeting might be called to plan or identify an appropriate strategy. In addition to the requirements above, a good strategy or planning meeting is one that reaches decisions, identifies actions relating to these decisions and allocates tasks. The key is whether participants in general get something out of the meeting – clarification of a decision, problem sharing, resolution of an issue, or information – that they could not achieve in another way. Participants certainly know when they have experienced a bad meeting: it drags on, provides little or no new or useful information, or is dominated by a few people and may be intimidating.

For community organisations, the two key principles are making decisions democratically and sharing information. These principles can conflict with the need to get things done as quickly as possible. It may be necessary to compromise between dealing with the business of the meeting in a reasonable time and allowing sufficient time for people to gain information, reflect, discuss and come to a consensus. Sometimes another meeting may be called to discuss a particular issue, but this can use up time and energy, leaving little for other tasks.

Community development workers learn to live with this situation, knowing that patience in listening to others and sharing information is part of a democratic society; that is, democracy requires time, patience and commitment. However, they also point out that when information is shared openly, all options are explored and decisions are made democratically, the participants in the decision-making process are more likely to ensure that a decision is effectively executed than if they had been coerced into accepting it.

Establishing a committee

When establishing a committee, the sponsoring community organisation or community group decides on its terms of reference, its activities and its composition in terms of numbers and categories of membership. More formal community organisations call for nominations and hold an election for representative positions. Some community organisations have standing office-bearers, such as chairperson and secretary; others rotate these positions. Some community organisations make a clear separation between policy and execution (actually carrying out the tasks). For example, a committee of management may make policy and the workers carry out the policies in their daily activities (often known as the **governance model** of community management). In other committees, however, some members are involved in executive tasks, as well as policy decisions. Committee work involves strong commitment to a community organisation or group, its causes and programs. Significant energy and time is required, both for unpaid and paid workers (even paid workers are not compensated fully for their involvement). People who join community-based committees must be able to work well with a range of other people; they need to develop knowledge of the principles of community development and community structures, as well as skills in committee processes. Finding such people can be a difficult task. It can be easier if the community organisation is clear about its philosophy and what is expected of the members of the committee. Some community organisations expect all members to contribute equally to the working of the committee. Others accept that committee members have different levels of input, but emphasise the importance of clarifying individuals' expectations and ensuring that all members are valued.

Committees of management

In Australia, most community organisations have some kind of committee of management. The rationale for this is to ensure that an organisation has a strong community base and is accountable to its community. Membership of a committee of management can include, for example, participants in programs run by the community organisation; other members of the local community such as community activists, youth and ethnic representatives; local MPs and councillors, the editor of a local newspaper; paid and unpaid workers in the community organisation; and representatives of funding bodies. Committees of management should have balanced gender, age and ethnic representation, and a mixture of old and new members.

The formal purpose of a committee of management is to ensure that the organisation is working well and achieving its goals. Under the governance approach discussed in chapter 2, a committee of management will not be involved in the day-to-day running of the organisation, but it should be informed as to how activities are going generally. The Victorian Council of Social Service (VCOSS, 1991) sets out eight key responsibilities for committees of management:

1 *The overall role*: overseeing the operations and activities of the organisation to make sure it fulfils its aims. This includes the smooth operation of the management group – in other words, 'the buck stops here'!
2 *Legal responsibilities:* meeting the requirements of a range of federal, state and local government laws and regulations on such matters as incorporation, insurance, permits, licences, copyright, defamation, occupational health and safety, awards and taxation.
3 *Financial responsibilities:* ensuring that there are adequate funds for the operation of the organisation, that the organisation works within the limits of these funds, that records are kept and funds accounted for. These responsibilities include the development of a funding strategy, obtaining funds, drawing up budgets, monitoring expenditure, bookkeeping, financial statements and audits, negotiating funding and service agreements, reporting on the use of funds.
4 *Personnel:* designing jobs; developing job descriptions; recruiting, training, supervising and supporting staff; disciplining and dismissing staff. Responsibilities include occupational health and safety issues and the development of employment policies.

5 *Premises and equipment:* ensuring that premises, facilities and physical resources are provided and maintained so that the services can be provided properly and safely.
6 *Planning and policy:* making sure that the guidelines and a framework are provided so that everyone in the organisation knows where it is headed, what it aims to achieve, and how each job fits into the overall plan.
7 *Promotion and marketing:* raising awareness and publicising the organisation, its aims, its services and its achievements. The credibility of the organisation with service users, funders, policy makers and the wider community depends on how well this is done.
8 *Reporting and accountability:* informing and involving consumers, members and the wider community. Funders and policy makers also need to be kept informed about the organisation and its achievements.

VCOSS also reminds us that any organisation needs to determine which decisions can be made by staff, coordinators, subcommittees and the committee of management. From a community development perspective, it is imperative to add participants and users of services and programs to this list and, of course, as a structure becomes more collective in style, then more egalitarian processes will be adopted. VCOSS (1991:12) advises that organisations should determine where the responsibilities of the management group stop and those of paid workers start. Members of a management committee are each responsible to the other members, as in a collective. The group as a whole should maintain its independence from narrow interest groups and political parties, and must be wary of co-option on the part of funding and other powerful bodies.

A committee of management has several advantages: it is a vehicle for input from the community, a wide range of knowledge and skills is contributed by members of varying backgrounds and it promotes accountability from the workers to the committee of management, and from the committee of management to the workers, participants and funding bodies. On the surface, committees of management appear to be an ideal basis for a good community organisational structure.

However, over the last 10 years the responsibilities of members of committee of management have increased and the time required to undertake the tasks well has become progressively more onerous. Committees of management are required to take on increasingly complex responsibilities and tasks, including greater fiscal responsibilities, risk-assessment and legal responsibilities. Members and aspiring members are increasingly required to enrol in the many courses now available that set out in detail the roles and responsibilities of committees of management (see, for example, PilchConnect). To carry out the functions for which they are formed, associations have rules about how they will operate. These rules can be unwritten but are usually written down formally as a *constitution* or *rules*. Increasingly, community organisations are formally incorporated. Many legal firms offer pro bono assistance to community organisations to help with the legal tasks.

There are also endless tales of disastrous policies, fruitless meetings, infighting, self-interest, incompetence, lack of interest and bullying of staff. Members of committees are sometimes driven by their own political agendas, rather than by working for a community. Some committees are stacked with middle-class professionals of Anglo-Celtic background and function as elitist clubs, working against the interests of the disempowered members of society. Some committees slip into a hierarchical mode of operation because this is the only way they know.

Overall then, a number of factors contribute to the difficulties faced by committees of management and they are not always easy to resolve. However, some suggestions and warnings can be put forward. A good committee of management must represent the community, as defined, as far as possible. It should encourage the open and full participation of all those involved in the community organisation in order to enable participants and workers to cooperatively control and develop programs. When committees of management are predominantly male or of middle-class or professional backgrounds, they need to make a determined effort to redress gender or class imbalance (if necessary, by resigning) and understand the perspectives of working-class women of non-English-speaking backgrounds, for example.

From a community development perspective, the central issues for committees are who are the members, are they clear about their roles and responsibilities, how accountable are they to the community at large and what powers do they have over workers?

Ward (1991) points out that it is contradictory to ask community development workers to adopt community development practices in their contact with the community while the organisation itself maintains a hierarchical structure. Policies should belong not to management or staff but to the organisation as a whole. Ward (1991:13) emphasises that greater participation by all will improve the effectiveness of any service and this means working as a team:

> Never do anything without involving others – there is always another point of view and there is always someone else available to assist or at least give you an opinion.

In maintaining committees, it is important that membership tasks are clear both to prospective members of the committee and to other members of the organisation, including workers and participants. Members of the committee should be clear about their expectations. Long-term members should help new members and inform them about the functioning of the committee. The role of chair, whether semi-permanent or rotated, must be clear; a good chairperson is invaluable to a committee of management. In addition, the conditions and term of membership of a committee of management must be well understood. Recruitment of members for committees is a demanding task. This is particularly so because, as VCOSS (1991:66) points out, oppressed and disadvantaged people often lack the time and confidence to participate, yet these are the very people who should be members of a committee of management.

Deliberative democracy

Notwithstanding all the emphasis on committee work and committees of management, in the last few years there has been a growing interest in exploring a new process for information sharing and decision making, which undercuts the hierarchical structures that still operate in most community organisations. This process involves **deliberative democracy**.

To understand the importance of deliberative democracy, it is useful to begin with five principles that underpin commitment to all deliberative processes. First is the commitment to deliberation itself. Deliberation involves discussing matters of public and mutual interest and concern as peers in order to learn about the topic or issues and other people's interest, opinions and perspectives (Cohen, 1999:215). In regard to human rights, for example, Ife (2001:118) points out that involvement in discussion of what constitute human rights is itself a specific human right. Deliberation is set up when people talk to each other in some kind of structured situation. It involves listening to and taking account of the views of others. It involves weighing up the consequences and costs of various options, including the consequences of one's own views (Social and Civic Policy Institute, 2000). Deliberation 'is distinguished from other kinds of communication in that the deliberators are amenable to changing their judgements, preferences, and views during the course of their interactions, which involve persuasion rather than coercion, manipulation, or deception' (Dryzek, 2000:1). That is, people involved in deliberation must want to increase their understanding of a topic, to reflect on what they know and exchange ideas.

An important line of influence here comes from the tradition of critical theory, which we have discussed previously. We have already encountered Habermas's idea of **instrumental rationality** (the capacity to identify specific ends and to achieve these by rational means). Instrumental rationality involves specific strategies for achieving goals. Communication is instrumental when it involves one party trying to force or convince another party to do something, as in a debate or a political contest. Political parties engage in this type of **promotional communication**. But not all communication and action is instrumental in this way. Human action also involves communication for the purpose of understanding, which is sometimes called **dialogical communication**. Dialogical communication involves communication directed at sharing information, interpretations and ideas, rather than promoting a particular viewpoint. According to Habermas, **communicative competence** occurs when communication is free from coercion, manipulation, deception and self-deception. Deliberative democracy is based on a commitment to achieving this form of communicative competence.

Second, deliberative democracy requires that citizens have the *opportunity* to critique policies and decisions, exchange ideas and participate generally in the democratic process. Thus, democratic legitimacy has come to be linked with 'the ability or opportunity to participate in effective deliberation on the part of those subject to collective decisions' (Dryzek, 2000:1).

The third principle of deliberative democracy concerns the value of public conversation and public identification of topics that need to be discussed, including problems and issues. As Warren (2001:81) notes, 'Silence serves the wealthy and powerful well, and public argument is one of the few resources through which poorer and weaker members of society can exert influence'. Warren adds that public discussion can be a powerful tool in setting the parameters of public debate. Thus, deliberative democracy needs to take place in a public space, such as a public forum.

The fourth principle is a commitment to the view that all humans have the capacity to contribute to knowledge and to learn. The authors of a handbook on deliberation comment on the value of reflection for participants in deliberation:

> Many who participate will reflect on their own views, the reasoning behind them and, in the context of hearing others' differing views, may have second thoughts and become more appreciative of what lies behind others' views. People learn that they are capable of understanding complex issues and reaching reasonable judgements about what to do (Social and Civic Policy Institute, 2000:15).

The final principle is a commitment to reciprocal recognition of individuals as speakers exchange ideas and views. This is perhaps the most difficult principle to achieve, given unequal power relations and the extent to which some groups in society are continually marginalised and devalued.

Doing deliberative democracy

A number of instruction pamphlets and booklets explain how to 'do' deliberative democracy, including those produced by the National Issues Forums and the Kettering Foundation in the USA and the Social and Civic Policy Institute in New Zealand. These have influenced the discussion below. Some programs of deliberative democracy are concerned with learning and exchanging ideas, while others involve attempts to deal with disagreements by finding common ground from which the protagonists can work towards solutions. While there is variation in the processes of deliberative democracy, there are some common themes.

- First, the process is assisted by a facilitator, who might be appointed prior to the deliberative process or be elected by the participants. The facilitator follows the rules and guidelines agreed to by the participants. The facilitator outlines the goals of the deliberative process, including the purpose of identifying and discussing choices, rather than debating and 'winning'. The facilitator must remain neutral throughout the process.
- Second, rules and guidelines must be agreed upon. These might include such rules as everyone being given the opportunity to speak as well as not speak, no one person will dominate the discussion and listening is as important as speaking.
- Third, the topic or problem must be named in a way that is clear and easy to understand. For example, the topic might involve suggestions about a policy change, such as whether the age of obtaining a driving licence should be lowered or whether the local council should provide recycling bins in each neighbourhood. The topic might also be based on a desire for information, such as about how refugees are treated in Australia or about unemployment in regional Australia. Sometimes this stage is called 'framing the topic or issue'. As the booklet *Public Politics in Practice* (Social and Civic Policy Institute, 2000:19) points out, framing an issue is important because it draws attention to understanding how the issue is presented, rather than jumping straight into a conclusion or solution. Too often problems that affect us are defined by experts with so-called solutions. Politicians and the media focus on the debate about the solution, rather than the problem that underlies the solution. The reason why the problem is an issue for people who are affected by it in different ways often gets lost. There are several ways of approaching the framing process. For example:

Processes and practices

- In some deliberative processes, the whole group is involved in this stage of framing the topic or problem, while in other processes a specific 'framing team' is established.
- In some deliberative processes, the framing stage might take a number of weeks or even months, and involves a detailed research process in which data collection, interviewing and analysis are undertaken. In other cases, particularly when there is a sense of urgency, participants might be given a couple of days to pull the material together.

• Fourth, once the topic or problem is named, then approaches can be set out. If the topic involves a clear issue, such as the legalisation of cultivation of marijuana, then three or four approaches might be identified: for example, (1) retaining the status quo (turning a blind eye), (2) liberalising the law or (3) getting tough (zero-tolerance approach). In regard to the specific approaches, a number of questions could be asked:

- What is appealing about this resolution?
- What are the (good and bad) consequences?
- Do you have a favoured resolution? If so, which is it?
- Do you have a view on this particular approach to the topic or problem? If so, what experiences have led you to this view?
- What are the pros and cons of each approach?

• Fifth, much of the process of deliberation involves investigating the various responses to the issues or problems. Certain questions are used at this stage of the deliberation, including:

- What is your interest in the topic or problem? or When you think about this issue what concerns you?
- What are people saying about the topic or problem?
- What is being done about the topic or problem (by you, your community and government)?

The aim of this step is both to get the participants to articulate their often implicit interest in the topic or problem (of course, in many cases this might be minimal), to locate their interest in the wider context and to also allow them to step back from arguing over the topic or problem. This approach encourages people to take on a public perspective, as they consider the choices and options. Once responses are articulated, several more questions could be posed to each of the participants.

- Do you have any views on this particular approach to the topic or problem? If so, what are they?
- What experiences have led you to this view?
- What are the pros and cons of each approach?

If the deliberation is about resolving a problem, the following questions could be asked:

- What are the various solutions to the problem?
- What are the pros and cons of each solution?

- Do you have a favoured solution? If so, which?
- What is appealing about this solution?
- What are the arguments against this choice?

- Sixth, once the issue or problem has been examined from all angles (a litmus test here is to reflect on whether the participants are learning new things or the discussion has become repetitive), then the facilitator can begin to bring the views and lines of argument together, by asking:

    - What are the common points in understanding the topic or problem?
    - Is there any agreement on direction (for example, for policy changes)?
    - If other participants have different views, are you prepared to accept trade-offs? If so, where?

- Finally, the last stage in the deliberative process is reflection. Questions that might be asked in this stage are:

    - Did your views change in the process? If so, why?
    - What were and are the sticking points?
    - What did you learn?

Criticisms of deliberative democracy

It is useful to also note some of the critiques of deliberative democracy, of which there are six major ones. The first criticism is that while engagement in deliberation as a process is a valuable part of community development, some practitioners point out that getting the process of deliberation right is not sufficient to 'change society'. They argue that any process of deliberation must be followed up with social action. We consider social action in the following chapter.

The second criticism is the assumption that participation is always good (see Elster, 1997:13). We have already noted this issue in the previous chapter and we take it up again in chapter 10. The view presented in this book is that people must always have the choice of participating or not participating in a discussion.

The third criticism involves the problem of ensuring reciprocal exchange and understanding, and respect for all parties when there are power differentials and differences in confidence, skills and knowledge. For example, the whole process of reciprocal exchange requires the ability to form and articulate views. Some people feel that they just do not have the knowledge or confidence to express specific views or understandings. This is a valid criticism and it is relevant for all decision making in community development. In an ideal world, the issues of unequal power and differentials in knowledge and skills would not exist or at least would be minimised. In unequal societies such as ours, several strategies can be used to lessen such power differentials. These are, first, to remember that all people have many things that they can offer others. People have different skills and knowledge and this can affect the way others see and respond to them. Second is that good facilitators can make a profound difference in the effective development of deliberative democracy. They must ensure that the aims of deliberation are understood and maintained. They can draw out the range of views and make sure that everyone in a deliberation session is valued and listened to.

The fourth criticism is based on the insight that mutual exchange requires reciprocal trust, especially when discussion requires honest sharing of experiences and openness of views. Again, the two strategies noted above are responses to this criticism.

Fifth, as Elster (1997) points out, deliberative democracy is based on the assumption that group discussion and decisions are always wiser and better than decisions taken by an individual, based on reflection. In fact 'group think', even if it takes place in the context of equality and fairness, is not always necessarily better than an individual's thoughts. An appropriate response to this point is to accept it, but to point out the arguments for deliberative democracy as well.

Finally, a single forum does not change people's views. This is true, but once deliberation becomes a habit and a way of working through complex issues, it allows people to think as active citizens and to participate in a meaningful way in democratic processes.

In concluding this section we should not forget the important promise of deliberative democracy as a way of prefiguring other ways of doing things and challenging the catchcry of TINA (there is no alternative).

Life cycles in community organisations

The following case study highlights the way that community organisations change. They commonly go through a kind of life cycle, experiencing both spurts of energy and setbacks.

POVERTY ACTION PROJECT

Six people are meeting to discuss a new direction for a poverty action project. The project, centred on advocacy and support for low-income people, is now almost two years old. It began when a group of people in a local community – single parents, unemployed people, teachers, academics, financial counsellors, health workers and municipal councillors – met to discuss the issues of poverty and unemployment in their locality. They formed a working group, lobbied local politicians for support, and developed a submission for funds to establish a poverty action project. The project was successfully established with funding from the state government and a philanthropic trust.

The committee of management is active, with about 20 enthusiastic people turning up to the fortnightly meetings. More than 40 people are involved; there are two full-time workers and the resources are well used. The project is fully supported by the community and has a deserved reputation as being successful. It has been given funding for a second year.

About 18 months into the project, the two full-time workers had a disagreement and neither the workers nor the committee of management was able to resolve the conflict. One worker left after a good deal of acrimony and her supporters on the management committee resigned. She was replaced and for a while it seemed that the project had got a second wind. Several new people joined the committee and it looked as if the project would be funded for a third year.

However, two months after the new worker was appointed, the committee of management heard through the grapevine that refunding now appeared unlikely. They wrote to the funding bodies requesting clarification, but received noncommittal answers.

Then the local council, which had provided free accommodation for the project, asked the workers to move from their shopfront to a room at the back of the shire offices, which they did reluctantly. The number of people using the resources dwindled, as did attendance at meetings. The project is now about to lose its funding and paid workers.

The remaining enthusiasts want the project to continue. They argue that there are not many programs involved in advocacy for people with low incomes, and there is a continuing need for such programs. Perhaps they should look at different strategic directions? The discussion turns to the question of how to develop an alternative direction and new sources of funding to cover the project's costs. While the office is still provided free by the local council, the telephone, stationery and mail must be paid for and, without paid workers, all activities will be on a voluntary basis. Several of the participants in the meeting say that they are prepared to contribute their own money to pay for the telephone, stationery and mail. Then the question arises as to how the project could be staffed with unpaid workers while it finds a new direction. It becomes clear that the project cannot operate with unpaid workers. A decision is made to dissolve the project, and a small group is formed to oversee the dissolution.

The history of this project follows the pattern of initial interest and enthusiasm, then establishment and maintenance of the project, followed by a second (or third or fourth) wind, a setback and finally an (informal) evaluation, in this case resulting in dissolution of the project.

Community organisations typically begin as small groups with relatively informal structures. The extent to which the structure becomes more formalised depends on how the organisation develops. Organisations may disband at any point in their life cycle. Some common reasons are:

- they have achieved their objectives
- they see no way of achieving their objectives
- the members move on to another group, organisation or issue
- the members are burnt out and there are no new members
- the organisation is torn apart by internal conflict
- resources, including funds, have dried up or are not available
- the organisation has lost its identity, rationale and legitimacy.

Some continue as small organisations of, say, two workers. Others grow to 20 to 30 workers in one community centre, forming part of a national network. Several environment groups, for example, are of this type.

Roberts (1991) presents an example of a life cycle of community organisations in four stages:

- *Innovation stage:* people recognise or experience a particular need, problem or opportunity and join forces as an informal group to discuss the issue. Roberts comments that this stage is one of energy and enthusiasm.

Processes and practices

- *Establishment stage:* group members agree to work together in order to achieve their objectives. They identify what resources are needed, such as equipment and premises, and develop a membership base and both formal and informal structures.
- *Maintenance stage:* as the group becomes established, there is a sense of achievement. The focus is on maintaining and extending facilities. Roberts points out that structure can become a blockage during this stage and the organisation can lose a sense of direction.
- *Evaluation stage:* the group evaluates what it has done and learnt, and embarks upon forward planning. The organisation may be identified as an established cause and find it difficult to attract funds during this time. Any group, of course, may dissolve at any point in its development, skip a stage, linger too long at one stage or even stagnate (see figure 6.3).

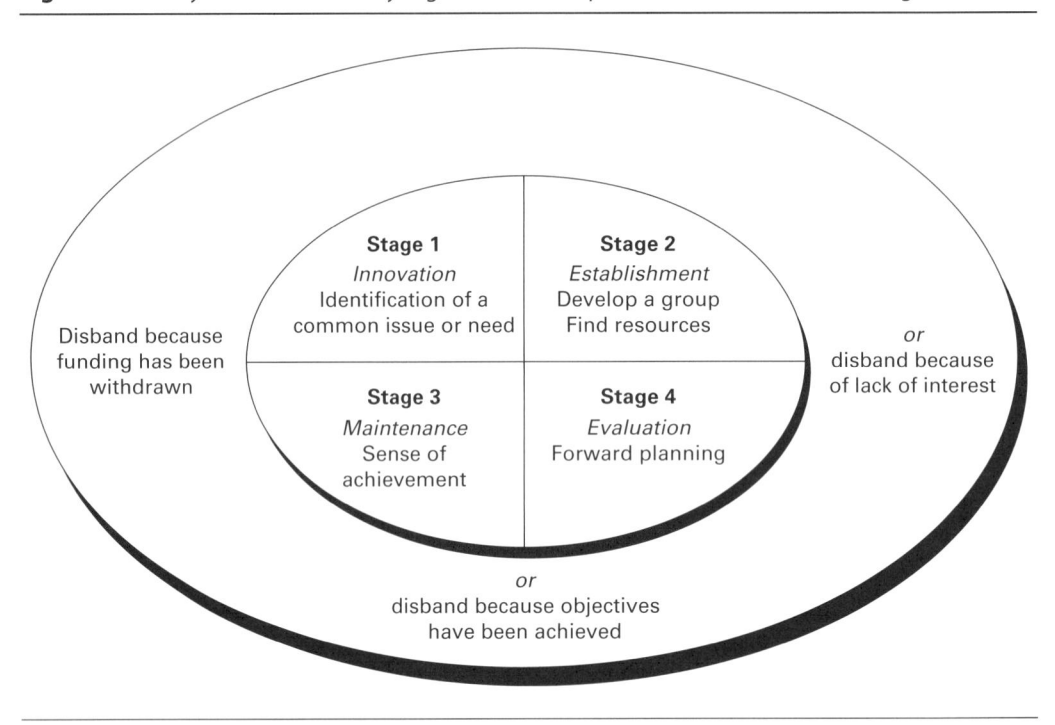

Figure 6.3 *Life cycle of a community organisation and possible reasons for disbanding*

Stage 1 — Innovation — Identification of a common issue or need
Stage 2 — Establishment — Develop a group, Find resources
Stage 3 — Maintenance — Sense of achievement
Stage 4 — Evaluation — Forward planning

Disband because funding has been withdrawn
or disband because of lack of interest
or disband because objectives have been achieved

Of course, the cycle is not closed. Community organisations, consistent with the principle of community development, use open processes that are based on flexibility and adaptability. The direction of the organisation can change at any time in its development. As Ife (2010) reminds us, community development processes and organisations deal with a reality that is not linear and tidy. It is messy, contradictory and often chaotic.

Resource sharing, co-location and amalgamation

Sometimes, after reviewing their priorities and identifying gaps in their resource base, community organisations decide to join with other organisations in ways that will facilitate the sharing of resources. Sometimes the sharing is developed as a partnership, while at other times it involves full amalgamation. In this section we discuss three main ways by which an organisation can share resources with other community organisations: establishing community networks, co-locating and amalgamating.

Community networks are formed when three or more community organisations decide to set up formal or informal contacts, which might be based on commonality in purpose and goals, a desire to share information or resources, common concerns about issues, or lobbying activities, for example. Community networks are maintained through regular meetings, newsletters and more recently through email and other computer-based links, such as sharing a home page on the Internet.

Co-location occurs when two or more community organisations agree to occupy a common location, usually sharing resources such as telephone and computer services, photocopiers and even staff. Each organisation retains its own operating procedures, funding sources and management structure.

Amalgamation occurs when two or more community organisations join together legally to form one organisation with common operating procedures, funding sources and a single management structure (see Management Support and Training Unit, 1993).

In the context of government policy to increase productivity and efficiency, the idea of economies of scale continues in discussions between community organisations and government funding bodies, and a number of community organisations have considered ways of collaborating with other organisations and sharing resources. However, this option has to be dealt with carefully, as collaboration can also be seen to be breaching the National Competition Policy.

Responsibilities of community organisations

Increasingly, government departments have made incorporation a condition of funding, and today all but the small informal community organisations are incorporated. An incorporated committee is legally separate from the individuals who are members, so the personal liability of committee members is limited. The organisation, rather than its individual members, can be sued and can own property. The incorporated organisation, being a legal entity, can enter into contracts. It retains its legal identity regardless of internal changes in staffing, committee membership and direction.

A community organisation must ensure that there are sufficient funds to maintain its operation, and that funds are accounted for. Tasks include the proper keeping of records, preparing budgets, monitoring income and expenditure, and preparing financial reports. Community organisations often elect or appoint treasurers to handle these matters. From a community development perspective it is preferable for all workers, committee members and participants to understand and have input into budgetary matters. They decide collectively how money is to be handled, agreeing, for instance, on the limits of petty cash claims.

Industrial disputes

Many confused and bitter industrial disputes have occurred in community organisations. There are several reasons for this, relating to the whole context in which community organisations and their workers operate. For example, disputes that arise over rates of pay, back-pay and leave entitlements are often related to poor and insecure funding of community organisations. Overtime is often thought of as volunteer work or time. For example, coordinators are surprised when workers demand pay for 'staying back'. In the following sections we consider further some of the factors in industrial disputes.

Unpaid work or volunteerism

The whole issue of unpaid work is a thorny one in community development. As discussed in chapter 2, the community services sector has some of its roots in the traditional charity approach to social issues, involving volunteer charity workers helping the poor and needy. Some aspects of this approach linger, manifested in encouragement of volunteer (unpaid) workers to 'give back to society'. It is also manifested in the expectation that because of their moral commitment to what they do, workers will often accept below-average wages and give extra time voluntarily. It often happens that a community development worker chooses to, or is coerced into, working some of their time without pay, and this undermines hard-won pay and conditions that are laid down in industrial awards. The use of volunteers can also devalue the skills necessary to community development work. In addition, unpaid workers or volunteers themselves can be exploited by paid workers.

Over the last 20 years, interest in the role of volunteers or **volunteerism** in the community services sector has grown and there now is a veritable industry of volunteer recruitment and management. On one hand, as indicated above, volunteerism can be used cynically as unpaid labour and a way of getting young people 'job ready'. For example, young people are enjoined to undertake volunteer work, not because they might be committed to an issue, but because in an instrumental way volunteer work assists them to get paid employment. On the other hand, community organisations are full of people, mainly women, who developed the confidence and skills for paid work through their unpaid activities. Indeed, volunteer work can be empowering for marginalised groups who lack the confidence and experience to take on a paid job. Many women who have been isolated during their childrearing years, for example, are empowered through volunteering experience: they begin as a participant in a program at a community house and progress to volunteer, part-time worker and eventually full-time coordinator.

In addition, many people genuinely 'want to give something back' to their community, without any financial reward, in appreciation for what they have gained by living there. One resolution of this dilemma of unpaid work undermining paid work is to clarify the goals, strategies and main functions of an organisation; develop job profiles and duty statements; and identify which key tasks should be done by volunteers and which by paid workers, making sure that the employment policy is consistent with the appropriate award. In regard to volunteers, it is useful to apply the definition of volunteering developed by Volunteering Australia (2005) whereby formal volunteering 'is undertaken to be of benefit to the community and the volunteer; of the volunteer's own free will and without coercion; for no financial payment; and in designated volunteer positions only'.

Chapter 6 Community organisations

From this perspective, volunteers, including students on placement, cannot take on tasks that are essential to the functioning of the organisation and its programs or which appear on the duty statements of workers. However, this does not guarantee that volunteers are not used to carry out tasks that should be done by paid workers. In times of funding constraints, many organisations can survive only by using unpaid workers. The effect of maintaining an organisation on this basis can be to demonstrate that it can function with inappropriate funding and to undermine its long-term prospects and the tasks it fulfils. Some organisations have policies that either exclude unpaid/volunteer labour or minimise its use to a limited number of student placements and to explicit political activities, such as the organisation of a protest meeting.

This leads us to two different ways of thinking about volunteerism. First, and perhaps most importantly, it would seem that nearly everyone involved in community development, regardless of whether they are in paid community development work or not, undertakes unpaid/volunteer labour as activist citizens or as a form of civic participation at some point in their lives, such as when they join a school committee, go to a local meeting, protest over a political issue, or join an advisory group. They participate as active citizens and their time is given voluntarily with the intention of benefiting the community. Second, while much volunteerism is set within a neo-liberal (individualised and instrumentally self-interested) framework or a charity framework (within a patronising top-down approach that emphasises the moral virtue of the giver), there is scope for a community development approach. Take the following example.

MT INDIRRI NEIGHBOURHOOD COUNCIL

Mt Indirri Neighbourhood Council (MINC), a network of community organisations, developed an ambitious strategic plan that offered to resolve some of the local issues and problems. The community members were so impressed with the plan that a number of them approached MINC offering their skills and time as active citizens. Given that MINC had never had volunteers or a volunteer policy, it was reluctant to accept the offer. It established a small committee of interested community members to thrash out the issues. The upshot of two meetings was the following recommendations:

- to establish a standing volunteer/active citizen committee
- to write a draft volunteer/active citizen committee policy, setting out the principles of a volunteer program and details of where unpaid labour would be used and how
- to produce an education kit for people who want to be involved in volunteer/active citizen activities, explaining their legal entitlements and responsibilities
- to develop a website listing details of activities in which people giving their time and skills could be involved.

These recommendations were put to a large meeting organised by MINC. The consensus was to proceed with all recommendations; however, there were a number of dissenters, including those who saw volunteerism as an excuse to bring in unpaid and un-unionised labour. The meeting then agreed to develop the policy and initiate a trial of the active citizen program.

Six months later, the program is not only up and running, but is thriving. In the review of the program, the following key factors were identified as contributing to its success:

case study

- Rather than use the term 'volunteer', MINC decided to talk about citizen participation and active citizenship and to stress the point that all people could be active citizens. This shifted the emphasis from a small group of the 'well-off' helping the 'less well-off' to active citizenship involving people working together in a multitude of ways.
- Active citizens were those involved in activist endeavours such as campaigning on environmental issues, as well as those providing services.
- The process of sharing citizenship commitments also involved community ownership of the program – thus outcomes suited to the community's needs – and shared responsibility among all members of the community.
- The matching of skills and time commitment of the participants was enabled by the up-to-date website detailing needs, so allowing them to choose how much they wanted to be involved.
- The up-to-date education kit enabled participants to be informed about their legal rights and responsibilities.

Management and workers

An important reason for the complexity of industrial disputes in the community sector is the ambiguous and confused nature of relations between employers and employees. Even where there are clear lines of accountability between employed staff and the committee of management, the committee members are often not thought of, either by the staff or by themselves, as 'the bosses'. When things go wrong, accusations often fly in all directions about bad or weak management or lack of staff respect for committee decisions. The members of a committee of management may be participants in programs run by the organisation, or, in the case of a collective, they may be the workers themselves. Consequently, the roles of employer and employee are not always clear. Moreover, the basis of the employer–employee relationship is not one of authority or intimidation, as tends to happen in large organisations and in the private sector. In many cases, the workers are better qualified than the members of the committee of management that employs them. Of course, the cliche that an organisation is as good as its human resources is true for community-based organisations. Appropriate workers are essential. There is no foolproof way of ensuring that the right workers are employed, but there should be a clear rationale for each job; a clear job description, duty statement and advertisement; and appropriate working conditions and salary. This goes a long way towards clarifying the expectations of a community organisation for a particular job. Also needed are a comprehensive orientation to the job and the organisation, a strong support system, a welcoming atmosphere, a clear system of accountability and appropriate procedures for the resolution of disputes.

Policies and procedures

One way of resolving such issues in community organisations is to have clear guidelines about the roles and responsibilities of committees and of workers. It is particularly important to have clear statements about the jobs that are undertaken in an organisation.

In fact, regardless of policy about unpaid work, community organisations should clarify what jobs are being done and need to be done and how they are allocated among workers (both paid and unpaid). Most organisations have documents that state the rationale, principles and objectives that guide activities. These often provide the basis for a constitution, but an organisation needs more detailed information on the tasks and roles of workers' positions. *Tasks* are everyday components of a particular job (such as opening the mail); *roles* are overall activities in an organisation (such as coordinator) – both must be clearly spelt out. From a community development perspective, daily decisions about what jobs need to be done and how, as well as specification of tasks and roles, should be made by the workers themselves rather than just allocated from above.

Many organisations have developed general employment booklets, comprising policies and procedures on the design of jobs and duty statements; job training and release for study; advertising; temporary, permanent, full-time and part-time positions; interviews, appointments and orientation; counselling and dismissal. These are all important ingredients in a good organisation, regardless of its structure.

A policy and procedures manual can also explain:

- how policies are made, recorded, communicated, evaluated, amended and deleted
- policies about information storage and retrieval
- policies regarding privacy
- budgeting processes
- operation of committees
- reporting processes
- procedures for financial and legal transactions.

A policy and procedures manual is important for newcomers to the organisation, for individual workers and for participants who want to know how to do something. Procedures and policies of any kind, of course, should be changed when appropriate. Such a manual should not control the organisation by laying down unchangeable rules. A good manual is one that is easy to read and frequently updated. The problem here, of course, is the labour needed to prepare frequent updates.

Creative community organisations

Much of this chapter has focused on the many factors that constrain and regulate community organisations. Before we conclude the chapter we should note that such constraints and regulations do not necessarily preclude alternative creative ways of 'doing things'. They might make this difficult, but it is still possible to organise more collectively and to be accountable to a community. As Anheier and Leat (2002) point out in a discussion of factors that make philanthropic trusts and foundations dynamic entities, it is still possible to establish creative organisations. They argue that resourcefulness and problem-solving capacity based on an open mind are they keys to the development of a **creative organisation**. A creative organisation begins with such questions as 'Why is this so?' and 'How can this be done differently?' Drawing on the work of Kanter (1983), they identify the characteristics of innovative organisations as:

- accepting that their programs will involve a significant amount of uncertainty – for example, the outcome of a program is not easy to predict
- making the commitment to being daring and taking risks – there is chance that the program might fail
- being prepared to work at the margins, rather than in the mainstream
- being committed to putting time and resources into innovation, knowing that innovations are knowledge-intensive and typically controversial
- being committed to looking outward and cooperating with others
- being committed to reaching across established boundaries, cultures, fields and sectors, and to bringing 'freshness'
- being prepared to learn from both failure and success.

We have already touched on some of these ideas in previous chapters. In a situation in which a community organisation is driven primarily by the need to generate funds to adequately resource its programs, it is often difficult to think in terms of constructing a 'creative organisation'. But this should not undermine the preparedness to think about ways of developing any community organisation into a creative one.

Summary points

- Community development takes place in groups of people who come together because of a common interest or concern. In this chapter we have focused on relatively formal community organisations; however, the discussion also applies to the activities of informal groups with common interests and concerns.
- Formal community organisations are not-for-profit, autonomous or semi-autonomous from government, and constructed around issues and programs.
- Despite methodological problems and lack of agreement about the dimensions of the community sector, studies indicate that the sector contributes significantly to the economy and to the development of civil society.
- Every organisation has a structure by which it works in terms of who does what, why, when and where; how decisions are made; and the nature of authority in the organisation. Community development workers are critical of hierarchical, bureaucratised and patriarchal organisational forms.
- From a community development perspective there is much that is anti-democratic and disempowering about bureaucratic and new managerialist processes.
- Many community organisations have, or aspire to have, organisational forms that follow a cooperative collective model. A collective approach to organisation is based on the view that all participants should contribute and that the structure should facilitate equality of power, status, tasks and responsibilities.

- Community development work invariably involves committee work. It is thus important to understand committee structures and processes, and to develop them to meet the needs of specific community organisations.
- Community development work involves meetings. It is important to understand meeting structures and processes, and to ensure that they are effective and appropriate to community development needs.
- Interest is growing in a decision-making process that aims to establish an informed community that is competent to resolve issues and conflicts democratically. This is often known as deliberative democracy.
- Community organisations have life cycles of innovation, establishment, maintenance and evaluation.
- Members of community organisations should understand the legal and other responsibilities of the organisation and never forget their responsibility to their communities.
- Many confused and bitter disputes arise in community organisations. Community organisations should have clear guidelines about the roles and responsibilities of workers (paid and unpaid) and committee members.
- The principles and processes of the operation of community organisations must be accessible to the communities they serve. They should be written down in an easy-to-read format. As well as a constitution and brochures that provide information about the organisation, a policy and procedures manual can be developed.
- Despite all the constraints, community organisations should, where possible, aspire to be creative.

Key terms

- bureaucratic organisation
- civil society organisations
- collective model
- committee of management
- communicative competence
- corporate bureaucracy
- creative organisation
- deliberative democracy
- dialogical communication
- governance model
- instrumental rationality
- line management
- non-government (or non-governmental) organisations (NGOs)
- non-profit/not-for-profit organisations
- operating rationale
- performativity
- policy and procedures manuals
- procedural bureaucracy
- promotional communication
- scientific management
- Taylorism
- third sector organisations
- vertical and horizontal organisation
- voluntary associations
- volunteerism

Exercises

1 List the different terms used to describe what we in Australia generally recognise as community organisations.
2 What kinds of data are available on the third sector?

Processes and practices

3 What is an operating rationale and what types of operating rationales do community organisations have?
4 Describe the principles of bureaucratic management.
5 What criticisms of bureaucratic management are relevant to community development work?
6 What are the consistencies and inconsistencies between bureaucratic organisation and new managerialism?
7 What type of organisational structure is appropriate to community development?
8 Why are committee work and meetings important in community development? What are some of the criticisms of committee work and meetings?
9 What is deliberative democracy? What is its relevance to community development?
10 List the stages that a community organisation might move through.
11 List the main ways that an organisation can share resources with other community organisations.
12 What are some reasons for industrial disputes in community organisations?
13 What is meant by the idea of a creative community organisation?
14 What community development processes and principles were evident in the Toolac Community House case study?

Further reading

Anheier H & Leat, D (2002) *From Charity to Creativity: Philanthropic Foundations in the 21st Century*. Comedia, United Kingdom.

Brown, K, Kenny, S & Turner, B (2000) *Rhetorics of Welfare: Uncertainty, Choice and Voluntary Associations*. Macmillan, London.

Cohen, J (1999) 'Trust, voluntary association and workable democracy: the contemporary American discourse of civil society', in M Warren (ed.) *Democracy and Trust*. Cambridge University Press, Cambridge, pp. 208–48.

Dryzek, J (2000) *Deliberative Democracy and Beyond: Liberals, Critics, Contestations*. Oxford University Press, Oxford.

Elster, J (1997) 'The market and the forum: three varieties of political theory', in J Bohman and W Rehg (eds) *Deliberative Democracy: Essays on Reason and Politics*. The MIT Press, Cambridge, Massachusetts.

Ferguson, K (1984) *The Feminist Case Against Bureaucracy*. Temple University Press, Philadelphia.

Ife, J (2001) *Human Rights and Social Work*. Cambridge University Press, Cambridge.

Kettering Foundation (2000) *A Handbook on Deliberation – Public Politics in Practice*. Kettering Foundation, Dayton, Ohio.

Landry, C. et al. (1985) *What a Way to Run a Railroad: An Analysis of Radical Failure*. Comedia, London.

Lyons, M (2001) *Third Sector*. Allen & Unwin, Crows Nest, NSW.

Productivity Commission (2010) *Contribution of the Not-for-Profit Sector*, Productivity Commission Research Report, Australian Government, Canberra.

Pusey, M (1991) *Economic Rationalism in Canberra*. Cambridge University Press, Cambridge.

Roberts, J (1991) *The Committee Members' Voluntary Handbook*. Information Australia, Melbourne.

Salamon, LM, Anheier, HK, List, R, Toepler, S, Sokolowski, SW and Associates (1999) *Global Civil Society: Dimensions of the Nonprofit*

Sector. The Johns Hopkins Center for Civil Society Studies, Baltimore.

Sennett, R (2004) *Respect: The Formation of Character in a World of Inequality*. Penguin, London.

Warren, ME (2001) *Democracy and Association*. Princeton University Press, Princeton.

Watson, S (ed.) (1990) *Playing the State: Australian Feminist Interventions*. Allen & Unwin, Crows Nest, NSW.

Weblinks

International non-profit organisations on Twitter
twitter.com/cornyman/non-profit-organization
www.communityorganizer20.com/2009/07/30/five-ways-nonprofit-organizations-can-really-connect-on-twitter/

Legal information for community organisations
www.pilch.org.au/legal_info/
www.lawhandbook.sa.gov.au/ch06s01.php

Non-profit organisations
www.pathwaysaustralia.com.au/Guide_About.asp
www.arnova.org/

Productivity Commission's Contribution of the Not-for-Profit Sector research report
www.pc.gov.au/projects/study/not-for-profit/report

Social entrepreneurship
www.sbs.ox.ac.uk/centres/skoll/Pages/default.aspx
www.socialenterprise.org.uk/pages/about-social-enterprise.html

CHAPTER 7

Activities and practices

Overview

In this chapter we consider in more detail some of the activities that a community development practitioner can expect to undertake. We review what approaches and activities make for good community practice. A case study of the first few weeks of a community development job is followed by a consideration of tasks of community development work. In our analysis of the tasks we begin by discussing ways of making contacts, encouraging involvement, identifying spaces for 'giving voice' and involvement, building trust and respect, and the importance of networks. We then discuss teamwork and what makes for good teamwork. Communication is central part of good community development and we explore this in some detail. Community organisations are increasingly sensitive to public image and we review the role of public events and publicity in community development, and consider the role of new media. The final sections of the chapter explore social policy development, lobbying, advocacy and conflict management.

Introduction
What makes good community development practice?

While answers to the question of what makes good community development practice vary according to political and theoretical perspectives – and there is no magic formula for community development practice – it is possible to identify some general themes. Clearly, a good community development worker is driven by a commitment to community development principles. Although this is obvious, it is worth emphasising because, caught up in the day-to-day activities of navigating regulations, negotiating funding bodies, maintaining a community organisation and identifying resources, workers can forget about the broad principles that underpin their work.

Community development workers have certain capacities and skills, such as the ability to undertake symbolic–analytic work. Some of the capacities are contradictory and not all of them are required in any one job. The hallmark of community development work is the ability to respond in an appropriate way to a particular situation. People utilise different capacities, according to their own experiences and their theoretical perspective. For example, a woman influenced by ideas of postmodern feminism might prioritise the need to be irreverent and creative, and to take risks and break rules if necessary, because she holds the view that we need to think and act in ways that break with commonplace thinking. An attribute of good community development practice that is often commented on is the importance of 'making yourself redundant'. For example, paid community development workers should not see their work primarily in terms of a secure job and continual employment. For unpaid community development activists, of course, community development is not a job. It is a method, a process and a set of practices driven by a commitment to change that 'makes things better'.

Community development work also requires curiosity, dedication and enthusiasm. Curiosity can begin with the question, 'Why?' For example, a community development worker in a rural area in which employment is mainly in the timber industry will need to ask why so many community members are committed to logging, despite the obvious harmful effects on the local rainforests and local fauna. Similarly, a practitioner will persist in asking such questions as why a local community organisation folded, or why this particular community welcomed refugees while another is hostile.

As Murphy (2006) points out, however, dedication, enthusiasm (and good intentions) are not enough by themselves to ensure the success of a community project: 'Ideas have to be shared, supported and developed … All those involved have to work well together'. Murphy (2006) also identifies some key personal dispositions that are assets in community development practice, including the value of patience (overnight success is rare) and being dedicated but not obsessed. Referring to ideas for good community projects, he suggests keeping an eye on the long-term benefits of any project and being flexible in approach – for example, accepting that projects change direction.

As well as understanding the objectives, attitudes and approaches that are required for community development work, practitioners must be able to carry out a variety of specific activities. For this they need a range of knowledge, abilities and skills. We have already outlined these in chapter 1. In this chapter, we discuss further how these are manifested in various aspects of community development work.

In a useful handbook, Wates (2000:11) identifies activities and practice principles that underpin successful community engagement in planning for their future. These activities and principles also apply to community development work in general. Some of the key activities and principles he promotes are listed below:

Accept different agendas	Have fun
Accept varied commitment	Involve all those affected
Agree rules and boundaries	Involve all sections of the community
Avoid jargon	Learn from others
Be honest	Ensure local ownership of the process
Be transparent	Maintain momentum
Be visionary yet realistic	Use a mixture of methods
Build local capacity	Record and document
Encourage collaboration	Respect cultural context

Flexibility	Respect local knowledge
Follow up	Share control
Go at the right pace	Think on your feet
Go for it	Trust in others' honesty
Visualise	Use local talent
Walk before you can run	Work on location

Types of activities

During a period of a week, a community development worker may respond to community requests to:

- prepare a submission for funding an additional program at the community centre
- talk to a group of residents about changes to social security legislation
- write a regular column for a local newspaper on coming events at the community centre
- respond to a request to identify appropriate emergency accommodation for young people in the locality
- advise on establishing a food cooperative, including any legal, financial and municipal constraints and regulations
- address a local organisation of people from culturally and linguistically diverse backgrounds about equal opportunity issues in the local council
- attend a meeting of local housing workers to advise on additional sources of funds
- take phone calls from other agencies who are seeking up-to-date information on such matters as domestic violence, cooperatives and action research
- work with local councillors on a strategy plan for community building in the region
- work on a committee with local trade union representatives to organise a meeting to explain new industrial relations laws to the local community.

While community development work does not include individual casework, workers often talk with local community members about the resources and options that are available to them in times of personal difficulty. A community development worker builds up a range of information and develops the analytical skills to make sense of this information over a period of time. The ability to discern informal power structures, networks and hidden political agendas comes from experience and from local knowledge gained in day-to-day conversation. Some community development workers identify so much with the problems and issues facing a community that they can lose the sense of perspective that dispassionate analysis provides. This is not to say that community development practitioners do not identify with the people with whom they are working and should never be passionate about their work, but they should be able to recognise their passion and what its effects might be.

Chapter 7 Activities and practices

As indicated in various parts of this book, as a community development worker you need sufficient information not only for your own activities but also to be able to respond to the community's needs for information. This requires the ability to develop **empirical knowledge**, or observable concrete knowledge, of how a community works and what affects it (such as facts and figures on unemployment, demographic profiles and the number and types of services available). It also requires the ability to understand hidden and overt power relations at the macro level, such as the effects on the local community of government policy and global trade agreements, and the micro level, which is sometimes known as local knowledge.

We will now consider how local knowledge is built up by examining some of the activities in which new community development workers might be involved when they enter the field.

VERONICA'S NEW JOB

Veronica is the successful applicant for a position of community development worker at a domestic violence resource centre. She has experience of working in women's refuges, has undertaken feminist research into domestic violence and has read widely on feminist theory and analysis. Before applying for the job, she read the job description carefully and used her contacts to find out how this particular resource centre functioned, the staff turnover rate and the future security of funding. Her contacts reinforced her view that the resource centre is a good place to work: it runs effectively, it is not overly bureaucratic and it has relatively secure funding.

In her interview for the job, Veronica had some queries about the details of the job description. She suggested some minor changes, which were accepted by the resource centre's collective. After the interview she took notes in her diary of what was said at the interview and her impressions. These notes summarised the rationale and principles of operation of the resource centre; the working conditions; the tasks, skills and abilities required; and her suggested modifications to the job description. On receiving the offer of the job, Veronica elaborated her diary notes and added an action column. Her notes are presented in table 7.1.

Veronica spends the first days of her new job familiarising herself with the centre by looking at the written material, including the history, day-to-day operation, filing system, recording system, minutes of meetings, policies and processes. Where possible, she chats with other workers about their views of the organisation and its programs, successes and failures, issues and problems. She also attends meetings.

On the basis of this information, during her third week at the centre, Veronica presents to the collective for comment a list of her objectives, an action plan and timeline for specific tasks such as organising a workshop, and a timetable for her day-to-day activities. At the top of her list of specific tasks is making contacts, followed by organising a workshop on domestic violence and developing self-help and support groups. There is considerable discussion about this work plan at the collective meeting, which Veronica finds very constructive. With her plan now developed, Veronica is ready to put it into practice.

In this case study, Veronica articulates and reflects upon the day-to-day nature of the job. It is important to do this when taking up a new job, but also to move as soon as possible to the concrete tasks. We now consider some of these.

Processes and practices

Table 7.1 *Notes for new job*

Notes on new job, 22 March	
Work context	*Action*
Rationale, objectives and principles of operation of resource centre are feminist; collective approach; aimed at working towards social change to empower women and children	Review origins of agency
Hours of work and salary according to CD Workers' Award?	Check with union
Core tasks	*Action*
Participate in the development of the centre's operations	Re-read constitution
Attend weekly two-hour workers' meeting	Ascertain funding sources
Attend monthly wider collective meeting (approximately three hours)	Ask to see agendas
Do three two-hour phone shifts for referral and follow up (if phone calls)	Scan statistics and trends reflected in intake data
Organise workshops on domestic violence	Check other agencies' experiences
Assist in the development of domestic violence self-help and support groups	Liaise with self-help groups
Undertake research on the needs of domestic violence survivors	Check other agencies' experiences
Build up a resource collection of books, articles and brochures on domestic violence and support for survivors	Check on what already exists Obtain reference lists from all courses or subjects in this area
General administrative tasks as decided in conjunction with the collective (e.g. filing, photocopying)	
Other tasks	*Action*
Undertake local needs assessment	Check on any previous needs assessments
Assist with review of centre's activities	Any previous review?
Work with the collective to ensure that the centre has a welcoming and friendly atmosphere for workers and participants	Enquire about evaluation processes within the agency
Contribute to the establishment of new programs	Identify priorities and time plan
Write submissions	
Lobby for funds	
Speak at public meetings	Review agency's public relations leaflets, etc.

Table 7.1 *(Continued)*

Notes on new job, 22 March

Assist in the coordination and organisation of state and regional seminars, conferences and meetings on domestic violence	Check calendar for other agencies' events (including rural areas)
Prepare newsletters, reports, handbook and training programs on domestic violence	Search for literature at local and university libraries and key agencies
Liaise with other agencies	
Assist in planning and participate in annual general meeting	Review reports of previous annual general meetings
Other duties as decided in conjunction with the collective	
Accountability	*Action*
Be responsible to the collective as equal members	
Attend weekly workers' meeting	Document and follow up issues arising from the meeting
Write reports to monthly wider collective meeting	Include report in agenda for the meeting
Write record of hours worked	Check standard timesheets
Skills and experience	*Action*
Ability to work on domestic violence issues from a feminist perspective	Form links with feminist community services collective
Ability to work within a feminist collective	
Ability to organise workshops for women	
Well-developed written and verbal communication skills	Check all written material with colleagues
Action research skills and experience	Attend Friends' Participatory Action Research meetings
Ability to network with other agencies	
Experience in administration in community organisation	Timetable sessions to update statistics and computer records

Making contacts

In community development work, one of the early tasks is always making contacts, or networking. For community development practitioners coming from outside the community, it is important to develop trust and build alliances with other people, link into existing formal and informal networks, tap into local knowledge, and respect and learn from the accumulated experience of the members of the community. For those who are already involved in the community it is equally important to extend existing contacts and to be continually learning from community members. Twelvetrees (1982:23–8) points to the need to take any opportunity to make or renew a contact, to learn how to listen and notice, to be prepared to give of yourself and to reflect on what people say (and don't always take things at face value).

An important component in all contact-making is to 'plug into' local networks, and to build up a picture of the way networks operate (for example, through bonding and bridging social capital). One early activity is to construct an inventory of local associations using word of mouth, libraries, shire offices, web searches, local newspapers, phone book or local community directory. Since the 1970s there have been profound changes in the ways we make, maintain and extend contacts, mainly resulting through the arrival of the Internet. The following case study sets out some of the some of the important changes in networking and communication tools since the 1970s.

CHANGING DIMENSIONS OF NETWORKING

In 2010, we asked Bob, a rural outreach community development worker located in a large regional town in western Queensland how his practice has changed since he began work as a community development practitioner in the 1970s. Bob began by reflecting on his expanding networks and the ways in which he had communicated with the people he worked with.

'My networks have expanded exponentially since the 1970s,' he told us. 'I seem to be communicating and working with many more people today, perhaps five times as many, but I generally don't know people as well as I once did. Interestingly, some of the people I liaise with overseas I know better than the people that I liaise with who live and work a few kilometres away. Both then and now, I have to cover an area hundreds of square miles. In the 1970s, as much as I could, I actually drove out to visit the communities and stay for a couple of days. Occasionally I got a lift out by plane, such as when the government officials flew out or ranchers were going to check their stock. I also used the phone to talk to individuals in their communities, but the phone line was sometimes down.

Records, such as minutes of meetings, were kept in handwritten files, although sometimes, such as when I had a report to do, I typed these up on that old typewriter out the back. In town here, information about what was happening in Australia came through on the news, on the radio and the two TV channels we had here then. And of course there's the newspapers. But I didn't get to hear much about things happening outside Australia, except when there was a major event, such as the American withdrawal from Vietnam. I never met anyone who lived outside Australia, although there were some Greek and Italian migrants working in town.

Today things are very different. Everyone I work with has a mobile phone. To organise a meeting we SMS each other. All the communities I work with have computers. Where they have access to the Internet they get their news and knowledge of the world from it. The type and amount of information I can access is unbelievable. Once people have Internet access they can also email each other. We are now also using Skype for virtual "face-to-face" meetings and discussions. One of the criticisms I have of the current government is that they promised to roll out high-speed broadband across the country but that has not happened yet. We are all looking forward to that whenever it happens. It will make such a difference.

I now have networks of people across the world with whom I am in regular contact though email. I know so much more now I can tap into the work of such groups as Witness and Human Rights Watch. The younger staff are all on Facebook and Twitter.

I now keep my files on the computer. I use proformas for writing submissions, doing evaluations, reporting on activities and the finances (for example, using especially generated flow charts). I now send all these to Canberra and Brisbane via email, when once I would have to send them by post.'

We asked Bob about whether the way he prepares and produces newsletters has changed. 'In some ways yes; in other ways no,' he replied. 'We used to type our newsletters on that old typewriter over there, and sometimes even write them in longhand. We would then duplicate them on an ink contraption called a Roneo machine. All our printed material now looks so professional. We have a logo and design that we downloaded free from the Internet. We send out newsletters as email and also print in colour. Of course, we still send the newsletters out with the mail, and personally drop off batches. People like to meet us and talk about what is in the newsletters. We have always done this. And, of course, the collection of ideas and decisions about what is included are still done collectively as it was in the 1970s.'

For Alinsky (1972), tapping into local networks involves linking up with organic (or what he calls 'native') leaders. Usually the building up of an extensive network involves some form of **snowballing**, whereby contacts introduce the community development worker to new contacts, and so on. Snowballing is a very important part of developing networks. However, there are two caveats to the use of the snowballing technique. First, it is important to be sensitive to privacy issues. Requesting contact names can be embarrassing to the people who are asked and it can also put them in an unethical position. It is imperative to find out whether their contacts want to communicate. Some community development practitioners, even when introduced to community members through another member, will not make the first contact themselves. They always wait for members of the community to initiate the communication. Communication and involvement should not be forced on community members. Second, it is important to understand that restricting the snowballing method to just one network can be limiting. It tends to put the community development practitioner in touch with only one group of people. Finding out what the local issues are, attending local public meetings and going to where people congregate, such as local shopping centres or playgrounds, can help you to make new contacts and hear a range of different views.

Identifying spaces for giving voice and involvement

A concept that has come to be associated with community development over the last decade is **giving voice**. In the context of community development it means facilitating a place and a method by which ordinary people can express their ideas and views, and participate in discussion and debate about the directions of their communities and the policies that affect their lives. It involves finding or creating sites for public views, such as websites, community organisations, government consultations and the mass media. As Cornwall (2008) argues, there are two types of spaces for 'giving voice': spaces that are created through invitations and spaces that people create themselves. She comments further that invited spaces are often structured and owned by those who originally created them, and transferring ownership to others is not always easy. Community development practitioners have a role to play in finding ways of opening up both types of spaces. They will seek out existing spaces by extending membership of existing projects, for example, and they will work with communities to create new spaces; for example, through working with marginalised groups to develop their own forms of expression, such as in their own newsletter or a weekly column in the local paper, or having their own show on a community radio station.

Of course, giving voice needs to be nurtured. Having a place to express one's views is not the same as actually presenting one's views. Cornwall (2008) points out that being involved in a process in general is not equivalent to having a voice. People need to feel confident that what they say will be listened to and will not result in reprisal.

Earlier in this book we explored reasons why people don't want to become involved in community activities, whether it be in the form of comment or action. Community development workers should not take the high ground when it comes to their expectations of people's involvement in community issues. We live in societies that value individualism, competition and self-interest at the expense of solidarity and sharing – although, as suggested earlier, there is probably too much nostalgia about the assumed solidarity of past societies. We must be realistic about the extent to which we expect people to be involved in activities that we think are important.

It is incumbent upon community development practitioners to identify the reasons for non-participation and respond accordingly. For example, as suggested in chapter 5, people might correctly see participation as a sham, or be quite happy to see others take a lead role. Such standpoints must be respected. In a comprehensive book, Moore (1978), reflecting on the reasons why people obey or revolt, observes that the predominant response to oppression and suffering has been sectional, past-oriented and conservative. The naturalisation of an existing state of affairs pre-empts a sense of injustice and leads to notions of inevitability and psychological dependence. He argues that people must feel a sense of injustice and moral outrage; they must believe that there are real options and alternative futures for them. He points out that people must have some assurances that efforts to change things on their part can be effective.

What a community development practitioner can do is to ensure that as far as possible that there are real choices available as to whether someone wants to be involved, where and when, and importantly, at what level. It might be that a person will be deeply involved in one aspect of a project for a short period of time, and then withdraw to a broad advisory role later in the project. What is important is that people should feel relaxed about how they might be involved. They should not be stigmatised because they choose not to be 'included' in a particular activity.

Of course, the methods of getting people involved follow familiar principles of community development:

- ensure that everyone's interests are considered
- accept the diversity of viewpoints and do not force conformity
- ensure that everyone has a say
- clarify what is involved in participation
- hold meetings (informal and formal) and keep them open
- ensure that everyone knows what, where, when and how an activity takes place
- as far as possible, ensure democratic decision making
- ensure that something other than meetings actually happens
- keep in touch with all members
- keep the aims, objectives, strategies and action plans clear
- understand and accept that people have varying levels of commitment.

It must also be understood that making contacts is a long, slow process, which rarely produces immediate or direct results. As Twelvetrees (1982:35–6) points out:

> People participate when they are ready. The fact that you have contacted them at a certain point may well provide them with more knowledge than they had before. You may have sown seeds which begin to germinate at a later date.

Working with local government

Community development practitioners are increasingly working with and through local government. The following case study describes the actions of a community development worker in liaising with his local council to develop a regional health and safety plan. It explains how relationships between local communities and councils might take place and introduces some basic research concepts.

WARRAH PARK SHIRE HEALTH AND SAFETY PLAN

A state government has provided a local regional council, the Shire of Warrah Park (covering both rural and urban communities), with funds to develop a regional health and safety plan. The conventional way of developing plans in this council has been to draw up tender specifications, develop a list of preferred expert planners and provide each local company of expert planners with the opportunity to submit a tender for the contract. The winning tenderer then carries out the work.

However, the council has been newly elected and comprises two people committed to community development practices. They hold several meetings with Ahmet, a local community development worker, who persuades them to argue for a different approach to the development of the regional health and safety plan. In the past, the successful tenderers have always been from the capital city. They have come into the region for a matter of a few weeks, undertaken the work, presented the draft plan to the council members and several selected high-flyers in the region in a token consultation, and then returned to the city to prepare the final draft. In this process there has been no opportunity for real community participation and virtually no transfer of knowledge and skills to the region's community members.

On Ahmet's advice, the councillors committed to community development spell out another option for the development of a regional health and safety plan. This option both recognises existing skills in the region and develops new skills in community members, who are largely without any experience of research, planning and document writing. This alternative approach begins with contact with the local university to ask if they would be interested in providing advice and running some sessions on research skills and working in research teams, so that community members can learn ways of drawing out the information, checking it with the community, and preparing the health and safety plan. Unlike the previous approach, this option commits to the further skilling of community members.

The arguments for the alternative approach are persuasive and the council establishes a subcommittee to draw up a draft plan of the steps and timelines for the development of the plan. Maria, another community development worker in the council, is seconded to the project to facilitate the process. She contacts the university and academics from the health promotion, sociology, policy and planning areas come forward to work on the project. The subcommittee develops draft action plans and calls a series of open meetings, over three weeks, in different places to encourage broad community participation in the process. The meetings are facilitated by two other community development workers, Don and Liz, who have been asked by their organisations to become involved.

At these local meetings community members suggest alternatives and modifications to the draft. Two options are voted on, and one is clearly the favourite. This action plan involves the development of a database setting out all interest groups in the region, such as Indigenous groups, pensioners, different ethnic groups, rural workers and landowners; a call to all members of the community for expressions of interest in undertaking research training and joining research and report committees; and, third, the development of a list of people interested in participating in the project ensuring that, as far as possible, all groups in the community are covered. This action plan proceeds and is modified and adapted through new insights and suggestions.

A research team of 16 people is trained to do the research, and a secretariat of support staff is established by the council, with a number of existing council employees applying to work on the project. The first task for the research team is to refine the research questions (What do we want to know and why?) and develop a process for doing the research (the research design). The research team wants to involve as many people as possible so they suggest that data collection (through both questionnaires and interviews) takes place on the territory of the community members, including in parkland adjacent to housing estates and in community halls. They also request that refreshments be made available (paid for by the council) when the interviews take place. The response rate for attendance at the interviews is 81 per cent and for the return of the questionnaires is 70 per cent, both figures being well above the norm. More people become interested in the project and some join the research team. Others drop out. However, a momentum builds in the research. Large numbers attend the feedback sessions at which the draft findings of the research are presented for comment and reflection and a proposed analysis is recommended. While the council has implemented a longer and more complex process for developing its health and safety plan than in the past, this plan is more comprehensive and sustainable than those provided by the neighbouring councils.

This case study illustrates the importance of networking and the advantages of having a preparedness to take a participatory approach to the development of a plan for a local council.

Organising with communities

As mentioned elsewhere in this book, there are two ways in which community organising can take place: first, through the work of **organic leaders** – or what Alinsky (1969:64–5) calls **native leaders** – and second through the work of an external facilitator. In community development both forms of organising are generally involved. Alinsky (1972:98) emphasised how, when community organisers come from outside, they must establish their identity or, as he put it, 'get a licence to operate'. He points out that when external community development workers do not connect with 'native leaders', community organisations founder. The ability to work closely with a community, and to understand hidden agendas and the nature of underlying relationships, is particularly important. Formal community structures such as councils and committees of management can frustrate such understandings. Regardless of whether community development practitioners are organic leaders or external facilitators, the relationship between them and the community with whom they work with is critical.

Organic leaders can be the gatekeepers of access to the community. However, there is no guarantee that they represent the interests of their whole community, and it is important not to assume that they do. For one thing, the community is not a homogeneous entity: it is full of diverse interests. In addition, organic leaders may have gained their leadership by self-selection and self-selected leaders can be co-opted into power structures in order to gain status. The point remains, however, that gatekeeping does exist and organic leaders are important sources of information and contacts.

Building trust and respect

In recent years there has been growing interest in the erosion of trust and respect and the need to establish relationships and institutions that can generate relations based on respect and trust (see, for example, Sennett, 2004; Putnam, 2000). As indicated elsewhere in this book, the interest in developing stocks of social capital based on trust and mutuality, and strengthening social inclusion and volunteer participation in communities, has become an important goal of social policy. As social policy makers search for ways of strengthening trust, they cast their eyes on community development programs. This social policy interest can work to the advantage of community development workers but, as we note in this book, capacity building and social inclusion policies can also be constructed and applied in a top-down manner and taken on in cynical ways.

But what is trust? According to Offe (1999:47), 'Trust is the belief that others, through their action or inaction, will contribute to my/our well-being and refrain from inflicting damage upon me/us'. Now, community development workers entering the field are often informed by colleagues to expect many people in the community to be sceptical about the latest 'fashion' in community engagement and will doubt the overall value of community involvement and action. This warning of cynicism in the community is often only too true. How can community development workers respond?

Patience, humility, skill and, above all, respect for the community are essential when engaging with a community. It might also be useful to draw on the findings of feminist research. One productive method is self-disclosure: disclosing one's personal views and feelings and articulating self-doubt when one experiences it. Drawing on the feminist tradition, some community development workers advise that when they communicate with the communities with whom they are working, they should adopt the same style of communication that they would use when communicating with a friend. That is, they should think of themselves as a friend, rather than an outsider and expert professional, or someone exchanging a service. It is essential to give people plenty of room in deciding whether they wish to be involved in community activities or not. Overall, it is important to be forthcoming with information, but not to pressure people into joining a project or group. Only in this way is it possible to build up trust. Two final points need to be made. First, people rarely stay around in a project, campaign or organisation in which people continually argue, and criticise and distrust each other. This is not to say that people cannot disagree, but processes must be in place to ensure that, as far as possible, disagreements have productive outcomes. Second, people rarely stay around a project, campaign or organisation that continually loses. Victories, however small, can do wonders in getting and keeping people involved.

Developing teamwork

Community development is not something done by individuals alone. On their own, individuals can do very little to change the structures in which they live or the conditions of their existence – but collectively they can organise to modify and transform structures, to alter material conditions and to change how people view the world. This requires a strong concept of teamwork. Teamwork depends on mutual trust between people who might share many ideas, assets, activities and problems, but will probably not agree on every topic or issue. A good team has a group culture of listening, attending to and empathising with others in the group.

It makes collective decisions in order to resolve issues and, in an ideal situation, all members will accept these decisions, regardless of their personal feelings about a particular issue. A team is more likely to work if its purpose is clear; if procedures, tasks, roles and responsibilities are understood and developed collectively; if all its members feel wanted and valuable; if workers feel comfortable to express how they feel about issues and where they might agree or disagree, and their views are taken seriously and responded to. From this discussion we can draw out some themes that can assist effective teamwork.

It is important to remember that teamwork, while providing space for 'giving voice', and a site for practising democratic processes and validating people's views, is also a way of 'getting things done'. A group can become overly preoccupied with what is going on in the team that they become inward-looking. A team can also become 'bogged down' by trying to get complete agreement on an issue or action. Sometimes disagreement arises because of different values, theories and priorities. In such circumstances, the team can develop a deliberative process to draw out points of commonality or those in disagreement might leave. In a team no person is indispensable, no matter how skilled and knowledgeable they might be.

Identifying opportunities and tools

As discussed in chapter 2, since the early community development projects in the 1970s there have been profound changes both in Australia and internationally. Take, for example, the relentless processes of globalisation, the spectre of international terrorism, the growing awareness of climate change and the unprecedented development of new information technologies. Community development practice has had to deal with such changes. Perhaps the most successful practitioners have been those who have been able to analyse the changes dispassionately, with neither nostalgia for the past nor an uncritical embrace of each latest fad. What is needed is a response that considers new opportunities in a measured way. Sometimes new opportunities will be embraced and sometimes they will not.

The use of computers and the Internet has changed forever the way we access and organise information. This is not to say that computers and the Internet have no 'down side'. There are now many well-rehearsed critiques of our overreliance upon the computer, including how it re-shapes and sometimes undermines face-to-face and personal contacts. However, it is proving to be an effective tool, not only to gain knowledge and communication, but also for social action. The following case study describes how the Internet can be used to collect information and monitor government performance.

MYNEIGHBOURHOOD.MOORINBAH

Six months ago, a group of concerned people in a large regional town got together to discuss the many unfulfilled election promises made by both the state government and the local council to maintain and enhance local services. On the list of promises were the expansion of the local hospital, maintenance and improvement of local schools, maintenance of roads, the signposting of a bypass route to limit heavy transport through the centre of the town and the refurbishment of the public swimming pool. Their response was to establish a website, www.myneighbourhood.moorinbah, on which they could register concerns and post information on the unfilled promises, track queries and contacts made with the responsible state bodies and the responses (or otherwise) from these bodies. The Myneighbourhood group have expanded rapidly over the past six months. They have elected a coordinating committee that is responsible for checking the veracity, validity and legality of the information provided. The website is now widely accessed by the local community, the local media and government officials alike.

Appreciation of skills and resources

As mentioned in chapter 5, one of the failings of many approaches to capacity and community building is that they are deficit based (for example, when a community is deemed to lack capacity, and requires having its capacity 'built up' by external experts). The deficit-based approach, if used on its own, can have dire consequences for the confidence of a community. The asset-based approach (starting with the premise that numerous skills and resources already exist in a community) is a good way of starting with a positive outlook in community development work. An asset-based approach can be undertaken formally or informally. Formally, the community development practitioner might audit skills and useful resources in a community by undertaking systematic research with feedback mechanisms, or by organising a strategy meeting at which people list the skills and resources that they can offer. Informally, practitioners can identify community assets by chatting to people, asking if they can help on specific issues or campaigns.

Communication

As said previously, understanding the forms of communication and aspects of good communication is an essential skill for community development practitioners. It is beyond the scope of this book to enter into theoretical debates about the functions of language and the production of meaning. However, it is important to acknowledge how communication can influence power relations within community settings. Fairclough (2000:3), in emphasising the role of language in politics, argues that:

> Language has always been important in politics and in government ... Political differences have always been constituted as differences in language, political struggles have always been partly struggles over the dominant language, and both the theory and practice of political rhetoric go back to ancient times.

While it is clear that any utterance can have many meanings and interpretations, and both the communicator and the listener may never know all of them, the very fact of human society rests on the assumption of (a degree of) mutual understanding. It is helpful to think of language as a multiplicity of layers of meaning – living and shifting, often contradictory and ambiguous, and located in action and processes. Meanings are derived from the technical aspects of an utterance (such as tone of voice) and from its social context. Words are always circumscribed by situation and intentions that may not, and may never be, wholly transparent. Nevertheless, this does not negate the importance of being sensitive to the way words are used. Take, for example, the following case study, in which the discussion revolves around the hidden meanings of certain terms and their suitability to the specific context.

case study

WESTERN SUBURBS YOUTH RESOURCE CENTRE

The setting is a meeting in a youth resource centre, at which the committee of management is discussing the effects of funding cuts on staffing. Some members believe that the resolution to the staffing crisis is to undertake a campaign to recruit volunteers. Several members champion the use of volunteers, referring to a commitment to tapping into this 'unused resource' in the community. One member suggest that the 'unemployed could be tapped into'. Another member talks about how they should 'market' the whole idea of volunteerism and establish a management group to manage volunteers. Another group within this committee object to the terms and assumptions in the discussion. The use of each of the key terms is highlighted and there are heated exchanges about the appropriateness of their use. For example, should 'volunteers' be replaced by other terms such as unpaid worker, active citizen or civic participant, for these terms can refer to the same activity but have different connotations. Referring to 'volunteers' constitutes them as 'things' or 'objects' with instrumental value, rather than as active self-determining agents. The term 'unemployed' presents a stereotypical view of 'the other' as an object to be used. Finally, another member asks whether the discourse of marketing and the idea of managing volunteers is appropriate.

What then are the principles of good communication in community development? First, community development practitioners should be sensitive to the difference between **dialogical communication** and **promotional communication**. As noted in our discussion of deliberative democracy in chapter 6, dialogical communication involves communication directed at sharing information, interpretations and ideas, rather than promoting a particular viewpoint. Much of the political 'spin' of contemporary political parties, for example, is concerned with promotional communication (Fairclough, 2000:12). Second, from a community development perspective, it is important that, as far as possible, communication takes place in democratic and open contexts, free from constraints brought about by authoritarian relationships. The elements of the autocratic approach and the democratic approach to communication are presented in Table 7.2.

Table 7.2 *Styles of communication and teamwork*

Autocratic approach	Democratic approach
Moral high ground	*Equality*
I decide what the decisions are.	We share decisions.
I follow the regulations.	We respect differences.
I know what is best.	Everyone's experience is valuable.
One correct view	*A multiplicity of views*
I'm not interested in your views.	There is no one correct view.
I have the authority to decide.	We all take responsibility.
I can solve the problems alone.	
A supervisory role	*Mutual trust*
I expect you to conform.	We do not force conformity.
I am trying to catch people out.	We help each other.
I have the knowledge and expertise.	

Good communication enables ordinary people to participate and work collectively in groups. Alinsky (1972:81), for example, sees good communication as the most important skill for community organising:

> Communication with others takes place when they understand what you're trying to get across to them. If they don't understand, then you are not communicating regardless of words, pictures or anything else. People only understand things in terms of their experiences, which means that you must get within their experience. Further, communication is a two-way process. If you try to get your ideas across to others without paying attention to what they have to say, you can forget the whole thing.

We cannot overstate the importance of accepting the authenticity of people's own experiences; it is a mistake to put people down because their experiences are different from yours. Here we can refer to the pioneering practice of Freire.

Freire's view

As indicated, our understanding of the power of communication to transform consciousness in community development has been strongly influenced by the work of Paolo Freire (1972, 1976). Freire emphasises the connections between education, language and power. He argues that most education is for what he calls **domestication** or domination. He proposes new ways of thinking about empowerment and he develops a process for thinking about education for the purpose of **political literacy**. Freire's educational programs were based on what he calls the **conscientisation** of disempowered people to demand justice, dignity and participation. Community development has drawn from Freire the notion that it is important not only to accept oppressed people's lived reality, but also to deepen their awareness both of the socio-cultural reality that shapes their lives and of their capacity to transform it. Thus, an investigation into real issues and problems can lead to critical awareness, rejection of the idea of the world as unalterably given and a realisation of our capacity to transform our world. Effective communication is also essential because it enables ordinary people to conceive of themselves in different ways and to articulate an alternative and desired future state of affairs.

Freire's method of teaching has been used in many community education programs, including English programs for migrants of non-English-speaking backgrounds. In these programs, teachers have become facilitators or coordinators; they do not give lectures but engage in dialogue for the purpose of exchanging information. There are no students, but active group participants; no textbooks, but learning programs. Freire developed **cultural circles** in which topics of relevance within the experience of the participants were discussed. The cultural circles aim to change people's general awareness of their situations, and their perceptions of themselves as makers of their own history. In short, this approach to education aims to produce a thoroughly informed and politicised community. A number of education programs in Australia have adopted cultural circles.

Freire's approach has been criticised as patronising, but we can learn from him. Community development takes the view that oppressed people themselves should control the process of conscientisation and develop their own political identity, based on a questioning of the forces of domination. Understanding and empathy are essential for critical questioning and the transformation of commonsense views. Gramsci (1971) argues that the way people commonly perceive the world, or common sense, must be taken seriously, as common sense is very powerful in constructing and maintaining social relations and politics. But, as Gramsci also points out, it can also be made critical and can challenge dominant ideologies in a society. Common sense can thus be a cause of resistance.

Communication skills

In this section, we consider the attitudes and capacities that underpin effective community development communication. Eight key related characteristics can be identified:

- Community development workers should strive for empathy and genuineness.
- Community development workers should always be open to new knowledge and new ways of thinking about issues. For example, the starting point for communication

should be sharing information, interpretations and ideas (dialogical communication), rather than promoting a particular viewpoint.
- Effective communicative competence occurs when communication is free from coercion, manipulation, deception and self-deception.
- A community development worker must be sensitive to the context in which a particular project or program is taking place.
- It is essential to listen and attend to what is being said.
- A community development worker must be able to respond to what is being said.
- Community development requires assertion skills as a defence against domination and manipulation.
- The message being presented must be clear, the style of presentation must draw people's attention and the content of the message must be meaningful.

We now consider key characteristics in more detail.

What are the indicators of empathy and genuineness?

While empathy and genuineness are essential for affirming the validity of oppressed people's experiences, there is discussion about how to ensure these aspects of good communication. In chapter 1 we noted the importance of a community development worker understanding how the quest for emancipation is a mutual one. From the perspective of mutuality, empathy involves a profound respect for their/our viewpoint, feelings, beliefs and ways of living. According to Wadsworth (1997) it is an essential part of dissatisfaction with any conditions that impinge negatively on the critical reference group, and the commitment and determination to work collectively towards the best way of overcoming these conditions. Bolton (1987) contrasts empathy with apathy and sympathy. Apathy is the lack of feeling or concern – un-involvement. Sympathy is over-involvement, a feeling for the oppressed person expressed as 'oh, you poor thing'. Sympathy is often condescending and can weaken the receiver. There is a fine line between sympathy and empathy. Empathy is the ability to understand and feel another person's experiences pretty much as they understands and feel them, in a non-prejudicial and non-judgemental way. It is 'feeling with' rather than 'feeling for'. Empathy is linked with genuineness – an ability to express real thoughts, feelings, motives and values. In revealing ourselves, of course, we become vulnerable.

Ultimately, we can never know how far we are revealing our real thoughts, or how much we are really understanding another person: there is no one true reality for all humans. Community development workers agree that the ultimate philosophical questions about reality cannot be resolved or even clarified in their everyday practice, but they still emphasise the necessity of good faith, of always striving to be honest and open with oneself and others, and of aspiring to empathy and genuineness.

Sensitivity

Linked with empathy and genuineness is sensitivity to the particular context in which a community development program is operating. Sensitivity implies an understanding of the way things are done in a particular community, and action within these terms of reference. A person born into a particular community understands traditional customs and the language(s) spoken. Yet it has also been argued that outsiders have a fresh outlook on issues in a community and find it easier to remain aloof from any political infighting. Regardless of whether a worker is indigenous or not, sensitivity to the community context is always important. We examine how sensitivity is applied in two situations: rural communities and ethnic groups.

Those working in rural areas point out that the decline of the rural economy, together with the isolation of rural communities, puts extra strain on community development activities. Rural areas are disadvantaged in terms of the availability and choice of jobs, income, education and health resources, and because of the price of goods (Cheers, 1987). Isolation is often experienced both by workers and by the members of the community. Lack of transport, particularly public transport, can prevent participation so that meetings are poorly attended and young people cannot take part in programs. It has also been argued that isolation makes rural communities more conservative and parochial than urban communities. But conservatism, of course, exists in all communities. Militancy among farmers, in fact, can increase as a result of rural recession. In any case, 'conservative' and 'parochial' are relative terms and not very useful in guiding practice.

Whatever their views on the extent of differences between rural and urban life, the worker must be sensitive to rural isolation and its effects. In practising community development in a rural setting it is important to:

- understand the many situational difficulties faced by rural communities
- work at the pace of the community, whatever that pace may be
- understand the politics and tensions at the local level, including tensions based on race and ethnic differences
- identify existing resources and work with them
- understand how existing networks and processes operate and link in with them.

Some of the most successful community development programs in rural areas work by outreach, in the sense that programs move to the people, rather than the people going to the program. Examples are mobile libraries and travelling medical services, including vaccination programs and day hospitals.

Listening and attending

Another essential characteristic of good communication skills is listening to what people are saying. What people say in much of our normal conversation is ignored, misunderstood or quickly forgotten; rarely are the deeper meanings grasped or considered. From early childhood, people are taught to not listen. Children experience inattentiveness, put-downs and interruptions when they try to speak. This pattern of non-listening is picked up and continued in adulthood. Listening involves understanding and interpreting what others say; it is different from hearing, which is a physiological process (Bolton, 1987:32).

Listening requires attention to others, including the careful observation of body movements and non-verbal communication. Many of the guidebooks on good communication written for an English-speaking audience emphasise the importance of people facing each other and making eye contact. However, there are significant variations in meanings of body movements and non-verbal communication, even in English-speaking countries. In Western cultures, a good listener generally faces or even leans towards the speaker, makes eye contact and ignores distractions. Attention indicates that you are interested in what the other person has to say. However, in some cultures, making eye contact can be seen as a sign of disrespect. Sensitivity to cultural norms is important in understanding how to listen and attend. We take up the importance of cultural sensitivity and intercultural competence in the following chapter.

Responding

A skilled communicator responds reflectively. The listener restates the feelings, content and the main themes of the speaker in a way that demonstrates understanding and acceptance (Bolton, 1987). This feedback is essential for good communication. It demonstrates that the listener is interested in what the speaker has to say. Alinsky (1972) makes the point that when you have communicated successfully with another person their eyes light up and they make comments such as 'I know exactly what you mean' or 'I had something just like that happen to me once'.

Assertiveness

To be assertive is to maintain self-respect and to defend one's own and others' rights, values, concerns and space without abusing, manipulating or dominating other people. In other words, assertive people stand up for their beliefs, while respecting the rights of others. Assertion is not putting down, blaming, moralising, judging or threatening. It is stating clearly and honestly what you think and how you feel. Community development workers must assert themselves to prevent personalising and individualising issues and problems, to reject political agendas that are inconsistent with those of the community, and to reject misleading categories and labels. Community development workers are susceptible to being labelled as 'stirrers', 'lefties' and 'misfits', for example.

Clear presentation and ability to engage

Finally, community development workers should try to be engaging speakers, which means, as has already been emphasised, that they should have the ability to communicate within terms of reference that have meaning to the listener, so that the listener does not switch off. While there are occasions when community development workers use language as a weapon against the powerful on behalf of the powerless, they generally do not use language to intimidate or threaten.

Use complex terminology and acronyms only when you know that your listeners understand the terms. A spontaneous personal touch or self-criticism can lighten a speech, particularly to a large gathering. Confidence is the key to public speaking and in order to be confident you must be sure of what you are saying. This, of course, means doing your homework. It is essential to know your audience and get the information and arguments clear. It helps to rehearse out loud before you present them.

Bolton (1987) identifies a number of barriers to effective communication:

- avoiding the concerns of others
- judging other people and what they say, including criticising, name-calling and labelling
- providing ready-made simplistic solutions, through ordering, threatening, advising and moralising.

Cautionary notes

Several cautions are in order: while texts on good communication abound, good communication is not enough. For example, structural inequalities can often be easily glossed over by good communication. Politicians might blame 'poor communication' from the electorate about 'what they need' as the reason for failing to implement a policy, for example. What might appear to be good communication can evince a positive response, yet a positive response might belie what another party is actually thinking. Take, for example, the case study below that shows different readings of the experience of being interviewed about a funding application. As will be indicated in chapter 9, there can be many reasons for one group securing a tender or a grant, and it is not always easy to gain reliable information on the reasons for success or failure. Here, we are concerned with the ways that we read situations differently.

GRASSROOTS COOP

Grassroots Coop, an Indigenous cooperative organisation, has been shortlisted for a government tender to evaluate a community participation program in a remote Australian community. The coordinator, the chair of the management committee and a worker have driven to Alice Springs to present their case. The Grassroots Coop team has been coached by another group before they arrive for the interview. They have been told to be positive and upbeat, and to make eye contact with the interview panel members. Given this advice, they try to communicate their enthusiasm for the program and their excitement about the prospect of winning the tender to the interview panel. However, there is either no obvious response or what seems to be a negative response to them. There are no smiles, nods or cues, and the attempt at a joke by the representatives of the Grassroots Coop falls flat. The members of the interview panel ask a number of questions, which are posed in a hostile or patronising way. After the presentation, the team meets for coffee and discusses their interpretations of how the interview panel responded to their ideas. They remark that 'being upbeat' had been an absolute failure and that they should have been more deferential. Their unanimous view is that they have not won the tender.

At the same time, elsewhere in Alice Springs, a women's group has been told that they will probably secure a small grant to prepare a booklet on human rights for Indigenous women who have a disability. The women's group has been invited to a meeting with members of the community trust who are providing the grant. The trust has told it not to prepare anything especially for this meeting. When the two women representing the women's group arrive at the meeting, they realise that they know two of the members of the interview panel, who have flown up from Adelaide. While some probing questions are put by the grant team members, it is very much a casual affair, with smiles, nods and repartee between all those who attend. On leaving the meeting, the representatives of the women's group agree that its purpose was probably to officially confirm a decision that had already been made and that it was an easy grant to secure.

One week later both the Grassroots Coop and the women's group receive letters informing them of the outcome: the Grassroots Coop has won the tender, but the women's group has not secured its grant.

In the first perception, the interviewees were searching for some positive gesture, such as a smile or a nod of approval. However, the government interview panel interpreted their role as one of neutral professionalism, believing that it was important not to 'give anything away' during the interview. In fact, they were very impressed by the quality of the presentation and the track record of the applicants.

In the second example, the community trust gave out a number of signals that implied that the grant was already secure. For example, what was really an evaluating interview was (mis)represented as a meeting and the applicants were told not to especially prepare for the meeting. The meeting was casual, with many affirmations on the part of the community trust members, through nods, smiles and shared humour. What some commentators identify as the feminist tendency towards horizontal mutual relationships was seen as proof of having secured the grant.

Much of the literature on communication skills individualises communication. Its purpose is to ensure that individuals (often meaning professional communicators) are better equipped to cope with the world around them. Such an approach is not consistent with community development. Community development workers need to be good communicators not for their own gain, to fulfil their own personal desires or to gain respect and wield power as individuals, but to work with disempowered people to help them gain control over their lives and to facilitate the fulfilment of their needs.

Of course, communication skills are vital in the informal everyday relationships that form the basis of community development practice. They are also needed for official tasks, such as public relations, lobbying, conflict resolution, negotiation, publicity, submissions, action research and evaluation. In the remainder of this chapter, we discuss these tasks.

Public image

Increasingly, community organisations, groups and activists are advised to be sensitive about their public image. Public images vary – they can be virtually non-existent, shifting, negative or positive. They can be developed informally, through word of mouth and general reputation, or through more systematic strategies, such as logos, brochures and publicity events.

It is difficult but not impossible for a community organisation to throw off a poor image once it has been burdened with a bad reputation. If a community organisation has the image of being dynamic and worthwhile, people are more likely to join, decision makers are more likely to be influenced by it, and governments are more likely to fund it (MacNamara, 1991).

Community organisations cannot ignore their public image. Community development workers are sometimes advised to build public relations into the everyday activities, in the sense that members should be aware of how actions may be viewed by the public. This is not to propose that public opinion should drive the activities of an organisation. The public is not homogeneous; it has more than one opinion. Public opinion is not unambiguous and static; it is shifting and often contradictory. And of course, community organisations are accountable to their communities in the first instance rather than to some other (often media-constructed) external public.

Ward (1984) points out that the easiest way to envisage the sort of image a community organisation should present is to imagine what descriptions of it the members would like to see in the newspapers. In some cases, for strategic reasons, an organisation will want to impress a particular group, such as Labor politicians or local councillors. To suit different situations and audiences, a community organisation may wish to be thought of as respectable, threatening, needy or authoritative, for example.

A particular image requires an appropriate presentation. For example, a community organisation that wishes to emphasise that it has wide support may use a petition. If it wants to be seen as respectable, sensible, informed and authoritative, it will undertake sensible, respectable activities and support its claims and arguments with carefully prepared information and reports, evidence for its claims and perhaps a glossy presentation. It will secure endorsements from recognised community, political and business leaders, who might also be part of a management committee.

When, where and how an image is presented is a strategic issue. One starting point is the importance of keeping people informed of what the group or organisation 'is all about' in simple terms, using as many outlets as possible. We consider the outlets and methods in the following discussion.

Many methods are used in public relations:

- public meetings and public speaking (at a municipal council meeting, for example)
- publicity events, such as demonstrations, sit-ins and marches
- door-knocks
- seminars and conferences
- open days
- annual and other reports
- newsletters
- brochures and leaflets
- audiovisual presentations
- information stands at conferences, exhibitions etc. (including posters, banners, flags)
- festivals, fetes and bazaars
- websites
- videos
- books

- media publicity releases
- feature articles in newspapers and journals
- news conferences.

To create an image, workers identify relevant options such as resources, times and audiences, and develop a detailed plan of action around them. As there are a number of practical manuals on public relations, here we discuss only some of the aspects that are pertinent for community development.

Public meetings and public speaking

A public meeting to publicise the activities of a community organisation or to gain support for an issue, for example, can be counterproductive if it is poorly attended or badly organised. People attend public meetings if there is something happening locally that is important to them, or if there is a big-name speaker (Ward, 1984). People also attend through loyalty to a community organisation and to demonstrate a strong community feeling. When publicising the meeting, explain in user-friendly terms what the project is about (don't use acronyms or jargon). Depending on resources available, meetings can be publicised through existing networks, the local media, SMS messaging, posters, websites and emails, and letter-boxing with pamphlets. Increasingly email and the Internet are being used. Make sure that a contact person (with email address) is named in all publicity. The time, place, chairperson or facilitator, speakers, program, publicity and venue for a public meeting must be carefully planned. Venues should be chosen carefully, ensuring disabled access, public transport availability and car-parking facilities. Posters and photographs can encourage engagement with the topics or issues addressed at the meeting.

Tasks include organising a public address system, seating, disability access, posters and banners, publicity material and petitions. Visiting speakers should be well briefed on the topic and audience. Speakers should identify the issues being addressed and why, and present clear statements, free of jargon, pomposity and ramblings. Selective use of personal anecdotes and humour is generally appreciated. One useful suggestion is for the organisers of the meeting and speakers to greet people as they arrive to personalise the communication from the start of the meeting.

The role of the chairperson or facilitator is to facilitate the business of the meeting, without judging the views of the speakers, and to ensure that people are encouraged to speak without interruption. Their role is also to ensure that different views are expressed and heard, and responses elicited. Some meeting organisers ask the facilitator to sum up different positions during or at the end of the meeting. The chairperson needs to keep track of time and, where a clear agenda has been developed, keep to it.

Publicity events, social action and direct action

There are many reasons for organising a publicity event:

- to bring an issue to the attention of the public – both locally and more widely through mass media coverage

- to illustrate public support
- (sometimes) to embarrass decision makers, although this can also create hostility
- to reinforce the solidarity of supporters of an issue
- to provide an avenue for other people to show support
- to commemorate a particular event.

Organisers of publicity events try to use creative themes and activities, such as props, slogans and street theatre. Badges, red noses, hats, flowers (poppies) and red socks have all been successful methods of raising money and showing support for a campaign or a cause. Sometimes counter-events are organised, such as a tent embassy outside parliament house or a soup kitchen outside an expensive banquet.

The role of political action in community development was discussed briefly in chapter 2. Here, a distinction can be made between social action and direct action. Social action typically involves demonstrations and marches. Direct action, as Ward (1984) points out, goes beyond marching and speech-making to intervening in the way things are normally done. It can include the occupation of a site such as a forest or a building, setting up a picket line to prevent people passing, cutting down a fence around a prohibited area, or blockading a road. In some cases, such action is unlawful; the legal consequences should be carefully thought through.

Publicity events constructed around direct action must be dealt with more sensitively than other forms of public relations. It is through intervening in the way things are normally done that community organisations come to be identified as radical and their members as activists. For some organisations this is a desirable image, because it draws attention to the strong commitment of the members to a burning issue. For example, many green groups have sought such an image, when challenging logging of forests or protesting against the construction of a dam. In these situations, preparedness to live with a 'radical' image is an integral part of the organisation's commitment to transforming society, and is thought to indicate the heartfelt concerns and the integrity of the members. Demonstrating this integrity is more important to its members than the manufactured image of a mainstream or acquiescent organisation.

In all publicity events – whether general publicity, social action or direct action – it is helpful to prepare an action plan. This broadly follows the process set out in chapter 5. It involves clarifying the aims and objectives of the event, anticipating the best and worst possible results, developing a plan of action and schedule, identifying the tasks and designating people to carry them out. The strategic impact of any publicity event should be considered in an evaluation at the end of the event. As with general action plans, the choice of strategies and tactics will depend on the group's overall resources. However, a group organising social action and direct action should also identify who it wants to influence and analyse its overall standing and contacts with the public at large, powerbrokers, media and government. Inevitably the group will be queried about who its members represent and what are the sources of its legitimacy.

Because campaigns, including those organised around social and direct action, are concerned to bring about change, the organisers need to be very clear about what they want changed and why. Grant (1995) and Lamb (1997) have identified factors that contribute to successful campaigns. These are divided into organisational issues and external issues. Organisational issues include the stability of the organising group or organisation, the capacity to take decisions and resolve internal conflicts, the financial resources, the ability to apply pressure and sanctions to the target of the campaign, the ability to mobilise supporters and to construct and maintain alliances. Many of these factors are similar to those identified by Alinsky in the 1940s. External issues include the extent to which public opinion is favourable or neutral in regard to the issue at the beginning of the campaign, the public profile of the organisation or group promoting the issue, the public and especially media contacts.

New tools for communication and activism

With the continuing innovations in communication technology there are now new tools for organising actions and for getting a message out to the public. For example, SMS on mobile phones allows almost instant communication between people involved in a protest action. Mobile phones are now also being used to photograph and film demonstrations, including any physical violence on the part of protagonists and authorities, and human rights abuses as they occur.

Perhaps the most significant new information source for community organisations is the Internet. With its global reach, the Internet is a quick and cheap way of reaching people. In Australia, community organisations have embraced the Internet in a way that was not predicted 10 years ago. Nearly all have access to email and many organisations now have their own websites. Some community organisations have employed special web designers, but, increasingly, community organisations are constructing websites themselves (see, for example, www.how-to-build-websites.com/).

Several international networks, such as Witness and WikiLeaks, use the Internet to assist people globally to record or reveal human rights abuses, corruption and media manipulation. Witness, which is an international non-government organisation, donates video cameras and provides technical and tactical guidance to groups to record human rights abuses. Using documentation and compelling images, Witness partners with local organisations around the globe to give voice to ordinary people and to bring their stories to the attention of the decision makers, media and general public. A growing band of websites pass on leaks from insiders and whistleblowers; one such website is WikiLeaks, which *The Age* newspaper described as an 'online drop zone for whistle blowers'. For example, in April 2010, WikiLeaks released footage, leaked from the US military, of an American helicopter gunship killing Iraqi citizens and two Reuters journalists on a Baghdad street in July 2007. The role of the Internet in getting information out to the public and monitoring the activities of people in power is still evolving.

Other tools

Other ways of reaching the public include:
- door-knocks – which are regularly undertaken to canvass support for federal, state and local government elections. Some environmental groups door-knock to explain their

views on environmental issues and to secure subscriptions for newsletters and magazines. Community organisations tend to door-knock only when an issue is localised (such as the need for a pedestrian crossing) or as a way of gaining signatures on a petition.
- attendance at seminars and conferences – which can be useful for the purpose of having a presence and discussing issues. It is also a good way of making and renewing contacts and raising enthusiasm. Conferences, seminars and exhibitions are underutilised as a form of publicity for community organisations. Information stands – with posters, flags, brochures, leaflets and newsletters – can be eye-catching and informative.
- open days – which are part of the public relations program in large organisations, but are rare in small community organisations. Community organisations can make good use of a well-run open day.
- annual reports – which are part of the reporting system of any organisation and should also be thought of as a public relations exercise.
- brochures, leaflets and newsletters – there is debate about the value of the presentation: glossy and expensive-looking or less professional and more folksy? The latter has the advantages of being cheaper and not pretending to compete with a slick presentation but it may not grab the attention of potential readers.
- videos – these need to sound and look professional and their costs are relatively high. Community organisations, unless specifically funded to produce videos, are generally cautious about directing time and money to them.
- books and manuals – as publication requires large amounts of money and resources, usually only larger organisations produce them.
- festivals, fetes and bazaars – offer good general publicity, but they require a good deal of energy and resources and need to be carefully planned.

The mass media

Most people think of publicity as mass media coverage. Community organisations have become wary about the indiscriminate use of publicity events to get media coverage. Some community organisations reject contact with the mass media altogether, arguing that it is all based on a one-way communication that does not allow for proper dialogue. Others argue that it is a matter of organising an appropriate media event and the right reporter. Certainly the mass media is becoming more complex, and community organisations need to be increasingly sophisticated in their dealings with them.

Some community organisations opt to focus on media coverage from local newspapers, radio and television. Small regional or local newspapers are likely to cover community activities because local events are newsworthy to local communities. Community organisations can write letters, news releases and feature articles for local papers, or arrange to contribute a regular column. They sometimes have a regular program or appearance on local radio or television stations, particularly in rural areas.

When making a decision as to whether to contact the mass media to publicise an event, it is essential to be well informed. Community organisations need to develop contacts in the media, especially the local media. They should be able to write good media releases. Once a decision has been made to obtain media coverage for an event or program, it is important to plan what is to be said and why, by whom, where and when.

While these more traditional forms of media still exist, one view is that they are being replaced by whole new media constellations, which are fragmented and fluid. We consider these new constructions below, but before we do, we should consider the different theories of media. We begin with mass manipulation, pluralism and bureaucratic and democratic explanations of the operations of mass media, which set the background for the argument that the technologies of mass media are at once converging and yet are more global, democratic and diverse.

Mass manipulation

The model of mass manipulation, linked with Marxism, feminism and critical theory, holds that the mass media functions as part of the patriarchal, capitalist system and is driven only by the profit motive. It serves the interests of those in power in society and reinforces control by men, big business and other dominant groups in society, including the owners of the mass media. The mass media works to control what citizens think and do in the ways it selects, filters and presents information and the actual discourses it uses (Foucault, 1980) and by perpetuating dominant ideologies. According to this view, it is naive to believe that a radical community organisation, or even a critical structural perspective on society, will get a sympathetic or sustained hearing in the mass media. Critical theorists argue that the mass media serves to insert consumers into mainstream society in an uncritical way.

Langer (1980:13) points out that the influence of pervasive capitalist and patriarchal values is subtle, nuanced, ambiguous and even contradictory:

> Television news is not a 'neutral image' of reality or a 'window on the world' as professional newsmakers would have us believe, but derives from and reproduces the culturally dominant assumptions of our society. Situated within a framework of communicative power, it functions to selectively represent, classify and integrate patterns of occurrences into an acknowledged order which serves to perpetuate and reinforce conservative social values, structuring the reality of everyday life and imposing meaning on the social world … it performs a political function and becomes instrumental in the production of consensus and legitimacy.

Pluralism

The pluralist approach to the mass media holds that there is no conspiracy to select, interpret or present news in a way that supports the interests of the ruling groups in society. Most journalists argue that events and activities are selected for their newsworthiness. The pluralist view is that the media presents a plurality of opinions and takes a balanced (meaning two-sided) approach to controversial issues. Ultimately, many journalists argue, the public decides what is newsworthy. Distorted and manipulated news does not sell.

Bureaucratic framework

The bureaucratic theory of the mass media holds that the most important factor to influence the operation of the media is the day-to-day constraints of actually producing a television or radio program or a newspaper. Thus, the actual structure of a program or newspaper, the time available in which to prepare it and the resources available for its presentation are more important than the ideological positions of journalists or editors, or the imperatives of profit. This view holds that it is the bureaucratic constraints that dominate the media's methods of reporting events to the public.

The democratisation framework

One of the weaknesses of the approaches above is that they focus on the print and electronic media that developed in the second half of the twentieth century. At the beginning of the twenty-first century, the idea of the mass media is much more complex and needs to be grasped in the context of the rapidly developing and diverse forms of new technologies, which cannot be simply understood as controlling and unitary disseminators of knowledge to a passive audience. There are two important aspects of new structures and processes of the media. First, the convergence of new technologies, such as the bringing together of the capacity to store and access huge amounts of data, use of computer programs to analyse data, digitisation and high-speed data transfer mean that people have unprecedented choice in the sources of information. Technology convergence also means that phones can also simultaneously offer access to the Internet, email, social networking chat rooms such as Facebook and Twitter, and video-conferencing such as Skype.

Importantly, information technology, and group and interpersonal communication technology, can be accessed from many parts of the world. From one perspective, this unprecedented choice supports both the pluralist theory and the argument that the mass media is being democratised. Information is both limitless and uncensored. As the examples of Witness and WikiLeaks attest, access to the Internet opens up new ways of monitoring issues and concerns, and constructing new forms of resistance, through global exposure of abuses of power unthought of a couple of decades ago. Technologies such as the Internet can also be much more interactive than traditional media, as occurs in online chat rooms. Individuals can present their points of view through their own blogs. People can also work together to create popular websites aimed at the ordinary person, in which views and ideas for everyday activities are shared, such as recipes and tips for health, beauty, travel and ancestor tracing, just to name a few. Some of these websites, including Mumsnet, introduced in chapter 2, have turned to political matters as well. Politicians have begun to track the views presented through such websites to supplement, or even replace, the conventional market research that collects data on attitudes and voting intentions of the populace. While Mumsnet appears apolitical, it wielded significance influence in the lead-up to general election in Britain in 2010, and it a good example of politicians sitting up and taking notice of what 'mums' are saying.

What are the implications of new media for community development? First, in its democratising form, new media provides unprecedented access to knowledge. Second, it offers new methods and sites for resistance and fighting TINA (there is no alternative). Third, it offers new ways of presenting an organisation and for publicising a community concern. Political and other campaigns are now being waged on Facebook and Twitter as increasingly important sites for getting messages across. For example, the 2008 Obama election strategy made effective use of Facebook and mobile-phone-based campaigns, and political parties in the 2010 British general election made considerable use of Facebook and Twitter. In Australia, like the USA and the UK, more and more politicians have their own Facebook pages. For some commentators, having a website is now a 'must' for community organisations (see Dorner, 2002; Williams, 2000). Finally, more and more communities are using the Internet to monitor and report on the activities of those in power, as we saw in the Myneighbourhood.moorinbah case study above. However, against these more positive views of the forms and uses of the new media, we must also note how the Internet is being used for personal attacks on individuals and groups, such as through personal blogs. New communication technology is also being used for unprecedented surveillance of the lives of citizens, including through accessing an individual's use of the Internet (including Facebook and Twitter) and tapping mobile phones (see www.empowermentresources.com/).

Lobbying

Another way of organising public relations in community development is through lobbying. Community development workers need to understand the context of lobbying and how it takes place. Lobbying is a process, rather than an event; it is part of the networking role of a community development worker. In its broadest sense, to lobby is to raise general awareness about an issue. Its aim is to enlist support for a particular cause, event or program in order to influence, for example, forthcoming legislation. More specifically, the objective of lobbying is to persuade decision makers to pay attention to a particular issue or problem and to take, or not to take, particular actions. Here, we focus on lobbying to influence decision makers.

Lobbying can occur on various levels and through various strategies. Professional lobbyists are usually employed by large corporations or industry bodies. Large community organisations also employ professional lobbyists and include lobbying as part of their public relations. Such lobbyists monitor government legislation and regulations, build up public relations networks and develop media contacts. Small community organisations generally do not have the funds to pay professional lobbyists or public relations personnel; instead they lobby on particular issues.

In some instances, a community organisation is informing about an issue that seems relatively unimportant to decision makers. In other instances, lobbying reminds decision makers that there are opposing views on an issue. Where a decision maker is perceived to be sympathetic to the need or viewpoint of a community, the lobbying process can be focused on obtaining tangible results, such as an increase in funding.

As Reed et al. (1985:98) argue, politicians and other policy makers often take little action on their own account. They are subject to the winds of change – the harder the wind blows, the more they (can) change. Any group trying to influence a decision should provide decision makers with information and persuasive arguments about its point of view. A group can try to get directly to a decision maker, such as a government minister, but while this is possible at the level of local government, at the levels of state and federal government it has become increasingly difficult, given the many advisers, or 'minders', now surrounding politicians. As gatekeeping mechanisms become tighter, the networks a worker has with key people around politicians (such as advisers and media contacts) are increasingly important. Contact with those who influence decision makers forms a part of the everyday networking activities of a community development worker.

In lobbying, it is important to know what decisions can be made and by whom. For example, while it could be advantageous for a community organisation to gain support from the local member of parliament in regard to changing a bylaw, the local member is not the decision maker when it comes to bylaws; municipal councillors are. For legislative changes, such as those related to environmental issues, the relevant government departments, ministers and cabinet all must be lobbied. Lobbying requires good information, negotiation, communication and planning, and dedication and persistence.

However the first contact is made, it should be confirmed by a brief letter setting out what has been agreed. If the lobbying group is to meet with the decision makers, it gathers information about the case to be presented, such as the resources needed and available, and plans who will comprise the delegation, what to say and how to say it. It is useful to imagine how the decision makers will respond to the group, including their objections and possible counter-responses. Seasoned lobbyists see the key ingredients of success as being dedication and persistence. It is important that a lobbying group is genuine and clear about the benefits of the proposal.

When briefing decision makers, the proposal or case to be considered must be presented clearly and concisely, without jargon. Sekuless (1991) comments that any submission or presentation must be comprehensive enough to satisfy bureaucrats and concise enough to be quickly absorbed by politicians. He suggests that the essential points be crystallised into a one-page summary. Back-up material, such as facts, figures, photographs or petition, should be available. Ward (1984) advises arming your supporters with arguments that they themselves can use and offering to supply them with additional information (of course, you must supply this when requested). Follow-up and timing are important. Sekuless (1991) points out that members of parliament like to champion causes in their electorates and that the value of backbenchers should not be underestimated. Roberts (1991) reminds us that there are hidden factors at work in any situation in which lobbying takes place. These include trends and fashionable issues for government and funding bodies, and the hidden status and power hierarchy among decision makers. It is important to know 'who is who' at the time of any lobbying activity and the amount of available resources. In addition, the standing and reputation of a community organisation and its members can influence the reception of a lobby group that represents it. A community organisation with a poor image in the eyes of a government committee or funding body can find it hard to get a fair hearing, regardless of the importance of the issue to them.

Other activities
Social policy development

Community development workers are involved in policy making at a number of levels. First, all community organisations have some sort of policy about how they operate, as we discussed in the previous chapter. For example, they have accepted ways of performing their everyday operations, such as how meetings are run. In chapter 6 we discussed the importance of having a policy and procedures manual, setting out such things as a smoking policy, an equal opportunity policy and procedures for hiring and terminating staff. Second, at a higher level, community organisations and community development workers are influenced by government policies that frame what they do, such as policies about government–community partnerships or social policies such as those concerned with social inclusion. Finally, community development workers can influence the policies of other organisations and institutions, such as business corporations, funding bodies and local, state and federal governments.

Many texts are now available on social and public policy in Australia and it is beyond the scope of this book to discuss policy development and analysis in detail; however, it is useful to outline key themes for understanding the policy process.

Graycar (1976:5) points out that the term 'policy' may refer to:

- a set of general philosophical guidelines
- a series of recommendations or conclusions that come from authoritative or expert bodies within the policy process
- established procedures or conventions and networks of discretionary decisions that come from individuals who are implementing specific programs
- particular outcomes registered in the form of acts of parliament.

It is important for community development workers to understand the level, formality and purpose of a particular social policy. The content, formulation and delivery of social policy depend on the institutional context and the theoretical perspectives and values of the decision makers. When analysing the development of social policy, some general questions can be asked.

- What is the issue or problem being addressed and how is it constructed? Is it a problem of large numbers of people being unemployed or living in poverty or lacking satisfactory housing, for example? Who is seen to be responsible (or blamed) for these problems: the individuals themselves, their families, the education system or the social system itself?
- Is the policy based on strong non-consultative intervention into society? Is it participatory? Is it based on a laissez-faire model that supports the status quo?
- Why and for whom is the social policy being formulated? Are politicians making a gesture to show that they are doing something about the problem? Is the policy being developed on social justice principles? Is it a cost-cutting exercise? Is it a repressive mechanism to ensure that the poor and disadvantaged are kept in line? Is it based on blaming the victims, as a punishment for those who are disadvantaged?

- If the social policy involves an allocation of resources, questions arise: What is being allocated: rights, services or cash? To which groups in society are the resources being allocated? Are the groups defined by age, ethnicity, gender or class? Are the resources delivered through subsidies to the private sector, such as subsidies to businesses to employ young people? Or are resources delivered through community organisations? Are programs developed and run by government departments? Are projects put out to tender for private companies?

Social policies are either specific (targeted) or universal. For example, age pensions may be means-tested (specific) or, because all elderly people have made a contribution to society, paid to all (universal). Similarly, health and unemployment programs may be targeted. Unemployment benefits may be paid only to those who prove that they are actively seeking work.

The questions above should be considered by anyone who develops or analyses social policy. They are also important in lobbying to maintain or change existing social policy, for it is necessary to understand the nature of social policy in order to have some influence on how it is developed.

Advocacy

Advocacy is a presentation – verbally or in writing and supported by argument – in favour of a specific position, cause, person or group. In traditional welfare practice, advocates are seen as being more skilled than the person or people they represent. Thus, advocates have often been lawyers or academics who have been deemed to have special expertise. The aim of community development is to develop advocacy skills in all people, not just in the few who become experts. The community development viewpoint is that advocacy becomes group self-advocacy.

However, disadvantaged or oppressed people who lack the confidence to advocate for their group or cause may appoint someone to perform an advocacy role on their behalf. Community development workers who accept such a role must always be conscious of their responsibility to the group. They should be aware of the dangers in speaking for others. They must be sensitive to the disempowering effects of advocacy when they are presented as experts on the subject being discussed. They should aim to create situations in which people can speak for themselves, in their own voices.

The advocate must have a thorough knowledge of the background of the cause or case. This requires knowledge of the implications for policy, legislation and human rights. The advocate must know the appropriate forums. Arguments for a cause can be presented at conferences and to the media and cases may be taken to an administrative appeals tribunal, a social security appeals tribunal, the Human Rights Commission, an equal opportunity commission, a small claims tribunal, the ombudsman or a residential tenancies tribunal. For example, a tenancy worker may help to present a case to a residential tenancies tribunal; a financial counsellor may work with a consumer group to present a case to the small claims tribunal. Regardless of the forum, the presentation of the cause or case requires communication skills, including public speaking, and careful preparation of documents. It is helpful to plan a careful strategy to present the material, such as when to use scientific or emotive evidence.

Financial counselling

Financial counselling helps individuals or groups to manage their financial affairs. It appears to fit the traditional welfare approach rather than a community development approach to social problems. However, financial counsellors have increasingly taken on an advocacy role that is aimed at empowering people on low incomes, rather than changing them to adapt to their situation and counselling them on how to cope. Financial counsellors act as advocates in securing rights, changing laws and developing community education programs. Neville (1992) identifies six areas of activity for financial counsellors. They work with low-income people to provide information and act as advocates on:

- *government authorities and utilities:* gas, electricity, telephone, water rates, local council rates
- *income security:* social security entitlements and appeals; the impact of policy changes
- *housing:* rent increases and arrears; mortgage problems
- *consumer credit:* inability to pay, harassment of debtors, repossession
- *consumer rights issues:* pressure selling, defective goods and services
- *community education on taxation:* income tax returns, changes in taxation policy.

Both advocacy and financial counselling focus on the role of individual agents in challenging and changing forms of disempowerment. Another approach, however, is to consider the structural conditions, or more specifically, the structural impediments to self-determination. One such way of reorganising structures so that they can facilitate self-determination is establishing micro-credit programs that give groups of people access to small amounts of low-interest funds that might obviate the need for financial counselling and advocacy in the first place.

Conflict management

The remainder of this chapter discusses the management, negotiation and resolution of conflict. In one way, the history of the development of human societies is the history of social conflict. Conflict is part of being human. As Marx explained, it is the basis of social change – it cannot be avoided. Marxism takes the view that conflict, in the form of class struggle, has been the motor of history (Marx & Engels, 1967). It is through struggle that progress is possible. Yet humans do not generally enjoy conflict. Most people try to avoid it, seeing it as disruptive or destructive.

Understanding conflict

It is important to make sense of conflict and to deal with it. Indeed, dealing with conflict is part of the everyday activities of a community development worker. While conflict is an aspect of a vibrant community organisation, it can also be emotionally draining, disruptive and destructive. Conflict can be dealt with by solving the cause of the problem, by accepting the conflict or by resolving the conflict. In most cases, it is not advisable to respond to conflict by denying it, avoiding it or capitulating to the other side. However, there are occasions when a community development worker, as a first step, plays down or ignores a minor outburst or deals with it in an informal way, rather than fanning it by formalising a conflict resolution process. Community development workers experience different forms of conflict. Conflict may occur within the organisation, among workers or between workers and management. It may arise from differences between two community development organisations or between a community organisation and a funding or auspice body such as a government department or a peak organisation. Because it is not always possible or even desirable to resolve conflict, some community development workers prefer to use the term 'conflict management' rather than 'conflict resolution'.

Conflict management is seen as a challenging area for community development workers for a number of reasons:

- Community development workers are partisan to the community they work with. They are not neutral adjudicators. (This view, however, raises the question about whether any adjudicators can be neutral in any situation.) Particularly in a dispute between a community and a powerful organisation, such as a government bureaucracy, accusations of bias and non-objectivity are sometimes aimed at community development workers. As Alinsky (1972) points out, such accusations are to be expected, particularly in regard to what a powerful body may call unethical behaviour. However, the view of ethical or unethical behaviour depends on the political position of those making the judgement and the means available to different sides in the conflict at a particular time.
- It is generally assumed that there are two sides in any conflict. Community development does not accept the 'sacred two' that underlies what feminists have identified as the binary system underpinning our construction of reality. There can be many positions in any argument. Not only do protagonists hold different positions, but also each protagonist may hold contradictory views at any one time and change views during the conflict.
- Some conflict is just not resolvable, particularly when it has its source in differences in deep-seated values. Such differences exist, for instance, between feminist views and the belief that a woman's duty is to obey her husband and know her place in the home, or when religious differences mean irreconcilable clashes between two groups over how they live. In addition, resolution may be impossible when the dice are so loaded against the powerless that they cannot negotiate a satisfactory result. This occurs, for instance, when a multinational company closes a factory and takes its operation offshore (to obtain cheap labour in a developing country) despite pleas from the local community to maintain jobs. In this situation, conflict must be coped with rather than resolved.

- Community development does not always see conflict as a problem to be resolved. Some conflict is part of a healthy community; for example, when it is manifested in open and spirited debate at a public meeting. Conflict occurs in all aspects of our life and work. Alinsky (1972:21) comments: 'Change means movement. Movement means friction. Only in the frictionless vacuum of a non-existent abstract world can movement or change occur without that abrasive friction of conflict.'
- Some conflicts within organisations, particularly between committees of management and workers, are industrial problems to be dealt with by industrial tribunals. In these situations there may be little or no role for community development workers as such to resolve the conflict, because the issues are subject to industrial law. Disputes about severance pay, long-service leave, paid overtime and gradings are industrial issues. In these types of disputes the relevant union is the advocate for a worker who is a union member. Given the extent of these disputes in the social and community services industry, union membership is important.

Dealing with internal conflict

Because of the bitterness and acrimony engendered by many internal conflicts and disputes, some community organisations prefer to call in outside negotiators. However, as Rees (1991:108) points out, 'an immediate rush for outside help may mask the resources which exist within the disaffected group'. Many community organisations have their own policy and procedures for managing conflict. While no manual can guarantee successful conflict management, well-thought-out procedures can be helpful. In the following section, we discuss the processes that are involved in conflict management.

Processes

Conflict management generally proceeds through several steps:

- Identify and analyse the problem or issue and the protagonists.
- Get the protagonists to agree to meet together. A typical process here is to call the parties together, each with a co-worker as advocate.
- A meeting takes place.

Take, for example, an ex-prisoners' support group that has set up a halfway house in an outer suburb. Local residents set up a picket outside the house to put pressure on the group to move it to another suburb. The analysis can proceed on several levels:

- the rights of ex-prisoners versus the rights of others in the neighbourhood
- the knowledge and perceptions of the protagonists
- the power(s) of the groups involved.

The community development worker analyses the situation at all these levels to identify the problems. The next step is to persuade the protagonists to meet and share their views honestly and openly. The community development worker needs to provide good reasons as to why they should meet, explaining to each group the pros and cons of meeting and not meeting. If the protagonists refuse to meet, there is stalemate and possible recourse to legal action.

If protagonists do meet, it is crucial to obtain agreement on the process of the meeting and then to find common ground. All parties must understand what the options are in achieving a negotiable outcome. All parties articulate their viewpoints and their preferred outcomes. Often the suggested outcomes are constrained by the context and lack imagination. A skilled facilitator has the ability to go outside the terms of reference to find creative solutions.

At the negotiating meeting, the communication skills described in the previous section are important. Put yourself in the shoes of your adversaries and try to see things from their point of view. It is counterproductive to belittle or insult opponents in a personal sense, although a quick, witty response to any name-calling on their part can unnerve the other side.

Negotiation

Let us now consider some of the important aspects of negotiation for community organisations. In face-to-face negotiations over a conflict, community organisations must carefully consider how to develop and present their case. For example, they should decide how many people will attend the negotiation meeting for their side. (This must be more than one, but a large group can intimidate the other side or allow the group to be ridiculed as being incompetent.) The participants must also be clear about their positions and strategy; the bottom line, a point at which they will concede no more; and ambit claims (what they ask for but do not expect to achieve). They need to identify their strengths and weaknesses and how to argue their case (including what arguments they will keep up their sleeve until late in the negotiation). When preparing for a negotiation, it is useful to think creatively, going outside the terms of reference and identifying new ways to approach and resolve issues.

Needs approach

Bolton (1987) suggests what he calls a needs approach to problem solving. Conflict can be resolved by identifying why a problem occurs in terms of the needs of the protagonists. Most of the time people think about problems in terms of conflicting solutions, but it is more productive to begin with an analysis of what the problem is and why a group or person wants a particular solution. Bolton gives the example of a group of nuns in dispute over who has the use of their one car. The source of the dispute is the need for transport. He points out that when the problem is seen in terms of the need for transport, there are several solutions.

In applying the needs approach to problem solving in community organisations, you begin from an understanding of people's need for control over their lives. The basis of conflict is often a belief that something has happened that has reduced one's control or rights. In the case of the halfway house, the ex-prisoners are concerned about their right to return to society. The neighbours feel that they have no control over the situation. They feel threatened in terms of personal security and the value of their homes. To counter this, evidence could be provided (if available) to show that property values in other suburbs have not fallen when ex-prisoners' halfway houses have been established, and that there was no increase in security problems for local residents. In direct response to the fear of loss of control, the ex-prisoners' support group may offer the neighbours several positions on the management committee of the halfway house. In turn, local community groups could ask ex-prisoners to join.

Bargaining power

Much of the literature on conflict management assumes that all the parties hold positions of equal power, and that the context is neutral in regard to power relations. This is not always so, particularly in the case of the relationship between a community organisation and official decision-making and funding bodies. People working in community organisations tend to see themselves as the underdogs in negotiations with officials. They may even succumb to decisions with which they do not agree for pragmatic reasons. The notion that 'those who hold the purse-string have the power' is sometimes invoked here.

Community development workers are seen to be industrially and politically weak because they have little to bargain with in their dealings with governments. But this is not always so, especially when they have skilled negotiators. Community organisations can develop skills that enable them to have some bargaining power in negotiations with groups that appear to hold all the power and control of the political agenda.

A perspective on the bargaining power of community development workers is provided by comparing the social and community services industry with nursing. They play similar roles in maintaining the social infrastructure of society. Nursing has generally been regarded as a tame occupation: nurses are professionals who, like Florence Nightingale, are so dedicated to their work that they can never be disruptive. Community development workers, similarly, are dedicated to their communities. The ultimate bargaining power of community development workers is to withdraw their services and disrupt community sector programs. They are reluctant to do this because of the harmful effects on community members.

It is argued that it is possible to withdraw from official services and programs while maintaining support in unofficial ways. Such a strategy would need to be carefully thought out and would require a high degree of solidarity throughout the sector. Opponents of this strategy argue that industrial action could precipitate the demise of small radical community organisations.

Like nurses, community development workers carry out activities and programs that are important to society. The degree of perceived importance may be considerable, for instance, in an electorate that is a swinging seat. The closure of a successful organisation or program can be an embarrassment to official decision makers, especially when there is media coverage.

Summary points

- A good community worker is driven by a commitment to community development principles and to resourcing and empowering communities.
- Community development work involves a range of activities that vary according to the situation.
- On starting a job in a community organisation, it is important to become familiar with the workings of the organisation and the local community. This requires the ability to develop knowledge of how a community works and what affects it.
- Using an asset-based approach is a good way of starting with a positive outlook in community development work.
- In community development work, one of the early tasks is making contacts, or networking. It is important to develop trust and build alliances with other people, to link into existing formal and informal networks, to tap into local knowledge and to respect and learn from the accumulated experience of the members of the community. As local knowledge builds up, it will be possible to identify spaces for giving voice and involvement.
- While encouraging involvement, it is important to understand why people may or may not become involved in their community.
- Community development requires a strong concept of teamwork. On their own, individuals can do very little to change the structures in which they live or the conditions of their existence – but collectively they can organise to modify and transform structures, alter material conditions and change how people view the world.
- To develop teamwork, it is important to have good communication skills, including empathy and genuineness, listening and attending, responding, assertiveness, clear presentation and an ability to engage.
- The public image of a community organisation develops informally, by word of mouth, and more systematically, through websites, brochures and media events.
- With the continuing innovations in communication technology there are new tools for organising actions and getting the message out to the public.
- In using public relations strategies, it is important to understand the theories of the media.
- Community development workers engage with government policies and develop their own policies.
- Community development work involves lobbying. Lobbying is a process, rather than an event: it is part of the networking role of a community development worker.
- Community development practitioners are also involved in advocacy work. Advocacy is a presentation – verbally or in writing and supported by argument – in favour of a specific position, cause, person or group. However, workers should be aware of the dangers in speaking for others.
- Human conflict is an integral part of our world. It is also an integral part of community development work. Community development workers are involved in the management, negotiation and resolution of conflict.

Key terms

- advocacy
- conflict management
- conscientisation
- cultural circles
- dialogical communication
- domestication
- empirical knowledge
- financial counselling
- giving voice
- native leaders
- organic leaders
- political literacy
- promotional communication
- snowballing

Exercises

1. Assume that you are interested in applying for a position as a community development worker in a large community organisation concerned with issues of homelessness. Before applying you want to know more about what the position entails. What questions would you ask?
2. You are new to a job and a community. List the activities you would carry out and the principles you would follow to make contact with people in this community.
3. What is snowballing and why can it be an important part of community development? What are some of the ethical issues concerning snowballing?
4. What is 'giving voice' and why is it an important part of community development?
5. List the activities and principles that are important for teamwork.
6. What are the principles of good communication?
7. Explain what is involved in education for domestication.
8. 'To suit different situations and audiences, a community organisation may wish to be thought of as respectable, threatening, pathetic or authoritative.' Explain this statement.
9. List some of the ways of reaching the public to promote an organisation's activities.
10. 'Different theories of the role of mass media in contemporary society influence the way community development practitioners think about their relationship with media organisations.' Discuss this statement.
11. What factors are important when organising to lobby a decision maker about an issue that is important to your community?
12. What is the relevance of social policy to community development?
13. How well do advocacy and financial counselling fit with community development work?
14. List the steps and principles that are used in community development practice in the management of conflict.
15. Referring to the case studies 'Changing dimensions of networking', 'Warrah Park Shire health and safety plan' and 'Myneighbourhood.moorinbah', list some of the different forms of communication and participation used by community development workers.
16. Referring to the case studies 'Western Suburbs Youth Resource Centre' and 'Grassroots Coop', explain why it is important to understand the meanings and intents of words and communication.

Further reading

Alinsky, S (1972) *Rules for Radicals*. Vintage, New York.

Bolton, R (1987) *People Skills*. Simon & Schuster, Brookvale, NSW.

Cunningham, S & Turner, G (2002) *The Media and Communications in Australia*. Allen & Unwin, Crows Nest, NSW.

Dorner, J (2002) *Creative Web Writing*. A & C Black, London.

Flew, T (2003) *New Media: An Introduction*. Oxford University Press, South Melbourne.

Foucault, M (1980) *Power/Knowledge: Selected Interviews and Other Writings, 1972–1977*, (ed.) C. Gordon. Harvester Press, Brighton.

Freire, P (1972) *Pedagogy of the Oppressed*. Penguin, Harmondsworth, Middlesex.

Lamb, B (1997) *The Good Campaigns Guide*. NCVO, London.

MacNamara, J (1991) *The Public Relations Handbook for Clubs and Associations*. Information Australia, Melbourne.

Reed, H, Cameron, D & Spinks, D (1985) *Stepping Stones: Crossing the River of Local Group Despair. A Management Training Manual for Community Groups*. Community Management Training Scheme, Hurstville, NSW.

Twelvetrees, A (1982) *Community Work*. Macmillan, London.

Wadsworth, Y (1991) *Everyday Evaluation on the Run*. Action Research Issues Association, Melbourne.

Ward, S (1984) *Organising Things*. Pluto Press, London.

Wates, N (2000) *The Community Planning Handbook*. Earthscan, London.

Williams, R (2000) *The Non-Designer's Web Book: An Easy Guide to Creating, Designing and Posting Your Own Web Site*, (2nd edn). PeachPit Press, New Jersey.

Weblinks

Community activism
http://actnow.com.au/

International networks
www.witness.org/index.html
http://wikileaks.org/

Public participation methods
www.peopleandparticipation.net/display/Methods/Home

CHAPTER 8

Understanding and responding to difference

Overview

In this chapter we discuss the importance of diversity and difference in community development practice. We consider how identity and difference are constructed and how we locate people within specific groups. One of the problems in identifying the characteristics of a group is the way that we generalise these characteristics to all members of the group. This problem is known as *essentialism*. However, generalisation can also help us to know how to relate to different groups. We begin by considering some of the theoretical understandings of the backdrop to racism and fear of certain kinds of foreigners, or what is known as *xenophobia*. We review how theorists have generalised differences within cultural groups and how these generalisations assist in developing cross-cultural competence. We discuss the elements of cultural understanding and the importance of cross-cultural competence in community development work.

In the second half of the chapter, we examine constructions of the idea of disability and issues in working with people with a disability, including discriminatory practices. We conclude with a discussion of good practice in communicating with people who have a disability through a specific impairment.

Introduction

Community development practitioners encounter diversity and work with difference in myriad ways in their everyday activities. For example, they will note that the many different experiences and life chances for men and women differ, just because they are identified as male or female. Men and women have different access to job opportunities and this affects their income and standard of living. Women are more likely to be involved in unpaid voluntary work than men. Community development practitioners observe these features of our society when involved in unemployment support programs and family violence programs, for example. Women's disadvantage is exacerbated if they are of a culturally and linguistically diverse (CALD) background or if they have a disability. When a woman is identified as different because she is a Muslim or lesbian, for example, this can lead to prejudice in terms of employment opportunities and social acceptance. Lesbian women and gay men present a challenge to those who maintain that there are immutable male and female characteristics that are transgressed by homosexuality. Fear of this transgression can be manifested in discriminatory practices.

In the 1970s, community development practitioners made sense of disadvantage and discrimination through class and gender analysis informed by Marxism and feminism, and political strategies were developed around these theoretical perspectives. In the twenty-first century, class and gender analyses are still useful lenses through which we can make sense of many of the aspects of disadvantage. However, over the past 30 years, there have been additional insights into difference and new practices have developed around these insights. And, as noted in chapter 3, there have also been new ways of understanding disadvantage other than through a single lens such as Marxism and feminism. These new perspectives, insights and practices have focused around ideas of **intersectionality**, difference, identity and **intercultural sensitivity**. In this chapter we explore some of these new perspectives on difference and disadvantage. We begin with the idea of intersectionality, followed by a discussion of difference and identity formation. Most of the chapter, however, is concerned with analysing three specific markers of difference that community development workers are concerned with, often on a daily basis. These are 'race', ethnicity and disability. We investigate how difference based on 'race', ethnicity and disability is constructed.

Intersectionality

Intersectionality refers to the multiple intersections of factors contributing to privilege, subordination and oppression. As Bilge and Denis (2010) note, it emerged out of critiques of the single-issue agendas of social movements, such as feminist movements, in which one dimension of subordination is prioritised over all others. Peurkayastha (2010) argues that understanding the intersections of 'race', class, age, sexuality, gender and other social hierarchies represents one of the most important theoretical shifts over the last few decades.

In relation to the position of women, transnational feminists have pointed out that Western feminists's account of subordinated women in the developing world assumes that the types of hierarchy between men and women that exist in the West are universal. This approach glosses over the ways that other forms of domination cut in, such as internal structuring through class, clan or caste relations, or indeed through Western imperialism itself.

Difference and identity formation

When communicating with other people we bestow on them an identity that is predicated on our view of the similarities and differences between us. In many ways, our identity is largely given to us, or ascribed, through our family and class situation and our (often allotted) job (or non-job) for life. However, individuals have always had a part in constructing their own identity. They construct for themselves certain images, both consciously and unconsciously (see Goffman, 1959). In chapter 3 we commented on the problem of stereotyping, involving generalisations about a person or a group on the basis of selective and one-sided assumptions. In contrast to this one-sided view, in the contemporary world identity tends to be more fluid and fragmented (see Bauman, 2000, 1995). Indeed, we change our identities and the group to which we 'belong' according to context and, at any one time, we may present a number of identities. It is important to understand that one's identity is not fixed, nor is it homogeneous. It is being continually made and remade in what is known as a reflexive way whereby people examine, reflect on and respond to what happens to them and, in so doing, also shape their own identities and the world around them. In chapter 3 we also discussed the way that postmodernists focus on the fragmented and discontinuous character of our life experiences.

These are some of the reasons why we should be wary of the tendency to stereotype when we are communicating with people who have been identified with a particular group, such as members of an ethnic group or a group with a particular disability. To generalise about a person's identity on the basis of one feature of that person's life not only involves stereotyping, but also falls into the theoretical trap of essentialism. More will be said about essentialism below. For the moment, it is enough to be aware that essentialism refers to a tendency to reduce identity to some core elements from which all other aspects of one's life are derived. While ideas of disadvantage can be understood through the lenses of disability and ethnic difference, we must be sensitive to how preconceptions and gross generalisations affect how we relate to each other, make sense of difference, and construct and respond to disadvantage.

The focus of this chapter is on difference that is embedded in membership of three types of groups based on **'race' identity**, **ethnic identity** and **disabled identity**. Difference in the first two groups – 'race' and ethnic identity – clearly relates to the idea of culture. Here, people are perceived to be different because they belong to different cultural groups. In the case of 'race', cultural differences, such as valuing efficiency over friendship, are linked to physical differences, such as skin colour. From an uninformed racist perspective, physical differences indicate identity in culture, personality and even intelligence. Ethnicity can also be indicated by physical appearance, but is more often understood through ideas of cultural difference. Difference because of disability is also identified through physical appearance or behaviour and, like 'race' and ethnicity, the differences it draws attention to can impact profoundly on a person's quality of life. All three forms of difference are basically social constructions used to distinguish between people and these constructions all have the power to determine life chances and how people relate to each other. Most community development practitioners will at some time in their work be involved in cross-cultural practice and in issues or programs concerned with 'race', ethnicity and disability.

At this point, it is important to note a paradox that exists at the heart of how we understand and respond to difference today: we know that individuals are different in thousands of ways – including the minute details of physical appearance, experiences, skills, abilities and knowledge – yet only some of these differences are selected as important for identity and group membership. That is, identity and group membership are social inventions, involving the aggregation of features of human existence that are often chosen arbitrarily. Thus, we know that the group identity that is used to categorise human beings is not immutable.

The construction of 'race', ethnicity and disability

We know, for example, that there is no genetic basis to differences that are ascribed to 'race' and that the biological notion of 'race' does not explain human behaviour (Abercrombie, Hill & Turner, 2000). As Hall (2000) points out, the concept of 'race' is being erased; it is no longer a serviceable concept in its unreconstructed form. We also know that the decision as to who might be categorised as 'disabled' is not as clear-cut as it might at first appear to be. Just because someone is defined as part of a specific racial, ethnic or disabled group, it does not mean that it is possible to draw conclusions about that person, or that there are not profound differences within racial, ethnic or disabled groups. The complexity and differentiated aspects of these categories suggest that the three ways of categorising people into groups should be abandoned, for using the group category distorts the reality and complexity of identity, social membership and social organisation.

On the other hand, however, acknowledging, making sense of and responding to difference and group categories is important for three reasons. First, identification with and bestowed membership of any of the groups mentioned above has far-reaching implications for life chances, including access to resources, relationships and even human dignity. As Garner (2010:ix) comments:

> Race is a fiction that we turn into a social reality every day of our lives. It lies at the heart of the complex, historical and multifaceted sets of social relationships to which we attach the label 'racism'.

Indeed, the categories of 'race', ethnicity and disability work on personal, structural and global levels to organise our social, economic and political world. As Knowles (2003:1) states:

> race and ethnicity operate on the surface and in deep structures of our world. Intricately woven into the social landscapes in which we live, race is all around us: a part of who we are and how we operate. It is outside on the streets and inside ourselves. It is part of the way the world operates.

For example, in Australia, 'race' and ethnic differences lurk behind our fear of 'Middle Eastern terrorists' and our fear of asylum seekers, who are presented as 'foreign hordes' intent on 'invading our shores'. In regard to disability, actual mental or physical impairment can significantly affect how a person can go about their life. The way that our physical environment is organised, for example, makes for all sorts of difficulties for people who use a wheelchair or who have a hearing impairment. So what might be called the **ideology of difference** has real efficacy in setting up frameworks within which human lives are constructed, whether we like it or not.

Second, it is important to acknowledge difference. Acknowledging and responding to difference is important for human rights and other political, cultural and social reasons. It is a person's and a group's human right to maintain their own cultures and cultural identity, including the right to freedom of thought, conscience and religion and the right to freedom of opinion and expression (United Nations, 1948). Political development through democracy requires the right to freedom of identity, speech and association. Social and cultural freedoms require acceptance of diverse ways of doing things. Indeed, acknowledgement of these rights has been the basis of what has come to be known as the 'politics of identity' and the 'politics of recognition'. For example, some of the major new social movements since the 1980s have been organised around questions of identity, including gay and lesbian rights, and the right to cultural expression.

It is important to understand that categories of difference – including the three categories, 'race', ethnicity and disability – are social constructions. Developing and using these constructions provide a means for dominant groups to subjugate less powerful groups, but they are also a way that groups might self-identify a difference as a basis for solidarity and political mobilisation, such as in the case of the Black Power movement and disability action movements.

However, in regard to community development, we must be able to develop appropriate practices that acknowledge the complexity of difference but do not render us incapable of developing effective communication, programs and strategies for different groups. To this end, it is proposed that 'race' and ethnicity are understood on the basis of cultural differences and identity, and disability is understood as a differentiated and flexible category. That is, practitioners can work both with and against racial, ethnic and disability categories, acknowledging both the lived experiences resulting from these categories and the 'treacherous bind' of accepting them as immutable reality (see Gunaratnam, 2003; Radhakrishnan, 1996).

Cross-cultural competence

Cross-cultural competence refers to the ability to successfully form, foster and improve relationships with members of a culture different from one's own. It aims to avoid cultural blindness or the assumption that all people are the same. At the same time, it is important not to fall into the trap of believing that there so many differences that we cannot understand or relate to other people at all. Cross-cultural competence is based on a commitment to actively seeking information about different ways of doing things and applying and incorporating this information in practices. It is based on an understanding of the values, perceptions, social structure, norms, mores, and verbal and non-verbal communication strategies of other cultures (see University of Michigan Health System, 2006).

There are no shortcuts to understanding the appropriate forms of communication between and within cultures. There are, however, some paths through which community development practitioners can learn about the many ways that cultures operate and can understand the diversity of human life, both between and within cultures. We can ask questions when we are trying to understand the complexity of the signals we send to each other when we communicate. In the previous chapter we discussed key communication skills: empathy and genuineness, sensitivity, listening and attending, responding, assertiveness, respect and self-respect, clear presentation and an ability to engage. In order to develop these skills it is necessary to understand the contexts in which the communication is taking place.

Contextual considerations

The context in which difference is constructed in Australian society today is most broadly thought of as a multicultural one. There are many meanings of **multiculturalism**. For our purposes, we can understand the term in several ways. First, multiculturalism can refer to the mix of people from different countries (demographic make-up) or the mix of different cultures and traditions in a society (such as food, dress and norms). Second, multiculturalism can refer to an approach to difference that is based on values of tolerance, respect and equality of opportunity. Finally, there are multicultural policies that aim to support the recognition of and respect for difference, and that are often framed by a commitment to harmony between different groups. Australia is often presented as a model of harmonious multicultural policies because, despite occasional well-publicised tensions between different ethnic groups, in the post–Second World War period in general there has been social cohesion between people coming from many different cultures.

However, there are two important challenges to this image of Australia as a harmonious egalitarian multicultural society. The first challenge has developed in the wake of the 'war on terror', which we have noted in previous chapters and discuss further below. Anxiety about possible threats to security and social cohesion whipped up by the media and some politicians (such as the fear of asylum seekers arriving by boat) can confront commitment to multicultural policy. In part, such anxiety has contributed to the shift to policies for social inclusion that we discussed in chapter 5. The second and most important challenge arises out of the immeasurable damage to the lives of Indigenous Australians, or Aboriginal and Torres Strait Islander peoples, caused by the attitudes, activities and policies of non-Indigenous Australians. For over two centuries, non-Indigenous Australians have destroyed the lives, cultures and livelihoods of Aboriginal and Torres Strait Islander peoples. Even today, attitudes towards Indigenous people continue to undermine all the principles of recognition and respect for different cultures that are embedded in the very idea of cross-cultural competence.

This reveals the somewhat disingenuous nature of multicultural policy in Australia, but Indigenous Australians are not just 'one other culture' in the multicultural mix that is contemporary Australian society. As the first Australians, they have a special place in Australian society. They understand and work with the land in ways that are often very difficult for Europeans to grasp. Their culture – or more correctly, their many cultures – of course, predate European colonisation by at least 60 000 years. Many languages have been identified, although today only 20 are recognised as strong (Nathan, 2007). Today Indigenous Australians live in large capital cities – for example, as inner urban dwellers; in regional towns and cities; and in remote rural areas, often in very isolated communities. Many traditions have been lost through assimilationist policies. But many traditions remain, and some are being revived and reinvigorated. Indigenous Australians now mostly live in and move between at least two cultural traditions: their traditional culture and Western culture.

The contexts of racism and xenophobia

Since 2000, some events in Western societies – the terrorist attacks perpetrated in the name of Islam, and the racial tensions that have spilled over into riots in Europe, the United Kingdom and Australia – have contributed to an increasing global emphasis on the importance of understanding difference and identity based on racial and ethnic categories. In Australia, there have always been tensions between Indigenous and non-Indigenous people based on the gross inequalities between the two groups, the virtual annihilation of many Indigenous cultures and the profound marginalisation of Indigenous communities. However, racism is not restricted to the relations between Indigenous and non-Indigenous Australians. It is also found in behaviour, attitudes and communication between Anglo-Celtic Australians and other groups differentiated on the basis of physical appearance and culture. In addition to explicit forms of racism, such as in name-calling, graffiti and physical assault, we can find many forms of subtle racism that influence who you will sit next to on a bus, who you will listen too and whether you will make an effort to hear people with an accent.

Community development practitioners are often at the frontline of these racial and ethnic tensions. It is therefore important that they understand how identity is constructed, the importance of difference, the contexts in which racism and xenophobia arises and their causes, as well as the principles of cross-cultural communication and practice. In the following section, we consider how the anxiety generated in a risk society and the construction of the Other have come together in a potent mix that provides fertile ground for the development of xenophobia.

Risk and the Other

We have already discussed the idea of risk society in some detail in chapter 3. Important here is understanding the ways that risk is connected with the fear of others. In Australia, European relations with Indigenous Australians have been underpinned by the construction of what sociologists have theorised as the 'Other'. The construction of the Other is a convenient artifice that has a long history. As Lupton (1999a:123) argues, notions of 'otherness' are central to ways of thinking and acting in regard to risk. **The Other** is someone who is different from the self – 'often someone who is strange'.

The idea of the Other has found expression in the idea of a 'clash of cultures'. For example, the 'war on terror' can be located in the theory of a new global political divide, which is based on culture rather than a dominant economic regime, and in which the major clashes are between 'civilisations' (Huntington, 1996). According to this theory, the major clashes at the beginning of the twenty-first century are between Christianity and Islam. The construction of the stereotype of terrorists as Muslims has fed the already heightened fear of Islam (see Kenny, Mansouri & Spratt, 2005). The implications of this stereotype for Muslim Australians have often been devastating. Their lives have become much more difficult, they have been required to justify their religious beliefs and they have had to deal with verbal insults and, in some cases, physical abuse. Working to recommit communities to multiculturalism in this context has been quite a challenge for community development practitioners.

The exoticised Other

The Other can be the object of 'exoticness'. In exoticising another culture, we not only focus on what makes it different, but also see it as strange, bizarre, fantastic or romantic. In the **exoticised Other**, we 'see' only the aspects of the culture that we wish to see, such as the food or physical symbols of the culture, and ignore the fundamental reality of discrimination and alienation experienced by people of that culture within mainstream society. In Australia we have numerous examples of how different cultural habits are exoticised. Exotic food from Asia has been embraced in Australian cuisine. The cultural artefacts of different cultures are displayed in the living rooms in middle-class suburbs. The art of Indigenous Australians is now being sold throughout the world – but is the exoticisation of the culture of Indigenous Australians of any benefit to them? This is an important question, which of course can only be answered by Indigenous Australians. The case study below, however, highlights some of the dimensions of the issue.

BUSH TUCKER FOR TOURISM OR THE RECLAMATION OF HERITAGE?

We are attending a meeting of Indigenous elders in a remote settlement in Central Australia. One member of the community has just returned from Darwin where he had been negotiating with a tourist company to develop a cultural tourism project that will bring in overseas visitors to learn about 'bush tucker'. The tourist company had been very enthusiastic about the project and could foresee further development into an export venture. A feasibility study revealed significant interest from European travellers who were looking for more than a traditional holiday. They wanted a genuine cultural experience and nothing could be more exotic than a visit to a settlement in the desert, camping by a waterhole, learning about traditional customs and having daily trips into the bush to identify traditional edible plants. According to the elder who had returned from Darwin, this could solve some of the problems faced by the inhabitants of the settlement. It would generate much-needed income and would provide employment. It seemed to be an opportunity that they could not afford to miss. However, there were serious reservations about the proposed project. Did the community really want outsiders snooping around the settlement? One woman comments that it would make them all feel like they were in a zoo, being observed as strange, exotic specimens. A younger man comments that such ventures are part of the 'commodification' of Indigenous culture. Another woman argues that the integrity of their customs is more important than the money. After much discussion it was decided that members of the settlement would be prepared to host a small group of people on a trial basis, and all visitors would be required to attend a briefing session in Darwin at the beginning of the tour.

Is non-Indigenous appreciation of the art, customs and food of Indigenous Australians based on a genuine appreciation of Indigenous cultures or a patronising, exoticising perspective? Paintings by Indigenous people are being sold at auction internationally and reaping large profits for non-Indigenous art dealers. Indigenous community development practitioners are working with their communities to reclaim their ownership of their artwork, not for the money but in order to reassert their heritage.

The Other as threat

Because of difference, the Other can also be a source of anxiety and even threat. 'Risky others' can also be the object of blame. But the construction of the Other offers more than this; it offers a way of ordering our world for us. The dichotomy between self and the Other offers a framework for setting boundaries between categories of people. Yet, as with all ordering through binary divides, the comfort afforded by the dichotomy between self and the Other is not guaranteed, for this dichotomy also generates its own anxieties and fears (see Lupton, 1999b; Bauman, 1991; Douglas, 1985).

First are the anxieties resulting from the transgression of boundaries of 'the self' and 'my world' by the Other or 'the stranger'. The fear of a stranger transgressing the norms and security of 'my world' is clearly evident in the discourse of alienated Indigenous youth and the 'foreignness' of other cultures in our midst – which, in Australia has presented as the growing unease with and criticism of multiculturalism – and the constructed anxiety concerning asylum seekers, who, according to the two main political parties in Australia, threaten the integrity of Australian borders.

Second are the anxieties resulting from the existence of anomalous and ambivalent categories that do not fit neatly into a relevant binary divide. For example, the fear resulting from the threat of terrorist acts in Australia and the London bombings in July 2005 is particularly uncomfortable as it is underpinned by an understanding that, in the case of the London bombings, the bombers both were 'of us' (clearly members of British society) and 'not of us' (that is, strangers transgressing British norms and way of life). They were anomalous agents. Similarly, in Australia, the popular support for increased powers of the state to fight terrorism is underpinned by an anti-terror discourse that draws on the threat of the stranger transgressing the norms and security of 'my world' and being both 'of us' and 'not of us'. Contemporary fears of transgression of the boundaries of 'my world' by the Other and fear of the 'stranger within' give succour to xenophobia in the popular media. But they are also given academic legitimacy in the ideas of 'the clash of civilizations' (see Huntington, 1996).

Orientalism

Another potent ingredient in the nexus between risk and otherness is **Orientalism**. Said's (1978) reflections upon Orientalism have provided the most influential analysis of the idea and its power. Orientalism refers to an academic study of the Orient – a style of thought that is based on a distinction between 'the Orient' and 'the Occident' (the West) – and a corporate institution for dealing with the Orient, for describing it, authorising views about it and dominating it (Said, 1978:3–4). For Said (1978:202–3):

> The Orient that appears in Orientalism, then, is a system of representations framed by a whole set of forces that brought the Orient into Western learning, Western Consciousness, and later, Western Empire.

In Australia many people, including journalists and politicians, see people from Asia and the Middle East in Orientalist terms, as foreigners who have strange and bizarre customs, who can both enrich and threaten the dominant Anglo-Celtic culture. The guardians of Anglo culture, including some conservative parliamentary leaders and journalists, focus on the element of threat. They present 'the Oriental' as someone to be monitored and assimilated into the so-called 'Australian way of life'.

It is important for community development practitioners to understand the Orientalist approaches of some opinion leaders. Practitioners should be aware of ways that people can exoticise and demonise others who are identified as foreigners or strangers. Indeed, community development practitioners need to be alerted to how risk society can frame how *they* think about people who are different and how *they* can be affected by the fear of the Other. But this is only a starting point. They also need to have the skills to penetrate and undermine the divide between 'us' and 'them'. These skills are formed in cross-cultural practice.

Cross-cultural practice

Understanding the principles of cross-cultural practice is especially important for community development practitioners. In the context of globalisation, whereby we are increasingly required to communicate across cultures, we should all be striving for intercultural and cross-cultural competence and, in a society as diverse as Australia, good intercultural practice is imperative for any community development practice. It is important to understand differences in cultures so that we may be informed about appropriate behaviour on our part in different situations and avoid being offended or shocked by the practices of other cultures. Following is a case study of how cultural differences affected a process involving the submission of funds for an Australian-Government-funded project.

CAPACITY BUILDING IN SOUTH-EAST ASIA

The setting is a medium-sized non-government organisation called Development for Peace in a capital city in a South-East Asian country. This NGO has a partnership with a community organisation in Australia called Asia Watch, which has resulted in a number of successful community development programs in South-East Asia, funded by local and national governments. This is the first time Development for Peace has applied to a Western government for funding. The Australian Government, through its embassies in the region, has advertised a tender for local NGOs to set up programs for capacity building.

The Development for Peace organisation has decided to tender for this project. If it wins the tender, it will be able to run workshops in more parts of Asia. However, while many of its workers have studied in Australia, Development for Peace does not feel confident about writing the tender. It has therefore entered into an agreement with Asia Watch to assist in writing the tender submission. Asia Watch will also help in the project management if the tender is successful. There is a short timeline of three weeks to write the tender. Gathering the required information is a demanding task for Development for Peace. It has not undertaken evaluations of previous projects and has not kept copies of positive references, so it has to chase them up. On the advice of its Australian partners, the coordinator of Development for Peace has informed the local Australian contact office that it will be submitting a tender. In the conversation the coordinator tries to find out what is required to win the tender, but with no success. She is told that all information is available in the tender specifications. She interprets this as an indication of the probable failure of the NGO's submission.

The submission is due at an office in the Asian city at 4.30 pm on a Friday. The joint writing team completed the tender submission on the Friday morning, emailed a copy to the Australian office and was able to print it by 1.00 pm. The Australian members of the writing team assumed that this meant that the final documents would be hand-delivered before the deadline of 4.30 pm. Two weeks later, the person who had offered to deliver the document rings Asia Watch in Australia to ask if they had heard anything. They had not. He explained that he had not actually delivered the hard copy of the tender when it was due because the budget needed to be changed. He had always been able to submit applications a couple of days after the deadline to local funding agencies, so he had not been concerned this time. However, when he had attempted to deliver the document four days later to the Australian office, they had refused to accept it. He then remembered that the email with the original submission had been sent, so they could revert to this anyway. So could Asia Watch put pressure on the Australian embassy to ensure that the tender was successful and, at the same time, ask them to change the budget?

In Asia Watch in Australia, a newly appointed community development worker, Lin, was able to observe the process and note the different experiences, practices, perceptions and expectations. Three main differences stood out. First, that the Development for Peace coordinator took the refusal of the Australian official to discuss the process and criteria for success as a sign of the probable failure of its submission. (Asia Watch did not take it as a sign of failure.) Second, the Development for Peace team are used to deadlines being loose and being able to submit a late application. As Asia Watch have learnt in Australia, deadlines are strictly adhered to. Similarly, in Australia, once a submission is written and submitted, it cannot be changed. Finally, having an 'off the record' chat and using contacts is an acceptable practice in the context in which Development for Peace operates. Officially, this is frowned upon in Australia. However, as Lin, who has worked in NGOs in both South-East Asia and Australia, points out, while officially in Australia 'everything is formal and above board', she has observed that, as in South-East Asia, 'who you know' can influence the outcome of a tender. What is said officially is often not what actually happens. Lin believes that in South-East Asia, people are just more honest about the importance of 'who you know'.

This case study indicates the importance of understanding these different experiences, practices, perceptions and expectations – that is, the cross-cultural issues at play. What we witness here are two different official approaches to presenting an application for funds. Tender requirements, contracts, tight timelines, specified deadlines, no exceptions, impersonal relations and no personal approaches are the official protocols that have been developed in Australia. Of course, as indicated by Lin, there are exceptions, but these are usually unknown and certainly not publicised.

It is useful to examine some of the cross-cultural differences. First is the issue of the meaning of time. Meeting deadlines for submissions has long been a key part of the tender regime in Australia. Officially, there are no exceptions for communities who have a different view of the importance of time and deadlines. The practices familiar to Development for Peace were much more relaxed. Thus, second, are the differing elements to projects. Even though Development for Peace has undertaken many projects, it has not been required to evaluate these and it has never sought letters of support or recommendations from the people with whom it has worked. In Australia, NGOs have learnt the importance of having positive evaluations and collecting positive references and recommendations. For Development for Peace, the budget is just a general indication of how the funds would be spent and can be altered at any time. Third, from the perspective of Development for Peace, an email is as good as a hard copy, even though the Australian funding agency had specified that the submission of a hard copy was essential. Fourth, the attempt on the part of Development for Peace to get more information was read as 'putting pressure' to get favoured treatment by the secretary at the Australian office. Finally, the experience of Development for Peace was that, even if the process of submission struck difficulties, it could all be resolved through personal approaches. In Australia, such personal contact after submission is seen to be putting undue pressure on the formal and legal process.

Cultural understandings

Why is it important to understand different cultures? To answer this question, we begin with the idea of culture. The concept of culture applied in this book is drawn from key anthropological and sociological usages. The term 'culture' is used:

- as a collective noun: 'for the symbolic and learned, non-biological aspects of human society, which include language, custom and convention, by which human behaviour can be distinguished from other primates' (Abercrombie, Hill & Turner, 2000:83)
- to refer to a way of life: 'social groups may be differentiated from each other by their differing attitudes, beliefs, languages, dress, manners, taste in food, music or interior decoration, and a host of other features which comprise a way of life' (Abercrombie, Hill & Turner, 2000:83).

O'Sullivan (1994:1), in a useful handbook, points out that our experience of different cultures can bring interest and enjoyment, as well as difficulty, discomfort or even conflict. O'Sullivan argues that the focus of intercultural and cross-cultural competence should not be to be nice to one another, or to change the culture of others or our own culture, or even to increase a person's level of tolerance (although these effects may occur). The focus should be on respecting the validity of other cultures and becoming a skilled intercultural communicator. To achieve this, it is necessary to have awareness, knowledge and skills.

Cross-cultural understanding means being sensitive to cultural assumptions, norms and mores, including our own. It means respect for other cultures and respect for those who do things differently to 'the way we do'. It means being able to communicate across cultural lines. *Norms* are agreed expectations of behaviour that are deemed appropriate to the social situation. Norms are guidelines about appropriate conduct, involving correct or proper behaviour. *Mores* also involve expectations of correct or proper behaviour, but are more prescriptive than norms. The requirement to observe mores is a stronger regulatory force in society than norms.

A number of issues should be addressed when we set out to understand other cultures. Some texts assume that it is possible to fully understand other cultures, but such an assumption is problematic. Social anthropologists often spend decades living in another culture and still point out that they can never understand all the aspects of the other culture. The difficulty of understanding other cultures, of course, is exacerbated once we try to understand a plurality of cultures. Perhaps, more importantly, is the problem of **essentialism**. As suggested previously, essentialism involves over-generalisation, so that the complexity of a cultural or social phenomenon is reduced to some key definitive factors that hold within them the essence of the phenomenon and thus stand for all the other aspects of a culture. In effect, essentialism of a culture minimises the internal differences within that culture.

There has been considerable discussion in both academic and practice contexts of the issue of essentialism. Two main arguments have been used to support at least some degree of essentialism. The first argument, noted above, holds that it is impossible to understand how different cultures operate unless we have some way of classifying the range of cultures, and classification always involves some form of essentialism. In this chapter, we consider some of the approaches of two influential writers, Hall and Hofstede. Second, from the perspective of political struggle, **identity politics** accentuates difference and reclaims or asserts difference; to do this, it draws out common features of existence that pertain to specific groups. Identity politics involves a struggle for recognition of and respect for difference. Here, moderate essentialism can be used as a tool for exposing prejudice and for garnering solidarity among disadvantaged and marginalised groups, such as Indigenous, feminist and disability groups. As indicated above, one way of moderating the slide into essentialism when we are involved in cross-cultural communication and practice is to locate actions and activities within the framework of cultural norms and mores, rather than as part of a person's identity within a 'race', gender or ethnic group. While expectations are linked with the idea of 'proper' behaviour, there is usually no strong social sanction about failure to abide by a norm. In contrast, mores are prescriptive standards for regulating behaviour that are supported by strong social sanctions for non-compliance.

From the work of Hall (1976, 1959) and Hofstede (1994), we can compile themes that should be considered when working with and for people who have different cultural experiences. In the following section, we discuss how Hall and Hofstede analyse cultural differences, norms and mores, using the concepts of space, time and context; monochronic and polychronic, and high-context and low-context cultures; individualist versus collectivist values; power distance; masculine or feminine value orientation; and uncertainty avoidance.

Understanding cultural difference
Space, time and context
Hall (1976, 1959), a social anthropologist, was interested in how different cultures construct ideas of space and time, and how these ideas can have profound implications for behaviours and practices. He points out that cultures can have different approaches to

privacy and private space. While in many cultures it is important to have private individual space and conversations are kept at a low volume, people in other cultures, such as traditional French and Italian cultures, are comfortable with noisy and crowded environs.

In a useful discussion of Hall's work, Hooker (2003) reflects on how in Germany where privacy and private space are very important, office doors are usually kept closed and, when doors are left open, it is considered rude for people who are passing to look in. In Japan, people can be private with only a flimsy partition or even with no partition at all in an office or even a public bath, where individuals do not acknowledge the presence of others. In community development organisations in Australia, having a private office and keeping one's door closed is often seen as an exclusionary practice, even when it is done for the practical purpose of getting some 'quiet time' to finish a task. Community development organisations tend to use partitions to separate spaces, and observe the privacy of people working within their 'own space'. And yet it is important to understand that there are alternative cultural norms whereby close proximity between people, even in a working situation, is perfectly acceptable.

There are also differences in ideas of public and private spaces. In Russia, for example, public spaces are opulent and private spaces, such as private apartments, are small and modest. The decor of the underground rail system in Moscow, with its marble and chandeliers, is an example of public opulence. Hooker (2003) draws our attention to the construction of space in Arab cultures, whereby private spaces are spacious and public places are crowded. In conversation, people in Arab cultures are comfortable with close proximity, whereas people in English-speaking cultures often prefer some distance between speakers.

Monochronic and polychronic cultures

Hall (1976) distinguishes between **monochronic and polychronic cultures**. People of British and northern European mainstream cultures tend to be monochronic, in that time is clearly segmented and in each segment are specific activities. People divide the day into these specific segments, which follow a lineal pattern. For example, they go to work, make appointments, attend meetings, meet deadlines, go home at around the same time on weekdays and have specific time set aside for leisure. Activities, including leisure, are organised well ahead of time. Punctuality is important and disruption of schedules is seen as a sign of rudeness. Deadlines must be met, as observed in the Development for Peace case study on page 316.

In monochronic cultures, time is measurable. A watch is an essential part of people's management of their lives. Time is a thing not to be 'wasted', so we ensure that we take our mobile phone or a document to read just in case we are early for a meeting. This allows us to save or catch up on time. Indeed, people fret about time that is 'lost', such as when we are caught in a traffic jam. Such wasted time needs to be 'made up' (see also Hooker, 2003). Thus, monochronic cultures are task-oriented and characterised by the approach identified as instrumental rationality that we discussed in chapter 2. Hall traces some interesting implications of this approach for organisational structures. In organisations dominated by monochronic cultures, tasks, projects and program management are the focus. Rules, policies, flow charts and organisational charts provide the framework for activities. For guidance, managers and workers consult rules and policies rather than other people. Because time is so important, workers and managers undertake courses on time-management so that they can get more done every day.

Polychronic cultures, such as in South America, southern Europe, India, South-East Asia and the Middle East, do not have such a tight lineal segmentation of time. Unlike monochronic cultures, time is flexible in polychronic cultures. People can be involved in a number of activities at the same time. Coordinators and project managers can interact and work with many people at once. As Hooker (2003) points out, time is elastic in polychronic cultures. Queues and punctuality are often eschewed and activities are often organised at the last minute. Organisations in polychronic cultures focus on relationships and people management rather than program management. Thus, the personal approach to winning funds can be more important than responding to all written requirements, as in the Development for Peace case study. In polychronic cultures, nurturing relationships, such as with family, is more important than keeping schedules. Meetings cannot be rushed in order to keep to a schedule. For Australians working in places dominated by polychronic cultural norms, the process of obtaining information and permits can be a long one. Tracing the whereabouts of documents, knowing who to talk to and even finding out where one can collect the correct forms can be very frustrating.

Hooker (2003) adds a caveat to this characterisation of monochronic and polychronic cultures. In any cultural environment, both monochronic and polychronic elements might occur together; for example, in predominantly polychronic China, people are usually on time.

There are elements of polychronic culture in community development practice in Australia today, such as the lack of commitment to punctuality often evidenced at the start of meetings, the refusal to rush meetings in order to keep to a schedule and the emphasis on relationship management, sometimes at the expense of the focus on program management. But in the context of the dominance of monochronic culture, these habits are often frowned upon by funding bodies and even workers in other fields. Indeed, community development programs today are usually dominated by monochronic norms and practices, because community development work takes place in situations framed by neo-liberal and managerialist theories and principles, and their corollary, the contract culture.

What can we learn from all this? As suggested above, understanding the ideas and manifestations of different constructions of time and space assists us to understand our assumptions about how best to work with other people. Indeed, in the settings in which community development practitioners operate, it is important to be sensitive to the types of attitudes and practices that indicate monochronic or polychronic cultural norms. If it is clear that either type of culture is dominant, then it is useful to have an understanding of and acknowledge appropriate practices. The question of whether someone should always adhere to these practices is a significant one and requires thoughtful and informed decisions on the part of a community development practitioner. In making such a decision, it is important not to be caught in the trap of 'culturalism'; that is, accepting all the norms and mores of another culture, because these are seen to be an authentic part of the culture.

Processes and practices

The idea of culturalism is taken up in chapter 10. The position taken in this book is that it is always necessary to be sensitive to cultural norms and mores, including one's own. It is also always important to make an informed decision about how to respond to norms and practices. For example, in situations in which the norms of monochronic cultures dominate, it is important to be on time and respect schedules, to focus on the task at hand (knowing when to answer your mobile phone in a meeting, for example), and have clear objectives, particularly in the short term. In situations in which the norms of polychronic cultures dominate, it is important not to interpret lateness as a sign of disrespect or lack of commitment. If people are involved in two or more activities at once, don't see this as a personal affront. It can be helpful to depersonalise the actions of others. As Hooker (2003:29) comments:

> For those of us used to the dominance of monochroculture, practise patience. For example, when waiting for others who are late for a meeting, use the time to reflect on the day's activities, rather than fret about time lost. Allow for flexibility in organising meetings or the outputs of your work. Some community development workers suggest clarifying both time and expectations. For example, when organising a meeting time it can be helpful to ask 'Does this mean 10.00 am for 10.00 am or 10.00 am for 10.30 am?'

High- and low-context cultures

Hall (1976) also developed a typology for understanding cultures through analysing the dominant social framework. A social framework can be high context or low context. He argues that in **high-context cultures**, such as Asian, Mediterranean and Arab cultures, the context of communication and information is very important. It is important to look for implicit meanings. Non-verbal communication is carefully observed. For example, children are taught to look for cues in facial expressions, gestures and physical distance. In contrast, in **low-context cultures**, such as exist in mainstream cultures in northern Europe, North America and Australia, communication of information tends to be explicit, and people feel that there is less need to understand the context of the message in order to understand the message itself. Australians dominated by Anglo-Celtic traditions tend to seek directions when in an unfamiliar place. We read notices and obey instructions. An example of this focus on explication in community development work in Australia is the increasing use of service agreements and formal contracts, setting out the tasks to be undertaken, performance levels required, forms of evaluation, risk-management strategies and conflict-management processes. As Hooker (2003) points out, in low-context cultures it is now common that for something as apparently simple as hiring a bicycle it is necessary to enter into a contract. In community development work in Australia, hiring a hall for a meeting, a projector or casual staff usually requires a formal contract to be signed. Hooker (2003) also notes that when tasks and obligations are written down, it is easy to regulate others. When people feel no need to write down the details, they rely on social understanding and unwritten norms and social cues.

For community development practitioners, it is important to understand how some groups want all transactions recorded and responded to, while others hold in disdain any preoccupation with formal or even informal recording and written proposals and responses.

As instrumental rationality and concerns about risk and 'covering one's tracks' intensify in Australian society, we are progressively required to document and check our activities and accept that we might (or must) be subjected to scrutiny and surveillance. Accepting these practices is difficult enough for those of us who have been taught to operate within a low-context environment, but is often even more unpalatable for those of us brought up in a high-context cultural environment.

Geert Hofstede's typologies

Perhaps the most influential classification of cultures has been developed by Geert Hofstede, who has set out a schema for understanding cultural difference using four dimensions: **individualism or collectivism**, **power distance**, **masculine or feminine**, and **uncertainty avoidance**. We consider each of these in turn below.

Individualism and collectivism

For Hofstede (1994:51):

> Individualism pertains to societies in which the ties between individuals are loose: everyone is expected to look after himself or herself and his or her immediate family. Collectivism, as its opposite, pertains to societies in which people from birth onwards are integrated into strong, cohesive in-groups, which throughout people's lifetime continue to protect them in exchange for unquestioning loyalty.

In collectivist cultures, the key unit is the group. Loyalty and group rights are highly valued. Identity is connected to the group. The individual consults the group before making decisions. Priority is given to the group above the individual. Patience is important. Individualist cultures focus on independence, self-reliance and speaking one's mind. They tend to be competitive, and impatience is accepted and common. In applying the individualism or collectivism typology, Hofstede acknowledges that the distribution of individualism or collectivism varies within cultures as well as across cultures. However, it is possible to discern cultural patterns within countries that indicate general tendencies towards individualism or collectivism. According to Hofstede's research, America, Australia, the United Kingdom, Canada, the Netherlands and New Zealand are strongly individualistic. Central and South American countries such as Panama and Colombia, and Indonesia, Pakistan, Taiwan and South Korea are strongly collectivist.

Power distance

Hofstede (1994:28) defines power distance as the extent to which the less powerful members of institutions and organisations within a country expect and accept that power is distributed unequally.

The concept of 'institutions' covers families, schools, communities and organisations. Power distance can be measured through questions designed to elicit how far people of lower status are prepared to question people of higher status. Hofstede's first important research on cultural difference analysed the response of white-collar employees in different countries working for IBM. This research indicated that in organisations in cultures in which there is high power distance, employees accept the power and dominance of superiors and often prefer it to a less autocratic or paternalistic relationship. Bosses are autocratic or paternalistic and workers consider themselves as dependent. Communication is top-down, filtered and quite restricted.

In organisations in cultures where there is low power distance, there is a small gap between the powerful and the less powerful. Workers are not afraid to contradict their bosses, and communication is less restricted and is two-way. Decisions are made on a consultative basis. In such situations, the relationship between boss and workers is more one of interdependence. In countries in which there are high degrees of power distance – such as Malaysia and India and those in the Middle East – there is significant emotional distance between workers and bosses, and children are typically required to be obedient and respectful of parents, teachers and their elders. Countries where there is a low power distance – such as those in the English-speaking world, the Nordic countries and the former West Germany – cultivate two-way discussions between parents and children and teachers and children. As indicated above, low power distance countries are also rule-based.

Masculine or feminine

Hofstede uses the idea of masculine to stand for attitudes, behaviours and practices that are assertive, competitive and tough. Femininity stands for caring, tenderness and cooperation. Masculine and feminine traits, as cultural traits, are social constructions and can vary between societies, and as indicated in chapter 3, men and women both have mixtures of masculine and feminine as cultural traits. In Hofstede's research, his indicators of masculinity are clearly found in Austria, Japan, Venezuela and Italy. His indicators of femininity are clearly found in the Nordic countries, Costa Rica and the former Yugoslavia. Interestingly, according to Hofstede, America, Australia and New Zealand are clustered together towards the masculine end of the masculinity–femininity scale.

Uncertainty avoidance

Uncertainty avoidance is defined by Hofstede as the extent to which the members of a culture feel threatened by uncertain or unknown situations (1994:113). This feeling is expressed in nervousness, a desire for rules and procedures and the need for predictability. According to Hofstede's research, the countries that demonstrate the highest degrees of uncertainty avoidance include Greece, Portugal, Guatemala, Uruguay, Belgium and Japan. The lowest degree of uncertainty avoidance is found in Jamaica, Sweden, Denmark, Hong Kong and Singapore. Australia is roughly in the middle of the uncertainty avoidance index.

Criticisms of Hofstede's classifications

Some intercultural practitioners find Hofstede's classifications useful, while others reject them because of their essentialism, oversimplifications and methodological weaknesses. Supporters of Hofstede's type of classificatory approach argue that it is a useful tool for understanding not only the differences between cultures, but also the reasons for the differences. It is a framework for workers when they do not have the time to learn all the differences and nuances of other cultures. Opponents of the use of a classification approach emphasise the problem of essentialism. They point to the ways that norms and mores change and to the significant differences within cultural groups.

From a somewhat different perspective, some commentators point to the processes of globalisation and, in particular, the reach of Western – particularly American – cultural norms (see Hooker, 2003:10). The discussion of the putative 'Westernisation' of the world is complex and beyond the scope of this book. There is, of course, evidence of the spread of global capital and, as a corollary, the spread of some of the cultural icons of global capital, such as fast-food chains with their own global branding and the global reach of sports fashion equipment. However, even these so-called global cultural forms are differently composed in different cultures. Take, for example, McDonald's. There are a number of variations in recipes and presentation: pork is not on any menu in Muslim and Jewish regions, chillies are used in Asia and an 'Ozzie' burger with beetroot has been offered in Australia.

At a deeper level, empirical research reveals that below surface appearances, traditional ways of doing things are remarkably resilient in all corners of the globe. Indeed, as indicated in chapter 2, an intensification of localism often accompanies globalism. The forces of globalisation can be both adapted to fit in with local cultures or rejected, while at the same time local cultures are strengthened as a reaction and a defence against the imposition of foreign ways of doing things.

There continue to be both supporters and opponents of the classificatory approach to understanding cultures. The standpoint in this book is that we should be sensitive to the tendencies towards over-generalisation and oversimplification in work such as Hall's and Hofstede's, and it is imperative to remember that cultural traits and habits are fluid. However, the categories that Hall and Hofstede have developed do underline the importance of sensitivity to cultural differences. They offer pointers for our own understandings as community development practitioners about how we develop intercultural skills.

Some community organisations construct checklists to help workers develop sensitivity to cultural differences. Three types of checklists are provided in the following figures. Figure 8.1 on page 326 is an example of a checklist drawn up by one community organisation to remind people of some of the principles of working interculturally. It sets out reminders of actions, thinking and approaches to avoid (things not to do), and attitudes and understandings to keep in mind (things to do). Figure 8.2 on page 327 is a checklist that has been used in an inner-urban multicultural community centre. It prompts workers about what to consider when responding to different cultural groups. If communication in an organisation is hampered by difficulties in language, the tips listed in figure 8.3 on page 328 are helpful.

Cosmopolitan cultures and identities

Linked with the commitment to cross-cultural competence is the idea of developing cosmopolitan cultures and identity. A **cosmopolitan culture** is a living process. It

Processes and practices

Figure 8.1 *Cross-cultural competence checklist*

Things not to do

- ☐ think that because something is very different it is abnormal, inferior, weird or wrong
- ☐ be so afraid of saying the wrong thing that you say nothing
- ☐ assume that there is one (right) way – yours – of doing things
- ☐ stereotype by automatically assuming that because a person appears to be a member of a specific 'race', ethnic or social group, for example, that they will act in a certain way

Things to do

- ☐ learn from generalisations about cultures, *but* don't use these generalisations to stereotype – all humans are multifaceted
- ☐ understand the importance of both verbal and non-verbal communication (non-verbal communication involves eye contact, facial expressions, gestures, silence and use of physical space)
- ☐ keep at it – work with others as much as you can (and if there is a breakdown in communication, try to find the source of it)
- ☐ accept that you might need to work at the edge of your comfort zone
- ☐ in the first instance, suspend judgement
- ☐ as far as possible, respect the views of others, even if you disagree with them
- ☐ be aware of power imbalance
- ☐ understand yourself
- ☐ always present information in relevant community languages
- ☐ if necessary, ensure that a professional (and appropriate) interpreter is available
- ☐ be sensitive to gender differences in norms, mores and communication
- ☐ as far as possible, respect cultural differences
- ☐ be sensitive to non-verbal communication
- ☐ be sensitive to different behaviour between men and women
- ☐ avoid saying 'you people', 'you Muslims', 'you . . .'
- ☐ learn whether it is appropriate or not to make eye contact
- ☐ learn what is the appropriate distance to stand when speaking to a particular person (status, age and gender can influence this)
- ☐ learn whether it is appropriate to overtly disagree or break into the conversation, and whether moments of silence are expected
- ☐ learn whether it is appropriate to cover your mouth when eating
- ☐ ask people how they want to be communicated with – ask 'What do I call you?'
- ☐ ask individuals and groups 'How are things usually done in this situation?'
- ☐ Ask 'Are you happy doing things this way?'
- ☐ Ask 'If you are not happy, how would you like to do things differently?'
- ☐ remember that words can be used differently in different situations (for example, yes might mean no)

retains as much cultural diversity as possible and provides spaces where this cultural diversity can be expressed, such as multicultural festivals and organisations. The citizen in such a cosmopolitan culture is a polyglot who can move comfortably between the cultures, often embracing these cultures but through the prism of what Turner (1999) calls 'cool commitment'. Cool commitment occurs when, for example, there is an interest in and support for a custom but the commitment is restrained and dispassionate.

Before we conclude this section it is useful to consider the case study on page 328 of a town that set out to develop effective cross-cultural relationships.

Figure 8.2 *Checklist of questions about cultural traditions*

How do members of this group address each other (verbally and non-verbally)
- as family?
- as equals/friends?
- as unequals, such as from adult to child?
- as the same or opposite gender?

When meeting someone for the first time
- should I address the person I am talking to by their family name or their first name?
- should I make direct eye contact or not?
- should I be formal in my conversation?
- should I talk about myself to get trust or will this embarrass them?

How do members of this group respond to a compliment (verbally and non-verbally)
- as family?
- as equals/friends?
- as unequals?
- as the same or opposite gender?

How do members of this group apologise (verbally and non-verbally)
- as family?
- as equals/friends?
- as unequals)?
- as the same or opposite gender?

How important are order and regularity in activities and tasks to the members of this group?
- for example, do they follow a set weekly pattern of work and leisure?

Do the members of this group consult rules and policies in order to decide what to do?

How important is hierarchy to this group? Do they prefer instructions (such as notices and handouts) or consultation?

How important is patience to this group?

How important is loyalty to the group versus independence and self-reliance?

How competitive are the members?

Is assertiveness valued or frowned upon?

Do members accept the power and dominance of superiors?

Is conflict acceptable or to be avoided at all costs?

Are members prepared to contradict and criticise superiors (including 'bosses')?

How strong are masculine and feminine values?

Processes and practices

Figure 8.3 *Checklist for communication between people who speak different languages*

- ☐ Offer to provide an interpreter, if necessary.
- ☐ Give the speaker your full attention.
- ☐ Be comfortable with silence and long pauses.
- ☐ Be patient.
- ☐ Be aware of non-verbal cues that may signal a lack of understanding.
- ☐ Concentrate on what is being said (this will help overcome the barriers of accents).
- ☐ Speak clearly and slowly.
- ☐ Be aware of your own prejudices and how they may interfere with your ability to listen.
- ☐ Remember that communication styles differ.
- ☐ Do not shout or yell at people who are having difficulty understanding you. This does nothing to clarify your message.
- ☐ Keep questions clear and simple.
- ☐ Ask one question at a time.
- ☐ Allow people to finish sentences and thoughts for themselves.

case study

AN INTERCULTURAL PRACTICE

The setting is a rural town with a long-established tinned fruit industry. The town has decades of experience of people from different cultures settling there, often after first visiting the area as fruit-pickers or working in the canneries. Many of these workers, who have included people of Italian, Greek and Turkish backgrounds, settled alongside the traditional Koori owners of the land and the English-speaking population who began arriving in the 1850s. In more recent years, people of Muslim backgrounds have also settled in the town. At first, many of the people living in the town saw the new arrivals, many of whom were refugees from Iraq, as a threat to local ways of doing things, particularly when the women wore the headscarfs, or hijabs, signifying that they were 'different'.

After reports of several experiences of abusive language being directed at the new settlers, a committee of local community organisations, inter-religious groups, local councillors and teachers was formed to exchange ideas on how to ensure that the town's commitment to multiculturalism could be maintained and strengthened. A number of policies and strategies were put in place. The religious leaders of the town agreed to hold interfaith religious services, which are now held every three weeks and are well attended.

The local schools designed special hijabs in school colours that enabled schoolgirls to participate in all sports, so now most schools have Muslim girls in the girls' soccer teams. Middle Eastern cafes and restaurants have opened up, with the encouragement of the local council, and community organisations now meet in these places, as well as in the existing Greek and Italian cafes. The local council has prepared a calendar that marks significant dates for all the local communities. The town is proud of its arts festival, which involves all members of the community. The two-day festival highlights the importance of the traditional owners of the land and respect for their culture. It also presents features of other cultures, including those of the Scottish, Italian, Greek, Turkish, Albanian, Fijian and Iraqi settlers. Year 8 students at a local high school undertook a project that involved talking to local people about how they greet each other. They produced booklets outlining the ways that people greet each other, setting out similarities and differences within and between cultures. Year 7 students produced a mural on human rights.

For each new group of arrivals, the council has established a 'buddy system', whereby local families get to know and support a family of new arrivals. The buddy system also operates in the local schools and the TAFE college. Members of the system work together collectively to ensure that there is not only respect for different cultures, but also interaction between them.

Indigenous and non-Indigenous relations

As suggested above, Australians need to pay special attention to Indigenous and non-Indigenous relations. There is history of 'community development' projects in Indigenous communities that have been quite problematic. For example, the federal Community Development Employment Projects (CDEP) held out the promise of community development processes through which to facilitate community action supporting the needs and aspirations of the communities. However, in general, CDEPs have been organised around a narrow agenda. They have been set up and controlled by government, with the major aim of increasing the work readiness and employability of Indigenous people by building individual skills and capacity to take up work where opportunities arise, as has been suggested by Centrelink. From a community development perspective, of course, top-down control is not appropriate to the development of any community. The people who will best understand what is going on in a community are those who are already part of the community. This is not to argue that in all cases it is inappropriate to have non-Indigenous workers working alongside Indigenous people. But it does mean that they need to understand their role very carefully.

If a non-Indigenous person is involved in an Indigenous community development program, on what basis do they work? We can begin with the community development principles of understanding and respecting. Understanding an Indigenous community means, in the first place, understanding the meaning of the idea of community. In chapter 2 we considered how the criteria varies for what is considered a community. This understanding is particularly important when working with Australian Indigenous communities. As Hunt and Smith (2007; cited in Abdullah & Young, 2010) point out, the central feature of an Aboriginal community is kinship ties, and not, for example, shared geographical location. Indeed, an Aboriginal community, defined by the members themselves, might be spread over different Australian states. And yet, as Abdullah and Young (2010) discuss, many programs, including community development programs, continue to provide funds for programs that are geographically based. And as we noted in our discussion of social inclusion in chapter 2, social inclusion policies continue to ignore the rich networks of kinship ties that provide high degrees of bonding social capital among Aboriginal communities when they socially exclude such communities. Indeed, the mutual support existing within these kinship networks is labelled as nepotism, or at least inappropriate, in the eyes of non-Indigenous administrators.

Understanding can also be demonstrated by acknowledging that there are different ways of 'knowing', as argued by Briskman (2007) and Connell (2007). Another failure to understand Indigenous populations is evidenced in the narrowly instrumental and performance-based framing of programs for Indigenous communities (see Ife, 2010). In contrast to the lineal logic upon which performance indicators are constructed, development in Indigenous communities is conceptualised in more cyclical ways, and through narratives and yarns (Lynn et al., 1998). Respect, which as Huggins (2008) points out is central to good relationships between Indigenous and non-Indigenous Australians, can be demonstrated by acknowledging the pervasive policies, past and present, of oppression and discrimination towards Indigenous Australians (Briskman, 2007) and the role of Indigenous Australians as the historical custodians of the land. For example, when working with Indigenous peoples to develop plans, finding out who are the current custodians and contacting them to discern communication protocols and the appropriate wording of acknowledgement in any written report is essential (Huggins, 2008). In a useful book, Walsh and Mitchell (2002) set out ways that Indigenous people can be supported in planning how they can best use and care for their land. To begin with, like all community development work, it is important that community development practitioners, whether already part of a group or as newly arrived workers, know as much as they can about the Indigenous community they are working with. As discussed in chapter 7, this, of course, does not mean that such knowledge consists of one view, or that Indigenous cultures are frozen in time (Hunt, 2008). As with all cultures, Indigenous ways of life are multidimensional (Briskman, 2007). There are usually many views about how a community works and what the major traditions are.

However, there are some general agreements that we can note here. There are two key ideas about how Indigenous peoples think of themselves and how they relate to each other. First, as suggested above, is the importance of family and kin. Connections between family not only define identity, but also have traditionally set out who can be married, who are to be avoided and who have obligations to each other. Second is the importance of country. Knowledge of who a person is in relation to land and heritage has been a central aspect of Aboriginal culture. In non-urban areas, for example, knowledge of hunting methods and protocols, and which groups have responsibility for particular sacred places and care of tracks has been passed on through generations.

Practice in Indigenous projects

In their useful discussion of cross-cultural approaches to decision making on Aboriginal lands, Walsh and Mitchell (2002:16) have prepared a list of critical success factors in planning and running Indigenous projects:

- The planning is driven by and the project controlled by local Indigenous people.
- The project is operated by a cohesive social group.
- All involved have access to appropriate information.
- There is acceptance by decision makers of each other's goals and responsibilities.
- Effort, and not just output and outcomes, is rewarded.
- Workers practise in a way that suits the pace and style of local people.
- There are sufficient resources for the project.
- There is technical support (for example, financial and management support) for the project.
- Genuine partnerships between local people and support agencies are developed.

Local ownership and control require participatory processes. As indicated in chapter 5, participatory approaches are not without their challenges. Walsh and Mitchell (2002) investigate the particular challenges that affect participatory approaches in the Northern Territory. For example, in regard to land use, they comment that even when Aboriginal groups do plan and agree on land use, it is often difficult to relay their aspirations to government, NGOs and donor agencies. It is important to understand the use of speaking and listening in

Aboriginal culture, which is preferred to writing and reports. Aboriginal people can become frustrated with the non-Aboriginals' insistence on documentation rather than seriously listening to what is being said. When the written word is translated from local Aboriginal discourses it is often framed in a way that is different to non-Aboriginal approaches. Thus, visual communication is essential. Walsh and Mitchell (2002:39) discuss how maps, drawings and games can be used in workshops as the basis for discussion. But this is sometimes seen as childlike by non-Aboriginal people, who will not take the time to listen to what Aboriginal people are saying by these means (Walsh & Mitchell, 2002). Underlying this advice, of course, is the importance of respecting different ways of doing things and working with people on the basis of their existing assets and their needs as they see them.

In an attempt to recognise the mistreatment of Aboriginal and Torres Strait Islander peoples, and to express remorse for the indignity and degradation they have suffered, in 2008 the newly elected federal Labor government, under the leadership of the then prime minister Kevin Rudd, presented an historic 'Apology' to Australia's Indigenous people. The Apology also expressed a resolve to establish new types of relationships between Indigenous and non-Indigenous Australians, which would not be based on gross inequalities but instead would be based on mutual respect, resolve and responsibility. There has been considerable discussion of the Apology. For many, it signified recognition of past injustices and was a symbolic first step towards new relationships. For others, as it stands, the Apology has been no more than a 'good soundbite'. It is meaningless until it is supported by real action. For example, the ideas of mutual respect, mutual resolve and mutual responsibility ring hollow when there is unilateral state intervention to control the lives of people living in Indigenous communities. One outcome has been that Indigenous Australians were identified as being in need of becoming socially included (social inclusion was discussed in chapter 5). From a community development perspective, the extent to which Australia offers a future that involves 'equal partners, with equal opportunities and with an equal stake in shaping the next chapter in the history of ... Australia', as promised in the Apology, will rest on whether there is real respect for Indigenous Australians and their ways of doing things, and real control of resources in their communities. It remains to be seen what will finally eventuate out of the Apology, but in 2010 the prospect of real practical respect for Indigenous Australians as equal partners, with equal opportunities, does not look hopeful.

Before we finish this discussion, we should summarise key ideas for practice. Those involved in community development with different cultural groups should:

- understand and respect the background and culture of the people they are working with
- not lump different groups together (for example, just because English is not their first language)
- not ignore differences within ethnic groups themselves
- listen carefully to what people are saying (including through interpreters)
- identify structures and processes that discourage the participation of ethnic groups
- be aware that 'race' and ethnicity are not static concepts, and customs change
- understand how racism affects the daily lives of people.

It is important to always question stereotypical views and be critically aware of our own practices. We should ask whether a particular practice, skill, explanation, program, structure or process is appropriate to the needs of the community with whom we are working. Has the community decided on how things should be done or have we constrained their views and activities because of our ethnocentrism?

Disability and difference

In this section we consider another form of difference that is important in community development: the concept of **disability**. Disability is a significant marker of difference, and one that is often overlooked in the discussions of diversity and identity. Disability, of course, is located in the construction of the body. One of Foucault's (1979, 1963) important contributions to social theory has been his work on the construction and deconstruction of the body. Hancock and Garner (2009:36) consider how, for Foucault, the body is the 'locus where the minutest social practices link up, intertwine, and connect to larger organizations of power'. It is continually worked on to construct self-identity and physical self-regulation.

Like ethnicity and 'race', the construct of a 'disabled' person also falls into the trap of essentialism, of assuming that all people with a disability can be grouped together. In fact, disability is just one of many experiences that humans have. All humans will experience some sort of disability in their lifetime; however, some people will experience a physical or mental impairment that means that they will be labelled 'disabled'. Marks (2001:169) argues that

> disabled people are socially constructed as dependent, primarily because the social and built environment is designed for non-disabled people. People with a disability are then expected to integrate into the 'ablist' world.

In this way, disabled people are treated as clients or patients who should be grateful and compliant, rather than as active citizens and consumers with rights and duties.

One of the first things that community development workers might notice when working with people with a disability is the varying conceptions of what it means to have a disability, and how these conceptions affect programs and strategies to improve people's lives. As Cocks and Stehlik (1996:10) state:

> The manner in which society thinks about people with disabilities strongly influences the way they are treated ... If the predominant view is that people with disabilities are ill and diseased, they will be treated within service systems that function as hospitals ... If people with disabilities are thought of as a menace – as indeed they have at various times in history – their treatment will reflect that belief and services will detain and punish them ... Historically, people with disabilities were regarded as being different to ordinary people and the nature of that difference was seen as undesirable.

Disability is a complex idea that arises when several factors come together: difference, specific functional impairments and social barriers to participation and wellbeing. Impairment is defined as a 'missing, damaged, deficient or weakened body part or function' (Miller & Sammons, 1999:26). For example, someone who uses a hearing aid has hearing impairment and someone with arthritis has impaired movement. Disability refers to an inability to perform one or more major life activities because of impairment and the inability of social structures and processes and, in some instances, medical knowledge and practice to respond to the needs generated by this impairment. Major life activities include caring for oneself, being able to move freely, having intact senses, communicating with others, using mental processes and maintaining relationships (Miller & Sammons, 1999:26–7). Responses to the disabled individual include stereotyping, social isolation and social exclusion. When a person with a disability is also a woman or is from a culturally and linguistically diverse community, the levels of disadvantage, social isolation and social exclusion are intensified. From a community development perspective, it is essential to understand how the idea of disability is constructed, the forms of discrimination against people who are identified as disabled and the barriers to their social inclusion. It is also important, of course, to identify and act on ways of overcoming discrimination and social exclusion.

Hackney (1996) identifies a number of approaches to disability. The **medical model** focuses on functional impairments. It involves diagnosis, treatment, therapy and, where applicable, a cure. 'Medical' treatment for people with a disability has at times included incarceration in asylums and isolation in specific hospital wards. The **charity model** also 'treats' people who are disabled, not by medical intervention but by doing 'good work' to help them. Charity involves giving and helping 'the unfortunate' on a moral basis and often has religious undertones. It perceives a person with a disability to be an object of pity. From this perspective, disability is also a deficiency and even a tragedy. The charity approach sees disabled people as passive citizens requiring altruistic support. In the framework of the undeserving and deserving poor, people who are disabled tend to be placed in the category of deserving poor, because they have no control over their impairments. The charity model of welfare is discussed in some detail in chapter 6. Both the medical model and the charity model are conceptualised as relations between 'abled-bodies' and 'disabled-bodies', involving asymmetrical power relations whereby the professional expert (such as a doctor or social worker), the charity worker or family member speaks and decides for them.

The **social model** emphasises the social construction of disability and 'the disabling barriers of prejudice, discrimination and social exclusion' (Morris, 2001:2). Thus, rather than asking what is wrong with the individual, the social model of disability traces the ways that people are constructed as disabled and questions the structures of society that maintain the disadvantage of those who are labelled disabled, such as the design of public transport or the way that banking is organised.

Once disability is analysed sociologically, it opens the way for an approach that affirms the common humanity of people with disabilities and identifies the rights of people with disabilities to welfare support. The **welfare state approach** offers professional and standardised services as a right for people with a disability, but it still constructs them as passive citizens who are supported by welfare professionals, and it can easily slide into the 'disability as tragedy' standpoint.

It is only in organisations that see people with disabilities as active citizens, whose positions in society have been constructed socially and who have human rights, that community development is possible. As Hackney (1996) points out, the disability rights and independence movement emerged in Australia in the 1970s. It drew on the 'independent living skills' movement in America, particularly the refusal of Vietnam

Processes and practices

case study

ACTION ON RIGHTS DISABILITY CENTRE

We are sitting in the meeting room of a disability action centre in an inner-urban area in an Australian capital city. This Action on Rights disability centre has been designed as a purpose-built construction by a firm of leading Australian architects, who took seriously the requirement to apply community development methods in the scoping and design stage of the brief. At all stages of the design, they worked with members of the centre to ensure that access and communication, and use of equipment, workstations, meeting rooms and informal spaces, were facilitated. The architects understood that they also had to ensure that the spaces were not overly designed so that they became sterile, because people wanted a friendly and welcoming atmosphere as well as useful spaces.

The members of the Action on Rights disability centre are proud of their building and of the actions that they are involved in. However, they also understand that the respect for people with a significant disability within the centre is not mirrored outside the centre. A group of four visitors is discussing recent experiences of discrimination while shopping and travelling on public transport.

One member of the group suggests that she would record their stories (in written and audio forms) and produce a small booklet of their experiences to explain to others what it is like to be labelled a disabled person. Another person argues that such a booklet could draw attention to disability differences in a way that would lead to patronising sympathy for the 'plight of the disabled'. He states that he is sick and tired of being patronised and assumed to be the object of charity. He wants action to change things. Discussion ensues about what such action could be. The group considers the value of targeting places where people are discriminated against, such as a local shopping centre. A young woman points out that the group really needs to know its rights. Another asks what their rights are and which rights apply to which situations.

At this point, a long-standing member of the centre enters the room and the group asks her what help the centre can offer. It has extensive information on the legal rights of people with a disability, setting out conventions and laws as well as non-legal protocols and checklists for different situations. She explains that the work in preparing a human rights kit was undertaken collaboratively. There is money to update it, and this was discussed at the last committee of management meeting, but no-one had the time to do it. She asks the group if they are interested in joining the reference group to update the human rights kit. All four visitors are interested.

---

veterans with disabilities to be excluded from a full and meaningful life. This model is sometimes called the **affirmation model**. The affirmation model is a working of the rights-based approach to include empowerment and diversity. In particular, it aims to give people with a disability the voice to articulate their experiences, both positive and negative, and to act for themselves as autonomous and independent people. The following case study indicates how an affirmation model might be applied.

The affirmation model is linked to the community development principles of empowerment, diversity, change and collective endeavour. It attempts to overturn the misguided approaches to disability that have dominated past efforts to respond appropriately to people with disabilities. Thus, it is this model that is generally applied in community development programs run by people with a disability.

While the affirmation model is preferable to the other models of disability, there remain two major concerns. First, for some, even the affirmation model continues to apply the misleading binary divide between people with and without disabilities. For example, some community development practitioners are still ill at ease even using the term 'person with a disability'. They point to how this label continues to stigmatise and separate certain groups of people. Like the other models of disability, it is an essentialist approach involving all the difficulties of essentialism. The affirmation model can also perpetuate, albeit unwittingly, the construction of the person with a disability as the Other. As with all differences that are collapsed into 'us/me' and 'the Other', it can challenge the security of 'our/my' way of doing things. The disabled Other can generate anxiety about how to deal with them. Antagonism can also result when the assumed boundaries of 'us' and 'them' are breached. However, the process of normalisation, through which people with disabilities are expected to integrate in the community, can also deny the different needs of people with different abilities and, most importantly, gives governments a way to abrogate their responsibilities to fund programs for people with specific disabilities.

Second is the issue of the concrete reality that some people do actually require someone to speak for them and to protect them. For example, Ife (2001) distinguishes between people who, because of intellectual limitations, have a reduced capacity to make decisions and represent their interests, and those who have a physical disability that does not reduce their capacity for decision making and self-advocacy. For the first group it is necessary to have a group or an individual advocating for them. For the latter group, it can be patronising and oppressive for someone (such as a welfare professional) to speak for them.

How can community development practitioners respond to these concerns? There are several answers. First, it is imperative that community development workers are sensitive to the issue of essentialism and understand the diversity of skills and interests among people with a disability. A community development practitioner can refuse to accept the idea of the binary division and to use the patronising language of disability, while simultaneously acknowledging and responding to the special needs of different groups of people with disabilities and their history of oppression. Second, it is still possible to affirm the experiences of people with a disability and to understand how affirmation can be the basis of resilience and solidarity among people with a disability.

Third, the role of a community development program is to break down the barriers to participation and a meaningful life, to counter discrimination, to build confidence in those who have a disability and to work with disability groups to establish structures, processes and practices that maintain dignity and self-determination. This involves responding to the needs of disability groups as they see them and maximising their autonomy. In the case of people for whom self-advocacy is more difficult, it might be necessary to have an advocate to ensure that their interests are secure. A person with a communication disability might also need support from an advocate to ensure that their wishes are listened to and, as far as possible, fulfilled.

Fourth, community development practitioners working in a disability program need to understand how the different models of disability inform how a disability program is constructed and implemented. They also need to understand the range of actions available to counter exclusion and discrimination. In Australia the task of identifying and ensuring that human rights are respected is facilitated by several important legal supports. For example, the Disability Discrimination Act (DDA) is a mechanism for complaint and redress following, or in anticipation of, direct and indirect discrimination and workplace harassment. The DDA is a landmark piece of legislation, which protects the rights of people with a disability. It is one of a suite of federal human rights acts; others include the *Human Rights and Equal Opportunity Commission Act 1986*, the *Racial Discrimination Act 1975, the Sex Discrimination Act 1984* and the *Age Discrimination Act 2004*. The Human Rights and Equal Opportunity Commission (HREOC) administers this legislation. The DDA complements equal opportunity legislation in each state and territory that addresses discrimination on a variety of grounds, including disability.

Finally, it is important to develop principles for communication that can reinforce or add to the dignity of disabled people. In the following section, we consider some of the principles that community development practitioners can use when communicating with people who have some form of disability (see figure 8.4), as well as some strategies they can employ to address the disadvantage and discrimination they experience (see figure 8.5).

Many people feel uncomfortable around people with disabilities because they are unsure of what do, how they should respond and what might offend. Communication Rights Australia argues that the best strategy is to be sensitive and flexible. They point out that it is important to use the terminology 'person with a disability' because this emphasises the person, not the limitations or disability. The list in figure 8.4 offers pointers about appropriate communication styles.

When working with people who have a disability it is important for community development workers to develop strategies for dealing with issues of disadvantage and discrimination. Figure 8.5 is a list of actions that community development workers might

Figure 8.4 *Principles for communicating with people with disabilities*

To communicate with people with disabilities:

- always face the person you are addressing, rather than an interpreter, companion or carer
- remain at eye level whenever possible
- identify yourself
- for people who are visually impaired, ensure good lighting; walk alongside and slightly ahead of the person and allow them to choose whether to take your arm
- don't leave a visually impaired person without explaining what you are doing
- provide assistance only when asked
- don't patronise a person in a wheelchair by patting them on the head or shoulder
- push a wheelchair only when asked
- don't lean on or hang onto a wheelchair or other apparatus
- be patient – listen attentively to what is being said and do not try to finish sentences
- if you have not understood something, ask the person to repeat it
- to get the attention of someone who is deaf, tap the person on the shoulder or wave your hand
- face people who read lips, and keep hands, food and cigarettes away from your mouth
- ask people if they have understood; do not shout
- reword your sentences if you are not understood
- don't be afraid to ask questions when you are unsure what to do
- when preparing information, use a plain font such as Arial and at least a 16-point type size.

Source: Adapted from Communication Rights Australia (2005)

Figure 8.5 *Strategies to address disadvantage and discrimination arising from disability*

To address disadvantage and discrimination arising from disability:
- question existing assumptions and beliefs
- recognise that disabilities are part of everyone's life experiences
- recognise the diversity of the experience of disability
- understand the principles and application of anti-discrimination laws and UN conventions
- inform the groups that you are working with about their rights, which include the right
    - to have life protected
    - to be treated with dignity
    - to freedom of thought, movement, association and speech
    - to take part in the conduct of public affairs
    - to non-discrimination
    - to social participation
    - to economic wellbeing
- for people of diverse cultural backgrounds, ensure that relevant literature is available in community languages
- establish programs to educate communities about the experiences of people with disabilities and encourage people with disabilities to relate their experiences and achievements to the wider public
- promote the value of diversity
- ensure that community development principles are applied in all program development, including ownership of programs and collaborative decision-making by people with a disability.

use. Many of the points made about disability and community development can also be made about 'race' and ethnicity. Whether a community development practitioner is working with groups on discrimination and oppression because of 'race', ethnicity or disability, it is important to question existing essentialist assumptions. Community development practitioners can validate the views and activities of culturally and linguistically diverse communities and disability activist groups by promoting diversity in general. They can emphasise our common human rights and the dignity of all human beings. In their practice, community development workers can ask people with a disability and people from different cultural communities about what is important to them. They can ask if their organisation has specific protocols setting out guidelines for interaction and what strategic action, if any, they are interested in.

The issue of difference is clearly an important one in the twenty-first century. While lip-service is now being paid to accepting a diverse range of cultures and ways of doing things, there is also much alarm in the West about the threats from the Other, whether they be from demonised asylum seekers, people who come from different cultures, or other people who just 'look different' by way of physical appearance or dress, for example. If we are not to fall prey to the false notions of the threat of the Other, or the 'clash of cultures', then we need to be working very hard to understand and negotiate differences. In many ways we are just beginning this journey. There is still so much to be done.

Processes and practices

Summary points

- Community development practitioners work with diversity and difference in a myriad of ways in their everyday activities. The focus in this chapter is on difference identified through 'race', ethnicity and disability.
- All three forms of difference are basically social constructions used to distinguish between people and they all have the power to determine life chances and how people relate to each other.
- Identity and group membership are social inventions, involving the aggregation of features of human existence, which are often chosen arbitrarily. Thus, we know that the group identity that is used to categorise human beings is not immutable.
- When communicating with other people, we bestow on them an identity predicated on our views of both the similarities and differences between us. In some societies, identity is largely given to us; however, individuals have always had a part in constructing their own identity.
- The context in which difference is constructed in Australian society today is most broadly thought of as a multicultural one.
- Australians need to pay special attention to Indigenous and non-Indigenous relations.
- Cross-cultural competence refers to the ability to successfully form, foster and improve relationships with members of a culture different from one's own. It aims to avoid cultural blindness or the assumption that all people are the same. Understanding the principles of cross-cultural practice is especially important for community development practitioners.
- Two theorists who have set out classification models for different cultures are Hall and Hofstede.
- Cultures can be classified on the basis of differences in perceptions of space, time and context; acceptance and extent of unequal distribution of power; level of uncertainty avoidance; and the construction of individualism or collectivism, and masculine and feminine values.
- To assist in the development of cross-cultural competence, some community organisations have produced checklists and questions for the participants in their activities.
- Disability is an important marker of difference and one that is often overlooked in the discussions of diversity and identity.
- One of the first things that community development workers might notice when working with people with a disability is the varying conceptions of what it means to have a disability.
- Disability occurs when a person's life is affected by specific impairments and social barriers to participation and wellbeing.
- Responses to people with a disability include stereotyping, social isolation and social exclusion.
- From a community development perspective, it is imperative to understand how the idea of disability is constructed, the forms of discrimination against people who are identified as disabled and the barriers to their social inclusion. It is also important, of course, to identify ways of overcoming discrimination and social exclusion.
- The medical model focuses on functional impairments. It involves diagnosis, treatment and therapy and, where applicable, a cure.
- The charity model also 'treats' people who are disabled, not by medical intervention but by doing 'good work' to help them. The charity approach sees disabled people as passive citizens requiring altruistic support.

- The social model emphasises the social construction of disability and 'the disabling barriers of prejudice, discrimination and social exclusion'.
- The affirmation model is based on the community development principles of empowerment, diversity, change and collective endeavour and attempts to overturn the dominant misguided approaches to disability.
- The story of making sense of disability and the disadvantages experienced by people with a disability is still developing. Even in the affirmation model of disability there are still challenges and issues.

Key terms

- affirmation model
- charity model
- cosmopolitan culture
- cross-cultural competence
- disability
- disabled identity
- essentialism
- ethnic identity
- exoticised Other
- high-context cultures
- identity politics
- ideology of difference
- individualism or collectivism
- intercultural sensitivity
- intersectionality
- low-context cultures
- masculine or feminine
- medical model
- monochronic and polychronic cultures
- multiculturalism
- Orientalism
- 'race' identity
- power distance
- social model
- the Other
- uncertainty avoidance
- welfare state approach

Exercises

1 Why is it important for community development practitioners to be able to make sense of, and respond to, difference and group categories?
2 Explain what is meant by the term 'essentialism' and why understanding essentialism is important for community development.
3 What are some of the theoretical explanations of racism and xenophobia?
4 What is Orientalism and how can it affect intercultural understanding?
5 Outline some of the meanings of multiculturalism.
6 Referring to the work of Hall and Hofstede, list the themes that we should consider when working with and for people who have different cultural experiences.
7 What is cross-cultural competence and why is it important for community development practitioners?
8 What should you be aware of when communicating with people from a different culture?
9 What is meant by the terms 'cosmopolitan cultures' and 'cosmopolitan identities'?
10 Outline three approaches to understanding the construction of the idea of disability.
11 The role of a community development worker is to break down the barriers to participation and a meaningful life, to counter discrimination, to build confidence in those who have a disability and to work with disability groups to establish structures, processes and practices that maintain dignity and self-determination. How can they do this?

Processes and practices

12 Referring to the three case studies 'Bush tucker for tourism or the reclamation of heritage?', 'Capacity building in South-East Asia' and 'An intercultural practice', give reasons why community development practitioners need intercultural sensitivity.
13 Referring to the 'Action on Rights disability centre' case study, explain why an understanding of human rights is important for community development practitioners.

Further reading

Abdullah, J & Young, S (2010) 'Emergent drivers for building and sustaining capacity in Australian Indigenous communities', in S Kenny and M Clarke, *Challenging Capacity Building: Comparative Perspectives,* Palgrave, London, pp. 87–111.

Bauman, Z (1995) *Life in Fragments: Essays in Postmodern Morality.* Butterworth, Oxford.

Bauman, Z (2000) *Liquid Modernity.* Polity Press, Cambridge.

Bilge, S & Denis, A (2010) 'Introduction: women, intersectionality and diasporas', *Journal of Intercultural Studies,* Vol. 31, No. 1, pp. 1–8.

Cocks, E & Stehlik, D (1996) 'History of services', in J Annison, J Jenkinson, W Sparrow and E Bethune (eds) *Disability: A Guide for Health Professionals.* Nelson ITP, South Melbourne, pp. 8–30.

Garner, S (2010) *Racisms: An Introduction,* Sage, London.

Goffman, E (1959) *The Presentation of Self in Everyday Life.* Doubleday Anchor, Garden City, New York.

Gunaratnam, Y (2003) *Researching 'Race' and Ethnicity: Methods, Knowledge and Power.* Sage, London.

Hackney, S (1996) *Actions Speak Louder: Affirmative Action of Women with a Disability. A Resource Guide,* Disability Action Incorporated, at www.disabilityaction.asn.au/dawebsite/systemsadvocacy/actions.html.

Hall, ET (1959) *The Silent Language.* Anchor Books Doubleday, New York.

Hall, ET (1976) *Beyond Culture.* Anchor Books Doubleday, New York.

Hall, S (2000) 'Who needs identity?', in P du Gay, J Evans and P Redman, *Identity: A Reader.* Gage, London, pp. 15–30.

Hofstede, G (1994) *Cultures and Organisations: Intercultural Cooperation and its Importance for Survival.* HarperCollins, London.

Hooker, J (2004) *Working Across Cultures.* Stanford University Press, Stanford.

Huntington, S (1997) *The Clash of Civilizations and the Remaking of the World Order.* Simon & Schuster, London.

Ife, J (2001) *Human Rights and Social Work: Towards Rights-Based Practice.* Cambridge University Press, Cambridge.

Kenny, S, Mansouri, F & Spratt, P (2005) *Arabic Communities and Well-Being: Supports and Barriers to Social Connectedness.* Centre for Citizenship and Human Rights, Deakin University, Melbourne.

Knowles, C (2003) *'Race' and Social Analysis.* Sage, London.

Lupton, D (1999b) 'Introduction: risk and sociocultural theory', in D Lupton (ed.) *Risk and Sociocultural Theory.* Cambridge University Press, Cambridge, pp. 1–11.

Marks, D (2001) 'Disability and cultural citizenship: exclusion, "integration" and resistance', in N Stevenson (ed.) *Culture and Citizenship.* Sage, London, pp. 167–79.

Miller, N & Sammons, C (1999) *Everybody's Different: Understanding and Changing our Reactions to Disabilities*. Paul H. Brookes, Baltimore.

Morris, J (2001) 'Impairment and disability: constructing an ethics of care that promotes human rights', *Hypatia*, Vol. 16, No. 4, pp. 1–16.

O'Sullivan, K (1994) *Understanding Ways: Communicating Between Cultures*. Hale & Ironmonger, Sydney.

Radhakrishnan, R (1996) *Diasporic Mediations between Home and Location*. University of Minneapolis Press, Minneapolis.

Reynolds, S & Valentine, D (2004) *Guide to Cross-Cultural Communication*. Pearson Prentice Hall, New Jersey.

Said, E (1978) *Orientalism*. Pantheon, New York.

Turner, BS (1999) 'McCitizens: risk, coolness and irony in contemporary politics', in B Smart (ed.) *Resisting McDonaldization*. Sage, London, pp. 83–100.

Weblinks

Community activism
http://actnow.com.au/

Community Development Employment Projects (CDEP)
www.fahcsia.gov.au/sa/indigenous/progserv/families/cdep/pages/default.aspx
www.centrelink.gov.au/internet/internet.nsf/services/cdep.htm#cdep

Disability rights networks
www.disabilityrightsfund.org/resources-list.html

Refugee information and action groups
www.barc.org.au/cms/
www.safecom.org.au/pdfs/greens_refugee_action_kit.pdf
www.refugeecouncil.org.au/
www.womensrefugeecommission.org/

Rights of minority groups
http://wgar.wordpress.com/
www.hreoc.gov.au/disability_rights/
www.niot.org/get-local?gclid=CL2Z4rz2waECFRXWbwodnj-K_w
www.piac.asn.au/publications/pubs/Refugees.pdf
www.rawa.org/index.php

CHAPTER 9

Funding and research

Overview

In this chapter, we focus on two important activities in community development today: funding and research. We begin with a discussion of the processes of funding and research within the framework of accountability. We then discuss the ways of funding community organisations and community projects, and funding issues. This leads us to the role of submission writing in community development work and the question of what constitutes a good submission. Funding relations between government and community organisations are increasingly based on contractual arrangements. We explore the types of contractual arrangements, beginning with service or funding agreements. Selection of contractors often takes place through a competitive tender process, and contracts, service agreements and competitive tendering are outlined in some detail. The remainder of the chapter deals with social research. We begin with an overview of the types of approaches to social research and we indicate how approaches, theories and methods influence the development of a research design. Finally, we consider two types of research that are increasingly being required for community development: community needs studies and evaluation.

Introduction

This book locates community development in the social and political contexts prevailing in the first decades of the twenty-first century. Contextual factors include the changes to the welfare state and community relations with the state, as well as the continuing dominance of neo-liberal policies and new managerialism, with their emphasis on demonstrating the outputs and outcomes of community programs. This chapter discusses two important components of community development, funding and research. However, at the outset it is important to acknowledge that many of the processes and practices in funding and research run counter to community development principles. Some community development practitioners decide that complying with requirements of funding is too great an ask. Others work with the terms of reference but use resources to prefigure other ways of doing things. Deciding how to respond to the terms of engagement when seeking funds is a difficult. We begin by discussing accountability. Accountability – and its corollaries, demonstrating effectiveness, reporting, auditing, monitoring and evaluation – has perhaps become one of the mantras of government policy and sets up the framework in which funding and research take place. Community development workers and community organisations are under pressure to demonstrate that they are accountable and transparent in their activities. But what is meant by accountability?

Accountability, relevance and effectiveness

From a community development perspective, accountability, relevance and effectiveness must be understood in the context of the community with whom a community development worker or community organisation works with and for. Accountability is not dealt with primarily through outputs and outcomes that are externally generated and measured. While the outcomes of a project can be very important to communities, the prioritising of development processes and goals by communities mean different ways of practising accountability. For example, accountability might be considered in terms of democratic and participatory processes, asset recognition and development and information sharing.

This community development approach is often at odds with government views of accountability; that is, whenever government money is involved then accountability is to government, and government funding bodies establish the criteria for evaluating programs. The argument given is that the government is responsible for 'taxpayers' money'. The assumption here, of course, is that the government always knows what is best; that is, how to best spend so-called taxpayers' money. The possibility that taxpayers might actually favour funding democratic processes is not considered. Within the framework of accountability 'upwards', programs need to be evaluated and usually by external 'experts'. The criteria for evaluating programs is set out in terms of (usually measurable) outputs (such as immediate demonstrated improvements) and outcomes (longer-term changes). In addition, in recent years, community organisations have been under increasing pressure from governments and other funding bodies to prove effectiveness and efficiency. Since the 1990s, proving efficiency and effectiveness has required a tightening of strategies, structures and resource use in community programs, and proof of relevance through research. The emphasis, then, has tended to be on accountability constructed around the need to prove the worth of community programs to government, rather than to the community served by the programs. Given the different ways of thinking about accountability in government circles and community development, some community organisations have decided to eschew government funding altogether. As many philanthropic organisations have become corporatised, they too have followed the government lead and adopted government concepts and protocols for accountability. Interestingly, some community development workers have reported a preference for seeking funding from large corporations, which allow for more community ownership of programs and greater creativity in constructing innovative programs.

Governments have introduced a number of strategies that putatively demonstrate the value of community programs, including:

- rigorous reviews of programs, such as through reporting, audits and monitoring and evaluation
- the shift to contract-based funding, whereby an organisation is funded to perform specific tasks

- the introduction of competitive submissions and competitive tendering processes that specify tasks and require that each task is fulfilled by the organisation in order to receive funds.

The pressure for community organisations to prove the value of their programs to funding bodies manifests in a number of ways, involving:

- the clear articulation of objectives and strategies, and well-prepared submissions
- comprehensive research to demonstrate the relevance of programs and appropriate response to community need
- rigorous review and evaluation of programs.

Funding and resource allocation

There are three major forms of funding for community organisations.

- *Internal funding* or self-funding: Members of a community organisation work out ways to generate funds to establish and maintain or develop the organisation and its programs, such as for acquiring office equipment and producing newsletters, for example. Member-serving organisations, such as self-help groups, tend to rely on membership fees or contributions. There is some interest in adapting microcredit (small low-interest loans) principles to fund Australian grassroots projects.
- *External funding:* This can take a number of forms. First are grants (through contracts and/or a competitive tender process, for example) from government departments or statutory bodies. Community welfare organisations providing programs in Australia obtain the majority of their funds through state governments (Brown, Kenny & Turner, 2000; Salamon et al., 1999). Second, community organisations also receive grants from church and philanthropic organisations or the newly developing community trusts. Third, grants are also given by corporate sponsors, under corporate citizenship responsibilities or corporate social responsibility. Fourth, some community organisations, and particularly those concerned with local crises, such as bushfire relief and international aid, receive funds from public support through private giving. Australian research reveals that a significant number of international aid programs receive most of their funds from private giving (see Salamon et al., 1999). (Note that the Productivity Commission report (2010) on the sector argues for an extension of tax deductibility for private giving to all 'charitable institutions', including community organisations concerned with the wellbeing of communities.) Finally community organisations also embark on fundraising events or entrepreneurial activities.
- *User pays:* In public-serving organisations, people who attend programs or use the services of a community organisation are required to pay for these services on the principle of user pays. In member-serving organisations, members contribute funds and resources to maintain the organisation.

Chapter 9 Funding and research

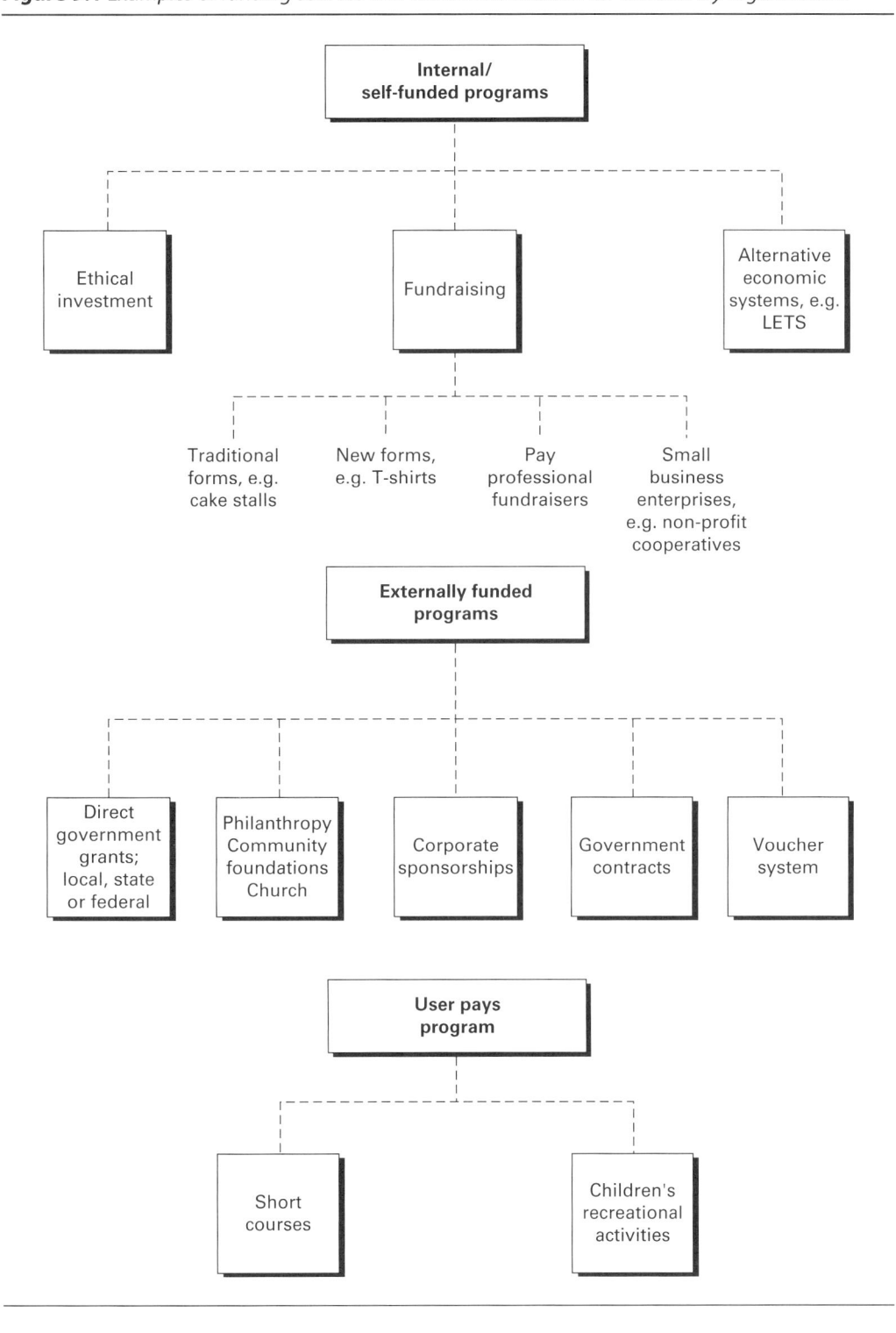

Figure 9.1 *Examples of funding sources and resource allocation for community organisations*

```
                    Internal/
                    self-funded programs
        ┌───────────────┼───────────────┐
     Ethical         Fundraising    Alternative
   investment                       economic
                                    systems, e.g.
                                    LETS
           ┌───────────┼───────────┬───────────┐
       Traditional  New forms,    Pay         Small
       forms, e.g.  e.g. T-shirts professional business
       cake stalls               fundraisers  enterprises,
                                              e.g. non-profit
                                              cooperatives

                    Externally funded
                    programs
    ┌───────────┬───────────┬───────────┬───────────┐
  Direct     Philanthropy  Corporate   Government   Voucher
 government  Community    sponsorships contracts    system
  grants;    foundations
local, state  Church
 or federal

                    User pays
                    program
              ┌───────────┴───────────┐
            Short              Children's
           courses             recreational
                               activities
```

Funding issues

The question of funding is a vexed one for community organisations. Here, we consider some of the main themes and issues of concern.

- *Priority:* How much time should be devoted to fundraising activities, such as writing submissions, preparing for **competitive tenders** or organising raffles, when this is at the expense of much-needed on-the-ground activities?
- *Compromises:* External funds have strings attached. Members of community organisations are painfully aware of their one-sided relationship with funding bodies; there is usually little scope for real negotiation over the conditions attached to funding. Moreover, despite the rhetoric of accountability to users, organisations tend to be placed in positions whereby their primary accountability is to the source of the funds. Some community activists argue that regardless of the form it takes, the funding game compromises their activist leanings. Their view is that community development can retain its activist integrity and accountability to the community only if it refuses to defer to any funding body; they reject funding that has strings attached.
- *Unpaid work:* Much of what community organisations do is possible only because a large amount of work is unpaid. How much should they rely on unpaid labour to keep a program going or to keep funding costs down?
- *Sustainability:* Sustainability has become increasingly important for community organisations. They are sensitive to the implications of overreliance on state funding, especially when this is short term and is increasingly for projects rather than to support infrastructure costs.

Some of the responses to the often insecure sources of state funding have included:

- using conventional forms of small-scale fundraising, such as raffles. Indeed, many funding bodies request that community organisations engage in fundraising activities to supplement their external funds.
- wariness of overreliance on large 'one-off' project grants. As Murphy (2006) points out, the larger the grant, the more difficult it is to sustain project activities when the funding has been spent.
- establishing a significant ongoing financial arm to their work, which they use to subsidise their community development activities. For example, they produce marketable products such as greeting cards and calendars.
- being involved in large-scale commercial ventures, not as a means to an end but as an end in themselves – so that the whole commercial project is also a community development project. For example, some Indigenous communities run ventures on a cooperative basis – for example, a 'bush tucker' cooperative – that involve teaching skills to local communities, providing employment and selling products.

Over the last decade, there has been interest in finding new forms and sources of external funding. Discussion here has taken three directions:

- First is a renewal of interest in the potential for philanthropic organisations to fund community programs. The disposable income of wealthy Australians is growing. Internationally, what the wealthy are doing and can do with their 'surplus' money, or 'generational transfer', is being discussed, although this is yet to occur in Australia. Philanthropy Australia, the peak philanthropy body, suggests that there are over 1200 trusts and foundations giving up to $500 million a year. A number of trusts give to one charity only and many make bequests, to hospitals, for example. Other charitable trusts have discretionary funds and provide grants to community programs. The annual directory of trusts, published by Philanthropy Australia, is a useful source of information on most Australian trusts and gives details of grants available. An interesting development in Australian trusts has been the number of community foundations established to foster local initiatives, particularly in rural areas.
- Second, as discussed above, is also a growing interest in working with the business world at both a local and wider level. For example, some community organisations in small rural towns are working in partnership with local businesses to run youth programs and refugee support programs. Larger corporations, under a commitment to corporate citizenship, are working with large community organisations to fund environmental programs or community arts projects, for example. In addition, there is now movement towards developing small-business enterprises that can either fully support or subsidise community projects in Australia, using the idea of social entrepreneurship.
- Finally, as noted above, adapting microcredit programs for Australian conditions is being discussed. Microcredit involves the giving of very small loans to small groups of people (rather than to individuals) for modest small-business projects. It is the responsibility of the group to ensure the repayments of the loan. We discuss microcredit in more detail below.

Coordinators in community organisations bemoan the time spent on accessing funds, but they continue to expend significant energy on writing submissions, embarking on small fundraising efforts, liaising with small businesses and corporations and developing entrepreneurial projects. Regardless of the stance taken by a community organisation about fundraising, it is important to understand how the main funding processes work. We now consider in detail self-funding, corporate sponsorship, philanthropic trusts and government funding.

Types of funding
Self-funding
Self-funding ranges from small traditional fundraising efforts to microcredit and to large business ventures such as non-profit cooperatives. One simple way to generate small-scale funds is to 'think smart' about the financial resources that the organisation already has. Ascertain whether the organisation is eligible for exemptions from payroll and sales tax. Thinking smart also includes investing available capital wisely, for example, and

considering the best interest rates at credit cooperatives and banks. Some organisations subscribe to **ethical investment** (see below). The principle of ethical investment is gaining support. While a significant amount of the investment available is in industries that are socially and environmentally destructive (in that they have unscrupulous employment practices and destroy the environment), it is possible to identify companies in which one can invest ethically. These are companies that:

- produce environmentally sound and socially useful products
- operate on the basis of industrial awards and fair employment practices
- use energy efficiently
- are equal opportunity employers
- take measures to ensure the occupational health and safety of their workers
- ensure worker participation.

As Mackenzie (1993) points out, by investing ethically you invest in industries that are likely to get strong support from consumers and help to secure a positive future for coming generations. Community Aid Abroad, the Australian Conservation Foundation and the YWCA Ethical Investment Trust have information on how to invest ethically.

Traditional fundraising methods include efforts such as those used by schools and hospitals, relying on unpaid (generally female) labour running cake stalls, raffles, fetes, bingo, for example. Contemporary forms are wine-bottling, fun runs and other sporting events, or music concerts. Funds can also be generated through paid membership drives; by selling T-shirts with logos, Christmas cards, badges, posters and tea-towels; and by offering fee-paying courses or workshops. Some organisations pay professional organisations to raise funds for them, usually for a one-off or annual project.

By establishing small-business enterprises such as non-profit cooperatives, some organisations have achieved a degree of independence and self-sufficiency. There are producers' cooperatives, trading cooperatives and community cooperatives (see Gardiner & O'Neil, 1991). They may be established with seeding money from government or other external funding sources, or they may be largely self-sufficient from their inception.

Financial arrangements for self-funding projects are often organised by credit unions and community banks. Some credit unions have membership criteria such as union membership, residence or income requirements. Because they are usually set up on social justice principles and are committed to their members or to the community they were set up to work with, credit unions and community banks are often preferred by community enterprises.

Microcredit and workers' cooperatives

The idea of **microcredit** is gaining international recognition as an effective way of providing small amounts of credit for community-based small businesses. In developing countries a model for microcredit for community projects was established by the Grameen (meaning 'rural') Bank in Bangladesh. The concept of the Grameen Bank was developed in the 1970s around the principle of lending money only to the very poor, charging low interest rates and requiring neither collateral nor guarantors. Borrowers are required to form active mutual support groups of five people, with one of these being leader. Each group must meet regularly with a bank worker. The majority of borrowers are women (about 97 per cent) and there is a 96–98 per cent repayment rate (Grameen Bank, 2010; Thas, 1992). In addition to lending money for income-generation activities, the Grameen Bank now also has a savings scheme and provides housing loans. While microcredit has been typically used in the developing world, there is now some interest in its application in the developed world. For example, the Grameen Foundation USA argues that microcredit can give the poor the tools they need to lift themselves out of poverty, so that they can reap the rewards of their own labour.

In Australia, there is still interest in the development of small-scale income-generating activities, especially in rural areas. There are numerous examples of community-based cooperatives and businesses that have gained financial and advisory support from local councils and credit unions and cooperatives. These include natural heritage tours owned and run by local farmers, cultural tourism ventures owned and run by Aboriginal groups, health food shops and other retail shops selling local produce such as eucalyptus products and dried wildflowers, and catering activities in cafes and other venues. Communities are increasingly looking for new forms of credit and banking that will lend small amounts of money to those who would be refused loans by the commercial banks, who would be charged high interest rates or who would need to provide collateral and/or guarantors.

The range of activities of workers' cooperatives covers many small-business activities. Examples of workers' cooperatives include a laundry service in a public housing estate, childcare centres and a handmade furniture business. Throughout Australia a range of community enterprises provide such services as publishing, printing, catering, computer training, tool hire, typing and office work, dancing and aerobics, bookshops, research consultancies, gardening and other home services, secondhand shops, carwashes and ethnic gift shops. There are food-buying cooperatives, credit cooperatives and rental housing cooperatives.

Business plans

Local cooperatives are usually established when a need for a material or service is recognised and some kind of plan has been developed to satisfy the need. Whatever the enterprise, it is important to have a well-thought-out **business plan**. The preparation of a business plan is similar to the process of strategy planning discussed in chapter 5. Most simply put, a business plan sets out the need for a service or product (market analysis), the segment of the market aimed for and the channels through which the product or service will be sold. It analyses how the service or product is currently provided, and identifies competitors and competitive advantage. It also includes a financial plan that estimates the capital required to get the initiative off the ground, borrowings needed, loan repayments, anticipated revenue and cashflow, and forecasts of profit and loss. Costs of equipment, staffing, energy and resources are taken into account. A schedule forecasts the point at which the enterprise will break even. As in any strategy plan, the resources and skills available are identified, as well as any likely facilitating and constraining factors.

In order to retain the community development perspective, members of a cooperative should participate in developing the business plan and establishing the broad organisational structure. Cooperative ventures, based on community development principles, must be environmentally appropriate and socially useful. Workers in the cooperative develop appropriate staffing, management and salary arrangements that meet the legal requirements. They decide how to distribute the income generated by the activities of the cooperative: for example, 70 per cent of income for salaries, 20 per cent for overheads and reserve funds, and 10 per cent distributed to other community programs.

A plethora of regulations covers fundraising and business activities, and it is important that community organisations understand them. In most states in Australia, government or independent organisations for cooperative research and small-business development provide advice and training for those wanting to develop cooperative ventures and other small businesses (see, for example, information provided by the Public Interest Law Clearing House, Victoria).

In a cooperative structure, self-funding enterprises and government funding can strengthen community development rather than undermine it. Cooperatives are based on equality of members, mutual support and a commitment to democratic participation and decision making. Capital and funds can provide for the collective benefit of all members. Sometimes such community enterprise projects are organised on a sliding scale of costs to subsidise low-income consumers.

Supporters of cooperatives are enthusiastic about the potential of cooperative ventures to help sustain a vibrant community sector. Small-business ventures run as workers' cooperatives offer (actual or potential) independence from government funding and, in addition, can create employment, either full time or part time, for community members. Yet many workers in community organisations doubt whether enterprise-based cooperatives can generate sufficient funds to maintain and develop a strong community sector.

Below we consider a case study of self-funding as an example of how a resourceful community can generate some of its own income.

SCENES FROM HISTORY

The setting is a neighbourhood house on the outskirts of a regional city. The neighbourhood house is situated on a two-hectare property that is operated as a small farm, with sheep, chickens, cows, ducks and goats.

In the house, a group of people are dressing up as squatters, settlers, traditional Murri Aboriginal people and convicts of the early 1800s. They are preparing for a visit to a local school to talk about what it was like to live in rural Australia during this time. Sometimes school groups visit the farm, where props of a specific historical period are set up.

'Scenes from History' was established two years ago, when a group of people met at the neighbourhood house to discuss how they could do something creative and generate income. In the group were two unemployed teachers; students from a local TAFE college, including several Murri Aboriginal students; environmentalists; and amateur actors. They all believed that history was exciting and could come to life if acted out by real people. They also believed that the story of how ordinary people lived, including the oppression of Indigenous people, women, minority groups, workers and peasants, was missing in many of the portrayals of local history.

They timidly approached local schools with the idea, and to their surprise were greatly encouraged to develop the project. Local community members helped the group prepare a business plan and the group decided that a small amount of money per student would be charged when the group put on a performance. They established a workers' cooperative. With a small arts grant, they were able to buy period clothes and develop their first sketch.

They now have requests to present sketches to a wide range of schools and have generated sufficient income to employ a part-time community arts worker, as well as provide income for themselves.

LETS

An alternative to enterprise-based cooperatives is the Local Employment and Trading System (**LETS**). First established in Canada, LETS enables community members to exchange goods and services, such as babysitting, carpentry, crafts, tools, submission writing, gardening, musical tuition, massage, plumbing and cooking. While based on the idea of barter, LETS is more complex and flexible. Traditional barter is a simple exchange between two parties that requires equivalences of value between the goods exchanged. Under LETS, if it is agreed that the value of the goods or services to be exchanged is not equal, then trading begins and, to ensure a fair exchange, dollars or local LETS points can be accumulated. For example, the person offering the more valuable goods or services in a transaction can be credited with a number of LETS points. In each transaction a small percentage is deducted as an administration fee, which is credited in LETS points to the people who do the bookkeeping. As Mackenzie (1993) points out, it all works like a big noticeboard or directory where people make known what goods and services they offer and what they are looking for, and then buyer and seller get together and agree on a price in LETS points. All transactions are documented and recorded in a computerised bookkeeping system. Monthly statements are sent out to members, and those wanting a product or service can get a LETS credit check done through the computer. The enthusiastic supporters of LETS argue that it promotes the idea that everyone has something to offer the community and it shows how neighbours can directly help one another. For them, while the brief of existing LETS programs is modest, it has the potential to provide much of the organisational and resource base for community organisations.

Issues in self-funding

There are both strengths and weaknesses in self-funding. Most importantly, self-funding can give a community organisation a degree of autonomy, which allows it to fund creative and radical projects that might otherwise not be funded. It also frees up community participants from some, although not all, of the reporting requirements of government funders, for example. However, a number of issues in self-funding should be understood by community organisations. The following case study describes how some of these issues arose in an Indigenous cooperative in central Australia.

BURRUMBA COOPERATIVE

The Burrumba Cooperative community development project is in a small community in Central Australia. The elders had obtained a small grant to document the extent to which bush tucker was available in the local area. They reported their findings to the local Land Council, who were amazed at both the depth of knowledge about bush tucker and the extent of edible food in the area. In particular, the elders had reclaimed the use of some Australian wattle varieties as a fast-growing nutritious food source in its form as acacia flour, which could be added to other flour products. The elders consulted with their community and collectively drew up a plan of action for developing a small-business venture, selling flour to local communities and running a small tourism enterprise introducing visitors to bush tucker. If they could develop these enterprises in a modest way, they believed that they could generate small amounts of income.

However, they were unprepared for what happened next. A visiting nutritionist from West Africa had heard about their use of the wattles and asked if she could visit the community. She became so excited about the potential of the plants that she immediately made contact with her colleagues in the European Union, who arranged a visit as well. The outcome of their visit was a joint West African–Australian project to grow and market several types of bush tucker. The problem then became one of how far the project might interrupt the local community. After three months of intense meetings and negotiation, the community has decided to undertake a small pilot program, which will be carefully controlled. The cooperative was initially reticent because of their experience in a similar project 15 years ago when all sorts of promises about purchasing goods made by the local community were not fulfilled, with the end result being almost the collapse of the community. If the cooperative can monitor and control this project it might have a better chance of success.

What are some of the general issues that community development practitioners should be aware of when they become involved in self-funding projects? The following is a checklist.

- A major issue for credit and workers' cooperatives is that they compete with other small businesses in a harsh business environment in which the majority of small-business ventures fail.
- The experience of the community organisations that have taken on fundraising is that it demands enormous amounts of time and energy at the expense of other projects and programs, and financial results are often disappointing. Cooperatives can become preoccupied with securing their workers' jobs and their own survival.
- Lack of capital, experience, research and marketing skills severely hinder the chances of success of any small business.
- The welfare of the community can suffer when cooperatives forget community development principles and become caught up in making money in order to survive.
- Most community organisations are wary of hiring professional fundraisers; they see them as using community organisations to get money for themselves.
- Fundraising activities are seen as a disguised form of user pays, in which low-income people are forced to pay for services that are their right.

- Requiring community members to pay for services is seen as further discriminating against the poor and disadvantaged.
- When communities use natural heritage or local cultural attractions as a means of generating funds – for example, from tourists – they are in effect setting up a relationship based on commodification between those who benefit financially from the income-generating activities, the local heritage and cultural environment, and the tourists. That is, the people running the income-generating projects tend to see tourists and their natural and cultural environment in narrow instrumental terms that revolve around how much money they can make from them, often at the expense of a genuine pride in the environment or because they wish to develop friendships with tourists (see Ife, 1995).
- By not applying for government funds, community organisations allow governments to abrogate their responsibility to maintain the social infrastructure and to protect and support all citizens. Governments already subsidise the wealthy in a variety of ways, including tax concessions (see Bryson, 1989). The wealthy are not made to feel guilty, but those who are powerless are often too embarrassed to request government support.

Corporate sponsorship

Some community organisations seek corporate donations or sponsorship for a specific purpose – such as getting office equipment from a furniture retailer – or for an event or program – such as being given financial support for a conference, festival or youth refuge. However, many community development workers feel uncomfortable about corporate funds on the basis that accepting them can compromise the principles of a community organisation and reduce its independence. While any financial support, regardless of its source, can lead to external control of a community program, community organisations are sensitive to the ways that corporate sponsorship, in particular, can be used by a company for the purposes of (sometimes tax-exempt) marketing.

Certainly, a link with a 'worthwhile' community organisation is a public relations achievement to be exploited by marketing and advertising. Of course, a big company is unlikely to support a small radical organisation, because this might result in little or even adverse publicity. Indeed, corporate sponsorship is much more forthcoming for established organisations such as opera companies, but less popular for more radical social groups such as human rights and Indigenous activist groups.

Other community organisations accept the value of corporate sponsorship, but choose companies for their sound environmental and management practices. As indicated above, some community organisations tend to accept goods and equipment rather than money. In the USA there are strong tax incentives for donating to a wide range of community organisations; in Australia tax incentives are more restricted.

Community organisations do not rely on corporate sponsorship for all their funds and resources. However, there is evidence of community organisations entering into 'partnerships' with corporations and local businesses so that a program operates through

Processes and practices

joint ownership of a project, and sometimes there is a three-way partnership between a government funder, corporate sponsor and local community organisation. The following case study indicates how such an arrangement can work.

PEAKE ESTATE PROJECT

The setting is a high-rise council housing estate in a low-income suburb in a capital city. The housing estate is characterised by the cultural diversity of its residents, high unemployment rates, high absenteeism from school and high crime rates. Many of the women are afraid to venture out at night. The estate has a 'bad reputation'. A community development worker, Paolo, is employed by the residents' committee, using government funds, with the major task being capacity and community building and to 'turn around' the bad reputation of the estate. He begins by talking to virtually all the residents, either individually or in small groups, about their fears and aspirations. What he finds out is that the adults want to find ways to work together across cultures and age groups, they want to be employed, they want a source of income other than social services, and they want their children to be 'off the streets'. The young people also want to 'do something'. They complain of being bored. Paolo begins by preparing a list of the residents' interests, developing a list or audit of community assets and identifying projects arising out of these interests. Many of the adults express interest in learning how to use computers, recognising that most of the younger residents already know very well how to use them. Could they match up the skills of the younger people with the needs of the older people? They speak to the younger people, most of whom are reluctant to 'teach the oldies'. However, a couple of young people see an opportunity to get access to computers to develop their interest in animation and so agree to participate in the program.

The problem now is the lack of computers. Paolo, a middle-aged man, has had a number of past jobs, including working with computers, and he has a wide network of contacts in the computer industry. He asks several of his contacts to provide laptop computers and, somewhat to his surprise, he is pleased to find that his contacts are happy to assist. With some trepidation, Paolo organises his first class, with two young people teaching a group of women. It is a great success and over the next weeks more young people join the group as teachers and a waiting list for students is set up.

One of the adults was a graphic designer in his country of origin. He teaches himself web design and then passes these skills to other residents. They begin to produce professional and stylish notices and posters, and then a website for the Peake Estate. Other community organisations come with requests and offer to pay. The residents use their own resources to develop a business plan and a strategy plan, and to learn how to fulfil legal requirements, including insurance requirements. Within a year Peake Estate has established a thriving small business that operates out of a small office, offering computer training to local community groups and subsidising the leisure activities of the Peake Estate residents.

The residents have managed to draw together existing community skills, government funds, corporate sponsorship and a small business development. This case study illustrates how a community group can use a number of existing resources to develop a successful community project.

Philanthropic trusts and foundations

Many community organisations feel more comfortable with funding support from **philanthropic trusts** or **community foundations** than from direct corporate sponsorship. Philanthropic trusts are developed when individuals or families decide to give or leave (tax-deductible) funds (private assets) for the public good. Decisions on where, when and how much to give are largely private affairs in philanthropy. For example, a family philanthropic trust might be committed to giving to a set charity once a year or it might use a specific grant-giving process.

Because of their emphasis on the development of communities, community trusts can provide a new source of funds for community development activities. A community foundation is set up with the purpose of attracting (tax-deductible) money from donors, which then goes into a public fund that is to be used for the good of a specific community. According to the Community Foundations Gateway (2005) this

> provides a permanent and growing source of funding, with the income earned each year being returned to the community as annual grants to deductible gift recipients or other tax deductible entities. In addition, the community foundation through the charitable company or trust can support wider charitable purposes.

The aim of a community foundation is to 'provide a cost effective mechanism to enable individuals, families, corporations and business to carry out their philanthropic aims' (Community Foundations Gateway, 2005) and:

- expand the pool of philanthropic funds in the foundation
- promote effective giving by providing support, expertise, research and advice to donors
- promote awareness of significant community and social issues, and grant funds to worthy charitable projects
- work collaboratively with communities, donors and others to ensure the foundation is effective
- make it easier for people to give during their lifetime and see the results of their benefaction in the community
- manage and invest funds prudently to achieve fund growth and good returns
- help build the local community
- provide an opportunity for the community to be an active part of long-term planning for its own needs and aspirations.

Yet there is also the view that, like corporations, philanthropic trusts and foundations are also little more than tax shelters for the privileged to pursue some favoured charity (see Anheier & Leat, 2002). From this perspective, philanthropic organisations allow governments to abrogate their responsibilities for the welfare of citizens. However, unlike corporations, philanthropic trusts are often not transparent in their policies of giving. Some critics argue that philanthropic trusts and foundations are elitist, undemocratic and unaccountable.

Processes and practices

One of the problems with this view is that it generalises about all philanthropic trusts. While some might be elitist and unaccountable, many are not and offer a way of gaining funds for innovative and even 'risky' projects that governments would be unlikely to fund, such as projects to assist asylum seekers or champion gay rights. From this perspective, philanthropy involves the leverage of private money for public benefit.

A number of people champion the potential of philanthropic and community trusts as a source of creative endeavour. For example, Anheier and Leat (2002:14) comment on the potential for creative foundations:

> They are the factories of ideas that bring about and facilitate innovation in the broadest sense. The creative foundation is a private problem-solving institution for public concern.

It is therefore important to understand the types of philanthropic trusts, what they can and can't do and what is the size of their grants. For example, some trusts have a clear brief to fund only certain types of projects, such as those for the hearing impaired or for childcare. Some trusts give money to support programs, while others actually develop and run programs themselves. Funds are generally quite small (around $5000 to $10 000) and competition for funds from philanthropic trusts, in particular, is keen. While the reserve (or corpus) of funds in existing trusts is growing in Australia – unlike in the USA – we do not have a strong culture of bequests from individual or corporate benefactors for community-based programs.

From the viewpoint of those working in philanthropic trusts, grant-givers have to make a number of decisions. Drawn from the work of Anheier and Leat (2002), the following list outlines some of the competing policy decisions considered by grant-givers. Should grant-givers:

- focus on alleviating symptoms or understanding the causes, and aim for structural reform and government policy change?
- be independent from government or work with government to achieve greater leverage?
- subsidise government activities?
- maximise the control of the donors or allow needs and recipients to have primacy?
- remain true to the founder's preference or respond to new needs and opportunities?
- stress professionalism and due process or leave space for innovative or untidy thinking?
- take risks?
- maximise money in order to give more or ensure smooth and well-funded administration of the trust or foundation?

Applying for grants

Tips for those who are considering applying for funds from philanthropic trusts (see Timmons, 1992) are listed below.

- Obtain information about the activities, processes and funding rounds of trusts to ensure which ones are relevant.
- Check to see if the trust has guidelines for writing submissions.
- Seek information on priorities for funding, such as whether particular issues or types of organisation are given preference.

- Ensure that your submission is clear, brief and easy to read.
- Make sure that you know your field and what other organisations are doing in this field.
- Apply to more than one trust or funding body, indicating to each that this is what you are doing.
- Seek an opportunity to meet with trust representatives – in a covering letter, for example – but do not be too pushy. It is not inappropriate to meet over lunch, but the emphasis should be on matters that are relevant to the submission.
- Be business-like and realistic in your budget, and include details such as appropriate award rates and levels.
- Don't use ambit claims to inflate costs, and indicate where you are prepared to cut back activities if necessary.

As indicated above, non-government funding sources are not all the same; their rationales or philosophies vary. Some specific funding bodies, including philanthropic trusts and churches, actively support community development. Some are overtly feminist. Others are flexible and open to persuasion about the worth of new and different kinds of community-based programs. More work could be done to reinforce a favourable understanding of community development projects, and to shift the terms of reference of funding programs towards community development by, for example, demonstrating support for community organisations and showing how well the programs work.

Government funding

As indicated above, in general, governments are the major source of funds for community organisations and programs, although, as Lyons (2001:36) points out, some community organisations receive no direct government funds (see Lyons, 2001). There has been increasing emphasis on local governments providing funds, sometimes acting as conduits for state government money for community building and capacity building programs, for example. While community needs always exceed the resources available from the state, funding bodies are increasingly demanding that the programs they fund be effective, efficient and accountable. Each government funding program has specific guidelines setting out criteria and procedures for allocating resources.

Most government bodies require written applications or submissions. These set out the need for a project or program; specify the goals, objectives and strategies; and outline a proposed budget. Government departments usually require completion of proforma applications that now include legal and organisational details of the group applying for the funds. Applications are generally evaluated and ranked by decision makers on the basis of specific funding criteria. Increasingly, government bodies call for tenders from community organisations and businesses to operate programs. However funds are allocated, community organisations must prepare submissions that set out the case for funding their programs. Whether their case is based on past performance, policy priorities or social indicators, it still requires rigorous research, argumentation and budgeting.

Processes and practices

Maher and Burke (1991) identified five major ways that governments in Australia allocate funds, to which a sixth can now be added.

- *Historical funding:* A community organisation that has existed for a number of years and is perceived to be meeting a need receives an annual grant based on the previous year's budget, plus an additional amount to take account of inflation.
- *Performance-based funding:* Funds are allocated on the basis of an evaluation of past performance. This approach is linked with both historical and submission-based funding.
- *Per capita funding:* Resources are allocated on the basis of the number of persons living in an area, without reference to the past performance of programs or special needs. Waste-recycling programs are often funded on this basis. The needs of particular groups, such as the elderly, are not taken into account.
- *Submission-based funding:* Groups identify and cost their resource requirements, and apply to funding agencies in writing or verbally. According to Maher and Burke, **submission-based funding** actually formalises political lobbying. Government departments usually advertise that there are funds available for a specific program and ask for submissions. In some cases they first call for expressions of interest, and select a number of these to develop more detailed submissions.
- *Needs-based funding:* This requires research to identify and rank criteria that measures need, such as demographic or social indicators and comparative need, and to determine where these specified needs are not being met. For example, a comparatively high percentage of teenagers in a community, together with a large homeless youth population and high teenage unemployment, could be the basis for funding for a youth refuge. A demographic profile of a community shows the distribution of ages, gender, ethnicity and other characteristics of the population. Researchers use social indicators to measure quality of life. For instance, suicide rates are seen as an indicator of the degree of social integration in a society, divorce rates as an indicator of family breakdown and unemployment rates as an indicator of general economic and social wellbeing.
- *Contracts and competitive tendering:* To this list should be added a sixth method, involving governments contracting-out or outsourcing activities, services, programs and projects. As indicated in previous chapters, one of the main shifts in government logic brought about by the ascendancy of neo-liberal thinking, managerialism and contractualism has been the development of new mechanisms through which governments fund community programs. These mechanisms involve the negotiation of programs and services and their provision on the basis of contracts – often won through the process of competitive submissions or competitive tendering – between the community organisation and the funder. Officially, funds are allocated according to policy priorities. These priorities may be set at a number of different decision-making levels; for example, they may be determined by cabinet, a government minister or by local government. In practice, however, funds are often allocated according to political agendas, perhaps as part of a strategy to win a marginal seat. Such decisions may

override formal processes for the allocation of funds, such as the demonstrated needs of a community or the quality of a submission.

This last point suggests that, in the actual processes of allocating resources to community organisations, funding decisions are made on the basis of a combination of these approaches. Below is a case study of how research, lobbying, set formulas and political agendas can bear on a decision to fund a particular program.

FUNDING GOVERNMENT PRIORITIES

A government minister responsible for social, community and health services is concerned about funding cuts in his portfolio areas. The department asks a research institute to develop a list of social indicators, such as unemployment rates, number of single-income families and number of old people in a locality. In conjunction with the research institute, the department allocates points to each of these indicators to develop a relative needs index.

The government is lobbied by interest groups, requesting that social and community sector programs be targeted on the basis of their group's special needs, such as childcare for single mothers, programs for unemployed Aboriginal young people, programs for elderly people of non-English-speaking backgrounds and increased provision of public housing programs designed to overcome rural isolation.

The department allocates funds to regions on the basis of a formula that takes into account demographic profile, policy priorities determined by cabinet and the minister, the relative needs index and submissions from lobby groups. In each region, a percentage of these funds is allocated to the community sector. Three priorities are chosen: health education for Aboriginal and Torres Strait Islanders, a program to reduce the isolation of those in rural poverty and a program to increase the number of childcare places in outer urban areas. Guidelines are established that set out the terms of reference, eligibility criteria, target groups, aims and objectives and the amount of funds available.

A funding round for these programs is announced. When submissions are received, they are ranked by a committee made up of representatives of the department, the representative organisations and the general community. The committee makes recommendations to the minister, who, after conferring with other ministers to minimise double-dipping by community organisations, announces the successful applicants.

Community organisations are painfully aware that success in funding for one organisation is often at the expense of others. The number of submissions for funding in the community-based sector varies, but requests for funding nearly always exceed the available funds, sometimes to the extent that fewer than 20 per cent of applications are successful. There is usually stiff competition between community groups for funds. Some communities prepare joint submissions for joint projects, but this approach can run into legal problems when it contravenes competition policy. Such an approach is consistent with community development, but does not resolve the problem of the shrinking cake and the increasing demand for community programs throughout Australia.

Corporate funding

In chapter 2 we noted the growing interest of the corporate sector in supporting and funding civil society. Corporations are now supporting community organisations in four ways:

- by offering services on a pro bono basis, such as lawyers helping organisations to set up trusts and foundations
- by funding community organisations and projects; for example, directly funding a community youth project or setting up an ongoing foundation for young people that is run by local community members
- by entering into partnerships with community organisations to fund community projects
- by funding philanthropic trusts that, in turn, fund community projects.

We have discussed some of the ambiguities of receiving corporate funds. What must be underlined here is the view of some community organisations that it is preferable to work with corporations than with government, because discussions with corporations are more open and frank than those with government bureaucrats and there is a more equal partnership. With the exception of some funding provided by philanthropic trusts, corporations tend to eschew the formal processes of calling for submissions in the way that governments do. Processes are often one-off and involve a close relationship between the corporate funder and the community funded. However, where a more formal process is used, it usually follows the type of submission process discussed below.

Extending taxation to the international arena

Given both the massive movements of finance and people around the globe daily, and the difficulties that many countries have in financing projects for the poor and disadvantaged, there has been some discussion of ways to fund government and non-government programs based on taxes collected from international financial transactions and travel. The best known of the proposals to generate taxes through a levy on international financial transactions has come to be known as the **Tobin Tax**, named after James Tobin, who proposed the introduction of a 0.5 per cent tax on all spot transactions on foreign exchange (Tobin, 1994). In the first instance, the funds from the tax could be used to eliminate the debts of developing countries. Funds could also be used by the United Nations for special projects. Supporters of this tax argue that it would serve to dampen speculative international financial movements but would not be large enough to deter serious international investment.

Of course, developing countries would be the urgent priority for the distribution of any funds collected through taxes on international financial transactions and travel, and correctly so. While Australian community organisations might bemoan the lack of funds and support from governments in a time of growing need for community development, health and education infrastructure and programs, Australia is still a rich country by global standards. We have the funds and resources to provide good community programs and a high standard of health and education. Whether we do have good community, health and education programs is largely a matter of whether governments decide to support them through funds and policy decisions. But is the power of governments to distribute the wealth of the country limited to Australia and other advanced capitalist countries? No. All governments have powers to establish policies that can assist with the concentration or redistribution of a country's wealth, however limited that wealth may be.

Citizen-directed taxation

One innovative way of testing whether the populace at large is satisfied with how governments spend taxpayers' money is based on the idea of **citizen-directed taxation** or budgets. With a modest change in the administration of tax returns, citizens could voluntarily decide on how a proportion of taxes (for example, 50 per cent) should be spent. Government budgets would be drawn up on the basis of citizens' preferences for government expenditure. In arguing for the introduction of citizen-directed tax, Wyatt (1995) states that it would mean that electors would become active citizens and partners in the process of government. The establishment of a process of citizen-directed tax could help to restore faith in governments and strengthen democracy.

Preparing submissions

Preparing submissions is an important part of community development work, not only to obtain funds or contracts, but also for the purposes of lobbying, research and media liaison. Table 9.1 (page 362) is a checklist of factors to consider when writing a submission.

From a community development perspective, a good submission is one that has empowerment as its focus – in rationale, aims, objectives and strategies, and in the very processes of its production. A good submission should be collectively produced and based on the widest participation. A good submission is, of course, also successful in achieving its aim, whether it is to obtain funds or to contribute to a change in government policy, for example. Submissions can express an opinion, identify a need, request a change in policy or ask for support in general (Roberts, 1985).

Roberts (1985:4) reminds us that, whatever the purpose of a submission, it should present a case that is achievable. It must be appropriate and acceptable to the people to whom it is directed, such as decision makers; the funding body; the community organisation and its participants; and the community in general. It is important to clarify why the submission is being prepared, and to specify exactly what is being sought, such as funds to run a new program or a letter of support from a member of parliament. Here we focus on submissions for funding, but the general principles are the same for any submission, including submissions to philanthropic trusts.

It is important to do your homework when preparing a submission. For funding submissions, find out about the funding body: its philosophy, mode of operation and guidelines for funding. If necessary, phone or visit the funding body. Link the submission with the terms of reference and policies of the funding body. The arguments presented in

Processes and practices

Table 9.1 *Writing submissions*

1 Why write a submission?

☐ to obtain funding	☐ to request withdrawal of a policy
☐ to request support for a program or campaign; for example, letter of support, funds, supporting vote	☐ to obtain publicity ☐ to advocate for a group
☐ to explain a need	☐ to clarify a problem or issue
☐ to express an opinion or concern	

2 Have we done our homework?

☐ What is currently happening in regard to the funds, needs, voting, policy, publicity, problem issue, etc.?	☐ Is the correct form or format used?
☐ Do we know about the group or individual to whom it is directed?	☐ Who are the key decision makers (that is, who holds the power)?

3 How is the submission produced?

☐ Is the submission produced on the basis of consultation? Is it produced collectively?	☐ Are the objectives clear?

4 Who is the submission aimed at?

☐ funding body	☐ another community organisation
☐ local councillors	☐ the media (newspapers, radio or television)
☐ members of parliament	☐ other members of the community

5 Does the submission cover relevant details?

☐ information on the submitting organisation	☐ evaluation procedures
☐ reason for the submission	☐ project management details
☐ support required (money, publicity, etc.)	☐ schedule
☐ who will benefit from the support	☐ a budget, including justification of each item
☐ aims and objectives	☐ existing program
☐ strategy plan	☐ existing resources
☐ observable indicators	☐ what is already being done?

6 The SMART test

Is the project:	☐ **S**imple? ☐ **M**easurable? ☐ **A**chievable? ☐ **R**ealistic? ☐ **T**ime-related?

the submission must be well researched, with accurate facts and figures, and display knowledge of existing research and relevant programs.

Many funding bodies use application forms for submissions for funding. If there is no official form, provide information on the:

- community organisation that is sponsoring or managing the project
- name, address, position and phone numbers of contact person(s)
- rationale or mission statement of the organisation
- management structure of the organisation
- outcomes and performance indicators
- performance review processes
- the organisation's incorporation status
- a brief history and description of related projects undertaken by the organisation
- the latest balance sheet and profit-and-loss reports
- resources, operating hours and details of staff, including brief curriculum vitae of staff involved in the project and how their track record is relevant to this particular project
- the title of the project
- its general rationale or purpose
- why there is a need for the project
- the key objectives of the project, including target groups (that is, the specific groups of people for whom the project is developed)
- how the proposed project fits the philosophy, aims and policies of the community organisation
- strategies for achieving these objectives
- how the project will be managed
- how the project will be reviewed and evaluated
- a detailed budget, including justification of each item of expenditure.

For the rationale of the project, it is useful to include information on the nature and scope of the problem or issue to be addressed. If appropriate, refer to relevant government policies, what is currently being done about the problem in the area and who the project will benefit.

The objectives of the project must be clearly stated and attainable within the resources and time available. For example, in a submission for funding for a youth refuge, it is unwise to claim that establishing the refuge will solve the problems of youth homelessness in the region; this statement assumes that it is possible to know the existing and potential extent of youth homelessness and that youth homelessness can be solved by establishing a youth refuge. A more modest claim is appropriate; for example, the submission could argue the need for a variety of responses to issues of youth homelessness, based on analysis of demographic and other data. It could base its claim for a youth refuge on research with young people who have expressed an interest in helping to establish it, and argue that it will provide emergency accommodation for some young people. It is better to be overly modest, rather than over-ambitious, when making claims about the significance of a project.

To argue the case for funding any project, it is useful to begin with some fundamental questions:

- Why this particular project in this particular region at this particular time?
- What do we hope to have achieved when we have completed this project?
- Who will the project affect, in terms of advantages and disadvantages?
- Why should this particular organisation receive funds?

It is important to demonstrate to the funding body that you can actually carry out the proposed project. Thus, the submission should include information about your community organisation, such as its rationale, policies, organisational structures, decision-making processes, existing programs, resources and funding. If existing resources are to be used to assist the project, explain how. List the achievements of your organisation in areas related to the project and other areas. Specify the processes for reviewing and evaluating the project. (Evaluation will be discussed later in this chapter.)

When writing the submission, keep in mind the audience – that is, the people who assess the submission for the funding body. Why are you applying to this particular funding body? How does this project relate to the rationale and guidelines of this funding program? In some cases, considering these questions leads a community organisation to abandon a submission, perhaps rejecting the hierarchical structure required by the funding body.

The extent of detail required in a submission varies. Some funding organisations work on a two-stage process, with initial brief expressions of interest followed by detailed proposals. Some ask for a minimum of information in the actual submission and accept detailed appendices, including justification and details of the applying organisation. When a funding body does not specify the amount of detail required, it is important to ask about their expectations.

In the case of government funding, remember that government departments are often overburdened with submissions. Increasingly they use their own proforma, and often the process involves two stages: a preliminary stage setting out in broad terms the case for funding and selection of a few applications from this stage to go forward to full documentation. In the case of a preliminary 'two-pager' the following points should be included:

- this is the issue
- this is how it can be dealt with
- these are the required actions
- this is how much it will cost.

An example for a proposal for a research project might use the following structure:

- this is the issue
- this is the information we need or the action we will do to understand the issue
- this is what it could tell us
- this is how it can help
- this is how much it will cost.

Whatever format is used for the presentation of submissions, it is important that a draft be distributed to the workers and community members for comment. They should consider such matters as whether:

- the submission is readable
- the arguments are logical and well supported
- the research is convincing
- the links are clear between the proposed project and the rationale and policies of both the funding body and the applying organisation
- the objectives and strategies are appropriate
- the expectations of achievements are realistic.

The process of developing a submission should at all stages be an open one and include, if at all possible, other community organisations that are prepared to share their knowledge and experiences.

Service agreements and funding agreements

Governments have been making increasing use of contractual arrangements between community organisations and the specific funding department. Contracts usually take the form of detailed service or funding agreements between the funding body and the funded community organisation. Like a submission, a **service agreement** contains a rationale for the program, objectives, strategies, expected achievements and a budget. It also usually sets out the exact requirements of the funding body, including the outputs and outcomes of the project or program, mutual responsibilities and obligations of the parties, lines of accountability, dispute resolution procedures and processes for evaluation and review. Service agreements also specify the accountability requirements for the program and its finances, so funded organisations must have a system of accountability and procedures for settling disputes. Government departments often have standard agreements, but details can be tailored to suit the requirements of the program and funded organisation.

It is important to understand the concepts of output and outcome, for these usually need to be specified in service agreements or funding agreements. As suggested earlier, output refers to activities or processes that are the measurable effects of a project, such as the commonly used measure of how many people accessed a program, or how much new knowledge was generated through a piece of research, or a specific new policy or how many people joined a campaign after a public meeting. That is, outputs are the actual accomplishments that occur in order to achieve outcomes. Outcomes are the desired changes that the program or project will eventually accomplish. For example, the outcome of a community information program on ways of saving water might be a decline in water consumption, or the outcome of a new policy to combat racism might be that there is less overt racial tension in a community (indicated through a decrease in racially motivated violence).

According to the proponents of service agreements, they facilitate the coordination of programs in the community sector and increase the effectiveness, efficiency and accountability of community-based programs, particularly in regard to financial accountability, program planning and administration. It is claimed that they streamline procedures and minimise paperwork and red tape.

Service agreements have had a mixed reception in the community sector. The process for applying for funds is tightly structured and largely controlled by funding bodies. Programs are usually shaped by the particular requirements set out in the service agreement, which preclude real negotiations with funding bodies. These funding requirements erode the abilities of community organisations to work with and be accountable to their communities, as well as undermine their internal capacities, in what Ignatieff (2003) calls 'capacity sucking-out'. For some community organisations, the whole process of contracting-out and signing up to service agreements is a process of risk management, whereby governments contract out risk. Many funding agreements stipulate that risk assessment and risk management strategies must be in place and boards of management must ensure that community organisation activities are well covered by insurance policies (Verity 2004). Community development workers point out that to measure output in quantitative terms restricts the way that community organisations go about their work and deflects attention from, or even undermines, the importance of processes and practices in community development. Yet other community organisations, which have experienced no difficulty with the service agreement itself, find the process of evaluation constraining and time consuming. Thus, many community organisations argue that statements about independence are just empty rhetoric, and that community organisations have no real bargaining or negotiating power.

Interestingly, some community organisations' experiences of service agreements have been very satisfactory. Such organisations report that service agreements have helped them to clarify and articulate goals and strategies, and the negotiations have been fruitful on both sides. Some community development workers report that they have taken part in frank and open discussions about conflicting expectations of what proposed programs will cost and achieve, and some funding bodies have improved their opinions of the community organisations. Some community development practitioners argue that with service agreements, community organisations at least know where they stand in regard to available funds and expectations. It seems that, regardless of whether funding arrangements for the community sector continue to be based on service agreements or some other similar formula, identifying and achieving desired outcomes will continue to be emphasised.

The message from this analysis is that community organisations should consider the focus of any service agreement they are entering into. For example, the service agreement may focus on enhancing or proving efficiency, ensuring accountability to the funding body or the community, clarifying objectives or setting measurable outcomes. When developing a formal or informal submission or service agreement for a funding body that does not work with any community development principles, there is probably not much scope for changing the terms of reference of the submission. As we have seen, power relations in regard to funding are one-sided and often set by external political agendas. Yet the fact that funding bodies have requirements for their own purposes does not absolve community organisations from their responsibility to identify and prioritise the needs of a community within their terms of reference.

Competitive tendering

Service agreements and funding agreements helped set the stage for the profound changes to how governments fund community organisations that took place in the first half of the 1990s. These changes were based on the central themes of neo-liberalism, including a commitment to developing an enterprise culture, faith in the superiority of the private sector to deliver more-efficient and more-productive programs than the public sector, new managerialism, and above all, the principle of competition. According to the supporters of neo-liberalism, competition is the mechanism by which the cost of services will be held down and the quality of services improved. For example, in neo-liberal theory, when organisations are placed in a competitive relationship to win the contract to run a program or to offer a service rather than automatically receive funds from year to year, the quality of the program or service will be improved.

To understand the strength of the commitment to contracts and competitive tendering in governments it is helpful to note the sea change that has taken place in economic policy in Australia since the 1990s, from a protectionist approach to an emphasis on open markets and competition. As King and Maddock (1996) point out, by 1992 there was broad agreement among all governments on the need for a national competition policy based on a commitment to eliminate anti-competitive behaviour and ensure that all market players were covered equally by the rules of market conduct. These agreements formed part of the terms of reference of the Independent Committee of Inquiry into National Competition Policy, chaired by Professor Fred Hilmer. In 1993 the report of this committee, the Hilmer Report, was released. By 1995 a bill supporting the principles of competition as laid down in the Hilmer Report was passed in federal parliament and supported by all Australian governments. The commitment to competition policy has continued into the twenty-first century.

A central feature of competition policy, and one that has had significant implications for community organisations, is that the sanctions against anti-competitive behaviour should be extended as far as possible from the private business sector to all service providers and government enterprises. That is, like the private business sector, community organisations and government departments are prohibited from acting in ways that might give them monopoly market power; for example, by having a statutory government monopoly, by colluding with other community organisations and government departments, by price-fixing through government regulations or by providing information selectively. There has been a steady process of eliminating 'government monopolies' through the removal of regulations, privatisation of government instrumentalities and the opening up of the work of government departments to other departments and the private sector. As King and Maddock (1996:39) argue, the objective of competition policy is to improve economic efficiency and productivity for the purpose of increasing Australian living standards and community welfare.

There are many difficulties in putting faith in competition as the mechanism by which the quality of life in Australia will be improved. These have been touched on in previous chapters and are discussed further in chapter 10. However, regardless of community development concerns and a weakening of competition policy over the past 10 years, many aspects of how governments relate to community organisations have been determined or influenced by competition policy. Most important of these is the competitive submissions and tendering for contracts to deliver government services and run government-funded community programs.

A competitive arrangement occurs when services are contracted-out – that is, a contract is awarded to an outside party to perform work – or when, after participating in a competitive process, there is an in-house agreement for other departmental personnel to perform work.

A competitive process might be narrow or broad. The narrow approach is evident when government departments approach a number of organisations to see if they are interested in putting in a submission to undertake a project. The competition is then between the organisations that present a submission. The broader approach is when a public notice advertising the tender and calling for submissions or expressions of interest is prepared and promulgated. All submissions conforming to the tender process are then considered and the contract awarded to one of the tenderers.

The focus on a competitive tendering process as the main or best way of making decisions about funding has diminished in the last few years, but many of the competition principles underlying competitive tendering remain the same. In the following sections we consider these, as well as setting out some of the specific tasks involved in preparing a competitive tender.

What is involved in the competitive tendering process and how is it different to a submission-based process of applying for external funds? First, as Wilson (1996) has pointed out, competitive tendering has shifted the emphasis on performance to what has been identified as a more 'business-like approach', with business plans and tight budget monitoring. When considering the nature of tenders it is important to understand the terms **tenderor**, **tenderer**, **tender specifications** and **tender briefs**. The tenderor prepares the tender brief and determines the successful tenderer. The tenderer applies for the tender. If the tenderor is a government department, for example, instead of preparing and distributing submission guidelines, the personnel in the department responsible for the tendering process will prepare tender specifications or tender briefs.

The starting point for understanding the logic of tenders is to acknowledge the emphasis on the commercial nature of the tender process (in which the information and communication are highly confidential, submitted as 'commercial in confidence') and the requirement that the tenderor specify exactly what is wanted. The tender specifications detail the expectations of the project, such as inputs, outputs and outcomes; the level of service required; and the selection criteria for choosing the successful tenderer.

Usually neither the tender specifications nor the tender brief provide instructions on budgets, although a tender specification may include schedules of rates and general levels of funding. It is up to the tenderer to provide detailed budgets, remembering that cost is a central factor in deciding who will be the successful tenderer. Because of the emphasis on following 'business practice', tenders are usually required to provide a sound business plan, setting out where money and other resources (equipment and in-kind activities, for example) will come from and how the money will be spent.

Costing is usually done on the basis of what is sometimes known as a **unit price** for each unit of service. A unit of service can be hours or days, people or products, or a mixture of these. For example, a unit might be an hour of financial counselling, a one-hour domestic violence workshop or an hour of a migrant English course. It might also refer to the placement of one person in emergency accommodation, spending one day with three young people undertaking outreach work or producing a policy document on a specific issue. The costing for the delivery of the unit includes direct costs, such as labour and material cost per unit; and indirect costs, such as insurance, rent, wear and tear on resources, and general administration and infrastructure costs. Unlike submission writers, the tenderer is expected to calculate where the project will break even (that is, cover all direct and indirect costs) or produce a surplus and, if necessary, work out ways of reducing costs to ensure that the program does break even.

Preparing a tender

The information required in the tender will be set out in the tender specifications (sometimes called a request for tender or RFT). As with submissions, the following information about the tenderer and the project is usually required:

- name, address, position and phone numbers of contact person(s)
- information on the community organisation sponsoring or managing the project
- the incorporation status and other legal details pertaining to the community organisation, such as insurance policy details
- the rationale or mission statement of the organisation
- a brief history and description of related projects undertaken by the organisation
- the latest balance sheet and profit-and-loss reports
- the management structure of the organisation
- resources
- operating hours
- outcomes and performance indicators
- performance review processes
- other programs run by the organisation
- staffing of the organisation
- the operating budget of the community organisation.

The tender submission will also include information on the project:

- the title of the project
- name, address, position and phone numbers of contact person(s)
- the general rationale and purpose and specified outcomes
- how the project fits with the philosophy, aims and policies of the community organisation

- the key objectives of the project, including target groups
- strategies for achieving these objectives
- details of tasks in the project, including how they will take place and who will do them
- details of outputs and indicators outcomes
- detailed timelines
- how the project will be managed
- how the project will be reviewed and evaluated
- unit costs
- a detailed budget, including justification of each item.

In addition, tenders usually require:

- an executive summary (a summary of the project, including the aims and objectives, resources, capabilities and unique qualities of the tenderers)
- a general forward plan (for example, three-year and five-year plans), including an operational plan that includes policies and procedures; a marketing plan that includes an analysis of who the target groups are, the current supply of services and how this project will access them; a financial plan that shows how finances will be managed; a service delivery plan showing how services will be delivered; and a risk management plan outlining possible risks and how they will be managed
- information on the insurance policies held by the organisation, bankers and solicitors
- cash-flow projection for the organisation during the period of the tender, including a break-even analysis
- information setting out compliance with regulations
- information on units of service
- information on sources of finance
- information on quality assurance (including the specification of standards and how a high quality of service will be measured and maintained).

Quality assurance, best practice and benchmarking

In the context of discussions about Australia becoming a globally competitive economy, there has been an increasing focus on ideas of **quality assurance**, **best practice** and **benchmarking**. Now, quality assurance and best practice requirements have been extended to many community services and programs. Quality assurance means that a program will operate in accordance with specified 'standards' – which does not necessarily mean that the product or service itself will be of a 'high standard'. In broad terms, a standard or benchmark specifies the best levels of activity, production, service or outcome to which a project or program aspires. Standards can be set on the basis of quality accreditation schemes established by governments or independently of governments, reference to international benchmarks (such as quality of life indicators), or consultation with participants in programs and customers of services. Standards are set by those who have the power to identify what a standard is, and how it should be measured, and of course, standards are not once and for all.

Community development workers in many parts of Australia have begun to consider the hard question of whether they are prepared to participate in the process of competitive submissions and tendering in order to gain funds or whether, in the interests of their integrity, they would do better to leave the funding arena altogether. Those who have made the decision to participate report mixed results for their programs. Some community development workers have commented that, once an organisation has won funding, gained know-how about how to write submissions and tenders, and established a name for itself, the funding process is actually simpler and the program less controlled by the funding body than under previous funding mechanisms. Some of these workers also argue that the cultural shift to accountability to 'customers' is consistent with the community development focus on facilitating the needs of the community. The focus on a 'can-do' approach to providing programs can generate new and exciting ways of responding to community needs, without being hamstrung by endless regulations and red tape. For other workers, the experiences are less favourable. They report less control of community projects by community members, more regulations, shortfalls in funding, more unpaid work and redundancies, more red tape and increased scrutiny of their activities. Moreover, because current funding is short term and security of funding disappears altogether, there is increased anxiety and insecurity for workers, and this makes long-term (sometimes yearly) planning very difficult.

Interestingly, the Productivity Commission's report *Contribution of the Not-for-Profit Sector* acknowledges that the regulatory framework for the sector is costly for not-for-profit organisations. It is 'complex, lacks coherence [and] sufficient transparency' (Productivity Commission, 2010:xxiii). The report comments on 'inadequate contracting processes', including 'overly prescriptive requirements, increased micro-management, requirements to return surplus funds and inappropriately short-term contracts' (Productivity Commission, 2010:xxiv). It argues for legislative proposals to reduce reporting burdens, alignment of contracts with the period required to achieve agreed outcomes and streamlined contracting processes. Whether, and how far, the recommendations of the Productivity Commission are taken up in practice by government will be borne out over the next decade.

Research

When arguing the case for funding a program on the basis of need or when lobbying for the development of policies for effective settlement of refugees, for example, community development workers undertake research to support their arguments. On one level, research is an everyday activity through which we collect and interpret information that can throw light on a question, problem or issue under discussion.

On another level, however, research is a complex process that depends on theories and assumptions about how the world works, and how we know about this. In recent years, formal and sophisticated research has become increasingly important in community development.

In the context of community development, research is useful because it helps us to understand why something happens and how to maintain or change some aspect of our practice or our social, political, economic or cultural environment. Research might also take place for the purpose of identifying and analysing an unmet need or to evaluate the success of a project. Examples of community development research projects follow.

- A women's group interviews survivors of violence with a view to improving police and community service processes for dealing with domestic violence.
- An activist organisation evaluates its recent campaign to establish more childcare centres in a region.
- A migrant resource centre interviews newly arrived refugees in order to understand their experiences and provide the best services possible.
- A community health centre evaluates its programs.
- A neighbourhood house investigates why a local group from culturally and linguistically diverse backgrounds does not use its resources.
- A youth drop-in centre undertakes a needs assessment to comply with the requirements of a funding body.
- An environment group investigates how to establish an education program to encourage people to recycle their rubbish.
- A multicultural group of parents, teachers and students investigate why there is a rise in racial tensions in a multi-racial school.

For the purpose of community development research, we need to know how information is collected (including **qualitative** and **quantitative research** methods), how to analyse the data and how to use the data and the analysis.

Research issues

The emphasis on research – to support an argument, demonstrate a need or evaluate a program, for example – has had a varied response from community organisations. Concerns regarding research include:

- Research is yet another requirement that diverts time and energy from running programs and organising action.
- Research further disempowers the powerless, who are generally the 'object' of the research.
- Emphasis on research is indicative of the professionalisation of community development work, and is an attempt to bring it into line with other academic professions.
- The requirement for workers to undertake research can discriminate against the employment of those workers who have no formal education.

These concerns are well founded. It is clear that social research has been used to disempower ordinary people through 'researching down', whereby the poor become the objects of study by middle-class professionals, who examine, analyse and even experiment with the habits and lifestyles of working-class people.

It is therefore important that community development researchers are sensitive to the issues of the relevance and politics of research. They should begin by ensuring that their research takes place within the overall context of community development principles. To begin with, community development research is **action research** insofar as its ultimate aim is to improve society, by shaping our understanding and engagement with the world to make it better (Blackshaw, 2010:49). It might do this by identifying different ways of knowing and seeing things, by using data and analysis to expose injustice to intervene in policy decisions, or to identify assets and needs, for example. For many supporters of action research, it must also be democratic, insofar as it is based on the co-generation of knowledge (researchers and researched together, as one and the same people); it should involve active participation of all who are involved; it should be equitable in that it acknowledges the equal worth of all people; and it should be liberating in that it frees people from oppressive and controlling conditions (Blackshaw, 2010:49–50).

Community development researchers should be conscious that, even when it is informal, research can be two-sided. It can be used both to intimidate and disempower ordinary people, as well as to empower people by providing knowledge, to expose injustices and to raise consciousness of issues. In all research activities, a community should consider who the research is ultimately for, and why it should be undertaken in the first place.

Elements of research

Before we move on to discuss the knowledge and skills that community development workers need in order to undertake competent research, we will recapitulate the six key elements in the community development process discussed in chapter 1.

- *Information:* Ensure that community members, including those who are researching and being researched, have access to information about the nature, purpose and expected outcomes of the research. As noted in chapter 1, this might involve obtaining detailed information and advice from specialist experts, such as demographers and lawyers, when they have necessary specialised knowledge.
- *Authenticity:* Accept the authenticity of the lives of those people who are being researched, and ensure that they are able to express their views in their terms of reference.
- *Vision:* Design settings in which people reflect upon their experiences, develop a critical awareness of their lives and identify alternative ways of doing things. It is in this element that they begin to consider possibilities for action and change.
- *Pragmatism:* Those involved in the research explore and discuss openly the factors that constrain the possibilities for action and change.
- *Strategy:* Identify strategies for change that are based on the findings of the research.
- *Transformation:* This is fully underway when these strategies are carried out, but it also occurs throughout the research process.

All of these elements are found in different forms and at different stages in community development research (see figure 9.2 on page 374).

Processes and practices

Figure 9.2 *Elements of the community development research process*

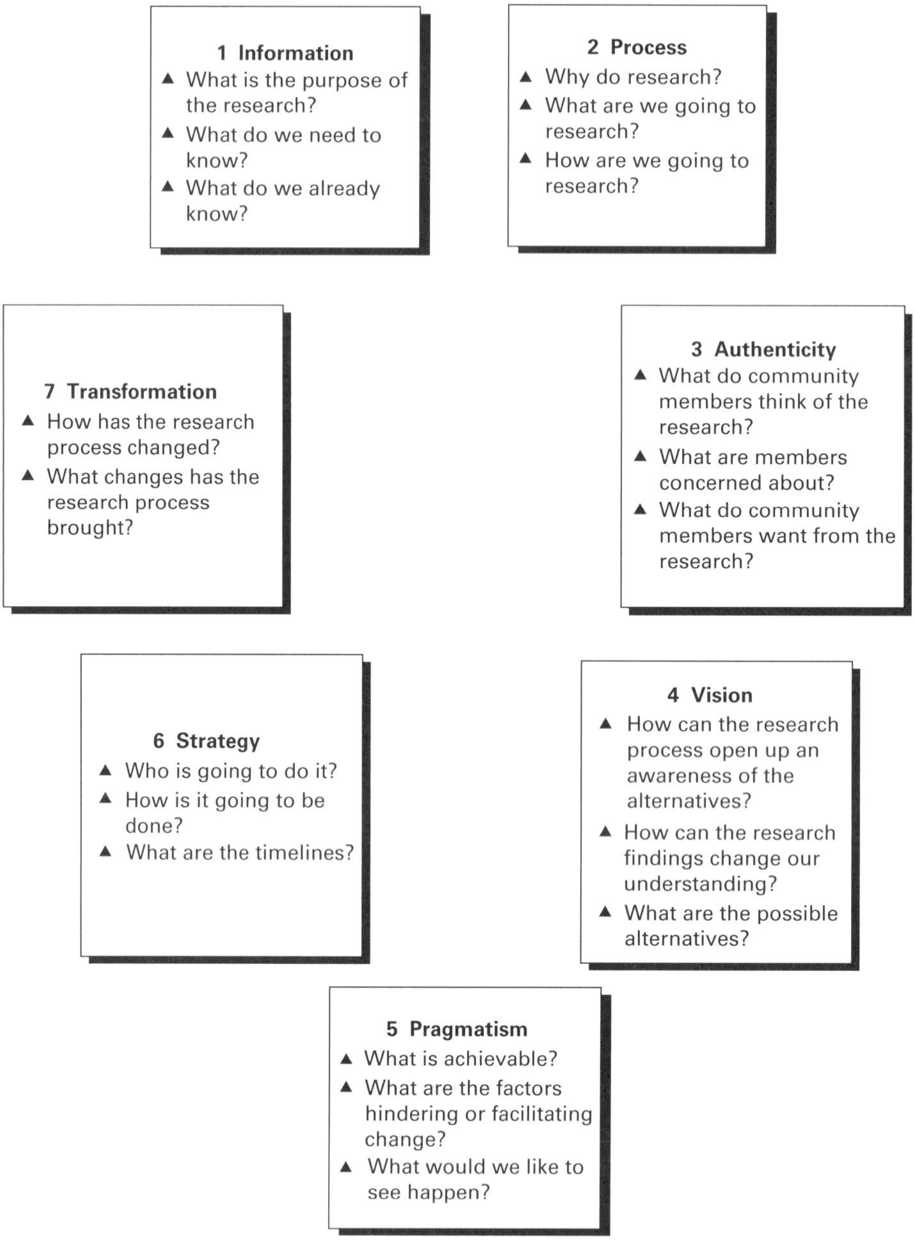

1 Information
- What is the purpose of the research?
- What do we need to know?
- What do we already know?

2 Process
- Why do research?
- What are we going to research?
- How are we going to research?

7 Transformation
- How has the research process changed?
- What changes has the research process brought?

3 Authenticity
- What do community members think of the research?
- What are members concerned about?
- What do community members want from the research?

6 Strategy
- Who is going to do it?
- How is it going to be done?
- What are the timelines?

4 Vision
- How can the research process open up an awareness of the alternatives?
- How can the research findings change our understanding?
- What are the possible alternatives?

5 Pragmatism
- What is achievable?
- What are the factors hindering or facilitating change?
- What would we like to see happen?

In regard to formal social research, a community development researcher should always raise questions about the purpose of the research, who controls it and in whose interests it is being carried out. In some instances the information required is already available, so the proposed research is unnecessary. Researchers should also consider what they expect to come out of the research, including its best and worst possible results, and they should be cautious about the use of their findings.

Collaboration, participation and ownership

As indicated above, whatever the subject matter of a research project, the community should own and, as far as possible, participate in the research process. The collaboration, participation and partnership necessary for community development research can take various forms. In full participatory research, the researchers and the researched become one; that is, people research themselves and their own experiences. A number of community organisations and local councils are committed to facilitating local community members to undertake their own research. For example, homeless young women learn how to interview and record data so that they can then interview other homeless young women. In another form of participatory research, the researchers immerse themselves in the group, situation or experience of the people they are researching. In both these situations, community development researchers strive to capture the experiences and authenticity of people's everyday lives and to feel at one with them.

Whatever form participatory research takes, it involves those who are in some way the subject of the research in the research process. For example, a community researching possible local employment programs might train and employ people who are unemployed or it might set up a steering or management committee comprising a majority of people who are unemployed and looking for work, as well as people who have had experience of local employment programs and representatives from the funding body, and state and local government departments. At all stages of the research process there is feedback and consultation between the researchers, the steering committee and the broader community.

Researchers need to go back frequently to those being researched and ask such questions as: Does this make sense to you? Would you put the question another way? In the case of recommendations, researchers can ask: If things changed in this way, do you think it would make a difference to your lives?

Wadsworth (1997) identifies the commitment to those who are being researched as the **critical reference group** perspective. Community development research attempts to involve all those affected by the research process, and the researcher is accountable to this group. Often it is the critical reference group that initiates the research.

Sometimes, however, the research is initiated by community organisations in order to fulfil the requirements of funding bodies or to persuade decision-making bodies to change policies. There is often tension between the requirements of funding bodies and the interests of a critical reference group, but this does not absolve the community development worker from ensuring that decisions about research and the research process are made collectively.

Funding bodies have tended to prefer facts and figures (quantitative data) to qualitative interview data as the basis of research. After examining the case for and against complying with a funding body's requirements for quantitative research, the critical reference group may decide to jettison the research and forgo this particular source of funding.

Approaches to research

While it is beyond the scope of this book to consider in detail the debates in research methodology, we can identify central precepts and approaches in social research that can be of use to community development practitioners.

Processes and practices

Community development research is concerned with getting information about 'what is going on', making sense of this information and using the information. Before we start to collect information we need to be clear about what we will accept as 'knowledge' and how we will make sense of or analyse the information. In a useful discussion of what counts as knowledge, Crotty (1998:8) explains the concept of **epistemology** and why it is important. He points out that epistemology deals with the question of how we know what we know. There are two broad approaches: first, what is often identified as **objectivism** and, second, what is identified as **constructionism**. Objectivism holds that there is 'an objective reality out there', and humans can discover this reality and its meaning as 'objective truth'. In contrast, constructionism rejects the view that there is single objective truth waiting for us to discover. As Crotty (1998:8–9) points out, in constructionism:

> Truth, or meaning, come into existence in and out of our engagement with the realities in our world. There is no meaning without a mind. Meaning is not discovered, but constructed.

Objectivism underlies a theoretical perspective known as *positivism*, which has been a dominant force in social research methodologies. In needs assessment and evaluation research, for example, objectivism and positivism are linked with a commitment to the use of value-neutral and scientific research methods to gain 'the truth'. In this context, practical research might be seen to be best undertaken by outside experts, who can be 'objective' and 'scientific'. In the case of an evaluation, for example, outside 'experts' can point out irrationalities, inconsistencies and ineffective practices. Objectivist approaches also utilise quantitative methods, where the objects of research are put into units that are measurable (sometimes known as **metrics**). Indentifying the number of people who live in an area and the percentage of these that want more public transport involves measurement, for example.

While there are many criticisms of the positivist approach to research, there are important uses of this approach, particularly when there is a need for comparative data. For example, the use of good indicators (such as numbers and percentages of positive responses to a new community program) can provide communities and funding bodies with one source of information on how well a program is working. There are some other useful applications of quantitative data in community development, such as measuring whether wellbeing has deteriorated or improved in a community through analysis of health data. Indeed, quantitative indicators – such as mortality rates, quality of life indicators, health and environmental statistics – can be useful for community development purposes to indicate a need or demonstrate how aspects of society have improved or deteriorated. Thus, there are situations when community development practitioners will use objectivist approaches as long as it is understood that quantitative data, like all data in the social sciences, is not the 'final truth' – like all information, it can be manipulated to suit certain purposes. Notwithstanding the arguments for using positivist quantifiable approaches, many social researchers note the range of criticisms and difficulties with these and lean towards the constructionist approach.

In a community development framework, reality is not once and for all. As commented above, it can also be seen as socially constructed. This involves both engaging with the external world and interpreting this world through the development of meanings. Of course, from this standpoint, meanings are not created by individuals in a vacuum – what Crotty (1998:43) calls 'out-and-out subjectivism'. They are created collectively. In order to understand meanings it is important to locate these in historical and cultural contexts. The perspective in this book is that both the objectivist or positivist approach and the constructionist approach have a place in community development research.

It is important to think carefully about which approach might be adopted for a particular piece of research. Such factors as timelines, available resources and the purpose of the research will influence the choice of approach and methods.

Preparing for a research project

Community development researchers should understand the theories, concepts and assumptions that underpin research and how they determine the actual research questions and methods. For example, they should:

- recognise the theoretical perspectives where they apply
- consider ethical issues such as confidentiality, and political issues such as the use of the research findings
- suggest options in regard to research methods and facilitate the collective choice of the most appropriate.

Choice of style and methods depends on the research questions and goals, theoretical underpinnings (for example, feminists tend to use qualitative research) and the subject matter of the research. In much social research, several methods are used.

In order to facilitate decisions about appropriate methods, community development researchers need to understand the debates over the use of quantitative data (such as statistics) and qualitative data (such as biographies) and know why and when these are appropriate to different research questions. They must be competent and rigorous in technical areas, such as developing a clear research question and appropriate research design.

A research design sets out how the research question will be tackled. It states

- what information will be collected and from whom
- the sampling procedures: how to choose a representative group (or not representative group) of the population being studied
- use of primary sources (such as interviews) and secondary sources (such as Australian Bureau of Statistics data).

A competent researcher can identify where and how to obtain data, interpret and analyse the data, summarise findings and make recommendations on the findings.

Researchers need to decide whether they will use primary data, such as interviews undertaken by the researcher, or secondary data, such as data collected by someone else (based on prior interviews), including government statistics and reports. In many cases researchers use both primary and secondary sources, and indeed a range of methods. This approach is sometimes called **triangulation**. Once the sources are identified, researchers need to plan where and when the data will be collected. If the data is primary and the method is qualitative a decision needs to be made as to how the data is collected. Is it to be through interviews? And if interviews, will these take the form of a free-flowing open conversation or use a checklist or a tighter structure? Or will data be collected through formal questionnaires filled out in private?

Some organisations now have ethics protocols for anyone undertaking research. Ethics protocols usually require a plain language statement to be given to those involved in the research, setting out the purpose of the research, the type and form of information that will be requested by the participants, and the understanding that participants can withdraw at any stage of the research. The ethics statement might also include a statement to the effect that all information will be anonymous (no one person is identifiable) or that all reports will be sent to participants for checking.

Community development practitioners should have a good practical understanding of research methods, and in particular what options are available for data collection and analysis, and what mistakes in logic and method to avoid. In regard to the latter point, it is important to avoid the mistakes of causality and representativeness. The **mistake of causality** occurs when research assumes that just because two activities occur together, or in succession, this necessarily means that one caused the other (see David & Sutton, 2004: 25–6). However, statistical calculations can be undertaken to analyse what any correlations might mean and whether there is a significant correlation. The ability to undertake such calculations can be learnt from research methodology textbooks. Similarly, a finding about views of a small group of people who offer to participate in a project on climate change, for example, does not mean that it reflects what all people in the community think. The issue of representation is an important one. Selection of participants in a research project involves **sampling**, and there are many texts dealing with sampling procedures, including ones that set out statistical calculations (de Vaus, 1985).

Indeed, there are many excellent general texts on research and research methods, including informative introductory books that explain these skills (see, for example, McNiff & Whitehead, 2009; Coghlan & Brannick, 2005; David & Sutton, 2004; Payne & Payne, 2004; Booth, Colomb & Williams, 2003; Williams, 2003; Bernard, 2000; Stewart & Cash, 1994; Hakim, 1987; de Vaus, 1985; Bulmer, 1986, 1984). It is important that community development practitioners have a good practical understanding of research methods. For a more complex analysis of quantitative data, however, community development practitioners often employ more-experienced data analysts.

Community assets and needs studies and evaluation

In order to meet the requirements for supporting community-based programs, strategic planning, accountability and review, community development workers commonly undertake three types of applied research: **community assets research**, **community needs studies** and **evaluation research**. In the following sections we discuss these in some detail.

Interest in community assets and needs studies has grown over the past decade, particularly with the growing awareness that funding of programs should be based on an understanding of the underlying assets and needs of a community rather than on historical precedent or skills in writing submissions. Interestingly, a cursory look at the literature on community assets and needs reveals that not much has been written on needs studies and even less on assets research.

While for some practitioners, needs-based funding is both too deficit-oriented and too positivistic to be appropriate to community development, for others it can provide measurable indicators of need, which are used to prioritise groups or localities for funding. When these indicators are linked with assets, they can provide an overview of both strengths and needs of communities.

The asset-based approach

We have mentioned the importance of an asset-based approach in various parts of this book. One approach is to begin with an asset inventory. Below are some of the key categories in building an asset inventory:

- *a capacity inventory*, such as caring for elderly people
- *a skills inventory* – skills people have learnt in the home, workplace, community organisation and community in general, such as computer, gardening and music skills
- *community organisation experiences and skills*, such as organising sports teams and protest action
- *business experience*, such as driving a truck and running your own business from home.

Another way of undertaking an asset-based initiative is to ask people to offer their skills and capacities, without listing what these might be. In this way there is more scope for creatively developing an asset inventory.

Needs studies

As discussed in this book, most funding bodies and government policy development take a deficit approach to understanding how communities work, often beginning with a process of comparing the respective claims of geographical areas or community organisations. From this perspective, it is argued that needs-based funding is consistent with principles of equity and social justice.

Needs studies have produced their own terminology. A needs study is a generic term for a general study of the overall needs of a specific group. **Needs identification** and **needs assessment** refer to the identification of a group's needs for services. **Needs-based planning** proceeds beyond assessment to develop indicators of need, to collect information that is perceived to reflect needs and to determine priorities for program planning.

Needs-based planning is often driven by the neo-liberal imperative of a lean public service, dedicated to efficiency. As a result, many community organisations are sceptical about the value of community needs studies to community development. However, an understanding of assets and needs can provide an overview of a community as a better starting point for resource distribution than the requirement to 'spend money' (because of availability of a given resource) or historical practice, or even because of a well-written submission.

The aims of a community assets and needs study are to find out what assets and needs exist, so that a community group or organisation can decide which assets should be developed, identify what needs it is dealing with and assign priorities to them. Funding bodies can know exactly what needs they are funding. Community assets and needs studies are also an important of the development of strategic plans in community organisations.

On first appearance, the process of needs assessment seems straightforward. However, on further probing we find that the concept of needs is both a political and complex one. For example, Fraser (1989) draws our attention to how needs interpretation and needs satisfaction are politicised, defined by the powerful, and so often work against the interests of women. She points out that

> needs talk functions as a medium for the making and contesting of political claims: it is an idiom in which political conflict is played out and through which inequalities are symbolically elaborated and challenged (Fraser, 1989:161–2).

Fraser's view of the politics of needs is borne out by much of the research on needs in Australia. This research has often drawn on the work of Bradshaw (1972), who defines four types of need:

- *normative needs:* defined by experts on the basis of their knowledge
- *felt needs:* articulated directly by community members themselves
- *expressed needs:* manifested by some kind of action, such as a demand for a service, putting one's name on a waiting list or a petition
- *comparative needs:* based on a comparison of resources, or lack of them, between communities.

Normative needs

The normative approach to needs analysis is underpinned by an objectivist or positivist view of the world. **Normative needs** are used by experts, including academics, professional human service workers and public administrators as a measure of what a community needs. Kettner et al. (1990:48) point out:

> By definition, the term normative implies the existence of standards of norms. When we add the concept of need, we posit the existence of some standard or criterion established by custom, authority, or general consensus against what the quantity or quality of a situation or condition is measured.

The Australian Council of Social Services (ACOSS) lists basic human needs as:

- housing
- health (absence of disease)
- education
- material goods and services (including income and credit access)
- leisure
- employment
- mobility and transportation
- opportunities to pursue and express personal values
- civil and legal rights and services

- political participation and power
- personal social services
- safety (Southern Regional Community Health Research Unit, 1991:11).

In a community needs assessment, a study of normative needs could begin by consulting professionals in a local area, such as social workers, doctors, local councillors and other people with relevant knowledge, such as members of a local action group. Information is obtained through questionnaires, in-depth interviews or discussion panels.

On the basis of the views of so-called experts, social indicators are often established as measures of wellbeing of a community. These include such factors as the incidence of disease and suicide and other morbidity rates, access to public transport, employment rates and average levels of income. One commonly used indicator of wellbeing is the poverty line, which is usually based on a calculation of the income required by a family to maintain an adequate standard of living. The measurement of poverty is complex, and significant debate continues about whether to measure it in terms of income or in terms of what is required to fulfil basic human needs. There have been numerous attempts to identify low income as the basis of poverty, but of course this depends on household composition and living patterns. Nevertheless, income level remains the most commonly used indicator of poverty.

Felt needs

Felt needs are those articulated by the people with the needs. They are what people say when they are surveyed about their needs. Surveys range from simple to sophisticated in technique, but they do not attempt to shift people's consciousness. They treat such consciousness as given.

Maher and Burke (1991) and Kettner et al. (1990) criticise the widespread use of felt needs as a measure of community needs, arguing that the perceptions of community members are often limited by the harsh day-to-day realities of survival. Maher and Burke (1991) claim that experts are likely to have knowledge that is not available to community members. Kettner et al. (1990:49) argue that a fine balance must be maintained between the professional's judgement of client needs and potential service users' (consumers) perceptions of what those needs are, 'because consumers might express what in reality are symptoms of problems and not causes'. They add that actively soliciting consumers' perceptions of their needs is likely to raise the expectations of consumers. In their critiques of felt needs, these writers ultimately privilege the expert's perceptions of needs over those of disadvantaged people.

From the community development and feminist viewpoint, of course, a survey of felt needs is not inferior to the normative needs approach, because it accepts the integrity of the views of disadvantaged people. Consideration of felt needs is consistent with the feminist principles that take women's lived experiences seriously, and do not patronise women from a patriarchal, all-knowing expert point of view.

Expressed needs

Expressed needs are those that are translated into a specific action, thus demonstrating an unmet need. Measures of an expressed need for a service may include waiting lists, protest meetings or a petition. The expressed needs approach appeals to planners since it can often be quantified (for example, numbers on waiting lists for public housing). However, such measures may understate need, especially if there is stigma attached to the use of a service (see Maher and Burke, 1991:255). It can also be argued that expressed needs reflect the interests of the most articulate or powerful lobby groups, rather than overall community needs.

Comparative needs

Comparative need is linked to normative need. The comparative needs approach is often favoured by funding bodies when allocating funds to geographic areas or demographic groups. In calculating comparative need, funding bodies compare the need for programs in different localities on the basis of demographic data and social indicators such as a poverty line. Kettner et al. (1990:50) comment:

> In some instances this can mean that a poor community that already is receiving many resources might be favoured over a more affluent community with fewer resources if it can be demonstrated that the relative unmet need is greater.

The comparative approach rests on precedence: existing community services are compared with services in other communities. Felt and expressed needs are articulated by the people with the needs, whereas most comparative and all normative approaches begin from the viewpoint of people other than those who have the needs, and are based on secondary data. The values and theoretical opinions of the experts are rarely examined, let alone questioned. In none of the four approaches are humans seen as agents making and changing their own society. That is, existing reality is taken as given. There is no notion of transformation. This raises problems for community development research, which is dedicated to transformation through the empowerment of ordinary people.

Theories of human needs

Discussions of the way we identify and measure human needs are underpinned by philosophical ideas about human life. Within these debates, the central concerns relate to what it is to be human:

- physical survival
- participation in social and cultural life
- personal autonomy and some control over one's life
- the overall capacity for fulfilment.

In order to survive, humans require their lives to be sustained and maintained. They need food, shelter, clothing and protection from physical harm. But being human, as the previous list by ACOSS shows, is more than just physical survival. Doyal and Gough (1991:69) point out that humans also

> have to be able to participate in a cultural form of life. In practice, this means they must have the physical, intellectual and emotional capacity to interact with fellow actors over sustained periods in ways which are valued and reinforced in some ways.

For Doyal and Gough, humans need to be able to reflect critically upon their situation and to change the rules of their social environment. These writers identify this ability as *critical autonomy*. To have critical autonomy is to have cognitive and emotional control and the political freedom to participate in democratic political processes. Goulet (1985) argues that, as well as physical survival and autonomy, humans need a sense of self-esteem, dignity and self-worth. Maslow (1962) argues that humans must be able to self-actualise and that they need to have a sense of fulfilment.

Freire (1972) argues that humans can only be fulfilled when they have a critical awareness of the world in which they live and their role as agents in this world, and when they are prepared to act upon this critical awareness. This requires control not only of decision making but also of problem-posing. It means that ordinary people must be able to identify problems as they see them, rather than as selected and interpreted by external experts (as occurs, for example, in community needs studies that are based upon the normative approach).

In Australia, Ife (2002) has emphasised the importance of human rights discourse in all community development. Human rights also draw attention to the question of what it is to be human. We are beginning to think about how needs assessments can be informed by human rights. That is, in identifying and satisfying needs we can work from the question of what our rights are, and the obligations of the state to ensure that these rights are fulfilled. This is not to say, of course, that rights are given from above, once and for all, but to accept that the process of defining and achieving rights should take place within the context of ongoing discussion of universal human rights themes (see Ife, 2002:67).

While a number of books set out approaches and methods for undertaking assets- or needs-based research, there is a lacunae of research that brings these two approaches together. At best we can draw on the philosophical discussions of need that link capacities and insights, such as critical autonomy and critical awareness, with a social, political, cultural and economic environment that facilitates the fulfilment of needs. From this perspective, we all have capacities. As Sen (1999) as pointed out, we need the freedom to develop these capacities.

Community control

From a community development perspective, it is not a matter of just individual capacities and individual freedom. Communities have collective capacities and collectively require freedom for their development. They cannot have freedom if they do not collectively own the processes of assets and needs identification. That is, community needs studies involve continuing processes owned by the community itself. These processes should find space for what Fraser (1989) calls oppositional forms of 'needs talk', which allow for needs to be 'politicised from below'. A number of methods can be used to ensure that the elucidation of community needs is an ongoing process, involving time for reflection (including philosophical and theoretical reflection), feedback, information exchange, strategy development and action. Community members should have control of the ways that needs are identified and satisfied.

Following is a case study of the development of a community plan based on a needs assessment. It involves a decision by a local council to skill local people to undertake research.

WEST BAY COMMUNITY PLAN

case study

West Bay council has been given an $86 000 grant to develop a community plan. The West Bay community support committee decided to check with other regional councils how they developed their community plan. They were advised that the quickest and easiest way of proceeding was to contract consultants to undertake the whole process. External experts could research the needs of the community, using existing profiles such as those based on census data, and develop the plan within six weeks. This plan could then be presented at a public forum and any additions could be made within a timeline of another two weeks. Add to this the employment of a multimedia designer to develop a brochure, posters and a website (taking another two weeks) and the final plan would take 10 weeks.

West Bay community support committee considered this procedure and rejected it. They had discovered that the local residents were extremely hostile to the plan; in fact, the plan based on the employment of consultants actually never got off the ground as there had been no resident input into its development. They decided that their community plan process would skill the community to research their own needs. They established a community development committee with the majority of the membership being non-council community members. They then drew up a database of all community groups and organisations, as well as identifying all categories of people in the council area, based on age, gender, socioeconomic status and cultural background. To ensure that all people in the community were included, they also identified who might be excluded in such a process, such as elderly non-English-speaking residents, and where this might occur. The committee wanted to make sure that all members of the community could have a say. This process took one week.

Next, instead of employing outsiders, they called for expressions of interest from residents to attend a training session to learn how to do community research. Fourteen people responded. A research training program was set up, run by in-house council researchers. All participants in the research training team were paid. The training took a demanding two weeks and, at the end of the period, there were 11 members left.

A community needs research design was developed, beginning with a focus on felt needs. This took one week. The sample was to be the whole population and the data was to be collected in focus groups, from a sample of people in in-depth interviews (ensuring that all categories of people were interviewed) and a questionnaire (distributed to all residents in the major languages in the council area). Preparation and piloting of the interviews and the questionnaire took three weeks. Because the trained resident interviewers were part of the community, they worked with their specific communities to ensure smooth communication. Focus groups were held in local neighbourhoods, as part of a sausage sizzle paid for by the council. These focus groups discussed existing needs, but also involved a 'healthy visions' workshop. The data-collection period took four weeks.

At the end of this period, there had been a 67 per cent response rate – an impressive rate for research of this nature. The analysis of the new data took three weeks. It was supplemented by the use of existing community data (normative, comparative and expressed needs). The first draft of the community plan took three weeks to prepare. It was based on the various needs analyses, a strategic assessment and a SWOT analysis.

It was distributed in summary form to all residents, who were given two weeks to respond. During this time, the multimedia presentation templates were drawn up. The responses were summarised and presented at an open forum. At this meeting there were disagreements about the emphases of the plan, but in general it was well received. The council researchers went out of their way to accommodate any dissenting views. The final draft took another two weeks to write and was received positively within the community. While the whole research process had taken 20 weeks, the outcome was a workable community plan based on the real needs of the community members.

This case study indicates two different ways of doing community research. The second approach took more time, but it did involve the local community and allowed for the community members to be skilled in research methods and took the views of the community seriously. The notion of transformation is central to an approach to community needs assessment variously called **healthy visions methodology** or **future visions workshop**. The method is to imagine a future healthy community in terms of how it looks, what people do day to day, how people produce and distribute goods, and how people relate to each other. Participants also identify what they think is good about their community as it is. The aim of such a workshop is to deal with problems, needs and solutions in a creative way and to shift people's consciousnesses, so that they begin to consider alternative future options for their communities.

The community development approach to assets and community needs studies uses broad theoretical insights and information from the normative and comparative approaches, but the processes involved, the interpretation of needs and the outcomes of the research should be largely controlled by communities themselves. Before we leave this discussion, one critical point should be made. Community assets and needs research can harness the expertise in a community, take a lot of effort and raise expectations, but this involvement and effort can come to nothing if those who allocate resources decide to reject the results of the research. As Doyal and Gough (1991:308) point out:

> Taken in isolation, the participatory, community-oriented approach to welfare politics has serious limitations and the need remains for a strong and representative central authority. The dangers are well known. In a society of pervasive inequality and unmet needs, greater participation can at best act as a figleaf to cover the powerlessness of the poor. At worst, it aggravates their deprivation and limits their power still further.

Linking needs assessments with strategic plans

This insight into the effects of assets assessment and community needs assessment that is undertaken as a discrete activity underscores the importance of linking assessments with strategic plans. This can be understood in the framework of two types of questions asked in community development work. One set of questions is on the theme of what is needed in a community; the other is on the theme of what we are going to do about these needs. Thus, it is important not just to identify needs or critical issues, but also to develop a plan that sets out strategies for what we want to do about the needs and critical issues and how we are going to get there. The case study above illustrates this as well as how a decision to skill local people to undertake research can be put into action.

Evaluation

In community development, evaluation involves the review and assessment of programs and projects. In some quarters, evaluation has come to be seen as a cure-all for all the difficulties that face community organisations and as a means by which funding bodies can scrutinise funded programs. Yet evaluation, of course, is a form of research and has all the complexities of any research project. In this section we begin to unpack some of these complexities.

Evaluation might involve a final overview and judgement of a program or it might be an ongoing process involving monitoring and then a final overview and judgement. It is important to understand the difference between evaluation and monitoring. Monitoring involves tracking the development of a project. It requires establishing systematic processes for 'keeping an eye on how things are going', such as weekly meetings in which workers reflect on the activities of the organisation. While it involves the collection of data, and reports may be written, these tend to be views about what a program looks like at a particular point. They may include suggestions for fine-tuning, but this is where monitoring shifts into evaluation. Evaluation occurs when descriptions are used for both judgement and intervention purposes. That is, evaluation involves specific questions that are then used for interventions; for example, 'How are things going?', 'What's the impact of the project or program?', 'Are we achieving our goals?', 'What are we doing right?' (or 'What is the project doing right?') and 'What are we doing wrong?'

As Rubin (1995) points out, evaluation uses information gathered during monitoring, and it then considers the effectiveness and impact of a project – against performance indicators, for example – with a view to improvement.

Why undertake an evaluation?

There are several perspectives on the purposes of evaluation. A useful way of categorising these is outlined by Chelimsky and Shadish (1997:10). They identify three broad rationales or orientations:

- evaluation for *accountability* (for example, to find out if a program has achieved its goals efficiently and effectively)
- evaluation for *knowledge* (for example, to understand how a program is operating)
- evaluation for *development* (for example, to find ways of strengthening a community organisation).

While, of course, in any one evaluation project these three purposes will be mixed together, it is usually possible to discern a dominant reason for undertaking monitoring and evaluation work.

When to evaluate?

When should an organisation evaluate? This is a common question, with several answers. There is strong support for including a monitoring process in all programs, as a process of reflection and to check actions against proposed milestones in a project. In some cases, community organisations have no choice about when to undertake a monitoring or evaluation exercise – for example, the terms of a contract might require that formal monitoring takes place every three months or that a less formal report be submitted to a funding body every fortnight. In other situations, community organisations have discretion as to when they monitor and evaluate their activities. They might decide to have an informal weekly meeting to discuss 'how things are going' or a more formal meeting with a set agenda, reflecting on goals set and goals achieved each week. Increasingly, funding bodies require a formal evaluation at the end of a project. However, the end of a project might be after six months or after five years.

Often an evaluation is undertaken when things go wrong, or when there is a loss of direction, with a view to clarifying priorities and reorganising. Yet many writers argue that this is the worst time to undertake an evaluation, for several reasons. First, because it tends to focus on the minutiae of the organisation, missing the big picture, and, second, because it tends to be reactive, rather than proactive, perhaps undertaken in a context of panic as a knee-jerk reaction rather than as thoughtful reflection. In such a context creative thinking can also be stifled.

Thus, such writers advise that the best time to monitor or evaluate an organisation or project is when things are going well. In a relaxed context, it is argued, evaluation can consider the options in a thoughtful way, focusing both on what can be learnt from the past and what is innovative for the future. There is no pressure to defend past actions or focus on why things went wrong. The idea of taking stock and developing in new directions when things seem to be going well is championed by Handy (1994), who argues that we should start rethinking and reorienting directions before our organisation reaches its peak and before enthusiasm for a program or project peters out. Wadsworth (1997) reviews the different times at which evaluation can take place and argues for the development of a **culture of evaluation**, whereby evaluation is integrated into our everyday activities.

A culture of evaluation

Wadsworth espouses the value of seeing evaluation as a natural element of ordinary daily activities, and building a culture of evaluation, with continual cycles of reflection and clarification. She comments:

> The better we are at daily informal reflection and the more of us that do it, the better we will – as part of the group and the services we work with – be able to think clearly about the value of what we are doing and wanting to do it collectively (Wadsworth, 1991:47).

A culture of evaluation involves working up hunches, trying out ideas and modifying them, observing and listening. It involves asking the questions: What are we trying to do here? What is making me feel uneasy here? In community development, researchers, whether they are members of the community or brought in from outside, should ensure that information is shared by all those involved in a project and options for transformation are clarified.

Open enquiry and audit review

In chapter 5 we noted the audit approach to evaluation. It is now time to discuss in more detail the difference between the **open enquiry** and **audit review** approaches to evaluation. Wadsworth (1997) describes how the open enquiry approach probes practices in order to extract assumptions and intentions. This approach can open up new formulations and new ways of thinking about what an organisation wishes to achieve. It contrasts with the closed nature of the audit review, whereby the failure to achieve objectives can become a problem to be solved rather than an opportunity to challenge original objectives and think in new ways. The open enquiry approach to evaluation can also be linked with the constructionist approach to research in general. Wadsworth argues for what she calls the 'grounded or naturalistic' approach to evaluation. This involves 'finding out about the meanings that are real to people'. With this approach, we 'check carefully for what we are hearing – not assuming too quickly that we understand' (Wadsworth 1997:16). Marsden and Oakley (1995) point to the importance of using evaluation as a way of challenging existing interpretations, arguing that the interpretative approach to evaluation assumes that truth is relative and that evaluations are fundamentally about control over direction and resources.

The audit review

In the audit review approach, evaluation research begins when we notice a discrepancy between what we expected and what actually occurred (Wadsworth, 1997). The research process consists of reflecting on this discrepancy, talking about why it happened, and deciding what to do about it. For example, an audit evaluation includes considering whether an expectation or objective was inappropriate in the first place, and clarifying the values that underlie the objectives and strategies. The audit review usually begins with the questions:

- What did we set out to achieve?
- Did we achieve these objectives?
- What are the signs that we achieved what we set out to do?

    The review then proceeds to another set of questions:

- What are we not doing (that we could do or would have liked to have done)?
- What are we doing that we should not be doing?

    The open enquiry approach proceeds by posing problems. It starts with the questions:

- How are we going?
- How is this group going?

- Are things working well? In what ways?
- What is the value of what we are doing?
- What are the signs of things working well or not working well?
- How could we improve things?
- What could we do better?
- How could we do more of what we are doing right? (Wadsworth, 1997:34)

In community organisations much of the evaluation, particularly evaluation initiated by government, continues to use the audit review approach.

Performance review

Official audit reviews often take the form of a **performance review**. In community services, a performance review is an assessment of programs in terms of whether they meet their objectives and how they can be improved. Like all audit reviews, performance reviews focus on the questions: What were our objectives? How far did we achieve these objectives and why? What could we do to improve the objectives and/or achievement of the objectives?

Performance reviews are generally based on **performance indicators** that measure the degree of achievement of objectives. For example, suppose the objective of a community education course is to increase the English skills of migrants of non-English-speaking backgrounds. A performance indicator is the percentage of people who successfully complete the course. Both the percentage and the phrase 'successfully complete a course' need further definition. The percentage might be set at 80 per cent of enrolment and 'successful completion' could mean, for example, obtaining a pass in a test at the end of a course. Thus, the performance goal is that at least 80 per cent of people who enrol in the course pass the test. The performance review would examine the actual success rate to see whether the performance goal had been met and usually it would suggest a course of action to reduce future discrepancies between expectation and actuality.

Performance is generally assessed in the following terms:

- *appropriateness:* provides the best way of achieving the desired objective
- *efficiency:* makes good use of time and resources to achieve the objective
- *effectiveness:* the degree to which the objective is actually achieved.

Thus from the point of view of many funding organisations, performance reviews measure efficiency: how time, resources and money are used. They do not consider whether communities are actually better off as a result of a program.

Community organisations accept the need to review and evaluate programs in the context of objectives. However, there are concerns about the simplistic and often technocratic approach to performance measurement and evaluation, particularly by government departments. For example, a community organisation can identify the number of referrals it receives in a week or the number of people attending programs, but such figures may not really reflect the organisation's effectiveness. It is difficult to measure the effects of programs in terms of, for example, a suicide that did *not* happen.

The tasks of community development are complex and interrelated, but performance indicators require them to be broken down into simple measurable activities. When performance review is controlled by bureaucrats for auditing purposes, there is a tendency for community organisations to respond defensively. They may, for example, hide weaknesses for fear of losing funding, rather than identifying the weaknesses and responding creatively and productively.

Criticisms of evaluation

It would be fair to say that alongside the continuing interest in evaluation there is also continuing criticism of the approaches to and uses of evaluation reports. The major thrust of the criticism has been directed at the use of evaluation as a form of control. For example, House (1990:19) has commented:

> Two major problems currently confront evaluation practice. First, evaluation is being used more and more as an instrument of control and accountability by increasingly centralized and hierarchical government authorities; and second, the extensive use of evaluation activities inside the bureaucracies means that evaluation activities are removed from public and peer scrutiny and increasingly subject to the pressures that exist within those organisations. Given these two trends, the possibility exists that evaluations can be used as an instrument for control rather than as a means of democratic enlightenment.

A similar line of critique as that of the preoccupation with evaluation is located in the analysis of contemporary forms of audit. For example, according to Power (1997), contemporary societies are investing more and more in 'an industry of checking'. This checking is part of an administrative style of control, based on the formal scrutiny of 'audit'. However, for Power, the value and effectiveness of the 'audit principle' is questionable. The logic of evaluation can be located in the context of an approach to 'doing things' that we identify in this book as instrumental rationality and technocratic consciousness, in which social issues and problems become technical concerns, and political and moral terms of reference are hollowed out. In the narrow instrumental terms of reference, programs, justifications or critiques of programs tend to be valued only on the basis of efficiency and productivity, which become ends in themselves. All these concerns are important, particularly when one thinks about evaluation from a community development perspective.

In concluding this section, we should add one final word on social research. As indicated above, any form of social research, when undertaken from a community development perspective, can open up new ways of seeing things. It can reveal injustices and discrepancies and it can raise the consciousness of members of a community. When it is participatory and based on action, it can help to emancipate and empower people. Evaluation can provide an honest appraisal of what is going on in a particular practice, organisation or process; it can throw light on where things are going right and wrong; and it can establish a basis for thinking about how things could be improved. However, social research can also be top-down – it can be looking for problems, or deficits. It can be used as a tool for the powerful, for example, by making the 'subjects' of research feel uncomfortable or inferior. Community development practitioners should always think carefully before undertaking research. They should consider why the research needs to be done, who is doing it, who is owning it and how it will be done. Once a decision is made to undertake a research project, every effort should be made to ensure that the processes are rigorous and the research is undertaken with integrity.

Summary points

- Community organisations are under increasing pressure to prove their effectiveness, relevance and efficiency.
- Community development projects are primarily accountable to the communities they serve.
- Community projects and organisations draw on different sources of funds.
- A number of issues are involved in funding arrangements for community organisations, including how much energy to expend getting overall funding, short timelines, insufficient funds, the use of unpaid labour, the weakness of community organisations in relation to funding bodies, and the issue of compromising activism to ensure funding.
- Preparing submissions is an important part of community development work for the purposes of influencing funding bodies, lobbying, researching and liaising with media, as well as articulating aims, objectives and strategies. It is necessary to know how to write submissions.
- Service agreements and funding agreements require a new approach to submissions in community organisations. There is some ambivalence among community development workers about the value of service agreements to the community.
- Funding arrangements between funding bodies and community organisations are increasingly structured and negotiated on the basis of formal contracts.
- Contracts usually take the form of detailed service or funding agreements between the funding body and the funded community organisation.
- Alongside the introduction of contractual arrangements has been the policy of using a competitive tendering process to choose which community organisations will be funded to deliver programs and projects.
- The Productivity Commission's report *Contribution of the Not-for-Profit Sector* acknowledges that the regulatory framework for the sector is costly for not-for-profit organisations.
- Research involves the collection and interpretation of information.
- Community development workers should know about the various approaches and methods in social research and the theories that underpin them.
- Identification of community assets and needs is an important activity in community development work.
- There is increasing pressure on community organisations to evaluate their programs. Community development workers should understand the ways of evaluating projects and programs, and issues in evaluation.

Processes and practices

Key terms

- action research
- audit review
- benchmarking
- best practice
- business plan
- citizen-directed taxation
- community assets research
- community foundations
- community needs studies
- comparative need
- competitive tenders
- constructionism
- critical reference group
- culture of evaluation
- epistemology
- ethical investment
- evaluation research
- expressed needs
- felt needs
- future visions workshop
- healthy visions
- methodology
- LETS
- metrics
- microcredit
- mistake of causality
- needs assessment
- needs identification
- needs-based planning
- normative needs
- objectivism
- open enquiry
- performance indicators
- performance review
- philanthropic trusts
- qualitative research
- quality assurance
- quantitative research
- sampling
- service agreement
- submission-based funding
- tender briefs
- tender specifications
- tenderer
- tenderor
- Tobin Tax
- triangulation
- unit price

Exercises

1. What are some the meanings of accountability today and why is accountability important?
2. Describe major forms of funding for community organisations.
3. List some of the main funding issues faced by community development workers.
4. Describe the forms of self-funding and list some of the strengths and weaknesses in self-funding.
5. List some of the factors that a philanthropic organisation has to consider when it is distributing funds.
6. List the major ways that governments in Australia allocate funds.
7. Make a checklist of factors you should consider when writing a submission.
8. What are service agreements and funding agreements? How can these affect community development?
9. What are the principles underpinning competitive tendering? How does competitive tendering affect community development work?
10. Make a checklist of factors you should consider when writing a tender.
11. Identify three situations in which a community development practitioner would be required to undertake research.
12. What are some of the key issues in research from a community development perspective?
13. What is an assets inventory and a community needs study and why are such studies important for community development work?
14. What are some of the choices in approach and method that a community development practitioner makes when undertaking an evaluation?
15. Referring to the case studies 'Scenes from history', 'Peake Estate project' and 'Funding government programs', identify some of the challenges for community development practitioners in obtaining funds.

16 Identify the elements of participatory research evident in the case study 'West Bay community plan'.

Further reading

Anheier, H & Leat, D (2002) *From Charity to Creativity: Philanthropic Foundations in the 21st Century. Perspectives from Britain and Beyond*. Comedia The Round, Bournes Green.

Booth, W, Colomb, G & Williams, J (2003) *The Craft of Research*, 2nd edn. The University of Chicago Press, Chicago and London.

Bulmer, M (ed.) (1984) *Sociological Research Methods*. Macmillan, London.

Crotty, M (1998) *The Foundations of Social Research: Meaning and Perspective in the Research Process*. Allen & Unwin, St Leonards.

David, M & Sutton, S (2004) *Social Research: The Basics*, Sage, London.

de Vaus, DA (1985) *Surveys in Social Research*. Allen & Unwin, Sydney.

Fraser, N (1989) *Unruly Practices: Power, Discourse and Gender in Contemporary Social Theory*. University of Minnesota Press, Minneapolis.

Ife, J (2002) *Community Development: Community-based Alternatives in an Age of Globalisation*, 2nd edn. Pearson Education, Frenchs Forest.

Kettner, PM et al. (1990) *Designing and Managing Programs: An Effectiveness-based Approach*. Sage, London.

Lyons, M (2001) *Third Sector*. Allen & Unwin, Crows Nest, NSW.

Marsden, D & Oakley, P (1990) *Evaluating Social Development Projects*. Oxfam, Oxford.

McGuire, L (1997) 'Service delivery contracts: quality for customers, clients and citizens', in G Davis, B Sullivan and A Yeatman, *The New Contractualism*. Macmillan, South Melbourne, pp. 102–18.

McNiff, J & Whitehead, J (2009) *Doing and Writing Action Research*, Sage, London.

Payne, G & Payne, J (2004) *Key Concepts in Social Research*. Sage, London.

Power, M (1997) *The Audit Society*. Oxford University Press, Oxford.

Productivity Commission (2010) *Contribution of the Not-for-Profit Sector,* Productivity Commission Research Report, Australian Government, Canberra.

Rubin, F (1995) *A Basic Guide to Evaluation for Development Workers*. Oxfam, Oxford.

Stewart, C & Cash, W (1994) *Interviewing Principles and Practices*. Brown & Benchmark, Madison, Wisconsin.

Tandon, R (1990) 'Partnership in social development evaluation: thematic paper', in D Marsden and P Oakley, *Evaluating Social Development Projects*. Oxfam, Oxford, pp. 96–101.

Timmons, G (1992) 'Philanthropic trusts: the 10 most asked questions', *Community Quarterly*, No. 23, pp. 17–21.

Tobin, J (1994) 'A tax on international currency transactions', *UNDP Human Development Report,* 1994. Oxford University Press, New York.

Wadsworth, Y (1997) *Everyday Evaluation on the Run*, 2nd edn. Allen & Unwin, Sydney.

Williams, M (2003) *Making Sense of Social Research*. Sage, London.

Wilson, K (1996) 'Demystifying the tendering process', *Community Quarterly*, No. 42, pp. 44–7.

Processes and practices

Weblinks

Funding and research for community organisations

www.community.gov.au/Internet/MFMC/community.nsf/pages/
    section?opendocument&Section=Funding%20and%20Grants
www.ourcommunity.com.au/funding/funding_main.jsp
www.aph.gov.au/library/intguide/sp/spgrants.htm
www.philanthropy.org.au/seekfund/index.html
www.fahcsia.gov.au/sa/families/pubs/SFCSevaluation/sfsc-toolkit/Pages/default.aspx
www.pilch.org.au/
www.grantslink.gov.au/
www.terena.org/publications/files/TERENA-brochure.pdf

Levels of funding provided by trusts and foundations in Australia

www.philanthropy.org.au/research/faq.html#restrfdn
http://philanthropywiki.org.au/index.php/Giving_In_Australia.

Grameen Bank

www.grameen-info.org/

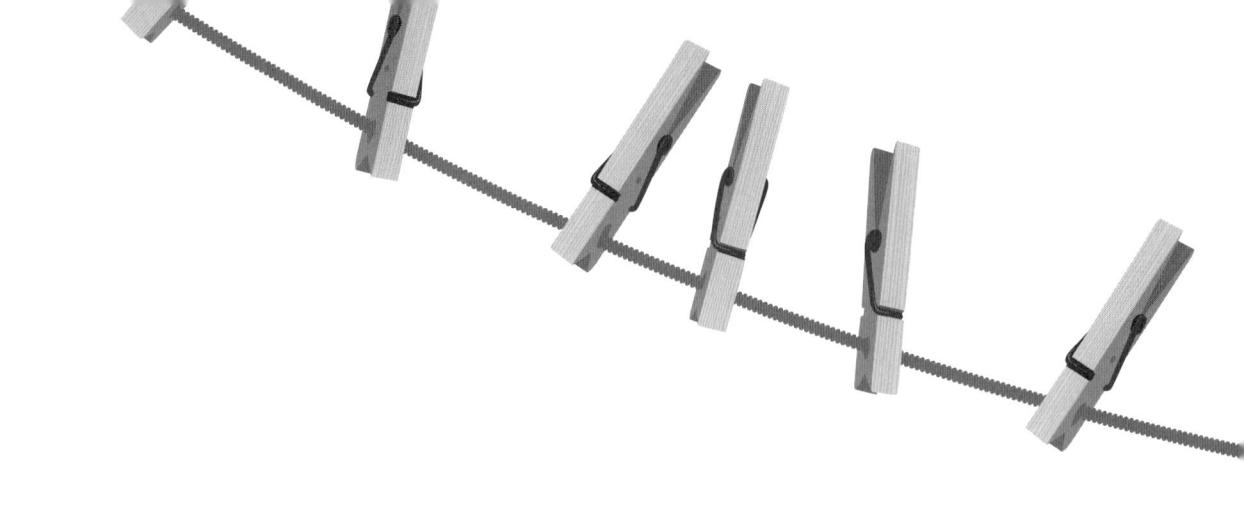

PART 3

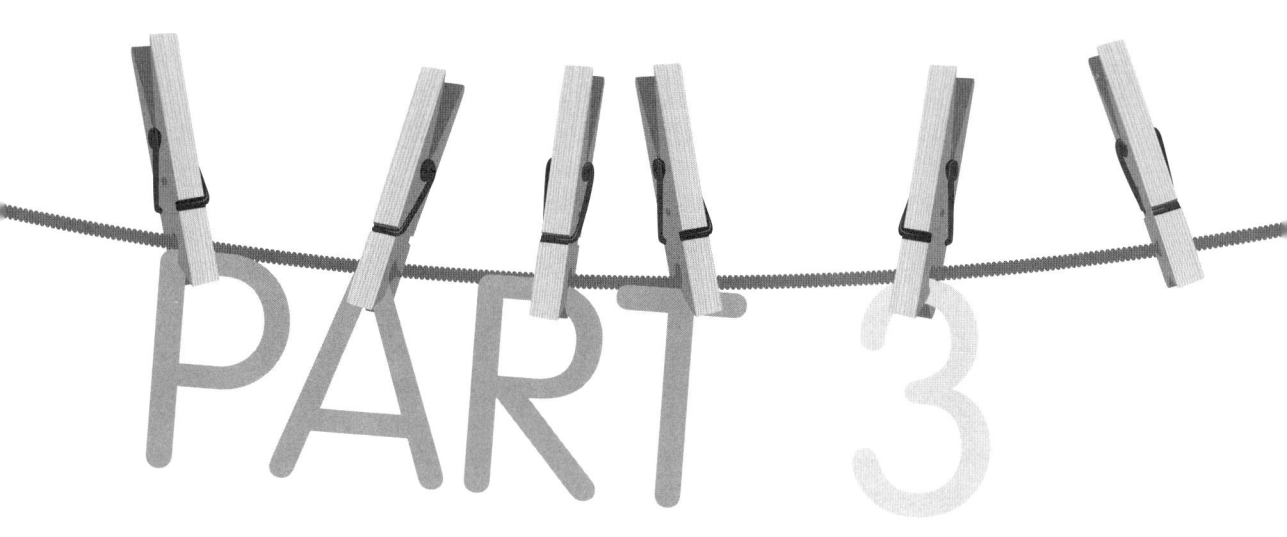

Contradictions

| **Chapter 10** | Difficulties and dilemmas | 398 |
| **Chapter 11** | Challenges for the twenty-first century | 424 |

CHAPTER 10

Difficulties and dilemmas

Overview

In this chapter we consider key difficulties and dilemmas in community development. We open the chapter with a comment on the idea of orthodoxy and we consider and critique the idea of 'pure' community development. The chapter proceeds to consider a number of tensions in community development practices, including contradictory expectations of community development practitioners, professionalism versus activism, freedom versus equality, nostalgia versus avant-gardism, facilitator or leader and freedom versus equality. We reflect on the issue of parochialism and how community development practitioners often overlook the power differentials in their work. The challenges of engagement with the state follow. Some of the critiques of community development practice, including co-option and exploitation of the community are noted. Ambiguities of globalisation are discussed, followed by a note on concerns about fundamentalism. The chapter concludes with discussion of how to deal with the pressures of everyday practice.

Introduction

In this book we have argued that community development comprises a challenging set of ideas, principles and practices. It requires an understanding of shifting contexts, engagement at different levels of society, dealing with dilemmas, maintaining flexibility, and at times making unpalatable choices and compromising. Community development operates in the context of both constraining and facilitating factors. These have led to some soul-searching on such questions as: What is a successful community development program? At what point am I not effective? How far should I compromise? There are no clear-cut answers to these questions. However, an important starting point is critical reflection, particularly in regard to our own assumptions and orthodoxies. We begin with a discussion of the orthodoxy of 'pure' community development.

'Pure' community development

Perhaps the most obvious of the orthodoxies of community development is the idea that we can draw a boundary around certain practices and motivations and call those falling within the boundary pure, real or genuine community development. 'Pure' community development is evidenced when a community development worker refuses to work collaboratively with welfare workers involved in individual counselling or with a government department that provides financial support on the proviso that in addition to community development activities, funds are used to train young people for work. The idea of **'pure' community development** raises some tricky political, theoretical and practical issues. In its strongest form it sets community development within a framework of moral certainty, where right and wrong are always easy to identify. This approach can be linked with what Miller (2004a:200) identifies as the **heroic school of community organising**. It is tempting to adopt the heroic approach. Yet there are difficulties. Attitudinally, heroic community development can slide into self-righteousness and self-legitimating discourses, eroding the humility needed for the mutuality and trust underpinning community development. Humility is also important in the light of the experiences of failings of community projects and community organisations. As DeMars (2005:2) points out, while community organisations do sometimes achieve more than expected, they frequently achieve much less. The ambitious claim that citizen empowerment primarily comes about through involvement in community organisations is betrayed by research undertaken by Demos in the United Kingdom (Leighton, 2009), which reveals that empowerment is linked to education and occupation, just as much as to local participation. In a practical and political sense there is the problem of who decides on what belongs in the category of 'pure'. Political history is full of claims for pure or authentic practice that are used as a way of keeping critics and challengers at bay.

Yet, of course, sensitivity to the issues involved in designating certain practices and motivations as 'pure' community development does not mean that we should reject all ideas of boundaries and slide into postmodern relativism, in which the core commitments of community development ultimately evaporate. The position taken in this book is to be wary of claims by people that they are practising 'pure' community development. However, as we have also discussed in this book, some core commitments are essential to community development work:

- the collective empowerment of communities to be able to identify and develop the assets they have, and to be able to make informed and deliberative decisions about the issues that affect them, their problems as they see them and how they wish to resolve them
- the resourcing of communities in such a way that they have real options for the control of their future
- community development practitioners and activists work to ensure that empowerment means that their role becomes redundant.

These commitments can be manifested in many ways and situations. A response that attempts to steer a path between the idea of a unitary 'pure' community development and an 'anything goes' relativism is to identify different models or types of community development. That is, while there are distinct values, principles and goals that underpin all community development, there are different ways of achieving the goals. For example, Miller (2010) notes the disagreements regarding strategies for advancing the cause of social justice. He identifies a divide between those who adopt a community organisation or action model, based on the view that change occurs only through conflict, and those concerned with community building, based on ideas of consensus building and social inclusion. Further, he warns that without an understanding of the realpolitik, such competing strategies are in danger of being reduced to little more than rhetoric.

Other commentators note the problematic influence of neo-liberalism on community development strategies (Geoghegan & Powell, 2009), which we can see in the engagement of community development in contractual social service work and the adoption of neo-liberal-based social entrepreneurship. Then there is the form of community development that keeps faith with a naive communitarianism: it focuses optimistically on the power of a community based on mutuality, trust and security, with good social capital to undertake community development projects (Geoghegan & Powell, 2009). Community strengthening, community building and neighbourhood renewal programs invoke this kind of community development.

There is continuing commitment to the idea that community development is, first and foremost, an activist pursuit, that offers a public space and practices whereby ordinary people can collectively source different kinds of information, obtain knowledge, debate ideas and options, resist domination and challenge neo-liberalism (Geoghegan & Powell, 2009). Finally, there is the view that the old notion of community development organised around the quest for the secure community – whether it be in the form of trusting and harmonious social relationships, or in the newer pursuits of the Transition Towns movement – is misguided, because we have moved beyond the possibility of living all our lives in self-contained local communities and any simple communitarian view of how the world should work. From this viewpoint, in its place we need a type of community development that has broken out of the narrow confines of localist endeavour and the nostalgic search for the secure, homogenous and harmonious community. We can identify this model of community development as the cosmopolitan model. Cosmopolitan community development does not aspire to be pure. It begins by accepting that there are common principles in community development, but we must also validate difference and embrace different ways of 'doing things'. Cosmopolitan community development is based on the view that we must understand that humans share a collective future (Beck, 2006).

Of course, what these different approaches indicate is that, as practised, community development has many faces. Several of the approaches discussed above might be operational in one project. Moreover, as a living pursuit, community development is continually changing. Of course, whatever view or approach is taken, we need to subject our practices, motivations and principles to critical scrutiny, probing for their continuing relevance and, of course, all the time keeping a judicious eye out for the pretensions of gatekeeping.

Contradictory themes and expectations

While some community development workers see claims for 'pure' community development to be a key issue, others have focused on the difficulty of working in a context in which there are different expectations of what they could and should do; for example, when the models of work require different attitudes and practices. A persistent concern of those working in community programs is how to deal with the inconsistent requirements of their work and the shifting contexts in which they operate. Many practitioners are trying to make sense of the daily frustrations and dilemmas arising out of contradictory aims and practices in their organisations. For example, on one hand, community development workers are told that good community development requires change, innovation and creativity, while on the other hand they are required to bureaucratically account for all their actions in auditing regimes. Workers in long-standing activist organisations have commented that more and more time is spent on paperwork, whether it be in terms of financial reporting requirements for local government, monitoring and evaluation requirements for international aid agencies or democratic accountability procedures required by membership organisations. These reporting requirements mean less and less time for social action. Tensions arise when workers involved in advocacy work have to do more and more service provision as agents of government in order to subsidise their major commitment to work on activist issues.

The 'professionalisation' of community service work also impacts upon community development workers. Although lip-service is paid to the value of working organically, and the contributions of unpaid workers or volunteers, in practice there is a strong 'credentiallist creep' whereby those with formal educational qualifications, rather than the grassroots representatives, are the ones listened to and offered paid work. In this chapter we discuss some of these tensions. We present them as they are presented in everyday work: namely as binary opposites. However, this does not preclude workers practising what might be seen as incompatible activities together, at the same time.

Activism versus professionalism

The discussion above leads us to the question of whether professionalisation, in the sense of a formal qualification, a commitment to a profession or expected level of competency, undermines the activist drive of community development. In their everyday work, community development workers are cautioned against too much action without analysis, which becomes mindless action, and too much analysis without action, which is paralysing. Three notions of community activism are implicit in the debate.

- First is the notion of the activist as organic grassroots organiser who has developed as a natural leader – or as Alinsky (1972) puts it, native leader – in a community. This person may or may not be in some kind of paid position as a community worker, and does not identify as a professional in the traditional sense. Those who support the view that 'real' community work can only be carried out by grassroots activists assume that activism is incompatible with training, qualifications and professionalism. An activist community development worker derives power from organisational knowledge and networking skills, rather than from credentials.
- Second is the radical activist who comes from outside the community, who identifies as a political activist but depends on work in another occupation; that is, radicalism is undertaken outside employment. This position holds that radical activism and professional community development work do not mix.
- Third is that community activism and professionalism are compatible, although working in institutions with outside funding can restrict the extent of activism. This is the prevailing view in Australia today.

  The dilemma of activism versus professionalism is evident in the follow case study.

Contradictions

> **case study**
>
> ### YALBANI COMMITTEE OF MANAGEMENT
>
> The setting is a meeting of the committee of management of the Yalbani Youth Centre. There is a lively debate in the meeting about the appointment of a new person as coordinator of the centre. The majority of members of the management committee are young people themselves and they are seeking a person who will maintain the high standing of the Yalbani Youth Centre in the community, while at the same time will challenge the reactionary and racist views of some of the local authorities.
>
> The meeting is almost equally divided between those who support John, an applicant from outside the area, who has a university degree in multimedia, has made an acclaimed film with young people and is halfway through a law degree, and those who support Pete, who has lived all his life in the area and is known and respected by local young people. Two years ago, Pete was involved in a sit-in at the local school where a teacher had been reprimanded for his racist attitudes and practices. The pupils had had enough, and demanded that the school 'get rid of him'. They were successful in their demand. Pete had picked up a bit of a reputation then as someone not to be taken lightly.
>
> In answer to the question of how he would deal with accusations of police harassment of local Indigenous young people, John responded that he would 'play it by the book'. He would organise a delegation to meet with the police and present facts and figures. He would show the young people's perspectives through a human rights documentary made by young people. He would ensure that the 'good name' of the centre in the community would continue, through teaching local young people to write their own column in the local newspaper and to produce professional-looking brochures. John has worked with young people before, and has a good track record in facilitation. For example, he had been successful in saving a youth centre from threat of closure.
>
> In contrast, Pete, in answer to the question about police harassment, replied, 'There's been lots of talk and it's got us nowhere'. For Pete it was now time to confront the police in a more assertive way; for example, by getting the local media on side, by using Facebook and Twitter and, if necessary, by organising protest action. He commented that he might not have any degrees, but 'I've certainly got the respect of much of the community for my forthright approach and my organising skills. I can certainly get things done'. In this case, it was Peter who got the job.

In this case study, the applicants offered different approaches to the job. There is no definitive answer as to who is the 'best' candidate, because this depends on the priorities at the time.

Freedom versus equality

As part of the left tradition, community development is committed to increasing equality in terms of access to resources, information and opportunity, and to freedom, in terms of choice and diversity. Yet one of the arguments that runs throughout political philosophy is that freedom and equality are contradictory precepts. While it is beyond the scope of this book to enter this complex philosophical debate, it is important to identify the dimensions that relate to community development. From the Right comes the view that attempts to bring about equality undermine freedom. For example, any government that promotes equality must redistribute resources; this impinges on the freedom of those who own the disproportionate resources by taking resources away from them. There are contradictions within the concept of freedom. It is obvious that the complete freedom of one individual impinges on the complete freedom of another. However, thinking about this apparent contradiction depends on how one understands both equality and freedom. For example, without equality of access to resources and opportunities, freedom is not possible. That is, freedom depends on equality in access to resources; it requires the redistribution of resources based on the principle of social justice, so that people can have real choices in their lives. And in the context of a development perspective, Sen (1999) argues that freedom is both constitutive of development and instrumental to it: instrumental freedoms include and require political freedom, economic resources and social opportunities. From this perspective, the issue is a paradox rather than an irreconcilable contradiction.

Nostalgia versus avant-garde

In chapter 2 we discussed how the nostalgic yearning for the traditional gemeinschaft notion of community is a burden when it drives community development activities. As Bauman (2001) contends, this 'feel good' community is an imaginary place, a 'paradise lost', that we construct because of our insecurity and need for comfort. Indeed in the 1980s, Bryson and Mowbray (1981) argued that the idea of community operates as a false elixir for social problems. The quest for the soothing community also diverts attention away from the dark side of security and comfort, the side that is fearful of difference and undermines the possibilities for a new cosmopolitan culture. This dark community is one where trust of strangers is eroded. It is, according to Bauman (2001:4), a place where we do not let strangers in and where we abstain from 'acting strangely' and 'thinking odd thoughts'. Yet this pursuit of a 'paradise lost' is still evident in some community building projects and in localist practices (Connors & McDonald, 2010; Mowbray, 2004).

In the light of all the critiques of the homogenous, stable and secure community, it would seem wise to embrace the world of change, uncertainty and fluidity (Bauman, 2001, 2000). Yet the brave new world of independently minded, floating community development activists is not without its own problems. In our discussion of Reich's symbolic analysts in chapter 5, we reflected on how elite symbolic analysts lose their roots and no longer feel any empathy with the people still operating within the confines of more traditional communities. But there is another problem with the instruction to live with uncertainty and embrace change. This is that we can become so enchanted with change that we will adopt any new trend and accept uncritically the new spin or jargon. The avant-garde can be just as hollow as the nostalgia for 'lost' community. If community development is to be able to sustain its energy, both avant-gardism, when it adopts every new trend for its own sake, and nostalgia for lost community should be avoided.

Localism as parochialism

Localism refers to small-scale interchanges, usually within certain limited spaces. In community development, 'local' continues to be bestowed with a positive connotation and there are good reasons for this. Local activities and exchanges are flexible, responsive and manageable. Local knowledge is often more useful and authentic than the knowledge of outsiders, especially in the context of social research (participatory action research, for example). The idea of 'local' is often contrasted favourably with 'global', or more specifically with globalisation. Yet, like its conceptual cousin 'community', local is not necessarily more enlightened than global. Local can consist of an inward-looking or myopic approach to the world. Local can be authoritarian and based on patronage, and as with 'community', the term 'local' tends to homogenise the types of relations within it, thus concealing internal differences and conflict (Mowbray, 1984; Repo, 1977). Localism can also have nostalgic effects. The yearnings for an unreconstructed notion of traditional community can promote parochial and reactionary politics. Doyal and Gough (1991:308–9) remind us that

> any local, community-based, small-scale form of need-satisfaction can foster 'insider' conceptions of human need and inhibit the growth of generalisable notions based on a wider collective identity. The politics of empowerment can mean accepting a variety of racist and sexist policies, or schemes which discriminate against outsiders. Provision by and for different communities can blind people to the common needs they share with others and monitoring is needed to ensure that serious harm does not result from too much emphasis being placed on the perceptions and preferences of particular groups.

A focus on the local can be out of touch with the increasingly global nature of the culture in which we live. For example, it can direct attention away from understanding the macro-contexts of inequalities. When it is privileged over the global, it can undercut the possibility of cosmopolitan culture and global solidarity in fighting oppression and human rights abuses.

Responses to parochialism

There are several responses to parochialism in community development practice.

- Community development workers must be sensitive to tendencies to ignore other communities and other ways of thinking and to ostracise people from different backgrounds, those who think differently and those who do not want to be involved in community affairs. The role of community development is to ensure that if and when members of a community want to become involved they can, and to be ready to offer alternative views and information when requested.
- Although we live in an increasingly global world, local power structures are not insignificant. The practice of prefigurative politics is important and the adage 'think global, act local' is still relevant.
- As we saw in the discussion of community needs studies in chapter 9, it is important to accept the existing relations and viewpoints of ordinary people (element of authenticity), to ensure access to information and ways of understanding it (element of information) and to offer different visions and different practices to transform knowledge and lived relations.

- It is important to remember that people are never completely preoccupied with the local. They are more likely to hold mixed or contradictory values in which they simultaneously endorse and reject parochial views (see Abercrombie, Hill & Turner, 1980).
- When community development workers disagree with the views of a community, they should state and explain their position. Some, when confronted with prejudice and discrimination in a community, refer to the Universal Declaration of Human Rights (see the Appendix). In the last instance, a community development worker who is unable to accept the views that prevail in the community (for example, on a matter of racial discrimination) should withdraw from the particular project about which there is contention. This could happen, for example, when a worker perceives the community they are working with to be racist or when they cannot accept the treatment of women in a particular group. If there is continual disagreement over a range of programs and issues, then the community development worker should resign.

None of these responses to parochialism is perfectly satisfactory, but social and political life does not have perfect responses. The point remains, however, that in general it is necessary to begin any community development work accepting ordinary people as they are and trusting them. Those who cannot do this find community development practice difficult, if not impossible.

Forgetting about power

In their efforts to prove their value, legitimate their work, facilitate community harmony and secure funds, community development practitioners often overlook the hard question of power differentials. This happens in three ways. First, they overlook power differentials within a community and how people have different levels of confidence, arising from gender, class and ethnicity structures. Second is the sense of power differentials between communities, such as between poorer, marginalised communities and wealthier ones. Finally there are power differentials between government and communities and the corporate sector and communities. Many community-based programs, including those championing social inclusion, community strengthening and neighbourhood renewal, can deflect attention from these power differentials. Even the commitment to focusing on assets rather than on deficits in a community, in the asset-based approach to community development, glosses over issues of power. A questioning and probing approach to power and power differentials (a power lens) in all our transactions is one way to be reminded of power issues.

Forgetting the state

There is also the difficult issue of how far we should bypass the state in our community development activities. There are certainly good reasons to avoid the state where we can, particularly when there is a heavy burden of overregulation. In addition, community development places self-determination rather than passive top-down state welfare at the centre of its activities. However, self-determination can be practised as 'self-responsibilisation', whereby self-determination requires communities to find their own resources with little or no support from the state. This approach to self-determination is underpinned by the processes of individualisation, discussed in chapter 2. However, this does not necessarily mean that we can avoid the state altogether. An alternative way of engaging the state involves practising facilitated self-determination, whereby the state assists with resources and structures that give communities real choices in their planning and directions.

Democratic decision making

It is often argued that the community is the best site for democracy because it is in people's interests to come to a consensus about issues. In fact, consensus decision making has its own problems. Community organisations have been destroyed by failed participatory democracy, bitter infighting and paralysing conflicts. In focusing on democratic process at the expense of achieving a goal or winning a struggle, community organisations can get bogged down in destructive debates and meetings without decisions. Moreover, as Cochrane (1986) points out, we cannot just assume that decision making in communities is democratic. Decisions at the community level can be influenced by petty self-interest, bickering and jockeying for power. As suggested above, community affairs can be insular and parochial and this can make the community an inappropriate site for developing new forms of democracy. An ostensibly open, tolerant structure with free-ranging activities can enable the most articulate and active people in a community organisation to dominate and, as Keane (1988:22) puts it, 'enjoy the freedom to twist the arms of the weaker'. Decisions can be made on the basis of personal loyalties, without recourse to agreed processes for structured decision making.

Responses

There are a number of responses to these tensions in the relationship between community organisations and democracy. The first response is directed at the tension between the principle of democratic discussion and the necessity of getting things done. Even though, in the first instance, democratic decisions can take longer to make than decisions based on authoritarian principles, if all the parties affected by a decision or policy participate in its making, they are much more likely to accept it and work to make it effective. This is likely to result in long-term efficiency.

The second response is to refer to human history. While there is symmetry between community development and democracy today, we should not expect it to be all smooth sailing as we try to ensure that democratic ways of thinking permeate community organisations. Community development forms a part of political thinking that is trying to change the nature of social relations, if not the whole direction of society. It thus confronts structures, approaches, power relations and procedures, such as patriarchal ones, that have been entrenched throughout human history. The process of change is slow, contradictory and often bothersome. In this context, many community development workers have been overly optimistic about the efficacy of community development to create new social relations.

The third response is to accept that community development is full of conflict and dilemmas, but to reject that these are problematic. If the processes involve everyone having an equal say, and if conflict is dealt with openly and honestly, and all this takes more time because of open and democratic processes, so be it. The final response is to attempt to reconcile the principles of democracy, participation, consensus, diversity and tolerance of conflict with the demands of efficiency and effectiveness by weighing them up in particular situations. Such an approach characterises community development as the art of compromise.

Too much talk?

Can there be too much talking and theorising in community development? The answer is yes. While we have argued for a sound understanding of the theoretical underpinnings of community development, and the need for informed discussion, talking and theorising are certainly not substitutes for activity and action. This point is brought home only too clearly is times of post-disaster recovery. For example, in the aftermath of the Victorian bushfires in February 2009, it was often the armed forces, with their logistical skills and immediate access to resources such as tents and food, that were able to respond to the articulated needs of survivors. The brief of army personnel in such situations is to respond immediately to an emergency; their actions are rarely part of a long-term strategy, and not 'complicated' by lengthy discussion or complex development theory. What we learn from this experience is how community development practitioners need to have good strategic skills to be able to identify needs and choices and to be able to put these to the survivors in a clear way. A logistically feasible plan needs to be constructed quickly in such situations, and can be unnecessarily forestalled by too much discussion and 'consultation'.

Neo-liberalism and the mantra of competition

As discussed throughout this book, particularly important challenges have arisen out of the pervasiveness of neo-liberal thinking and practice over the past two decades. Drawing on Bauman's (1998) idea that civil society is like the 'agora' – originally a place for political assembly in Ancient Greece – Geoghegan and Powell (2009) argue that today the main enemy of civil society, and thus community development, is still neo-liberalism. They explain that this is because the neo-liberal world view holds that civil society should be subservient to the economy, or more specifically, to the development of capitalism. Geoghegan and Powell (2009) question how far community development can sit alongside neo-liberalism.

We have examined how neo-liberalism favours a competitive ethos that aims to ensure individual incentive and keep costs down. This preoccupation with cost and securing the cheapest programs has led to a focus on standardised programs, emphasising throughput and output at the expense of offering diverse programs, and ensuring that the principles of empowerment, social justice and human rights are maintained. Alongside the precepts of neo-liberalism, the adoption of new managerialism as a way of managing community and government organisations has meant that processes based on collective and democratic decision making have become difficult or impossible to implement.

Neo-liberal policies championing the effectiveness of competition have led to the process of competitive submissions and tenders in order to win contracts for funds to establish and run community programs. Contractual regimes stifle flexibility in programs because they narrowly circumscribe the scope and 'deliverables' of a project. As indicated earlier in this book, the practice of contracting-out has posed considerable dilemmas for community development organisations. As governments in Australia have embraced the principles of contracting-out and have shifted their funding mechanism to competitive submissions and tendering, community organisations are being forced to make decisions about whether they will participate in competitive tendering processes or face the possibility of losing government and other external funding altogether.

What factors influence such a decision? The first set of factors is concerned with the principles that underpin competition policy and the ideological context in which competitive tendering has been introduced. These factors engender profound difficulties for community development. Competition undermines collaboration and cooperation, sharing and trust as the normative principles of economic and social development. The second set of factors is concerned with whether competitive tendering offers any openings for community development practices. On one hand, the willingness of government departments to allow community organisations to run programs that might previously have run as entirely as in-house government operations has been welcomed by some community organisations, who have argued, for example, that their closeness to the grassroots can mean more responsive and less bureaucratic community programs. On the other hand, contracting-out means that communities are more obliged to take responsibility for any failures in the programs that they operate, even when there is less financial and other support from governments. Moreover, contracting-out does not necessarily mean that communities have more independence from government regulation and oversight, because governments still control the terms of reference of a community program – and the policy process in general.

The third set of factors relates to an empirical question. Regardless of the rhetoric and principles of competitive tendering, is there any evidence that establishing programs through competitive tendering is any better than previous ways of organising and distributing funds and programs? This is a complex question. To answer it fully we need to explain exactly what is meant by 'better' and to access reliable data. Within the framework of competition policy, 'better' means more productive, more efficient and a higher quality of service. But these terms have different meanings in different contexts.

For example, increasing productivity usually refers to some notion of producing more with the same, or even fewer, resources. In the framework of competitive submissions and tenders, productivity can be measured by counting the number of units produced or serviced, and relating this number to time and the resources used. The more units you produce or service, the higher the productivity. However, in the social and community services industry, in the case of a financial counselling program, for example, an indicator of the success of the program might be that a worker services fewer people because fewer people need financial counselling, perhaps because their past 'counselling' has been successful. That is, it could be that the more units (people) you see, the less successful is the program. Similarly, from a community development perspective, quality can be defined in terms not just of safeguards to ensure that certain quality assurance processes are adhered to, or that consumer satisfaction is guaranteed (as occurs in competitive tendering), but also in terms of flexible criteria that are set by the community itself and measured on the basis of the extent to which communities own and control the way that services are actually provided.

Additionally, when a community development worker spends a considerable amount of time in meetings and on the telephone, and there are no tangible outcomes, this may appear to be an inefficient use of time (the unit-cost output is not measurable). However, time spent networking and passing information to community members can pay off in times of stress and conflict in a community and when hard decisions have to be made about where to put resources, for example. When people have been part of the information sharing and have been involved in discussion and decision making, they are more likely to go along with the final (sometimes unpalatable) decisions, because they understand the issues. More time spent on discussion and consultation at the beginning of a conflict can be more efficient than quick decisive decision making that requires less time in the short run, but more time in the long term.

Performativity, competency and training

New managerialism has embedded an organisational culture that focuses on and rewards individual activity. In this culture, based on the performance of individuals – or performativity – managers and workers are constantly evaluated on the basis of how they carry out prescribed functions. For example, they are expected to produce 'results' and show initiative. Managers must drive an efficient and productive workforce. Their output should be measurable. A corollary to this approach to work has been the development of competency standards, whereby attitudes, aptitudes, skills and outputs for different jobs are broken down into specific tasks and ability to undertake such tasks is measured and evaluated. To ensure that tasks are fulfilled to the correct standard, professional training is required and there has been an explosion of training courses in the community sector over several decades. Indeed, a response to many of the challenges in undertaking community service work is the introduction of specific training programs for specific competencies. Mostly training programs are paid for and offered 'in-house', although many are explicitly commodified insofar as they are offered as fee-paying courses. As discussed in chapter 5, there are different forms of competency, some of which are problematic from a community development perspective.

But in the context of the community development principles of mutuality and shared knowledge, the idea that workers should meet competency standards constructed by external consultants, and that individuals should become credentialled through specific training programs, clearly challenges the bottom-up, holistic approach of community development. It is very difficult to take a collectivist stand in regard to performativity, individual competency and training. Some community development practitioners attempt to balance their effectiveness in their work by using what are called 'metrics' to measure their output (such as higher usage and satisfaction levels with recreational activities after the employment of a youth worker) with an emphasis on democratic process, rather than measurable output.

Compliance regimes

In chapter 2 we discussed the concept of risk society and the growth of regulatory power as a response to the focus on risk and risk management. More and more of the activities of community development practitioners are subjected to new **compliance regimes** of public policy and funding bodies. The establishment of compliance regimes is at the same time both a sign of the erosion of trust and an effective form of top-down control. Within a compliance culture we are required to accede to protocols, rules and regulations, often under the rationale of protecting us and our organisations against risk – or perhaps more accurately against litigation. Compliance is more or less guaranteed through quality assurance methods, and proof of our compliance is obtained through audits and evaluations.

The new compliance regimes are rarely challenged, because they are presented as a mechanism to guarantee transparency and accountability, and provide assurances that community organisations are not abusing the trust invested in them by communities. That is, there are sound reasons for requiring community organisations to put quality assurance mechanisms in place and subject themselves to audits and evaluations, and indeed for community development practitioners to spend an inordinate amount of their time preparing reports and ensuring that policies and practices comply with a wide range of regulations. However, as Power (1997:123) points out, the audit explosion is becoming 'an industry of empty comfort certificates'.

As suggested in chapter 6, the increasing power of compliance regimes (or what is sometimes known as the culture of compliance) is at odds with the injunction to be creative and innovative in conceiving and developing programs. In the context of the risk society, the compliance regime is an effective form of social control and presents a significant challenge to the flexibility required for community development work. Perhaps, most importantly, the new compliance regimes signal the development of a new strain of authoritarianism in Australian society.

Community development practitioners might respond to compliance regimes by posing the following questions: Where is the evidence of its efficacy? Does it ensure transparency? Do communities want the compliance regimes? Why are compliance regimes set in place by the powerful (funders and governments)? Who audits these auditors? What actually are the best mechanisms for transparency and multiple reciprocal accountabilities?

Co-option

Community development practitioners have to deal with three forms of co-option. First, there is the personal co-option that threatens when practitioners need the support of those in more powerful positions, for funding or policy changes, for example. They need to be legitimate in the terms of reference set by powerbrokers. A second related form of co-option occurs when the state contracts-out functions and service delivery to community organisations that then operate as service instruments of proxies for the state. For example, co-option can occur when practitioners work for or in partnership with high-powered government officials, or shift their prime accountability to their employers.

The third form of co-option that workers must deal with is more abstract. It involves understanding the differing interpretations of concepts that, on first sight, are located in the left community development tradition, such as citizenship, social capital, social entrepreneurship and even community. The meanings of these concepts change according to who is using them and the context in which they are used. That is, they can become **co-opted discourses**. Citizenship, for example, can be invoked to draw attention to human rights or, within the framework of obligation, to the one-way 'mutual obligation' of the unemployed to fulfil their constructed obligations to the state. Active citizenship can be invoked to refer to participation, opposition and resistance within the political process or, as in the case of many of the third way policy orientations, to refer to the need for citizens to take responsibility for finding and gaining employment. The 'to-ing and fro-ing' over meaning and ownership of these concepts, and others such as 'globalisation' and 'community', reveals the ways in which the processes of co-option and incorporation are taking place today.

Newspeak or spin

Concepts that form what is known as **newspeak or spin** are more clearly ideological in the sense that they distort and conceal critical understanding and experiences of reality. Several publications have identified these concepts and revealed how they can be used to control public perceptions. For example, Fairclough (2000) alerts us to how the Blair Labour government in Britain developed its own language, starting with the idea of 'new' Labour. Fairclough provides a list of Labour-preferred expressions, including the notion of 'public–private' in preference to the term 'privatisation', 'reform' rather than 'changing' or 'restructuring', and 'downsizing' or 'rationalisation' rather than 'sacking'. In Australia, Watson (2003) discusses the use of what he calls **weasel words**; that is, words that have had their meaning sucked out and are used to distort and confuse. They include such terms as 'enemies of the people' for political dissidents and 'free trade' (which is rarely open, free or equitable) to champion the promises of 'global capital'. Management-speak is full of 'weasel' cliches such as core values, stakeholders, deliverables, drivers and operational. Wheen (2004) identifies the new concepts as 'mumbo-jumbo' and places this language, and its lack of critical reflection, in the context of an attack upon the logic of reason and indeed the whole Enlightenment tradition. Wheen (2004:7) comments, 'The sleep of reason brings forth monsters, and the past two decades have produced monsters galore. Some are manifestly sinister, others seem merely comical'.

While we have always had these kinds of concepts, we seem to have more difficulty in demystifying them today.

The volunteering industry

A considerable amount of community development activity, whether it be organising a protest march, or sitting on a management committee, or responding to emails at a neighbourhood house, is only possible because of the dedicated work of unpaid workers, or volunteers. In chapter 6 we noted how volunteering can be understood as a way of bringing in unpaid workers to undertake jobs that should rightly be paid. However, during the last decade, acts of volunteering are no longer organised as small, quite casual forms of civic engagement. Volunteers need police checks and sometimes training. For example, many management committees now require members to have attended workshops on their legal responsibilities and training on risk assessment and insurance requirements. Volunteers are often managed by paid professionals. Young people and those looking for work are instructed to undertake unpaid or volunteer work as preparation for paid work, and because such activity 'looks good' on their curriculum vitae. We are seeing the construction of what might be described as a **volunteering industry**, involving courses for volunteers and paid professionals whose job it is to recruit, organise and manage volunteers. There is little that community development practitioners can do about the requirements of police checks, risk assessment and the legal obligations of management committees – and probably most would agree with such requirements anyway. However, the managerialist imperative in the volunteer industry is problematic for community development. It conceptualises volunteers and unpaid workers as subjects to be recruited and directed by expert managers as external helpers in a way that undercuts mutuality and collective endeavour.

Moral superiority of the oppressed

People who have been oppressed, disadvantaged, excluded and marginalised from the mainstream of society tend to have a special claim to authenticity, and even 'moral righteousness', that is not available to those whose lives have been in safe, secure environments. In community development, the disadvantaged and oppressed are the Other, whose life experiences give them valuable and special insights into the nature of the world. From the traditional Left, this view draws on the idea that the working class has an uncontaminated view of the world, because it has no vested interest in ideological manipulation that serves to support the status quo. As Marx and Engels (1967:120–1) stated, the working class, unlike the ruling class, 'have nothing to lose but their chains'. This view of the superiority of the oppressed, disadvantaged, excluded and marginalised rests on a class analysis. In contrast, another approach to the claim that the oppressed or disadvantaged have a special authenticity demands that they be respected and listened to. This approach is informed by constructs of ethnicity and race. In particular it is influenced by the idea of non-Europeans as the Other, who are not only different but also exotic, as noted in chapter 8.

While community development prioritises activities that address the need for equality and thus, first and foremost, champions the rights and needs of the oppressed and disadvantaged, practitioners should also be sensitive to tendencies to romanticise the people with whom they are working. It is important not to 'enshrine the poor' (see Alinsky, 1972) and anyone, including people who are oppressed, can hold backward-looking and paternalistic views (Croft & Beresford, 1984). Some people argue that empowerment has a dark side to it: people who have been oppressed are likely to be reactionary when they finally achieve some power. We must be cautious in bestowing upon the disadvantaged the role of historical agents who will pave the way for the establishment of the new society.

Moreover, there are some conceptual and strategic weaknesses in any approach to working with communities that prioritises the interests of certain groups on the grounds of their superior authenticity. First, it works on oversimplistic binary divides – of the authentic and the inauthentic, of the morally superior and morally inferior. Second, it also homogenises each side of this divide. It sees power and knowledge as a zero-sum game rather than something that occurs throughout society, involving a multiplicity of forms of domination. Third, in regard to the expectation that the oppressed and disadvantaged are the bearers of history, there remains debate about whether the search for a particular historical agent is misguided and whether identifying an ethnic group, gender or class as the agents of social change is strategically very important. Indeed, while people who are disadvantaged and oppressed can be differently informed, they are not necessarily better informed. As indicated above, they can have reactionary politics.

Culturalism

Linked to the need to be sensitive to the assumption of the moral superiority of the oppressed is the assumption of culturalism, first mentioned in chapter 8. Culturalism refers to the view that whatever happens in a community, if it is an authentic and traditional part of their culture, then an outsider has no right to criticise it. Culturalism often involves the privileging of traditional knowledge over 'imported' or foreign knowledge. However, the question arises as to whether culturalism applies in all situations. As discussed in this book, it is important that community development practitioners understand and acknowledge the integrity of other cultures and are able to respond appropriately to diverse cultural practices. Yet this does not mean that a community development worker must accept all cultural practices. In an informative discussion of culturalism, Ife (2001:68) comments:

> [Culturalism] is the assumption that if something is a cultural tradition this makes it above criticism and somehow sacrosanct. Culturalism reifies culture, and in effect allows the continuation of the most abusive and oppressive practices, all in the name of cultural integrity.

Culturalism often involves the privileging of traditional knowledge over new or hybrid knowledge. Ife (2001) points out that the culturalist position makes two false assumptions about culture: first, that cultures are static and, second, that they are monolithic. In fact, cultural traditions are both diverse and continually changing. The acceptance of another cultural tradition in the name of cultural sensitivity can ignore or even deny criticism within the 'other culture'. Of course the criticism of another culture can indeed be fraught with the problems of apparent patronisation and arrogance. Making a decision as a worker either to remain silent or to speak out when you disagree with practices in another culture can be really difficult. From a community development perspective, one way of dealing with this issue is to ask two questions: 'Are people in the other culture critical of this practice as well?' and 'Does the practice contravene human rights conventions (such as in the case of patriarchal practices that undermine the human rights of women)?'

Facilitator or leader?

We have stressed that community development workers facilitate rather than lead, that they are accountable to the community they are working with and for, and that they must ensure that members of the community speak for themselves in their own words and in their own terms of reference. We have also argued that community development workers should not construct themselves as the heroines and heroes of the community. Yet while it is all very well to talk about being accountable to the community, of making oneself redundant and not presenting oneself as a spokesperson, it is often difficult to do this in practice. Practitioners work in locations where people have been oppressed and repressed, often for generations, and they often find that members of the community expect them to take the initiative. They are expected to speak for the community, to chair meetings and to ensure that information is disseminated, for example. In fact, many of these tasks are part of the job description of a community development worker, as in the case of an advocacy worker.

How do community workers know when they have taken on the role of leader in the community rather than facilitator? If it happens, what can they do about it? There is no clear answer to these questions. However, if when a community development worker leaves a project it collapses, this might indicate that the worker had taken on too much leadership (yet it might also indicate that the project was misconceived). In addition, community development workers can be alert to ways that one can unconsciously take on leadership roles; for example, by talking on behalf of the community, by being the person to organise meetings, and by writing reports for the community (because it is easier and faster to do so). Yet speaking for others can undermine the confidence of less assertive people and deny them the option of setting their own agendas. The following case study is an example of a context where taking a leadership role is easier than being a facilitator.

HERRON CREEK COMMUNITY PLANNING PROJECT

Denise has just been informed that she is the successful candidate for a position as coordinator of a community planning project in a large country town. While she had been 'born and bred' in the town, she has spent the last 20 years as a community development worker in Uganda. One of the things that she has been really looking forward to, now that she is back in Australia, and in her own town, is that the structure of the program means that she can really be a facilitator. She is certainly known to the local people as 'one of them' and she assumes that she will have no difficulty standing back, and setting up the structures and processes for community-led initiatives. Before she begins the job, she walks around her old haunts to get to know the locals who live in the area today. She makes an appointment to speak to the current community development worker, who is taking early retirement. While the warm welcome Denise receives is very heartening, she is somewhat uneasy about what she hears. Margy, the retiring worker, confides that while she has tried to step back and encourage community control of local projects, this has been very difficult, because local people have been reluctant to take the lead. It has been much easier for Margy to do it all for them. 'I know I shouldn't have,' she says, 'but with all the pressures I've been under, it has been quicker for me to initiate programs, develop strategies and do all the planning myself. Where the community comes in is to check it all before I send it to council.' A similar picture emerges when Denise talks to community members. 'Margy has been an absolute gem in the community. Without her many of our projects would have collapsed,' they tell Denise. This scenario is not unique. With all the pressures on workers today, the temptation to take control when encouraged by communities is difficult to resist.

One way of thinking about this inclination to 'speak for' communities is to bring in the elements of authenticity, information and vision once again. The authenticity of people's experiences and views forms the basis of any engagement with community development. In order to make choices, people in a community need access to a wide range of relevant information about issues that concern them. Here the role of a community development worker is to provide this information. The element of vision requires the community to think about how things could be done differently. Here a skilled facilitator becomes important and the line between facilitator and leader becomes most blurred. The facilitator needs self-awareness and a self-questioning attitude.

Alinsky (1972) offers ways of thinking about this dilemma when he distinguishes between a leader and an organiser. Leaders go on to build and hold power for themselves to fulfil their desires, while organisers have as their goal the creation of power for others to hold. Similarly, Freire reminds us of the importance of community control of the definition of issues as the basis of transformation.

Exploiting the community

A community development worker's role is to empower ordinary people so that their job becomes redundant. Some critics point out that this principle is only token. Ironically, the strengthening of feelings of community, popular initiative and an increased rate of change rarely result in redundancy for community development workers. The strengthening of a community creates confidence and power, which enable community members to discover rights, clarify issues and identify new needs for community development work.

Some writers contend that special interest and lobby groups have infiltrated communities and community programs for their own purposes, and in so doing, have excluded 'real' consumers and the 'genuine' poor. Foreshadowing arguments put forward by the neo-liberal think tank, the Institute of Public Affairs, Browning (1990) argues that many self-styled public-interest pressure groups usurp and disempower ordinary consumers, rather than work on their behalf. His argument centres on the contention that some community groups falsely claim to have a mandate from the ordinary people to whom they are accountable. He claims that activists use this supposed mandate to their own advantage, surviving on government subsidies and taxpayers' money.

This argument is compatible with the views of Hayek (1960), who proposes that the power vested in government representatives leaves them open to blackmail by organised groups. Hayek regards this as a 'fatal defect' in liberal democracies. The neo-liberal view is that decisions about the distribution of resources should be decided by the market. This view ignores how the market is itself manipulated, and therefore also advantages some groups while it disadvantages and disempowers others.

It is true that some community groups are controlled by special interest groups, and that groups with more resources and 'pull' with politicians (through being able to employ lobbyists, for example) gain unfair advantage over groups that lack the resources. Indeed, this is an issue for community organisations. It is also true that some groups are dominated by a self-styled leader or spokesperson, and as discussed above, locating the line between leading and facilitation is difficult.

However, special interest groups and even self-styled leaders can have a mandate from participants in community organisations. They often champion minority interests, but these interests are not manufactured or distorted. The very existence of advocacy is based on the inequality of resource distribution in a society and results from the requests of oppressed groups and the need to present a case for those who are excluded from accessing resources.

Public-interest groups are not alone in receiving government subsidies: businesses and private entrepreneurs also receive public monies through such mechanisms as tax relief for superannuation contributions (see Bryson, 1989). Rather than imputing sinister motives to those involved in public-interest groups, it is pertinent to consider how far the needs of communities are tailored, reconstructed and deflected by community organisers and government bureaucrats because of resource constraints and political pressures.

In a way, Browning's logic is the same as the narrow Marxist instrumentalist view of the state as a tool of the bourgeoisie used against the interests of the working class. In Browning's argument, community organisations are tools of the Left, used to put pressure on the state to develop policies against the interests of capitalist enterprise. Both arguments miss the complexity and contradictory nature of relations between the state and civil society.

At various times, situations do come to light whereby members of community groups use funds for their own pecuniary interests. The evidence suggests that such cases are rare and, of course, we can find such examples in all institutions and in all occupations.

The ambiguities of globalisation

In chapter 2 we discussed different interpretations of globalisation and we considered how globalisation affects community development. As noted, the term 'globalisation' can refer to the tentacles of global capital, whereby large powerful corporations operate across different countries of the world, influencing the internal politics of nation states and setting agendas for capital and labour relations. The global financial crisis beginning in 2008 has negatively affected the incomes of ordinary people around the world, and yet the power of international capital has been left largely unscathed. On the other hand, communities have unprecedented access to knowledge of what's happening globally and many new globally connected communication tools and organising methods. Indeed, if globalisation is understood as referring to the multiplicity of links and interconnections that transcend nation states, it can be seen as a new way of thinking about how civil society actors can work together – through the Internet, for example – forming transnational networks and alliances. In this way globalisation offers much to community development practitioners.

Local communities can tap into alternative forms of information and knowledge. They can join international activist movements by 'thinking globally, acting locally', such as occurs in the relocalisation movements. However, as Bauman (2004) points out, the globalisation of capital also means the shunting of problems made by global corporations (unemployment and environmental harm, for example) away from global corporate responsibility to the local level, where dealing with the issues becomes a community responsibility.

The rise of fundamentalisms

Community development is placed in the intellectual tradition of the Enlightenment, with its focus on science and reason. The growth of community development in the 1970s linked community development principles and practices with not only the Left, but also the optimism of modernity. Through reasoning and the methods of science, humans could be propelled into a just, equal and enlightened world. For the Left, evidence and logic were the key to the efficacy of any strategy. Much of the debate about a better future revolved around the question of how communist or capitalist economics could get us there. The arrival of postmodern ideas and theories challenged the confidence of those championing the precepts of modernity, but postmodernist critique has done little more than modify the most ambitious and optimistic claims of science. Community development practitioners now need to understand how the commitment to evidence and reason has been attacked from quite another direction. The attack has come from the rise of new forms of **fundamentalism**. Fundamentalism refers to strict adherence to orthodox beliefs, such as the doctrines of religions or political parties.

Of course there has always been fundamentalist thinking. Today we have two kinds of renewal of fundamentalism: secular and religious. To some extent, secular fundamentalism is evident in the blind faith in scientific 'progress', such as the faith in nuclear energy. In addition, the beliefs in the 'right' of the neo-conservative agenda, with its commitment to neo-liberal economics and the self-righteous might of America, are based on fundamentalist thinking. Mann (2003) points out that the new form of fundamentalist thinking is what he calls **ethno-nationalism**. Ethno-nationalism is based on a belief of an ethnic group that it has the right to its own state, purged of all other ethnic groups. It was the basis of the belief that Rwanda should be only for the Hutus and Afghanistan be purged of people of Hazara ethnicity.

Overlaid on these forms of fundamentalism, and often linked, is religious fundamentalism, which is beginning to take on transnational and even global forms, particularly when religious beliefs have been hijacked for political purposes. Mann (2003) points to the powerful effects of the mixing of ethno-nationalism and religious forms of fundamentalism, as in Chechnya and parts of India and Indonesia. Religious fundamentalism is found in Christianity, Judaism, Hinduism and Islam. The religious fundamentalism of Islam has been the subject of most attention, because of its link with terrorism. Terrorism and risk society make a volatile mix. They have led to government injunctions to report 'suspicious' behaviour and to anti-terrorism laws that give police and security agents increased powers to search private premises, hold citizens without charge and deny the right to legal advice and support.

Ali (2002), who writes about the links between the neo-conservative Western agenda and the rise of religious fundamentalism, dissects the history of Islamic engagement with the West. He comments on the misguided aspects of the Western response to violent Islamic fundamentalism:

> If Western politicians remain ignorant of the causes and carry on as before there will be repetitions. Moral outrage has some therapeutic value, but as a political strategy it is useless. Lightly disguised wars of revenge waged in the heat of the moment are not much better. To fight tyranny and oppression by using tyrannical and oppressive means, to combat a

single-minded and ruthless fanaticism by becoming equally fanatical and ruthless, will not further the cause of justice or bring about a meaningful democracy. It can only prolong the cycle of violence (Ali, 2002:3).

Sadly, these comments have proved to be only too prophetic in some parts of the world.

Responding appropriately to the new forms of fundamentalism and its effects will be a major challenge to community development in the coming years. We do not as yet understand how this cycle will play out or its dimensions. What we can do is learn as much as we can about the contexts and forms of fundamentalism, understand how fundamentalism is manifested in communities and continue our work to sustain tolerance, respect and global networking between diverse communities.

The demands of everyday work

The critiques, difficulties and dilemmas that we have discussed in this chapter set the context for the everyday activities of community development practitioners. Juggling these is no easy task. Workers are under great pressure to achieve results, to explain why they are doing things and to act in accordance with their principles. Overall, in their everyday tasks and practices, they are demanding of themselves and their colleagues. They also face increasing demands and conflicting expectations from co-workers, committees of management, funding bodies and their communities at large, and from subgroups within each of these.

Discussing feminist action from a post-structuralist perspective, Lather (1991:31) reminds us that, 'Awareness of the complexity, contingency and fragility of the practices that we invent to discover the truth about ourselves can be paralysing.' The effects of these pressures are expressed in a number of ways. Some workers feel obliged to take personal responsibility for everything that goes wrong, including financial disasters, planning mistakes and breakdown of interpersonal relations in a community organisation. As Shields (1991) notes, community development workers can become 'hooked on bad news'. They may unconsciously seek out information that maintains a state of indignation, or even panic, in a community organisation.

Other workers become so enthusiastic that their commitment to community development work takes on a religious fervour, or their whole identity becomes fused with their work. In an overloaded work environment, they tend to believe that they are the only ones who can do the job properly, and they place greater and greater pressure on themselves. Some believe that if they work just a little harder, they will stem the demands of the job; thus, they take on more and more tasks and set up an expectation that they will never say no. The approach is also manifested in the tendencies of workers to become supercritical of their own practices and those of their colleagues, expressed in concerns about co-option or even betrayal of the principles of community development. Bryan explains this predicament thus:

> We just assume that the mission is more important than our personal needs. This is where a fundamental contradiction sets in. Those of us who are burn-out prone are also sensitive people who have feelings, want to be liked and recognised, and wish to do worthwhile things for other people. We want to do well and look good in the eyes of our peers, but unfortunately our peers

are usually in the same dilemma. They also play down personal needs … This usually means that competition thrives between us … Purity tests abound as to who is the better environmentalist, feminist, civil rights advocate or socialist (Bryan, quoted in Shields, 1991:123).

Burnout

If the pressures become prolonged and stress levels rise, burnout is often the result. Burnout is a failure of the interaction between capacity and environment. For some people, it is a temporary experience of tiredness, but for others it is a major crisis with profound emotional and physical effects. Sufferers lose their sense of purpose or direction; they oscillate between a mounting sense of urgency and obsession with small tasks; they experience panic, negativity, cynicism and withdrawal. Physical symptoms include deep exhaustion, lethargy and susceptibility to illness.

Many books advise how to deal with stress, but few of them address the type of stress that occurs in people who are committed to social change. Shields (1991:125) describes how stress touches all levels of our being as community development workers:

> Involvement is not something that one can neatly close the door on at 5 pm. In fact, for a lot of activists it might be a case of literally opening the door to the home-cum-office-cum-action headquarters: papers on the bed, meetings round the kitchen table … Operating in this way means there's no getting away from it. Though all this activity has the potential to enrich our lives, it is this feature of unceasing demands which creates much fuel for burn-out. It also leads to deterioration of relationships. After-hours phone calls, night organising of meetings, weekend activities and work-related visitors infringe on the time with children or partners. Parties become just another venue to talk shop ('networking').

Managing stress and learning from failure

We cannot prevent burnout resulting from this type of stress, for it is inherent in the work that community development workers do. However, there are some strategies for managing burnout and stress. There are also ways that we can learn from failures and disappointments. We begin by considering some of the strategies for managing stress.

- Acknowledge that you are having difficulties, such as doing the work, keeping up commitment, balancing home and work life.
- Apply community development principles to yourself. Do not fall into the trap of blaming the victim (in this case, yourself). Do not focus attention on such questions such as 'Where have I gone wrong?' Instead, focus on what structural, ideological and political factors have led to the situation, and ask what can be done to change these.
- Work collectively. Share your feelings about the difficulties with the people you are working with. Talk things through. Discuss strategies. Even if your audience is hostile (and it generally is not) at least you have been able to articulate what is going on and to communicate this to co-workers.
- Celebrate what is going well; feel good about victories, however small.
- Take time out. Make sure that you put time aside each day to do something different from your work activities, such as physical activity or meditation. While it is a cliche, and

Contradictions

in community development work it is often hard to accept, it is true that no-one is indispensable. If things are not done while you are not there, and even if the organisation is in a state of collapse because of your absence, so be it – it may well collapse anyway. It is important to remember that there is no end to the tasks to be completed and issues to be resolved, however hard you work. In a larger organisation, of course, it is possible to delegate work and this is central to a community development worker's job.

- Specify what is going right and why, and what is going wrong and why. In particular, there is a host of reasons why things go wrong: lack of clarification of aims and objectives; lack of clear structure, including lines of accountability; lack of planning and strategy; weak committee structures and meetings; failure to articulate expectations (your own and those of other workers); lack of communication; interpersonal politics; and, finally, but certainly not the least of the difficulties, having to operate with very limited resources.
- Think strategically and act strategically. Consider why you are doing something and what its overall purpose is in terms of aims, objectives and strategies. It may well be that a particular task, such as attending a meeting, has lost its overall value to your work. You may need to reassess your job description, alter timelines or even redesign your job to make your tasks more achievable. For example, community organisations often seriously underestimate the time needed for a research project or an evaluation. Speak to other community workers who have undertaken similar projects to get an idea of the amount of time that should be set aside.
- Lighten up! Keep a sense of perspective and humour and do not seek personal salvation through your work. Alinsky (1972:25) urges us to keep in mind Goethe's enjoinder that

> conscience is the virtue of observers and not of agents of action; in action, one does not always enjoy the luxury of a decision that is consistent both with one's individual conscience and the good of mankind [sic]. The choice must always be the latter. Action is for mass salvation and not for the individual's personal salvation. He who sacrifices the mass good for his personal conscience has a peculiar conception of 'personal salvation'; he doesn't care enough for people to be 'corrupted' for them.

'Heroic' failure

As the old adage goes, learning from failure can be far more instructive than learning from success. Yet there is very little written in community development and related literature about how we can learn from failure. Miller (2004b:148) points out the interesting paradox that while 'eternal optimism' is at the heart of community development work, in their everyday practices workers are concerned with the apparent failures of communities and neighbourhoods (the need for neighbourhood renewal), the erosion of community (the need for capacity building to correct community deficits), exclusion (the need for policies of inclusion), social disadvantage (the need for structural change to redress issues of disadvantage) and powerlessness (the need for strategies of empowerment). Indeed,

> the objects of intervention are those who have been unable to succeed within contemporary capitalism, the losers in the economic and social stakes when all around the message is that winning is the prize offered to everyone (Miller, 2004b:149).

Miller's discussion reminds us that in community development there are many types of failures and most community development practitioners have experiences of some of the following examples:

- failure to work with the community; for example, where a group of outside 'experts' impose themselves and their views on a community in a top-down manner
- interpersonal conflict within a community program, and clear processes for dealing with conflict have not been identified
- intimidation of those who disagree and failure to hear opposing views of 'how things should be done', which allow tensions to fester, leading to schisms in the community
- planning and organisational weaknesses; for example, when a community organisation fails to identify and carry out the activities necessary to maintain the organisational infrastructure
- failure of resources; for example, when a community organisation does not have the necessary resources to fulfil the requirements of a community project
- being caught in the politics of 'rescue' (maintaining the status quo) at the expense of the politics of 'transformation' (moving on, shifting the terms of reference) (see Miller, 2004b:149)
- failure to reflect on and learn from mistakes, so that such mistakes are repeated.

Of course, the identification of success and failure depends on definition. In these instances failure is conceptualised as the binary opposite to success, as a zero sum. All community programs probably have some elements that could be seemed to be 'successful' and some elements that could be deemed 'failures'.

In concluding this chapter, it is important to restate that if the reality of community development seems messy and contradictory, this is not a fatal flaw. Reality is always messy, contradictory and full of paradox. If community development is to be a living, creative and challenging activity – whether undertaken as a formal occupation or as social activism – it must be seen in the context of a changing world. In the final chapter we consider further the question of the compatibility between the themes of community development and those that dominate the contemporary world.

Summary points

- Critical reflection is an important part of community development, particularly in regard to our own assumptions and orthodoxies.
- Community development workers should be aware of the major critiques, difficulties and dilemmas in community development work.
- It is important to understand the issues associated with the idea of 'pure' community development.
- Community development practitioners are affected by different and often contradictory expectations.

Contradictions

- A continuing tension in community development work is the issue of whether practitioners are professionals or activists.
- Community development practitioners should understand how localism can equate with parochialism and be able to respond to this critique.
- As well as being a way of empowering members of a community, consensus decision making has its own problems.
- It is important to understand the power differentials setting the backdrop to our work.
- While community development work can be compromised by over-involvement with the state (as a state proxy), it can also be facilitated by the state.
- Community development work is constrained when it takes place in the context of neo-liberal economics, particularly because of the ideological commitment to competition as the motor for economic and political development.
- Community development workers are increasingly caught in the web of new compliance regimes.
- An understanding of the assumptions and issues underlying the idea of the moral superiority of the oppressed is useful for community development practitioners.
- While community development is premised on the principle that practice involves facilitating, not leading, there is often a fine line between facilitation and leadership.
- Workers need to be mindful of the criticism that their role involves exploiting community problems rather than helping to resolve them.
- While theory and discussion are central to community development, they are not sufficient in themselves. Discussion must be translated into activity and action.
- Community development workers should be aware of the ambiguities of globalisation.
- Community development practitioners should be sensitive to culturalism – the view that if something is a cultural tradition it is above criticism and somehow sacrosanct.
- It is important to understand the new political conjunctures and particularly the development of new forms of fundamentalism.
- While everyday community development work is demanding and stressful, there are strategies for responding to these demands.

Key terms

- co-opted discourses
- compliance regimes
- ethno-nationalism
- fundamentalism
- 'heroic' failure
- 'heroic' school of community organising
- localism
- newspeak or spin
- 'pure' community development
- volunteering industry
- weasel words

Exercises

1. Why is the idea of 'pure' community development problematic?
2. List some of the contradictory expectations of community development work.
3. Explain the view that localism is parochialism. What are the responses to this view?
4. Why is understanding power important for community development?
5. In what ways can community development workers be co-opted?
6. List the challenges and dilemmas for community development practitioners presented by having to work within a context dominated by neo-liberal principles, structures and processes.

7 Are community activism and professionalism compatible?
8 What are the differences between leading and facilitating?
9 Why is the relationship between volunteerism and community development sometimes an uneasy one?
10 In what ways could community development workers be seen to exploit a community?
11 In what ways does globalisation facilitate, constrain and threaten community development?
12 Why is fundamentalism a threat to community development?
13 List some issues confronting community development practitioners in their everyday work.
14 What is meant by 'heroic' community development?
15 Referring to the 'Yalbani committee of management' case study, list the factors that would be most important from your perspective in deciding which applicant would be the best person for the job. How would you think about the issue of professionalism versus activism in this context?
16 Consider the situation facing Denise in the 'Herron Creek community planning project' case study. How would you handle the pressures to continue as a leader rather than a facilitator?

Further reading

Ali, T (2002) *The Clash of Fundamentalisms*. Verso, London.

Bauman, Z (2004) *Wasted Lives: Modernity and its Outcasts*. Polity Press, Cambridge.

Fairclough, N (2000) *New Labour: New Language*. Routledge, London and New York.

Friedman, J (1987) *Planning in the Public Domain: From Knowledge to Action*. Princeton University Press, New Jersey.

Ife, J (2001) *Human Rights and Social Work: Towards Rights-Based Practice*. Cambridge University Press, Cambridge.

Mann, M (2003) *Incoherent Empire*. Verso, London.

Miller, C (2004a) 'Community practices in Australia', *Community Development*, Vol. 39, No. 2, pp. 199–201.

Miller, C (2004b) 'Community development as the pursuit of human rights: the new direction of travel?', in *Community Development, Human Rights and the Grassroots Conference Proceedings*. Melbourne, pp. 141–58.

Power, M (1997) *The Audit Society: Rituals of Verification*. Oxford University Press, Oxford.

Watson, D (2003) *Death Sentence: How Cliches, Weasel Words and Management-Speak are Strangling Public Language*. Random House, Scoresby, Victoria.

Wheen, F (2004) *How Mumbo-Jumbo Conquered the World*. Harper Perennial, London.

Weblinks

Australian Services Union
www.asumembers.org.au/sacs/main-page

Transition Towns movement
www.transitionnetwork.org/
http://transitiontown.com.au/

CHAPTER 11

Challenges for the twenty-first century

Overview

What does community development look like at the beginning of the twenty-first century? Its promises are still seductive and many. The challenges are still immense. In this final chapter we return to the discussion of the role of community development in Australia in the second decade of the twenty-first century. At one level we can be pleased with the progress of community development over the past 40 years. In some ways, the current context validates the principles and practices of community development. Yet there remain many constraints. In this chapter we identify successes, constraints and possible choices and directions for the future.

Introduction

Contemporary Australian society appears to be full of paradox. It is a society that is largely nonchalant about the discrepancies between the very rich and the poor. Middle Australia is concerned about exorbitant property prices, yet exults the outstanding record of economic growth and the weathering of the global financial crisis. While anxiety about the global terrorist threat has subsided in Australia, there is still concern about asylum seekers arriving by boat, and Australians in general have supported government policies that result in harsh treatment of asylum seekers. At the same time, they give generously to victims of natural disasters in the developing world, such as the victims of recent tsunamis. While there are some notable sceptics, generally there is heightened acceptance of climate change and the role of humans in environmental destruction, yet at the same time most Australians are ambivalent about the need to contain carbon emissions and seem to turn a blind eye to the destruction of rainforests and unrestrained mining. Moreover, anger about the exploitation of the environment and cheap labour in our region is rarely translated into active solidarity with people on the ground in neighbouring countries.

As argued in the previous chapter, community development is full of challenges. At its best it pushes the boundaries of conventional thought and offers new ways of doing things. Community development practitioners champion the authenticity and rights of people who are marginalised and excluded. They aim to do this, not as welfare professionals or even as advocates, but more as fellow travellers. They contest unjust power. Yet their critiques of social complacency and the hypocrisy of politicians (who talk social justice and human rights, yet in practice do very little to change things), render community development workers as outsiders to the main game of power politics.

In the ways that it challenges prevailing orthodoxies, community development can be thought of as a construction of heresy. By and large, community development practitioners like to wear the badge of heresy, as it signals that the wearer will not be content to accept the status quo and is not afraid of opposition or conflict. However, the position taken in this book is that, hopefully, alongside the aspirations for an edgy, radicalising community development is sensitivity to the pretensions of a pure or heroic community development that we discussed in the previous chapter. It is also important to acknowledge that for some community development practitioners, the radicalising character of community development, insofar as it places community development at the margins of political and social life, leaves it in a weak position to deal with the world of realpolitik. For others still, what lies at the heart of community development is the art of compromise. From this position community development practitioners need to know when to fight and when to give in. In order to survive, practitioners often need to comply with regulations that they deem unnecessary. They have to work within agendas and terms of reference not set by them.

These challenges have been a part of community development since its early days in Australia in the 1970s. But in many ways, the last 40 years of community development can also be seen as a success story. What has emerged out of the early visions of community development is a robust set of precepts and practice. In the following section we discuss some of the visions and actualities of community development during this period.

Beware what you wish for . . .

When the idea of community development was just 'taking off' 40 years ago, the community development vision was of a society in which ordinary people had a real say in what they thought was important in their lives; in which politicians and government bureaucrats listened to the views of those at the grassroots; in which people's different assets and needs were understood; in which community services were framed by human rights considerations and all people felt respected and included in society, regardless of colour, ethnicity or (dis)ability; and in which community development was an accepted and effective way of facilitating collective self-determination and redressing power imbalances and social exclusion.

In some ways, we have come a long way since the 1970s. While it has not disappeared, the top-down approach of governments has become less comfortable to politicians and bureaucrats, evidenced by the strengthening discourses of 'listening' and 'consulting' with ordinary people. Indeed the language of empowerment, social inclusion, participation, partnerships and capacity building is now common in government policies and corporate citizenship programs.

Yet is this kind of endorsement of community development really what we wished for? This is a difficult question to answer, because it calls for both thinking retrospectively and for evidence of real change. Certainly we wished for the empowerment of ordinary people. The establishment of many community development, community strengthening and community renewal programs in Australia over the past 10 years would suggest that there has been a growing respect for the principle of empowerment. We wished for validation of the civic involvement of people in their communities. Grassroots involvement has become very important in local policy making. The work of unpaid contributors to social development in communities is now being validated through the celebration of volunteerism. We wished for recognition of the contribution of community organisations. Community organisations have gained unprecedented acceptance as key players in society, and are now entering into partnerships with governments. The contribution of community organisations, not only as civil society actors but also in terms of their contribution to the economy, is increasingly recognised, as witnessed by the Productivity Commission's (2010) report *Contribution of the Not-for-Profit Sector*. Some of the larger community organisations are now advising on and even assisting in the framing of government policy. We also wished for recognition of the injustices meted out to Indigenous Australians over almost 250 years, and Kevin Rudd's historic apology to Indigenous Australians in 2008 has indicated some change in awareness of the oppression perpetrated by non-Indigenous settlers.

From the perspective of some community development practitioners, there have been real changes to how ordinary people think of their rights, their capacities to collectively 'own' local processes and identify needs, and their power to exert pressure on decision makers to act on climate change. Other practitioners argue that these successes have little relevance to community development because they are largely top-down and deficit-based; they do not demonstrate any changes in power structures or any real ownership of community assets and processes by community members. For yet other practitioners there are successes, but the price of these successes is high. This is because in the process they have become handmaidens to the state and business, with community development programs operating, at best, at the margins of political and social life. Finally, there is the view that we have expected too much of community development. In its own way it can make a difference to the lives of thousands of Australian, usually in just small ways, by validating their views, facilitating collective endeavour and opening up new perspectives, for example. In different ways, all these responses contribute to our understanding of community development in the twenty-first century. All should be understood in the context of the constraints upon community development programs and the challenges facing workers. We consider these in the following section.

Constraints and challenges

The major constraints and challenges facing community development practitioners are:

- First is the continuation of neo-liberal and managerialist policies that circumscribe the activities of community development practitioners – perhaps the two most important developments to watch are the continuing commercialisation of community programs and organisations, as they seek legitimacy in the eyes of government bureaucrats, philanthropic and business organisations in their efforts to secure funding; and the relentless push for applying new managerialist techniques to community organisations, including top-down professionalised management. A major challenge is to generate funds and resources without fully embracing the precepts and assumptions of neo-liberalism. Some community organisations will eschew (or continue to eschew) government funds and commercial endeavours, while others will attempt to balance acceptance of government funds and commercial endeavours with critique of the principles, practices and effects of neo-liberalism.

- The second constraint arises out of the contradictory expectations of community development work, which can be explained in part by the way that practitioners are required to work within different operating rationales, as discussed in chapter 6. The major challenge is to understand how operating rationales can push in opposite directions and for practitioners to decide which direction is the most appropriate for each specific context. It is here that practitioners will be required to balance the principles and practices of community development with pragmatism. There is no set formula for resolving such issues, other than the need to be well informed and to understand the specificity of the situation.

- The third constraint is the use of language – two key aspects of the complex and ideological use of language affect community development practitioners today. First, commentators have revealed the extent to which language is being used as newspeak or spin (see chapter 10); that is, when it is used for promotion rather than deliberation, and when it is presented opportunistically to hide the real interests and justify the actions of governments, businesses and even community organisations. Spin can be all the more pernicious when it involves the opportunistic use of community development ideas without any commitment to the empowering processes and practices of community development, such as when governments insist on community programs being creative and innovative, while at the same time offering such narrow terms of reference in contracts that creativity and innovation become impossible. The other aspect of language to which community development practitioners need to pay attention is the mixed messages of co-opted discourses (also discussed in chapter 10). It is important to avoid embracing such discourses in an unexamined or uncritical way. Unpacking co-opted discourses is a major challenge for practitioners, in particular because they are now expected in submissions for funds and in evaluations and reports.

- The final constraint starts with how the idea of risk society is now being moulded to strengthen the authoritarian tendencies of the state. It works in three ways. First, the concept of risk society has facilitated a preoccupation with more government regulations, audits and evaluations. These risk management strategies are overlaid on the existing plethora of regulatory, checking and other surveillance processes. Second, risk society has often provided fertile terrain on which to develop intolerant, distrustful and xenophobic attitudes to strangers. These attitudes are beginning to undermine the long-held commitment to multiculturalism in Australia. Third, it has provided a rationale for increasing government control and surveillance in general. There will be continuing legal requirements to obey regulations and undertake audits and evaluations. It is important to critique the assumptions and red tape involved in these regulatory practices, while at the same time maintain accountability and evaluate what we do as community development practitioners. A major challenge for community development is to continue to critically scrutinise the construction of risk society, to ensure that community development practice is based on cross-cultural competence and, of course, to refuse to treat the stranger, such as the Islamic Other, with suspicion.

Directions for community development

It is clear that community development practitioners are facing a range of new challenges. There is no easy way of responding to these challenges or identifying the opportunities for community development. However, while there is no 'once and for all' way of dealing with the shifting frameworks in which we operate, continued critical analysis and activist endeavour is essential if community development is to truly empower, maintain a critical edge and withstand capture by the state and the market. A key theme in this book is that community organisations can continue to provide appropriate venues from which to launch symbolic, ideological and micro-structural challenges to the ongoing subjugation that occurs in everyday life and the concentration of power that occurs locally, nationally and, increasingly, transnationally.

Here, we consider some possible directions and choices for community development over the next five to 10 years.

- *Security or risk taking*: In regard to the general orientation of community development for the next five to 10 years, there are two different paths. We can seek security in existing practices and frameworks or we can explore new possibilities and new ways of doing things and, in this way, we can choose to take risks.
- *Strengthening global activity*: While commitment to working from the grassroots level is the hallmark of community development, how we work at this level is not straightforward. The idea of grassroots work used to refer to local activity in the geographical sense, but today the term 'grassroots' can apply to organic work that links people within and across nations. Here, we propose a small heresy: what we need now in community development is not more localism, but more globalism. That is, we need to be learning from each other across nations and cultures. Practitioners should do this in order to call upon inspirational and salutary lessons for their local practice. We need more international solidarity with the millions of practitioners and their NGOs. Indeed, community development should be a transnational and multinational actor in itself.
- *Strengthening activism*: We need to strive continually to understand where the strategic opportunities for action lie. As discussed in this book, activism is based on the divide between existing dominant power structures and opposition to these power structures. Activism requires concrete activities that are deliberately directed to some form of change in the dominant power structures and relations. Activism can involve risk-taking in the context of exploring new possibilities and new ways of doing things, as noted above, or it can involve defensive action through conventional forms of protest.

What will be important for the next few decades is to sustain the activist strand in community development work, although in the immediate future this might well become increasingly difficult.

- *Leading cross-cultural competence*: As the movement of people from different class and cultural backgrounds intensifies, two broad responses are possible. First, the host group can demand that the newcomers reject their cultural background and integrate into the host culture through assimilation. Alternatively, the host group can decide to adopt multicultural policies based on respect for difference. Community development, of course, is based on a commitment to the latter, but this does not mean sliding into a postmodern relativism, or culturalism, where 'anything goes'. This is because community development holds to certain modernist principles, emanating from the humanist tradition (see chapter 3). In bringing together a respect for cultural diversity and the humanist idiom of modernity, community development provides a framework for the much-needed understanding and demonstration of cross-cultural competence. Over the coming decade, community development can have an important role in showing people how to live effectively as cross-cultural citizens.

- *Demonstrating the power of deliberation and negotiation in conflict situations*: As discussed in chapter 1, there are several ways we can deal with conflict. We can resort to violence; the conflicting parties can be segregated; one party can exit, or be banished; or we can engage in deliberation and negotiation. The community development approach, of course, involves deliberation and negotiation. Humans as a whole do not seem to have come very far in finding ways of resolving conflict that are not based on zero-sum game (win/lose), resulting in segregation, banishment or violence. There is an important role for community development in demonstrating the effectiveness of conflict management through dialogue. But this dialogue should involve more than just rhetorical or symbolic resolutions. It requires democratic discussion based on democratic principles and organisation, real power sharing and equal sharing of resources. Democratic decision making requires communication that is oriented to sharing information, rather than influencing and persuading. It requires a new deal between the public and the politicians that is based on honesty, openness and mutual respect (Giddens, 1994; Coote, 1998; Franklin, 1998). As Coote (1998) points out, the democratic path means that politicians will let the public know the limits of their own knowledge and reveal the interests lying behind their decisions. The democratic path also requires governments to facilitate the development of institutions and policies that are committed to sharing information and dialogue.

- *Gathering and telling stories*: The discussion above suggests some general directions for community development in the next 10 years. However, community development practitioners are in many ways an impatient group. They wish to know what can be done immediately. Many actions are possible in regard to 'what can be done on Monday morning' and it is hoped that the examples provided in this book will provide some inspiration for new programs, actions and strategies. However, if there is one set of actions that could be recommended for 'Monday morning', it would be to start gathering and telling stories about their encounters – thousands of them – of community development projects in Australia and around the world. We need to share the experiences of these projects: particularly the things that went right or the things that went wrong. They might showcase good examples of how community development can work – we need to understand how and why projects do and don't work. They will often offer different ways of doing things. Today, we can draw on thousands of community development projects to demonstrate the rich diversity of ways we can respond to issues; develop alternative prefigurative politics, such as deliberative democracy; and show how we could organise our lives differently. In such demonstration projects we can show how community development practices and programs can be at the forefront in the fight against TINA (there is no alternative).

If our balance sheet takes account of the reasons to celebrate and the constraints under which we operate, and is mindful of the orthodoxies that we can slip into, we can have a more nuanced, ambiguous stocktake of community development today. The nuanced, ambiguous picture is a good place to start in our voyage into the future.

Summary points

- Australian society at the beginning of the twenty-first century is full of paradox, as is community development.
- We have a number of reasons to celebrate the role of community development in Australia today.
- Many community development principles and practices are accepted in development activities in Australia.
- The community development vision 40 years ago was of a society in which ordinary people had a real say in what they thought was important in their lives.
- There have been both advances in, and new challenges to, community development since the 1970s.
- Community development practitioners have to operate within the context of many constraints and they face many challenges.
- A major constraint is the continuing dominance of neo-liberalism.
- Community development practitioners have to respond to the contradictory expectations of what they will achieve and what is identified as co-opted discourses.
- Community development practitioners have to work in contexts dominated by newspeak or spin.
- The context in which community development practitioners work is also affected by the construction of contemporary society as risk society.
- Risk society provides a suitable ideological framework in which to develop new regulatory and surveillance processes.
- Risk society also provides fertile terrain for intolerant, distrustful and xenophobic attitudes.
- In mapping some directions for community development in the next five to 10 years, we can seek security in existing practices and frameworks or we can explore new possibilities and new ways of doing things – that is, we can choose to take risks.

- We need to be continually striving to identify where the strategic opportunities for community development action lie.
- The position taken in this book is that we need more globalism – that is, we need to be learning from each other across nations and cultures.
- Community development plays an important part in showing people how to respond and celebrate difference. It can have an important role in showing people how to live effectively as cross-cultural citizens.
- There is an important role for community development in demonstrating the effectiveness of conflict management through dialogue.
- One important way of renewing community development is to share experiences of community development and to tell stories of where things went right or wrong.

Exercises

1 List the promises of community development, the constraints under which it works and the challenges it faces.
2 List the concepts and ideas that are used to explain the value of community development to society today.
3 Note the options for the future of community development in the next five to 10 years. Which of these directions do you think will be the most important?

Further reading

Coote, A (1998) 'Risk and public policy: towards a high-trust democracy', in J Franklin (ed.). *The Politics of Risk Society*. Polity Press Cambridge, pp. 9–22.

Fairclough, N (2000) *New Labour, New Language*. Routledge, London and New York.

Watson, D (2003) *Death Sentence: How Cliches, Weasel Words and Management-Speak are Strangling Public Language*. Random House, Scoresby, Victoria.

Wheen, F (2004) *How Mumbo-Jumbo Conquered the World*. Harper Perennial, London.

Appendix

Universal Declaration of Human Rights, 1948

Preamble

Whereas recognition of the inherent dignity and of the equal and inalienable rights of all members of the human family is the foundation of freedom, justice and peace in the world.

Whereas disregard and contempt for human rights have resulted in barbarous acts which have outraged the conscience of mankind, and the advent of a world in which human beings shall enjoy freedom of speech and belief and freedom from fear and want has been proclaimed as the highest aspiration of the common people.

Whereas it is essential, if man is not to be compelled to have recourse, as a last resort, to rebellion against tyranny and oppression, that human rights should be protected by the rule of law.

Whereas the peoples of the United Nations have in the charter reaffirmed their faith in fundamental human rights, in the dignity and worth of the human person and in the equal rights of men and women and have determined to promote social progress and better standards of life in larger freedom.

Whereas Member States have pledged themselves to achieve, in cooperation with the United Nations, the promotion of universal respect for and observance of human rights and fundamental freedom.

Whereas a common understanding of these rights and freedom is of the greatest importance for the full realisation of this pledge.

Now, therefore

The General Assembly

Proclaims this Universal Declaration of Human Rights as a common standard of achievement for all peoples and all nations, to the end that every individual and every organ of society, keeping this Declaration constantly in mind, shall strive by teaching and education to promote respect for these rights and freedom and by progressive measures, national and international, to secure their universal and effective recognition and observance, both among the peoples of Member States themselves and among the peoples of territories under their jurisdiction.

Article 1

All human beings are born free and equal in dignity and rights. They are endowed with reason and conscience and should act towards one another in a spirit of brotherhood.

Article 2

Everyone is entitled to all the rights and freedoms set forth in this Declaration, without distinction of any kind, such as race, colour, sex, language, religion, political or other opinion, national or social origin, property, birth or other status.

Furthermore, no distinction shall be made on the basis of the political, jurisdictional or international status of the country or territory to which a person belongs, whether it be independent, trust, non-self-governing or under any other limitation of sovereignty.

Appendix

Article 3
Everyone has the right to life, liberty and the security of person.
Article 4
No one shall be held in slavery or servitude; slavery and the slave trade shall be prohibited in all their forms.
Article 5
No one shall be subjected to torture or to cruel, inhuman or degrading treatment or punishment.
Article 6
Everyone has the right to recognition everywhere as a person before the law.
Article 7
All are equal before the law and are entitled without any discrimination to equal protection of the law. All are entitled to equal protection against any discrimination in violation of this Declaration and against any incitement to such discrimination.
Article 8
Everyone has the right to an effective remedy by the competent national tribunals for acts violating the fundamental rights granted him by that constitution or by law.
Article 9
No one shall be subjected to arbitrary arrest, detention or exile.
Article 10
Everyone is entitled in full equality to a fair, and public hearing by an independent and impartial tribunal, in the determination of his rights and obligations and of any criminal charge against him.
Article 11
1 Everyone charged with a penal offence has the right to be presumed innocent until proved guilty according to law in a public trial at which he has had all the guarantees necessary for his defence.
2 No one shall be held guilty of any penal offence on account of any act or omission which did not constitute a penal offence, under national or international law, at the time when it was committed. Nor shall a heavier penalty be imposed than the one that was applicable at the time the penal offence was committed.
Article 12
No one shall be subjected to arbitrary interference with his privacy, family, home or correspondence, nor to attacks upon his honour and reputation. Everyone has the right to the protection of the law against such interference or attacks.
Article 13
1 Everyone has the right to freedom of movement and residence within the borders of each State.
2 Everyone has the right to leave any country, including his own, and to return to his country.
Article 14
1 Everyone has the right to seek and to enjoy in other countries asylum from persecution.

Appendix

2 This right may not be invoked in the case of prosecutions genuinely arising from nonpolitical crimes or from acts contrary to the purposes and principles of the United Nations.

Article 15
1 Everyone has the right to a nationality.
2 No one shall be arbitrarily deprived of his nationality nor denied the right to change his nationality.

Article 16
1 Men and women of full age, without any limitation due to race, nationality or religion, have the right to marry and to found a family. They are entitled to equal rights as to marriage, during marriage and at its dissolution.
2 Marriage shall be entered into only with the free and full consent of the intending spouses.
3 The family is the natural and fundamental group unit of society and is entitled to protection by society and the State.

Article 17
1 Everyone has the right to own property alone as well as in association with others.
2 No one shall be arbitrarily deprived of his property.

Article 18
Everyone has the right to freedom of thought, conscience and religion; this right includes freedom to change his religion or belief, and freedom, whether alone or in community with others and in public or private, to manifest his religion or belief in teaching, practice, worship and observance.

Article 19
Everyone has the right to freedom of opinion and expression; this right includes freedom to hold opinions without interference and to seek, receive and impart information and ideas through any media and regardless of frontiers.

Article 20
1 Everyone has the right to freedom of peaceful assembly and association.
2 No one may be compelled to belong to an association.

Article 21
1 Everyone has the right to take part in the government of his country, directly or through freely chosen representatives.
2 Everyone has the right of equal access to public service in his country.
3 The will of the people shall be the basis of the authority of government; this will shall be expressed in periodic and genuine elections which shall be by secret vote or by equivalent free voting procedures.

Article 22
Everyone, as a member of society, has the right to social security and is entitled to realisation, through national effort and international cooperation and in accordance with the organisation and resources of each State, of the economic, social and cultural rights indispensable for his dignity and the free development of his personality.

Appendix

Article 23
1. Everyone has the right to work, to free choice of employment, to just and favourable conditions of work and to protection against unemployment.
2. Everyone, without any discrimination, has the right to equal pay for equal work.
3. Everyone who works has the right to just and favourable remuneration ensuring for himself and his family an existence worthy of human dignity, and supplemented, if necessary, by other means of social protection.
4. Everyone has the right to form and to join trade unions for the protection of his interests.

Article 24
Everyone has the right to rest and leisure, including reasonable limitation of working hours and periodic holidays with pay.

Article 25
1. Everyone has the right to a standard of living adequate for the health and well-being of himself and of his family, including food, clothing, housing and medical care and necessary social services, and the right to security in the event of unemployment, sickness, disability, widowhood, old age or other lack of livelihood in circumstances beyond his control.
2. Motherhood and childhood are entitled to special care and assistance. All children, whether born in or out of wedlock, shall enjoy the same social protection.

Article 26
1. Everyone has the right to education. Education shall be free, at least in the elementary and fundamental stages. Elementary education shall be compulsory. Technical and professional education shall be made generally available and higher education shall be equally accessible to all on the basis of merit.
2. Education shall be directed to the full development of the human personality and to the strengthening of respect for human rights and fundamental freedom. It shall promote understanding, tolerance and friendship among all nations, racial or religious groups, and shall further the activities of the United Nations for the maintenance of peace.
3. Parents have a prior right to choose the kind of education that shall be given to their children.

Article 27
1. Everyone has the right freely to participate in the cultural life of the community, to enjoy the arts and to share in scientific advancement and its benefits.
2. Everyone has the right to the protection of the moral and material interests resulting from any scientific, literary or artistic production of which he is the author.

Article 28
Everyone is entitled to a social and international order in which the rights and freedom set forth in this Declaration can be fully realised.

Article 29
1. Everyone has duties to the community in which alone the free and full development of his personality is possible.

2   In the exercise of his rights and freedom, everyone shall be subject only to such limitations as are determined by law solely for the purpose of securing due recognition and respect for the rights and freedom of others and of meeting the just requirements of morality, public order and the general welfare in a democratic society.
3   These rights and freedom may in no case be exercised contrary to the purposes and principles of the United Nations.

Article 30

Nothing in this Declaration may be interpreted as implying for any State, group or person any right to engage in any activity or to perform any act aimed at the destruction of any of the rights and freedom set forth herein.

References

Abdullah, J & Young, S (2010) 'Emergent drivers for building and sustaining capacity in Australian Indigenous communities', in S Kenny and M Clarke, *Challenging Capacity Building: Comparative Perspectives*, Palgrave, London, pp. 87–111.

Abercrombie, N, Hill, S & Turner, BS (1980) *The Dominant Ideology Thesis*. Allen & Unwin, London.

Abercrombie, N, Hill, S & Turner, BS (2000) *The Penguin Dictionary of Sociology* 4th edn. Penguin, London.

Alford, J & O'Neill, D (1994) *The Contract State: Public Management and the Kennett Government*. Centre for Applied Social Research, Deakin University Press, Geelong.

Ali, T (2002) *The Clash of Fundamentalisms*. Verso, London.

Alinsky, S (ed.) (1969) *Reveille for Radicals*. Vintage, New York.

Alinsky, S (1972) *Rules for Radicals*. Vintage, New York.

Althusser, L (1977) *Lenin and Philosophy and Other Essays*. New Left Books, London.

Anheier, H & Leat, D (2002) *From Charity to Creativity: Philanthropic Foundations in the 21st Century. Perspectives from Britain and Beyond*. Comedia The Round, Bournes Green.

Arnstein, S (1969) 'A ladder of citizen participation', *Journal of the American Institute of Planners*, Vol. 35, No. 4, July 1969, pp. 216–24.

Australian Bureau of Statistics (2006) *ABS General Social Survey. Summary Results, Australia*, ABS Catalogue No. 4159.0, Australian Government Printer, Canberra.

Australian Government (2009a) *National Compact between the Australian Government and the Third Sector – Consultation Report*, http://fahcsia.gov.au/sa/communities/pubs/national_compact_consultation/Pages/p1.aspx.

Australian Government (2009b) *A Stronger, Fairer Australia*, Social Inclusion Unit: Department of the Prime Minister and Cabinet, Canberra, socialinclusionunit@pmc.gov.au.

Baldry, E & Vinson, T (eds) (1991) *Actions Speak*. Longman Cheshire, Melbourne.

Balloch, S & Taylor, M (2001) 'Conclusion—can partnerships work?', in S Balloch and M Taylor, *Partnership Working: Policy and Practice*. The Policy Press, Bristol, pp. 283–8.

Barker, J (2003) *The No-Nonsense Guide to Terrorism*. New Internationalist and Verso, London.

Barrett, M (1980) *Women's Oppression Today*. Verso, London.

Battin, T (1991) 'What is this thing called economic rationalism?', *Australian Journal of Social Issues*, Vol. 26, No. 4, December, pp. 294–307.

Bauman, Z (1991) *Modernity and Ambivalence*. Polity Press, Cambridge.

Bauman, Z (1995) *Life in Fragments: Essays in Postmodern Morality*. Butterworth, Oxford.

Bauman, Z (1998) *Globalization: The Human Consequences*, Polity Press, Cambridge.

Bauman, Z (2000) *Liquid Modernity*. Polity Press, Cambridge.

Bauman, Z (2001) *Community: Seeking Safety in an Insecure World*, Polity Press, Cambridge.

Bauman, Z (2004) *Wasted Lives: Modernity and its Outcasts*. Polity Press, Cambridge.

Beaumont, J (1987) *Mastering the Meeting: All You Ever Wanted to Know about Meetings*. Information Australia, Melbourne.

Beck, U (1992) *Risk Society: Towards a New Modernity*. Sage, London.

Beck, U (1994) *Ecological Political Politics in an Age of Risk*. Polity Press, Cambridge.

Beck, U (1999) *World Risk Society*. Polity Press, Cambridge.

Beck, U (2000) *The Brave New World of Work*. Polity Press, Cambridge.

Beck, U (2006) *The Cosmopolitan Vision*, Polity Press, Cambridge.

Beck, U & Sznaider, N (2006) 'Unpacking cosmopolitanism for the social sciences: a research agenda', *The British Journal of Sociology*, Vol. 57, No. 1, pp. 1–23.

Bernard, HR (2000) *Social Research Methods: Qualitative and Quantitative Approaches*. Sage, Thousand Oaks.

Bilge, S & Denis, A (2010) 'Introduction: women, intersectionality and diasporas', *Journal of Intercultural Studies*, Vol. 31, No. 1, pp. 1–8.

Blackburn, R (ed.) (1991) *After the Fall*. Verso, London.

Blackshaw, T (2010) *Key Concepts in Community Studies*. Sage, London.

Bobbio, N (1986) *Which Socialism?* Polity Press, Oxford.

Bobbio, N (1996) *Left and Right: The Significance of a Political Distinction*. Polity Press, Cambridge.

References

Boddy, M & Fudge, C (1984) *Local Socialism*. Macmillan, London.

Bolton, R (1987) *People Skills*. Simon & Schuster, Brookvale, NSW.

Bookchin, M (1986) *Toward an Ecological Society*. BlackRose, Manfred–Buffalo.

Booth, W, Colomb, G & Williams, J (2003) *The Craft of Research*, 2nd edn. The University of Chicago Press, Chicago and London.

Bourdieu, P (1977) *Outline of a Theory of Practice*. Cambridge University Press, Cambridge.

Bourdieu, P (1985) 'The forms of capital', in J Richardson (ed.) *Handbook of Theory and Research for Sociology of Education*. Greenwood, New York, pp. 241–58.

Bowman, C (1990) *The Essence of Strategic Management*. Prentice-Hall, Hemel Hempstead.

Bradshaw, S (1972) 'The concept of social need', *New Society*, Vol. 20, pp. 641–3.

Braverman, H (1974) *Labor and Monopoly Capital: The Degradation of Work in the Twentieth Century*. Monthly Review Press, New York.

Briskman, L (2007) *Social Work with Indigenous Communities*. The Federation Press, Melbourne.

Brown, K, Kenny, S & Turner, B (2000) *Rhetorics of Welfare: Uncertainty, Choice and Voluntary Associations*. Macmillan, London.

Brown, K, Onyx, J & Kenny, S (2008) Active Citizenship and the Third Sector. Unpublished research report.

Browning, B (1990) *The Network: A Guide to Anti-Business Pressure Groups*. Canonbury Press, Melbourne.

Bryson, L (1989) 'The role of the SACS industry in meeting social needs and in generating employment', in J Wisemen and R Watts (eds), *From Charity to Industry*. PIT Press, Bundoora.

Bryson, L & Mowbray, M (1981) '"Community": the spray-on solution', *Australian Journal of Social Issues*, Vol. 16, No. 4.

Buckman, G (2004) *Globalisation: Tame it or Scrap it?* Zed Books, London.

Buckmaster, L & Thomas, M (2009) 'Social inclusion and social citizenship – towards a truly inclusive society', Research Paper No. 08, 2009–10, Australian Government Publishers, Canberra.

Bulmer, M (ed.) (1984) *Sociological Research Methods*. Macmillan, London.

Bulmer, M (1986) *Social Science and Social Policy*. Allen & Unwin, London.

Burgmann, V (1993) *Power and Protest Movements for Change in Australian Society*. Allen & Unwin, St Leonards.

Burkett, I (2008) 'There's more than one 'E' in community development: linking ecology, economy and equality in the re-localisation agenda', *New Community Quarterly*, Vol. 6, No. 2 Winter, pp. 2–11.

Burkhart, PJ & Reuss, S (1993) *Successful Strategic Planning: A Guide for Nonprofit Agencies and Organisations*. Sage, California.

Callinicos, A (2001) *Against the Third Way*. Polity Press, Cambridge.

Camilleri, J, Christoff, P, Frankel, B & Wiseman, J (1989) *New Economic Directions for Australia*. PIT Press, Bundoora.

Campfrens, H (ed.) (1997) *Community Development around the World: Practice, Theory, Research, Training*. University of Toronto Press, Toronto.

Carr, DK, Hard, KJ & Trahant, WJ (1996) *Managing the Change Process: A Field Book for Change Agents, Consultants, Team Leaders and Reengineering Managers*. McGraw Hill, New York.

Castells, M (2000) *The Rise of the Network Society, The Information Age: Economy, Society and Culture*, Vol. I. Blackwell, Oxford.

Castells, M (2004) 'Informationalism, networks, and the network society: a theoretical blueprinting', in M Castells, (ed.) *The Network Society: A Cross-Cultural Perspective*. Edward Elgar, Northampton, MA.

Cauchi, J & Murphy, J (2004) 'What's wrong with community-building!: It's much worse than we thought', Community Development, Human Rights and the Grassroots Conference Proceedings. Centre for Citizenship and Human Rights, Deakin University, Geelong, pp. 44–66.

Chambers, R (2005) *Ideas for Development*, Earthscan, London.

Chaskin, RJ, Brown, P, Venkatesh, S & Vidal, A (2001) *Building Community Capacity*. Aldine De Gruyter, New York.

Cheers, B (1987) Linking Formal Personal Support Services with Natural Support Services in Remote Areas. Paper presented at the 57th ANZAAS Conference, James Cook University of North Queensland.

Chelimsky, E & Shadish WR (eds) (1997) *Evaluation for the 21st Century: A Handbook*. Sage, Thousand Oaks, CA.

Chomsky, N (2003) *Understanding Power*. Vintage, London.

References

Clarke, J, Hall, S, Jefferson, T & Roberts, B (1976) 'Subcultures, cultures and class: a theoretical overview', in S Hall and T Jefferson (eds) *Resistance Through Rituals*. Hutchinson University Press, London.

Clarke, J & Neuman, J (1997) *The Managerial State*. Sage, London.

Cleaver, F (2001) 'Institutions, agency and the limitations of participatory approaches to development', in B Cooke and U Kothari (eds) *Participation: The New Tyranny*. Zed Books, London and New York, pp. 36–55.

Cochrane, A (1986) 'Community politics and democracy', in D Held and C Pollitt (eds) *New Forms of Democracy*. Open University, Sage, London.

Cockburn, C (1977) *The Local State*. Pluto Press, London.

Cocks, E & Stehlik, D (1996) 'History of services', in J Annison, J Jenkinson, W Sparrow and E Bethune (eds), *Disability: A Guide for Health Professionals*. Nelson ITP, South Melbourne, pp. 8–30.

Coghlan, D & Brannick, T (2005) *Doing Action Research in Your Own organisation*, 2nd edn. Sage, London.

Cohen, J (1982) *Class and Civil Society: The Limits of Marxian Critical Theory*. Martin Robinson, Oxford.

Cohen, J (1983) 'Rethinking social movements', *Berkeley Journal of Sociology*, XXVIII, pp. 99–113.

Cohen, J (1999) 'Trust, voluntary association and workable democracy: the contemporary American discourse of civil society', in M Warren (ed.) *Democracy and Trust*. Cambridge University Press, Cambridge, pp. 208–48.

Cohen, J & Arato, A (1995) *Civil Society and Political Theory*. MIT Press, Cambridge.

Communication Rights Australia (2005) 'Communication tips', at www.caus.com.au.

Community Foundations Gateway (2005) 'About community foundations', at www.philanthropy.org.au/community/aboutcf.html.

Connell, R (2007) *Southern Theory: The Global Dynamics of Knowledge in Social Science*, Allen & Unwin, Crows Nest, NSW.

Connors, P & McDonald, P (2010) 'Transitioning communities: community, participation and the Transition Town movement', *Community Development Journal*, in press.

Considine, M (1996) 'Market bureaucracy', *Labour and Industry*, Vol. 7, No. 1, June, pp. 1–28.

Considine, M & Painter, M (1997) 'Introduction', in M Considine and M Painter (eds) *Managerialism: The Great Debate*. Melbourne University Press, Melbourne, pp. 1–11.

Cooke, B & Kothari, U (2001) 'The case for participation as tyranny', in B Cooke and U Kothari (eds) *Participation: The New Tyranny*. Zed Books, London and New York, pp. 1–15.

Cooley, C (1909) *Social Organisation*. Scribners, New York.

Coote, A (1998) 'Risk and public policy: towards a high trust democracy', in J Franklin (ed.) *The Politics of Risk Society*. Polity Press, Cambridge, in association with the Institute of Public Policy Research, pp. 9–22.

Cornwall, A (2008) 'Unpacking "participation": models, meanings and practices', *Community Development Journal*, Vol. 43, No. 3, pp. 269–83.

Corpwatch (2010) 'Greenwash fact sheet 2001', www.corpwatch.org/article.php?id=242.

Cox, E (1995) *A Truly Civil Society*. 1995 Boyer Lectures. Australian Broadcasting Corporation, Sydney.

Craig, G, Derricort, N & Loney, M (eds) (1982) *Community Development and the State*. Routledge & Kegan Paul, London.

Craig, G, Mayo, M & Sharman, N (eds) (1979) *Jobs and Community Action*. Routledge & Kegan Paul, London.

Croft, S & Beresford, P (1984) 'Poor politics', *New Socialist*, October, pp. 57–9.

Croft, S & Beresford, P (1989) 'User-involvement, citizenship and social policy', *Critical Social Policy*, No. 26, Autumn, pp. 5–18.

Crotty, M (1998) *The Foundations of Social Research: Meaning and Perspective in the Research Process*. Allen & Unwin, St Leonards.

Curno, P (ed.) (1978) *Political Issues and Community Work*. Routledge & Kegan Paul, London.

Daly, M & Silver, H (2008) 'Social exclusion and social capital: a comparison and critique', *Theory and Society*, Vol. 37, No. 6, pp. 537–66.

David, M & Sutton, S (2004) *Social Research: The Basics*. Sage, London.

Davis, S & Watts, R (1987) 'The nature of community development work: knowledge, skills, objectives and work style: a job profile', in Broadmeadows College of TAFE, Community Development Course, Accreditation Submission. Broadmeadows College of TAFE, Victoria.

Davis, S, Elin, L & Reeher, G (2002) *Click on Democracy*. Westview Press, Boulder, Colorado.

Davis-Meehan, E (1996) *The Power of Positive Planning: A Strategic Planning Kit for Even Better*

References

Service Delivery. Family Support Services Association of NSW, and ITRAC, Wyong Shire, NSW.

de Beauvoir, S (1972) *The Second Sex*. Penguin, Harmondsworth.

de Vaus, DA (1985) *Surveys in Social Research*. Allen & Unwin, Sydney.

de Wit, B & Meyer, R (1994) *Strategy, Process, Content, Context: An International Perspective*. West, St Paul.

DeMars, W (2005) *NGOs and Transnational Networks: Wild Cards in World Politics*, Pluto Press. London.

Demetrious, K (2004) 'What's the point of corporate responsibility?', *The Corporate Citizen*, Vol. 4, Issue 2, pp. 20–21.

Derrida, J (1978) *Writing and Difference*, Routledge, London.

Dickey, B (1980) *No Charity There: A Short History of Social Welfare in Australia*. Nelson, Melbourne.

Donnison, D (1991) *A Radical Agenda: After the New Right and the Old Left*. Rivers Oram Press, London.

Dorner, J (2002) *Creative Web Writing*. A & C Black, London.

Douglas, M (1985) *Risk Acceptability According to the Social Sciences*. Routledge & Kegan Paul, London.

Doyal, L & Gough, I (1991) *A Theory of Human Need*. Macmillan, London.

Dryzek, J (2000) *Deliberative Democracy and Beyond: Liberals, Critics, Contestations*. Oxford University Press, Oxford.

du Sautoy, P (1966), 'Community development in Britain?', in G Craig, K Popple and M Shaw (eds) (2008) *Community Development in Theory and Practice. An International Reader*. Spokesman, Nottingham, pp. 28–32.

Dunleavy, P & Hood, C (1994) 'From old public administration to new public management', *Public Money and Management*, July–September, pp. 9–16.

Durkheim, E (1960) *The Division of Labour*. Free Press, Glencoe.

Eade, D (1997) *Capacity Building: An Approach to People-Centred Development*. Oxfam, Oxford.

Eade, D & Williams, S (1995) *The Oxfam Handbook of Development and Relief*, Vol. 1. Oxfam, Oxford.

Elliott, A (2009) *Contemporary Social Theory: An Introduction*, Routledge, Abingdon.

Elster, J (1997) 'The market and the forum: three varieties of political theory', in J Bohman and W Rehg (eds) *Deliberative Democracy: Essays on Reason and Politics*. The MIT Press, Cambridge, Massachusetts.

Engels, F (1884) *The Origin of the Family: Private Property and the State*. International, New York.

Ernst, J (1994) 'Privatisation, competition and contracts', in J Alford and D O'Neill (eds) *The Contract State: Public Management and the Kennett Government*. Centre for Applied Social Research, Deakin University Press, Geelong, pp. 101–35.

Etzioni, A (ed.) (1993) *New Communitarian Thinking: Persons, Virtues, Institutions and Communities*. University Press of Virginia, Charlotteville.

Etzioni, A (1995) *The Spirit of Community*. Fontana, London.

Fairclough, N (1992) *Discourse and Social Change*. Polity Press, Cambridge.

Fairclough, N (2000) *New Labour, New Language*. Routledge, London and New York.

Feher, F & Heller, A (1983) 'Class, democracy, modernity', *Theory and Society*, Vol. 12, No. 2, pp. 211–44.

Ferguson, K (1984) *The Feminist Case Against Bureaucracy*. Temple University Press, Philadelphia.

Fine, R (2007) *Cosmopolitanism*. Routledge, London and New York.

Fiske, J (1989) *Reading the Popular*. Allen & Unwin, Sydney.

Foucault, M (1963) *The Birth of the Clinic: An Archeology of the Human Sciences*. Tavistock, London.

Foucault, M (1969) *The Order of Things: The Archeology of the Human Sciences*. Vintage, New York

Foucault, M (1979) *Discipline and Punish: The Birth of the Prison*. Vintage, New York.

Foucault, M (1980) *Power/Knowledge: Selected Interviews and Other Writings*, 1972–1977, C Gordon (ed.). Harvester Press, Brighton.

Franklin, J (1998) 'Introduction', in J Franklin (ed.) *The Politics of Risk Society*. Polity Press, Cambridge, pp. 1–8.

Fraser, N (1989) *Unruly Practices: Power, Discourse and Gender in Contemporary Social Theory*. University of Minnesota Press, Minneapolis.

Freire, P (1972) *Pedagogy of the Oppressed*. Penguin, Harmondsworth, Middlesex.

Freire, P (1976) *Education: The Practice of Freedom*. Writers and Readers Publishing Cooperative, London.

Friedman, M (1962) *Capitalism and Freedom*. University of Chicago Press, Chicago.

References

Gardiner, K & O'Neil, M (1991) *Dollars and Sense*. Youth Accommodation Coalition of Victoria, Fitzroy.

Garner, S (2010) *Racisms: An Introduction*. Sage, London.

Gee, CD & Lankshear, C (1995) 'The new work order: critical language awareness and "fast" capitalism texts', *Discourse: Studies in the Cultural Politics of Education*, Vol. 16, No. 1, pp. 5–14.

Geoghegan, M & Powell, F (2009) 'Community development and the contested politics of the late modern agora: of, alongside or against neo-liberalism?', *Community Development Journal*, Vol. 44, No. 4, pp. 430–48.

Gibney, M (ed.) (2003) 'Globalizing rights'. The Oxford Amnesty Lectures 1999. *Community Development Journal*. Oxford University Press, Oxford.

Giddens, A (1994) *Beyond Left and Right: The Future of Radical Politics*. Polity Press, Cambridge.

Giddens, A (1998a) *The Third Way: The Renewal of Social Democracy*. Polity Press, Cambridge.

Giddens, A (1998b) 'Risk society: the context of British politics', in J Franklin (ed.) *The Politics of Risk Society*. Polity Press, Cambridge, pp. 23–34.

Giddens, A (2002) *Where Now for New Labour?* Polity Press, Cambridge.

Giddens, A (2009) *The Politics of Climate Change*. Polity Press, Cambridge

Goffman, E (1959) *The Presentation of Self in Everyday Life*. Doubleday Anchor, New York.

Goffman, E (1961a) *Encounters: Two Studies in Sociology of Interaction*. Bobbs-Merril, Indianapolis.

Goffman, E (1961b) *Asylums: Essays on the Social Situation of Mental Patients and Other Inmates*. Doubleday, New York.

Goffman, E (1967) *Interaction Ritual*. Anchor Books, New York.

Goodin, RE (1992) *Green Political Theory*. Polity Press, Cambridge.

Goulet, D (1985) *The Cruel Choice*. University Press of America, Lanham.

Grameen Bank (2010) 'Grameen Bank at a glance', www.grameen-info.org/index.php?option=com_content&task=view&id=26&Itemid=0.

Gramsci, A (1971) *Selections from the Prison Notebooks*, Q Hoare (ed.) and G Nowell (trans.). Laurence & Wishart, London.

Grant, W (1995) *Pressure Groups, Politics and Democracy in Britain*, 2nd edn. Harvester, Hemel Hempstead.

Graycar, A (1976) *Social Policy: An Australian Introduction*. Macmillan, Melbourne.

Gunaratnam, Y (2003) *Researching 'Race' and Ethnicity: Methods, Knowledge and Power*. Sage, London.

Gyford, J (1985) *The Politics of Local Socialism*. Allen & Unwin, London.

Habermas, J (1971) *Toward a Rational Society*. Heinemann, London.

Habermas, J (1974) *Theory and Society*. Heinemann, London.

Habermas, J (1976) *Legitimation Crisis*. Heinemann, London.

Habermas, J (1981) 'New social movements', *Telos*, No. 49, pp. 33–8.

Habermas, J (1983) 'Modernity: an incomplete project', in H Foster (ed.) *Postmodern Culture*. Pluto Press, London.

Hackney, S (1996) *Actions Speak Louder: Affirmative Action of Women with a Disability. A Resource Guide*. Disability Action Incorporated, www.disabilityaction.asn.au/dawebsite/systemsadvocacy/actions.html.

Hakim, C (1987) *Research Design*. Allen & Unwin, London.

Hall, ET (1959) *The Silent Language*. Anchor Doubleday, New York.

Hall, ET (1976) *Beyond Culture*. Anchor Doubleday, New York.

Hall, S (2000) 'Who needs identity?', in P du Gay, J Evans and P Redman (eds) *Identity: A Reader*. Sage, London, pp. 15–30.

Hancock, B & Garner, R (2009) *Changing Theories: New Directions in Sociology*. University of Toronto Press, Toronto.

Handy, C (1994) *The Empty Raincoat*. Arrow Business Books, London.

Hardy, J (1981) *Values in Social Policy: Nine Contradictions*. Routledge & Kegan Paul, London.

Harvey, D (1989) *The Condition of Postmodernity*. Blackwell, London.

Hatten, KJ & Hatten, MJ (1988) *Effective Strategic Management: Analysis and Action*. Prentice-Hall, New Jersey.

Hayek, FA (1960) *The Constitution of Liberty*. Routledge & Kegan Paul, London.

Held, D (2004) *Globalising World? Culture, Economics, Politics*. Routledge, London and the Open University.

Held, D & Pollitt, C (eds) (1986) *New Forms of Democracy*. Open University, Sage, London.

Hillery, GA (1955) 'Definitions of community: areas of agreement', *Rural Sociology*, No. 20.

References

Hilmer, F (1993) *Independent Committee of Inquiry into Competition Policy in Australia: National Competition Policy*. Australian Government Publishing Service, Canberra.

Hindess, B (1987) *Freedom, Equality and the Market: Arguments on Social Policy*. Tavistock, New York.

Hirst, P (1994) *Associative Democracy: New Forms of Economic and Social Governance*. Polity Press, Cambridge.

Hirst, P & Thompson, G (1996) *Globalization in Question*. Polity Press, London.

Hofstede, G (1994) *Cultures and Organizations: Intercultural Cooperation and its Importance for Survival*. HarperCollins, London.

Hooker, J (2003) *Working Across Cultures*. Stanford University Press, Stanford.

Horkheimer, M & Adorno, T (1972) *Dialectic of Enlightenment*, J Cumming (trans.). Herder & Herder, New York.

House, E (1990) 'Participant introductory comments', in MC Aitkin, *Debates on Evaluation*. Sage, Newbury Park, California.

Huggins, J (2008) 'The 1967 referendum ... four decades later', *New Community Quarterly*, Vol. 6, No. 1, pp. 3–5.

Hunt, J (2008) 'Strengthening Indigenous community governance for sustainability: using Indigenous principles in a community development approach', *New Community Quarterly*, Vol. 6, No. 1 pp. 18–23.

Hunt, J & Smith, D (2007) *Indigenous Community Governance Project: Year Two Research Findings*, Working Paper 36/2007. Centre for Aboriginal Economic Policy Research, Australian National University, Canberra.

Huntington, S (1996) *The Clash of Civilizations and the Remaking of World Order*. Simon & Schuster, New York.

Ife, J (1995) *Community Development: Creating Community Alternatives—Vision, Analysis and Practice*. Longman, Melbourne.

Ife, J (2001) *Human Rights and Social Work: Towards Rights-Based Practice*. Cambridge University Press, Cambridge.

Ife, J (2002) *Community Development: Community-based Alternatives in an Age of Globalisation*, 2nd edn. Pearson Education, French's Forest, NSW.

Ife, J (2004) 'Linking community development and human rights', Community Development, Human Rights and the Grassroots Conference Proceedings, Melbourne, pp. 84–93.

Ife, J (2009) *Human Rights from Below: Achieving Human Rights through Community Development*, Cambridge University Press, Cambridge.

Ife, J (2010) 'Capacity building and community development' in S Kenny and M Clarke (eds) *Challenging Capacity Building: Comparative Perspectives*, Palgrave, Basingstoke, pp. 67–83.

Ignatieff, M (2001) *Human Rights as Politics and Idolatry*. Princeton University Press, Princeton.

Ignatieff, M (2003) *EmpireLite: Nation-Building in Bosnia, Kosovo and Afghanistan*. Vintage, London.

Jamieson, D (2007) 'Justice: The heart of environmentalism', in R Sandler and P Pezullo (eds) *Environmental Justice and Environmentalism – The Social Justice Challenge to the Environmental Movement*, MIT Press, Cambridge, Massachusetts and London, pp. 85–102.

Jochum, V (2003) *Social Capital: Beyond the Theory*. National Council for Voluntary Organisations, London.

Johnson, J & Murton, B (2007) 'Re/placing native science: Indigenous voices in contemporary constructions of nature', *Geographical Research*, Vol. 45, No. 2, pp. 121–9.

Jones, C & Novak, T (1999) *Poverty, Welfare and the Disciplinary State*. Routledge, London.

Jones, D & Mayo, M (eds) (1974) *Community Work One*. Routledge & Kegan Paul, London.

Joyce, P & Woods, A (1996) *Essential Strategic Management: From Modernism to Pragmatism*. Butterworth Heinemann, Oxford.

Kanter, RM (1983) *The Change Masters*. Simon & Schuster, New York.

Keane, J (1988) *Democracy and Civil Society*. Verso, London.

Keat, R (1991) 'Introduction: Starship Britain or international enterprise?', in R Keat & N Abercrombie (eds), *Enterprise Culture*. Routledge, London.

Kemshall, H (2002) *Risk, Social Policy and Welfare*. Open University Press, Buckingham.

Kennedy, R (1982) *Australian Welfare History*. Macmillan, South Melbourne.

Kenny, S (2004) 'Non-government organisations and contesting active citizenship' in G Patmore (ed.), *The Vocal Citizen*. Arena, Fitzroy, pp. 70–85.

Kenny, S (2007) 'Reconstruction in Aceh: building whose capacity?', *Community Development Journal*, Vol. 42, No. 2, pp. 206–21.

Kenny, S (2008) 'Community development and environmentalism: the dilemmas of being a good ecological citizen', in *Community Development and Ecology Conference, Refereed Conference Proceedings*. Melbourne, pp. 214–29.

Kenny, S (2010) 'Reconstruction through participatory practice?' in M Clarke, I Fanany and S Kenny (2010) *Post-Disaster Reconstruction: Lessons from Aceh*. Earthscan, London, pp. 79–106.

Kenny, S, Mansouri, F & Spratt, P (2005) *Arabic Communities and Well-Being: Supports and Barriers to Social Connectedness*. Centre for Citizenship and Human Rights, Deakin University, Victoria.

Kettner, PM, Moroney, RM & Martin, MM (1990) *Designing and Managing Programs: An Effectiveness-based Approach*. Sage, London.

King, S & Maddock, R (1996) *Unlocking the Infrastructure: The Reform of Public Utilities in Australia*. Southwood Press, Sydney.

Knowles, C (2003) *Race and Social Analysis*. Sage, London.

Kothari, U (2005) 'From colonial administration to development studies: a postcolonial critique of the history of development studies', in U Kothari, *A Radical History of Development Studies: Individuals, Institutions and Ideologies*. Zed Books, London, pp. 47–66.

Kretzmann, J & McKnight, J (1993) *Building Communities from the Inside Out. A Path Toward Finding and Mobilizing a Community's Assets*. ACTA Publications, Stokie.

Kuhn, T (1962) *The Structure of Scientific Revolutions*. University of Chicago Press, Chicago.

Lamb, B (1997) *The Good Campaigns Guide*. NCVO Publications, London.

Landry, C et al. (1985) *What a Way to Run a Railroad: An Analysis of Radical Failure*. Comedia The Round, London.

Langer, J (1980) 'The structure and ideology of the "other news" and television', in P Edgar, *The News in Focus*. Macmillan, Melbourne.

Latham, M (1998) *Civilising Global Capital*. Allen & Unwin, Sydney.

Latham, M (2001) 'The Third Way: an outline', in A Giddens (ed.) *The Global Third Way Debate*. Polity Press, Cambridge, pp. 35–45.

Lather, P (1991) *Feminist Research in Education: Within/Against*. Deakin University Press, Geelong.

Laufer, W (2003) 'Social Accountability and corporate greenwashing', *Journal of Business Ethics*, No. 43, pp. 253–61.

Le Grand, J (1990) 'The state of welfare', in J Hills (ed.) *The State of Welfare: The Welfare State in Britain Since 1974*. Oxford University Press, London, pp. 338–62.

Leat, D (2000) 'Making partnerships work: typologies and conditions', in Third Sector and State Partnerships Conference Proceedings. Centre for Citizenship and Human Rights, Deakin University, Geelong, pp. 51–62.

Lee, P & Raban, C (1988) *Welfare Theory and Social Policy*. Sage, London.

Leggett, M (2009) Practical application of community development principles at Wadeye in the Northern Territory: lessons from a case study on the re-emergence of Thamarrurr, a traditional form of governance and the Council of Australian Governments Whole of Government Trial. Unpublished thesis, Deakin University.

Leighton, D (2009) *The Power Gap: An Index of Everyday Power in Britain*, Demos, London.

Lenin, VI (1971) *State and Revolution*. International, New York.

Levitas, R (1998) *The Inclusive Society? Social Exclusion and New Labour*. Macmillan, Basingstoke.

Levitas, R (2004) 'Let's hear it for Humpty: social exclusion, the third way and cultural capita', *Cultural Trends*, Vol. 13, No. 2, pp. 41–56.

Ling, T (2000) 'Unpacking partnerships: the case of health care', in J Clarke, J Gewirtz and E McLaughlin (eds), *New Managerialism, New Welfare?* Sage, London, in association with the Open University.

London Edinburgh Weekend Return Group (1980) *In and Against the State*. Pluto Press, London.

Lukes, S (1974) *Power: A Radical View*. Macmillan, London.

Lupton, D (1999a) *Risk*. Routledge, London.

Lupton, D (1999b) 'Introduction: risk and sociocultural theory', in D Lupton (ed.) *Risk and Sociocultural Theory*. Cambridge University Press, Cambridge, pp. 1–11.

Lynn, R, Thorpe, R & Miles, D (1998). '"Murri way!" – Aborigines and Torres Strait Islanders reconstruct social welfare practice'. Report on Aboriginal and Torres Strait Islander helping styles in social welfare practice in North Queensland. Townsville, Centre for Social Research, James Cook University.

Lyon, D (2001) *Surveillance Society: Monitoring Everyday Life*. Open University Press, Buckingham.

Lyon, D (2003) *Surveillance after September 11*. Polity Press, Cambridge.

References

Lyons, M (2000) 'The impossibility of public–private partnerships under quasi-market funding regimes: Australian case', Fourth International Research Symposium on Public Management, April. Erasmus University, Rotterdam.

Lyons, M (2001) *Third Sector*. Allen & Unwin, Crows Nest, NSW.

Lyons, M & Hocking, S (2000) *Dimensions of Australia's Third Sector*. Centre for Australian Community Organisations and Management, University of Technology, Sydney.

Lyotard, J (1984) *The Postmodern Condition*. Manchester University Press, Manchester.

MacCannell, D (1992) *Empty Meeting Grounds: The Tourist Papers*, Routledge, London.

Macintyre, S (1985) *Winners and Losers*. Allen & Unwin, Crows Nest, NSW.

Mackenzie, J (1993) *The HOPE Generator, or Bicarb and Beyond: Effective and Enjoyable Action for a Sustainable Way of Life*. HOPE Victoria, Mansfield.

MacNamara, J (1991) *The Public Relations Handbook for Clubs and Associations*. Information Australia, Melbourne.

Maher, C & Burke, T (1991) *Informed Decision-Making: The Use of Secondary Data Sources in Policy Studies*. Longman Cheshire: Melbourne.

Management Support and Training Unit (1993) *From Good Intentions to Good Practice*. Victorian Council of Social Service, Melbourne.

Mander, J & Goldsmith, E (1996) *The Case against the Global Economy: And the Turn to the Local*. Sierra Club Books, San Francisco.

Mann, M (2003) *Incoherent Empire*. Verso, London.

Manteaw, B (2008) 'From tokenism to social justice: rethinking the bottom line for sustainable community development', *Community Development Journal*, Vol. 43, No. 4, pp. 428–43.

Marks, D (2001) 'Disability and cultural citizenship: exclusion, "integration" and resistance', in N Stevenson (ed.) *Culture and Citizenship*. Sage, London, pp. 167–79.

Marsden, D & Oakley, P (1990) *Evaluating Social Development Projects*. Oxfam, Oxford.

Marshall, TH (1950) *Citizenship and Social Class*. Cambridge University Press, Cambridge.

Marshall, TH (1981) *The Right to Welfare, and Other Essays*. Heinemann, London.

Marx, K (1977) *Selected Writings*, D McLellan (ed.). Oxford University Press, Oxford.

Marx, K & Engels, F (1967) *The Communist Manifesto*, Introduction by A. J. P. Taylor. Penguin, Harmondsworth.

Marx, K & Engels, F (1976) *The German Ideology*. Progress, Moscow.

Maslow, A. (1962) *Toward a Psychology of Being*. Van Nostrand, New York.

Mathews, J (1989) *Age of Democracy*. Oxford University Press, Melbourne.

Mayo, M (2008) 'Community development, contestations, continuities and change', in G Craig, K Popple and M Shaw (eds) *Community Development in Theory and Practice: An International Reader*, Spokesman, Nottingham, pp. 13–27.

Mayo, M & Taylor, M (2001) 'Partnerships and power in community regeneration', in S Balloch and M Taylor, *Partnership Working, Policy and Practice*. Policy Press, Bristol, pp. 39–56.

McGrew, A (1992) 'A global society?', in S Hall, D Held and T McGrew (eds) *Modernity and its Futures*. Polity Press, in association with The Open University, Cambridge, pp. 61–116.

McNiff, J & Whitehead, J (2009) *Doing and Writing Action Research*. Sage, London.

Meadows, DH, Meadows, DL & Randers, J (1992) *Beyond the Limits—Global Collapse or a Sustainable Future*. Earthscan, London.

Merton, RK (1949) 'Discrimination and the American creed', in R McIver (ed.) *Discrimination and National Welfare*. Harper & Row, New York.

Metcalfe, A (1990) 'Myths of struggle: the metaphor of war and the misunderstanding of class'. Paper delivered to the Socialist Scholars Conference, Sydney University of Technology, October.

Michels, R (1959) *Political Parties*. Dover, New York.

Migliore RH, Stevens, RE, Loudon, DL, Williamson, SG & Winston, W (1995) *Strategic Planning for Not-for Profit Organizations*. Haworth Press, New York.

Miliband, D (ed.) (1994) *Reinventing the Left*. Polity Press, Cambridge.

Miller, C (2004a) 'Community practices in Australia', *Community Development Journal*, Vol. 39, No. 2, pp. 199–201.

Miller, C (2004b) 'Community development as the pursuit of human rights: the new direction of travel?', *Community Development, Human Rights and the Grassroots Conference Proceedings*. Melbourne, pp. 141–58.

Miller, C (2010) 'Developing capacities and agency in complex times', in S Kenny and M Clarke, *Challenging Capacity Building: Comparative Perspectives*. Palgrave, London, pp. 21–40.

Miller, N & Sammons, C (1999) *Everybody's Different: Understanding and Changing our

Reactions to Disabilities. Paul H. Brookes, Baltimore.

Mishra, R (1984) *The Welfare State in Crisis*. Harvester Press, London.

Moore, B (1978) *Injustice: The Social Bases of Obedience and Revolt*. Pantheon, New York.

Morgan, P (1998) *Capacity and Capacity Development – Some Strategies*. Political and Social Policies Division, Policy Branch, Canadian International Development Agency, Quebec.

Morris, J (2001) 'Impairment and disability: constructing an ethics of care that promotes human rights', *Hypatia*, Vol. 16, No. 4, pp. 1–16.

Mowbray, M (1984) 'Localism and hegemony in contemporary Australian social policy'. Paper delivered at the 54th ANZAAS Congress, May, Canberra.

Mowbray, M (1985) 'The medicinal properties of localism: a historical perspective', in R Thorpe and J Petruchenia (eds) *Community Work or Social Change?* Routledge & Kegan Paul, London.

Mowbray, M (2004) 'The new communitarianism: building great communities or brigadoonery?', *Just Policy*, No. 32, June, pp. 11–20.

Muetzelfeldt, M (1994) 'Contracts, politics and society', in J Alford and D O'Neill (eds) *The Contract State: Public Management and the Kennett Government*. Centre for Applied Social Research, Deakin University Press, Geelong, pp. 136–57.

Mune, M (1989) 'Implausible dreams: community work and the human services'. Paper delivered to AASW 21st national conference, Townsville, Queensland.

Murphy, J (2006) *Great Ideas to Make Your Community Project Successful*. Mornington Peninsula Community Connections, The Triple A Foundation, Wellington.

Mythen, G (2004) *Ulrich Beck: A Critical Introduction to the Risk Society*. Pluto Press, London.

Naess, A (1989) *Ecology, Community and Lifestyle*, D Rothenberg (trans.). Cambridge University Press, Cambridge.

Naess, A (2002) *Life's Philosophy: Reason and Feeling in a Deeper World*. University of Georgia Press, Athens, Georgia.

Nathan, D (ed.) (2007) 'Aboriginal languages of Australia', www.dnathan.com/VL/austLang.htm.

Nederveen Pieterse, J (2001) *Development Theory, Deconstructions/Reconstructions*. Sage, London.

Neville, L (1992) 'More than a passing interest', *Community Quarterly*, No. 23, pp. 28–33.

Nussbaum, M & Sen, A (eds) (1993) *The Quality of Life*, Clarendon Press, Oxford.

O'Connor, J (1973) *The Fiscal Crisis of the State*. St Martins Press, New York.

O'Shaughnessy, T (1999) *Capacity Building: A New Approach*. World Vision, Melbourne.

O'Sullivan, K (1994) *Understanding Ways: Communicating Between Cultures*. Hale & Ironmonger, Sydney.

Offe, C (1984) *Contradictions of the Welfare State*. Hutchinson, London.

Offe, C (1999) 'How can we trust our fellow citizens?', in M Warren (ed.), *Democracy and Trust*. Cambridge University Press, Cambridge, pp. 42–87.

Onyx, J & Bullen, P (2000) 'Measuring social capital in five communities', *Journal of Applied Behavioural Science*, Vol. 36, No. 1, pp. 23–42.

Osborne, D & Gaebler, T (1993) *Reinventing Government: How the Entrepreneurial Spirit is Transforming the Public Sector*. Plume, New York.

Paddon, M (1993) 'Taking contracting seriously: the current debate in the UK and Europe', in J Coulter (ed.) *Doing More with Less: Contracting Out and Efficiency in the Public Sector*. Public Service Research Centre, Kensington, NSW, pp. 62–71.

Pakulski, J (1991) 'The shrinking state'. Paper delivered at the Annual Conference of the Australian Sociology Association, December. Murdoch University, Perth.

Papadakis, E (1990) 'Privatisation and the welfare state', in B Hindess (ed.), *Reactions to the Right*. Routledge, London.

Payne, G & Payne, J (2004) *Key Concepts in Social Research*. Sage, London.

Peavy, F (1994) *By Life's Grace*. New Society, Philadelphia.

Peurkayastha (2010) 'Interrogating intersectionality: contemporary globalisation and radicalised gendering in the lives of highly educated South Asian Americans and their children', *Journal of Intercultural Studies*, Vol. 31, No. 1, pp. 29–48.

Pierson, J (2002) *Tackling Social Exclusion*. Routledge, Abingdon.

Pin-Fat, V (2000) '(Im)possible universalism: reading human rights in world politics', *Review of International Studies*, Vol. 26, pp. 663–74.

Piven, FF & Cloward, RA (1971) *Regulating the Poor: The Functions of Public Welfare*. Vintage, New York.

Popple, K (2008) 'The first forty years: the history of the *Community Development Journal*'. *Community Development Journal*, Vol. 43, No 1, pp. 6–23.

References

Powell, D (2006) 'Technologies of existence: the indigenous environmental justice movement', *Development*, Vol. 49, No. 3, pp 125–32.

Powell, F & Geoghegan, M (2006) 'Beyond political zoology: community development, civil socciety and strong democracy', *Community Development Journal*, Vol. 41, No. 2, pp. 128–42.

Power, M (1997) *The Audit Society: Rituals of Verification*. Oxford University Press, Oxford.

Pretty, J (1995) 'Participatory learning for sustainable agriculture', *World Development*, Vol. 2, No. 8, pp. 1247–63.

Productivity Commission (2010) *Contribution of the Not-for-Profit Sector*, Productivity Commission Research Report, Australian Government, Canberra.

Pusey, M (1991) *Economic Rationalism in Canberra*. Cambridge University Press, Cambridge.

Pusey, M (2003) *The Experience of Middle Australia: The Dark Side of Economic Reform*. Cambridge University Press, Cambridge.

Putnam, RD (1993) *Making Democracy Work: Civic Traditions in Modern Italy*. Princeton University Press, New Jersey.

Putnam, RD (2000) *Bowling Alone: The Collapse and Revival of American Community*. Simon & Schuster, New York.

Putnam, RD (ed.) (2002) *Democracies in Flux: The Evolution of Social Capital in Contemporary Society*. Oxford University Press, Oxford.

Radhakrishnan, R (1996) *Diasporic Mediations between Home and Location*. University of Minneapolis Press, Minneapolis.

Reed, H, Cameron, D & Spinks, D (1985) *Stepping Stones: A Management Training Manual for Community Groups*. Community Management Training Scheme, Hurstville, NSW.

Rees, S (1991) *Achieving Power*. Allen & Unwin, Sydney.

Rees, S & Rodley, G (eds) (1995) *The Human Costs of Managerialism*. Pluto Press, Leichhardt, NSW.

Reich, R (1992) *The Work of Nations*. Vintage, New York.

Repo, M (1977) 'The fallacy of community control', in J Cowley et al. (eds) *Community or Class Struggle*. Stage 1, London.

Ritzer, G (2000) *Contemporary Sociological Theory and its Classical Roots: The Basics*. McGraw Hill, New York.

Ritzer, G (2004) *The Globalization of Nothing*. Pine Forge Press, Thousand Oaks.

Roberts, J (1985) *Successful Submission Writing*. Information Australia, Melbourne.

Roberts, J (1991) *The Committee Members' Voluntary Handbook*. Information Australia, Melbourne.

Rossouw, AMM (1996) *Community Development: A Concept for Social Change and Development*. University of Port Elizabeth, Republic of South Africa.

Rowbotham, S, Segal, L & Wainwright, H (1979) *Beyond the Fragments*. Merlin Press, London.

Rubin, F (1995) *A Basic Guide to Evaluation for Development Workers*. Oxfam, Oxford.

Rubin, H & Rubin, I (1992) *Community Organising and Development*, 2nd edn. Macmillan, New York.

Said, E (1978) *Orientalism*. Pantheon, New York.

Salamon, LM & Anheier, HK (1996) *The Emerging Nonprofit Sector: An Overview*. Manchester University Press, Manchester.

Salamon, LM, Anheier, HK, List, R, Toepler, S, Sokolowski, SW & Associates (1999) *Global Civil Society: Dimensions of the Nonprofit Sector*. The Johns Hopkins Center for Civil Society Studies, Baltimore.

Sanderson, I (1993) *Management of Quality in Local Government*. Longman, London.

Sarkar, S (1999) *Eco-Socialism or Eco-capitalism? A Critical Analysis of Humanity's Fundamental Choices*. Zed Books, London.

Sassoon, AS (1987) *Women and the State*. Allen & Unwin, London.

Scott, CD & Jaffe, DT (1991) *Empowerment: Building a Committed Workforce*. Crisp, California.

Scott, D (1981) *Don't Mourn for Me—Organise!* Allen & Unwin, Sydney.

Seabrook, J (1982) *Unemployment*. Quartet, London.

Seers, D (1969) 'The meaning of development'. Paper presented at the 11th World Conference of the Society for International Development, New Delhi.

Sekuless, P (1991) *Lobbying Canberra in the Nineties: The Government Relations Game*. Allen & Unwin, Crows Nest, NSW.

Sen, A (1999) *Development as Freedom*. Oxford University Press, Oxford.

Sennett, R (1998) *The Corrosion of Character: The Personal Consequences of Work in the New Capitalism*. WW Norton, New York.

Sennett, R (2004) *Respect: The Formation of Character in an Age of Inequality*. Penguin, London.

Shearman, D & Smith, J (2007) *The Climate Change Challenge and the Failure of Democracy*. DEA Publications, Praeger, Connecticut.

References

Shields, K (1991) *In the Tiger's Mouth: An Empowerment Guide for Social Action*. Millennium, Newtown, NSW.

Simon, R (1991) *Gramsci's Political Thought: An Introduction*. Lawrence & Wishart, London.

Singer, P (1993) *How Are We to Live? Ethics in the Age of Self-Interest*. Text, Melbourne.

Skoll Centre for Social Entrepreneurship (2009) 'Is there a new way of addressing the big social issues? More on social innovation', www.sbs.ox.ac.uk/centres/skoll/research/Pages/socialinnovation.aspx.

Smart, B (1990) 'Modernism, postmodernism and the present', in B Turner (ed.) *Theories of Modernism and Postmodernism*. Sage, London.

Smith, BC (1998) 'Participation without empowerment: subterfuge or development', *Community Development Journal*, Vol. 33, No. 3, pp. 197–204.

Smith, B (2004) 'Rhetoric or reality: has 'community' delivered for Aboriginal people in remote Australia?, in Community Development, Human Rights and the Grassroots Conference Proceedings. Centre for Citizenship and Human Rights, Deakin University, Geelong. pp. 252–5.

Social and Civic Policy Institute (2000) *Public Politics in Practice*. Social and Civic Policy Institute, Wellington, New Zealand.

Social and Community Services Industry Training Board (1990) *Social and Community Services Industry Training Plan*. SACS Industry Training Board, Hawthorn.

Social Enterprise Coalition (2010) 'About social enterprise', www.socialenterprise.org.uk/pages/about-social-enterprise.html.

Southern Regional Community Health Research Unit (1991) *Planning Healthy Communities*. Southern Regional Community Health Research Unit, Bedford Park, SA.

Spandler, H (2007) 'From social exclusion to inclusion? A critique of the inclusion imperative in mental health', *Medical Sociology Online*, Vol. 2, No. 2, at www.medicalsociologyonline.org/archives/issue22/spandler.html.

Spencer, H (1964) 'The evolution of societies', in A Etzioni and E Etzioni (eds) *Social Change: Sources, Patterns and Consequences*. Basic Books, New York.

Stacey, M (1969) 'The myth of community studies', *British Journal of Sociology*, Vol. 20, pp. 25–49.

Stanton, A (1989) 'Citizens of workplace democracies', *Critical Social Policy*, No. 26, Autumn.

Steger, M (2003) *Globalization: A Very Short Introduction*. Oxford University Press, Oxford.

Stern, N (2006) *The Economics of Climate Change*. The Stern Review, Cambridge University Press, Cambridge.

Stewart, C & Cash, W (1994) *Interviewing Principles and Practices*. Brown & Benchmark, Madison, Wisconsin.

Stewart-Weeks, M (2001) 'Voice and the Third Sector: why social entrepreneurs matter', *Third Sector Review*, Vol. 7, No. 2, pp. 23–40.

Tam, H (1998) *Communitarianism: A New Agenda for Politics and Citizenship*. Macmillan, Basingstoke.

Taylor, P & Mayo, M (2008) 'Editorial', *Community Development Journal*, Vol. 43, No. 3, pp. 263–8.

Thas, A (1992) 'The Grameen Bank, replicating a success story', *Community Quarterly*, No. 23, pp. 33–7.

Thomas, D (1983) *The Making of Community Work*. Allen & Unwin, London.

Thorpe, R (1985) 'Community work and ideology: an Australian perspective', in R Thorpe and J Petruchenia (eds) *Community Work or Social Change*. Routledge & Kegan Paul, London.

Timmons, G (1992) 'Philanthropic trusts: the 10 most asked questions', *Community Quarterly*, No. 23, pp. 17–21.

Tobin, J (1994) *A Tax on International Currency Transactions*. UNDP Human Development Report. Oxford University Press, New York.

Todaro, MP (1994) *Economic Development*. Longman, New York.

Toennies, F (1987) *Community and Association*. Michigan State University Press, Michigan.

Tomlinson, J (1999) *Globalisation and Culture*. Polity Press, Cambridge.

Touraine, A (1981) *The Voice and the Eye*. Cambridge University Press, Cambridge.

Touraine, A (1988) *Return of the Actor*. University of Minnesota Press, Minneapolis.

Turner, BS (1986) *Citizenship and Capitalism*. Allen & Unwin, London.

Turner, BS (1999) 'McCitizens: risk, coolness and irony in contemporary politics', in B Smart (ed.), *Resisting McDonaldization*. Sage, London, pp. 83–100.

Twelvetrees, A (1982) *Community Work*. Macmillan, London.

United Nations (1948) *Universal Declaration of Human Rights*. United Nations General Assembly.

References

United Nations Development Programme (1996) *The Copenhagen Alternative Declaration*. UNDP, Copenhagen.

United Nations Development Programme (1997) *Capacity Development*. Technical Advisory Paper 2, July. Management Development and Governance Division, UNDP, New York.

University of Michigan Health System (2006) 'Program for multicultural health', at www.med.umich.edu/multicultural/ccp/basic.htm#continuum.

VCOSS (1991) *Community Management Handbook*. Victorian Council of Social Service, Collingwood, Victoria.

Verity, F (2004), 'Building stronger communities – "risky" business in an environment of rising public liability insurance?', *Just Policy*, No. 32, June, pp. 11–20.

Volunteering Australia (2005), *Definition and Principles of Volunteering*. Volunteering Australia, Melbourne.

von Kaufmann, KH (2002) *The Enemy of Nature: The End of Capitalism or the End of the World*. Zed Books, London.

Wadsworth, Y (1991) *Everyday Evaluation on the Run*. Action Research Issues Association, Melbourne.

Wadsworth, Y (1997) *Everyday Evaluation on the Run*, 2nd edn. Allen & Unwin, Crows Nest, NSW.

Wainwright, H (2003) *Reclaim the State: Experiments in Popular Democracy*. Verso, London.

Walsh, F & Mitchell, P (2002) *Planning for Country. Cross-cultural Approaches to Decision-making on Aboriginal Lands*. Jukurrpa Books, Alice Springs.

Ward, D & Mullender, A (1991) 'Empowerment and oppression in an indissoluble pairing for contemporary social work', *Critical Social Policy*, No. 32, Autumn, pp. 21–30.

Ward, J (1991) *Community Development Tactics: Parts I and II*. Victoria College Press, Burwood, Victoria.

Ward, S (1984) *Organising Things*. Pluto Press, London.

Warren, ME (2001) *Democracy and Association*. Princeton University Press, Princeton.

Wates, N (2000) *The Community Planning Handbook*. Earthscan, London.

Watson, D (2003) *Death Sentence: How Cliches, Weasel Words and Management-Speak are Strangling Public Language*. Random House, Scoresby, Victoria.

Watson, S (ed.) (1990) *Playing the State: Australian Feminist Interventions*. Allen & Unwin, Sydney.

Weber, M (1946) *From Max Weber: Essays in Sociology*, HH Girth and CW Mills (eds). Routledge & Kegan Paul, London.

Wellman, B & Gulia, M (1999) 'Virtual communities as communities: net surfers don't ride alone', in M Smith and P Kollock (eds) *Communities in Cynberspace*. Routledge, London, pp. 167–94.

Wheen, F (2004) *How Mumbo-Jumbo Conquered the World*. Harper Perennial, London.

Wild, RA (1981) *Australian Community Studies and Beyond*. Allen & Unwin, Sydney.

Williams, M (2003) *Making Sense of Social Research*. Sage, London.

Williams, R (2000) *The Non-Designer's Web Book: An Easy Guide to Creating, Designing and Posting Your Own Web Site*, 2nd edn. PeachPit Press, New Jersey.

Wilson, E (1977) *Women and the Welfare State*. Tavistock, London.

Wilson, K (1996) 'Demystifying the tendering process', *Community Quarterly*, No. 42, pp. 44–7.

Winter, I (ed.) (2000) *Social Capital and Public Policy in Australia*. Australian Institute of Family Studies, Melbourne.

Woodcock, G (1962) *Anarchism*. Penguin, London.

Woolcock, M (2001) 'The place of social capital in understanding social and economic outcomes', *Canadian Journal of Policy Responses*, Vol. 2. No. 1, February, pp. 11–17.

Wyatt, M (1995) 'A glimmer of hope: community empowerment through tax reform', *Community Quarterly*, No. 36, pp. 10–14.

Yates, H & Jochum, V (2003) *It's Who You Know That Counts: The Role of the Voluntary Sector in the Development of Social Capital in Rural Areas*. NCVO, London.

Young, I (1990) 'The ideal of community and the politics of difference', in L Nicholson (ed.) *Feminism/Postmodernism*. Routledge, New York.

Young, IM (1983) 'Justice and hazardous waste: the applied turn in contemporary philosophy bowling green studies', *Applied Philsosophy*, No. 5, pp. 171–83.

Index

AAP *see* Australian Assistance Plan
ABCD *see* asset-based community development
accountability 15, 137, 233–4, 343–4, 346, 365, 371
action plans 217–19, 220
action research 373
active citizenship 25–6, 67, 129–30
activism 291–2, 428–9
    activist approach (strategic development) 206–7
    activist model (community organisation) 233–4
    versus professionalism 401–2
advocacy 298–9, 416
affective action 117
affirmation model (disability approach) 334–5
amalgamation 256–7
anarchism 143–4
Apology 332
assertiveness 285
asset-based approach (communities) 190–1, 205–6, 379
asset-based community development (ABCD) 206, 209–10
associative democracy 56–7
asylum seekers 184
attending/attention 284–5
audit review 211, 388–9, 390
Australian Assistance Plan (AAP) 44
authenticity 34, 373–4, 415
autonomy 56, 57, 61, 111, 335, 383

bargaining power 303
barter 351
benchmarking 370–1
best practice 370–1
binary division 335, 412
bluewashing 76
bonding social capital 126
bottom-up development 41–3
bourgeoisie 95
bridging social capital 126
bureaucracy 238–40, 294
burnout 419

campaigns (political) 290–1
capacity building 316–17
    approaches 194–6, 199
    case study 196
    community capacity building 193–202
    and community development 198–202
    criticisms 197
    elements and framework 197–8
    indicators of increased capacity 201–2
    mutual capacity building approach 196
    performance monitoring 194–5
    in practice 197–8
    principles 200–1
    projects 194–6
capital 8, 60, 95, 125–30, 277–8, 325
capital–labour relation 95
capitalism 93, 95, 97, 98, 101–2, 109–10, 157–9
    global capitalism 114–15, 416
    master capitalist 144
    state monopoly capitalism (stamocap) 145
CDEP *see* Community Development Employment Projects
centralisation/decentralisation 61, 111, 167–8
charity model 232–3, 333
citizen-directed taxation 361
citizenship 25–7, 67, 235
    active citizenship 25–6, 67, 129–30
    corporate citizenship 16, 75–7
civic engagement 42
civil labour 129
civil society concept 128–30, 142, 229
class struggle 54
coercion 180
collaboration 375, 408
collective action 28, 47–9
collective endeavour 69–70, 228, 334–5
collective models (community organisations) 242–4
collectivism 323
co-location 256–7
committees
    committee of management 242, 247–9
    committee work 244–54
    establishing 246–9
    meetings 245–6, 289
    policy and procedures 260–1
commodification 160, 353
communication 280–7, 330–1, 407
    case studies 272–3, 280, 286–7
    communication styles and teamwork 281
    communicative competence 250
    within and between cultures 311–12
    dialogical communication 250, 281
    Freire's view 282
    and globalisation 61–2
    involvement and giving voice 273–5
    non-verbal communication 285
    principles 336
    promotional communication 250, 281
    public speaking 289
    skills 287–303
    and technology 294
    tools 291–2

Index

communism 95
communitarianism 47–50
community 44–53, 124, 190–1, 300
    case study 54
    and communitarianism 47–9
    community capacity building 193–202
    community control of needs studies 383–6
    community foundations 355–7
    concept of community 8–12, 44–53, 127, 197, 329
    exploiting the community 415–16
    feminist critiques 50
    gemeinschaft/gesellschaft dichotomy 46, 47, 50–1, 403
    organising with communities 277
    as a site 45–6
    social and community services industry 14–16
    socialist perspective 49–50
    in sociological theory 46–7
    as study object 45
    usefulness debate 51–3
    virtual communities 9, 50–1
community assets research 378–9
community development
    activism versus professionalism 401–2
    activities 266–303
    building trust and respect 277–8
    and capacity building 198–202
    community backdrop 44–53
    conflict management 299–303
    constraints and challenges 426–8
    contexts 7–8, 41–79, 208–10
    cosmopolitan model 400
    defining 8–13
    directions 428–30
    diversity 21, 307–37
    domains 36
    elements 33–8
    feminist contribution to 104
    freedom versus equality 402–3
    funding 342–91
    giving voice 273–5, 278
    global backdrop 58–65
    and green perspectives 111–15
    heroic school of community organising 399
    history 41–3
    as international practice 16–17
    key themes 5–7
    language and discourse 115–21, 410–11, 427
    localism as parochialism 404–5
    making contact 271–3
    Marxist influence 92–3
    modernity and postmodernity 119–21
    nature 2–38
    new themes, concepts and theories 121–31
    nostalgia versus avant-garde 403
    opportunities and tools 279–80
    organising with communities 277
    policy backdrop 65–79
    political backdrop 53–8
    practice 16–17, 85–6, 174–224, 266–303
    principles 12–13, 21–32
    processes 32–8
    public image 287–96
    'pure' community development 398–400
    research 342–91
    resources 256–7, 279–80, 344–61
    settings 4–5, 284
    skills 279–80, 282–7
    and social movements 106–7
    and the state 137–68, 405–6
    teamwork development 278
    terminology 8–12
    theoretical perspectives 83, 86–115, 121–31, 407
    theory–practice relationship 85–6
    welfare backdrop 43–4
    working with local government 275–6
Community Development Employment Projects (CDEP) 329
community development workers 14, 76
    abilities 19
    advocacy 298–9, 416
    burnout 419
    and conflict 299–303
    employer–employee relationship 260
    facilitators versus leaders 413–15
    financial counselling 299
    'heroic' failure 420–1
    key skills 19–21
    link to levels of government 137–8
    and lobbying 295–6
    managing stress 419–21
    modernity and postmodernity 119–21
    and operating rationales 427
    roles 17–21
    social policy development 297–8
    tasks 17
    work demands 418–21
community needs studies 378, 379–86
community organisations 228–62, 426
    accountability, relevance and effectiveness 343–4
    appropriate structures 244
    case studies 229–30, 254–5
    collective models 242–4
    co-location and amalgamation 256–7
    committee work 244–54
    and community development work 13–17
    creative community organisations 261–2

Index

and democracy 406–7
funding 344–61
industrial disputes 257–61, 301
life cycles 254–7
and lobbying 295–6
models 231–7, 242–4
nature 230–44
partnerships with the state 149–51
public image 287–96
resources 256–7, 344–61
responsibilities 257–61
size of the sector 230–1
structures 237–44
compacts 149–50
comparative needs 382
competency 176–9, 409
communicative competence 250
cross-cultural competence 311–16, 429
types 177–9
competition 407–10
competitive tendering 346, 358–9, 367–71, 408–9
preparing a tender 369–71
quality assurance, best practice and benchmarking 370–1
tender specifications and briefs 368–9
'tenderor'; 'tenderer' 368
unit price 369
compliance regimes 410
conflict 29–30, 406–7, 409
conflict management 299–303
internal conflict 301–3
power of deliberation and negotiation 429
resolution 300–1
understanding 299–301
conscientisation 187, 282
consent 180
constructionism 376
consultation 188
contested terrain 141, 145, 149
contract state 141, 145–7
contracts/contracting out 13–14, 166, 358–9, 368, 407–8
contractualism 166
cooperatives (workers') 348–51, 352
co-option 410–11, 427
corporate bureaucracy 240
corporate citizenship 16, 75–7
corporate funding 360–1
corporate management 162
corporate social responsibility (CSR) 15–16, 75–7
corporate sponsorship 353–4
cosmopolitan cultures 325–8
cosmopolitanism 64, 65, 400
crisis management 158–9
critical autonomy 383

critical reference group 375
critical theory 93–4, 293
cross-cultural competence 311–16, 429
cross-cultural practice 29, 316–28
cross-cultural relationships 328
cross-cultural solidarity 6
CSR *see* corporate social responsibility
culturalism 322, 413
culturally and linguistically diverse (CALD) groups 4, 20, 307–8
culture
cosmopolitan cultures and identities 325–8
cultural circles 282
cultural understandings 318–28
culturally and linguistically diverse (CALD) groups 4, 20, 307–8
enterprise culture 71–2, 74–5
Geert Hofstede's typologies 323–5
high- and low-context cultures 322–3
intercultural sensitivity 308
monochronic and polychronic cultures 320–2
performance management 78–9, 194–5
term 'culture' 318

DDA *see* Disability Discrimination Act
deconstruction 85
deep ecology 108
deficit-based approach (communities) 190, 196
deliberative democracy 31–2, 249–54, 429
democracy 152, 246, 294–5
associative democracy 56–7
deliberative democracy 31–2, 249–54, 429
democratic approach to capacity building 195–6, 199
democratic decision making 406–7, 429
extending 167–8
liberal democracy 142–3
participatory democracy 16, 30–2
representative democracy 31
deregulation 69
'descending ladder of abstraction' 215
development
bottom-up development 41–3
and the freedom concept 11–12
the term 'development' 9–12
Development for Peace 318
devolution of responsibility 159, 160–1
dialogical communication 250, 281
difference 125, 307–37
case study 316–17
categories 309, 310–11
cultural difference 319–28
and identity formation 308–11
see also diversity

453

Index

direct action 290–1
disability 309, 310–11, 332–7
    approaches 333–5
    case study 334
Disability Discrimination Act (DDA) 336
disabled identity 309
disadvantage 22, 24, 43–4, 66–7, 138, 232–3
    class and gender analyses 308
    and moral righteousness 412–13
    see also poverty
discrimination 91–2, 336
    racial discrimination 85–6, 91–2, 313
distributive justice 113
diversity 28–9, 125, 184, 407
    in community development 21, 307–37
    culturally and linguistically diverse (CALD) groups 4, 20
    see also difference
domestication 282

ecology 107–11
economic determinism 95
economic rationalism 69–75
elite theory 142
emancipatory politics 2
empathy 282, 283
empirical knowledge 269
employer–employee relationship 260
empowerment 26, 179–87, 234, 240, 334–5, 361, 426
    case study 192–3
    and the human condition 185–7
    indicators 191–2
    in practice 190–3
enchanted workplace 74
engagement (communication) 285–7
Enlightenment period 116, 117, 118
enterprise culture 71–2, 74–5
entrepreneurship 70–2, 74, 347
    social entrepreneurship 14, 75, 236–7
environmental authoritarianism 111
environmental justice 112–13
environmentalism 107–8
epistemology 376
equalitarian societies 55
equality concept 402–3
essentialism 307, 309, 319, 325, 335, 337
ethical investment 348
ethics 348, 378
ethnicity/ethnic identity 309, 310–11
ethnocentrism 92
ethno-nationalism 417
ethno-specific organisations 20
evaluation 220–1, 386–91
    approaches 388–90

    criticisms 390–1
    culture of evaluation 387–8
    rationales 386
    when to evaluate 387
existentialist feminism 100
exoticised Other 314–15
expressed needs 381–2
external funding 344–5

facilitation 413–15
fair trade approach 113
Family Centre Project 43
felt needs 381
femininity–masculinity scale 324
feminism 50, 84–5, 99–104, 156–7, 239, 381, 418
    class and gender analyses 308
    and conflict 300
    contribution to community development 104
    eco-feminist perspectives (of green movement) 110–11
    and empowerment 192
    existentialist feminism 100
    feminisation of poverty 85–6
    feminist theory 24, 54–5
    feminist views of the state 154
    liberal feminism 100–1
    Marxist and socialist feminism 101–2
    and mass manipulation 293
    postmodern feminism 103–4
    psychoanalytic feminism 100
    radical feminism 102–3
    socialist feminism 101–2
financial counselling 299
Foucauldian analysis 116
fragmentation 61
free market 89
freedom concept 11–12, 402–3
functionalism 87–8
fundamentalism 417–18
funding (community organisations) 344–61
    compliance regimes 410
    funding agreements 365–7
    funding issues 346–7
    government funding 357–9
    self funding 344–5, 347–53
    submission-based funding 358, 361–6
    types of funding 347–61
    see also grants; service agreements
future visions workshop 385

Gantt charts 218
gemeinschaft/gesellschaft dichotomy 46, 50–1, 403
gender 99, 104, 308
generative politics 56–7

generic managers 73
genuineness 282, 283
giving voice 273–5, 278
global capitalism 114–15, 416
global financial crisis (GFC) 90, 145, 416
globalisation 17, 58–65, 113, 325, 428
    ambiguities 416
    contradictory processes 60–1
    forms 59–60
governance 69, 117, 146, 166, 246–7
government funding 357–9
governmentality approach (to organisation/management) 146, 167, 184–5
Grameen Bank 348–9
grammar of life 105–6
grants 344–5, 356–7
green movement 107–11
    and community development 111–15
    definition of nature 108–9
    eco-anarchist perspectives 111
    eco-feminist perspectives 110–11
    eco-socialist perspectives 109–10
    environmental authoritarianism 111
    green responses 108
    growth focus and technological progress 109
    relocalisation movement 114–15
greenwashing 76

healthy visions methodology 385
'heroic' failure 420–1
heroic school of community organising 399
hierarchical organisation (community organisations) 241
high-context cultures 322–3
historical funding 358
historical materialism 93
historicity 105
Hofstede's typologies (culture) 323–5
homogenisation 60–1
horizontal organisation (community organisations) 240–2
human agency 186
human condition 185–7
human needs *see* needs studies
human rights 8, 25–7, 57–8, 186, 335–6, 383, 433–7

identity 125, 308–11, 323, 330
    cosmopolitan cultures and identities 325–8
identity politics 319
ideological hegemony 181, 182
ideology 97, 180–3
    challenging 182–3
    ideological state apparatuses 144
    ideology of difference 310

impartiality 23
incorporation 257
independent state 140, 142–3
    see also state, the
Indigenous people 5, 312–13, 314–15, 352
    Apology 332
    Indigenous and non-Indigenous relations 329–32
    practice in Indigenous projects 330–2
individualisation 22, 71
individualism 323
industrial disputes 257–61, 301
industrialisation 46–7
information 33, 34, 246, 373–4, 415
    information technology 294
in-person services 177
instrumental rationality 118, 250, 323
integration 61
intercultural sensitivity 308
interlocking state 141, 144–5
internal conflict 301–3
internal funding 344–5
Internet 53, 61–2, 272–3, 279, 291
intersectionality 308
interventions 7–8, 9, 36–8

justice 8, 23–5, 112–14

knowledge 269–71

labour 94, 95, 129
laissez-faire state 142
leadership 277, 413–15
Left, the 55, 59
legislation 295–6, 336
legitimation crisis 158
LETS *see* Local Employment and Trading System
liberal democracy 142–3
liberal feminism 100–1
liberalism 88–90
liberation 30–2
line management 238
linking social capital 126
listening 284–5
lobbying 295–6
Local Employment and Trading System (LETS) 351
local government 154–5
    case studies 138, 275–6
localism 325, 404–5
London Edinburgh Weekend Return Group 139
low-context cultures 322–3

management
    committee of management 242, 247–9
    conflict management 299–303

Index

corporate management 162
crisis management 158–9
employer–employee relationship 260
line management 238
scientific management 238–40
managerialism
   'generic managers' 73
   new managerialism 32, 72–3, 239–40, 407, 427
manipulation 188, 189
   mass manipulation 293
market model (community organisation) 236
marketisation 159–62
Marxism 24, 54, 84–5, 92–8, 144, 239
   class and gender analyses 308
   critique of social welfare programs 95–6
   Marxist feminism 101–2
   Marxist philosophy 93–4
   and mass manipulation 293
   orthodox Marxist theory 96
   political struggle 96–7
   restructured theory and practice 97–8
   structure of societies and social change 94–5
   and the welfare state 156–7
   Western Marxists 96, 97
masculinity–femininity scale 324
mass media 292–5
   bureaucratic framework 294
   democratisation framework 294–5
   mass manipulation 293
   pluralist approach 293
master capitalist 144
medical model (disability approach) 333
meetings 245–6, 289
metanarrative 84
metrics 376, 409
microcredit 344, 347, 348–51
mistake of causality 378
mistake of lineality 205, 224
modernism 117–18
modernity 10, 27–8, 117–18, 119–21, 429
   instrumental rationality and technocratic consciousness 118
monochronic cultures 320–2
mores 318–19
multi-active society 129
multiculturalism 312–14
mutuality 409

native leaders 277
needs approach (problem solving) 302–3
needs studies 181–2, 378, 379–86
   case study 384–5
   community control of 383–6
   needs assessment and identification 379–80, 385–6

needs-based funding 358
needs-based planning 379–80
and strategic plans 385–6
theories of human needs 382–3
types of needs 380–2
negotiation 302, 366, 429
neighbourhood renewal 193–4
neo-authoritarian state 164–5
neo-liberalism 13–14, 66, 69–75, 88–90, 148, 165–6, 367, 400
   critique 89–90
   effects 162–4
   and the mantra of competition 407–10
   neo-liberal policy 426–7
   and the welfare state 156, 159
networking 271–3, 275–6, 291, 409
new managerialism 32, 72–3, 239–40, 407, 427
New Right 89–90, 161
newspeak or spin 411
non-government organisations (NGOs) 62, 229, 318
non-hierarchical organisation (community organisations) 242
non-participation 189–90
non-profit organisations 229
non-verbal communication 285
normative needs 380–1
norms 318, 325
not-for-profit sector 67, 78–9, 153, 229

objectivism 376
objectivity 23
open enquiry 211
open societies 30–2
operating rationale 232–7
oppression 412–13, 425
organic analogy 87
organic leaders 277
organisations (community) 13–17
Orientalism 315–16
orthodox Marxist theory 96
Other, the 313–14, 335, 337, 412
   exoticised Other 314–15
   as a threat 315
ownership 188, 375

panopticon vision 184–5
parochialism 404–5
participation 187–90, 274, 330–1, 407
participatory democracy 16, 30–2
participatory justice 113–14
participatory research 375
particularisation 60–1
partnership state 141, 148–51
   social investment state 152
partnerships 138, 149–51, 166, 188, 353–4

Index

passive citizenship 25–6, 67
patriarchy 54–5, 99–100, 102–3, 110–11
per capita funding 358
performance indicators 389
performance management 78–9, 194–5
performance review 389–90
performance-based funding 358
performativity 78–9, 240, 409
philanthropic trusts 347, 355–7
pluralism 235, 293
policy 65–79, 138
    committee policy and procedures 260–1
    competition policy 367
    compliance regimes 410
    economic policy 367
    neo-liberal policies 162–4, 407–10, 426–7
    policy and procedures manuals 237–8, 260–1
    privatisation policies 13–14
    social inclusion policies 66–9, 329, 332
    social policy 297–8
    top-down approach 68
politics 53–8
    campaigns 290–1
    and communication 250–1, 290–1
    emancipatory politics 2
    generative politics 56–7
    identity politics 319
    the Left 55, 59
    and lobbying 295–6
    political action 53–5, 290–1
    political literacy 282
    political struggle 96–7
    prefigurative politics 32, 96
    rethinking politics 56–7
    third way approach 152
polychronic cultures 320–2
postmodern feminism 103–4
postmodernism 103–4, 118–21
poverty 43–4, 156–7, 232–3
    case study 254–5
    feminisation of poverty 85–6
    see also disadvantage
power 415–16
    bargaining power 303
    case study 185
    centralised state power 163–4
    community as a site 45–6
    of compliance regimes 410
    empowerment 26, 179–87, 234, 240, 334–5, 361, 426
    ideas of power 179–83
    ideological state apparatuses 97
    and modernism 117–18
    power differentials 405
    power distance 323–4
    power imbalances 6
    power of example 12–13, 32
    'powerless people' 23–5
    practices and processes 183–5
PPPs *see* private public partnerships
pragmatism 35, 373–4
praxis 85–6
prefigurative politics 32, 96
private public partnerships (PPPs) 78–9
private sector organisations 13–14, 147
privatisation 13–14, 77–8, 159–62, 165, 166
procedural bureaucracy 240
production 24, 94, 177
professionalism 175–6
    versus activism 401–2
    professional training 409
project of modernity 10, 117–18
proletariat 94
promotional communication 250, 281
protagonists 291, 300, 301–3
psychoanalytic feminism 100
public image 287–96
public meetings 289
public speaking 289
publicity events 289–91
    mass media 292–5
purchaser–provider split 147

qualitative research 372
quality assurance 370–1
quantitative research 372

'race' identity 309, 310–11
racism/racial discrimination 85–6, 91–2, 313
radical feminism 102–3
radicalism 107
rationality crisis 158
reification 143
religious fundamentalism 417–18
relocalisation movement 114–15
representative democracy 31
repressive state apparatuses 144
research 342–91
    action research 373
    approaches 375–8
    community assets and needs studies and evaluation 378–86
    critical reference group 375
    elements 373–4
    issues 372–3
    preparing for a research project 377–8
    social research 374, 390–1
resources 256–7, 279–80, 344–61
respect (principle) 24, 277–8, 329–30
responding 285

Index

rights 334, 426
    human rights 8, 25–7, 57–8, 186, 335–6, 383, 433–7
risk 68, 75, 164–5, 366, 428
    case study 63
    and the Other 313–14
    risk society 62–3, 71, 122–4, 224, 240, 427–8
routine production work 177
rural renewal 193–4

sampling 378
scientific management 238–40
secular fundamentalism 417
self-determination 23, 26, 57, 234
self-funding 344–5, 347–53
    case studies 350–1, 352
    issues 351–3
self-governing voluntary associations 56–7
self-mobilisation 188
self-monitoring 185
sensitivity 283–4
service agreements 365–7
SMART analysis 218, 362
snowballing 273
social action 117–18, 290–1
social and community services industry 14–16
social capital 8, 125–30, 277–8
social change 94–5
social Darwinism 86–7
social entrepreneurship 14, 75, 236–7
social evolutionary framework 9, 86
social inclusion 6, 66–9, 329, 332
social interactionism 90–2
    stereotypes 91–2
social investment state 152
social justice 8, 23–5
social model (disability approach) 333
social movements
    and community development 106–7
    green movement 107–11
    social movement theory 105–15
social policy 297–8
social research 374, 390–1
social solidarity *see* solidarity
social welfare 95–6
socialism 49–50, 157
    eco-socialist perspectives (of green movement) 109–10
socialist feminism 101–2
societies 2–3
    civil society 128–30, 142, 229
    disadvantage in society 22, 24
    equalitarian societies 55

    multi-active society 129
    open societies 30–2
    and power imbalance 6
    progress in societies 11
    and respect 24
    risk society 62–3, 71, 122–4, 224, 240, 427–8
    southern theory 130–1
    spheres of society 99
    structure 94–5
    see also citizenship; state, the
sociological theory 46–7
solidarity 6, 47
    mechanical versus organic solidarity 46
southern theory 130–1
space concept 319–20
species-being 93
stamocap theory 145
state, the 137–68, 235, 405–6, 427–8
    approaches to understanding 139–55
    case study 153
    and community development 137–68, 405–6
    as a concrete object versus as a theoretical object 139–40
    as contested terrain 141, 145, 149
    contract state 141, 145–7
    a decentralised democratic and facilitative state 167–8
    definitions 139–42
    feminist views 154
    independent state 140, 142–3
    instrumental view 140, 143–4
    interlocking state 141, 144–5
    laissez-faire state 142
    models for the future 164–8
    neo-liberal state 159, 165–6
    partnership state 141, 148–51
    stamocap theory 145
    a supervising state 166–7
    surveillance state 141, 147–8
    theories 140–1
    welfare state 70, 155–64, 234–5, 333
state instrumentalism 140, 143–4
steering–rowing distinction 147
stereotypes 91–2
strategic plans 210, 385–6
strategy development 204–24
    action plans 217–19, 220
    aims and objectives 214–15
    approaches 204–8
    context and problem analysis 215–17
    elements 205–8
    evaluation 220–1
    issues and criticisms 223–4

Index

means and ends 222–3
processes and steps 212–13
reasons for undertaking 213–14
strategy and research 373–4
taking action 219–20
visions, missions, rationales and aims 211–12, 214–15
when to undertake 210–11
structural Marxism 95
submission-based funding 358, 361–6
subsidiarity 6
superfluous populations 163
surplus value 101
surveillance 124, 153, 164–5, 184–5
surveillance state 141, 147–8
sustainability 27–8, 64–5, 346
SWOT analysis 211, 216
symbolic–analytic services 177–8
sympathy 283
systematic planning for effectiveness approach (strategic development) 207–8

taxation 360–1
Taylorism 238
teamwork 278, 281
technocratic consciousness 118
technology 109, 118, 294–5
tendering *see* competitive tendering
terrorism 60, 147, 315
    war on terror 312, 313–14
there is no alternative (TINA) 32, 38, 295, 430
third way politics 152
third-sector organisations 13–17, 229, 230–1
    see also community organisations
time concept 317–18, 319–22, 409
TINA *see* there is no alternative
Tobin Tax 360
traditional action 117
transformation 35, 373–4, 385
triangulation 377–8
trust 277–8

trusts (philanthropic) 347, 355–7
'twinning' 151

uncertainty avoidance 324
understanding (principle) 329–30
unionism/unionisation 14, 55
Universal Declaration of Human Rights 433–7
universalisation 60
unpaid work 258–60, 346
user-pays 13, 34, 344–5

vertical gender segmentation 104
vertical organisation (community organisations) 240–2
Victorian Council of Social Service (VCOSS) 247–9
virtual communities 9, 50–1
vision 3, 35, 184–5, 373–4, 415
voluntary associations 56–7, 229, 258–60
volunteerism 232–3, 258–60, 426
    case study 259–60
    volunteering industry 411–12

wasted humans 74
weasel words 411
welfare 6, 43–4, 232, 233
    charity model 333
    consumers 161
    feminisation of poverty 86
    social welfare programs 95–6
    user-pays approach 13
    welfare state 70, 155–64, 234–5, 333
welfare state industry model (community organisation) 234–5
wertrational action 117
Western Marxists 96, 97
whistleblowing 291
workers' cooperatives 348–51, 352

xenophobia 307, 313

zweckrational action 117–18

WANT TIPS ON
NOTE TAKING?

DO YOU NEED TO WRITE
ESSAYS AND REPORTS?

FINDING IT HARD TO GET A GRIP ON
RESEARCHING AND REFERENCING?

WANT SOME EXTRA
HELP – DESIGNED
JUST FOR STUDENTS?

Visit your campus bookstore today!

Tertiary Studies - it's a new environment

Make sure you get the most out of your studies – and leave with the best possible marks!

Communication Skills Toolkit
Unlocking the Secrets of Tertiary Success
2nd edition

Jane Grellier • Veronica Goerke